# THE WHOLE INTERNET

## USER'S GUIDE

*Academic Edition*

### Ed Krol

Adapted by

## Bruce C. Klopfenstein, Ph.D.

Bowling Green State University

**INTEGRATED MEDIA GROUP**

*An Imprint of Wadsworth Publishing Company*

I(T)P® An International Thomson Publishing Company

PUBLISHING • SOFTWARE • RESEARCH

O'Reilly & Associates, Inc.

Sebastopol, California

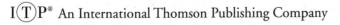
Belmont • Albany • Bonn • Boston • Cincinnati • Detroit • London • Madrid • Melbourne
Mexico City • New York • Paris • San Francisco • Singapore • Tokyo • Toronto • Washington

Editor: Kathy Shields

Assistant Editor: Tamara Huggins

Production: Gary Palmatier, Ideas to Images

Composition: Ideas to Images

Print Buyer: Karen Hunt

Cover Design: Edie Freedman

Cover Image: Adapted from the Dover Pictorial Archive

O'REILLY & ASSOCIATES, INC.
103 Morris Street, Suite A
Sebastopol, CA 95472
(800) 998-9938    (707) 829-0515
e-mail: *nuts@ora.com*  or  *uunet!ora!nuts*


Printed in the United States of America
1  2  3  4  5  6  7  8  9  10

For more information, contact Wadsworth Publishing Company:

Wadsworth Publishing Company
10 Davis Drive
Belmont, California 94002, USA

International Thomson Publishing Europe
Berkshire House 168-173
High Holborn
London, WC1V 7AA, England

Thomas Nelson Australia
102 Dodds Street
South Melbourne 3205
Victoria, Australia

Nelson Canada
1120 Birchmount Road
Scarborough, Ontario
Canada M1K 5G4

International Thomson Editores
Campos Eliseos 385, Piso 7
Col. Polanco
11560 México D.F. México

International Thomson Publishing GmbH
Königswinterer Strasse 418
53227 Bonn, Germany

International Thomson Publishing Asia
221 Henderson Road
#05-10 Henderson Building
Singapore 0315

International Thomson Publishing Japan
Hirakawacho Kyowa Building, 3F
2-2-1 Hirakawacho
Chiyoda-ku, Tokyo 102, Japan

ISBN 0-534-50674-7

# CONTENTS

CHAPTER THREE

# How the Internet Works

CHAPTER FOUR

# What's Allowed on the Internet?

CHAPTER SEVEN

# ELECTRONIC MAIL 107

CHAPTER EIGHT

# NETWORK NEWS ⎯⎯⎯⎯⎯⎯⎯⎯⎯⎯⎯⎯⎯⎯⎯⎯⎯⎯ 153

CHAPTER TEN

# FINDING SOMEONE 223

## CATALOG

# RESOURCES ON THE INTERNET     439

# FIGURES

## Chapter 14 — Other Applications      395

## Chapter 15 — Dealing with Problems      421

## Appendix B — International Network Connectivity      569

# Tables

# PREFACE

This is a book about the most important research tool available to students, teachers, and scholars: the Internet, the world's largest computer network, and the World Wide Web, a subset of the Internet that has truly made the Net accessible to anyone. In many ways, the WWW is to the Internet what Windows is to DOS. The Internet grew up on UNIX (an operating system known for being much less user-friendly than DOS), but the WWW has made it accessible to anyone, regardless of UNIX background. Let's be clear: You do not have to know UNIX to use the Internet or the WWW, and that assumption helped drive *The Whole Internet: Academic Edition.*

Borrowing from the second edition, this version is updated and revised with an academic user in mind and one who wants to become an expert user of the Internet's many incredible tools. All revisions were completed by Dr. Bruce Klopfenstein, a communication scholar from the social science tradition who has been teaching students how to use the Internet since 1985. To those of us who have been using the Internet for a long time, much of what we discuss has become commonplace. To get a sense of what the Internet is, and why this book is important, we need to take a few steps back.

About fifteen years ago, a minor revolution occurred when personal computers became common, and in the United States, they are now selling faster than television sets. The price/performance ratio continues to change at such a pace that computers are becoming economically accessible to more and more people and classrooms. Visionaries have talked about computers as information appliances: You could use your home or school computer to connect to the national news services, get stock reports, do library searches, even read professional journals or literary classics. Without much warning, heavy computer users have now moved from these great expectations to "Been there, done that, what's next?"

A revolution, by definition, is rare. Perhaps there has been a revolution in computing in which large, mainframe computing has been usurped by personal computing, whether on the desktop or the laptop. As of today, it appears that another revolution is reaching fruition, and that revolution is in computer networking. We are moving into a new era of information access and control, and what some contemporary visionaries see as the dawning of the *Communication* Age.

With the Internet, networking clearly came of age. The information resources that visionaries talked about as early as the 1940s are not just research topics that a few advanced thinkers can master; they are potentially as much a part of your life as other communication media like radio or television. Once you're connected to the Internet, you have instant access to a mind-boggling wealth of information that continues to grow from year to year. In some cases, you have to pay for access to it, but the tradition of media in the United States is commercial subsidization, and we are witnessing that today on the World Wide Web.

Through electronic mail and bulletin boards (called newsgroups in the Internet community), you can use a different kind of resource: a worldwide supply of knowledgeable people, some of whom are certain to share your interests, no matter how obscure. It's easy to find a discussion group on almost any topic, or to find people interested in forming a new discussion group. Although free advice is often worth what you pay for it, there are also plenty of well-informed experts who are more than willing to be helpful and giving of their time. In this sense, the Internet may be contributing to a renewal in the human spirit of individuals helping one another.

In the months since the second edition of *The Whole Internet* appeared, the Internet began to be superseded by the World Wide Web. Whereas the "information superhighway" seemed to be an overhyped cliché, the Web became perhaps the single most discussed topic in American popular culture. Now, everyone seems to want to get on. You can read about the Net daily in *USA Today,* the electronic daily edition of *Time,* or perhaps from the home page of CNN. Not only can you watch news items about the Net on your local TV station, you might even be able to download the story as a video clip; advertisements with "URLs," the electronic addresses of Web "home pages," have become commonplace. There are more and constantly improving resources: There's a whole new world of multimedia resources, including museums, exhibitions, art galleries, and shopping malls, that incredibly did not exist two years ago. Even the visionaries would be astonished by what we've achieved in such a short period of time.

Well, then, where do you start? Getting a handle on the Net remains a lot like what Ed Krol calls grabbing a handful of Jell-O—the more firm you think your grasp is, the more oozes down your arm. You don't need to deal with Jell-O in this manner to eat it, you just need the right tool: a spoon. And you need to dig in and start eating. The same is true of the Internet. You don't need to be an expert in telephone lines, data communications, and network protocols for it to be useful. No amount of hyperbole about the Net's limitless resources will make the Internet useful. You just need to know how to use some tools and to start working with them. There is no doubt, of course, that to be competitive in the academic world now, you really need competency on the WWW.

As for uses, they may be virtually (pun intended) limitless. They range from scholarly ones (you can read literary works analyzing Dante's *Divine Comedy*) to dissecting a frog, to participating in policy debates. Applications may be applied (agricultural market reports), recreational (ski reports for Aspen), or humorous (David Letterman's Top Ten list). It is also an amazing tool for collaboration: working with other people on your own magnum opus. In fact, Dr. Klopfenstein never met face-to-face the many other people who worked on this text (although he was an anonymous audience member in a packed house at which Tim O'Reilly and Ed Krol discussed the ins and outs of cyberspace).

In a sense, the origination of this book is a continuing tribute to the power and usefulness of the Internet. Mike Loukides, the editor, and Ed Krol met via electronic mail. Network users were clamoring to get Ed to update a help guide he wrote earlier, *The Hitchhiker's Guide to the Internet.* He was about to volunteer when Mike e-mailed him and asked, "How about doing it as a book?" This spurred a number of messages about outlines and time frames until both were finalized. The legalities and contracts were handled by the Postal Service; electronic contracts were too commercial for the Internet at the time, and are still too high-tech for courts to deal with. And we were on our way.

Shortly thereafter, Ed was shipped macro libraries to use in production, and began shipping chapters to Mike, all by e-mail. Mike would annotate, change, and ship them back to him by the same means. Occasionally, they would trade file directories, screen images, and illustrations. Except for the final review copies and illustrations, everything was handled via the Internet. The whole process was accomplished with less than 10 telephone calls.

Think for a minute about what this means. Traditional Post Office service between Illinois (where Ed lives) and Connecticut (where Mike lives) takes three days. If you want to pay extra, you can use a courier service and cut the time down to one day. But he could ship the entire book to Mike over the Net in a few minutes.

The academic edition worked much the same way. Bruce Klopfenstein was on an e-mail list where a "call for proposals" was posted. Seems there was interest in taking *The Whole Internet* and adapting it for academic use (the entrepreneurial O'Reilly and Associates was teaming up with the well-established Wadsworth academic publisher). As someone who had used it in class but wanted to make it more "newbie" accessible, Bruce wrote up a proposal and e-mailed it in. The proposal won out over a number of others. Had he not forgotten to mention to Kathy Shields from Wadsworth that BGSU was in Bowling Green, *Ohio,* they actually would have met in person to sign the contracts.

## ▪ *Audience*

This book is intended for any student (including adult learners) who wants to become an expert at accessing the Internet and World Wide Web's tremendous resources. It's a book for university, community college, and high-school students and teachers. This revision of the second edition into this academic edition was designed for those who want to use the network particularly for research applications. It is not intended in any way as an engineer's guide to internetworking, and you do not need to learn UNIX to use it. Some references to UNIX remain, but those that do are there only for the benefit of those who already know a little bit about UNIX or might choose to learn more. Some of the original UNIX-based examples from the original text remain, but they can certainly be ignored by most readers. The classroom instructor can help steer students clear of any sections that stray too far into the UNIX world.

Bruce believed in doing this revision that the user should want and be able to become an expert *researcher* on the Internet and the WWW. He sees the Web as a tool that can be exploited. The technologies of the Net, of course, are not exempt from scrutiny or criticism. The Web as a new communication medium is not in and of itself good or bad, but the same is not necessarily true of the applications placed on it. Those applications can and surely must be examined critically. This book focuses on the functionality of the Web for academic research purposes. The social impacts of this technology remain a vital topic for classroom discussion (and some chapter exercises are intended to spark in-class debate).

## ▪ *Approaching This Book*

Many users probably will want to get to Chapter 13 quickly. In it, the World Wide Web is discussed specifically, and we introduce Netscape Navigator 2.0b. The decision to go with Netscape Navigator was a simple one, given its dominance of the educational environment. Note that examples in other book chapters may show screen images in Netscape 1.1 because they were completed before 2.0b was available. We will watch for changes on the WWW that affect the users of this book, and you can expect to find them at the Wadsworth home page (URL: **http://www.thomson.com/wadsworth.html**) as well as the Whole Internet Catalog.

There are many ways to approach the Internet; likewise, there are many ways to read this book. For our first attempt at the academic edition, we have kept the chapter order intact. Here are a few suggestions for using them. If you are completely new to the Internet, start at the beginning and read to the end. You might want to pay particular attention to the *Resource Catalog,* which tells you what you'll find, and Appendix A, *Getting Connected to the Internet,* which tells you how to get connected. Chapter 13, which discusses the World Wide Web, may well be the best place to start. If you want, you can skim chapters 3 and 4, which explain how the Internet works and what's allowed; but please revisit these later.

Those familiar with the Internet but not as a user can skip to chapter 5; in this chapter we start discussing the basic utilities that you use on the Internet. An experienced Internet user who wants to get right at the searching tools might skip to chapter 9. Chapters 9 through 13 discuss the newest tools to come on the scene: Archie, some newer "white pages" services, Gopher, WAIS, and the Netscape Navigator WWW browser. Even if you've been around for a while, you may want to brush up on these. If you're not familiar with these tools, you really should be.

If you have used the Internet casually, read the first four chapters to get the background you may have missed; and then scan the Table of Contents for chapters whose topics are unfamiliar to you. If you do this, read the chapters in order, because many of the newer facilities (chapter 9 and subsequent chapters), build on each other. Appendix A discusses various ways of getting a connection, but it's worth inquiring locally if school access is not already available. If you want to get an idea quickly about what's available, look at the *Resource Catalog.*

If you think you are only interested in the WWW, dedicate yourself to using the other chapters. E-mail and especially network news (chapters 7 and 8) can be among the most valuable tools available to you. The WWW is clearly the hot topic today, but don't overlook the other established tools despite their plain vanilla wrapping.

## ▨ *Conventions*

In this book, we use the following conventions:

- ■ WWW addresses are printed in **bold**, preceded by "URL".
- ■ Command names are printed in **bold**; for example, **telnet** or **archie**.
- ■ Names of services or protocols are printed in UPPERCASE or with the initial letter capitalized; for example, TELNET or Archie.
- ■ Input typed by the user is printed in **bold**; for example, **get host-table.txt**.
- ■ Internet names and addresses are printed in **bold**; for example, **ora.com**.

- Menu titles and options are printed in **bold**.

- Filenames are printed in *italic;* for example, */etc/hosts.*

- Names of the USENET newsgroups are printed in *italic;* for example, *rec.music.folk.*

- "Variables"—placeholders that the reader will replace with an actual value—are printed in *italic.* For example, in the command **ftp** *hostname,* you must substitute the name of a computer on the Internet for *hostname.*

- Within examples, output from the computer is printed in `monospace` type.

- Within examples, text typed by the user is printed in `monospace bold` type.

- Within examples, variables are printed in `monospace italic` type.

- Within examples, explanatory comments are often placed in *italic* type.

## *Acknowledgments from Ed Krol*

A whole host of people helped with this book. First and foremost is my wife, Margaret. Without her support and help, it never would have come to pass. She read and corrected most of it, searched Gopher for resources, and tried things to see if my explanations really were sufficient for a computer professional to use the Internet. Also, she took over enough of the running of our home to give me time to devote to the project.

Next comes my daughter, Molly, who did without me in many ways for the better part of a year while I was writing. (This is Molly's second experience with computing fame—she was the toddler with a penchant for emergency-off switches, after whom "Molly-guards" are named in the "Hackers Dictionary.")

Then there is Mike Loukides, the editor, project leader, confidence-builder, and cheerleader, who dragged me, sometimes kicking and screaming, to the finish line. In the beginning, Mike helped me to think through just what the book needed to contain, and then made sure that everything made it in. Near the end, when Tim O'Reilly asked us to beef up the coverage of a couple of topics, Mike did most of the restructuring and wrote a significant part of the new material.

Next are all the people at the University of Illinois who helped. George Badger, the head of the Computing and Communications Service Office, for the support I needed with the project. Beth Scheid, for picking up some pieces of my real job while I was preoccupied with book-related problems. The real technical people, who answered some bizarre questions and made some of the examples possible: Charley Kline, Paul Pomes, Greg German, Lynn Ward, Albert Cheng, Sandy Seehusen, Bob Booth, Randy Cotton, Allan

Tuchman, Bob Foertsch, Mona Heath, and Ed Kubaitis. The faculty of the Graduate School of Library Science was also involved, especially Greg Newby, who had a number of suggestions about how to approach the searching tools of the Internet.

Two people were my test audience: Lisa German, a recent library science graduate, and Pat King, a then-neophyte system administrator. They knew little about the Internet when they began reading the book as it was written, chapter by chapter. They pointed out all the things that were used before they were explained or that were just plain explained too technically. Lisa also spent many hours visiting most of the notable anonymous FTP servers on the Internet, searching for resources. It's pretty amazing what someone with a knowledge of common cataloging words and phrases can do with Archie, but I guess that's what librarians are trained to do.

A large group of people read the book, or just pieces of it, checking for technical errors, inconsistencies, and "useful stuff that I left out." These included Eric Pearce, Robin Peek, Jerry Peek, Mitch Wright, Rick Adams, Tim Berners-Lee, Susan Calcari, Deborah Schaffer, Peter Deutsch, Alan Emtage, Chris Schulte, Martyne Hallgren, and Jim Williams. The book would not be anywhere near as useful without their help.

The interior design of the book, which is a departure from O'Reilly & Associates's previous books, was sparked by a comment of Dale Dougherty's. He thought it a shame that the standard dry "technical book" interior didn't live up to the whimsical promise of Edie Freedman's cover. Tim O'Reilly picked up on that comment, and insisted on a redesign to make the book and catalog more accessible to a non-technical audience. Edie actually developed the design (with her usual flair) and selected all of the illustrations for both the chapter dividers and the catalog. Her design work was not just something that happened after the book was done, but an integral part of how it turned out. The design was then implemented in **troff** by Lenny Muellner, something no sane person should be asked to do. It included the illustrations of Chris Reilley and the text copyedited by Rosanne Wagger, who corrected more typos than I thought existed. Together this crew turned a rough manuscript into a work of art.

For the second edition, Ellen Siever did a wonderful job of crash-editing, in addition to pulling together the list of service providers in Appendix A; Jennifer Niederst and John Labovitz created the print rendition of the *Resource Catalog* (from the online catalog for GNN ), using software developed by Terry Allen. Clairemarie Fisher O'Leary copyedited the *Resource Catalog* and assisted with production, Kismet McDonough performed the final production quality-control edit, Chris Tong updated the index, and Linda Mui verified the resources in the *Resource Catalog* under a lot of time pressure.

Finally, I'd like to thank the people at Yoyodyne Software Systems, especially John McMahon and John Vance Stuart, whose domain I invaded.

## ▦ *Acknowledgments from Bruce Klopfenstein*

Thanks to Ed Krol for creating this incredible "bible of Internet books." It is an honor and a privilege for me to take on his fine work and try to adapt it for students like mine. I hope to have the chance to make it still better pending feedback from the users.

As an academic chair serving in an era of organizational restructuring, I had to balance the demands of this project against my other professional obligations. When the work moved into high gear, I asked my faculty colleagues in the Department of Telecommunications at Bowling Green State University to give me the time it would take to make this book my top priority in the fall 1995 semester. If not for their incredible tolerance and understanding, as well as the implicit support of my dean and the director of our new School of Communication Studies, this project could not have been completed. Probably the one person who earned my greatest gratitude is our department secretary, Gail Deuschle, who more than anyone else "minded the store" while I was off for hours, days, and weeks in cyberspace getting this job done. Of course, everyone on campuses knows that the secretaries are the ones who really run academic departments.

Working with two publishers, Wadsworth and O'Reilly, sometimes seemed to have the many chiefs in search of enough Indians to get everything done. Nevertheless, I was impressed with the way these two organizations were able to come together on this project and, in the end, as my Ohio State doctoral adviser Joe Foley used to tell me, "Just get it done."

I literally don't know everyone who worked thousands of miles from me to get this book ready, but I do know some. Apologies to those I am overlooking here. Though I haven't met them either, thanks to the Cleveland Indians for reminding me there was more to life in October 1995 than finishing this book.

Mary Leal of O'Reilly was forever supportive of me and especially my students (including allowing me to pass out prizes in return for their invaluable help with ideas for the revisions). Dean Kohrs was one of those "tuned in" graduate students in my class who (in a welcomed way) often showed me up by demonstrating knowledge of yet another WWW technique with which I was just becoming familiar. He helped with screen images and anything else I threw his way with the caveat that whatever I was asking for was needed yesterday.

Nothing serves one better when the going gets tough (as it sometimes did) than a sense of humor, and I am particularly grateful for Gary Palmatier's witticisms as we worked under deadlines that everyone involved knew were impossible, but got the unwieldy manuscript ready for production. Elizabeth von Radics, copy editor, was always calm, ready for chapters at any hour or day of the week, and understanding even if a chapter came in just a little later than planned. Kathy Shields of Wadsworth was the slave driver, my personal e-mail alarm clock, reminding me when things were due, then reminding me again. Kathy also had the unenviable job of coordinating many tasks that were transparent to me in Ohio, even as I knew there must have been an occasional fire drill in California.

Of course, one's personal relationships are affected by projects that can engulf weeknights and weekends. I thank my wife, Keri Hurney, for allowing me the freedom and isolation I sometimes needed to work (not to mention use of her computer account that allowed me to **telnet** to BGSU without having to pay Ma Bell). This book is dedicated to our daughter, Laurel, whose use of an Apple IIe in first grade in 1995 reminds me how far we still need to go in making information tools available to students and teachers in public education, and to her unborn sibling, who will know what else I was up to the year he or she was conceived.

I hope this book is helpful, but know a future edition will benefit greatly from user criticism. We will have a Web site for use with this book that you will find at the Wadsworth home page, URL **http://www.thomson.com/wadsworth.html**. You might find some other valuable information at my personal home page, which is linked from URL **http://www.bgsu.edu/departments/tcom**. Let's not forget the ever-popular GNN's Whole Internet Catalog at URL **http://www.gnn.com/gnn/wic** that evolved with the first edition of this book.

Regardless of the enormous help given me in this exhilarating project, the responsibility for the manipulation of Ed Krol's text into what appears within this book rests with me. Let me know what you think by sending your comments to **klopfens@bgnet.bgsu.edu**.

# CHAPTER ONE

# WHAT THIS BOOK IS ABOUT

In the early 1900s, if you wanted to tinker with horseless carriages, you fell in with other tinkerers and learned by doing. There were no books about automobiles, no schools for would-be mechanics, no weekend courses. The market was too small for these training aids. In addition, there were good reasons to fall in with a group of experts: Early cars were so unreliable that they could hardly be called transportation. When your car broke down, you needed to fix it yourself, or have some good friends who could come to the rescue. You fiddled and asked questions of others. Soon you could answer questions for a novice. Eventually, you might become a highly regarded mechanic (a "guru"). When you got to this level, your car might actually become useful transportation, not just an expensive hobby.

In the early 1980s, the Internet (a network of computer networks that allows sharing of files) was in much the same state. The network had only a few thousand users. All of its users either had ready access to experts, or were experts themselves. Expertise was critical. The network was slow and unreliable. Its major purpose was not to help students and educators find information, but to help technicians learn how to build and use networks. Since then, the number of Internet users easily has increased a thousandfold; and thousands of new users are being added daily. The introduction of the World Wide Web (WWW or W3) accelerated this already frenetic pace (see "Growth of the World Wide Web," at URL **http://www.netgen.com/info/growth.html**; for a valuable timeline on the entire history of the Internet, see Robert Hobbes's Zakon's Internet Timeline v2.2, URL **http://info.isoc.org/guest/zakon/Internet/History/HIT.html**). These people use the network for their daily work and play. They demand reliability, and do not want to be mechanics. They want to be chemists, librarians, meteorologists, kindergarten teachers, students, or anyone else who happens to use the network. So now they demand documentation—something to read on the train to work to improve their job skills. They are increasingly computer literate, but not network literate. This book is about network literacy for the student and educator. We will tell you how to unlock the boundless resources available on the Net once you have an Internet connection.

## What an Internet Connection Means

If you ask someone, "Are you connected to the Internet?" you might get some strange answers. The question has a good, precise answer, but that is not what many people think about. For many people, the question "Are you connected?" is similar to the question "Do you shop at J.C. Penney's?" Shopping at J.C. Penney's means different things to different people. To some, Penney's is a store at the mall; to others, it is a catalog. Whether the answer to the question is yes or no probably depends on whether the respondent has been able to get what he or she wanted at Penney's, not the means by which the purchases were made.

The same is true of Internet connections. If I ask, "Are you connected?" the question you are likely to hear is, "Can I do the Internet things I want to do from my desktop?" For example, many people who use only electronic mail think they are directly connected to the Internet when, in fact, they are not. Before you get started, it's important to know what a connection means.

The Internet offers a wide range of services, and new services can be expected in the next few years. A partial list of these services includes electronic mail, bulletin boards, file transfer, remote login, index programs, and so on. To get the complete set of services, you should have a specific Internet "TCP/IP" connection (treat this as a buzzword right now—we'll get to what it means in a while). A TCP/IP connection to the Internet is like a Vulcan mind meld on *Star Trek*. Your computer is part of the network: Your computer is configured to contact every computer service on the Internet, though it may need some particular software to use some of them.

Anything that can happen between networked computers can occur. For example, if you want a file, you can move it directly to your desktop as in Figure 1-1. If you are interested only in some limited services, you do not necessarily need a full connection to the Internet. Commercial online providers like America Online, CompuServe, eWorld, and Prodigy changed attitudes in the mid-1990s by moving toward full Internet access. (For a detailed account of the various possibilities of being "on the Internet," see "Request for Comments: 1775" at URL **http://www.es.net/pub/rfcs/rfc1775.txt**; RFCs are the official document series of the Internet Advisory Board.)

We focus in this book on a direct connection to the Internet that bypasses other online intermediaries to the Net. That is, you can obtain an account on a computer connected

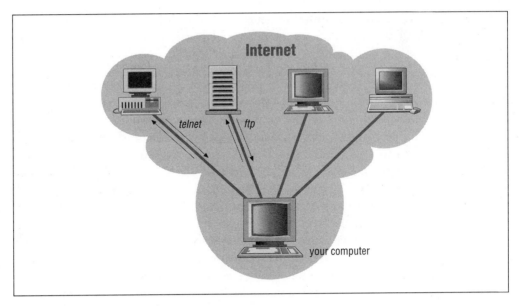

*Figure 1-1*    *A true Internet connection*

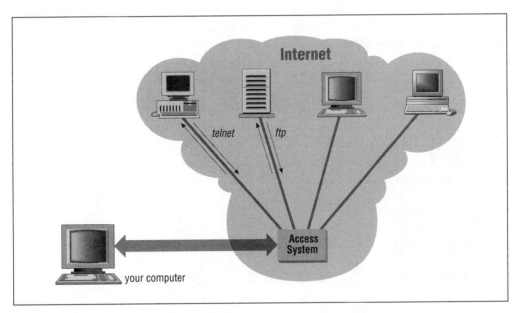

*Figure 1-2*    *A dial-up Internet connection*

to the Internet or do it through such an intermediary. Then you can use a terminal emulator to dial in from your computer to the Internet machine, log in, read mail, fetch files, and do whatever you want (Figure 1-2). In this situation it's fair to say, "I have access to the Internet" or, "I have an Internet connection," because you can do anything the Internet will allow you to do—on the remote machine.*

However, you technically cannot say, "My home computer is connected to the Internet," because it isn't. What's the difference? Well, once you've dialed in to your remote system, you can read and write electronic mail. But you can't send or receive electronic mail from your home system directly; you have to log in to some remote access point first. If you want to save an important mail message, you can save it on the remote system. To save it on your own computer's disk, you'll need to use your communications program to move that message file from the remote system back to your personal computer. Likewise, you can fetch a file from any of the Internet's public archives; but you still need to go through an extra step of moving that file from the access computer to your personal computer. You also can't automatically use any of the sophisticated applications that require a graphical display (like Netscape or Mosaic, discussed in chapter 13) via dial-up modem. Without proper setup, the access computer has no way to get the display information to your local PC. One step farther away, you can get limited access to the Internet. If you're a commercial online subscriber (e.g., America Online, CompuServe, or Prodigy), you may have varying degrees of Internet access.†

Although it's common for people in this situation to say that they're "connected to the Internet," they aren't in any real sense. With many connections, you are limited to the Internet interface provided to you. You may be able to use the most popular Internet services, but not all. The diffusion of information about the Internet and its services has served as a catalyst for the commercial online industry to move into full Internet access.

Some service providers offer software that covers up the limitations of not having a true Internet connection. The software allows you to move files or mail from your home computer to and from Internet sites in one operation. This gives the illusion of being on the Internet even though you may be really accessing it like a dial-up terminal. This is certainly better, but it still leaves you in the hands of the service provider as far as what you can or can't do. The real acid test of being on the Internet versus accessing the Internet is, "If I find out about a new or better Internet application program, can I just put the software on my home computer and use it?" Let's be specific: If you can run Netscape or Mosaic, you probably can do everything the Internet will let you do.

It doesn't really matter if you are on the Internet, accessing the Internet, or using an alternative network to get to the Internet so long as you can do what you want to do. If all you care about is e-mail, then an account on a timesharing computer with Internet

*Of course, the remote (Internet) computer might not have some useful program installed. You'll have to talk that system's manager into finding it and installing it. You may need to install something else on your home PC.

†A UNIX user who uses UUCP for electronic mail and news is in the same boat. UUCP is an ancient way of configuring a UNIX computer to automatically dial up another UNIX computer and transfer files. This is the basis for a very popular mail service.

access will suffice and is likely to be cheaper. If you want to use all the latest and greatest features, you probably won't be satisfied without a full connection. You and your pocketbook have to pick. The problem is that Net surfing is addictive. You may think today that all you want is e-mail. Through e-mail, you'll find out you are missing something else, so you may want to add that service. With access to that service you'll learn more about another, and the process can become a seemingly endless loop.

## Getting Connected?

Here's the good news: You may already have an Internet connection and not know it. Most Internet users have a connection through school or work. Their university or business is connected to the Internet, and they use it for work or for pleasure. If your school is not already on the Internet, it probably is looking into how to get a connection. If not, telephone companies and cable television operators are joining existing online providers to offer Internet access. A clear trend that is emerging is that Internet access is becoming more widespread from multiple providers. As the system moves from public into private hands, however, the more likely it is that individual users will be charged for this access.* Most university students have ready access to the Internet once they get a computer account. If you're school or office is not on the Internet, ask the obvious question: "Why not?" Internet access has moved beyond the domain of large research organizations (including universities) and into small colleges and local school systems.

If you're not already connected, there are many ways to get connected. These range from large, fairly expensive solutions that are appropriate for large universities to relatively low-cost solutions that are appropriate for small school, business, or home. No matter what level you're at, Internet access always comes via an "access provider"—an organization that provides for a price. There are access providers for every level of service from expensive dedicated Internet connections to inexpensive dial-up connections for home users. Appendix A, *Getting Connected to the Internet,* lists many (though not all) access providers and the types of service they provide. It also gives you some hints as to how an individual may be able to get connected for little personal cost.†

## Something for Everyone

The usefulness of the Internet parallels the history of computing, with a lag of about 10 years. In the early 1980s, personal computers brought computing from the realm of

---

*Cable and telephone operators also bring two different perspectives on billing possibilities. Both charge flat monthly fees for existing services, but telephone companies (like online service providers) are also experienced in charging per minute of use.

†The definitive guide to buying an Internet connection is Susan Estrada's book *Connecting to the Internet,* published by O'Reilly Associates.

technical gurus to the general public: "the rest of us," as Apple said in their advertisements. The Internet is currently making the same transition rapidly.

As with personal computers (or, for that matter, automobiles), the Internet made the transition from an expert's plaything to an everyday tool through a "feedback loop." The network started to become easier to use—in part because the tools were better, in part because it was faster and more reliable. Of the people who were previously scared away from the Internet, the more venturesome started to use it. These new users created a demand for new resources and better tools. The old tools were improved, and new tools were developed to access new resources, making the network easier to use. Now another group of people started finding the Internet useful. The process repeated itself; and it's still repeating itself.

Whatever their sophistication, Internet users are, as a whole, looking for one thing: information. They find information from two general classes of sources: people and computers. It's easy to forget about the Internet's "people" resources, but they're just as important (if not more so) as the computers that are available. Far from being a machine-dominated wasteland, where antisocial misfits sporting pocket protectors flail away at keyboards, the Internet is a friendly place to meet people just like you. You're a potential network user if you are:

- A science teacher who needs to remain current and develop curricula
- A Unitarian-Universalist minister in a town of fundamentalists, looking for some spiritual camaraderie
- A criminal lawyer who needs to discuss a case with someone who has a particular kind of legal expertise
- A first-year college student looking for the latest online hints about how to prepare a better writing composition
- An eighth grader looking for others whose parents don't understand real music

For these people and millions more, the Internet provides a way of meeting others with shared interests. It's possible to find an electronic discussion group on almost any topic, or to start a new discussion group if one doesn't already exist. These topics related to both personal and profession interests. The Internet also provides people with access to computer resources. The science teacher can access a NASA-funded computer that provides information—past, present, and future—about space science and the space program. The minister can find the Bible, the Koran, and the Torah, waiting to be searched for selected passages. The lawyer can find timely transcriptions of U.S. Supreme Court opinions in Project Hermes (URL: **http://www.law.cornell.edu/supct**).* The

---

*URL represents "Uniform Resource Locator." In this case, **http://www.law.cornell.edu/supct** tells you this is a hypertext link from the Internet domain named **www.law.cornell.edu** and the directory (or "folder") named */supct*).

eighth grader can discuss musical lyrics with other eighth graders, or can appear to be an expert among adults. After all, who is the one who knows the lyrics?

This is just the beginning. Because of its history, the Internet is especially replete with sources of interest to specialists in computing and networking. This is quickly changing as the Internet is introduced to a vast number of users outside that particular specialty. A large part of this book is a catalog of information sources you can access through the Internet. In creating this catalog, we picked as broad a range of sources as possible, to show that the Net really does have something for everyone. If we cataloged every resource on the Internet, the book would be huge, and much of it would be telling you about different software repositories. While we cover our share of software repositories, anyone can find software (if you can't, this book will show you how). What's harder is finding the many gems waiting for your personal discovery.

The nice thing about all this is that you can browse on your terms. When trying something new in person, you're likely to be plagued by doubts. You hear about a bridge gathering at the community center, and think "Am I good enough?" "Am I too good?" "Will my ex-wife be there?" On the network, you can:

- Devote as much or as little time as you like
- Become casual acquaintances or fast friends with someone
- Observe discussions or take part
- Walk away from anything you find objectionable, or fight every wrong

If you like, you can make your collected works of poetry available to anyone who would like to read them. There is very little risk, so you might as well try.

## What You Will Learn

Just as there is no one use for the network, there is also no one way to use the network. The graphical user interfaces to the World Wide Web (WWW) like Netscape, Chameleon, and Mosaic make navigating the Internet easier than ever. Each uses the basic tools of the Internet that are covered in this book. If you use every chapter in this book, you will become an expert Web user. You will know how to access every common thing on the network, and you'll know how to get the software needed to do the uncommon things. That knowledge will still represent only one way. New and different software packages will become available. Your school or business may select its standard approach, but there is no general standard just yet. The good news is that Internet services are becoming dramatically easier to use for novices. Unlike the inaccessibility of the 1980s, Internet users now choose between easily adopted tools.

Many people view the Internet as the Interstate Highway System for information. You can drive cross-country in a sports car, a pick-up truck, or a jalopy—they all can get you there. This book takes you on a tour in a 1985 Chevy Impala. A Chevy may not be as sexy or fast as a Porsche, but it does offer you a comfortable ride to your destination. You won't get stuck in Outback, Montana, because the one mechanic in town has never seen a metric wrench. In particular, here's what we will cover:

- How to log on to other computers on the Internet (**telnet**). Many computers are "publicly available" for various kinds of work. Some of these computers allow anyone to use them; for some, you have to arrange for an account in advance. Some of these computers can be used for "general purpose" work; others provide some special service, like access to a library catalog or a database.

- How to move files from one computer to another (**ftp**). There are many public archives scattered around the network, providing files that are free for the taking. Many of these archives provide source code for various computer programs, but other archives hold recipes, short stories, demographic information, and so on. You name it, and you can probably find it (or something reasonably close).

- How to send electronic mail to other people who use the Internet. This is one of the first reasons users had to get online, and it remains so. The Internet provides global electronic mail delivery.

- How to read and participate in group discussions (USENET news). There are discussion groups for topics ranging from the obscure to the bizarre to the practical. USENET is a wonderful example of how the Internet can meet both personal and professional needs.

- How to locate various network resources, ranging from people to software to general databases ("white pages," Archie, Gopher, WAIS, World Wide Web). One of the Internet's paradoxical problems is that it's too rich; there are so many resources available, it can be difficult to find what you want, or to remember later where you found it. A few years ago, the network was like a library without a catalog. The "cataloging" tools are now being put into place and improving steadily almost from month to month. We'll tell you how to use the new and exciting tools (and some older, less exciting tools) to locate almost anything you might possibly want, ranging from people and software to sociological abstracts and fruit-fly stocks.

With these tools, you'll have the network at your fingertips. There are many different versions of all of these tools, and the earlier ones were based on the UNIX operating system, a very threatening system for general users (UNIX is to current graphical interfaces like Mosaic as DOS is to the PC interface Windows). Internet users as late as the early 1990s had to learn basic, keyboard-oriented UNIX software. Just as Windows users who know DOS are more dangerous than those who don't, Internet users who have some knowledge of basic UNIX commands have some advantages over those who don't. While several references to UNIX will be helpful, for the most part we will avoid getting into UNIX in any great detail (see UNIX Documentation and Tutorials, URL **http://www.ece.uc.edu/ece/information/unixman.html**, for more information on UNIX).

For the most part, what you can do on the Internet is defined by the network itself, not by the software you run on your computer to gain access. Using a mouse and pull-down menus makes the network easier to use, but it really doesn't let you do anything you couldn't do with a character-oriented display and keyboard. Limiting use to a character display is advantageous when you have a slower link to the Internet and/or you do not need to see graphical information. By including some references to UNIX, we're expanding what you can do. The trend clearly is away from the old "command line" interface (e.g., typing in UNIX commands to navigate a system on the Internet) to the "point-and-click" interface of Apple Computer and Microsoft Windows.

## *What If I Never Used UNIX?*

It doesn't matter if you don't know UNIX. The Internet is not UNIX. There are two parts to using the network: running programs on your computer to access the Internet and using those programs to do things across the network. For a PC/DOS user, the program that lets you connect to another system for an interactive terminal session is no different from any other PC/DOS program.

The program's name is **telnet**, so you might type:

```
A: telnet
```

This looks just like starting WordPerfect or Lotus. The same is true for any other brand of computer.

For your edification, here's the comparable UNIX command:

```
% telnet
```

Fewer and fewer PC users are faced with the bother of typing commands to initiate software applications. You're far more likely to be looking for a **telnet** icon at which to point with your mouse and click than you are to type in the **telnet** command. Even the "platforms" (e.g., Windows or Macintosh) are becoming more and more transparent. If you can use Netscape for Windows, you shouldn't have much trouble using Netscape on a Macintosh. The commands you use may be slightly different, to make them more like a "normal" command on your computer system, but when and why you use which command will remain the same. If an example shows that you start the **ftp** program (you use this to move files), connect to a file archive on some computer, and retrieve a certain file; then on a PC/DOS computer, you need to do those same steps in the same order. If you know how to run standard software on a computer, and if you read this book, you should be able to use the Internet. If you are interested in learning more about UNIX, there are many other guides available including the original version of this text. We tried to skip the UNIX details, but include some explanation of what's going on. You might even be able to guess what you should do in an emergency and/or be in a better position to solicit help from your Internet support staff (whether school or commercially oriented).

## What You Need

You need three things to explore and use the Internet: a desire for information, the ability to use (or willingness to learn to use) a computer, and access to the Internet. Desire for information is the most important. That's what the Internet offers: the information you want, when you want it—not "details at noon, six, and ten, stay tuned." Without that desire, this book's contents won't impress you. If I say, "Let's check the agricultural markets, the special nutritional requirements of AIDS sufferers, ski conditions, and home beer recipes," and you reply, "So what?" then you're not ready. If your response is, "How?" then the Internet is for you. A "pioneer's" explorer spirit also helps. You need to be willing to ask, "What's in here?" when faced with a new source on the Net. Remember the worst-kept secret about using the Net: It's fun.

You use the Internet with a computer. You don't have to be a computer scientist to use it. This book is not a tutorial on how to use a PC, Mac, or computer workstation. You need to be able to operate your local system, run existing programs, and understand what files are. Some computer jargon might help, but mostly you need a couple of very basic buzzwords:

*bit*        The smallest unit of information. A bit can have the value 1 or the value 0. Everything in computing is based on collecting hunks of bits together, manipulating them, and moving them from place to place. For example, it takes 8 bits to represent a standard alphabetic character.

*K*          A suffix meaning "about 1,000," derived from the Greek "kilo." For example, 8.6K characters means 8,600 characters. In computing, K may refer to 1,000 or 1,024, depending on the context, but who cares? For our purposes, "about 1,000" is good enough.

*click*      A verb meaning "to select something with a mouse." Sliding a mouse around on the desk moves an arrow on the screen. Programs that use a mouse frequently display simulated "push-buttons" on the screen. You activate those buttons by positioning the arrow on the button you want to push, and pressing the button on the mouse. This is commonly called "clicking" that button.

*URL (Uniform Resource Locater)*

An identifier that tells a World Wide Web browser the name of a desired site and the protocol for reaching it (hypertext, file transfer, TELNET, and others we will discuss soon). A typical Web URL is **http://www.bgsu.edu**, the home page for Bowling Green State University.

If we did our job in writing this book, you will learn what you need to know along the way and how to find out more about what's available at the time you are using this book.

Finally, you need an Internet connection. This book is oriented toward someone who has a connection and needs to know how to use it. That connection can take a variety of flavors, and they are getting easier to install (if necessary) and use. If you already have a connection, you can skip the next section. If you don't have a connection, Appendix A discusses how to get one. Many commercial providers are making access to the Internet technically (if not financially) available to anyone who wants it. You may find that your school or public library has the best available Internet link at no direct cost to you. Most colleges and universities offer computer accounts that allow students to use the Internet, and the day is coming when accounts may be given to entering students when they register for the first time.

## ■ *How This Book Is Organized*

Technical information is condensed as much as possible. You need not be a telecommunications whiz to take full advantage of the resources available on the Internet and WWW. The days of "command line" Internet use appear to be dwindling as browsers are becoming the dominant Internet interface of the near future.

### *Unique Features and In-Text Learning Aids*

As noted, this text is published with a companion WWW site, where new tools and exercises are available for students. This allows us to keep the material as fresh as possible.

The second author of this book is a social scientist, not a computer or information scientist. The needs of less-technical users remain the key for this text.

Some figures for this book are available as URLs on the World Wide Web. Here again, the Wadsworth WWW site at **http://www.thomson.com/wadsworth.html** is your key to updated links.

We have included expanded coverage of commercial services available on the Internet for research purposes. The focus is on research applications for the students and faculty. We hope this combination of an introduction to the Internet and WWW with the focus on research applications makes this book especially valuable to its users.

We have included an expanded glossary especially for new users, academics, and researchers. Additional online links to dictionaries of related interest are included as well.

This book is organized to allow the student to use it according to his or her local Internet access capabilities. If a graphical user interface is readily available, it may be wise to get to those chapters first. If you are limited to a dial-up modem and a text-based interface, then use the other chapters first. We begin with some history and technical theory. We'll keep the background material to a minimum—just enough so you can understand how the Internet evolved into what it is today. We discuss how the Internet works, limiting the technical information to mostly hand-waving explanations. This is useful information that will add to your overall understanding of the Internet. If you get into a bind and have to guess at what is going on or what to do next, nothing helps more than a feel for how things work. If you would like to know more about the history of the Internet or its technology, there are other books and online material that go into more detail.*

Most of the text discusses how to use the tools that allow your computer to find information on the Internet. We've tried to focus on what you're likely to do and why— not just on which knob to turn and which button to push, but *why* you need them. Some attention is paid to some relatively "fuzzy" but ultimately practical, issues: What's allowed and what isn't? What's polite and what isn't? What's the best way to find the kind of information you want?

A resource catalog for use with this text is available online via Wadsworth's Web site (URL **http://www.thomson.com/wadsworth.html**). This site allows us to include the latest links to tools on the World Wide Web.

The number of WWW sites grew exponentially into 1995 (URL: **http://www.nw.com/ zone/hosts-graph-log.gif**). No printed list is truly current because of both the new items constantly being added and the fluid nature of Internet sites (addresses can change often). This can be your place to start. Start at someplace interesting and begin to look and wander. It's amazing what you will find. If you still don't think the Internet is for you, press on. The Internet is a tool waiting to be exploited.

---

*The best of these is probably Douglas Comer's book *Internetworking with TCP/IP: Principles, Protocols, and Architectures* (Prentice Hall). Technically, it's quite advanced, but it's the standard work on the topic.

# ■ *Exercises*

**1.** Although not literally necessary, everyone working on the Internet should have an electronic mail (e-mail) account. Your instructor will tell you how to register for one. As a warm-up exercise, get the documentation needed to compose e-mail to the instructor. If possible, create an alias for him or her; an alias is a nickname that you can use so that an entire e-mail address is not needed each time you want to send e-mail to an individual.

Here's a sample "getting acquainted" message you can send, if asked, to your instructor.

- Your preferred name (i.e., including nickname), major, and class

- Your computer experience (classes, Mac/Windows, software expertise)

- Your current Internet expertise

- What you expect to get out of this class

- Something unusual about you that will help others remember your name

**2.** The growth of the Internet in the 1990s has been remarkable. What factors led to that dramatic growth? What differentiates the growth of Internet users in the 1990s from the much slower growth that occurred in the 1980s?

**3.** How many people do you think will eventually be using the Internet on at least a weekly, if not daily, basis? Why might some people not be using the Internet in the next few years? What are your concerns about being able to become an Internet expert?

**4.** The Internet is a communication technology. One approach for understanding the acceptance of a communication technology is the "diffusion of innovations." Go to the library and find the definitions for "innovation attributes" of relative advantage, compatibility, complexity, trialability, and observability. Suggest one way you might investigate each attribute as it relates to the potential use (adoption) of the Internet.

**5.** Computer operating systems today such as the Macintosh, Windows, and others employ the "graphical user interface": Point with a mouse at an image on the screen and click to start the application. Learning to use the Internet may assume some personal computing expertise on your part. Your school may well have tutorials that you can use (**http://www.leeds.ac.uk/ucs/docs/beg2/beg2.html** is an example WWW tutorial on how to use Windows from the University of Leeds).

Using the operating system of choice for your class purposes, be sure you know how to do the following things (independent of using the Internet):

- Format or initialize a blank diskette (preformatted disks may be purchased at little if any additional cost)
- Find various applications on the machine, such as a word processor (e.g., Word or WordPerfect), and a separate text editor (e.g., SimpleText on Macintosh and Notepad on Windows)
- Toggle between applications
- Cut text from one application window and paste it into another
- Print and save a file
- Print and save an entire screen or specific window

CHAPTER TWO

# WHAT IS THE INTERNET?

*What Makes Up the Internet?*
*Who Governs the Internet?*
*Who Pays for It?*
*What Does This Mean for Me?*
*What Does the Future Hold?*

T he Internet was born about 25 years ago (see Zakon, 1995, URL **http://info.isoc.org/guest/zakon/Internet/History/HIT.html**), out of an effort to connect a U.S. Defense Department network called the ARPAnet (named for the Advanced Research Projects Agency, URL **http://www.arpa.mil**). The ARPAnet was an experimental network designed to support military research. This included research on how to build networks that could withstand partial outages (like nuclear attacks) and still function. The idea was to create a network that would function even if some links were inoperable.

In the ARPAnet model, communication always occurs between a source (server) and a destination (client) computer. The network itself is assumed to be unreliable; any portion of the network could disappear at any moment (backhoes cutting cables are more of a threat than bombs). It was designed to require the minimum of information from the computer clients. To send a message on the network, a computer simply had to put its data in an envelope, called an Internet Protocol (IP) packet, and "address" the packets correctly. The communicating computers, not the network itself, were also given the responsibility for ensuring that the communication was accomplished. The philosophy was that every computer on the network could talk, as a peer, with any other computer.

Internet developers in the U.S., UK, and Scandinavia, responding to market pressures, began to put their IP software on every conceivable type of computer. It became the only practical method for computers from different manufacturers to communicate. This was attractive to the governments and universities, which did not have policies saying that all computers must be bought from the same vendor. Everyone bought whichever computer they liked and expected the computers to work together over the network. IP was embraced as a standard by which various machines regardless of operating system could communicate with one another.

At about the same time as the Internet was coming into being, Ethernet local area networks (LANs) were developed. LAN technology matured quietly until roughly 1983, when desktop workstations became available and local networking exploded. At about the same time, many companies and other organizations started building private networks using the same communications protocols as the ARPAnet: namely, IP and its relatives. It became obvious that if these networks could talk together, users on one network could communicate with those on another; everyone would benefit.

One of the most important of these newer networks was the NSFNET, commissioned by the National Science Foundation (NSF), an agency of the U.S. government. In the late 1980s, the NSF created five supercomputer centers at major universities. Up to this point, the world's fastest computers had been available only to weapons developers and a few researchers from very large corporations. By creating supercomputer centers, the NSF was making these resources available for any scholarly research. Only five centers were created because they were so expensive that they had to be shared. This created a communications problem: They needed a way to connect their centers together and to allow the clients of these centers to access them.

At first, the NSF unsuccessfully tried to use the ARPAnet for communications. The NSF decided to build its own network, based on the ARPAnet's IP technology. It connected the centers with 56,000-bits-per-second* telephone lines. Users pay for these telephone lines by the mile. One line per campus with a supercomputing center at the hub adds up to many miles of phone lines. Regional networks were created to help save on cost. In each area of the country, schools would be connected to their nearest neighbor. Each chain was connected to a supercomputer center at one point, and the centers were connected together. With this configuration, any computer could eventually communicate with any other by forwarding the conversation through its neighbors.

This solution was successful—and, like any successful solution, a time came when it no longer worked. Sharing supercomputers also allowed the connected sites to share a lot of other things not related to the centers. Suddenly these schools had a world of data and collaborators at their fingertips. The network's traffic increased until eventually the computers controlling the network, and the telephone lines connecting them, were overloaded. In 1987 a contract to manage and upgrade the network was awarded to Merit Network Inc., which ran Michigan's educational network, in partnership with IBM and MCI. The old network was upgraded with faster telephone lines (by a factor of 20) and faster computers.

---

*This is roughly the ability to transfer two full typewritten pages per second. That's slow by modern standards, but was reasonably fast in the mid-1980s.

The process of running out of horsepower and getting bigger engines and better roads continues to this day. Unlike changes to the highway system, however, most of these changes are not noticed by the people trying to use the Internet to do real work. Like the telephone network, changes occur constantly even though they usually are transparent, if not unknown, to the user. For our purposes, the most important aspect of the NSF's networking effort is that it allowed everyone to access the network. Up to that point, Internet access had been available only to researchers in computer science, government employees, and government contractors. The NSF promoted universal educational access by funding campus connections only if the campus had a plan to spread the access around. Everyone attending a four-year college could become an Internet user.

The demand keeps growing. Now that most four-year colleges are connected, secondary and primary schools are lining up to connect to the Internet. Libraries, too, are getting their links in place. Internet-literate college graduates have talked their employers into connecting corporations to the Internet. All this activity points to continued growth, networking problems to solve, evolving technologies, and job security for networkers. The next logical stage of Internet growth will be from the home market.

## What Makes Up the Internet?

What it is exactly that the Internet comprises is a difficult question; the answer changes over time. Ten years ago the answer would have been easy: all the networks, using the IP protocol, that cooperate to form a seamless network for their collective users. This would include various federal networks, a set of regional networks, campus networks, and some foreign networks.

More recently, some non-IP-based networks saw that the Internet was good. They wanted to provide its services to their clientele. So they developed methods of connecting these "strange" networks (e.g., BITNET, DECnets, etc.) to the Internet. At first these connections, called *gateways,* merely served to transfer electronic mail between the two networks. Some, however, have grown to translate other services between the networks as well. Are they part of the Internet? It depends.

## Who Governs the Internet?

In many ways, the Internet is like a church: It has its council of elders, every member has an opinion about how things should work, and you can either take part or not. It's your choice. The Internet has no president, chief operating officer, or Pope. The constituent networks may have presidents and CEOs, but that's a different issue; there's no single authority figure for the Internet as a whole.

The ultimate authority for where the Internet is going rests with the Internet Society, or ISOC (URL: **http://www.isoc.org**). ISOC is a voluntary membership organization whose purpose is to promote global information exchange through Internet technology. It appoints a council of elders, which has responsibility for the technical management and direction of the Internet.

The council of elders is a group of invited volunteers called the *Internet Architecture Board,* or the IAB (URL: **http://www.iab.org/iab**). The IAB meets regularly to "bless" standards and allocate resources, such as addresses. The IAB is responsible for Internet standards; it decides when a standard is necessary, it considers the problem, adopts a standard, and, appropriately enough, announces it via the network. The IAB also keeps track of various numbers (and other things) that must remain unique. For example, each computer on the Internet has a unique 32-bit address; no other computer has the same address. How does this address get assigned? The IAB worries about this kind of problem. It does not actually assign the addresses, but it makes the rules about how to assign addresses.

As in a church, everyone has opinions about how things ought to run. Internet users express their opinions through meetings of the Internet Engineering Task Force (IETF). The IETF (URL: **http://www.ietf.cnri.reston.va.us**) is another volunteer organization; it meets regularly to discuss operational and near-term technical problems of the Internet. When it considers a problem important enough to merit concern, the IETF sets up a "working group" for further investigation. Working groups have many different functions, ranging from producing documentation, to deciding how networks should cooperate when problems occur, to changing the meaning of the bits in some kind of packet. A working group usually produces a report. Depending on the kind of recommendation, it could just be documentation that is made available to anyone wanting it, it could be accepted voluntarily as a good idea that people follow, or it could be sent to the IAB to be declared a standard.

If you go to a church and accept its teachings and philosophy, you are accepted by it, and receive the benefits. If you don't like it, you can leave. The church is still there, and you get none of the benefits. This analogy fits the Internet. If a network accepts the teachings of the Internet, is connected to it, and considers itself part of it, then it is part of the Internet. It will find things it does not like and can address those concerns through the IETF. Some concerns may be considered valid, and the Internet may change accordingly. Some of the changes may run counter to the religion and be rejected. If the network does something that causes damage to the Internet, it could be excommunicated until it mends its evil ways.

# ▨ *Who Pays for It?*

The old rule for when things are confusing is "follow the money." Well, this will not help you to understand the Internet. No one pays for "it"; there is no Internet, Inc., that collects fees from all Internet networks or users. Instead, everyone pays for their part. The NSF paid for NSFNET. NASA pays for the NASA Science Internet. A college or corporation pays for its connection to a regional network, which in turn pays a national provider for its access.

There is a myth that access to the Internet is free. It is not; someone pays for every connection to the Internet. Many times these fees are not passed on to the actual users, which feeds the illusion of "free access." An increasing number of users know very well that Internet access is not free: Many users pay monthly or hourly charges for Internet access from home at speeds up to 56K bits per second (the same as the original network backbones). Right now, the fastest growth areas for the Internet are small businesses and individuals, and these users are very aware of the price. As the Internet is commercialized, users will be able to see exactly how much their access is costing. For the time being, students may pay for their access only indirectly. The historical precedent of allowing students to use computers without direct charges, however, may not continue into the future.

# ▨ *What Does This Mean for Me?*

The concept that the Internet is not a network, but a collection of networks, means little to the end user. You want to do something useful: find a research source, run a program, or access some unique data. You should not have to worry about how it is all stuck together. Consider the telephone system—it is an internet, too. Pacific Bell, AT&T, MCI, British Telecom, Teléfonos de México, and so on, are all separate corporations that run pieces of the telephone system. *They* worry about how to make it all work together; all you have to do is dial. If you ignore cost and commercials, you should not care if you are dealing with MCI, AT&T, or Sprint. Dial the number and your call goes through. You care who carries your calls only when a problem occurs. If one switch breaks, only the company that owns the switch can fix it. Different phone companies can talk to each other about problems, but each phone carrier is responsible for fixing problems on its own part of the system. The same is true on the Internet. Each network has its own Network Operations Center (NOC). The operations centers talk to each other and know how to resolve problems. Your site has a contract with one of the Internet's constituent networks, and its job is to keep your site happy. If something goes wrong, they are the ones to inform. If it is not their problem, they'll pass it along.

# ■ *What Does the Future Hold?*

Here is a question that can be answered. There's no need for a crystal ball. Planning is an important function for the Internet powers-that-be. IAB and the IETF meeting discussions help set a future course. Most people don't care about the long discussions; they only want to know how they'll be affected. So here are highlights of the networking future.

## *New Standard Protocols*

In noting how the Internet started, we mentioned the Organization for International Standardization and their set of protocol standards. Well, they finally finished designing it. Now it is an international standard, typically referred to as the ISO/OSI (Open Systems Interconnect) protocol suite. Many of the Internet's component networks allow use of OSI today. There is not much demand—yet. The U.S. government has taken a position that government computers should be able to speak these protocols. Many have the software, but few are using it yet.

It is really unclear how much demand there will be for OSI, notwithstanding the government backing. Many believe that because the current approach is not broken, there's no need to fix it. Just as they are becoming comfortable with what they have, a new set of commands and terminology loom with the new standard. Currently there are no real advantages to moving to OSI. It is more complex and less mature than IP, and hence does not work as efficiently. OSI does offer hope of some additional features, but it also suffers from some of the same problems that will plague IP as the network gets much bigger and faster. It is clear that some sites will convert to the OSI protocols over the next few years. The question is: How many?

## *International Connections*

The Internet has been an international network for a long time, but it extended only to the United States' allies and overseas military bases. Advancing technology and global politics have converged to allow the Internet to spread worldwide. It is currently in more than 80 countries (see **http://www.openmarket.com/info/internet-index/ currentsources.html**), and the number continues to increase. Eastern European countries longing for Western scientific ties have wanted to participate for a long time, but were excluded by government regulation. Now that the Iron Curtain no longer exists, they're well represented. Third world countries that formerly did not have the means to participate now view the Internet as a way to raise their education and technology levels.

In Europe, the development of the Internet used to be hampered by national policies mandating OSI protocols, regarding IP as a cultural threat akin to EuroDisney. Outside of Scandinavia (where the Internet protocols were embraced long ago), these policies prevented development of large-scale Internet infrastructures. In 1989, RIPE (Reseaux IP Europeens) began coordinating the operation of the Internet in Europe; today, about 25 percent of all hosts connected to the Internet are located in Europe.

At present, the Internet's international expansion is hampered by the lack of a good supporting infrastructure; namely, the telecommunications infrastructure (telephone system). In both eastern Europe and the third world, state-of-the-art phone systems are lacking. Even in major cities, connections are limited to the speeds available to the average home anywhere in the U.S.—9,600 bits per second. Typically, even if one of these countries is "on the Internet," only a few sites are accessible. Usually, this is the major technical university for that country. However, as phone systems improve and commercial access providers expand into new markets, this will change, too.

## Commercialization

Many big corporations have been on the Internet for years. For the most part, their participation has been limited to their research and engineering departments. The same corporations used some other network (usually a private network) for their business communications. Businesses are now discovering that running multiple networks is expensive. Some are beginning to look to the Internet for "one-stop" network shopping. They stayed away in the past by policies that excluded or restricted commercial use. Most of these policies have fallen by the wayside. Now, corporations may use the Internet as a tool to solve any appropriate business problems.

This should be especially good news for small businesses. Motorola or Standard Oil can afford to run nationwide networks connecting their sites, but Ace Discount Software cannot. If Ace has a San Jose office and a Washington office, all it needs is an Internet connection on each end. For all practical purposes, they have a nationwide corporate network, just like the big boys.

## Privatization

Right behind commercialization comes privatization. For years, the networking community has wanted the telephone companies and other for-profit ventures to provide "off the shelf" IP connections. That is, just as you can place an order for a telephone jack in your house, you could do this for an Internet connection. You order, the telephone installer leaves, and you plug your computer into the Internet. The telephone companies historically stayed with the telephone business and out of the home networking business. By default, the federal government stayed in the networking business.

Now that large corporations have become interested in the Internet, the phone companies have started to change their attitude. They and other profit-oriented network purveyors complained that the government ought to get out of the network business. After all, who best can provide network services but the phone companies? They've got the ear of a lot of political people, to whom it appears to be reasonable. Phone company personnel today are learning about the Internet very quickly.

Since the Clinton administration focused talk of the "national information infrastructure" when its term began, even more players have become involved. The cable TV companies have realized that they too own wire capable of carrying digital signals; that wire already extends into many homes in the U.S. The cable industry has proposed solving the privatization problem by creating its own network with no government investment required. Their network would piggy-back on the existing investment in cable TV. It remains to be seen what will come of this initiative. Cable operators have been slow to show direct involvement in the Internet. It is clear that cable TV companies are interested in applications that are being introduced to the Internet community: interactive home shopping, video games, and so on. Members of the cable industry have less experience in traditional uses of data networking and do not have the track record of reliability that telephone companies and computer network providers have.

Although most people in the networking community think that privatization is a good idea, there are some obstacles in the way. Most revolve around funding for the connections that are already in place. Many schools are connected because the government pays part of the bill. If they had to pay their own way, some schools might have to cut spending elsewhere. Major research institutions would certainly stay on the Net; but some smaller colleges might have more limited access, and the costs could be prohibitive for most secondary schools (let alone grade schools). What if the school could afford either an Internet connection or a science lab? It is unclear which one would get funded. The Internet has not yet become a "necessity" in many people's minds. When it does, expect privatization to come quickly.

We are quickly moving from the era when the network itself was the project, to an era when the network is a tool being used in "real" projects. This is changing the way that governmental subsidies for networking are being distributed. Rather than funding a network connection to a campus, school, agency, or corporation, subsidy money is moving to project budgets. The people who run the projects can then buy Internet services from a variety of vendors in the open marketplace. This makes a lot of people nervous, because it threatens an existing flow of money (something near and dear to the recipients' hearts).

On the other hand, it is probably the only practical way to merge public money and private money into one pool big enough to keep the Internet expanding into the more rural parts of the world.

Well, enough about the history of the information highway system. It is time to walk to the edge of the road, hitch a ride, and be on your way.

## ■ *Exercises*

**1.** Mass media systems and content in the United States have traditionally been subsidized by advertising. This is now occurring with the Internet. What are some implications of commercial sponsorship of the Internet for content made available to end users? Commercial broadcast television in the U.S. is dominated by entertainment programs. Explain why you think this either will or will not happen with the commercialization of the Internet.

**2.** Starr Roxanne Hiltz and Murray Turoff wrote a seminal work, *The Network Nation,* in 1978 (Reading, Mass.: Addison-Wesley) about computer-mediated communication. They made the following predictions about the future of human communication via computer. Although forecasting serves a purpose at the time of the predictions, it can be enlightening to see how well expectations were met. Can you find contemporary evidence to support or refute these predictions from 1978? What can we learn about expectations for the future of the Internet from this?

- Computerized conferencing will be a prominent form of communications in most organizations by the mid-1980s.
- By the mid-1990s, it will be as widely used in society as the telephone today.
- It will offer a home recreational use that will make significant inroads into TV viewing patterns.
- It will have dramatic psychological and sociological impacts on various group communication objectives and processes.
- It will be cheaper than mails or long-distance telephone voice communications.
- It will offer major opportunities to disadvantaged groups in the society to acquire the skills and social ties they need to become full members of the society.
- It will have dramatic impacts on the degree of centralization or decentralization possible in organizations.

- It will become a fundamental mechanism for individuals to form groups having common concerns, interests, or purposes.

- It will facilitate working at home for a large percentage of the workforce during at least half of their normal work week.

- It will have a dramatic impact upon the formation of political and special-interest groups.

- It will open the doors to new and unique types of services.

- It will indirectly allow for sizable amounts of energy conservation through substitution of communication for travel.

- It will dramatically alter the nature of social science research concerned with the study of human systems and human communication processes.

- It will facilitate a richness and variability of human groupings and relationships almost impossible to comprehend.

# CHAPTER THREE

# How the Internet Works

*Moving Bits from One Place to Another
Making the Network Friendly*

Knowing how things work allows you to make sense out of some of the hints you will find in this book. This understanding will help avoid the path of learning by rote. Lest you be frightened away, we will explore this with a maximum amount of hand waving. If you want to know more, there is no lack of reference material on the subject (e.g., see "Internet Protocol Frequently Asked Questions" at URL **http://web.cnam.fr/Network/TCP-IP** or Network Working Group Request for Comments 1180: A TCP/IP Tutorial at URL **http://www.cis.ohio-state.edu/htbin/rfc/rfc1180.html**).

In this section, we will look briefly at packet switched networks and the basic protocol that governs Internet communication: TCP. This makes up the network's building blocks. When you add the Domain Name System (DNS) and a few applications on top of it, it becomes something useful. It is something that you will be using indirectly for your entire Internet career.

## ■ *Moving Bits from One Place to Another*

Modern networking is built around the concept of "layers of service." The physical level consists of wires and hardware. A layer of basic software shields you from the problems of hardware. Add another layer of software to give the basic software some desirable features. You continue to add functionality and intelligence to the network, one layer at a time, until you have something that is friendly and useful.

When you try to imagine what the Internet is and how it operates, it is natural to think of the telephone system. The telephone network, however, is a *circuit switched* network.

When you make a call, you get a part of the network dedicated to you. Even if you are not using it (for example, if you are put on hold), your piece of the network is unavailable to others wishing to do real work. This leads to underutilization of a very expensive resource—the network.

A better model for the Internet is the U.S. Postal Service. The Postal Service is a *packet switched* network. You have no dedicated piece of the network. What you want to send is mixed with everyone else's stuff, put in a pipe, transferred to another post office, and sorted out again. Although the technologies are completely different, the Postal Service is a surprisingly accurate analogy to keep in mind.

## *The Internet Protocol (IP)*

A wire (or other telecommunications medium) carries data from one place to another. The Internet can get data to many different places globally. Computers called *routers* link networks together on the Internet. These networks are sometimes Ethernets, sometimes Token Rings, and sometimes telephone lines, as shown in Figure 3-1.

Telephone lines and Ethernets are equivalent to the trucks and planes of the Postal Service. They are the means by which mail is moved from place to place. The routers are postal substations; they make decisions about how to route data ("packets"), just like a postal substation decides how to route envelopes containing mail. Each substation or router does not have a connection to every other one. If you put an envelope in the mail in Dixville Notch, New Hampshire, addressed to Boonville, California, the Post Office

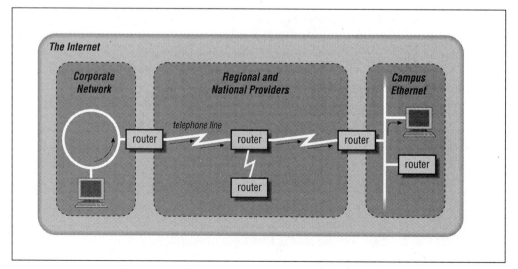

*Figure 3-1    Internet hardware*

does not reserve a plane from New Hampshire to California to carry it. The local Post Office sends the envelope to a substation; the substation sends it to another substation; and this process is repeated until it reaches the destination. That is, each substation needs to know only what connections are available and what is the best "next hop" to get a packet closer to its destination. In the case of the Internet, a router looks at where your data is going and decides where to send it next.

How does the Net know where your data is going? If you want to send a letter, you need to put the paper into an envelope, write an address on the envelope, and stamp it. Just as the Post Office has rules that define how its network works, there are rules that govern how the Internet operates. The rules are called *protocols.* The Internet Protocol (IP) takes care of addressing, or making sure that the routers know what to do with your data when it arrives. Sticking with our Post Office analogy, the Internet Protocol works just like an envelope (Figure 3-2).

Some addressing information goes at the beginning of your message; this information gives the network enough information to deliver the packet of data.

Internet addresses consist of four numbers, each less than 256 (two to the eighth power). When written out, the numbers are separated by periods, like this:

```
192.112.36.5
128.174.5.6
```

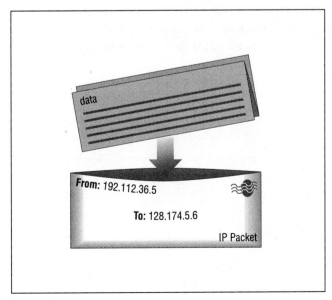

*Figure 3-2   IP envelopes*

The address is made up of multiple parts. Because the Internet is a network of networks, the beginning of the address tells the Internet routers what network you are part of. The rightmost part of the address tells that network which computer or host should receive the packet. This numbering scheme is similar to a telephone number that also goes from most general to most specific beginning with country code, area or city code, and local exchange and number. Like a telephone, every computer on the Internet has a unique, numbered address under this scheme.

Let's return to the postal analogy. Consider the address "50 Kelly Road, Hamden, CT." The "Hamden, CT" portion is like a network address; it gets the envelope to the right local Post Office, the Post Office that knows about streets in a certain area. "50 Kelly Road" is like the host address; it identifies a particular mailbox within the Post Office's service area. The Postal Service has done its job when it has delivered the mail to the right local office, and when that local office has put it into the right mailbox. Similarly, the Internet has done its job when its routers have delivered data to the right network, and when that local network has given the data to the right computer on the network.

For many practical reasons (notably hardware limitations), information sent across IP networks is broken into bite-sized pieces, called *packets*. The information within a packet is usually between one and about fifteen hundred characters long. This prevents any one user of the network from monopolizing the network. It also means that when the network is overloaded, its behavior gets slightly worse for all its users: It does not crash while a few heavy users monopolize it.

One of the amazing things about the Internet is that on a basic level, IP is all you need to participate. If your data is put in an IP envelope, the network has all the information it needs to get your packet from your computer to its destination. Now, however, we need to deal with several problems:

- Most information transfers are not limited to fifteen hundred characters.

- Things can go wrong. The Post Office occasionally loses a letter; networks sometimes lose packets, or damage them in transit.

- Packets may arrive out of sequence. If you mail two letters to the same place on successive days, there is no guarantee that they will take the same route or arrive in order. The same is true of the Internet.

## The Transmission Control Protocol (TCP)

TCP is the protocol that is used to get around these problems. What would happen if you wanted to send a book to someone, but the Post Office accepted only letters? You could rip each page out of the book, put it in a separate envelope, and dump all the

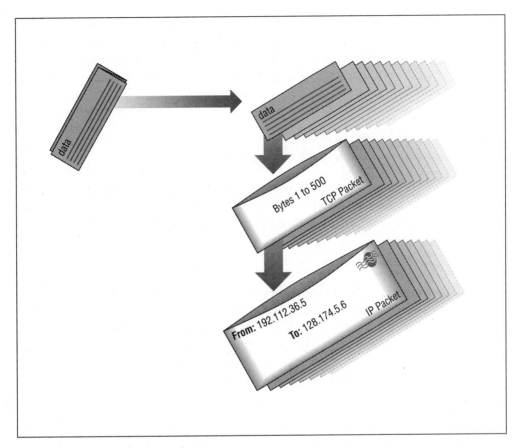

***Figure 3-3***    *TCP packet encapsulation*

envelopes in a mailbox. The recipient would then have to make sure all the pages arrived and paste them together in the right order. This is what TCP does.

TCP takes the information you want to transmit and breaks it into pieces. It numbers each piece so receipt can be verified and the data can be put back in the proper order. To pass this sequence number across the network, it has an envelope of its own that has the information it requires "written on it" (Figure 3-3). A piece of your data is placed in a TCP envelope. The TCP envelope is, in turn, placed inside an IP envelope and given to the network. Once you have something in an IP envelope, the network can carry it.

On the receiving side, a TCP software package collects the envelopes, extracts the data, and puts it in the proper order. If some envelopes are missing, it asks the sender to retransmit them. Once it has all the information in the proper order, it passes the data to whatever application program is using its services.

This is a slightly utopian view of TCP. In the real world not only do packets get lost, they can also be changed in transit by glitches on telephone lines. TCP also handles this problem by requesting a retransmission if necessary. TCP creates the appearance of a dedicated wire between the two applications, guaranteeing that what goes in one side comes out the other.

# Making the Network Friendly

Now that we can transfer information between places on the network, we can start working on making the Internet more friendly. This is done by having software tailored to the task at hand, and using names rather than numbered addresses to refer to computers.

## The Domain Name System

Fairly early on, people realized that addresses were fine for machines communicating with machines, but humans preferred names. It is hard to talk using addresses (who would say, "I was connected to 205.217.107.0 yesterday"?) and even harder to remember them. Computers on the Internet were given names for the convenience of their human users. The preceding conversation might become, "I was connected to CNN yesterday and …". All of the Internet applications today let you use system names rather than host addresses.

Of course, naming introduces problems of its own. For one thing, you have to make sure that no two computers connected to the Internet have the same name. You also have to provide a way to convert names into numeric addresses. You can give a program a name, but it needs some way to look that name up and convert it into an address (like looking someone up in the phone book).

In the early days, dealing with Internet names was easy. The NIC (Network Information Center) set up a registry. Users would send in a form electronically, and the NIC would add it to the list of names and addresses it maintained. This hosts file was distributed regularly to every machine on the network. The names were simple words, every one chosen to be unique. If you used a name, your computer would look it up in the file and substitute the address. When the Internet grew, so did the size of the file. There were significant delays in getting a name registered, and it became increasingly difficult to find names that were not already used. Also, too much network time was spent distributing this large file to every machine contained in it. Clearly, a distributed, online system was required to cope with the rate of change. This system is called the *Domain Name System* or *DNS*.

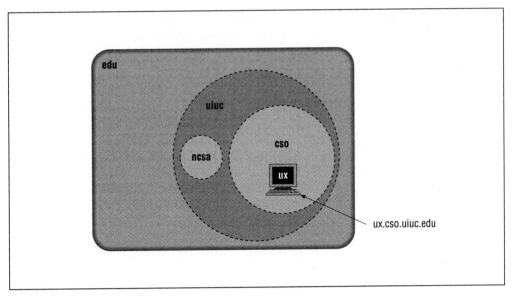

*Figure 3-4   Domain authority*

### The Domain System Structure

The Domain Name System administers names by giving different groups responsibility for subsets of the names. Each level in this system is called a *domain*. The domains are separated by periods:

```
ux.cso.uiuc.edu
nic.ddn.mil
yoyodyne.com
```

There can be any number of domains within the name, but you will rarely see more than five. Like a telephone number from left to right, each domain is larger than the previous one. In the name **ux.cso.uiuc.edu**, **ux** is the name of a host, a real computer with an IP address (Figure 3-4). The name for that computer is created and maintained by the **cso** group, which happens to be the department where the computer resides. The department **cso** is a part of the University of Illinois at Urbana Champaign (**uiuc**); **uiuc** is part of the national group of educational institutions (**edu**). So the domain **edu** contains all computers in all U.S. educational institutions; the domain **uiuc.edu** contains all computers at the University of Illinois, and so on.

Each group can create or change whatever lies within it. If **uiuc** decided to create another group called **ncsa**, it could do so without asking anyone's permission. All it has to do is add the new names to its part of the worldwide database, and eventually everyone who needs to know will find out about the new name (**ncsa.uiuc.edu**). Similarly, **cso** can buy a new computer, assign it a name, and add it to the network without asking anyone's permission. If every group from **edu** on down plays by the rules and makes sure that the names it assigns are unique, no two systems anywhere on the Internet will have the same name. You could have two machines named **fred**, but only if they are in different domains (for example, **fred.cso.uiuc.edu** and **fred.ora.com**).

It is easy to see where domains and names come from within an organization like a university or a business. However, where do the "top-level" domains such as **edu** come from? They were created by *fiat* when the domain system was invented. Originally, there were six highest-level domains (see Table 3-1).

*Table 3-1    Original High-Level Domains*

| Domain | Usage |
|--------|-------|
| com | For commercial organizations (i.e., businesses) |
| edu | Educational organizations (universities, secondary schools, etc.) |
| gov | Governmental organizations, non-military |
| mil | Military (army, navy, etc.) |
| org | Other organizations |
| net | Network resources |

As the Internet became an international network, a way was needed to give foreign countries responsibility for their own names. To this end, there is a set of two-letter domains that correspond to the highest-level domains for countries. Because **ca** is the country code for Canada, a Canadian computer might be named:

```
hockey.guelph.ca
```

There are almost 300 country codes; about 150 of those countries have some kind of computer networking. There is a list of the country codes in Appendix B, *International Network Connectivity,* in case you want to see where mail you received came from.

It's worth noting that the U.S. has its own country code, although it has not been used much; in the U.S., most network sites use the "organizational" domains (such as **edu**), rather than the "geographical" domains (such as **va.us**—Virginia). One computer may even have both kinds of names just for completeness. There is no way to "convert" between organizational names and geographical names. For example, although **uxc.cso.uiuc.edu** happens to be in Urbana, Illinois, USA, there is not necessarily a name **uxc.urbana.il.us**.

### Domain Name System Hints

There are a few common misconceptions that you may encounter dealing with names. Here are "truths" to prevent those misconceptions from taking root:

- The pieces of a domain-style name tell you who is responsible for maintaining the name. It may not tell you anything about who maintains the computer corresponding to that IP address, or even (despite the country codes) where that machine is located. It would be perfectly legal for me to have the name **oz.cso.uiuc.edu** (part of the University of Illinois' name space) point to a machine in Australia.

- The pieces of a domain name do not even necessarily tell you on what network a computer is located. Domain names and networking often overlap, but there is no necessary connection between them; two machines that are in the same domain may not be on the same network. For example, the systems **uxc.cso.uiuc.edu** and **ux1.cso.uiuc.edu** may be on different networks.

- A machine can have multiple names, and names (unlike addresses) are portable. This is especially true of machines that offer services, where the service may be moved to a different computer in the future. People wanting the particular service use the same name, no matter which computer is providing the service. Names that symbolically refer to a service are aliases for the unique "canonical name" or *cname* of a computer. You will see symbolic names frequently as you wander about the Internet.

- Names are not necessary for communication. Unless the error message you receive is "host unknown," the name worked fine. A message like "host unknown" means your system could not translate the name you gave it into an address. Once your system has the address in hand, it never uses the name again.

- The problem with addresses is that they are tied to a network. If the computer providing a service is moved from one building to another, its network, and hence its address, is likely to change. The name, fortunately, need not change. The administrator needs only to update the name record so that the name points to the new address. Because the name still works, you do not particularly care if the computer or function has changed locations. We can be reasonably sure that **www.mci.com** will take us to MCI (until and unless MCI changes its company or service names).

The Domain Name System may sound complicated, but it is one of the things that make the Internet a comfortable place to live. You will quickly begin to decipher Internet addresses. The real advantage of the domain system is that it breaks the gigantic worldwide Internet into a set of manageable pieces. Although hundreds of thousands of computers are "on the Net," they're all named; and the names are organized in a convenient, perhaps even rational, way, making it easier for you to remember the ones you need.

## ▨ *Exercises*

**1.** Explain what is meant by a dedicated line. The telephone network itself has been in the process of converting from old analog technology (one phone call literally ties up one phone line) to digital technology using packets (bursts of digital information) typical of computer networks. Can you explain how a digital telephone system increases the overall capacity of the telephone network by not requiring a dedicated line for each phone call?

**2.** *Bandwidth* in networks refers to the amount of data that can be carried (in bits per second) by a channel. The unit of measure is hertz (cycles per second). One television channel (6 megahertz) equals nearly 10,000 telephone channels (3 to 3.5 kilohertz). What are some possible implications of this for cable television operators offering Internet services into homes and businesses?

**3.** The Internet Archive is housed at Ohio State University (URL: **http://www.cis.ohio-state.edu/hypertext/information/rfc.html**). This collection includes The Internet Request For Comments (or RFC) documents, the written definitions of the protocols and policies of the Internet.

If you are able to reach a WWW address, try this one:

> `http://www.cis.ohio-state.edu/htbin/rfc/rfc1206.html`

which brings you to this table of contents:

```
Network Working Group                              T. Socolofsky
Request for Comments:  1180                             C. Kale
Spider Systems Limited January 1991
A TCP/IP Tutorial
Status of this Memo

This RFC is a tutorial on the TCP/IP protocol suite, focusing particularly on
the steps in forwarding an IP datagram from source host to destination host
through a router. It does not specify an Internet standard. Distribution of this
memo is unlimited.

Table of Contents
1. Introduction
2. TCP/IP Overview
3. Ethernet
4. ARP
5. Internet Protocol
6. User Datagram Protocol
7. Transmission Control Protocol
8. Network Applications
```

```
 9. Other Information
10. References
11. Relation to other RFCs
12. Security Considerations
13. Authors' Addresses
```

Is this document accessible (understandable) to a new Internet user? What else is there of possible interest to new Internet users?

**4.** WWW commercial domain names are best if chosen in a way that makes it easy for users to find them. For example, a typical WWW domain name is **www.company.com.** Is there a **www.apple.com** or a **www.ibm.com**? How might these companies use additional domain names to take users to more specific areas?

# CHAPTER FOUR

# WHAT'S ALLOWED ON THE INTERNET?

*Legal Implications*
*Politics and the Internet*
*Network Ethics*
*Ethics and the Private Commercial Internet*
*Security Consciousness*

Before talking about how to use the Internet, we must first examine what is allowed on the network. This complex issue is influenced by law, ethics, and politics. How these interrelate, and which is paramount, vary from place to place (or, in Net terms, from site to site). Remember that the Internet isn't a network—it's a network of networks—each of which may have its own policies and rules. Lest you give up before starting, the rules are reasonably uniform, and you'll be safe if you keep a few guidelines in mind. Fortunately, these guidelines aren't terribly restrictive; so long as you stay within them, you can do whatever you want. If you are in doubt about what is permissible at your site, contact your network provider to find out. It may be possible to do what you want, but it's your responsibility to ask. Ignorance of the policies is no excuse for inappropriate behavior. Let's look at some key issues you need to consider when using the Internet.

## ▉ *Legal Implications*

Three areas of the law affect the Internet:

- Federal subsidies pay for large sections of the Internet. These subsidies exclude purely commercial use.

- The Internet is not just a nationwide network, but a truly global network. When shipping anything across a national boundary, including bits, export laws come into effect and local laws change.

- Whenever you are shipping software (or, for that matter, ideas) from one place to another, you must consider intellectual property and license issues.

## Research, Education, and Federal Support

Many of the networks in the Internet are sponsored by federal agencies. Under federal law, an agency may spend its budget only on things that it is charged to do. For example, the U.S. Air Force can't secretly increase its budget by ordering rockets through NASA.

These same laws apply to the network—if NASA funds a network, it must be used for space science. As a user, you may have no idea which networks your packets are traversing, but they must fall within the scope of each network's funding agency.

Actually, it's not as bad as it sounds. A few of years ago, the folks in Washington realized that multiple parallel IP networks (NSFNET, NASA Science Internet, etc.—one network per federal agency) was an unnecessary duplication of resources. Legislation was passed to create the National Research and Education Network, or NREN. This was to be a portion of the Internet dedicated to supporting research and education that was common to all federal agencies. This means that you can use the NREN* to do basic research and education, or in support of research and education.

The importance of the clause "in support of research or education" cannot be overemphasized. This provision legitimizes important ways to use the network that might seem inappropriate. For example, if a vendor markets software that is used in research or education, it can distribute updates and answer questions through electronic mail. This usage is considered "in support of research or education" *(RE)*. The vendor cannot use the NREN for business functions, such as marketing, billing, or accounting. For this, it must use a commercial part of the Internet.†

Lately, a lot of attention has been focused on the NII (National Information Infrastructure). The NII is a large and relatively vague proposal for nationwide networking. It could be considered a long-term plan for the NREN's direction; it could be considered a replacement for the NREN. The fact is, right now, no one really knows. There are many players (including the current network providers, phone companies, cable TV companies, and even electric power companies) trying to make sure the chips fall in their territory. There is little discussion about the NII in this book because we're examining the network that exists now, not the one that might exist in a few years. The NII will have a major impact on networking in the U.S., but until the smoke clears, we won't know what that impact is. Everyone involved is promising easier access, lower prices, and higher data rates, and this seems to be an inevitable trend. The more unpredictable element is the interplay of various political factors.

---

*Actually, the NREN is a real network that hasn't yet been built. The bill also authorizes this traffic on existing federal networks. The correct term for what we have now is the *Interim Interagency NREN*.

†A copy of the official NSFNET acceptable use policy is included in Appendix C, *Acceptable Use*. It is one of the most restrictive with regard to commercial use. If your usage is acceptable to NSFNET, it is likely acceptable to the other networks as well.

## Commercial Use

When your site arranged for its Internet connection, someone needed to tell the network provider whether the connection would be use for research and education or for commercial purposes. Assuming your site decided it is research and education, your network traffic is routed to prefer subsidized NREN routes. If yours were a commercial site, your traffic is routed over private routes. Network access fees depend on these decisions; commercial use is generally more expensive than research and education because the former is not subsidized. Only someone in your network administration can tell you whether commercial dealings are allowed over your connection. If you are using a university account, it's safe to assume commercial use is forbidden.

Of course, many corporations join the Internet as research and education sites. This is appropriate, since the motivation for joining the Internet is often research. For example, a seed company may wish to do joint soybean research with a university. Many corporate legal departments, however, decide to declare their connections commercial. This ensures that there will not be a legal liability in the future, in case some uninformed employee uses the research connection for commercial work. To many businesses, the added fees are well worth the peace of mind.

There are a number of commercial Internet providers: Advanced Networks and Services (ANS), Performance Systems International (PSI), and UUNET to name a few. Each of these companies developed its own market niche and its own national network to provide commercial Internet services. In addition, state and regional networks carry commercial traffic for their members. There are connections between each of these and the federally supported networks. Using these connections and some creative accounting agreements, all of these networks interoperate legally.

## Export Laws

Whether you know it or not, exporting bits falls under the auspices of the Department of Commerce export restrictions.* As a virtually seamless global network, the Internet is very easy to use for exporting items without your knowledge. A body of networking legal research will continue to grow as new problems are uncovered. Although not giving legal advice, we try here to sketch what is required to keep Internet use legal. If after reading this you have concerns about your use, seek competent legal help.

---

*This is strictly a U.S.-centric discussion. Other laws apply to servers in other countries.

Export law is based on two points:

- Exporting anything requires a license
- Exporting a service is roughly equivalent to exporting the pieces necessary to provide that service

The first point is fairly obvious: If you ship, carry, transfer a file, or electronically mail anything out of the country, it needs to be covered by an export license. A loophole called a *general license* allows you to export anything that is not explicitly restricted and is readily available in public forums in the United States. Anything you can learn from walking into a conference or classroom that does not have security restrictions is probably covered by the general license.

The list of restricted items, however, has a lot of surprises and does cover things that you can learn as a student in any university. Networking code and encryption code might be restricted, based upon their capabilities. At times, one item of concern results in regulations that are then written to cover a much wider area. For example, during the Persian Gulf War, it was more difficult to knock out Iraq's command and control network than anticipated. It turned out they were using commercial IP routers that worked, as designed, to find alternative routes quickly. Suddenly, exporting any router that could find alternate routes became a concern for national security.*

The second point is even simpler. If exporting some hardware such as a supercomputer is not allowed, remote access to that hardware within this country is prohibited as well. System operators must be careful about granting access to "special" resources (like supercomputers) to people in foreign countries. The exact nature of these restrictions depends, of course, on the foreign country and (depending on the world political scene) can change quickly. When investigating their potential for legal liability, the consortium that runs the BITNET (CREN) came to the following conclusions:† A network operator is responsible for illegal export only if the operator was aware of the violation and failed to inform proper authorities; the network operator isn't responsible for monitoring your usage and determining whether or not it's within the law. Network personnel nationwide probably are not snooping through your packets to see what you are shipping overseas, but the U.S. government has pushed the notion of keeping the network open for its checking where deemed appropriate. If a network technician sees your packets and knows

---

*This story may actually be a network "urban legend." Everyone on the Net talked about this situation, but when verification was sought, a definitive source could not be found.

†The actual legal opinions are available on the network; see the *Resource Catalog* under "Law—Corporation for Research and Educational Networking." NAFTA makes regulating access between North American countries less relevant (see Alexandra Field, "Current Developments in the FCC: Telecommunications and the NAFTA." *Law & Policy in International Business* 1994, v. 25 n. 3, p. 1145–1151).

they are obviously in violation of some regulation, the technician is obliged to inform the government.

## *Property Rights*

Property rights can also become an issue when you ship something to someone else. The problem gets even more confusing when the communication is across national borders. Copyright and patent laws vary greatly from country to country. You might find on the network a curious volume of forgotten lore whose copyright has expired in the U.S. Shipping these files to England might place you in violation of British law. Know who has the rights to anything you give away across the network. If it is not yours, make sure you have permission before giving something away.

The law surrounding electronic communication has not kept pace with the technology. If you have a book, journal, or personal letter, you can ask almost any lawyer or librarian if you can copy or use it in a particular manner. They can tell you whose permission you need to obtain. Ask the same question regarding a network bulletin board posting, an electronic mail message, or a report in a file available on the network, and they will throw up their hands. Even if you knew whose permission to obtain and obtained that permission via electronic mail, it's not clear whether an e-mail message offers any useful protection. Be aware that this is a murky part of law that is likely to be hammered out in the next decade. Please note that property rights can be a problem even when using publicly available files. Some software available for public retrieval through the Internet must be licensed from the vendor. For example, a workstation vendor might make updates to its operating system software available via anonymous FTP. You can easily get the software, but in order to use it legally you must hold a valid software maintenance license. Just because a file is there for the taking doesn't mean that taking it is legal. As for your own materials, a simple rule of thumb applies: Anything you make available online is likely to be available to an unintended user.

## ▉ *Politics and the Internet*

Many network users view the political process as both a blessing and a curse. The blessing is funding. Subsidies provide many people with a utility they could not afford otherwise. The curse is that their individual actions are under constant scrutiny. Questionable uses of the Internet can become the target of political attack. The digitized centerfold accessible via the Internet can suddenly become the focus of an editorial entitled "Tax Dollars Fund Pornography Distribution."* This causes everyone responsible for the Internet's funding to commit undesired expenditures of energy on "damage control."

---

*Something like this actually happened. The files were slightly more explicit than centerfolds, and it did jeopardize the funding of the entire NSFNET.

The Internet does have many political supporters, including members of Congress (including Newt Gingrich), the Clinton administration, educational leaders, and heads of federal agencies. They support the Internet because it benefits the country: It increases the United States' ability to compete in international research and trade. A state-of-the-art computer network allows the research and educational process to speed up; because of the Net, researchers and their students can develop better solutions to technical problems. As is typical in the political world, there are also those who do not see the benefits as readily. The millions of dollars spent on the network are likely to come under additional scrutiny as the Republican-controlled Congress looks to privatize where possible (public broadcasting is another example).

The bottom line in the politics of networking is that political support for the network is broad, but relatively thin. Any act that can cause political waves might radically change it. The best approach is for all users to respect the intent of the Internet and to do their best to avoid abusing it.

## ■ *Network Ethics*

For the novice network user, the apparent lack of ethics on the network is fairly disquieting. The network is actually a very ethical place, but the ethics are often learned through experience. To understand this, consider the term "frontier justice." When the West was young, there was a set of laws for the United States, but they were applied differently west of the Mississippi River. Today the network is on the frontier of technology, and "frontier justice" seems to apply here too. You can delve safely, provided you know what to expect. The two overriding premises of network ethics are:

- Individualism is honored and fostered
- The network is good and must be protected

Notice how these are very close to the frontier ethics of the West, where individualism and preservation of lifestyle were paramount. Let's look a bit more at how these points play off each other on the network.

### *Individualism*

In society, everyone may claim to be an individual, but often their individualism is compromised by the need for a sufficiently large group that shares their concerns. This is called critical mass. You may love medieval French poetry, but trying to start a local group to discuss it would be difficult. You probably won't be able to find sufficient interest from people who are willing to meet often enough to support a chain of discussions. In order to at least get some interaction for your love, you join a poetry society with more general interests—perhaps one on medieval poetry in general. Maybe there's only one poetry society in town, and it spends most of its time discussing bad pseudoreligious verse. That's the problem with critical mass. If you can't assemble enough people to form a group, you suffer. You may join a larger group out of necessity, but it may not be what you want.

On the network, "critical mass" is two users. You can interact when you want and how you want (assuming sufficient telecommunications lines). Geography is irrelevant. A colleague can be anywhere on the network (virtually anywhere in the world). Therefore, a group, no matter how specific, is possible. Even competing groups are likely to form. Some groups may choose to "meet" by electronic mail, some on bulletin boards, some by making files publicly available, and some by other means. People are free to operate in the manner they like.

Since no one needs to join a large group to enjoy critical mass, everyone is part of some minority group. Everyone is equally at risk of being singled out for persecution or electronic "flaming." Many Internet users want to avoid any threat of outside censorship, because that could result in the Net's becoming less useful.

Of course, individualism is a two-edged sword. It makes the network a nice place for finding diverse information and people, but it may tax your personal code of appropriate and inappropriate material. People have many differing opinions about acceptable behavior. If you put your machine on the network, you should realize that many users feel that any files that they can get to are fair game to retrieve. After all, if you didn't intend to make them available, you shouldn't have put them there. This view, of course, has no basis in law, but it brings us back to the "frontier justice" analogy.

## *Protecting the Internet*

Frequent users find the Internet extremely valuable for both work and play. Since access to the Internet frequently comes at no personal, direct expense (or very little), they view this valuable resource as something that must be protected. The threats to the Internet come from two sources:

- Excessive use for unintended purposes
- Political pressures

The NREN is being built with a purpose. A company's commercial connection to the Internet has a purpose. Chances are no one will prosecute a person who uses these connections for unintended purposes, but it is still discouraged by other means. If you use an employer's computer for a bit of personal business, such as balancing your checkbook, it will probably be ignored. Likewise, small amounts of network time used for unintended purposes will likely be ignored. (In fact, many seemingly unintended uses, say a high school student playing a game across the network, might actually qualify as intended. She must have learned a lot about computing and networking to get that far.) It is only when someone does something blatant, perhaps organizing a nationwide multiuser dungeon game day on the network, that problems occur.

Unintended use also takes the form of ill-conceived supported usage. The network was not built to be a substitute for inadequate local facilities. For example, using an exported disk system halfway across the world because you have no space on your computer's hard drive is unacceptable. You may need the disk to do valuable research, but the cost of providing that storage across the network is outrageous. The network was designed to allow easy access to unique resources, not gratuitous access to common ones.

Heavy network users and network providers are not stodgy. They enjoy a game as well as the next guy. They are also not stupid. They read news. They work on the network regularly. If performance goes bad for no apparent reason, they investigate. If they find that the traffic in a particular area has gone up a hundredfold, they will want to know why. If you are the "why" and the use is unacceptable, you will probably get a polite electronic mail message asking you to stop. After that, you may get some less polite messages; finally, someone will contact your local network provider. Where fees are based upon traffic, this problem will be that much more of a concern.

Self-regulation is important because of the politics that surround the network. No reasonable person could expect the network to exist without occasional abuses and problems. However, if these problems aren't resolved within the network community, but are thrown into newspapers and Congress, everyone loses. To summarize, here are some areas that are considered politically damaging to the network and should be avoided:

- Excessive game playing
- Excessive ill-conceived use
- Knowingly denying others access while using the Net for trivial purposes
- Hateful, harassing, or other antisocial behavior
- Intentional damage or interference with others (e.g., the Internet Worm*)
- Publicly accessible obscene files

It is difficult to justify the NREN's budget to Congress if "Sixty Minutes" is doing a feature on network abuse the Sunday before the budget hearings.

---

*The Internet Worm was a program that used the Internet to attack certain types of computers on the network. It would gain unauthorized access to computers and then use those computers to try to break in to others. It was a lot like a personal computer "virus," but technically it is called a worm because it did not cause intentional damage to its hosts. For a good description, see *Computer Security Basics* (Russell and Gangemi), O'Reilly & Associates.

## Ethics and the Private Commercial Internet

In the previous few sections, we talked about the political and social climate that got the Internet to where it is today. However, the climate is changing. Every day the percentage of Internet funding that comes from the federal government grows smaller and smaller because of increased commercial usage. It is the government's goal to get out of the networking business and turn over the providing of Internet services to private industry. The obvious question is: If the government is getting out of the Internet business, do I still have to play by its rules? There are two issues to be dealt with, one personal and one commercial.

On the personal side, if you get your connection through a school, employer, Free-Net, or anyone else who is paying for that access, they may still require you to follow a set of policies. You may have to give up some freedom to prevent losing your subsidized network connection. It's your responsibility to find out what your network provider considers "acceptable use." The issue on the commercial side is trying to do business in tune with the Internet's culture.

Although the culture is under stress and changing all the time, there was until quite recently a core sentiment on the Internet against blatant commercialism. Sending an electronic mail message advertising a product to everyone on the Internet remains an affront to most users. The Internet culture isn't necessarily opposed to advertising, but it demands that you view advertising as an information service. There would be nothing wrong, in terms of policy or culture, with an auto manufacturer putting up a server with pictures of its cars, technical data sheets, and information about options. If an Internet user wanted to buy a car, he could comparison-shop from his terminal, decide what he wanted, and visit one dealer, rather than three, to do a test drive. Many users would welcome this kind of service, and many such resources are coming online each month.* In the future, you might even be able to do your test drive over the Internet via a virtual-reality simulation. If we become deluged with unsolicited e-mail selling everything from vinyl siding to sexy underwear, the market for intelligent interpreters that eliminate such messages will grow quickly.

## Security Consciousness

A computer connected to the Internet is not, in itself, a much different security problem than a machine you can dial in to with a modem. The problems are the same; it's the magnitude of the problem that changes. Anyone can dial a known modem number and try to break in to a system. There are three mitigating factors: The computer's phone

---

*O'Reilly & Associate's *Global Network Navigator* (GNN), for example; for information, send e-mail to **info@gnn.com**.

number need not be widely known; if the intruder is outside your local calling area, a long-distance charge will be assessed; and there is only one interface that can be attacked.

If you are on the Internet, the mitigating factors are gone. The general address of your network is easily found, and an intruder would only have to try a few host numbers before stumbling onto an active one. In principle, this is still no worse than computer services that provide dial-in access to their machines through toll-free 800 numbers. The problem is that those services have staff who focus on security, and there is still only one point from which to break in: the ASCII terminal port. On the Internet, someone could try to break in through the interactive terminal port, the file transfer port, the e-mail port, and so on. Someone can pull a workstation out of the box and put it on the Internet without thinking about security at all. He or she plugs the machine in, turns it on, and it works. The job is done, until someone breaks in and does something that causes harm. In the long run, it is less time-consuming to put a little thought into security beforehand than to deal with it after the fact.

Start by having the right attitude toward security. Believe that it is your workstation's responsibility to protect itself, and not the network's job to protect it. A network provider can restrict who may talk over your connection. However, that probably isn't what you want, because it strips away much of the Internet's value. Most of this book describes how to reach out to random places and find valuable sources. A network conversation is a two-way pipe. In order to take advantage of the Internet, you must be a part of it. This puts your computer at risk, so you need to protect it.

Security on the Internet is really a group effort by the whole community. One technique that break-in artists use is to break in to a chain of computers (e.g., break in to A, use A to break in to B, use B to break in to C, etc.). This allows them to cover their tracks more completely. Even if there's nothing of use on your computer, it's a worthwhile intermediary for someone who wants to break in to an important system.

Discussing security and rumors of security problems is a bit tricky. To tackle the task of investigating a purported problem, finding a solution, and informing people without making the problem worse, the government has funded an organization named *CERT:* the Computer Emergency Response Team. CERT does a number of things. It investigates security problems, works with manufacturers to solve them, and announces the solutions. It also produces a number of aids to allow people to assess the security of their computers. CERT prefers to work with site security personnel but will, in an emergency, field questions from anyone. If you feel you are out in the woods alone and must talk to someone about security, you can contact them via electronic mail at:

    cert@cert.sei.cmu.edu

There are four ways in which network machines become compromised. In decreasing order of likelihood, these are:*

- Valid users choosing bad passwords
- Valid users importing corrupt software
- Illegal users entering through misconfigured software
- Illegal users entering through an operating system security flaw

You can draw one very important conclusion from this list. It is well within your ability to protect your system. Let's look at what you can do to stay out of trouble.

## Passwords

Most people choose passwords for their convenience. Unfortunately, what is convenient for you is also convenient for the hacker. CERT believes that 80 percent of computer break-ins are caused by poor password choice. When it comes to passwords, computers break in, not people. Some program spends all day trying out possible passwords. You can easily make it very difficult to guess the right password. Most password crackers start with common words from the dictionary and simple names. Here are some suggestions on choosing a good password:

- Is at least six characters long
- Has a mixture of uppercase, lowercase, and numbers
- Is not a word
- Is not a set of adjacent keyboard keys (e.g., QWERTY)

It is hard for many people to create a password that will meet all these criteria and still be easy to remember. One common thing is to pick the first letters of a favorite phrase, such as *FmdIdgad* (Frankly my dear, I don't give a damn).

## Importing Software

The following story illustrates the second most common source of security problems:†

> Two Cornell University undergraduates were arrested for computer tampering. They tampered with a Tetris-style game on a public server at the school. When played, the game would appear to work normally, but would cause damage to the machine running it. It was spread throughout the world by computer networks. The FBI is investigating and expects further charges to be filed ...

---

*A good place to look if you want to learn more about security issues is RFC1244 and the CERT server machine (see the *Resource Catalog* under "Security"). Also, see *Computer Security Basics* (Russell and Gangemi) for a general discussion of security issues, and *Practical UNIX Security* (Garfinkel and Spafford) for UNIX-related system administration issues. Both are published by O'Reilly & Associates.

†This story is a paraphrase of an article in the newsgroup *clari.biz.courts,* February 26, 1992.

This is a classic "Trojan horse" program: something threatening hidden in a gift.

Whenever you put software on your machine, you place it at risk. Sharing software can be a great benefit. Only you can decide whether the risk is worth it. Buying commercial software entails minimal risk, especially if you buy from reputable vendors. On the network there are no assurances. What can you do to make using it as safe as possible? Here are some rules of thumb:

- Try to use official sources. If you are after a Microsoft software update, it's safer to get the code from a machine whose name ends with **microsoft.com** than **hacker.hoople.usnd.edu**.

- Be aware that even "public domain" or "free" software can be risky.* You have to decide how much risk you are willing to live with.

- Before installing the software on an important, heavily used system, run it for a while on a less critical computer. If you have one machine on which you do your life's work and another that is only used occasionally, put the new software on the second machine. See if anything bad happens.

- Do a complete backup of your files before using the software. If you're using a PC or Macintosh, use a virus checker to test the integrity of any software you get from the Net.

*Remember:* Only files that are executed can cause damage. Binary files are the most dangerous; source code is much safer. Data files are never a threat to a computer—though you should be aware that data files may be inaccurate.

## Misconfigured Software

Some system software has debugging options that can be turned on or off at installation or startup time. These options are occasionally left enabled on production systems—either inadvertently, or so the developers can get in at a later time (for example, if you start having problems) and see what's going on. However, any hole that's large enough to let a legitimate software developer in can also let a cracker in. Some break-ins (including the Internet Worm) have occurred through these means. Make sure that, unless needed, debugging options are turned off on system software. Most vendors configure their operating systems to run everything right out of the box. This makes it easier to install; if all the options are turned on automatically, you don't have to run around figuring out which are needed. Unfortunately, this practice also makes it easier for someone to break in.

---

*We do not, of course, mean software produced by the Free Software Foundation. That software is trustworthy—at least in its original state. We'll repeat the first point: It's worth making sure you get an official copy of the sources.

## System Software Flaws

The competition in computer operating systems can lead to market introduction before all possible problems are discovered. Operating system flaws are either found and fixed, or "workaround" procedures are developed quickly. A computer manufacturer doesn't want his product to get a reputation as an easy mark for break-ins. The bigger problem comes after the manufacturer takes corrective action. You need to get the update and install it before it will protect anything. And you can install software updates only if you know that they exist. Therefore, you need to keep up with the current state and release of your operating system. The easiest way to do this is to maintain a dialog with your software support staff. It's also worth watching newsgroups and mailing lists where your system is discussed. We cover that in the chapter on USENET newsgroups.

## What If My Computer Is Violated?

The first question to ask is really, "How will I know if my computer is violated?" Someone who breaks in tries to be as discreet as possible, covering his tracks as he goes. Once you discover him, you should take corrective action. So, how do you discover a break-in?

Most people don't take advantage of security information provided regularly by their computer. Let's say that your machine tells you, "Last login 06:31 26 Jan 1996." Can you remember when you last logged in? Probably not exactly. But you might notice that a login at 6:30 A.M. was strange, given your usual work habits. This is how many break-ins are discovered. The process often starts when someone simply "feels" that something is wrong. For example:

- I don't think I logged in then
- The machine feels slow today
- I don't remember deleting or changing that file

If something like this happens, don't just say, "Oh well" and move on. Investigate further. If you suspect that you have been the target of a break-in, there are a few things your system administrator should investigate. That process will not start automatically if you don't alert someone to your concerns. Act quickly to get help; do not try to proceed on your own. Don't destroy anything before you get help. Don't do another disk dump onto a standard tape or diskette backup yet—the backup tape you are overwriting may be the last uncorrupted one around. Don't assume that closing one hole fixes the problem. When a break-in artist gains access, the first thing he will do is cover his tracks. Next, he'll create more holes to maintain access to your system.

All of this may sound frightening, but don't let fear paralyze you. After all the cautions I've given, paralysis might sound like a good option. However, the non-networked world is full of dangers, too; if you become overzealous about eliminating danger, you'll spend the rest of your life in a cocoon. Most people don't intentionally subject themselves to dangers that they could easily minimize, and they try to live with the dangers that they can't minimize. They wear seat belts; they don't stop traveling. In the network's world, you need to do the same thing. Make sure your password is good, be careful about installing public domain software, watch your system so that you'll be aware of a break-in if one happens, and get help if you need it.

## ▣ *Exercises*

**1.** *Time* magazine's July 3, 1995, issue carried a disturbing cover story: "On a Screen Near You: Cyberporn," by Philip Elmer-DeWitt. This article is typical of many that appeared as Internet accessibility grew into the mainstream in the 1990s.

Do you believe the Internet should be allowed the same First Amendment rights and protections given to newspapers? Why or why not? If not, should a newspaper be held to a different standard when it begins publishing on the WWW?

**2.** The vast resources available on the Internet may be likened to those found in a huge bookstore, newsstand, library, or even a video store. Selected material may be personally objectionable to some people in any of these outlets whether it be pornographic or political. What precautions, if any, are taken by each outlet to monitor access to materials? Are there corollaries for Internet access to personally objectionable material?

**3.** What new technologies are being introduced that will allow parents to monitor what their children access online?

**4.** What virus-checking program(s) do you have on the computer you are using to access the Internet? How is it used? What happens if a virus is detected?

**5.** The Internet was originally intended for and dominated by research applications. How has the commercialization of the Internet changed this?

**6.** Find five different Internet service providers in your area (off campus). What do they charge as a setup fee? How many hours per month does the subscription cover? What is the hourly charge beyond that? What Internet services are provided? What other services are included? What is their statement on subscriber privacy?

**7.** The Electronic Frontier Foundation (URL: **http://www.eff.org**) is a good resource for privacy-related information. Using this and other sources, what are five top privacy concerns related to the Internet today? How is security related to privacy?

CHAPTER FIVE

# REMOTE LOGIN

*Simple TELNET*
*What's Really Going On*
*TELNET Command Mode*
*Non-standard TELNET Servers*
*TELNETing to IBM Mainframes*

I n the next few chapters, the basic tools for using the Internet are introduced. Many of these tools are now integrated into the World Wide Web, but direct experience with them will both allow you to better utilize the Net and troubleshoot on your own whenever you experience difficulties. Just as the Windows user is better off knowing something about DOS, the expert Net user is better off knowing the tools of the Internet.

Here is an overview of Internet tools:

- **telnet** is used for logging in to other computers on the Internet including online library card catalogs and other kinds of databases.

- **ftp** allows you to move files back and forth. This tool is most useful for retrieving document and software files from public archives that are scattered around the Internet. This is called "anonymous FTP" because an account with a user ID is not needed for the computer being accessed. Anonymous FTP is covered in chapter 6, *Moving Files: FTP.*

- Electronic mail lets you send and receive messages, and is, of course, one of the most established tools on the Internet. The Internet's approach to e-mail is discussed in chapter 7, *Electronic Mail.*

- USENET News is a system that lets you read (and post) messages on any of thousands of topic-oriented bulletin boards or "newsgroups." USENET is the world's largest bulletin board service and potentially one of the most valuable communication and research tools available via the Internet. We discuss it in chapter 8, *Network News.*

These are the Internet's basic services. After chapter 8, we discuss a different kind of service: how to search through all of the vast material that's available to find what you need. An obstacle to the new Internet user is that information on the Net is not well coordinated or organized. There are incredible resources, but there is no central coordination to help find what you want. In the past few years, however, developers have made tremendous progress in sorting out the chaos and providing tools to help you find what's interesting.

## ▧ *Simple TELNET*

TELNET is the Internet's remote login protocol. It lets you sit at a keyboard connected to one computer and log on to a remote computer across the network. The connection can be to a machine in the same room, on the same campus, or in a distant corner of the world. When you are connected, it is as if your keyboard were connected directly to that remote computer. You can access whatever services the remote machine provides to its local terminals. You can run a normal interactive session (logging in, executing commands), or you can access many special services: You can look at library catalogs, find out what's playing in Peoria, access the text of *USA Today,* and take advantage of the many other services that are provided by different hosts on the network.

The simplest way to use TELNET is to type:

```
%  telnet remote-computer-name
```

at the "command level" (this example shows a UNIX system command prompt: %). If you're using some other computer system (such as DOS, VAX/VMS, or a Macintosh), the command will be fundamentally the same, though the details might be slightly different.) Here's a very basic example:

```
%  telnet sonne.uiuc.edu
Trying...

Connected to sonne.uiuc.edu.
Escape character is '^]'.

SunOS UNIX (sonne)

login: krol                                    logging in to remote system
Password:                                      password not echoed by the system
Last login: Sat Sep  7 17:16:35 from ux1.uiuc.edu
SunOS Release 4.1(GENERIC) #1:Tue Mar 6 17:27:17 PST 1990
sonne% ls                                      command executed by remote system
Mail         News           development        project1
sonne% pwd                                     command executed by remote system
/home/sonne/krol
sonne% logout                                  logout from remote system
%                                              back to local system
```

We told TELNET to find a remote computer named **sonne.uiuc.edu**. After finding the computer on the Internet, it started a "terminal session." Once this session starts, the dialog appears to be the same as if you were at a terminal connected to that host.* In particular, you must log in and log out just as if you were directly attached to that computer. After you have logged in, you can give any commands that are appropriate for the remote system; because **sonne.uiuc.edu** happens to be a UNIX system, all of the standard UNIX commands (such as **ls** and **pwd**) are available. When you log out from the remote system, **telnet** quits. Any further commands will be executed by your local system.

That's really all that TELNET is: It's a tool that lets you log in to remote computers. In the course of this chapter, we'll discuss a number of fancy TELNET commands and options, and we'll see that you can use it to access some special-purpose "servers" with their own behavior. But the simple **telnet** command above (plus an account on the remote computer) is all you need to get started.

## ▨ *What's Really Going On*

Let's take a deeper look at what happens when you start a TELNET session. An application consists of two pieces of software that cooperate: the *client,* which runs on the computer that is requesting the service, and the *server,* which runs on the computer providing the service. In your case, if seeking a connection to another computer, you are the client whereas the remote computer is the server. The network, using either TCP (Transmission Control Protocol) or UDP (User Datagram Services), is the medium by which the two communicate. The client, which is the program that began running on your system when you typed the **telnet** command, must:

- Create a TCP network connection with a server
- Accept input from you in a convenient manner
- Reformat the input to a standard format and send it to a server
- Accept output from the server in a standard format
- Reformat that output for display to you

---

*TELNET may not communicate your exact terminal specification to the remote host. You might have to do something to set the terminal specifications after you log in if you see some kind of error message. Check your local user help guides for more information.

The server software runs on the machine delivering the service; if the server is not running, the service is not available.* When it is ready to accept requests, a typical server:

- Informs the networking software that it is ready to accept connections
- Waits for a request in a standard format
- Services the request
- Sends the results back to the client in a standard format
- Waits again

A server must be able to handle a variety of clients, some running on the same kind of computer, and some running on IBM/compatible PCs, Macintoshes, Amigas—whatever happens to be out there. To make this possible, there is a set of rules for communicating with the server. This set of rules is generally called a *protocol.* In this case, since it is a protocol used between pieces of an application, it is called an *application protocol.* Anyone can write a client on any type of computer. So long as that client can communicate across the network to the server and can speak the protocol properly, it can access the service. In practice, this means that your Macintosh (or IBM PC, etc.) can use TELNET and the other Internet tools to do work on an incredible number of different systems, ranging from UNIX workstations to IBM mainframes. As a user, this all seems transparent, but there is actually much going on over the Internet connection.

An application protocol usually allows the client and server to differentiate between data destined for the user, and messages the client and server use to communicate with each other. This is frequently done by adding a few characters of text onto the beginning of each line. For example, if the server sends the client a line that begins with the characters "TXT", the rest of the line is data to be passed on to the screen. If the line begins with "CMD", it is a message from the server software to the client software. Of course, you never see any of this; by the time the message gets to you, the control information is stripped off. So let's get back to looking at how all this relates to TELNET.

## ■ *TELNET Command Mode*

TELNET has more features than our first example would lead you to believe. The clue to this was the message:

```
Escape character is '^]'
```

TELNET sends any character you type to the remote host, with one exception: the *escape character.* If you type the escape character, your **telnet** client enters a special command mode. By default, the escape character is usually **CTRL-]**. Do not confuse

---

*On UNIX systems, servers are often called *daemons,* system jobs that run in the background all the time. These "silent helpers" wait for their services to be required and when they are, spring into action.

this with the ESC key on your keyboard. The TELNET escape character can be any character that you will never want to send to the remote system. The ESC key on the keyboard represents a special character that you frequently need to send to remote systems to flag commands. Remember that there are exceptions: The escape character is not always **CTRL-]**. **telnet** clients that run on machines with slick interfaces generally use menus or function keys instead of an obscure escape character.

You can also enter the command mode by typing **telnet** alone, with no machine name following it. When you're in command mode (no matter how you got there), you will see the prompt:

```
telnet>
```

This means that TELNET is waiting for you to type a command. Typing a question mark (?) will get you a list of the commands available:

```
telnet>  ?
Commands may be abbreviated.  Commands are:

close       close current connection
display     display operating parameters
mode        try to enter line-by-line or character-at-a-time mode
open        connect to a site
quit        exit telnet
send        transmit special characters ('send ?' for more)
set         set operating parameters ('set ?' for more)
status      print status information
toggle      toggle operating parameters ('toggle ?' for more)
z           suspend telnet
?           print help information
```

Although there are a number of commands, and even more subcommands (try a **set ?** sometime), only a few are generally used:

**close**          Terminates the connection that currently exists or is being created. It automatically disconnects you from the remote system; it may also quit from TELNET if you specified a hostname with the **telnet** command. This command is useful if you get into a bind across the network and want to get out.

**open** *name*          Attempts to create a connection to the named machine. The name or address of the target machine is required. Most TELNETs will prompt for a machine name if it is not specified. Note that you must close any existing connection before opening a new one.

**set echo**          Turns local echoing on or off. *Echoing* is the process by which the characters you type appear on-screen. Usually, the remote computer is responsible for sending the character back to your terminal after it receives it. This is called *remote echoing,* and is generally considered more reliable, because you know that the remote system is receiving your keystrokes correctly. *Local echoing* means that the local computer (in this case, your **telnet** client) sends the characters you type back to the display screen. Because remote echoing is more reliable, TELNET usually starts with echoing turned off. To turn it on, enter command mode and type the **set echo** command. To turn it off again, just type **set echo** again. (This is a "toggle" command, which is like a light switch: giving the command repeatedly turns echoing on or off.)

How do you know whether local echoing should be on or off? If local echoing is turned off and it should be on, any characters you type will not be echoed; you won't see the commands you send to the remote system, but you will see the output from these commands. If local echoing is turned on and it should be off, you'll see every character you type twice. In either case, the solution is the same: Enter command mode and type **set echo**.

**set escape** *char*          Sets the escape character to the specified character. You will usually want to use some kind of control character, which you can either type "as is" (for example, if you want to use **CTRL-b**, just type **b** while holding down the CTRL key), or by typing a caret (^) followed by the letter (for example, **^b**). It is important that your escape character be a character that you'll never need to type while doing your normal work. This can be a problem—many programs (the *emacs* editor in particular) assign meanings to virtually every key on the keyboard. The ability to change the escape character is really useful if you are running daisy-chained applications. For example, you **telnet** from system A to system B, log in, and then **telnet** to system C. If what you are doing on system C goes bad, and if the escape characters are the same, there is no way to break the B-to-C connection; typing the escape character will always put you into command mode on system A. If you use a different escape character for each TELNET session, however, you can choose which one to put into command mode by typing the appropriate character. This applies not only to **telnet**, but also to other applications with escape characters, like terminal emulators (for example, the popular **kermit** program).

**quit**                     Gets you out of the **telnet** program gracefully.

**z**                        Temporarily suspends the TELNET session to allow other commands to be executed on the local system.

**Carriage Return**          Without issuing a command (a blank line in command mode) returns you to your session on the remote machine from command mode. In addition, many of the other commands implicitly take you out of command mode.

Here's a sample session in which we log in to **sonne.uiuc.edu**, go into command mode for a few commands, and then return to **sonne**:

```
% telnet sonne.uiuc.edu
Trying...
Connected to sonne.uiuc.edu.
Escape character is '^]'.

SunOS UNIX (sonne)

login: krol                                           logging in to remote system
Password:
Last login: Sat Sep  7 17:16:35 from ux1.uiuc.edu
SunOS Release 4.1(GENERIC) #1:Tue Mar 6 17:27:17 PST 1990
sonne% ls
Mail        News          development        project1
sonne% pwd
/home/sonne/krol sonne% CTRL-]                         enter telnet command mode
telnet> ?                                              print help message
Commands may be abbreviated. Commands are:

close       close current connection
display     display operating parameters
...                                                    several commands omitted
z           suspend telnet
?           print help information
telnet> set escape ^b                                  change escape character
escape character is '^B'
sonne% pwd                                             back to sonne; give a command
/home/sonne/krol
sonne % logout                                         and quit
%                                                      back to local system
```

Note that the **set** command implicitly takes you out of command mode. If it did not, you could just enter a blank line to get back to the remote system, **sonne**.

# ◼ *Non-standard TELNET Servers*

I may have given the impression that TELNET is useful only for logging on to other computers. This is not strictly the case. It also means that when you connect to a computer using TELNET, you will not get the normal login prompt, with which we hope you are familiar by now. There's one variation of a "non-standard" server that's worth knowing about. Sometimes you get a standard login prompt; then you use a specific login name (such as "library") to start a special application program. You're still using the standard TELNET server.

You get whatever the writer of the service wanted to give you. So, you need to approach these services with a bit more caution.

- Almost every special-purpose server is different. Some have good user interfaces; some have horrible user interfaces. What you get is what you get. Most have help facilities (some useful, some not so useful).

- Most servers will ask for a terminal type of some sort when you enter. "VT100" is probably the most common choice—many terminal emulators, and most window systems, use it. If you do not know what kind of terminal to ask for, if your terminal is not represented, or VT100 does strange things, fall back to the basic "hardcopy" or "dumb" choices.

- On their first screen, most servers will tell you how to log out, or terminate your session. Look for this information when you start a session; that will keep you from getting stuck. Of course, you can always use TELNET's escape character to get out of a session. **Ctrl-]** is the usual choice. Watch the screen when you complete a TELNET connection to see if other escape sequences are offered.

## *TELNET to Non-standard Ports*

Requiring that you dedicate a computer to a non-standard service limits non-standard servers to applications where user-friendliness is paramount. However, there's another solution to this problem that strikes a compromise between friendliness and capital investment. What you really want to do is use the user's existing **telnet** client program, but write a special application server without preventing the serving machine from offering normal TELNET services. This can be done, but to understand how, you need to know a bit more about how the Internet works. Since most computers provide many different servers (for **telnet** and other applications), there needs to be a way for the software communicating with the network to decide which server is to handle a request. This is accomplished by assigning each server a specific port number as identification. When the server starts running, it tells the network software which port it is responsible for servicing.* When a client program wants to connect to some service, it must specify both the address (to get to a particular machine) and a port number (to get to a particular service on that machine). Frequently used applications have standard port numbers assigned to them; TELNET is assigned to port 23, for example.†

Now we can see how to use a standard client for another application—all we need is some way to make use of another port number. Private applications have to use an unassigned port that the client and server agree upon. If we write our non-standard server and tell it to listen to some other port (say, for example, port 10001) and if we can tell users to "connect" their **telnet** client to port 10001 on our machine, we're home free.

In fact, there are many such applications scattered around the Internet. When applications are provided over non-standard ports, the documentation about the service (or the person telling you to use it) must tell you which port to use. For example, let's try to use the Weather Underground, which provides access to weather information for cities across the United States. Its entry in the *Resource Catalog* looks like this:

```
Access via: telnet madlab.sprl.umich.edu 3000
```

This tells you to "connect to **madlab.sprl.umich.edu** using **telnet**, but do not use the default port (23); use port 3000 instead." The non-standard port number is just added to the end of the **telnet** command. Here is the actual session accessing that service:

```
%  telnet madlab.sprl.umich.edu 3000
Trying 141.213.23.12 ...
Connected to madlab.engin.umich.edu.
Escape character is '^]'.
---------------------------------------------------------------------------
*                         University of Michigan                          *
*                         WEATHER UNDERGROUND                             *
---------------------------------------------------------------------------
*                                                                         *
*           College of Engineering, University of Michigan                *
*           Department of Atmospheric, Oceanic, and Space Sciences        *
*           Ann Arbor, Michigan  48109-2143                               *
*           comments: ldm@cirrus.sprl.umich.edu                           *
*                                                                         *
* With Help from:  The National Science Foundation supported Unidata Project *
*                  University Corporation for Atmospheric Research         *
```

---

*These are "virtual" ports that are used by software to differentiate between various communications streams. Do not confuse them with terminal ports, SCSI ports, and the like, which are actual hardware plugs.

†On BSD UNIX systems, the standard port numbers can be found in the file */etc/services*. Standard port number assignments are documented in an RFC titled "Assigned Numbers." At the time of this printing, this number is RFC 1700, but it gets updated periodically; newer versions will have a different number.

```
*                    Boulder, Colorado  80307-3000                 *
*                                                                  *
*      Commercial, for-profit users should contact our data provider,   *
*      Alden Electronics, 508-366-8851 to acquire their own data feed.   *
*                 comments: ldm@cirrus.sprl.umich.edu              *
*                                                                  *
-------------------------------------------------------------------
*   NOTE:----------> New users, please select option "H" on the main menu:   *
*                    H) Help and information for new users         *
-------------------------------------------------------------------

Press Return for menu, or enter 3 letter forecast city code:

                    WEATHER UNDERGROUND MAIN MENU
                    *****************************
                     1) U.S. forecasts and climate data
                     2) Canadian forecasts
                     3) Current weather observations
                     4) Ski conditions
                     5) Long-range forecasts
                     6) Latest earthquake reports
                     7) Severe weather
                     8) Hurricane advisories
                     9) National Weather Summary
                    10) International data
                    11) Marine forecasts and observations
                    12) Ultraviolet light forecast
                    13) K-12 School Weather Observations
                    14) Weather summary for the past month
                     X) Exit program
                     C) Change scrolling to screen
                     H) Help and information for new users
                     ?) Answers to all your questions

                         CITY FORECAST MENU
        ---------------------------------------------------
                     1) Print forecast for selected city
                     2) Print climatic data for selected city
                     3) Display 3-letter city codes for a selected state
                     4) Display all 2-letter state codes
                     M) Return to main menu
                     X) Exit program
                     ?) Help

                         Selection:1

            Enter 3-letter city code: cle
```

```
Weather Conditions at 11 PM EDT on 23 AUG 95 for Cleveland, OH.

Temp(F)     Humidity(%)     Wind(mph)     Pressure(in)     Weather
======================================================================
  68            83%          SSW at 8        30.11          Clear
ASHTABULA-CUYAHOGA-ERIE-LAKE-LORAIN-
INCLUDING THE CITIES OF...SANDUSKY...LORAIN...CLEVELAND...
PAINESVILLE...ASHTABULA
919 PM EDT WED AUG 23 1995
 TONIGHT...CLEAR EARLY WITH SOME CLOUDINESS SPREADING IN LATE. LOW
60
TO 65. SOUTHWEST WINDS LESS THAN 10 MPH BECOMING NORTHWEST BY
DAYBREAK.
 THURSDAY...PARTLY CLOUDY IN THE MORNING...THEN MOSTLY SUNNY. HIGH
AROUND 80. NORTHWEST WINDS 5 TO 10 MPH BECOMING NORTHEAST.
 THURSDAY NIGHT...MOSTLY CLEAR. LOW 55 TO 60.
 FRIDAY...MOSTLY SUNNY. HIGH IN THE UPPER 70S.


             ***********************
             State extended forecast
             ***********************


   EXTENDED FORECAST...
```

There are two things worth noting about this session. First, rather than receiving the usual login prompt, you ended up right in the middle of an application. Every non-standard server has its own set of commands. You need to read the screens carefully to learn how to use them. Most servers tell you fairly early in the session how to log out and how to access its help facility. In this case, you enter a carriage return to get to the main menu and then an **H** to get to help information.

Second, because you never saw a login prompt, you never had to log in nor did you need an account on **madlab.sprl.umich.edu** to use the service. Of course, the non-standard server can have its own login procedure; you may need to register with some authority to use the service, and that authority may want to bill you for your usage. Many services remain free and open to the public.

In this example, we used TELNET to connect to a non-standard port and thus accessed a special service. In practice, you will see both solutions: non-standard TELNET servers that use the standard port (port 23) and are therefore dedicated to a particular task, and non-standard servers that use a non-standard port. Our *Resource Catalog,* and other databases of network resources, tell you when a non-standard port is necessary.

## ■ *TELNETing to IBM Mainframes*

If you've used computers for very long, you've probably come to expect IBM mainframes to exhibit their own behaviors, just to confuse the rest of the world. Watch someone use an IBM mainframe, for example, to perform statistical analyses. TELNET is no exception. So far as TELNET is concerned, we can divide IBM applications into two classes: "line-mode" applications and "3270" (or "full-screen") applications. We'll consider each of them separately.

Line-mode applications are more or less what you're used to. *Line mode* means that the terminal sends characters to the computer one line at a time. This is the way most common terminals behave, and it's the way TELNET normally behaves. Line-mode applications do not present a problem. (You might have to issue the **set echo** command to **telnet**, since line-mode applications sometimes do not echo the characters you type.) You can **telnet** to an IBM system, start your application, and everything will work normally.

Some IBM systems are more challenging, such as the 3270. First, what does "3270" mean? For a long time, IBM computers have used a proprietary full-screen terminal known as a 3270. The *3270* was designed to make data entry (filling in forms, etc.) easier for the user and less of a load on the system. Therefore, it has many features that you will not find on garden-variety terminals: protected fields, numeric fields, alphabetic fields, etc. There are also several special-purpose keys, notably *programmed function* (PF) keys, which may have special commands tied to them. The terminal operates on block transfers, which means that it does not send anything to the host until you press the ENTER key or a PF key; when you do, it sends a compressed image of the screen changes since the last transmission. Obviously, then, a 3270 application is going to require some special handling. It is usually possible to use a 3270 application in line mode, but it will be pretty unpleasant.

To use a 3270 application on its own terms, you really need a "terminal emulator" that can make your system act like a 3270 terminal. In many cases, the IBM mainframe that you're connected to will provide the terminal emulation itself. In this case, you can use the usual TELNET to connect to the computer. When TELNET connects, the mainframe will ask you what kind of terminal you are using. After you tell the system your terminal type, you're ready to go. You do not need to do anything special, but you do need to know what the special keys are on your terminal, so read on.

If the host you contact does not provide some kind of 3270 emulation, you need to use a special version of TELNET that has an emulator built in. This version is called **tn3270** ("telnet 3270"). First, how do you know when you need **tn3270**? If you **telnet** to a system and see a message like this:

```
% telnet vmd.cso.uiuc.edu
```

```
Trying 128.174.5.98...
Connected to vmd.cso.uiuc.edu.
Escape character is '^]'.
VM/XA SP ONLINE-PRESS ENTER KEY TO BEGIN SESSION .
```

you know you're talking to an IBM mainframe. Two flags should give you a clue to this. One is the string "VM" in the message (or it might say "MVS"); these are the names of IBM operating systems. The other clue is that the message is entirely in capital letters, which is common in IBM-land. (Of course, there are other operating systems that do all their work with uppercase letters.) In this case, you should be able to use the computer system with regular TELNET, but it will be cumbersome; **tn3270** will probably work better.

You should also try **tn3270** if something funny happens to your session:

```
%  telnet lib.cc.purdue.edu
Trying 128.210.9.8...
Connected to lib.cc.purdue.edu.
Escape character is '^]'.
Connection closed by foreign host.
```

TELNET managed to connect to the remote system, but something went wrong, and the remote system gave up. In this example, the remote system is so entrenched in the 3270's features that it quit and closed the connection when it found you were not using them. (*Note:* Many things can cause a connection to close immediately; this is only one of them.)

In this case, using **tn3270** gives you completely different results. Here's how you start:

```
%  tn3270 lib.cc.purdue.edu
Trying...
Connected to lib.cc.purdue.edu.
```

Then the screen clears and you see:

```
                                             THe Online Resource      TOO1
        Choose from the list below by typing the   TTTTTTTTTTTTTTTTTTT      \
        name displayed to the left of your choice.  T                      //
                                                     T  H H  OOO  RRR    //
        Some choices may lead to other lists.        T  HHH  O O  R R   //
                                                     T  H H  OOO  R R   \
                                                                         \par

                              MAIN MENU
                       CATALOG  Purdue Catalogs
                       INDEX    Journal Indexes
                       REMOTE   Other Library Catalogs
```

```
                        Press ENTER to go directly to PCAT

------------------------------------------ + Page 1 of 8 -------------
HELp                 Select a database label from above    <F8> FORward
                     NEWs  (Library System News)

Database Selection:
```

This is more like what the designer of the THOR system wanted.

Using a system in 3270 mode usually involves "filling in the blanks" and hitting PF keys or ENTER to get work done. You get to the blanks you want to fill in by moving the cursor to them and typing. When you want to send the completed form to the computer, you hit ENTER. Optional commands can be executed by hitting PF keys rather than ENTER. The bottom of the screen frequently lists the functions that are available through the PF keys; they often vary, depending on what you are doing. If the screen gets too full, or if the system prints an "important" message, the keyboard will lock until the screen is cleared using the CLEAR key. Obviously, this is not your run-of-the-mill terminal.

**tn3270** is the only practical way to use some machines on the network, but it is confusing. The first problem is finding the program. Sometimes it is a funny mode of TELNET; if your **telnet** client detects that it is talking to an IBM system, it may start talking **tn3270** automatically. (It's worth noting that this general trend describes what's happening to most interfaces between you, the user, and that electronic tool you wish to use on the Internet.) With some versions of TELNET, you may find a **tn3270** option in the command menu, or you may be able to specify it in the command line. For example, in a popular old DOS version of the client, the normal line-mode **telnet** command is **tn**. It looks like this:

```
C: >  tn vmd.cso.uiuc.edu
```

This translates into being at the DOS prompt C:>, **tn** is the command, and **vmd.cso.uiuc.edu** is the destination.

If you want to do full-screen (3270-style) **telnet**, you use a slightly different command: We need the **tn -t 3278** option. (3278 is one of IBM's variations on the 3270 theme—it's the same, as far as we're concerned):

```
C: >  tn -t 3278 vmd.cso.uiuc.edu
```

On most systems, **tn3270** is a stand-alone program. If you need it, try typing **tn3270** and see if it starts. **tn3270** is currently part of the normal distribution of BSD 4.3 UNIX, but some older systems may not have it. It comes with most TCP/IP products for microcomputers. You can use Archie to locate a free copy of the software (for UNIX or any other system). See chapter 9, *Finding Software,* for information about how to use the Archie service.

Once you've found **tn3270**—or even if the mainframe is taking care of 3270 emulation for you—you need to figure out how the 3270's special keys have been mapped onto your keyboard. There is no agreement on how to do this; it differs from system to system. That is, some implementations map the PF keys to the numeric keypad that's to the right of the keyboard (PF1 being 1, PF2 being 2, etc.); other emulators map the key sequence PF1 to ESC 1; still others use the special function keys that are often placed above the keyboard.

In this book, we cannot describe the different variations that you might encounter, because it is determined by the person who installed the emulator or **tn3270** you are using, another example of the chaotic nature of the Internet. We can tell you what you need to know and how to "feel" your way around. You need to know what keys move the cursor, clear the screen, and transmit the PF key and "reset" key codes.* In addition, make sure you know how to escape to command mode, so you can close the connection if things go wrong. This should be similar to the regular **telnet** program's escape command.

If you are lucky, the program's documentation, or the person who installed the program, might be able to provide a key map. If not, here are some hints to help you:

- Make sure that you identify your terminal correctly. (If you are using an ADM 3A terminal and the computer thinks you are using a VT100, things will be really confused.)

- To position the cursor, first try the arrow keys, if they exist on your keyboard. If there are no arrow keys, or if you try the arrow keys and the cursor does not move, try the h, j, k, l keys (just like the UNIX text editor *vi,* if you are familiar with that). Failing that, the TAB key almost always works. It takes you to the next field you can type into. By using TAB repeatedly, you can move the cursor around, albeit inconveniently.

- ENTER is usually the carriage return or the ENTER key near the numeric keypad.

- To find the function keys: first try any keys marked F1, F2, etc., (or PF1, PF2, etc. if you have them). You are looking for the screen to change or for a message such as "PF4 Undefined" to appear. (This message means you have successfully sent a PF key but that no command has been assigned to it.) If that doesn't work, try the numeric keypad, or the sequence ESC *number* (e.g., try typing **ESC 1** to

---

*Reset unlocks the terminal after you have typed something illegal. Some implementations do not support reset.

send PF1). If you still have no luck, you need to search for the key map (as described below).

- To clear the screen, try **CTRL-z, CTRL-l** (lowercase "L," not the digit one), or **CTRL-HOME**. One of these should work.

- Implementations running on menu-driven workstations sometimes use menu items to send special keys.

If these hints did not help and you are using regular TELNET to contact the host (i.e., if the terminal emulator is running on the remote system, not your local system), you're out of luck. Try to contact the help desk for the remote computer and ask for a copy of their key mappings. If you are using **tn3270**, there is one more thing you can try: Look around for a file named *map3270* (or something similar), either in same directory as the program, the system area or folder, or the */etc* directory. It should contain a list of terminal types and, for each terminal type, the key sequences that do good things. Unfortunately, its form is fairly unreadable.

A final word of caution: There are many **tn3270** programs that do not work well in more specialized IBM applications. You may find that your version of **tn3270** works just fine doing mundane things on an IBM system (e.g., electronic mail, editing files, etc.), but as soon as you start the big software package you really wanted to use, it dies with a message:

```
Unexpected command sequence - program terminated
```

This is because the original **tn3270** program, which is the basis for a lot of implementations, could not handle certain correct, but infrequent, 3270 control codes. Therefore, **tn3270** will work correctly until you try to run a program that uses one of the codes that it cannot handle. There is only one solution to this problem: Try to get a better, usually newer, version of **tn3270**.

## Exercises

Remember that there are two addressing schemes used on the Internet. The IP address is a unique numeric representation of a computer's location within a network. It comprises four sets of numbers separated by periods. By contrast, the domain name is a unique alphabetic representation of a computer's location within a network. The IP address **192.54.81.18** and the domain **name pac.carl.org** are equivalent. IP addresses can change, whereas domain names usually stay the same. For this reason, the domain name is more commonly used when describing an Internet address and most worth keeping over time. Here's a way to learn what the IP address of an Internet domain name is:

## *IP Address Resolver*

Mails you IP address of site. (body: site address)

```
resolve@cs.widener.edu
dns@grasp.insa-lyon.fr (body of letter: help)
```

*Examples of requests:*

To request the IP address for **pac.carl.org**, e-mail this message to **resolve@cs.widener.edu**:

```
ip pac.carl.org
```

To request the domain name for the IP address **192.54.81.18**, e-mail this message to **dns@grasp.insa-lyon.fr**:

```
host 192.54.81.18
```

## *Electronic Frontier Foundation*

A variety of interesting **telnet** examples may be found at the Electronic Frontier Foundation's (Extended) Guide to the Internet on the WWW at **http://www.eff.org/papers/eegtti/eeg_96.html#SEC97**.

*Example:* TELNET session to Colorado Alliance of Research Libraries, a large number of library-related databases and a periodical document delivery service.

```
telnet pac.carl.org

Trying... Connected to CSI.CARL.ORG, a TANDEM running GUARDIAN.

WELCOME TO CSI.CARL.ORG [WINDOW $ZT2.#PTY233P]
T9553D20 TELNET SERVER 14APR95 VERSION ABP
Available Services:
EXIT    PAC
Enter Choice>
```

*Example:* A **telnet** seminar from HomeCom Communications:

```
http://www.homecom.com/seminar/telnet.html
```

Try the following and see if you get the University of Michigan's Department of Atmospheric, Oceanographic and Space Sciences weather forecasts. What happens if you leave 3000 off of the address?

```
telnet: madlab.sprl.umich.edu 3000
```

CHAPTER SIX

# MOVING FILES: FTP

*Getting Started with FTP*
*FTP Command Summary*
*Anonymous FTP*
*Handling Large Files and Groups of Files*
*Special Notes on Various Systems*
*Last Words: Some Practical Advice*

Often, you will find information via a search tool (such as Archie or Infoseek) on the Internet that you want to have a copy of for yourself. You need, for example, the text of a recent Supreme Court opinion. You found a tutorial on photochemistry that looks useful. You discovered some free software that just might solve all your problems, and you want to try it. In each case, you need to move a copy of the file to your local system so you can manipulate it there. The Internet tool for doing this is **ftp**.

**ftp** is named after the application protocol it uses: the *File Transfer Protocol (FTP)* (see URL **http://ds.internic.net/rfc/rfc959.txt**). As the name implies, **ftp**'s job is to move files from one computer to another. It does not matter where the two computers are located, how they are connected, or even whether or not they use the same operating system. Provided that both computers can "talk" the FTP protocol and have access to the Internet, you can use the **ftp** command to transfer files. Some of the nuances of its use do change with each operating system, but the basic command structure is the same from machine to machine.

Like **telnet**, **ftp** has spawned a broad range of databases and services. You can, indeed, find anything from legal opinions to recipes to free software in any number of publicly available online databases, or archives, that can be accessed through **ftp**. For a sampling of the archives that you can access with **ftp**, go to URL **http://hoohoo.ncsa.uiuc.edu/ftp**. If you are a serious researcher, you will find **ftp** invaluable; it is the common "language" for sharing data.

**ftp** is a complex program because there are many different ways to manipulate files and file structures. Different ways of storing files (binary or ASCII, compressed or uncompressed, etc.) introduce complications and may require additional thought to get things right. First, we will look at how to transfer files between two computers on which you have an account (a login name and, if needed, a password). Next, we will discuss anonymous FTP, which is a special service that lets you access public databases without obtaining an account. Most public archives provide anonymous FTP access, which means that you can get files from the archive without arranging for a login name and an account in advance.

## Getting Started with FTP

First, we will consider how to move files between two computers on which you already have accounts. Like **telnet**, **ftp** requires that you specify the machine with which you would like to exchange files. This can be done with the line command:

```
% ftp  remote-machine-name
```

This starts the **ftp** program and connects to the named machine.

When **ftp** makes the connection with the remote computer, you will be asked to identify yourself with a login name and password:

```
% ftp sonne.uiuc.edu
Connected to sonne.uiuc.edu.
220 sonne FTP server (SunOS 4.1) ready.
Name (ux.uiuc.edu:krol): krol              send login name krol
331 Password required for krol.
Password:                                  type the password; it isn't echoed
230 User krol logged in.
```

With some operating systems, such as DOS and the Macintosh system, **ftp** may not ask for a password; it may only demand a login name, because there is no password security on the system. On these machines, protection from unwanted access is usually handled by disabling the FTP server software.

If you respond to the "name" prompt with a carriage return, many versions of **ftp** will send the login name that you are using on the local system. In the above example, the name of the local system and the default login name are shown in parentheses (**ux.uiuc.edu:krol**). Therefore, as a shortcut we could have typed a carriage return instead of the full login name. The login name you use will determine which remote files you can access, just as if you were logging in to it locally. However, remember that you have to use a login name and password that are appropriate for the remote system.

After the remote system has accepted your login name and password, you are ready to start transferring files. **ftp** prints an ftp> prompt to prompt you for further commands. **ftp** can transfer files in two directions. It can take a file on the local machine (the one initiating the transfer) and **put** it on the remote machine; or it can **get** a file from the remote machine and place it on the local machine. The **get** and **put** commands have the syntax:

```
ftp>  get  source-file destination-file
ftp>  put  source-file destination-file
```

The *source-file* is the name of the existing file you want; *destination-file* is the name of your newly created copy. The *destination-file* name is optional; if it is omitted, the copy is given the same name as the source file. In the following example, we start by logging in to machine **ux.uiuc.edu** under the name **edk**. We transfer the file *comments* from the machine **sonne.uiuc.edu** under login name **krol**'s default directory to the originating machine. Then we transfer the file *newversion* to **sonne.uiuc.edu**, renaming the new copy to *readthis:*

```
ux login:    edk
                                        send login name edk to ux
password:                               type the password; it isn't echoed
Welcome to ux.uiuc.edu
ux%  ftp sonne.uiuc.edu
Connected to sonne.uiuc.edu.
220 sonne FTP server (SunOS 4.1) ready.
Name (ux.uiuc.edu:edk):  krol          send login name krol
331 Password required for krol.
Password:                              type the password; it isn't echoed
230 User krol logged in.
ftp>  get comments                     request copy of file comments
200 PORT command successful.           be moved from sonne to ux
150 ASCII data connection for comments (128.174.5.55,3516) (1588 bytes).
226 ASCII Transfer complete.
1634 bytes received in 0.052 seconds (30 Kbytes/s)
ftp>  put newversion readthis          copy newversion to sonne
200 PORT command successful.           from ux; rename it as readthis
150 ASCII data connection for readthis (128.174.5.55,3518)
226 ASCII Transfer complete.
62757 bytes sent in 0.22 seconds (2.8e+02 Kbytes/s)
ftp>  quit                             end this session
221 Goodbye.
ux%
```

There are a few things worth mentioning about the example. First, knowing how to quit from any program is as important as knowing how to start it. When we finished transferring the files, we gave the **quit** command to terminate the **ftp** program. The command **bye** does the same thing. We also are assuming that we "knew" that there would be a file named *comments* on **sonne**. It is possible to look at the list of files on the remote machine. Note that **ftp** is fairly verbose; it gives you a lot of information about what it is doing. Unfortunately, the messages are rather arcane and inconsistent; **ftp** was designed before "user-friendliness" was invented. The messages begin with a "message number," which is unnecessary for our needs (as is the file transfer rate).

## Common Problems

What if you have a typo in your login? There are two ways to handle this. You can exit **ftp** and try again, or you can give the "**user** command," followed by your login name, to login again:

```
ux%  ftp sonne.uiuc.edu
Connected to sonne.uiuc.edu
220 sonne FTP server (SunOS 4.1) ready.
Name (ux.uiuc.edu:edk):  krol                     login name krol
331 Password required for krol.
Password:                                         type the password incorrectly
530 Login incorrect.
Login failed.
ftp>  user krol                                   start again with the login name
331 Password required for krol
Password:                                         this time, get the password right
230 User krol logged in.
ftp>
```

If your first attempt to log in fails, you get an ftp> prompt, but you can't do anything with it. You have to repeat the login process. Other things can go wrong, from misspelled host names to a crashed computer (e.g., "host not responding," "host unreachable," or "connection timed out"). If you misspell the name of the file you are trying to transfer, you will see a message saying "no such file or directory." If you try to get a file that you are not allowed to take, you will get an appropiate error message. Finally, some systems place file size limits on their users, or your disk may not have room for large files.

## Browsing on a Remote Machine

When using **ftp**, you frequently do not know exactly what files you want and where they are. There are a few useful commands and techniques to allow browsing on the remote machine. The basic commands to list directory information on the remote machine are **dir** and **ls**. The two commands have the same format (only **dir** or **ls** are required):

```
ftp>  dir  directory-name local-file-name
ftp>  ls   directory-name local-file-name
```

Both commands list the files in directory *directory-name* on the remote machine, sending that list to a local file (called *local-file-name*). Both arguments are optional. If you want the file list to appear on your screen instead, just omit "local-file-name" as an option.

The first "argument," *directory-name,* gives the name of the directories or files that you want listed. If it is omitted, **ftp** lists all the files in the current remote directory. The first argument may contain "wildcard" characters, which are very useful if you want to limit file lists. Wildcards may be interpreted somewhat differently, depending on what kind of computer you are trying to browse. On most computer systems, the asterisk (*) is a wildcard that matches any group of characters. For example, on many machines the command in **ftp**:

```
ftp>  dir test*
```

lists only files whose names begin with *test.* On computers running the UNIX operating system, **test*** would match filenames such as *test.one* and *test.txt,* in addition to filenames like *test1* and *test.* On computers running the VAX/VMS or MS-DOS operating system, the filename and extension are considered different entities, so **test*** may match only files with no extension (such as *test1* and *testout*). You may have to experiment to see what happens. You can try a wildcard in either the name, the extension, or both; commands like **test*.** match files beginning with *test* with no extension; *****.**txt** matches any file with the extension *.txt.*

Now, back to the basic listing commands, **ls** and **dir**. Their output should be quite different. The **ls** command, by default, gives you a simplified listing of filenames with no additional information. It is designed primarily for making a list of files that can be easily used as input to another program. It should look something like this:

```
ftp>  ls
150 Opening ASCII mode data connection for file list.
nsfnet
CIC
campus
scott
```

The **dir** command produces more complete information:

```
ftp>  dir
150 Opening ASCII mode data connection for /bin/ls.
total 2529
-rw———— 1 krol    cso     110 Oct 31 08:18 .Xauthority
-rw-r—r— 1 krol    cso     821 Nov 21 15:11 .cshrc
-rw———— 1 krol    cso      68 Mar  4  1989 .exrc
```

The output of the **dir** command looks like a full directory listing on the remote system. This is because the client tells the server to send the directory information; the server executes an appropriate command, and then sends the listing back to the client untouched. (Some poor **ftp** implementations use **dir** and **ls** commands synonymously.)

The ultimate in directory commands, which works only if the remote system is running UNIX, is **ls –lR**. This is a "recursive" listing; it lists all files in the current directory and, if there are subdirectories, lists the files in those subdirectories too. It continues until it has exhausted the subdirectories of the subdirectories, listing just about every file that you can get to with **ftp**. Output from this command looks like this:

```
ftp>  ls –lR
200 PORT command successful.
150 Opening ASCII mode data connection for /bin/ls.
total 2529
-rw————  1 krol   cso    110 Oct 31 08:18 .Xauthority
-rw-r—r—  1 krol   cso    821 Nov 21 15:11 .cshrc
drwx————  3 krol   cso    512 Oct  3  1989 iab
-rw-r—r—  1 krol   cso   2289 Jan  5 12:34 index

iab:                                      contents of iab directory above
total 51
-rw-r—r—  1 krol   cso  25164 Sep  1  1989 crucible
-rw-r—r—  1 krol   cso  14045 Oct  3  1989 iab
drwx————  3 krol   cso   1024 Jan  3  1990 ietf
-rw————  1 krol   cso  10565 May 15  1989

inarc iab/ietf:                           contents of subdirectory ietf of iab
total 416
-rw-r—r—  1 krol   cso  24663 Jan 17  1990 agenda
drwxr-xr-x 2 krol   cso    512 Jul 13  1989 reports

iab/ietf/reports:
total 329
-rw-r—r—  1 krol   cso  46652 Jul 13  1989 jun89
-rw-r—r—  1 krol   cso  53905 May 11  1989 mar89
-rw-r—r—  1 krol   cso  53769 Jun 15  1989 may89
-rw————  1 krol   cso  47429 Dec 15  1988 nov88

226 Transfer complete.
```

Be careful: It may produce large amounts of output. It is often a good idea to save the results of **ls –lR** in a file with the command:

```
ftp>  ls –lR  filename
```

So you do a few **dir** commands and see some files that are likely candidates to **get**. To see if a file is the right one, it would be helpful to take a quick look at it. Many **ftp** implementations provide this ability by invoking a minus sign (–) instead of a destination filename. Let's use another example to demonstrate this.

Project Hermes was started in May 1990 by the U.S. Supreme Court as an experiment in disseminating its opinions electronically. Starting with the 1993 calendar year, the

U.S. Supreme Court began disseminating opinions electronically on an official basis. A site at Case Western Reserve University (**ftp.cwru.edu**) has decisions available via **ftp**:

```
[6:52pm] bgsuvax > ftp ftp.cwru.edu
Connected to slc1.INS.CWRU.Edu.
220 slc1 FTP server (SunOS 4.1) ready.
Name (ftp.cwru.edu:klopfens): ftp
331 Guest login ok, send ident as password.
Password:
230 Guest login ok, access restrictions apply.
ftp> dir
200 PORT command successful.
150 ASCII data connection for /bin/ls (129.1.2.2,4585) (0 bytes).
total 63
drwxrwxr-x 26 105       staff        1024 May 17  1994 ArtOfProlog
drwxr-xr-x  3 root      daemon        512 Jun 15  1993 Mathematica
lrwxrwxrwx  1 root      daemon          7 Jul 23  1993 OH.Appeals.8th.dist ->
mercury
lrwxrwxrwx  1 root      daemon          6 Aug 12  1992 U.S.Supreme.Court ->
hermes
drwxr-xr-x  2 root      wheel         512 Mar 11  1992 adf
```

*...lines deleted...*

```
226 ASCII Transfer complete.
1306 bytes received in 0.63 seconds (2 Kbytes/s)
ftp> cd hermes
250 CWD command successful.
ftp> dir
200 PORT command successful.
150 ASCII data connection for /bin/ls (129.1.2.2,4590) (0 bytes).
total 236
-rw-r--r--  1 uucp      daemon      92448 Sep  5 15:24 Index
-r--r--r--  1 root      wheel         878 Feb  8  1993 README.FIRST
-r--r--r--  1 root      wheel        2255 Sep  8  1994 README.SECOND
-r--r--r--  1 root      daemon        998 Feb  8  1993 README.UPDATE
drwxrwxr-x  2 uucp      daemon      55296 Sep  5 15:24 ascii
drwxrwxr-x  2 uucp      daemon      23040 Sep  5 15:21 ascii-orig
drwxrwxr-x  2 uucp      daemon      10752 Jan 25  1994 atex
drwxrwxr-x  5 uucp      daemon        512 Aug  5  1993 briefs
drwxrwxr-x  2 uucp      daemon      40960 Sep  5 15:24 word-perfect
drwxrwxr-x  2 uucp      daemon      11264 Jan 25  1994 xywrite
226 ASCII Transfer complete.
658 bytes received in 0.19 seconds (3.4 Kbytes/s)
ftp> get README.FIRST -            This command displays the contents of README.FIRST
200 PORT command successful.
150 ASCII data connection for README.FIRST (129.1.2.2,4619) (878 bytes).
```

```
TO ALL USERS AND MEMBERS OF THE MEDIA:

Permission is hereby granted to download, reproduce, or re-
post any of the Supreme Court opinion files found on this system
PROVIDED NO CHANGES OR EDITING ARE MADE TO THE SUBJECT MATERIAL.
We would greatly appreciate it if source credit were given to
Case Western Reserve University.
...lines deleted...

226 ASCII Transfer complete.
remote: README.FIRST
898 bytes received in 0.15 seconds (5.7 Kbytes/s)
ftp> get README.SECOND -
200 PORT command successful.
150 ASCII data connection for README.SECOND (129.1.2.2,4631) (2255 bytes).
Thank you for your interest in Project Hermes and in receiving  U.S.
Supreme Court opinions electronically.

The U.S. Supreme Court opinions are immediately available from Case
Western Reserve University via "anonymous" ftp over the Internet from
host "FTP.CWRU.Edu". The files relating to the opinions are located
in the directory "hermes".

...lines deleted ...

226 ASCII Transfer complete.
remote: README.SECOND
2297 bytes received in 0.16 seconds (14 Kbytes/s)
ftp>
```

The **get** *filename* – (minus) command is especially useful for looking at "read.me" files that are very often located at **ftp** sites. The problem with this technique is that the entire file is transferred to your terminal; this can be more than you want to see. One solution in this situation is to try to suspend the output with **CTRL-S**; typing **CTRL-S** stops your computer from sending characters to the screen. To see more, type **CTRL-Q**, which lets your computer continue. **CTRL-S** and **CTRL-Q** are fairly standard "suspend" characters. Faster communications links are making the need to suspend scrolling less necessary today. If all else fails, send an interrupt to the server, telling it to stop sending (this is often the **CTRL-C** character). This cancels the current transfer after a delay in which the suspend command is received and acted upon by the remote computer.

## Directories in FTP

There are a number of commands in **ftp** to deal with file system directories—probably more commands than you'd ever need to use. There are so many commands because two sets of directories are involved during an **ftp** session: the working directory or folder on your local machine and the directory on the remote machine. Moving around the local directory depends upon the system you are using. Manipulating the remote directory is often more restrictive,* and is done using the "change directory" (**cd**) command:

```
ftp>  cd  directory
```

When you create a connection to a remote computer using **ftp**, you are initially placed in the same directory you would have been in if you had logged in to that machine directly. You are also governed by the file and directory access permissions allowed by the remote system (normally, not all files and directories are accessible for obvious reasons).

Perhaps the easiest way to get around this problem is to know the full directory path you need on the remote computer. If you know it, whenever you get lost you can just change directories to that path name to get back on familiar turf. If you forget what directory you are in, you can use the "print working directory" (**pwd**) command to find out. **pwd** returns the path of the current working directory:

```
ftp>  pwd
257 "/hermes" is current directory.
```

## ASCII and Binary Transfers

Now that you can change remote directories and find files, let's examine how to transfer data. **ftp** has two commonly used ways ("modes") of transferring data, called "binary" and "ASCII." In a *binary* transfer, the bit sequence of the file is preserved, so the original and the copy are bit-by-bit identical, even if a file containing that bit sequence is meaningless on the destination machine. For example, if a Macintosh transferred an executable file to an IBM VM system in binary, the file could not be executed on the VM system. (It could, however, be copied in binary mode from that VM system to another Macintosh and be executed there.)

*ASCII* mode is really an unfortunate misnomer: It simply should be called "text" mode. In ASCII mode, transfers are treated as sets of (keyboard) characters; the client and server try to ensure that the characters they transfer have the same meaning on the target computer as they did on the source computer. If a Macintosh file contains text, the file still would be meaningless on the IBM VM machine, because the codes used to represent characters on the Macintosh are different than those used on the IBM VM. In ASCII mode, **ftp** automatically translates the file from a Mac text file to an IBM VM text file: Hence the file would be readable on the IBM machine.

If you are confused by this, think of giving someone a journal article published in German. Binary mode would be equivalent to photocopying the article, in which case it is useless

---

*This is especially true if you are using the guest account, *anonymous*. We will discuss "anonymous FTP" extensively later in this chapter.

unless the recipient understands German. ASCII mode is equivalent to translating the article before giving it to the other person. In this case, it becomes useful to the person who does not understand the original German.

In the previous example, some of the messages made a big point of saying that this was an ASCII transfer. This is appropriate, because the two files we were transferring were both text files. We do not know what kind of machine we are taking them from, and we do not care; we just want to make sure that we can read the files on our machine. The following options are simple but important for understanding **ftp** file transfers:

- To make sure that **ftp** is in ASCII mode, enter the command **ascii**.
- To put **ftp** into binary mode, enter the command **binary**.

The command **image** is a synonym for **binary**; you will find that a lot of **ftp** messages use the phrase "image mode" or "I mode" when they mean **binary**. For example:

```
ftp> binary                    now we're ready to transfer a binary file
200 Type set to I.             I stands for "image," or "binary"
ftp> put a.out                 transfer a UNIX executable (binary)
ftp> ascii                     toggle to ASCII to transfer a text file
200 Type set to A.             A stands for "ASCII," or "text"
ftp> get help.txt              retrieve a text (ASCII) file
```

Even if you are transferring files between identical machines, you need to be aware of the proper mode for the type of file you are transferring. The **ftp** software does not know the machines are identical. So, if you transfer a binary file in ASCII mode, the translation will still take place, even though it is not needed. This may slow the transfer down slightly, which probably is not a big deal, but it may also damage the data, perhaps making the file unusable. If you know that both machines are identical, binary mode will work for both text files and data files.

This means that it is important to know what kind of data you want to transfer. Table 6-1 gives you hints for some common file types.

Many database and spreadsheet programs use a binary format to store their data, even if the data is inherently text. Therefore, unless you know what your software does, we recommend trying binary mode first for database or spreadsheet files. Then see whether or not the file you have transferred works correctly (if not, try ASCII mode).

For word processing programs, you can get a few additional clues. The so-called WYSIWYG word processors (word processors that have an elaborate display that matches the actual output very closely) usually store documents in a binary format. Some of these programs have a special command for writing text (i.e., ASCII) files that can be transferred in ASCII mode, but you may lose some formatting information. To look for

*Table 6-1* *Common File Types and Modes*

| File | Mode |
| --- | --- |
| Text file | ASCII, by definition |
| Hypertext (HTML) document | ASCII |
| Spreadsheet | Probably binary |
| Database file | Probably binary, possibly |
| ASCII word processor file | Probably binary, possibly ASCII |
| Program source code | ASCII |
| Electronic mail messages | ASCII |
| UNIX shell archive | ASCII |
| UNIX tar file | Binary |
| Backup file | Binary |
| Compressed file | Binary |
| Uuencoded or binhexed* file | ASCII |
| Executable file | Binary, but see below |
| PostScript (laser printer) file | ASCII |
| Picture files (GIF, JPEG, MPEG) | Binary |

*uuencode is a UNIX utility that we will mention in chapter 7, *Electronic Mail.* The UNIX UUCP utilities use it to encode binary files in an all-ASCII representation, which makes them easier to transfer correctly. **BinHex** is a similar utility used on DOS and Windows systems.

this option, try the **File**, **Save As** option and look for a prompt that allows you to pick "text only." The simpler (and older) word processors that do not have fancy WYSIWYG display capabilities typically store data in an ASCII format.

Executable files are generally binary files; however, there are exceptions. Programs that are executed directly by the processor are always binary. With some operating systems, scripts are called "command files." Scripts are always text files.

On the World Wide Web, many hypertext files are stored in a format called HTML, which stands for "Hypertext Markup Language." This is an ASCII format that is used by the WWW (described in chapter 13, *The World Wide Web and Netscape Navigator*). There are many places on the Net where various types of video images (weather maps, satellite images, etc.) are available.

The most important file formats for video images are called GIF and JPEG, both of which can encode elaborate multicolor images; and MPEG, which is used for "movies" (the MP stands for "motion picture"). These are all binary formats and should therefore be transferred in binary mode. You probably need extra software to view these files; that is also available through the Internet.

## Transferring Multiple Files

The **get** and **put** commands discussed earlier can transfer only one file at a time. On occasion, you want to transfer groups of files. To do so, you can use the "multiple" **mput** and **mget** commands. They have the syntax:

```
ftp>  mput   list of files
ftp>  mget  list of files
```

The **mput** command takes the files in the list and moves them to the remote system. The **mget** command moves files from the remote system to the local system. In both cases, the filenames will be the same on both the local and remote systems. The list of files can be arbitrarily long and can include wildcards.

The actual rules for how wildcards are expanded are more complicated than the **ftp** documentation suggests. You can usually use an asterisk (*) to match zero or more characters and forget about the complexities. (On UNIX systems, you can use a question mark [?] to match any single character.) You may have to do some experimentation or some careful reading of the documentation to see what works.* Here's a typical session using **mget** and **mput**, assuming we have accessed **ftp.isoc.org**:

```
ftp>  dir
200 PORT command successful.
150 ASCII data connection for /bin/ls  (129.1.3.43,3055) (0 bytes).
total 122
-rw-rw-r--   1 1034     1000
9480 Mar 27  1994 _A Brief History of the Internet
-rw-rw-r--   1 1034     1000
29608 Mar 27  1994 how.internet.came.to.be
-rw-rw-r--   1 1034     1000
21776 Mar 27  1994 short.history.of.internet
226 ASCII Transfer complete.
292 bytes received in 0.035 seconds (8.1 Kbytes/s)
ftp> mget *
mget _A Brief History of the Internet? y
200 PORT command successful.
150 ASCII data connection for _A Brief History of the Internet
(129.1.3.43,3051) (9480 bytes).
226 ASCII Transfer complete.
local: _A Brief History of the Internet
remote: _A Brief History of the Internet
9642 bytes received in 0.29 seconds (32 Kbytes/s)
```

---

*When you use **mput**, you are moving files from your local system to the remote system. The wildcards are expanded by your local system and use the local system's wildcard rules. When you use **mget**, you need to locate files on the remote system. In this case, **ftp** uses the remote system to see what, if anything, matches the wildcards. The wildcard rules that **mput** and **mget** obey may differ.

```
mget how.internet.came.to.be? y
200 PORT command successful.
150 ASCII data connection for how.internet.came.to.be
(129.1.3.43,3052) (29608 bytes).
226 ASCII Transfer complete.
local: how.internet.came.to.be
remote: how.internet.came.to.be
30181 bytes received in 1 seconds (28 Kbytes/s)
mget short.history.of.internet? y
200 PORT command successful.
150 ASCII data connection for short.history.of.internet
(129.1.3.43,3053) (21776 bytes).
226 ASCII Transfer complete.
local: short.history.of.internet
remote: short.history.of.internet
22140 bytes received in 0.49 seconds (44 Kbytes/s)
ftp>
```

Now let's try to "put" a group of files. This time, we will explicitly put two filenames on the command, just to show you that it can be done.

```
ftp>  mput myfile tblsz.c                           now try to put some files
mput myfile?  yes                                   first file: do I really want it?
200 PORT command successful.
150 ASCII data connection for myfile (127.0.0.1,1139).
226 Transfer complete.
local: myfile remote: myfile 2785 bytes sent in 0.03 seconds (91 Kbytes/s)
mput tblsz.c?  y                                    second file: do I really want it?
200 PORT command successful.
150 ASCII data connection for tblsz.c (127.0.0.1,1141).
226 Transfer complete.
local: tblsz.c remote: tblsz.c
975 bytes sent in 0.04 seconds (24 Kbytes/s)
ftp>
```

Note this difference between **put** and **mput**: The command we just gave, **mput myfile tblsz.c**, does *not* mean "put *myfile* on the remote system with the filename *tblsz.c*," as it would if it were the **put** command. It means "copy all the files listed to the remote system without changing their names."

**ftp** normally asks you whether or not you want to transfer each file; you have to type y (or **yes**, or press ENTER) to transfer the file.

Typing **n** (or **no**)* cancels the transfer. Being prompted for each file is annoying (particularly if you are transferring a large group of files), but it helps prevent mistakes.

---

*Actually, anything that begins with the letter "n" will do. In some implementations, anything that does *not* begin with the letter "n" is taken as a yes.

You can disable it with the command prompt. The whole group of files will be transferred without further intervention. Giving the prompt command again reenables prompting.

There are a few things to watch out for:

- Remember that **mput** does not allow you to specify a name for the destination file. All the names you list are interpreted as source files. If you want to place the files in a different directory on the remote computer, use the command **cd** to change to that directory before using **mput**. The same is true for **mget** commands.

- You cannot use **mput** or **mget** (or, for that matter, the regular **get** and **put**) commands to copy a directory. You can use them only to copy groups of plain files. Copying a directory yields unpredictable results. If you need to transfer a directory, create an archive of some sort and transfer the archive.

- You may find that the **mget**, with wildcards, does not always work properly; it appears to depend on whether or not the **ls** command is implemented correctly by the remote FTP server.

## FTP Command Summary

The following table summarizes **ftp**'s most useful commands. It includes all of the commands that we have discussed so far. These commands are available on most, if not all, **ftp** clients. **ftp** will show you the commands that are available on your particular client if you type **help**.

| | |
|---|---|
| **account** *info* | Supplies additional accounting or security information which must sometimes be given within a session. Later we will see a situation in which the **account** command is needed for accessing IBM mainframes. |
| **ascii** | Enters ASCII mode, for transferring text files. |
| **binary** | Enters binary mode, for transferring binary files. |
| **cd** *(remote-directory)* | Changes the working directory on the remote machine. |
| **close** | Ends the **ftp** session with a particular machine and returns to **ftp** command mode. After a **close**, you can open a connection to a new system or **quit** from **ftp**. |
| **delete** *filename* | Deletes the named file on the remote system. |

**dir** *(file destination)*    Gives a full directory listing on the remote machine. *file* and *destination* are both optional. *file* can either be a single file or a wildcard construction. The listing shows all filenames that match the specification. If *file* is omitted, the listing shows all files in the current remote directory. The *destination* is where the output should be put. It can be either a file on the local machine or a command through which to filter the file. If *destination* is omitted, the listing appears on the terminal.

**hash**    Tells **ftp** to print a pound sign (#) every time a block of data is transferred by a **get** or **put** command. Useful if you are not certain the network is working; it gives you a visual signal that data is actually moving. It is also lets you know that something's happening when you are transferring a very long file. If **ftp** is already printing hashes, the **hash** command tells it to stop.

**help**    Prints a short bit of documentation about the command.

**lcd** *(directory)*    Changes the default directory on your local machine to the named directory.

**ls** *(file destination)*    Gives a short directory listing on the remote machine. The arguments are the same as for **dir**.

**mget** *(file-list)*    Gets multiple files from the remote machine. The file list can be either a list of filenames separated by spaces or a wildcard construction.

**mput** *(file-list)*    Puts multiple files onto the remote machine. The file list can be either a list of filenames separated by spaces or a wildcard construction.

**open** *machine-name*    Connects to the named machine. This is useful if you want to **connect** to a new system after transferring files from another system. You must **close** your old connection first.

**prompt**    With **mget** or **mput**, the **prompt** command tells **ftp** to prompt you for confirmation before transferring each file. This is useful if you want to make sure you are not needlessly transferring files or (worse) overwriting files that already exist. If prompting is already enabled when you give the **prompt** command, **ftp** turns it off and transfers all the files without asking any questions.

pwd                     Prints the name of the current remote directory (print working directory).

quit                    Closes the connection, if one exists, and exits **ftp**.

**user** *username*     Sends the username to the remote machine to log in. This is useful if you typed your username or password incorrectly. Rather than closing the connection and opening a new one, you can try again by issuing a **user** command.

Most **ftp** implementations actually have 70 or 80 commands. Unless you have very special needs, the commands listed above will suffice.

## ◾ *Anonymous FTP*

So far, the facilities we have discussed make it difficult to make a file available for everyone to use. For example, if I wanted to distribute a software package, I'd have to put it on the system and then pass out login/password combinations to everyone who wanted to get the software. This would be a burden, particularly for the administrator, but also for the user.

*Anonymous FTP* bypasses this limitation. It allows users who do not have a login name or a password to access certain files on a machine. Of course, there are strong restrictions: Anonymous users can normally only **get** files (i.e., copy them); they cannot install new files or modify files that already exist.* There are strict limits on which files they can copy.

When anonymous FTP is enabled, you start **ftp**, connect to a remote computer, and give *anonymous* or *ftp* as your login name. **ftp** will accept any string as your password. It is generally considered good form to use your electronic mail address as the password. Some systems demand that you use a valid e-mail address before they will let you in. After signing in as *anonymous,* you are allowed to get those files that are placed there expressly for retrieval.

When you enter a system anonymously, you are placed at a particular spot in the remote directory system. That initial directory is the starting point for all anonymous FTP access. From there, you can move to subdirectories only by giving the name of the subdirectory, or move back from a subdirectory to its "parent" by using the .. argument. Positioning yourself by specifying a directory beginning with a slash ( / ), is usually not allowed.

---

*An archive manager can create directories that can be written by anonymous FTP users. Such directories are often used to let users submit articles or software for inclusion in an archive. If the archive manager has set up an incoming anonymous FTP directory, you can use **ftp**'s normal **put** and **mput** commands to place files there.

**cd /pub** has been redefined to mean "move to the *pub* subdirectory of the initial anonymous FTP directory." You can use **cd /** if you get lost in an anonymous FTP session and need to get back to your starting point. Your other option is to use **cd ..** repeatedly to move up to where you started. (The command **cdup** is a synonym for **cd ...**)

Remember, when you are using anonymous FTP, you are a guest on someone else's system. Sometimes there will be usage restrictions posted:

```
230-Available for anonymous ftp only between 5 pm EST 230-and 8 am EST.
```

These are displayed when you first log in. Please observe them.

Now for an example. You were browsing through the *Resource Catalog,* and ran across a document called *Not Just Cows,* a directory of useful agriculture-oriented Internet resources. The entry for this document gave the following access information:

```
ftp ftp.sura.net login anonymous; cd pub/nic;
get agriculture.list
```

This tells you to get a copy of the document via anonymous FTP from **ftp.sura.net.** Your dialog with **ftp** to get this resource would look like this:

```
%  ftp ftp.sura.net                                     start up ftp to the server
Connection opened (Assuming 8-bit connections)
<nic.sura.net FTP server (Version wu-2.4(1) Fri May 20 10:20:58 EDT 1994) ready.
Username: anonymous                                     anonymous login
331 Guest login ok, send email address as password.
Password: krol@ux1.cso.uiuc.edu                         password doesn't really echo
<                    BBN Planet, Southeast Region
<              FTP server running wuarchive experimental ftpd
<
<Welcome to the BBN Planet, Southeast Region FTP server. If you have
<any problems with the server, please try using a dash (-) as the first
<character of your password -- this will turn off the continuation messages
<that may be confusing your FTP client. If you still have problems, please
<send mail to systems@sura.net.
<
<Nifty feature:
<
<       Compressed files may be uncompressed by attempting to get the
<name without the .Z. Example: to get zen-1.0.tar.Z uncompressed one
<would get zen-1.0.tar.
<
<       Entire hierarchies may also be tarred and optionally compressed.
<To get, for example, the sendmail hierarchy tarred & compressed, one would
<get sendmail.tar.Z.
<
<Guest login ok, access restrictions apply.
```

```
NIC.SURA.NET>
NIC.SURA.NET>  cd pub/nic                             move to the directory
250-######WELCOME TO THE SURANET NETWORK INFORMATION CENTER##########
250-SURAnet                                  info@sura.net
250-8400 Baltimore Blvd.                     301-982-4600(voice)
250-College Park, Maryland  USA 20740-2498   FAX 301-982-4605
250-    Many of the documents available in this ftp archive are geared
250-towards the new user of the Internet. SURAnet has provided several
250-"How To" guides for network navigation tools such as, telnet, ftp,
250-and email. These "How To" guides are available in the directory
250 CWD command successful.
NIC.SURA.NET>  dir                                    list files
200 PORT command successful.
150 Opening ASCII mode data connection for /bin/ls.
total 4096
-rw-rw-r--  1 1115     120      122743 Jan  7  1994 agricultural.list
-rw-rw-r--  1 1048     120       27840 Apr 17  1992 archie.manual
-rw-rw-r--  1 1048     120       30500 Oct 14  1992 bbs.list.10-14
-rw-rw-r--  1 1048     120        1347 Nov 12  1992 bionet.list
-rw-rw-r--  1 1048     120       41580 Dec  8  1992 cwis.list
drwxrwsr-x  3 1048     120         512 Apr 20 22:28 directory.services
-rw-rw-r--  1 1044     120        1904 Jan  6  1992 farnet-recommendations
-rw-rw-r--  1 1048     120       15968 Oct 28  1992 holocaust.archive
-rw-rw-r--  1 1115     120        3650 May 15 21:45 how.to.get.SURAnet.guide
drwxr-sr-x  2 1115     120         512 Apr 10 16:03 infoguide
drwxrwsr-x  2 1142     120         512 Nov 14  1994 mailing.lists
drwxrwsr-x  2 1086     120         512 Oct 15  1993 monticello
-rw-rw-r--  1 1048     120       15474 Nov 11  1992 network.law.info
drwxrwsr-x  2 1048     120         512 Feb 10  1994 network.service.guides
                                         remainder of list deleted for space
<Transfer complete.
2302 bytes transferred at 65771 bps.
Run time = 10. ms, Elapsed time = 280. ms.
NIC.SURA.NET>  get agricultural.list NJC              move the file
200 PORT command successful.
150 Opening ASCII mode data connection for agricultural.list (85677 bytes).
226 Transfer complete.
local: NJC remote: agricultural.list
88383 bytes received in 2.8 seconds (31 Kbytes/s)
NIC.SURA.NET>  quit
221 Goodbye.
%
```

Let's examine the preceding example and see what happened. Once connected to **ftp.sura.net**, which was specified on the **ftp** command, *anonymous* (or *ftp*) is used as the login name. As a password, you send your e-mail address (it does not print when you enter it). Next you issue the **cd pub/nic** to move to the directory specified in the *Resource*

*Catalog* entry. The server responded with a message (all the lines beginning 250). Some newer FTP servers automatically display a file on your terminal whenever you enter a directory.\* This feature is becoming increasingly common; it is very helpful, because you do not have to search for a *README* or *INDEX* file to find out what is in the directory. After reading the introductory message, you list the files in the directory to see whether there is anything else you might want; finally, you get around to copying the file named *agricultural.list* on the remote computer to *NJC* on your home computer.

That is all there is to it. Anonymous FTP is just like regular FTP, except that you do not need a password. The home page associated with this book lists many FTP archives that you can access; the Archie service will give you much more information about what is available and where to find it.

## Handling Large Files and Groups of Files

Network users often need to transfer extremely large files, or large batches of files, across the network. You may need a large database, an archive of a discussion group, or a set of reports or documents. All of these tend to be large. In this section, we will discuss techniques for handling large files (compression) and ways to accumulate large groups of files into a single archive to make them easier to transfer. Because most anonymous FTP sites already store files as compressed archives, we will also discuss how to "unpack" such a file once you have transferred it to your system.

### Compressed Files

To reduce the cost of storage and transmission across the network, large files are frequently stored in *compressed format*. There are many techniques for data compression, and consequently a number of different compression programs that can be used. Text files run through a good data compression program can be reduced anywhere from 30 to 70 percent in size.

Moving compressed files across the network really is not a problem. They should always be treated as *binary* files. The problem is that getting the file to the target system is only half the battle. After it is there, you must uncompress it before it is usable. This may or may not be easy, because there is no one standard for compression utilities.

Compressed files are usually flagged by an unusual suffix or extension on the filename. The most common compression utilities are:

---

\*The initial message is stored in the file *.message;* you will see it in the directory listing.

*Table 6-2    Common Compression Programs*

| Compression Program | Decompression Program | File Suffix | Typical Filename |
|---|---|---|---|
| compress | uncompress | .Z | rfc1118.txt.Z |
| gzip | gunzip | .z or .gz | textfile.gz |
| pack | unpack | .z | textfile.z |
| Stuffit | unsit | .Sit | program.Sit |
| PackIt | unpit | .pit | report.pit |
| PKZIP | unzip41 | .ZIP | package.ZIP |
| zoo210 | zoo210 | .zoo | picture.zoo |

If you are looking at the files available on a remote system and see these suffixes, that is an indication that the files are probably compressed. The suffix gives you a hint about what utility should be used to uncompress it. The program you need to uncompress the file will vary depending on what kind of computer you are using and what kind of compression was used. This is only the tip of the iceberg; there are about as many compression programs as there are types of computers. A very useful chart is available via **ftp** (URL: **ftp://ftp.cso.uiuc.edu in directory /doc/pcnet**).

On UNIX, compression and uncompression are usually done using the **compress** and **uncompress** utilities. Let's take the file we just retrieved, *NJC*, check its size, and compress it:

```
% ls -l NJC*                                     list all files starting with NJC
-rw-r--r--  1 krol        61411 Dec 20 14:46 NJC
% compress -v NJC                                -v says tell me how much compression
NJC: Compression: 57% - replaced with NJC.Z
% ls -l NJC*                                     now I have a .Z file only
-rw-r--r--  1 krol        26230 Dec 20 14:46 NJC.Z
```

Now we have a file called *NJC.Z.* The original file was 61,411 characters long; the compressed file is only 26,230 characters long, for a savings of roughly 57 percent. This means that the compressed file will take less than half as much storage and half as much time to transfer from one computer to another. Let's uncompress *NJC.Z,* to make the original file again:

```
% uncompress NJC.Z
% ls -l NJC*
-rw-r--r--  1 krol        61411 Dec 20 14:46 NJC.txt
```

We have the same useful file back. Note that its size has not changed; the uncompressed file is still 61,411 bytes, just like the original.

## Moving a Whole Directory

When you are using **ftp**, you often want to receive a whole file structure: a directory or collection of directories, not just a single file. **ftp** really is not designed to do this effectively; it is not convenient to move 50 or 100 files at a time, and there are no standard commands for moving entire directories.

Although this situation comes up all the time, it is particularly common when you want to get a set of files from a remote FTP archive. For example, someone who distributes a free software package by putting it in an FTP archive usually needs to make dozens (maybe even hundreds) of files available. Rather than telling users to "**ftp** these 50 files," he or she usually uses a backup utility to aggregate all of these files into a single file (shown in Figure 6-1).

On the source computer containing the files to be distributed, the person responsible must copy all the files into one package. When someone gets the package, he or she

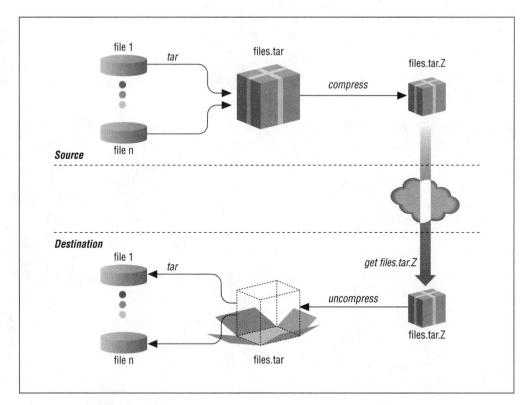

*Figure 6-1   Moving many files*

must open it up to get the group of files that are contained. On a UNIX system, this
single file is typically created using **tar**, as follows:

```
%  cd book                              let's see what's in the directory
%  ls                                   we plan to dump
README          ftp.2          news          tmac.Seffnuts
applications    ftp.bak        nut.guide     tmac.Sioc
%  cd ..                                move to parent directory
%  tar -cf book.tar book               dump directory book into book.tar
%  ls -l book.tar                      how big is book.tar
-rw-r--r--  1 krol       802816 Dec 21 06:35 book.tar
```

The directory to be packaged is called *book* and can be seen to contain a number of files.
From the parent directory of *book,* the **tar** command is used to create a file named *book.tar*
that contains all the data to be distributed. The file is quite large and is of no benefit to
the owner anymore (he has the directory already). It makes sense to compress it:

```
%  compress -v book.tar
book.tar: Compression: 60.13% -- replaced with book.tar.Z
%  ls -l book.tar*
-rw-r--r--  1 krol       321717 Dec 21 06:35 book.tar.Z
```

That uses only 40 percent as much disk space. The friendly system administrator now
puts this file into the anonymous FTP directory, where it can be fetched by anyone in
the world.

You may later decide you want to pick up the "book" package and install it on your
computer. You begin by using anonymous FTP to contact the server and retrieve
*book.tar.Z:*

```
%  ftp ux1.cso.uiuc.edu                          start an ftp to the server
Connected to ux1.cso.uiuc.edu.
220 ux1.cso.uiuc.edu FTP server (Version 5.60) awaits your command
Name (ux1.cso.uiuc.edu:): anonymous               log in as appropriate
331 Guest login ok, send ident as password.
Password:
230 Guest login ok, access restrictions apply.
Remote system type is UNIX.
Using binary mode to transfer files.                note binary mode
ftp> get book.tar.Z                                 get the aggregate dump file
200 PORT command successful.
150 Opening BINARY mode data connection for book.tar.Z (321717 bytes).
226 Transfer complete.
321717 bytes received in 2.4 seconds (1.3e+02 Kbytes/s)
ftp> quit                                           quit ftp
221 Goodbye.
```

You now have the compressed **tar** file; you only need to undo all the operations done to it to make it usable. Sometimes people are confused by the order of doing these multiple operations. You must undo them in exactly the opposite order they were performed to create the file. The rule of thumb is to do whatever it takes to handle the filename extensions right to left. So, with a file like *book.tar.Z,* you must first get rid of the *Z:*

```
%  uncompress book.tar.Z                         file is unusable until uncompressed
%  ls -l book*                                   now one file book.tar
-rw-r--r--  1 krol        802816 Dec 21 07:00 book.tar
```

Now you have an uncompressed **tar** file, *book.tar.* Get rid of the *tar* and you are done:

```
%  tar -xf book.tar                              extract all files in book.tar
%  ls -l book*                                   same file as before
-rw-r--r--  1 krol        802816 Dec 21 07:00 book.tar
book:                                            and a whole new directory
total 792
-rw-r--r--  1 krol          4630 Sep  3 10:43 README
-rw-r--r--  1 krol         14461 Nov 11 15:18 applications
                                                remainder deleted for space considerations
```

You will find the command **tar -tf** *filename* useful, too. This lists the files that are present in the **tar** file; by looking at the list, you can figure out whether or not you got the right file.

From time to time, you will see other complications. At some sites, extremely large archives are cut into many smaller pieces (usually 100KB or so). Each piece is typically assigned a two-digit decimal number, which is the last part of the filename. For example, you might see files named *book.tar.Z.01, book.tar.Z.02,* etc. Transfer all of these files to your system.

Some hints:

- Before you unpack a **tar** file, it is a good idea to give the command **tar -tf book.tar** to find out what files are contained. Make sure that unpacking the archive will not overwrite any files that you want. One drawback of **tar** is that it cannot rename files as it unpacks them; the names you see are the names you will get.

- You can combine the uncompress and unpack steps into one command with **zcat book.tar.Z | tar -xf -**. This way, you do not leave an extra temporary file lying around.

- An increasing number of archives are using the **gzip** program (GNU-zip) for compression, which uses the extension *.z* or *.gz.* The corresponding uncompress tool is called **gunzip**; and **gzip -d** corresponds to **zcat**. GNU-zip is free software that is distributed by the Free Software Foundation; their FTP archive is listed in the *Resource Catalog* in the "Computing" section. It may come with your system, but it probably does not; you will have to get your own copy.

### *Other Archival Utilities*

There are a few other archive types you may see from time to time. You may see archives created by various programs on DOS systems (FASTBACK, ZIP, PCBACKUP, etc.) or the BACKUP utility on VMS operating systems. Unfortunately, most archival tools are specific to one operating system. If you are using a Macintosh, you probably do not have a **tar** command, let alone a VMS BACKUP command. Likewise, if you are using a UNIX system, you probably do not have a DOS FASTBACK program. As a rule, therefore, an archive is useful only if you are unpacking it on the same kind of computer that created it. (The archive might be stored on another kind of computer, which is not important—so long as it is treated as a binary file.)

If the Internet presents some problems, it also gives you a way to resolve these problems (URL: **http://www.cis.ohio-state.edu:80/text/faq/usenet/compression-faq/top.html**). If you have the time and energy to search through the volumes of free software that are available on the Net, you may be able to find a program that will unpack a strange archive format on your system. (Chapter 9 tells you how to locate software.) Commercial software also is available for unpacking different backup formats.

## ▓ *Special Notes on Various Systems*

**ftp**'s biggest virtue is that it lets you move files among computers regardless of their type. In many cases, you do not need to know anything about the remote systems. However, this is not completely true; in practice, whenever you have two systems, you usually end up needing to know something (certainly not much, but something) about the remote system.

The problems are relatively minor, and typically have to do with the way the remote system specifies filenames. As much as possible, **ftp** uses a uniform, UNIX-like notation for filenames and addresses. This can be confusing, however, because **ftp** does not try to interpret **dir** listings and other output generated by the remote system: It just sends the command's output back to you verbatim. Deciphering the output from **ls**, **dir**, or any other command usually is not too difficult. It is fairly easy to find the filename, the file's size, and the last modification date, and that is usually all the information you care about. But you do need to know how to convert remote filenames into a form that **ftp** understands.

Here are a number of examples using **ftp** to access various kinds of systems that you will find as servers on the Internet. Remember that these are examples. There are many vendors of TCP/IP software for the Macintosh, Digital Equipment, and IBM computers. The server you are contacting might look a bit different from the examples we show here. Also, in most of the examples, the remote system tells you what kind of computer it is. This is not always the case. If you do not know what kind of system you are using, your best bet is to look for *README* files; there is often one that explains what archive you are looking at, what kind of a system you are using, and so on. If this does not work, do a **dir** and try matching the format to the examples.

## Target: Digital Equipment VMS Systems

VMS systems have a fairly feature-rich file structure. Logging in to one presents no particular problems:

```
%  ftp vaxb.cs.usnd.edu
Connected to vaxb.cs.usnd.edu.
220 FTP Service Ready
Name (vaxb.cs.unsd.edu:krol): anonymous          anonymous FTP
331 ANONYMOUS user ok, send real identity as password.
Password:
230 ANONYMOUS logged in, directory HSC1$DUA1:[ANON], restrictions apply.
Remote system type is VMS.
```

**ftp** was nice enough to tell you that it is talking to a VMS system, so you know what to expect. This is not always the case. The software necessary to take part in the Internet does not come automatically on VMS. A site wanting Internet access must buy a software package from one of several companies; the competing implementations are all a bit different. Another clue that you are communicating with a VMS server might be the word "Multinet":

```
220 ftp.unsd.edu MultiNet FTP Server Process 3.3(14)...
```

Multinet is the name of a popular software product for VMS systems; if you see it, you are probably dealing with a VMS server.

The complexity surrounding VMS lies in its file structure. We have been placed in a directory containing files accessible via anonymous FTP; the complete name of this directory is *HSC1$DUA1:[ANON]*. This name consists of two parts: *HSC1$DUA1* is the name of a disk; and *[ANON]* is a directory on that disk.*

---

*If we had been using regular **ftp**, rather than anonymous FTP, we probably would have been placed in a "default directory," which is similar to the UNIX "home directory." The home directory name would probably be *HSC$1DUA1:[KROL]*.

Now that we have logged in, let's try a **dir** command to see what is available:

```
ftp> dir
200 PORT Command OK.
125 File transfer started correctly
Directory HSC1$DUA1:[ANON]

AAAREADME.TXT;9   2-MAY-1991 15:45:51   730/2   (RWED,RE,,R)
ARTICLES.DIR;1   28-MAY-1990 10:20:14  1536/3   (RWE,RE,RE,R)
LIBRARY.DIR;1    30-APR-1991 11:13:06  1536/3   (RWE,RE,RE,RE)
WAIS.DIR;1        1-OCT-1991 10:21:16   512/1   (RWE,RE,RE,RE)
Total of 4 files, 1448 blocks.
226 File transfer completed ok
```

Each file consists of a name (e.g., *AAAREADME*), an extension (e.g., *TXT*), and a version number (e.g., *9*). Ignore the version number;* you will almost always want the most recent version of a file, which is what you will get if you pretend the version number does not exist. The extension tells you something about the file. *TXT* is the extension for text files, so these files may be read directly. Files with the extension *DIR* are directories. There are a number of other standard extensions, such as *FOR* for FORTRAN files, *EXE* for executable files, and *COM* for command files. The filenames will be listed in uppercase, but VMS does not care whether you use upper- or lowercase letters.

We see that the default directory for anonymous FTP has three subdirectories. Let's use **cd** to look at the subdirectory *wais.dir*. When you use **cd** to change directories, you use the directory name without the extension:

```
ftp> cd wais
200 Working directory changed to "HSC1$DUA1:[ANON.WAIS]"
```

Now our working directory is *HSC1$DUA1:[ANON.WAIS]*. Notice that VMS specifies a subdirectory by listing each subdirectory after a period within the brackets. So this subdirectory is roughly equivalent to the UNIX path *HSC1$DUA1/ANON/WAIS*. Likewise, it is equivalent to the DOS path *\ANON\WAIS,* on a disk named *HSC1$DUA1:.*

Unfortunately, the people who sell TCP/IP software for VAX/VMS systems do not agree about how the **cd** command should work, particularly when you want to move through

---

*All right, we will explain it. VMS has the peculiarity that it keeps old versions of your files, until you explicitly tell it to delete them. This can waste tremendous amounts of disk space, but it does make it easy to undo your mistakes.

multiple levels of directories. With some VMS FTP servers, you have to use a VMS-style directory specification, like this:

```
ftp>  cd [x.y.z]
```

If the FTP server you are using expects this syntax, then to move up a level, you must use the command **cdup**; the UNIX-style **cd ..** will not work.

Other implementations expect you to specify multiple directories using the UNIX "slash" notation:

```
ftp>  cd x/y/z
```

Which do you use? As we said, it depends on the software the FTP server is running. The easiest way to find out which syntax to use is to try one approach; if it does not work, try the other. No harm will be done if it does not work. If you want to be safe, you can move through one directory level at a time:

```
ftp>  cd x
ftp>  cd y
ftp>  cd z
```

This strategy works in either case. And, once again, you must omit the *.dir* extension from the directory's name whenever you use it in a **cd** command.

**get** and **put** work in the usual way. You must specify the extension as part of the filename. You can include the version number, but it is easier to omit it (unless you want an old version for some special reason).* In this example, we will move two levels down the directory tree and retrieve the file *waissearch.hlp* from there:

```
ftp>  cd wais/doc                          change to directory anon/wais/doc
200 Working directory changed to "HSC1$DUA1:[ANON.WAIS.DOC]"
ftp>  get waissearch.hlp                    get the file waissearch.hlp
200 PORT Command OK.
125 ASCII transfer started for
HSC1$DUA1:[ANON.WAIS.DOC]WAISSEARCH.HLP; (1076 bytes)
226 File transfer completed ok
1076 bytes received in 0.35 seconds (3 Kbytes/s)
ftp>
```

So long as you are not confused by the VMS-style file specifications, you should have no problems dealing with VAX/VMS systems.

---

*If you specify an old file version, be sure to specify a local filename. If you don't, you will probably end up with a filename that has a semicolon in it. The semicolon will really confuse UNIX, and probably is not too healthy for DOS or Windows systems.

## *Target: MS-DOS Systems*

MS-DOS systems look very much like other network servers. You log in using the normal
procedure:

```
%  ftp server.uiuc.edu
Connected to server.uiuc.edu.
220-server.uiuc.edu PC/TCP 2.0 FTP Server by FTP Software ready
220 Connection is automatically closed if idle for 5 minutes
Name (server.uiuc.edu:):  krol
331 User OK, send password
Password:
230 krol logged in
Remote system type is MS-DOS.
```

Note that the remote system tells you that you are connected to a system running DOS.

It is also fairly obvious how to interpret the output of the **dir** command:

```
ftp>  dir
200 Port OK
150 Opening data connection
        336         FS.BAT    Tue Dec 17 21:36:56 1991
          0         MBOX      Thu Nov 07 14:46:30 1991
        123         NS.BAT    Tue Jan 08 22:34:44 1991
<dir>           NETWIRE    Tue Jun 11 02:37:34 1991
<dir>           INCOMING.FTP  Tue Dec 17 21:42:24 1991
226 Transfer successful. Closing data connection
```

Filenames on a DOS computer consist of a filename (e.g., *FS*) and a three-character
extension (e.g., *BAT*). Subdirectories are flagged with the character string **<dir>** at the
beginning of their line.

When you are dealing with a DOS server, you may be confused by the way that it
handles directories. First, directories are disk-specific; you sometimes need to specify the
disk on which the directory resides. Disks are identified by a single letter followed by a
colon (:). The following **cd** command changed the "working disk" to the **h** disk:

```
ftp>  cd h:
200 OK
```

If you now do another directory command, you will see a different set of files:

```
ftp>  dir
200 Port OK
150 Opening data connection
<dir>               SYSTEM    Wed Dec 31 00:00:00 1980
<dir>               PUBLIC    Wed Dec 31 00:00:00 1980
226 Transfer successful. Closing data connection
```

Changing directories within a disk is done with a normal **cd** command, like the following:

```
ftp>  cd public
200 OK
```

This command changes to the subdirectory *public.* You can also move down multiple directory levels at once with a command:

```
ftp>  cd h:public/ibm_pc/msdos
200 OK
```

The trick is that DOS uses backslashes ( \ ) to separate directory levels. However, when you access a DOS server with **ftp**, the server will try to be Internet-compatible and accept the slash rather than the backslash. If you use a backslash (as an experienced DOS user would expect), you will get an error message:

```
ftp>  cd\h:public\ibm_pc\msdos
550 can't CWD: Error 2: No such file or directory
```

To add to the confusion, when you check the current directory, **ftp** prints the name using backslashes:

```
ftp>  pwd
250 Current working directory is H:\PUBLIC\IBM_PC\MSDOS
```

Once you are positioned in the directory where the file you want lives, moving the file works as expected:

```
ftp>  get config.bak
200 Port OK
150 Opening data connection
226 Transfer successful. Closing data connection
99 bytes received in 0.12 seconds (0.82 Kbytes/s)
```

The moral of the story is very simple. When you are accessing an MS-DOS system using **ftp**, use slashes instead of backslashes. With this in mind, you will not be confused.

## *Target: IBM VM Systems*

IBM VM systems require a little more special handling. Most of the special handling is needed because VM does not have a hierarchical filesystem. On VM, you have disks; each disk can have multiple passwords (one for read-only access and one for read/write access); and filenames are short but have two parts. When you **ftp** to a VM system and log in, it looks like this:

```
%  ftp vmd.cso.uiuc.edu
Connected to vmd.cso.uiuc.edu.
```

```
220-FTPSERVE at vmd.cso.uiuc.edu, 14:46:14 CST MONDAY 12/16/91
220 Connection will close if idle for more than 5 minutes.
Name (vmd.cso.uiuc.edu:krol):                          took the default name: krol
331 Send password please.
Password:
230 KROL logged in; no working directory defined. Remote system type is VM.
```

Once again, **ftp** was nice enough to inform you that the remote system is VM. It also tells you that, even though you are logged in, you cannot get at the files you want. The message "no working directory defined," which you see when **ftp** confirms that you are logged in, tells you that you are not ready to transfer files yet.

When you do a **cd** command on a VM system, you are really asking to get at another disk. Disks are functions of a login name and an address. So to cram this into a **cd** command, you need to say:

```
ftp>  cd  login–name.disk–address
```

For example, the command:

```
ftp>  cd krol.191
```

starts the connection to the disk addressed 191 of user krol. (You can find the names and addresses of the disks you normally use when logged in to a VM system by doing a **q disk** command while you are logged in.) A disk password is usually required; to supply the password, use the **account** command immediately *after* the **cd** command. Continuing the previous example:

```
ftp>  cd krol.191
550 Permission denied to LINK to KROL 191; still no working directory
ftp>  account j9876hoh
230 Working directory is KROL 191
```

Note that message 550 implies your **cd** command failed, even though it looked correct at the time. The **account** command, which you must give next, "fixes" the original **cd** command, so you can access files. Also, because your local system does not really know what the **account** command does on the remote computer, it makes no attempt to hide your password. Take precautions to make sure that others do not find out your password.

Now you have established a directory to work in. The output from a **dir** command looks like this:

```
ftp>  dir
200 Port request OK.
125 List started OK
ACCNT    LEDGER   V    80     59      5 12/20/90  9:04:24 LEN
AGENDA   MEETING  V    73     34      2  9/24/91 10:23:01 LEN
ALL      NOTEBOOK V    80   5174    233 12/10/91 15:17:11 LEN
```

Each filename on an IBM VM system consists of two character strings. Each string has at most eight characters. The first string is called the "filename" and the second is call the "filetype." Above, the filenames are in the first column (e.g., *ALL*), whereas the second column shows the filetype (e.g., *NOTEBOOK*).

If **dir** does not show you all the files you expect to see, it is because there is also a file mode (1 or 0) associated with a file. A file with the mode 0 is considered "private" and cannot be seen with the read password. If you give the write password, you can see all the files. Again, the read and write passwords are set by the owner of the disk.

The filename and filetype both must be specified if you try to move a file. Because both are variable length, you use a period (.) to separate the two. So:

```
ftp>  get all.notebook mbox
```

transfers the file *all* of type *notebook* to the file *mbox* on the local machine.

If you are doing anonymous FTP and the remote host is a VM system, you still have to give a **cd** command before you can access any files. You do not have to give a second password with the **account** command. When you actually **get** files, you must (as you'd expect) give a complete, two-part filename.

## *Target: Macintosh*

Using **ftp** to access a Macintosh server is fairly straightforward, once you get connected. Getting connected might be a problem if the Mac is on a network that dynamically assigns addresses. Many Macs are connected to *Localtalk* networks, which in turn are connected to the Internet through a gateway. Some Localtalk gateways assign Internet addresses to computers as they are turned on, taking addresses from a pool reserved for the Localtalk net. This means that the address or name of a machine might change from day to day; the address that works today might not work tomorrow. This is not usually a problem with public archives; anyone who configures their Macintosh as a public server usually makes sure that its address is assigned permanently. (Otherwise, complaining users would make his life miserable.) You are most likely to run into addressing problems when someone tells you to "grab this file from my Macintosh" on the spur of the moment. The system's owner gives you a numeric IP address, letting you grab the file—so long as he does not turn the system off first. Newer Macintoshes usually do not have this problem, because they can handle Ethernet cards and be connected directly to the Internet.

When you get connected to a Macintosh, **ftp** may ask you for a name; even if it does, it will not require a password. The name is used for logging purposes only.

```
%  ftp 128.174.33.56                              used an IP address this time
Connected to 128.174.33.56.                       rather than a name
220 Macintosh Resident FTP server, ready
Name (128.174.33.56:krol):                        send default name
230 User logged in
```

Doing a **dir** command will get a listing which looks like this:

```
ftp>  dir
Accelerator
Administration/
Applications Combined
Article T3 connections
```

There are two things to note about this listing. One is that subdirectories, which in the Mac world are called *folders,* are flagged by the trailing slash ( / ). The second is that filenames can have spaces in them, which requires special handling. If a filename contains spaces, you must put the entire name within quotes. For example:

```
ftp>  get "Applications Combined" applications
```

This gets the file *Applications Combined,* putting it into the file *applications* on the local machine. Aside from the Macintosh, most systems cannot properly handle names with spaces. Therefore, in this example, we made a point of specifying a local filename without a space.

Changing directories is handled in the usual way. The command:

```
ftp>  cd Administration
```

changes the current directory to *Administration.* If we wanted to move through multiple folders and subfolders, we would list the whole path separated with slashes:

```
ftp>  cd Administration/Personnel
```

## ▨ *Last Words: Some Practical Advice*

Because using **ftp** is fairly straightforward, it is easy to get enthralled with the power it puts at your fingers and lose sight of its limitations. Here are a couple of hints that you may find useful:

- **ftp** allows you to create, delete, and rename files and directories on a remote system. Treat this ability as a convenience to use occasionally, rather than a technique to use all the time. If you are making a lot of changes on a remote system, instead of moving files, it is probably easier to use **telnet** and do your changes as a timesharing session.

■ Directions about anonymous FTP are frequently sketchy. Someone will tell you "anonymous FTP to **server.public.com** and get the Whizbang editor, it is really neat." Servers set up for distributing free software (or other large public archives) frequently have many, many files stashed in various directories. If you cannot find what you are after, try looking for files in the default directory named *README, index, ls–lR,* or something similar. If you are lucky, you will find information about how the server is organized.

■ On UNIX, **ftp** allows you to make some convenient things happen by putting instructions in the *.netrc* file of your home directory. The *.netrc* file is usually used to give instructions for logging in to remote computers. You should not set up automatic logins for computers needing a private login name and password, because you should never put your password in a file. But if you use one anonymous FTP server frequently, say **ftp.sura.net**, you could bypass the login step by putting something like this in *.netrc:*

```
machine ftp.sura.net
login anonymous
password krol@ux1.cso.uiuc.edu
```

More information about this facility can be found in your FTP documentation.

■ When you copy a file with FTP, the file gets created with the standard access permissions that are used for any new file you create. If the file has special permissions on its originating system, they will not be preserved. In particular, if you transfer a file that requires execute permission (like *.plan* or *.Xsession*), you will have to give a **chmod +x** command before you will be able to use it.

■ Some FTP servers allow you to put extensions on filenames that are really file reformatting commands to the server. The two most common ones are **.tar** and **.Z**. For example, if a file named *program* exists, and you issue the command **get program.Z**, the server automatically compresses the file before the transfer. With the **.tar** ending (e.g., **get pub.tar**), the file or directory is converted to a UNIX **tar** archive before transmittal. This makes it possible to transfer an entire directory tree with a single command. As you might expect, the server does nothing special if a file with the suffix already exists. For example, if *program.Z* already exists, the server will give it to you as is, without trying to compress it.

These are extensions to the normal FTP service which will probably become more widespread in the future. Right now, they may work and they may not. If you use a server regularly, you might give them a try to see if they work.

■ Some clients get confused by the extensive messages new FTP servers send after **cd** commands. If nothing comes out after a **cd** command but you start seeing long messages after other commands, your **ftp** client may be getting confused. Here's what you might see:

```
%  ftp ftp.sura.net                                    start up ftp to the server
Connected to nic.sura.net.
220 nic.sura.net FTP server (Version 6.9 Sep 30 1991) ready.
Name (ftp.sura.net:krol):  anonymous              anonymous login
331 Guest login ok, send email address as password.
Password:  krol@ux1.cso.uiuc.edu                  password does not really echo
230 Guest login ok, access restrictions apply.
ftp>  cd pub/nic                                       move to the directory
250- ######WELCOME TO THE SURANET NETWORK INFORMATION CENTER##########
ftp>  get NJC                                          the following messages should
                                                       have been displayed before this line
250-SURAnet                          info@sura.net
250-8400 Baltimore Blvd.             301-982-4600(voice)
250-College Park, Maryland  USA 20740-2498     FAX 301-982-4605
250-   Many of the documents available in this ftp archive are geared
250- towards the new user of the Internet. SURAnet has provided several
250-"How To" guides for network navigation tools such as, telnet, ftp,
250-and email. These "How To" guides are available in the directory
250 CWD command successful.
```

Try disconnecting and logging in again, but this time prefix your password with a minus sign (–). The minus sign tells the new FTP server not to send the additional messages.

## ◼ *Exercises*

**1.** Examine the FTP session below. From the example, explain each step as we begin at the computer **bgsuvax** and make an FTP connection to **ftp.ora.com**. What is the purpose of **dir**? What does the step **cd pub** do? Where are the messages coming from that are displayed when we first connect to **ftp.ora.com** and then again when we execute the **cd pub** command?

```
[6:23pm] bgsuvax > ftp ftp.ora.com

Connected to amber.ora.com.

220 amber FTP server (Version wu-2.4(1) Fri Apr 15 14:14:30 EDT 1994) ready.
Name (ftp.ora.com:klopfens): ftp
331 Guest login ok, send your complete email address as password.
Password:
230- Welcome to the O'Reilly & Associates, Inc. FTP Archive.
230-
230- If your ftp client chokes on this message, log in with a '-' as the
230- first character of your password to disable it.
230-
```

```
230–  If you have problems with or questions about this service, send mail to
230–  ftpmaster@ora.com; we will try to fix the problem or answer the
230–  question.
230–
230–  Current local time is Wed Sep  6 18:24:04 1995
230–
230–Please read the file README
230–  it was last modified on Thu Jun 15 21:02:51 1995 – 83 days ago
230 Guest login ok, access restrictions apply.
ftp> dir
200 PORT command successful.
150 Opening ASCII mode data connection for /bin/ls.
total 10
–rw–r—r—   1 325      100            485 Jun 16 01:02 README
d—x—x—x   2 root     61             512 Jul 27 17:49 bin
dr–xr–xr–x   2 325      61             512 Nov 17  1994 dev
dr–xr–xr–x   3 325      61             512 Jun 15 18:13 etc
d–wxrwx——   3 ftp      100           1024 Sep  6 21:44 incoming
drwxrwsr–x   5 325      100           1536 Sep  6 02:15 outgoing
drwxrwsr–x  16 325      61            1024 Sep  6 11:46 pub
drwxr–xr–x   2 325      daemon         512 Oct 26  1993 published
dr–xr–xr–x   3 325      61             512 Nov 17  1994 usr
226 Transfer complete.
569 bytes received in 0.31 seconds (1.8 Kbytes/s)
ftp> cd pub
250–  This is the /pub directory, the place to look for most of the information
250–  you need. The names of subdirectories give a clue to what is inside;
250–  "Index" files in this directory and subdirectories have more information.
250–
250–  NOTE: Some files that were here in /pub have been moved to subdirectories.
250–  For a list of these files, read the README.moved file.
250–
250–Please read the file README.ftp
250–  it was last modified on Wed Jun 21 11:53:57 1995 – 77 days ago
250–Please read the file README.moved
250–  it was last modified on Wed Jun 21 11:42:34 1995 – 77 days ago
250 CWD command successful.
ftp> dir
200 PORT command successful.
150 Opening ASCII mode data connection for /bin/ls.
total 230
–rw–rw–r—   1 325      61             358 Jun 21 15:15 .message
drwxr–sr–x   2 115      61             512 Jun 21 15:41 .old_files
–rw–rw–r—   1 325      61            1112 Sep  5 19:03 Index
–rw–rw–r—   1 115      61            2592 Jun 21 15:53 README.ftp
–rw–rw–r—   1 115      61            1033 Jun 21 15:42 README.moved
drwxrwxr–x   2 325      61             512 Jul  6 19:54 bibliography
drwxrwsr–x  16 325      61             512 Jun  1 21:33 davenport
drwxrws—x   5 325      61             512 Sep  6 17:54 dist
```

```
drwxrwsr-x 13 325      61        512 Aug  2 21:29 examples
drwxrwxr-x  6 199     100        512 May  7 21:59 frame
drwxr-sr-x  3 325      61        512 Jun  8 1994  gnn
drwxrwsr-x  5 115      61        512 Jun 17 00:01 graphics
-rw-r--r-   1 325      61     204286 Sep  6 11:45 ls-lR.Z
drwxrwxr-x  2 325     100        512 Jul  7 00:30 mosaic
drwxrwsr-x  6 325      61        512 Sep  6 10:43 products
drwxr-xr-x  2 325      61        512 Dec 19 1994  twi
drwxrwsr-x  3 325      61        512 Jul  8 23:39 usenet
drwxrwsr-x  3 325      61        512 Jul 26 23:09 www
drwxr-xr-x  2 325      61        512 Apr 17 14:27 z-code
226 Transfer complete.
1227 bytes received in 0.44 seconds (2.7 Kbytes/s)
ftp> get README.ftp
200 PORT command successful.
150 Opening ASCII mode data connection for README.ftp (2592 bytes).
226 Transfer complete.
local: README.ftp remote: README.ftp
2642 bytes received in 1 seconds (2.6 Kbytes/s)
ftp> quit
221 Goodbye.
```

**2.** Look at the contents of the *README.ftp* file that was retrieved in the FTP session in the preceding exercise. Explain why this file was called *README.ftp* and why it could be helpful to you as an anonymous FTP user of **ftp.ora.com**.

```
[6:25pm] bgsuvax > dir README.ftp
-rw-r--r-   1 klopfens    2592 Sep  6 18:25 README.ftp
[6:25pm] bgsuvax > type README.ftp
Welcome to the O'Reilly & Associates FTP archive. Here are a few
things we'd like to tell you.

- Please do NOT do a recursive listing (a command like "ls -lR")
  from the root (top-level directory) of the archive. Recursive
  listings of the entire archive take a long time and slow down
  everyones' work. Instead, get the master index file, ls-lR.Z,
  from this directory. If you can't handle a compressed file,
  ask for the filename ls-lR instead; this server will uncompress
  the index before sending it (see below).

- This server can run the UNIX "tar" and "compress" commands
  automatically as you retrieve files and directories. Do this
  by adding or deleting the filename extensions ".tar" and ".Z",
  respectively, when you request a file or directory. For example,
  if a directory listing shows a long file named "Index" and
  you'd like to compress it before it is sent, use the FTP command:
     get Index.Z
  and the server will compress the file as it is sent (be sure you have
  chosen binary transfer mode). Or, if the directory "foo" has
```

```
several files in it and/or subdirectories, and you'd like to
receive the directory contents as a single tar archive file, type:
    get foo.tar
You can combine the two commands. Get a compressed tar archive of
the foo directory with the command:
    get foo.tar.Z
You can also do the opposite. For example, this server has a lot of
compressed tar files. If you want the file upt.oct93.tar.Z but you
don't have "uncompress" on your computer, you can use this command:
    get upt.oct93.tar
and the file will be uncompressed before it is sent. Unfortunately,
this server can't un-tar an archive and send separate files (yet).

In the same way, from a Web browser, create a URL by adding or
removing extensions. For example, if you want to view the compressed
file /pub/ls-1R.Z in your browser, tell the server to send it in
uncompressed format by giving your browser this URL:
    ftp://ftp.ora.com/pub/ls-1R

Note that these commands may not work if you use a graphical FTP
browser; it may only know how to ask for files listed in the
directory. In that case, use a plain command-line FTP program.

- Many of these example files are available on our Gopher server
  (gopher.ora.com) as separate, single files — instead of as a tar
  archive. This is handy when you want only a few of the files in
  an archive. We're working to expand this kind of service; if you
  have suggestions or comments, please send them!

Thanks. You can contact us by sending email to:   ftpmaster@ora.com
```

*Answer questions 3 through 10 for each FTP interface you will be using (e.g., FTP, Fetch, lynx, or graphical WWW browser). If you have trouble locating or connecting to an FTP site, try URL* **http://hoohoo.ncsa.uiuc.edu/ftp/intro.html** *for other options.*

**3.** The U.S. Library of Congress FTP site is **ftp.loc.gov**. What is the difference between a directory and a file? How can you tell? Why is the */pub* directory usually a good choice to begin on any FTP site? What is the difference between the *INDEX* file and the *README* file in the directory */pub?*

**4.** Use your WWW browswer to link to **ftp://ftp.loc.gov**. How can you change to the */pub* directory using your browswer?

**5.** Can you find the */pub/exhibit.images/1492.exhibit/README* file at **ftp.loc.gov**? What is located in the directory */pub/exhibit.images/1492.exhibit?* Look for both text files and binary files. List three image files. How does this site offer help you if you need a viewer to see image files located in this directory? Get an image file and view it locally.

**6.** What compression and uncompression software do you have at your disposal. If none, where can you find this software?

**7.** The U.S. federal government has an FTP server at **ftp.fedworld.gov** (see also URL **http://www.fedworld.gov**). Using anonymous FTP, log in to that site. Change to the */pub* directory and then change to the *commerce* subdirectory (i.e., */pub/commerce*). Look for either a *README* file or one called *00_index.txt*. What is in that file? How did you find out? How would you rate this site? How does it compare to what's available on the World Wide Web at URL **http://www.fedworld.gov**?

**8.** Using the computer platform of preference (e.g., Macintosh, Windows, or other), search the Internet for a compressed, executable software program you can download and run. For example, find software that will allow you to view image files. How can you locate such software? How do you know it's compressed? Explain simply but precisely how to retrieve it and uncompress it, and then demonstrate that it works.

**9.** How can you check what you download for viruses?

**10.** What are the differences between freeware, shareware, and "beta test" software?

CHAPTER SEVEN

# ELECTRONIC MAIL

**M**ost network users get their start by using electronic mail *(e-mail)*. After sending a few hesitant messages (frequently followed up by a telephone call to ask if the mail arrived), most e-mail users quickly become comfortable with the system. Your confidence, too, will grow after you have gotten past the first few awkward messages; you will be using mail frequently and with authority, customizing the system to meet your own needs and establishing your own mailing lists. Soon you will find that e-mail means much more than faster letters and memos. You can take part in electronic conversations about genetics, the job market, or virtually any topic imaginable.

How quickly you become comfortable with electronic mail has a lot to do with your knowledge of the medium and some basic technical decisions you make in choosing and using your e-mail system. There are any number of electronic mail programs for each kind of computer. To get enough background to describe good e-mail software, we will start out discussing general facilities of electronic mail, mail addressing, and how electronic mail works. After that, we will look at what features exist in e-mail packages. Finally, we will talk about how to use those features in concert to move files, take part in discussions, and deal with problems that you might encounter.

## ■ *When Is Electronic Mail Useful?*

Like any other tool, electronic mail has its strengths and weaknesses. On the surface, it appears to be just a faster way of delivering letters, memos, or their equivalent. To know when electronic mail is appropriate, think about how it differs from other communications

*Table 7-1    Comparison of Communication Techniques*

|                | Telephone   | E-mail      | Post         |
|----------------|-------------|-------------|--------------|
| Speed          | High        | Moderate    | Low          |
| Synchronized   | Yes         | No          | No           |
| Formality      | Varies      | Moderate    | Varies       |
| Accountability | Low         | Moderate    | High         |
| Conferencing   | Small group | Any to all  | One-way only |
| Security       | Moderate    | Low         | High         |

media. In some ways, e-mail is very similar to the telephone; in other ways, it is similar to traditional postal mail. Table 7-1 makes a quick comparison.

First, let's think about how quickly each medium gets a message from one point to another. The telephone offers immediate delivery and works at a fairly high communication speed. The time it takes to deliver electronic mail ranges from seconds to a day; and postal delivery can be overnight in the best case, but often takes several days. In telephony, the caller and the sender must be synchronized; that is, they must both be on the phone at the same time. E-mail and postal mail are both asynchronous; the sender sends when the time is ripe, and you read it at your leisure. This makes distance (e.g., time zones) and daily schedules irrelevant.

The delivery time for e-mail consists of two parts: the time it takes the network to deliver the message to your mail computer and the delay in your reading it once it is there. The first part is a function of how your mail machine is connected to the network. The second part is under your control. When electronic mail is delivered (and read) quickly, it can become almost as convenient and fluent as a personal conversation.

Formality and accountability are closely related. On the telephone, formality varies: With some people you are very formal; with others, very casual. The same is true of postal mail. You can take time to construct messages and multiple formats from which to choose (handwritten notes, typed business letters, etc.). These formats and other cues (e.g., a perfumed envelope) give signals regarding the purpose of the note.

E-mail is generally text-only. The medium developed before any style guides existed for it. Individual status is less apparent; the chief executive's e-mail address looks just like anyone else's. E-mail often is exchanged between parties at a rate approaching that of a conversation, and many people tend to drift into informality in their electronic messaging.

This can be a problem when it comes to accountability: The writer must take responsibility for his or her messages.

Written words historically have been used to hold writers more accountable for their actions than spoken words. Unrecorded spoken words can be disavowed fairly easily. This is not true of e-mail. If you try this with e-mail, anyone with a saved copy of the message in a file can bring it back to life. The only factor that reduces e-mail accountability is that the sender's identity can be spoofed. I could send you an e-mail with the return address **president@whitehouse.gov**, offering you a seat on the Supreme Court. Forging paper mail is possible, but it is much more difficult.

E-mail is unique in group communication. The telephone is limited to small groups. Conference calls allow groups to talk with each other. As the group gets larger, scheduling and setup get prohibitively difficult. At the other end of the spectrum, bulk mail is easy to use and can reach millions with little difficulty. The problem with mass mailings (aside from being a nuisance) is that all messages originate from one point and go to the whole group. Communication from any other point cannot easily be sent to the whole group. Electronic mail allows you to set up arbitrarily large groups, and any member of the group can communicate with the whole at any time. This is very useful both for disseminating information and for querying a group.

Finally, the security of electronic mail is generally low compared to other media. If care is taken with the post, a letter could remain within locked boxes or the Postal Service until it gets into the recipient's hands. If it is opened along the way, damage to the envelope normally makes the intrusion obvious. Telephone tapping requires access at one end or the other to intercept a conversation. Once a conversation makes it outside your building and into the telephone network, it is technically difficult for anyone to intrude without the phone company's help. E-mail, however, takes a fairly predictable route through computers, some of whose security may be questionable. There are error modes in which a computer is programmed to deliver an undeliverable message to a mail administrator. Administrators will not normally snoop or spread your message around, but still, if security is an issue, having your mail fall into the hands of someone else—even a responsible administrator—is unsuitable. "Privacy-enhanced mailers" try to encrypt the message to combat these security deficiencies, but they are not yet in general use. As a general rule, you cannot trust e-mail's security and you should not use it when security is an issue.

## ■ *Hints for Writing Electronic Mail*

If you read much e-mail, you will see many messages that should never have been sent and that the sender probably regrets sending. To prevent making such mistakes yourself, you should develop some electronic mail "etiquette." Creating good habits while you are beginning can prevent embarrassments later on. Here is some advice:

- Never commit anything to e-mail that you would not want to become public knowledge. Taking it to a not-inappropriate extreme, if you would not like to see it on the front page of the *New York Times,* don't put it on e-mail. You never know who may end up reading your e-mail message. This may be on purpose (e.g., if a coworker covers someone's e-mail while she is on vacation) or by mistake, either yours or a misbehaving computer's. The threat does not end when the mail is deleted from the mail system. E-mail messages are frequently caught in system backups and sit on tapes in machine rooms for years. With enough effort, an old message might be found and resurrected. This was how much of Oliver North's connection to the Iran-Contra affair was documented. There is nothing to prevent a recipient from saving your message for years.

- Never send abusive, harassing, threatening, or bigoted messages. Although abuse, harassment, and even bigotry are hard to define, there is one good rule of thumb: If a message's recipient complains, stop. E-mail can usually be traced to its originating machine, and systems on the Internet are liable for the misdeeds of their users. You do not want your system administrator (or the system administrator of your electronic mail link) to receive complaints about your activity. It could come back to haunt you.

- Writers frequently approach electronic mail as a friendly conversation, but recipients frequently view e-mail as a cast-in-stone business letter. You might have had a wry smile on your face when you wrote the note, but that wry smile does not cross the network. You also cannot control when the message will be read, so it might be received at the worst possible moment. Consider sitting around after class with a friend and saying, "You really blew that exam." You could judge his frame of mind before speaking, so you are sure he will take it jokingly. That same thing in e-mail, which he reads after just being deflated by the grade, comes off as "YOU REALLY BLEW THAT EXAM!"

- Be very careful with sarcasm. Consider this exchange with a coach:

    Coach: You worked with Sam a while ago. What would you think of promoting her to the starting team?

    To which you respond: She's a real winner!

Does she get the start? The answer could mean either that she played on winning teams before, or that she has not won anything since elementary school. There is no body language nor perhaps any personal knowledge on the recipient's side (e.g., she may not know that you are quite the wisecracker). Some help is available for these situations. For example, inserting a "smiley face" into a message can affect the meaning:

> She's a real winner! :-)

means, in this case, she has your endorsement. Another symbol is the wink that is analogous to a wink of the eye:

> Spencer and Laurel spent a long time last night working on the presentation. ;-)

The meaning of this sentence is left to the reader. There are many other "emoticons" that are used less frequently. A summary of them and their meanings is available at URL **http://www.eff.org/papers/eegtti/eeg_286.html** (see also David W. Sanderson (ed.), *Smileys,* (Sebastopol, Calif.: O'Reilly & Associates, 1993).

Aside from basic mail etiquette, there are other guidelines that, if followed, make e-mail easier to read and understand:

- Keep the line length reasonable (less than 60 characters). You want it to display on just about any screen. If the note is forwarded, it might be indented by a tab character (usually 8 columns). To avoid messages that may wind up as long, unwrapped lines at the other end, use the ENTER key.

- Use mixed case. Even though some operating systems do not understand lowercase letters, virtually all modern terminals can generate them. All-uppercase sounds harsh, like shouting. UPPERCASE CAN BE USED FOR EMPHASIS!

- Do not use text-formatting features of your terminal (bold, italics, etc.). These frequently send a string of control characters that wreak havoc on some types of terminals.

- Read your message before you send it, and decide if you will regret it in the morning. On most e-mail systems, once you send it, you are committed to it, although many systems allow you a second thought by prompting you for confirmation after you give the initial send mail command.

## How Electronic Mail Works

Electronic mail differs from the other applications we are looking at because it is not an "end to end" service: The sending and receiving machine need not be able to communicate directly with each other to make it work. This is known as a "store and forward" service. Mail is passed from one machine to another until it finally arrives at its destination. This is completely analogous to the way the U.S. Postal Service delivers mail; if we examine that, we can draw some interesting conclusions.

The U.S. Postal Service operates a store and forward network. You address a message and put it into a mailbox. The message is picked up by a truck and sent to another place and stored there. It is sorted and forwarded to another place. This step is repeated until it arrives at the recipient's mailbox. If the recipient's mailbox happens to be in a place where the U.S. Postal Service cannot deliver directly (e.g., another country), you can still send the message; the U.S. Postal Service will pass the message to the Postal Service of that country for delivery.

We can infer some observations about the Internet from this analogy. First, if you correctly address a message, the network will take it from there. You need not know much about what is going on. Messages also can be moved among the Internet and other mail networks. This is true, but the address required may be more complex in order to get to and through the international network.

Just as in the Postal Service, if the destination and source are not on the same network, there needs to be a place where the e-mail from one network is handed to the e-mail service of another. Points of connection between e-mail networks are computers called *application gateways*. They are called "gateways" because they can be viewed as magic doors between worlds; they are "application gateways" because they know enough about the e-mail applications on both sides to reformat messages so they are legal on the new network. To send mail through a gateway, you frequently have to give an address that contains information about both how to get to the gateway and how to deliver the mail on the other side. We discuss addressing in the following section.

Finally, before you can put a postal letter into a mailbox, you put it in an envelope. The same happens to e-mail, except that the "envelope" is called a *mail header.* The header is the **To:**, **From:**, **Subject:** stuff on the front of the message. Just as an envelope may get changed en route (e.g., a hand-scribbled "not at this address" here, a yellow sticker with a forwarding address there), the mail header gets stuff stuck into it while the message is traveling to help you figure out what route it took, just in case it does not get through.

## It's All in the Address

Whether your e-mail gets to its destination depends almost solely on whether the address is constructed correctly. (E-mail sometimes fails because machines or pieces of the network are unavailable, but usually the network tries to send mail for days before giving up.)

Unfortunately, e-mail addresses are a bit more complex than the simple host addresses we have seen so far.* They are more complex for several reasons:

- The e-mail world actually supersedes that of the Internet
- E-mail needs to be addressed to a person, not just a machine
- Personal names are sometimes included as comments in e-mail addresses

Let's start with the Internet's addressing rules. On the Internet, the basis for all mail is the domain name of the machine that is acting as a mail agent (the machine that is handling the addressee's mail; e.g., **bgnet.bgsu.edu**). In fact, this is all that the network, per se, is responsible for. Once it has delivered a message to the named machine, the network's task is over. It is up to that computer to deliver it the rest of the way.

The machine requires more information about further routing: at the minimum, the name of a user, but possibly extended information for routing the mail to another kind of network. To form an e-mail address, we use this additional information as a prefix to the destination system's domain name. In order to tell where one ends and the other starts, they are separated by an "at" sign (@). So, the form of an e-mail address is:

```
login-name@machine-name
```

For example, the e-mail address:

```
klopfens@bgnet.bgsu.edu
```

sends mail to someone whose login name is **klopfens** on a machine named **bgnet.bgsu.edu**. If you are lucky, regardless of where the person is in the world, all you need to do is specify that person's e-mail address for your message to be delivered.

Whether or not you are lucky depends on how smart the first few machines that handle your mail are. The Domain Name System also works for some non-Internet addresses, which usually have a network flag as their highest-level domains, rather than an organization type or a country. So long as your mail message encounters a machine that understands how to route this type of mail before encountering one that gives up on it, the mail will go through with no additional effort. There is only one way to find out: try it. If it doesn't work, you will find out fairly quickly, and no harm can be done.

Because more and more non-Internet computer networks are now accepting that the Internet is here to stay, it is getting easier every day to send mail to a user on these networks. Usually, you only need to take the user's e-mail address on his or her network

---

*An authoritative work on e-mail addressing is, *@#!%, The Directory of Electronic Mail Addressing & Networks*, O'Reilly & Associates.

and tack the name of the network on at the end. For example, if you know someone whose address on the Delphi network is **walthowe**, you can guess that his Internet e-mail address may be **walthowe@delphi.com**. Other providers allow new users to pick their own username. Sometimes the easiest way to find a friend or colleague's e-mail address is to simply telephone them and ask.

If your e-mail machine is not intelligent enough to deal with these addresses on its own, or if the address you have does not remotely look like an Internet address, you will have to intervene manually. Here are some hints that might help you to succeed:

### BITNET

BITNET addresses normally have the form *name@host*.**bitnet**. Change this address to something like *name%host,* and use that for the login name part of the address. Use the address of a BITNET-Internet gateway for the machine-name side (for example, **cunyvm.cuny.edu**). Separate the two with an "at" sign (@). For example, rewrite the address **krol@uiucvmd.bitnet** as **krol%uiucvmd@cunyvm.cuny.edu**.* If you are going to do this regularly, find out the best gateway for you to use from someone local.

### CompuServe

CompuServe addresses consist of two numbers separated by a comma. Change the comma to a period and use the result as the left-hand side of the address. To the right of the @, use **compuserve.com**. A CompuServe address of 76543,123 would become **76543.123@compuserve.com**. CompuServe users must be careful when sending Internet mail from their CompuServe account. *userid@hostname.domain* becomes *INTERNET:userid@hostname.domain.*

### Fidonet

Fidonet addresses consist of a first and last name and a set of numbers of the form *a:b/ c.d.* Separate the first and last names with a period (.) and send to p*d*.f*c*.n*b*.z*a*.**fidonet.org**. For example, send mail to Willie Martin at 1:5/2.3 by addressing it to **willie.martin@p3.f2.n5.z1.fidonet.org**. Some machines may still have trouble with an address like this. If yours does, try sending the message, using the above address, to the gateway machine: **willie.martin%p3.f2.n5.z1.fidonet.org@zeus.ieee.org**.

---

*This is a non-standard format for an address, known as the "BBN hack," but it is in common use, it is easy for people to understand, and it works. The standard way of doing this would be **@cunyvm.cuny.edu:krol@uiucvmd**.

### Sprintmail

Complete Sprintmail addresses look like *"John Bigboote"/YOYODYNE/TELEMAIL/US.* If the address is used within Sprintmail, it can be abbreviated to *John Bigboote/ YOYODYNE.* These two parameters are the person's name and organization; this is all you will get when someone gives you a Sprintmail address. These parameters are positional and need to be plugged into a command like the following:*

`/PN=John.Bigboote/O=YOYODYNE/ADMD=TELEMAIL/C=US/@sprint.com`

Even if the person only gives you the first two parts of the address, the complete address should be used when sending it to **sprint.com**. Sprintmail can ill afford to allow this addressing scheme to continue.

### MCImail

There are multiple ways of addressing MCImail. MCI mailboxes have both an address and a person's name associated with them. The address looks a lot like a phone number. If that is what you have, use that number on the left side of the @ and use the gateway name **mcimail.com** on the right side. For example: *1234567*@**mcimail.com**. If you are given the name of a person on MCImail, you can address it to: *firstname_lastname*@**mcimail.com**, like: **John_Bigboote@mcimail.com**.

### Delphi

We have already seen Delphi. To send mail to a Delphi user, add **@delphi.com** to the user's Delphi account name. For example, walthowe becomes **walthowe@delphi.com**.

### America Online

To send mail to a user on America Online, add **@aol.com** to the user's America Online account name. For example, Will Barber becomes **WillBarber@aol.com**. Note that AOL users can send e-mail to the Internet using Internet addresses (without any special prefixes).

### Prodigy

To send mail to a Prodigy member, add **@prodigy.com** to the user's account name. Will Barber becomes **WillBarber@prodigy.com**. Note that Prodigy users did have to pay extra to send Internet mail.

---

*An address like this is an X.500 style address. X.500 is an ISO standard form of addresses that no one really likes, but will likely be around for a long time.

## UUCP

For most users, these instructions will rarely be needed as we evolve beyond this system of addressing. Change the UUCP address, which looks like *name@host*.**uucp**, to *name%host*. Use that for the login name portion of the address. Use the address of a UUNET-Internet gateway as the machine name. Of course, separate the two with the @ sign. For example, a user receiving mail via UUCP from PSI, Inc., should be sent mail through **uu.psi.com**, like **johnw%yoyodyne@uu.psi.com**. You can ask your e-mail or system administrator for the address of a good gateway to use. You may be given a UUCP address in the following form: ...**!uunet!***host***!***name*. This is a UUCP "path"; it means "you figure out how to get the mail to the system named **uunet**, and then **uunet** will send it to host that will deliver it." Convert this to *name%host@gateway-machine*. You pick the proper gateway by examining the UUCP path address. If it has **uunet** as part of the address, you can use **uunet.uu.net**; if it has **uupsi** as part of the address, you can use **uu.psi.com**, etc. On very rare occasions, you may see gateway names other than **uunet** or **uupsi** in the path; you will have to figure out the Internet address of the gateway.

How do you send mail to other networks? For most networks, it is easy—like it is for Delphi. You just tack something on to the user's user ID on his net. (See Table 7-2.) We will tackle these easy cases first; then we will look at the more difficult ones.

## Acquiring Electronic Mail Addresses

Once you decide to jump into the e-mail world, you have to start collecting e-mail addresses. There is no national registry of e-mail addresses. There are a few specialized servers that one can peruse to look for someone's address. These servers are known as white-pages servers because they provide the electronic equivalent to the white pages of a telephone book. (Chapter 10 tells you how to use the common ones.) The easiest and best way to acquire these addresses is via information sent directly to you, be it a business card, a phone call, a postal letter, an e-mail message, or a newsgroup posting.

This method of acquiring e-mail addresses has two advantages over all others:

- You are fairly sure it is an e-mail address that is current and checked regularly. An address found in an index might be an old e-mail address used at a previous employer, or an address on a machine that no longer exists.

- If there are typically problems getting to the person's e-mail address, the address he gives out will probably reflect the best way to get to his machine. For example, if Joe's business card gives his e-mail address as **joe%bizarrenet@bizarregate.com**, that is the address you should try first.

*Table 7-2*  *Addressing Users of Other Networks*

| Network | Send Mail to | Notes |
|---|---|---|
| Alternex | *user*@**ax.apc.org** | |
| ALAnet | *user*%**ALANET@intermail.isi.edu** | American Library Assn. |
| Applelink | *user*@applelink.apple.com | |
| ATTmail | *user*@**attmail.com** | |
| BIX | *user*@bix.com | |
| CGNet | *user*%CGNET@intermail.isi.edu | |
| Chasque | *user*@chasque.apc.org | |
| Comlink | *user*@oln.comlink.apc.org | |
| Econet | *user*@**igc.apc.org** | |
| Ecuanex | *user*@ecuanex.apc.org | |
| eWorld | *user*@online.apple.com | |
| Genie | *user*@genie.geis.com | |
| GeoNet | *user*@**geo1.geonet.de** | For recipients in Europe |
| | *user*@**geo2.geonet.de** | For recipients in the United Kingdom |
| | *user*@**geo4.geonet.de** | For recipients in North America |
| Glasnet | *user*@**glas.apc.org** | |
| Greenet | *user*@**gn.apc.org** | |
| Nasamail | *user*@nasamail.nasa.gov | |
| Nicarao | *user*@nicarao.apc.org | |
| NIFTY-Serve | *user*@**niftyserve.or.jp** | |
| Nordnet | *user*@**pns.apc.org** | |
| Peacenet | *user*@**igc.apc.org** | |
| Pegasus | *user*@**peg.apc.org** | |
| Pronet | *user*@**tanus.oz.au** | |
| Web | *user*@web.apc.org | |

Sometimes when you try to glean e-mail addresses from mail you receive, you will see an address that looks like:

```
John Bigboote<johnb@yoyodyne.com>
```

This address is in a slightly more elaborate format than anything we have seen so far:

```
comments<email-address>
```

Adding comments to the e-mail address is a really nice thing to do. As in the example above, the comment is usually the addressee's name. Putting the name in a comment makes it a little more obvious to other recipients who also got the message. This is especially true if the person's e-mail address is computer generated, such as **ajzxmvk@uicvmc.bitnet**. If you get a message as part of a mail distribution list, and if the list's manager has included comments, you can look at the **To:** field and easily see who else got the message, even if the e-mail addresses themselves are not recognizable. (You might want to keep some of those addresses in case you want to send one of them a message later.)

## ▪ *Choosing an E-mail Package*

Electronic mail systems evolved in two separate environments: on wide area networks (WANs), where the goal was to provide a "least common denominator" service to everyone in the world, and on local area networks (LANs), where feature-rich service to a workgroup in a small area was the target. As a result, people on wide area nets were frustrated because e-mail was hard to use, but they could send e-mail to anyone. People on LANs were frustrated because they could easily send e-mail to virtually no one. As e-mail evolved, the WAN mailers added nicer user interfaces and features, whereas the LAN products added the ability to send over wide area networks. We have reached the point where most e-mail systems can exchange basic e-mail with any other e-mail system. This means that if you have a choice between e-mail packages, the decision will be made on the basis of how you plan to use e-mail and the extended features and comfort of the packages, not on connectivity.* When you decide how to approach e-mail, a number of questions will affect the decision:

- ▪ With whom are you going to be exchanging mail?

- ▪ How closely are you "tied" to them?

- ▪ What do you like in a user interface?

---

*That is not to say that some decisions will not cost more than others. Connecting a LAN-based mail system to the Internet may require a dedicated PC and some fairly expensive software.

- How much do you travel?
- Are you happy sending text, or do you want to send other data?

Many facilities are common to all mailers. Other features (like multimedia including digitized pictures and voice) can be used only when the sender and recipient both use similar mail software and operating system utilities. If your goal is to transfer all kinds of files between a small circle of colleagues with as little trouble as possible, you and your friends should agree on a single mail system and use it. If that is not a big concern, you should pick the e-mail software that you find the easiest to use and with which you can feel at home. That is, if you like Macintoshes, you should pick something that works, looks, and feels like a Macintosh. Your school may have a particular mail package or two that they especially recommend. This is important because those packages will be the one with which they can most help you.

If you are a frequent traveler, you should investigate systems that allow you to connect a portable computer to the network (even by dial-up) and download mail. You can then read your mail and queue new messages while disconnected from the network. The next time you connect to the net, the queued mail gets sent. So you could dial up in Chicago, download 20 messages, read and respond to them at 30,000 feet over Cleveland, queue your responses, and, finally, send the queued mail and pick up a new batch when you arrive in Florida for spring break. These systems are based on the Post Office protocol, or POP, which allows remote interaction between a workstation and a mail repository.

Pick your mail system to suit your needs. If your needs are not that great and you are mainly concerned with basic messaging, pick something that is free and that other people are using. **pine** is one such free software product that has become very popular in recent years.

## *The pine Program*

We focus now on the **pine** e-mail interface because of its popularity and because it has a useful help facility. Unlike UNIX mail, **pine**'s simplicity and its menu orientation allow many people to adopt it quickly. **pine** was designed at the University of Washington to be used by students (URL: **http://www.cac.washington.edu:1180/pine/index.html**).*

**pine** is a very basic and functional e-mail system that was designed for learning by trial and error rather than reading manuals. Although originally designed for UNIX, later

---

*The software to run **pine** is available from URL **ftp://ftp.cac.washington.edu**, in the directory */mail*. **pine** has been adapted to run on various operating systems; see the *README* file. For information on version history, see URL **ftp://ftp.cac.washington.edu/pine/docs/release-notes.txt**.

versions were devised for other operating systems including DOS. It runs in full-screen mode on standard ASCII terminals. This means it works over dial-up lines with simple VT100 emulation and on text-only terminals; it does not require a graphical display like Windows or Macintosh. **pine** uses Pico, a simple editor, for message composition. Pico is a very simple and easy-to-use text editor that allows paragraph justification, text cutting and pasting, a spelling checker, and other features.

Launch **pine** from your system prompt (% for UNIX, $ for Vax, etc.) by typing **pine** and pressing the ENTER key. You are greeted with a screen that summarizes the most common commands. With no other experience, you should be able to figure out where to go from here (see Figure 7-1). All the commands are single keystrokes. Using **I** to see your e-mail is not intuitive, but the command itself is obvious enough from the **pine** main menu.

To send an e-mail message, the command **C** for compose starts the process. Once again, this is not completely intuitive but it is easy to find on the opening screen. Once you press **C** for compose, **pine** takes you to a new screen. You simply type the address and subject where prompted. Once complete, pressing **CTRL-X** sends the message.

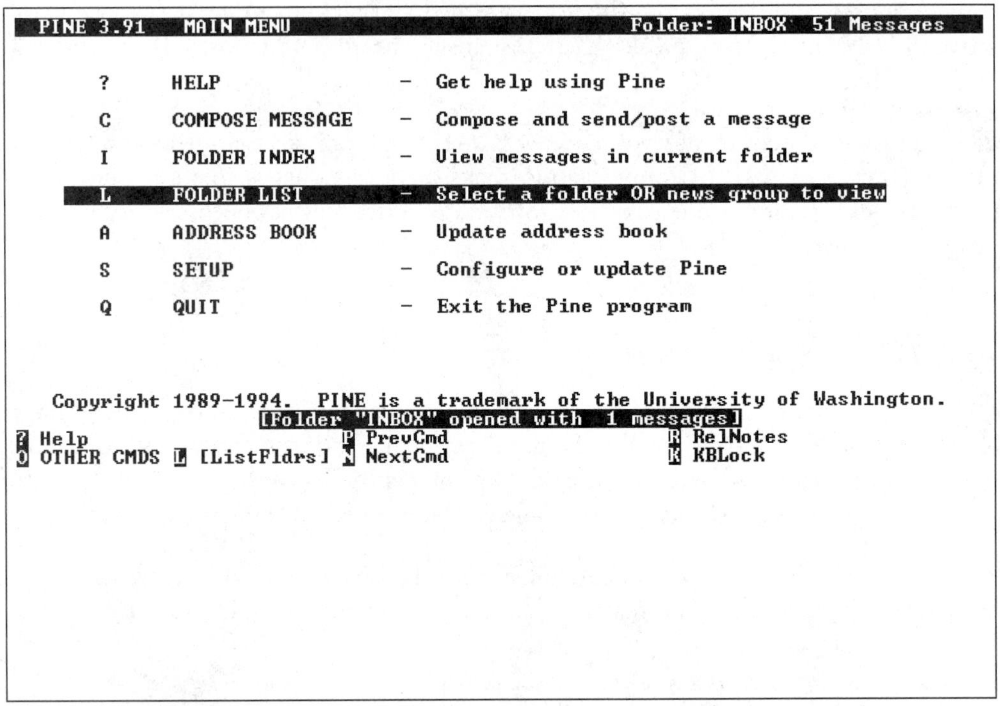

```
 PINE 3.91     MAIN MENU                      Folder: INBOX  51 Messages


         ?     HELP              -  Get help using Pine

         C     COMPOSE MESSAGE   -  Compose and send/post a message

         I     FOLDER INDEX      -  View messages in current folder

         L     FOLDER LIST       -  Select a folder OR news group to view

         A     ADDRESS BOOK      -  Update address book

         S     SETUP             -  Configure or update Pine

         Q     QUIT              -  Exit the Pine program



     Copyright 1989-1994.  PINE is a trademark of the University of Washington.
                       [Folder "INBOX" opened with  1 messages]
 ? Help                       P PrevCmd                        R RelNotes
 O OTHER CMDS  L [ListFldrs]  N NextCmd                        K KBLock
```

*Figure 7-1　Example pine main menu*

Note the help commands at the bottom of the screen in Figure 7-2. **CTRL-G** (depicted as ^G) takes you to a help menu. **CTRL-K** and **CTRL-U** can be used together to cut and paste text. If you would like more time to think about a message you are sending, **CTRL-O** postpones it without deleting it. These help keys change when you are using the headers to address and title your e-mail, and there is another selection when you are reading a message. If you use **pine** on a regular basis, the commands you use most often will begin to come quite naturally.

## *Sending Files via pine*

**pine** makes sending files from your home directory to a recipient simple. In the case of a text file, you can simply compose an e-mail message to that person and use **CTRL-G** to insert the file in the composition. In many cases, this is a quite reasonable procedure. The Internet world is moving rapidly beyond plain ASCII text, however, and that is where MIME (Multipurpose Internet Mail Extensions) comes in. MIME allows us to send files of various contents including software and images.

To elaborate on how we can use **pine** to send more than just text messages, we will use the example of appending an image file to an e-mail message. In this example, we will use the image of Hurricane Hugo from September of 1989. The file is named *HRAD_89092208.GIF\** (and is available from URL **http://lumahai.soest.hawaii.edu/** among others).

Pressing **C** from the **pine** main menu brings us to the e-mail entry template (Figure 7-2). The cursor is initially in the **To:** field. We type the destination address, and then use TAB, direction keys, or ENTER to move to other fields. When we get to the **Attachmnt:** field, we type the name of the file to send, in this case, *HRAD_89092208.GIF.* We typed only the filename; when **pine** notices that we had typed a complete filename, it adds the file size and the other information. That is all we have to do to send the image file; MIME does the rest. We then type a subject and the message text. When that is done, we press **CTRL-X** to send the message.

Now let's see what it looks like to receive this message (the example here comes from a colleague's account to **klopfenstein@opie.bgsu.edu**). We again start with **pine**'s main menu, which gives a command summary and tells us that there are messages waiting in the "inbox" including the hurricane item. Choose **I** to see mail in the current folder inbox. By positioning the cursor on the proper message and pressing **V**, the message is displayed (Figure 7.3).

---

\* *GIF (Graphics Interchange Format)* is a common format for storing color graphic images. Many of the images you find around the network are stored as GIF files (pronounced "jif").

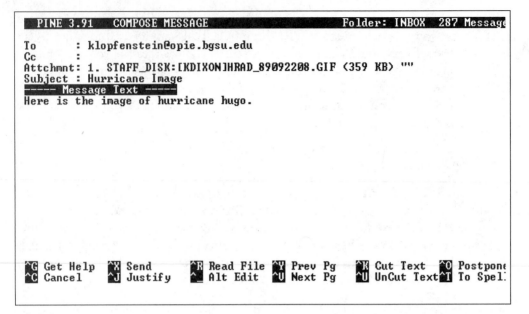

*Figure 7-2   pine composition screen*

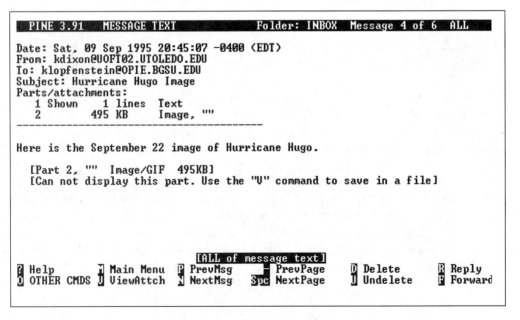

*Figure 7-3   pine displaying message received*

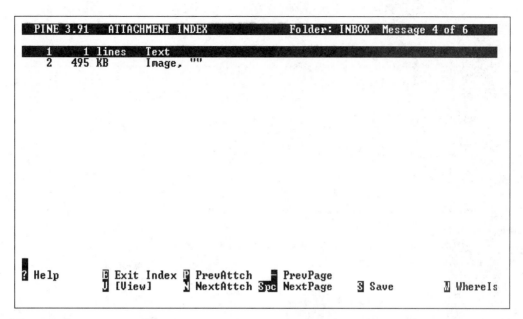

*Figure 7-4    pine view attachment*

As we would expect, **pine** displays the text portion of the message and says that the file *HRAD_89092208.GIF* is attached. It does not make sense to display it on a text-only screen, and **pine** also gives a hint about how to save the message. When this is attempted, **pine** prompts for a filename to call the appended image file received through e-mail (Figure 7-4).

**pine** can deal with two kinds of "object" files: binary files and GIF files. If the terminal supports graphics, we could view *HRAD_89092208.GIF* by pressing **V**. Otherwise, we can save the attachment in a file, which is done by pressing **S**. We can, of course, enter any filename we like. There is no encoding or decoding, no odd file formats to learn and understand.

**pine**'s other features are explained in the online User's Guide (URL: **http://www.cac.washington.edu:1180/pine/user-guide/index.html**). Table 7-3 gives an indication of the versatility of **pine** (note that help is available online from any **pine** screen for that screen's commands).

*Table 7-3    pine Screens/Modes*

## Message Text (viewing a message)

    Compose Message
    Folder Index
    Folder List
    Address Book
    Setup and Configuration

## pine Commands

    *Commands for Message Handling*
    Export and Save
    Take Address
    Reply and Forward
    Bounce (Remail)
    View/Save Attachment
    Flag as Important
    Select Message
    Apply and Zoom

    *Commands for Message Composition*
    Justify
    Cut and Paste
    Read-in File
    Attach File
    Postponing a Message
    Spelling
    Rich Headers

    *Other Commands*
    Whereis
    Full Headers
    Sorting a Folder
    Expunge/Exclude
    Next Interesting Message
    Jump to a Message
    Goto Folder

## Information Pages

    pine and Alternate Character Sets
    Syntax for IMAP Folders and Collections

**pine** is clearly worth exploring if it is available to you. This is particularly true if you have dial-up access from home with an older modem. Because **pine** is text-only, it can be fast (it is not slowed down by graphics transmission). If you use it, remember that each screen has a help command that describes the commands you can enter at that point.

# ■ *The UNIX Mail Program*

The UNIX **mail** program is the predecessor of user-friendly electronic mail packages. It gets the job done, but may be responsible for keeping people off the Internet until recently. UNIX mail is so unwieldy that **pine** was invented to overcome its obstacles to all but UNIX aficionados. UNIX **mail** does have advantages. With a few commands, you can use all of its basic features. Although you may never use the UNIX **mail** program, it provides a good basis for discussing how to use a mail system.* To start the **mail** program, give the command:†

```
% mail address-string
```

The *address-string* parameter is optional. If it is there, the command sends a message to those people listed in the address string. You can usually use either spaces or commas to separate different addressees in the list. If the address string is absent, mail enters command mode. One of the things you do in command mode is read your incoming messages.

## *Reading Your Mail*

To read your mail, enter command mode. If you do not have any mail to read, the program tells you:

```
% mail
No mail for krol
```

If you have messages waiting, **mail** lists the first 20 new message headers:

```
% mail
"/usr/spool/mail/krol": 5 messages 1 new
    1 LISTSERV@bitni        Fri Nov  8 16:02 128/6172 "File: "LISTSERV FILELI"
```

---

*If you want to get into a deep discussion about UNIX e-mail, look into **mh** and the whole book dedicated to its use (*MH and xmh: Email for Users and Programmers,* O'Reilly & Associates). For yet another approach to UNIX mail, consider Z-Mail, which was known as **mush** in an earlier incarnation (discussed in *The Z-Mail Handbook,* O'Reilly & Associates).

†Unfortunately, some UNIX systems have two different mail programs with almost the same name. The proper command may be **mailx**.

```
    2 LISTSERV@bitni      Fri Nov  8 16:08 164/9834 "File: "BITNODE FILELIS"
U   3 daemon@pit-man      Sat Nov  9 09:26  72/2817 "Reply from mserv re: s"
U   4 akida               Sat Dec 28 05:53  12/298  "Overthruster found"
>  N 5 buckaroo           Thu Jan  2 19:15  11/305  "Aliens in Grovers Mill"
    &
```

Each message has a status and a number. The status is flagged by the letter (or the lack of a letter) at the beginning of each line. These letters might be:

N               New message received since the last time you entered **mail** in command mode to read messages.

P               Signifies a preserved message, which you have read and decided to put back in your "in-basket" within this invocation of the **mail** program.

U               Unread message. New messages turn into unread messages if you exit **mail** without reading them.

**no letter**       The message was read and preserved in a previous **mail** session.

The message number is used in various commands to refer to that particular message (more on this when we talk about commands). Finally, notice that one message has a greater-than sign (>) pointing to it. This is the current message. If you give any commands without specifying a message number, the command applies to the current message.

The & that follows the message list is **mail**'s command prompt, telling you that it is waiting for you to type a command. You need to know only about four commands to read e-mail for fun and profit. Commands are usually single letters, but there are a couple that are longer to avoid ambiguity. To read messages, use the print command (**p**), which has the general format:

&   **p** *messages*

The *messages* parameter is optional. If you leave it off, the current message is displayed on-screen. The parameter can take one of the following forms:

&   **p 3**                      *display message #3*
&   **p 3-5**                    *display messages #3 through #5*
&   **p $**                      *display the last message*
&   **p 3-$**                    *display messages #3 through the last message*

All commands that allow a message number as a parameter operate in this same fashion. Remember that you can use $ to indicate the last message.

The print command is also the default command. So the following commands are the same:

```
&  3
&  p 3
```

Therefore, a carriage return with no command just prints the current message.

Unless you do something special, any messages you read while you are in a mail session get moved from your in-basket into the file *mbox* when you quit. The usual commands to change this action are:

**d** *messages*      Delete the messages specified (or the current one if not specified). This deletes those message numbers from the menu and deletes the messages themselves at the end of the mail session.

**pre** *messages*      Preserve the specified messages (or the current one if none are specified). That is, keep them in your in-basket, where they may be viewed in future sessions.

**q**      Exit the **mail** program.

## Sending UNIX Mail Messages

In this section, we will tell you how to originate a new e-mail message. You can also respond to a message that someone sent you; we will cover that later.

To send a message, either enter the UNIX **mail** command, followed by a list of addresses, or enter the **mail** command from within the **mail** program (i.e., after the & prompt). Both forms of the commands have the same syntax:

```
%  mail  address-list
```

— *or* —

```
&  mail  address-list
```

The *address-list* can be one or more addresses separated by commas. If the addresses are not full domain names, like **krol@ux1.cso.uiuc.edu**, the **mail** program usually completes the address by adding the domain of the machine it is running on. If **krol** has a mailbox on **ux1.cso.uiuc.edu**, then **mail krol** works fine on the computer **ux1.cso.uiuc.edu**. If you execute it on any other computer, it will fail, because it will try to send it to a user named **krol** on that same local system.

Next, **mail** prompts you for a subject:

```
%  mail johnb@yoyodyne.com
Subject:  Do you have the Overthruster
```

Enter a meaningful synopsis of the message as a subject. That and your name will be all the recipient has to decide on the priority to give this message.* After you type the subject, start typing the text of your message. You will not get another prompt. Here is how we completed the message we started above:

```
%  mail johnb@yoyodyne.com
Subject:  Do you have the Overthruster
John Warfin was wondering if you had acquired the overthruster yet?  He is
pretty excitable.
.
```

Notice the period in column one. A period on a line by itself signifies the end of the message to the UNIX **mail** program. When the message is completed, it is sent, and you return to whatever you were doing before issuing the command. That is, you return to the UNIX prompt if you sent your message from the UNIX command line; you return to **mail**'s command mode if you sent your message from command mode.†

## ■ *Common E-mail Features*

E-mail packages all have some common features that can be used when sending mail to any other mailer, some features that look similar but are implemented differently and therefore cannot be used with other kinds of mailers, and some features that are unique. Here are some common features of mail systems, what they do, and how much interoperability you can expect.

### *Universally Supported Features*

Aside from the basic ability to send mail, almost any e-mail facility gives you the following features, which can work with other mail systems.

---

*Not all **mail** programs prompt for the subject by default. Sometimes, you have to put a line reading **set ask** (or, for some versions, **set asksub**) into the file *.mailrc* in your home directory. We strongly recommend that you always put a subject on your message. That makes it much easier for the recipient (who may get hundreds of messages a day) to handle.

†You can use the **vi** editor to compose your message by giving the command ~v, putting the ~ in the first column on the screen. The ~v command starts the **vi** editor; if you have already typed part of the message, you should see it within **vi**. Use **vi** commands to edit your message; then, when you are ready, save the message and quit. You will be back within **mail**; type a period in the first column to end the message and send it. If you do not like vi, quit **mail** and give the UNIX command:

```
%  setenv EDITOR my-favorite-editor
```

where *my-favorite-editor* is the name of an editor you'd rather use. For example, if you like the **emacs** editor, give the command **setenv EDITOR emacs**.)

### Aliasing

*Aliasing* is the ability to define nicknames for people. To avoid typing complete Internet addresses, you can decide that **edk** is shorthand for **krol@ux1.cso.uiuc.edu**; if you then use **edk** as the recipient of a message, your system will substitute the complete address for you. Do not decide on aliases arbitrarily: Pick some convention and stick to it. Having an alias does not do you any good if you cannot remember or guess it. You may need to remember an alias even though you have not used it for a long time. It is common to use a first name, followed by the last initial, as an alias. It is also common to have nicknames that are tied to "functions," rather than a specific person (e.g., secretary or boss); over time, the person may change, but the function will remain the same.

With **pine**, you can put alias definitions in the address book. This is choice **A** from the **pine** main menu. As usual, **pine** will walk you through the process of entering a real name, nickname, and e-mail address.

### Folders

Folders let you save messages in an organized way. For example, you could have a folder for each project or class with which you are involved, and another called *personal*. As mail arrives, you can file it in the appropriate folder for future reference. These can usually be examined from within the mail-reading program, using the same facilities you would normally use to read incoming mail. You merely tell **mail** to read the mail in a folder instead of the incoming mail.

In **pine**, a folder is a file that contains messages stored in a format the **mail** program can understand. The file *mbox* or *mail* is where **pine** stores the message that you do not delete, preserve, or file elsewhere; in other words, the default folder. To create another folder or append to an existing one, use the **S** command and name the folder, new or existing, that you wish to use.

Switching to a different folder is accomplished with the **L** command from the **pine** main menu. When you switch folders, **pine** lists the contents of the new folder. This list looks just like the list that **pine** gives when you start the program. The folder name is visible in the upper-right corner of the **pine** screen. Once you are in a folder, you can use all of the normal commands (print, delete, etc.) to manipulate or read your archived messages.

### Forwarding

Within e-mail, *forwarding* has two slightly different meanings. First, forwarding means automatically sending all mail received by a particular login on one computer to another. This is particularly useful if you have accounts on several different computers.

So that you do not have to check mail on different computers constantly, you may want any mail sent to any of your accounts to be forwarded to the one where you normally read mail.*

Forwarding also means taking a message you have received and sending it on to someone else who might be interested. This can usually be done either in its entirety, or as a part of a message that you compose. **pine** makes this quite simple. To forward the current message, press **F**, and **pine** will prompt you for the recipient's address. Do not forget that forwarding e-mail can be very unethical if the message was not intended for anyone but you.

## Mailing text files

The various e-mail messages allow inclusion of a text file via electronic mail. You would like to keep the file intact and insert a copy of it into the message being sent. That way, the file will be immediately useful to the recipient, who does not have to use **ftp** to get it. You can also insert an explanation into the message, telling the recipient what to do with the file.

Keep in mind that a text file refers only to unformatted text. Files that are created by popular word processing software include various formatting commands that cannot be handled by text-only processor such as plain e-mail. You can get around this problem easily enough by saving your word-processed file as text-only. You will also need to be careful that your text-only output has line lengths no greater than what is allowed by your e-mail system. Otherwise you will end up with misaligned text that can be a great source of frustration to the recipient.

## Mailing lists

With electronic mail, it is just as easy to send a message to a group of people as it is to send a message to a single person. The facility that makes this possible is called a *mailing list*. It allows an alias or nickname to stand for a group of recipients; for example, the alias **class** can be defined as "all students in this course." When you send mail to the name **class**, the mail is actually delivered to everyone in the group.

---

*UNIX uses the file *.forward* to accomplish this. You create this in your *home* directory on each system from which you want mail forwarded. In the file, you place the mail address to which you want the mail sent. For example, the following *.forward* file is taken from **johnb**'s *home* directory at **yoyodyne.com**; it contains a single line:

    krol@ux1.cso.uiuc.edu

This file causes any mail sent to **johnb@yoyodyne.com** to be forwarded to **krol@ux1.cso.uiuc.edu**.

With many mailers, including **pine**, this is simple. You can create a list of recipients under one name by using the address book. This is tedious the first time the list is entered, but will save much more time in the long run.

**pine** expands the mailing-list name to a set of normal e-mail addresses. This means that the recipients' e-mail addresses will be listed in the **To:** part of the header. An important advantage of **pine** is the "blind copy" option from the e-mail composition screen. When the cursor is positioned in the address portion of the **pine** composition screen, press **CTRL-R**. One of the "new" options you will see is **Bcc:** for "blind carbon copy." **Bcc:** is just the same as the **To:** and **Cc:** (carbon copy) fields in the way the addresses are entered. The recipients listed here will receive a copy of your message, but there will be nothing in the message header as delivered that indicates the message was sent to others. Rather than creating another ethical dilemma, **Bcc:** was designed to save recipients from having to see a screenful or more of other list members' e-mail addresses. Just as individualized postal letters may get greater attention from recipients than a flyer that is clearly a mass mailing, a group e-mail message that appears to the user as intended only for him or her may receive a higher priority than one addressed to a multitude of recipients.

### Reply

*Replying* is a shorthand way of telling your mailer that you want to send a response back to the person who sent you a particular message. It saves you the trouble of typing the e-mail address. Your mailer typically copies the **From:** (or **Reply-To:**) field from the original message to create the **To:** line of a new message; to create the new **Subject:** line, your mailer just copies the original and adds **Re:** at the beginning to show that this is a response to an earlier message.

Replies can be tricky. Your mailer may not be able to convert the original **From:** field into something reasonable. Whether or not a reply will work correctly depends on whether the sender's return address is complete and acceptable to your mailer. If it does not work, you might need to look at the **From:** address and modify it, based on your experience (see "Acquiring Electronic Mail Addresses" earlier in this chapter). This should not be a problem very often.

### Commonly Supported Features

There are several common features that are supported by most mail programs. If your mailer supports any of these, you can use them when sending messages to any other mailer—regardless of its type.

## Carbon copies

All mailers let you put several addresses in the **To:** field of the header. It is frequently useful to differentiate between those to whom the message is primarily directed and those who receive it for their information. To do so, the mail-forwarding software recognizes that a line beginning with **Cc:** contains a list of addresses; anyone listed on the **Cc:** line will also receive a copy, just as if he or she were listed on the **To:** line. Thus, the **Cc:** field has the same meaning as the old cc: line on a business letter. Many mailers have a facility for creating a **Cc:** line automatically. If the mailer allows you to edit the header, you can create a **Cc:** line manually.

## Blind carbon copies

*Blind carbon copies* are copies sent to a list of readers, just like carbon copies. The header line that lists the recipients, however, is automatically deleted from the outgoing mail. None of the other recipients will know who (if anyone) received blind carbon copies. Because there is no record in the received message that these copies were ever sent, later actions that use data in the header (for example, replies to the message) will not include these recipients in their action.

## Signature files

*Signature files* are a way to append additional information to outgoing mail messages. They are often used to include information about who you are and how you can be contacted. The information is like that which you would see on someone's business card. You can set up a file that gives your name, postal address, phone number, FAX number, other e-mail addresses, and even a favorite quote (**pine** allows you to do this via its setup command). If the recipient cannot get e-mail back to you, the information in your signature file might be the only means at his disposal to get in touch with you. Keep it short and useful. Clever quotes in your signature can get annoying, particularly for people who get e-mail from you with any regularity.

## Unusual and Non-standard Features

The following features are found in some electronic mail packages, but cannot be assumed to be available to everyone. Some of them, such as attaching documents, are becoming more common because there are standard ways of doing them. Others, like notification of reading, will probably never become standard. As a result, you cannot assume these will work unless you know the recipient's mailer has the feature you need and is compatible with your mailer.

### Attaching documents

Some electronic mail systems allow you to mail files as separate entities along with a message. As we saw with **pine**, when you send a message to someone you can say, "send this file, too." When the message is read, the receiving mailer asks the person reading the message where the file should be stored. These files can be either binary or ASCII, and system information about the file is preserved in the move. For example, you could send a message saying, "Take a look at the spreadsheet I have enclosed and get back to me," and attach an Excel spreadsheet from a Macintosh. When the recipient reads the message and accepts the attachment, his Mac automatically creates an Excel spreadsheet file on his machine.

A facility called "multimedia mail" is related to attached documents. This extension allows you to send digitized voice and pictures as part of a message—together with other attachments (such as binary data). The new standard Internet way of doing this is called MIME; we will discuss it more fully later in this chapter. Remember, digitized sound and video take a lot of time to transmit and a lot of disk space to store.

### Notification of receipt

Notification of receipt automatically sends you a message when the mail you have sent is placed in the recipient's electronic in-basket. This prevents someone from denying that your e-mail was delivered.

### Notification of reading

This feature automatically sends you a message when the mail you have sent is displayed by the recipient. It does not mean that he actually read or understood it. It only indicates when it was displayed.

### Message cancel

*Message cancel* allows you to take back a message after you have sent it. This can be handy if you write a message and then wish (later) that you had not sent it. There's a limited window of time during which you can cancel a message. The length of this window varies with the message's destination (where the mail is going) and how the mailers are connected. If the message is sent to another user within the same mail system, it can usually be canceled until it is read. If it is addressed to an in-basket on another mail system, it usually cannot be retrieved after it has passed out of the sender's system. Rather than rely this as a solution, learn to use the postpone option in **pine**.

### *Sending Binary Data as ASCII*

At times, you want to send a binary file (for example, files from WordPerfect, disk dumps, etc.) through electronic mail. **ftp**, which is designed for transferring files, may not be possible or practical. E-mail can reach many places that **ftp** cannot: It can traverse networks that are not directly connected to the Internet, or networks that provide only mail service. In addition, **ftp** cannot send a file to many recipients; you may want to post an executable of your new newsreader to a large mailing list, in which case **ftp** will be impractical.

Electronic mail is a text-only medium. That is, it deals only with messages that are constructed from characters. Relatively few mailers allow you to send binary (i.e., non-text) files directly, and those that do probably are not compatible with each other, although MIME is establishing standards in this area.

With a little additional work, it's possible for any mailer to transmit a binary file, provided that both the sending and receiving computers have a utility to convert binary files into some ASCII representation. All UNIX systems have such utilities; one is called **uuencode**, and we will use it as an example below. Many other systems have an equivalent utility.

You need to find a program that converts a binary file into a printable character representation of the binary data. Most systems have this kind of utility available. **uuencode** comes with UNIX and is available in the public domain for PCs. **BinHex** performs a similar function in the Macintosh world. With these utilities, you can encode the file, turning the binary file into a textual representation. Once you have a textual representation, you can send it through electronic mail. The recipient takes the message, edits off the headers if necessary, decodes it, and has the original binary file. To make the recipient's life easier, say what you used to encode the file.

## *MIME: Multipurpose Internet Mail Extensions*

*MIME* is a specification for automatically sending objects other than text in e-mail messages (URL: **http://www.cis.ohio-state.edu/text/faq/usenet/mail/mime-faq/top.html**). It allows you to avoid **uuencode** and **uudecode**. Even if you and the recipient of a message are using different mail packages, if both packages are MIME-compliant, you should be able to transfer any kind of object you desire. Several packages are capable of handling MIME messages: **metamail** is one, Z-Mail (a popular commercial mailer that runs on many different systems) is another, and **pine** is another.

Although MIME is primarily a specification for attaching files to e-mail messages, for most people MIME is associated with multimedia, and their expectations go a little farther. MIME mailers usually know how to process several kinds of file attachments themselves; in particular, images, audio recordings, and movies. The ability to display any of these depends on your computer having the appropriate hardware and, most likely, some additional software. As compression technologies continue to progress, it will become easier to send digitized images, audio, and video.

At their most exotic, some MIME messages can even contain software that executes on your system. For example, you might receive a message about a breakthrough in curing the common cold. After you read the message, it automatically creates a new screen that displays a model of how the cure works. Although letting someone else execute software on your system sounds dangerous, there's a very clever bit of engineering here: This software is written in a special language that your MIME mailer understands, and it is not allowed to do anything that could possibly be harmful.

## What MIME Does

Let's look at a slightly less esoteric example that will give us some insight into what MIME really does. If you want to send someone an Excel spreadsheet, you can attach the spreadsheet file to your message as a document. If the recipient's e-mail package is not MIME-compliant, she will see something like this:

```
From e-krol@uiuc.edu Mon Jan  3 11:19:49 1994
Date: Mon, 3 Jan 1994 11:19:39 -0600
Message-Id: <199401031719.AA25021@ux1.cso.uiuc.edu>
X-Sender: krol@ux1.cso.uiuc.edu
Mime-Version: 1.0
Content-Type: multipart/mixed; boundary="=====_3514124==_"
To: ajzxmvk@ux1.cso.uiuc.edu
From: e-krol@uiuc.edu (Ed Krol)
Subject: Here is the spreadsheet
Status: RO
--======_3514124==_                          this is the normal text part
Content-Type: text/plain; charset="us-ascii"
Hi, Martha. Here's the spreadsheet you wanted.
--======_3514124==_                          this is the included file
Content-Type: application/mac-binhex40; name="Projected_Costs_List"
Content-Disposition: attachment; filename="Projected_Costs_List"
(This file must be converted with BinHex 4.0)
:&&"bEfTPBh4PC#"$EhOdFb"-DAOd!&K-8cOB3d9-!3!!!%!&!!!!!2`H#3)'!!!
!%!$f"9`!)!!+8QpcFb"@C@&MD#!J)#!J)#!J)#!J)#!J)#!J)!X#'!"@!`!
```

When MIME sent the message, it added some additional lines that are, essentially, directions to the recipient's mail package. Whether you are sending or receiving the message, you do not have to understand these directives; they are processed automatically. There is no way to tell in advance whether or not the recipient's system can process them.

If things work correctly, MIME will leave the decoded *Projected_Costs_List* file on the recipient's computer, with no additional work of coding or decoding necessary on the user's part. However, there's still a compatibility problem here. There are many MIME types. If your mailer is MIME-compatible, but it encounters an unfamiliar message type, you might see something like this:

```
This message contains data in an unrecognized format,
application/mac-binhex40, that can either be viewed
as text or written to a file.

What do you want to do with application/mac-binhex40 data?
1 -- See it as text
2 -- Write it to a file
3 -- Just skip it
```

In this case, you can salvage the message by saving the message (or just the offending part) in a file, and decoding it by hand—just as you would with an old-fashioned mailer. The MIME message will usually tell you what you need to do. In this example, you need to find a utility that can decode BinHex 4.0 files and use it to make the file readable.*
Remember: Just because you or your e-mail package managed to decode the message, it may not be usable on your computer. If you received the spreadsheet we sent in the example, you'd need to have Microsoft Excel on your computer to read it.

One other feature of MIME is that it can avoid sending a file unless the recipient wants it. Instead of putting the file into the mail message as an encoded insertion, it adds a directive telling the recipient's mailer how to **ftp** the file automatically. (Of course, the sender has to make sure that the file is available in an FTP archive somewhere). This feature lets you choose whether or not you want to receive a file; if you do not want the file, you save storage on your computer and reduce network traffic.

## ▓ *When Electronic Mail Gets Returned*

When electronic mail cannot be delivered, you normally get a message telling you why. This takes the format of a strange message in your in-basket. There are three common reasons for electronic mail to fail:

- The mail system cannot find the recipient's machine.
- The recipient is unknown at that machine.
- The mail can find the machine but still cannot deliver the message.

Let's investigate these causes one at a time.

---

*See "Computing/Compression and Archival Software Summary" in the *Resource Catalog*.

## *Unknown Hosts*

When you send a message to someone, the network tries to make some sense out of the information to the right of the @. If it cannot make sense of it, or if it cannot look up the address of the named machine, the mailer that gives up sends you a message saying that the host is unknown. Look at the following example, in which we encoded a binary program and sent it to **johnb@yoyodyne.com**. Assume that the net was unable to recognize the system **yoyodyne.com**. Eventually, you will get a returned message like this:

```
Sun Nov  3 09:03:18 1991
Date: Sun, 3 Nov 1991 09:02:57 -0600
From: Mail Delivery Subsystem <MAILER-DAEMON@uxc.cso.uiuc.edu>
To: krol@ux1.cso.uiuc.edu
Subject: Returned mail: Host unknown

   ----- Transcript of session follows -----
550 yoyodyne.com (TCP)... 550 Host unknown

      ----- Unsent message follows -----
Received: from ux1.cso.uiuc.edu by uxc.cso.uiuc.edu with SMTP id AA17283
   (5.65c/IDA-1.4.4 for <johnb@yoyodyne.com>);
Sun, 3 Nov 1991 09:02:57 -0600 Received: by ux1.cso.uiuc.edu id AA17906
   (5.65c/IDA-1.4.4 for johnb@yoyodyne.com); Sun, 3 Nov 1991 06:22:30 -0600
Date: Sun, 3 Nov 1991 06:22:30 -0600
From: Ed Krol <krol@ux1.cso.uiuc.edu>
Message-Id: <199111031222.AA17906@uxh.cso.uiuc.edu>
To: johnb@yoyodyne.com
Subject: The program you wanted.
```

You see a message from the MAILER-DAEMON on a machine named **uxc.cso.uiuc.edu**, which is an intermediate mail handler. Your mail was sent to this system *en route* to **yoyodyne.com**; this is where it ran into trouble. Past the header of the returned mail message, in a section marked "Transcript of session," you find a message that the host **yoyodyne.com** is unknown to the network. After this, you will usually find the unsent message itself. This saves you the trouble of reentering it (or remembering it).

What should you do when something like this happens? First, check the address: Is the name **yoyodyne.com** spelled correctly? Second, check whether the address is complete. When presented with an incomplete name like **yoyodyne**, many machines add a domain suffix automatically; they assume that the suffix should be the same as their own.

A variant of this problem occurs when people give out partial addresses, assuming that you will be able to figure out the rest. For example, someone might give you an address like **joe@turing.cs**. He is assuming that you know he's in the CS department of the University of Illinois. To a computer, **turing.cs** looks exactly like the complete name of

**turing** in Czechoslovakia (**cs** is Czechoslovakia's country code). If you are lucky, **turing.cs** does not exist, and you will get an "unknown host" message. First, you may need to finish the address yourself from your own knowledge of where the person really resides. Second, when you give your address to someone, always give a complete address; do not assume that your correspondents will figure out the rest.

It is also possible that your computer just does not know about the system to which you are sending mail. Some mailers have lists of valid hostnames that are not updated continuously. The target machine may just not be on the list. If you think this may be the problem, talk to whoever manages the mail system you are using. Similar errors may occur when you reply to someone's message. Some mailers fail to fill out their full name in the **From:** section of the header. The **From:** field gets copied to the **To:** field when you do a reply.

If none of these hints apply, you have no recourse other than calling the person to see if some other address might work better.

## Unknown Recipients

Now let's assume that your mail made its way to the correct host. Eventually, a machine forwarding your mail makes contact with the destination machine and tells it the recipient's name. What happens if the destination machine has not heard of the message's addressee? In this case, the returned mail header looks something like this:

```
>From daemon Mon Nov  4 14:44:31 1991
Received: by uxh.cso.uiuc.edu id AA08280
    (5.65c/IDA-1.4.4 for krol); Mon, 4 Nov 1991 14:44:26
Date: Mon, 4 Nov 1991 14:44:26 -0600
From: Mail Delivery Subsystem <MAILER-DAEMON>
Message-Id: <199111042044.AA08280@uxh.cso.uiuc.edu>
To: krol
Subject: Returned mail: User unknown Status: RO
    ----- Transcript of session follows -----
While talking to yoyodyne.com:
>>> RCPT
To:<johm@yoyodyne.com>
<<< 550 <johm@yoyodyne.com>... User unknown
550 johm@yoyodyne.com... User unknown
```

This failure is frequently caused by mistyping the username in the address. (That is what happened above; "john" is mistyped.) It is also possible that the username is correct, and the hostname is incorrect but legal. For example, if you address a message to **johnb@ux2** rather than **johnb@ux1**, you may get a "User unknown" message. The machine **ux2** exists, but there is no user **johnb** on it.

## *Mail Cannot Be Delivered*

The previous examples show the most frequent ways of failing, but if you are clever you may find others. You may see the message:

```
----- Transcript of session follows -----
554 <johnb@yoyodyne.com>... Service unavailable
```

This message tells us that the machine was not accepting electronic mail at this time. In this case, your best bet is to wait a while and try again, perhaps during normal working hours. In the previous cases, you would receive notification of the problem almost immediately. For example, if the destination host is unknown to the network, you will receive notification as soon as a system that's handling the mail tries to look up the destination and fails. This should happen in minutes or, at most, a few hours. There is an additional common failure mode in which the problem might not be known for days: The machine is known to the network, but unreachable. In these cases, the sending machine may try to send the mail for two or three days (or more) before it gives up and tells you about it.

## *Failures Involving Multiple Recipients*

So far, all of the examples of failures have been for mail destined for one person. It's easy to become confused when something goes wrong with mail sent to several recipients. The returned mail might look like this:

```
Subject: Returned mail: User unknown
Status: RO
    ----- Transcript of session follows -----
While talking to ux1.cso.uiuc.edu:
>>> RCPT To:<willie_martin@ux1.cso.uiuc.edu> <<<
550 <willie_martin@ux1.cso.uiuc.edu>... User unknown
550 willie_martin@ux1.cso.uiuc.edu... User unknown

    ----- Unsent message follows -----
Date: Thu, 7 Nov 1991 10:43:40 -0600
From: Ed Krol <krol>
To: krol@ux1.cso.uiuc.edu, willie_martin@ux1.cso.uiuc.edu
Subject: Willie do you exist?
```

Who got the mail and who did not? You can figure out the answer by looking at the "unsent message" section. The message was destined for both **krol@ux1.cso.uiuc.edu** and **willie_martin@ux1.cso.uiuc.edu**. The "Transcript of session" tells us it is having trouble with **willie_martin**, not with **krol**. You can conclude that **krol** received the message safely and that there is something wrong with **willie_martin**'s address. You need only resend the message to **willie** when you correct his address.

## Last-ditch Help

By convention, every computer that exchanges mail should have a mailbox named **postmaster** defined. Mail addressed to **postmaster** should be read by the e-mail administrator for the host computer. If you need any help with a particular machine, you can send a request to:

```
postmaster@machine-name
```

Some things you might consider sending a message to postmaster about are:

- Help finding the e-mail address for someone you know to be using that host
- Help finding the proper gateway for sending e-mail to external networks
- Complaints about the actions of someone on that host (e.g., harassing messages)

## Mail Lists and Reflectors

Aliases and address book lists allow e-mail users to send the same mail message to a group of recipients. For example, we can define a group name for a few people:

```
alias team johnb@yoyodyne.com, johnw@yoyodyne.com
```

After we have created this name, **team**, we can send a message to **team** and it will be delivered to both **johnb** and **johnw**. This is a natural way to implement group discussions through electronic mail. It works for small groups, or for personal groups that only you use. As the group grows and other people want to use the same group definition, it turns into a maintenance nightmare. Whenever anyone is added to or deleted from the group, everyone who wants to use the alias name must change his or her own personal definition. "Everyone" never does, so someone gets left out and does not receive a message, and there are problems.

You really want a centrally maintained mailing list so that you can make a single change that is effective for everyone. So long as you (or some other responsible person) maintains the mailing list, everyone, senders and recipients, will be happy. This is typically implemented by a mail reflector. A *mail reflector* is a special e-mail address set up so that any message sent to it will automatically be resent to everyone on a list. For example, let's assume that we have set up a mail reflector for **team**, rather than a simple alias. Now I can send a message to **team@yoyodyne.com**. The mailer on **yoyodyne.com** will take my message and resend it to **johnb** and **johnw**. It does not take much of a machine to act as a mail reflector, but it does take someone with system administrator privileges to set one up.* In this section, we will tell you how to use lists that other people have set up; we will not discuss how to create your own. Your local system administrator can help you do that (assuming he or she has the needed resources).

The mail reflector we discussed above works well for a private (though large) group. What if, rather than a private list of people, it were a list available to anyone who wanted to take part in a discussion? Suppose we want to allow anyone in the world who is interested in discussing multimedia to access the address **multimedia@hoople.usnd.edu**. From there the mail will be forwarded to all the other participating list members. You will receive everyone else's messages automatically; likewise anything you send to this address will be "broadcast" to multimedia enthusiasts worldwide.

For this to work, there must be a method for saying "Please add me to the list." Sending that message to **multimedia@hoople.usnd.edu** is not a reasonable solution. It sends the message to everyone on the list. Doing this may get you put on the list, but it is considered *extremely* bad form. Busy list members do not want to read your personal request to join the list, and may not be afraid to tell you so if you post that request to everyone on the list. Worse, the person who manages the list may not get your message at all. The list maintainer may be an e-mail administrator who does not follow the multimedia list itself.

The correct way to subscribe to a list depends on how the list is maintained. Historically, the Internet uses special addresses for administrative requests. Whenever you create a public mail reflector, you create a second mailbox on the same machine. This mailbox has the same name as the mailing list, with a suffix -**request** added. This special mailbox is "private"; anything it receives is not broadcast, but instead is sent to the mailing list's maintainer. So the correct way of subscribing is to send a message to:

```
multimedia-request@hoople.usnd.edu
```

This is still a bit of a chore for the list maintainer, who must read the requests and edit the list manually. A nice utility named **listserv** (URL: **http://www.earn.net/lug**) for maintaining lists (and more) without human intervention grew up in the BITNET community on IBM/VM machines.† Because BITNET **listservs** were accessible to both the BITNET and the Internet communities, they grew quite popular. So popular, in fact, that there has been a proliferation of **listserv**-like software running on all sorts of

---

*One of the reasons for this is that if you create multiple mail reflectors, which have each other as members, they could send messages to each other forever.

†BITNET is a message and file retrieval network that has been around for a long time within the educational community. It used to be a real network, with phone lines of its own. Although BITNET probably still has a few phone lines, it now uses the Internet to handle a lot of its traffic.

computers. Luckily, these packages, such as **listproc, mailserv** (URL: **http://iquest.com/ ~fitz/www/mailserv**), and **majordomo** (URL: **http://www.math.psu.edu/barr/ majordomo-faq.html**), accept a similar command set, so signing up for mailing lists is not quite as confusing as it might have been.

To subscribe to a mailing list that's managed by one of these automatic packages, you send a specially formatted message to a particular address on the computer that runs the mailing list. The "addressee" is often—but not always—the name of the program that's managing the list. For example, to subscribe to a pencil collector's list, you might send a message to **listserv@hoople.usnd.edu**. The messages would consist of one line, with no subject:

```
subscribe pencils your name
```

where **subscribe** is a keyword and **pencils** is the name of the group. *Your name* in the above example is strictly for documentation and the format does not really matter— though many groups will not let you sign up without giving your name. Be sure you send the subscription request from the account where you want to receive the mailings! The list processor gets your e-mail address directly from the message headers, so if you use the wrong account, the mail will go to the wrong place. Once you have subscribed, whenever anyone sends a message to **pencils@hoople.usnd.edu**, you will get a copy.*

If the mailing list were managed by **majordomo**, the address might be **majordomo@hoople.usnd.edu**; the message you'd send to subscribe would be identical. Similarly, if the mailing list is managed by **almanac**, you would send your subscription request to an address like **almanac@hoople.usnd.edu**. You'd send the same message, except that **almanac** does not require your personal name: The message would be simply **subscribe pencils**.

No matter who manages the list, the following rules hold:

- The address you send your request to probably serves many different lists: **listserv@hoople.usnd.edu** could maintain mailing lists for multimedia enthusiasts, pencil collectors, cat lovers, and fans of obscure Baroque composers.

- The address to which you send the subscription request and the address to which you send actual list postings are different. Many lists do not repost mail to the submitter. If you really want a copy, send a carbon copy to yourself.

---

*A few mailing lists add an additional step: They require "subscription confirmation." This means they will send you a standard message, requesting that you forward it back to them—possibly with some additional information. In any case, the message you receive should contain precise instructions about what to do.

## *Dropping Your Subscription*

Now that you can get on a list, how do you get off it, or *unsubscribe?* Mailing lists can be as annoying as any other form of junk mail. Unsubscribing is known in the **listserv** parlance as **signoff**, and is done by sending the following command to the list server:

```
signoff pencils
```

This subscribe/signoff pairing was viewed as a bit obscure by the developers of **majordomo** and **almanac**, who chose the obvious:

```
unsubscribe listname
```

for their lists. Of course, if you want to unsubscribe to an Internet-style mailing list, just send a message to the administrative (**list-request**) address.

If you want more information about what any of these automated mailing-list packages can do, send the message:

```
help
```

to any list server you can find—no matter what type of server it is. It will mail a help guide back to you. When you subscribe to a mailing list, the first message you receive will probably be a "form letter" describing the list in detail and telling you how to sign off. Make it standard procedure to save that letter.

This has been a lot of information. Let's summarize with a table. In Table 7-4, *hostname* is the computer that manages the list, and *list* is the name of the list.

*Table 7-4    Subscribing to Mailing Lists*

| List Type | Subscription Address | Subscription Message | Termination Message | Posting Address |
|-----------|---------------------|---------------------|---------------------|-----------------|
| listserv | listserv@*hostname* | **SUB**scribe *listname* <your real name> | **UNS**ubscribe *listname* or **signoff** *listname* | *listname*@*hostname* |
| listproc | listproc@*address* | **SUB**scribe *listname* <your real name> | **UNS**ubscribe *listname* | *listname*@*hostname* |
| majordomo | majordomo@*host* | subscribe <list> [<e-mail address>] | unsubscribe <list> [<address>] | *listname*@**majordomo** |

If this seems complicated, remember to simply send the e-mail message **help** to the subscription address (not the list itself). There really is no need to memorize commands. Remember that the trend is toward graphical user interfaces, and this will continue to put pop-up help menus within a click of the mouse.

If you think about what happens when a mail reflector is in operation, you will realize that it is not terribly efficient. If five people from the Yoyodyne corporation all subscribe to the **aliens** mail reflector at **hoople.usnd.edu**, five messages will be sent from **hoople.usnd.edu** to **yoyodyne.com** for every original message sent to **aliens@hoople.usnd.edu**. This sends unneeded, extra traffic across the Internet. There is a way to get around this suboptimal behavior and, also, make the list more responsive to local personnel changes. The system administrator for **yoyodyne.com** can create a local mail reflector that resends messages only to its employees (Figure 7-5).

Then he subscribes the Yoyodyne reflector's address to the national reflector at **hoople**. So, when a message gets sent to **aliens@hoople.usnd.edu**, one message is sent to **aliens@yoyodyne.com**, which resends it to the five subscribing employees.

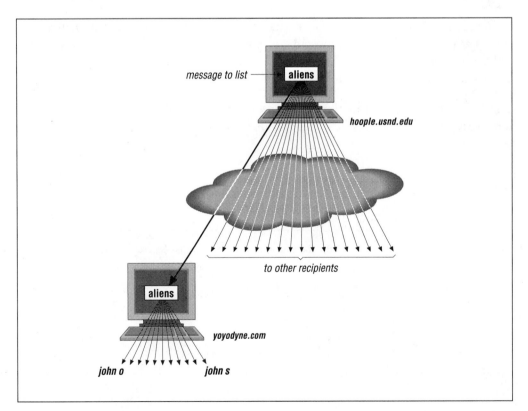

*Figure 7-5    Local mail reflectors*

Which mail list server is best for you? There may not be an absolute answer. A periodic posting at URL **ftp://ftp.uu.net/usenet/news.answers/mail/list-admin/software-faq** attempts to stay current with that question.

### Moderators and List Etiquette

A couple of final pieces of trivia about using mailing lists. First, some lists are moderated. With a *moderated* list, the messages are not automatically transmitted. Instead, a moderator first screens the messages to determine whether or not they are appropriate. This is usually not a big deal, but may lead to some delays in reposting. It also means that inappropriate or grossly impolite postings will be screened out—though the meaning of "inappropriate" depends on the tastes of the moderator and the expectations of the particular list.

Many mailing lists have their own etiquette rules. Some are free-for-alls; others have very strict standards about the behavior of their members. The form letter you get when subscribing will tell you what expectations the list has, if any. Be sure to obey these rules; do not make inappropriate postings.

Finally, be careful when responding to list messages. Some messages require personal responses to the original sender; for others, it's more appropriate to send your response to the list. For example, consider a meeting announcement requesting an RSVP. Your RSVP should be sent to the person requesting the information—do not expect that everyone on the list cares that you are coming. On the other hand, replies to requests for information of general interest (e.g., "Anyone know how to make a million dollars legally?") should probably be sent to the list. Be careful about using your mailer's reply command. Sometimes, your reply will go to the entire list by default; other times, replies are sent to the originator by default. Exactly what happens depends on how the mail reflector was set up. A mail reflector should set the message's **From:** line to the address of the reflector, and should insert a **Reply-To:** line containing the address of the original sender. If this is done, and if your mailer works correctly, the reply should go to the original sender. However, not all mail reflectors are set up correctly, and not all mailers handle **Reply-To:** lines properly. Only experience will tell you for sure. One thing about e-mail lists: You will hear about it, via e-mail, if you do something obnoxious.

## ■ File Retrieval Using Electronic Mail

Earlier, we discussed how you can use e-mail to send a file to someone else as a substitute for FTP. The reverse is also true in some special cases: You can, on occasion, use e-mail to request and receive files from FTP archives. This requires a special kind of server at the FTP archive site. You send this server a special message, telling it which file you want it to send. Upon receiving this message, the server gets the file and sends it back to you through the mail. The reason for this service is, again, so that you can retrieve files even if the server is on another network (such as BITNET) or over a UUCP connection. Archie services are also available via e-mail; these are discussed in chapter 9.

There are three ways of requesting files via electronic mail:

- Specialized "Internet-style" servers that give access to a specific set of files at one location.

- Mailing list servers, such as **listserv**, **majordomo**, and **almanac**, that give access to a specific set of files at one location. These are functionally equivalent to the Internet-style servers, but for historical reasons, they work differently. **listserv** is especially prevalent, because BITNET has no equivalent to FTP. Many **almanac** servers have cropped up recently.

- General FTP-mail gateways (**ftpmail** and **bitftp**). These servers allow you to send a message describing what you want to get. The server then performs anonymous FTP for you and mails the results back. This differs from the previous two in that **ftpmail** can get any publicly available file anywhere on the Internet.

If you have access to FTP, you will not need to use these facilities; it's easier to use FTP directly.

## Internet-style Servers

The first method of retrieval is used by Internet information repositories that have to be widely accessible. To get a file from one of these Internet-style servers, send a mail message to the server in which the message body contains the command **send** followed by the name of the file you want. For example:

```
%  mail mail-server@rtfm.mit.edu
Subject:
send usenet/comp.mail.misc/Inter- Network_Mail_Guide
.
Cc:
```

This message asks the machine named **rtfm** at MIT to send a copy of the file *usenet/comp.mail.misc/Inter-Network_Mail_Guide* back to the original sender (i.e., the **From:** line of the requesting message). If you do not have enough information, or if your request fails, a message with the command **help** as the body requests information about what facilities are available through that server. One common pitfall: Filenames on Internet servers are usually case-sensitive, so be careful to use capital and lowercase letters appropriately; you must match the filename exactly.

## *listserv-style Requests*

Here you will need to be cognizant of the kind of server you are using, because there are some differences both in syntax and interpretation of the commands you give to retrieve files.

### *listserv file retrieval commands*

The **listserv** commands for requesting files are similar to those used for mailing-list maintenance. Send your request to the name **listserv** on the machine providing the service. The message body should have lines of the form:

> **get** *filename filetype*

where *filename* and *filetype* are the two components that make up an IBM VM filename.* For example, assume you want to get a list of files that are available about BITNET network nodes. This list is in the file *bitnode filelist* and is available from the server **bitnic.bitnet**. To get the file, send the message:

> **get** z

to the address **listserv@bitnic.bitnet**. There are a couple of funny things that you will notice the first time you try to fetch something from a **listserv** server. You will receive at least two messages back: a message acknowledging the request and telling you it will be sent, and a message that contains the requested data. The data may arrive in multiple messages, because BITNET has a limit on the size of an individual message. If the file you want is too long, it will be divided into smaller chunks. Finally, with a **listserv** request, you do not have to worry about upper- and lowercase letters. **listserv** servers are not case-sensitive. All requests are converted into uppercase before being serviced.

### *majordomo file retrieval*

The commands to do file retrieval using **majordomo** are the same as those for **listserv**, with two differences:

- The files available are list-dependent
- The filenames are case-sensitive

On **listserv** servers, all the files available to be fetched are sitting there on the server in one big pool, so they must all have unique names. The authors of **majordomo** thought this was a problem, so **majordomo** software maintains a separate pool of files for each

---

*There is more about this in chapter 6, *Moving Files: FTP,* in the section "Target: IBM VM Systems."

mailing list it maintains. This implies that the server needs two pieces of information: the name of the file and the list that it came from.

The second difference is merely a result of **majordomo**'s UNIX background. On UNIX systems, upper- and lowercase characters are different. Therefore the file *REPORT* is a different file from *report*. You must type the filename you want exactly.

Now that the background is out of the way, we can look at the command you need:

> **get** *listname filename*

*listname* is the name of the mailing list, and *filename* is the file that you want sent to you. You put this in the body of the mail message and send it off, just as you would with **listserv**.

### *almanac file retrieval*

**almanac** servers work a little differently than the others. **almanac** servers are organized in terms of topic-oriented "folders." To get a list of the folders available at an **almanac** server, send the following message to the server:

> send catalog

Folders can have many files (and other folders) within them. Once you know what folders are available, you need to look inside the folders that interest you. To do so, send a command like:

> send *foldername* catalog

Finally, when you have a catalog that contains a file you want, send a request like this to get the file:

> send *foldername filename*

For example, to receive the document named *0001* from the folder *ers-reports,* send the command:

> send ers-reports 0001

Many folders and files have aliases, or shortened names that make requests more convenient. The catalog will show any aliases that are available. Aliases can be used instead of the file- or folder name. You can also use wildcards to request multiple files or groups of files, for example:

> send ers-reports "*"

retrieves all the files in the folder *ers-reports*. Beware—commands like this may retrieve many, many files. If you are paying for connection time, you may be in for a big bill!

For more information about what **almanac** does, send it a **help** message.

## *The FTPmail Application Gateway*

You can also request a file through e-mail by using an FTP application gateway called **ftpmail**. **ftpmail** may be used to retrieve files from any FTP server on the Internet. Requests to use the **ftpmail** service are made by sending messages to an FTPmail server. The original server was **ftpmail@decwrl.dec.com**, but several more have appeared. The server includes your subject text in the mail it returns to you, but otherwise ignores it—so you can use the subject line for your own reference. For example, let's assume that you are really into juggling and want to get a copy of the Juggling FAQ, available in the directory */pub/juggling* on the computer **cogsci.indiana.edu**. You might do the following:

```
% mail ftpmail@decwrl.dec.com
Subject: juggling FAQ
connect cogsci.indiana.edu        ftp from this computer
chdir pub/juggling                move to target directory
get FAQ                           request the file
quit
.
Cc:
```

You can get complete information about how to use **ftpmail** by sending it a message with the single word **help** in the body, but some of the more useful commands are listed here:

**connect** *(hostname login password)*

Specifies the host to contact. Each request must have one connect statement in it. If you do not list a *hostname* with the command, **ftpmail** assumes that the file is located on the host **gatekeeper.dec.com** (which is not a very good assumption). *login* and *password* are optional. If they are not given, they default to "anonymous" and your e-mail address.

**binary**

Specifies that the files are binary and should be encoded into ASCII before being transmitted. By default, the files are encoded with the **btoa** utility.

**uuencode**

Specifies that binary files should be encoded with **uuencode** rather than **btoa**.

| | |
|---|---|
| **compress** | Specifies that binary files should be compressed with the UNIX **compress** utility. |
| **chdir** *directory* | Change to the specified directory when the **ftp** connection is made to the server computer. |
| **dir** *directory* | Return a directory listing of the specified directory. If none is specified, return a listing of the current directory. |
| **get** *file* | Specifies the file to be sent to you from the FTP server via e-mail. |
| **chunksize** *number* | Specifies the maximum number of characters that will be sent in any one message. If a message is larger than the number specified (the default is 64,000), the file is split into as many messages as required for transmission. When you receive all the pieces, you have to reassemble them in order. |
| **quit** | Tells the server to terminate the request. |

The **ftpmail** utility will send you any file you request. It is up to you to tell it if it should treat it as a binary file. If it is binary and you do not tell it so, what you get will be useless.

## Other FTPmail Servers

The original FTPmail server at **decwrl.dec.com** is very heavily loaded—obviously because it fulfills a need. However, it may take days for it to respond. Their help file says that it may take a week or more. Therefore, some other servers have appeared that you might want to try. Table 7-5 lists some FTP–e-mail gateways we know about. It's a good idea to use a server that's close to you. In particular, avoid the European servers if you are not in Europe. It's a good idea to use a server that's located near you.

Now, how do you use these servers? Before doing anything else, get the help file. All of the servers respond to the single word **help** sent as the body of a mail message. That's the easy part.

Describing more than the **help** command is difficult, because the five servers we mention below have three different command sets! However, we can give you a couple of examples. That, plus the help file of the server you want to use, should get you started.

### FTPmail to IEUnet

Here's how to get the file we retrieved earlier from the IEUnet server. Send the following message to **ftpmail@ieunet.ie**:

```
begin
send cogsci.indiana.edu:/pub/juggling/FAQ
end
```

By default, the file will come back **uuencoded**, unless you specify some other encoding with the ENCODE command. You can include several **send** commands if you want. Note that the command includes the hostname, the directory, and the filename as a single string.

### BITFTP

The three BITNET servers, fortunately, have the same user interface. Here is how to get a file from them. Send the following message to **bitftp@pucc.princeton.edu**, **bitftp@vm.gmd.de**, or **bitftp@plearn.edu.pl**:

```
FTP cogsci.indiana.edu
USER anonymous
cd /pub/juggling
get FAQ
QUIT
```

You can include more **get** commands if you wish.

*Table 7-5* *FTPmail and BITFTP servers*

| Server | Location |
|---|---|
| **ftpmail@decwrl.dec.com** | United States |
| **ftpmail@ieunet.ie** | Ireland |
| **bitftp@vm.gmd.de** | Germany |
| **bitftp@pucc.princeton.edu** | New Jersey |
| **bitftp@plearn.edu.pl** | Poland |

## ▓ *Exercises*

*Answer the following questions for each e-mail interface you will be using (e.g.,* **pine**, *Eudora,* UNIX **mail**, *and/or others):*

**1.** What is your complete Internet e-mail address?

**2.** Send an e-mail message to another student in your class. In doing so, answer the following questions. How can you spell-check your mail message before sending it? Is a copy of the message automatically saved for you? Does your system allow "word wrap" that, like a word processor, does not require you to press ENTER whenever you reach the end of a line? Are you prompted after executing the **send** command before the message is actually sent?

**3.** Does your e-mail system have an address book? If so, explain how you can enter someone's complete e-mail address into your address book. What is the easiest (fastest) way to access that address when you are composing a message?

**4.** Explain how you can manipulate e-mail messages sent to you. How do you save, print, and delete an e-mail message?

**5.** Can you forward messages received to other users? Explain some of the dangers of forwarding others' e-mail messages. Why might you object to someone else forwarding your e-mail compositions?

**6.** How large is your e-mail box? What are its limits? If the answer is not readily apparent, whom can you contact to answer these questions?

**7.** Name a tool that is available to you for looking up others' e-mail addresses locally. Name three tools for looking up others' e-mail addresses globally via the Internet. (*Hint:* Try URL **telnet://info.cnri.reston.va.us:185**).

**8.** TILE.NET (URL: **http://www.tile.net/tile/listserv/index.html**) includes an enormous index of **listserv** lists. Use it to try to locate three **listserv** groups, one each of academic, professional, and personal interest. For each, list the simple directions for joining each list and those for broadcasting your contribution to each.

**9.** Repeat the previous exercise by using Indiana University's Mailing List archive (URL: **http://scwww.ucs.indiana.edu/mlarchive**) that adds **majordomo** and **listproc** lists to their collection of **listserv** lists.

**10.** Why might "lurking" (reading list messages without participating by adding your own) be desirable before you jump in with your own comments or questions?

**11.** Using one that is given to you or by locating one on your own, join a **listserv** discussion list. Before trying to join, answer these questions *carefully:* What is the Internet address for communicating with the electronic manager of the e-mail list? What is the Internet address for broadcasting a message you author to the entire list? How can you get off the list? *Note:* Your school may have a mailing list intended for local new users. If so, it may be well worth it to join that list.

**12.** E-mail has rapidly diffused throughout organizations including both universities and corporate entities in recent years. It often is used in a more casual manner than other forms of communication, particularly legal documents. How should e-mail messages be treated? If a supervisor promises an employee a promotion via e-mail, under what circumstances, if any, should this be treated as legally binding?

# NETWORK NEWS

The Internet is commonly known to be a source from which to find online libraries, documents, and other structured research tools. One of the most important elements of the Internet is simply its ability to put people in touch with one another. The Internet offers something particularly unique in the quest for knowledge: the shared expertise of its users. *Network news,* current discussion on several thousand different topic areas called *newsgroups,* is a key way in which this is accomplished.

The shared knowledge base of the Internet is not limited to professional information. You can just as appropriately ask, "What is the recovery rate for the operation my uncle is having?" as you can, "How do I set my printer to produce the right color?" On the surface, e-mail discussion groups seem to provide all you could possibly want for worldwide discussions. As you get into it, however, you find that there is a problem with the volume of messages. There are discussions in which you take part for work, and those in which you participate for recreation and enjoyment. Active e-mail discussion lists fill your mailbox quickly and can "hide" more important messages. Network news is a way to take part in even more discussions, yet keep them organized and separate from your mail.

News has another advantage: It is ideal for browsing and does not require daily use. If you are marginally interested in a topic, you can check the latest discussions once a month, or once a year. You do not have to subscribe to a mailing list, and you will not receive mail that is only vaguely interesting that you will have to delete. Of course, something about network news can turn many of these "marginal interests" into all-consuming passions. If electronic mail is the application that entices people to use the Internet the first time, net news is the application that keeps them coming back.

Network news is the Internet equivalent of a discussion group or a "bulletin board system" (BBS) like those on CompuServe or private dial-up facilities. The name is misleading in that it implies to a new user that it is a source of "news." An individual posting to a newsgroup is called an "article." Although many commercial and other sources of news are available on the World Wide Web, network news is really a global group of opinions posted on electronic discussion lists called newsgroups. Keep this in mind as we continue.

To the user, network news organizes discussions under a set of broad headings, the newsgroups. A newsreading program presents those discussions in an orderly way: a menu of classical music discussions, followed by a menu of multimedia discussions, followed by a menu of chemical engineering items, etc. Inside each newsgroup, there are usually multiple discussions going on under specific subjects. In the classical music newsgroup, you might see discussions of Beethoven's Ninth Symphony, breaking in reeds for an oboe, and Bach's children. All these discussions will be going on simultaneously.

The newsreader helps you keep everything in order. It keeps track of the items you have already seen and displays only new items that have arrived since your last session. Once the newsreader has shown you what articles are available for any topic, you can select and read the items that interest you. If you forget where you have seen something, you can search for an article based on its author, subject, or an author-given synopsis. You can also set up your newsreader to view or discard certain items automatically, based on the author's name or the article's subject.

As with most Internet applications, there are many newsreading programs from which you can choose. On nongraphical UNIX systems, the most common newsreaders are probably **rn**, **trn**, **nn**, and **tin**. The WWW and new graphical tools are relegating these command-line readers to computer specialists and have little to offer the general user. **rn** was written before there was much news flowing around. **trn** is a descendant of **rn** that supports threads; i.e., it lets you read news items in order within a topic. We will not discuss **trn** either, though it is a valuable, modern newsreader with a good set of features and was designed to be used in a busy news environment. **tin** is the newest of the four readers listed. It seems to be particularly popular among new users; many people feel that it is easy to use, but it does not sacrifice any of the functionality you get with **nn**.

There tend to be many similarities between different newsreaders, so looking at the commands and features of **nn** will give you a start on whatever newsreader you finally decide to use.* There are strong arguments among users about which newsreader is the best, and new ones are under development (see URL **news:news.software.readers**). The important thing is not whether or not you use **nn**, **trn**, **tin**, or a graphical or WWW program, but that you use a reader that supports threads. This makes following USENET

---

*__nn__ is a very complicated program; its entry in the UNIX reference manual is over 50 pages long, significantly longer than this chapter. We are introducing you only to the "important" ones.

discussions far more efficient. **nn**, **trn**, and **tin** all support threads, as do Newswatcher and many WWW browsers.

Newsreaders differ in how they organize and present the new articles. Which is best for you is a personal matter. Some people like to read magazines cover-to-cover, and some people pick and choose articles. The same is true of the news. **nn** is a "cover-to-cover" reader. If that is not your style, you might be interested in the **tin** program, which gives you a bit more freedom to jump around according to your whims.

## Newsgroups and News System Organization

Newsgroups are organized hierarchically, with the broadest grouping first in the name, followed by an arbitrary number of subgroupings. The name of each group is separated from its parent and its subgroups by a period (.), a notation you are probably familiar with by now. Newsgroup names are like telephone numbers in that they go from most general to most specific from left to right. So:

```
rec.music.folk
```

is a *rec*reational discussion, one that most people take part in for fun, in the general category of *music*. Specifically, it is a discussion of *folk* music.

What precise newsgroups are depends mostly on what computer your newsreader uses for its news server (see URL **http://www.w3.org/hypertext/WWW/LineMode/Defaults/ AboutNewsServers.html**. To understand this, we need to look a little at how news works. Figure 8-1 shows what the news system looks like to users. There is a newsreader that interrogates a news server to receive menus of articles and calls for the articles themselves as required. The server is known as an *NNTP* server (Network News Transfer Protocol). The server collects news from several places: USENET, local news sources, mail reflectors, and Clarinet. It holds these articles for a certain preset period (controlled by the server's administrator) and eventually discards them.

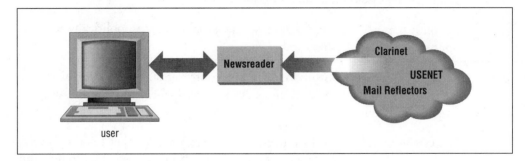

*Figure 8-1* *User's view of the news system*

Most of the server's newsgroups come as part of *USENET,* a set of newsgroups generally considered to be of interest globally. USENET is one of the most misunderstood concepts around. Here are some key points about USENET (see URL **http://www.cis.ohio-state.edu/hypertext/faq/usenet/news-newusers-intro/faq.html**):

- USENET is not a computer network
- USENET does not *require* the Internet
- USENET is not software
- USENET is a set of voluntary rules for passing and maintaining newsgroups
- USENET is a set of volunteers who use and respect those rules

USENET used to be made up of seven well-managed newsgroup categories. The rules for how to use, create, and delete groups have been around since before the Internet. (USENET predates the Internet; in those days, news was passed via regular dial-up connections. There are still many sites that participate in USENET in this fashion.) The seven "original" news categories are:

*comp*        Computer science and related topics. This includes computer science proper, software sources, information on hardware and software systems, and topics of general interest.

*news*        Groups concerned with the news network and news software. This includes the important groups *news.newusers.questions* (questions from new users) and *news.announce.newusers* (important information for new users). If you are new to USENET, you should read these to become comfortable with the interface.

*rec*         Groups discussing hobbies, recreational activities, and the arts.

*sci*         Groups discussing scientific research and applications (other than computer science). This includes newsgroups for many established scientific and engineering disciplines, including some social sciences.

*soc*         Groups that address social issues, where social can mean politically relevant or socializing, or anything in between.

*talk*        The *talk* groups are a forum for debate on controversial topics. The discussions tend to be long-winded and unresolved. This is where to go if you want to argue about religion.

*misc*        Anything that does not fit into the above categories, or that fits into several categories. It is worth knowing about *misc.jobs* (jobs wanted and offered) and *misc.forsale* (just what it says).

Servers may also have newsgroups they create locally. Any server administrator can create whatever groups he or she likes, corresponding to the interests of the server's users. These might include discussions of campus events, class newsgroups, local network outages, and employee announcements. Although these are local groups, they can still be passed to other servers that want to carry them. In a large corporation, each department might have its own news server; the servers would be able to pass the employee-announcements group among themselves. Of course, the servers would not pass groups like this to the outside world. Local newsgroups are named by the local server's administrator, who must choose names that do not conflict with other newsgroups.

To a user, the news system looks like Figure 8-1. In actuality, it is implemented as shown in Figure 8-2. A server's administrator makes bilateral agreements with other administrators to transfer certain newsgroups, usually over the Internet, between one another.

A site that provides your server with one or more newsgroups is known as a *news feed.* Certain servers will provide feeds for some groups, other servers for other groups. A server administrator may make any arrangements for news feeds from any servers that are necessary to provide the set of groups to be offered. Over the years, this has caused some useful local groups to be distributed almost as widely as the core USENET groups.

These widespread local groups are known as "alternative newsgroup hierarchies."\* Because they look like the USENET newsgroups (except that they have different names), the

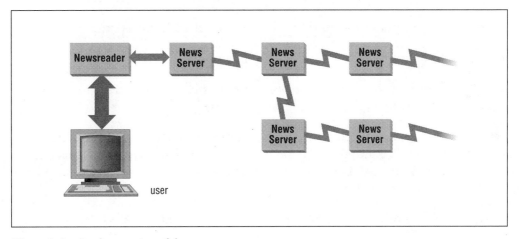

***Figure 8-2*** *Implementation of the news system*

---

\*If you are interested in a complete list of all official and alternative newsgroup hierarchies, you might check out the newsgroup *news.groups* (URL: **news:news.groups**). These lists are posted regularly there.

term "USENET" is frequently expanded to include these groups as well. The most common alternative newsgroups are:

*alt*  Groups that discuss "alternative ways of looking at things." There are a lot of truly bizarre newsgroups here. A more serious *alt* group, such as *alt.dcom.telecom,* is an alternative to a moderated newsgroup *comp.dcom.telecom.* Other important groups (like *alt.gopher*) were created here rather than going through the voting process required to create an "official" newsgroup. (These groups sometimes migrate to official newsgroups as their topics gain acceptance.) Other *alt* groups can be far off the mainstream, and reader discretion is advised.

*bionet* Groups of interest to biologists.

*bit*  The most popular BITNET **listserv** discussion groups.

*biz*  Discussions related to business. This newsgroup hierarchy allows postings of advertisements or other marketing materials; such activity is not allowed in other groups.

*can*  Groups that are Canada-specific have this as their area name. Although generally provided as an outlet for Canadian interests, these groups also offer a good way for Americans to learn more about our northern neighbors.

*clari*  Fee-based newsgroup interface to journalistic newswire services.

*courts* These groups cover court cases at the federal and state levels.

*de*   Technical, recreational, and social discussions in German.

*fj*   Technical, recreational, and social discussions in Japanese (some require software to display the Kanji character set).

*gnu*  Discussions related to the Free Software Foundation (FSF) and its GNU project. This includes announcements of new FSF software, new developments to old software, bug reports, and questions and discussion by users of the Foundation's tools.

*hepnet* Discussions primarily of interest to the high-energy physics community.

*ieee*  Discussions related to the IEEE (Institute of Electronic and Electrical Engineers).

*info*  A group of mailing lists on a wide variety of topics that are transformed into newsgroups.

*k12*    A group dedicated to teachers and students, kindergarten through high school. This category already has demonstrated great potential in the application of this interface in education.

*relcom*    Various groups originating in the former USSR (some require special software to display the Cyrillic alphabet).

*u3b*    Discussions related to the AT&T 3B computer series.

*vmsnet*    Discussions of Digital Equipment's VAX/VMS operating system and DECnet.

Several of these groups are *gatewayed:* in particular, the *bit, info,* and *gnu* groups. This is another way of creating newsgroups. The output of a mail reflector or a list server can be converted into a newsgroup. This allows people who would rather use the organizational facilities of news to take part in a mail reflector–style discussion without subscribing to the mailing list themselves. In other words, the user takes on the active role of reading a newsgroup as opposed to passively accepting e-mail messages. A few computers subscribe to a mailing list, reformat the mail so it is appropriate for the news system, and then distribute it to anyone who wants a news feed.

## Clarinet

Several commercial information services are distributed via network news. One example of this is Clarinet (URL: **http://www.clarinet.com/index.html**). The e.News service offers general, international, sports, technology, entertainment, and financial news, as well as special features and columns. Clarinet uses the news hierarchy to broadcast articles from the traditional wire services among other sources. For a server to offer this service, the organization that owns it must contract with Clarinet for the service; this contract places limits on where the server can distribute the Clarinet newsgroups. The distribution is usually limited to a particular corporation, campus, or workgroup. These newsgroups are prefixed by the header *clari* and include information of national and localized interests.

Clarinet is available via **telnet** remote login. Figure 8-3 shows what Clarinet accessed in this text-only environment. This is quite familiar in appearance to those who are accustomed to using USENET. Note that the authors of the postings are newswire services.

Following a trend in the delivery of information to desktops, Clarinet is also available via the Mac or Windows GUI. Figure 8-4 shows Clarinet as accessed by the WWW browser Mosaic. This interface may supplant pure newsreaders as the WWW continues its evolution. We will take a brief tour of those new newsgroup interfaces before returning to the general discussion of USENET.

*Figure 8-3    Clarinet news via telnet*

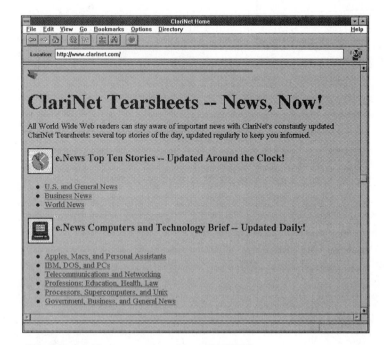

*Figure 8-4    Clarinet news via Mosaic WWW browser*

## Recent Browsers

### WinVN

WinVN is a Microsoft Windows and Windows NT–based newsreader. Like other newsreaders, it can be used to select, view, and write USENET news articles. WinVN can also be used to send (but not receive) electronic mail messages. WinVN offers the graphical user interface approach to USENET.

In normal operation, WinVN displays three types of windows: the main group-list window, which displays a list of all newsgroups; one or more group article-list windows, each of which displays a list of the articles in a newsgroup; and one or more article windows, which each displays an article. Double-clicking on a newsgroup or article name causes that item to be displayed in a separate window. WinVN is depicted in Figure 8-5 (from URL **http://www.ksc.nasa.gov/software/winvn/wvlarge.gif**).

When you want to write an article, WinVN opens a composition window for that purpose (see "Posting Articles" later in this chapter). Similarly, when you want to write an e-mail message, WinVN either opens a MAPI (Microsoft Mail) editor session or opens a composition window to accept your text. WinVN offers a very flexible, customizable newsreading environment typical of what is available on the WWW.

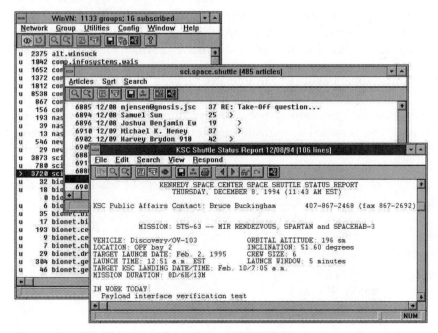

*Figure 8-5   WinVN newsreader via Mosaic WWW browser*

### *Newswatcher*

A popular tool for reading news on Macintosh computers is Newswatcher. (See URL **http://www.bgsu.edu/docs/Mac/newswatcher/newswatcher.html**).

All of these groups generate an amazing amount of network traffic; a typical server subscribes to more than 4,000 newsgroups and receives at least 50 megabytes per day. This leads to other limitations on which newsgroups are available from any particular server. A server administrator may choose not to accept a certain group because it is very active and eats up too much disk space. This also limits the amount of time old news items will reside on a server. It is possible to go back and read news items you passed by earlier, provided that the server has not yet deleted (or expired) the article. The amount of time that any article remains on the system depends entirely on how long the administrator feels those items can be stored. It varies from a few days to months and may be different for each group. This also means that if you go away on vacation, some items may come and go before you get a chance to read them. Fortunately, many important work-related newsgroups have their conversations archived at various places. The locations of these archives are usually announced via the group.

## ■ *Controlling News Access*

Censorship can be an issue with news feeds. Some administrators decide that some groups (especially in the *alt* category) are not for consumption by the server's clientele, and they choose not to carry them. Individuals who believe a newsgroup should be carried can appeal to the administrator and/or search for an alternative provider.

Gatekeeping is a complex topic and can lead to animated discussions about basic freedoms. There are many reasons why an administrator might decide not to offer a group; strictly speaking, censorship usually is not among them. A server administrator is the steward of a machine. That computer is owned by someone, and it has a purpose, aside from being a news server. The administrator walks a fine line between accepting as many newsgroups as possible and not diverting too many machine resources to news. Access to newsgroups that include large files of sexually explicit images must somehow be balanced with the machine's intended purpose. If disk space runs low and groups need to be cut, those groups may be among the first to be cut. You can suggest that *alt.sex* (or any other group) be carried, but not demand it. One final suggestion is to check "How to Receive Banned Newsgroups FAQ" at URL **http://www.cis.ohio-state.edu/hypertext/faq/usenet/usenet/banned-groups-faq/faq.html**. This document discusses the legal and technical issues surrounding newsgroup access.

# ◼ *Getting Started*

The biggest obstacle with starting to read the newsgroups is that your client software starts by offering you all newsgroups or none. You must configure your newsreader to access the news server before you will be able to read any newsgroups. Once configured, your client may subscribe you to *all* 4,000 or 5,000 of them. *Subscribe* is once again an unfortunate choice of words. You have access to all the newsgroups on your server whether you "subscribe" to them or not. Subscriptions will take you directly to the groups you have selected and will keep track of where you left off in your last session. You may go directly to an unsubscribed newsgroup, but there will be no record of where you were when you last read the group. Subscribing, therefore, simply gives you more control over a newsgroup.

Only a relatively few newsgroups will be of enough interest that you might want to read them on a daily basis (the traffic on a group may dictate how feasible it is for you to read it on, for example, a weekly basis). The old, straightforward approach is to unsubscribe to the groups one by one after you initially are subscribed to all in your first USENET session. Obviously, this process is cumbersome and tedious, requiring that you accept or decline a group some 4,000 or more times. Some UNIX users avoid this by simply using standard UNIX commands to read news directly without first subscribing.

If you look back to Figure 8-1, the computer running the newsreader has no news files on it. Whenever you read news, it asks the computer running the server for articles. Assuming you are not a UNIX expert, you will want to use an interface between you and the server: the client newsreader. We need to discuss how you get needed control over what you read. Newsreaders have different files and utilities for handling this problem; you may have to use your ingenuity to find out what works. Whatever you do, your first step will be the same: You must tell your computer which groups you want to view.

## *What Is a News Item?*

A news item is very similar to an electronic mail message. It has the same general parts as an e-mail message: a header and a body. The body of a news item is the message's text, just as you would expect. The header tells the news software how to distribute the item throughout the Internet and also tells you something about the item's contents. The header has information about the submitter, the subject, a synopsis, and some indexing keywords. The header information is used to build an index on news servers; this index allows the client readers to build menus and search for items of interest without having to pass around the complete set of articles. The header is built when you create a new item. You need not worry about its format, but you do need to provide the information. (The program you use to post the news will ask you for the information it needs.) You will see a header if you save an item in a file for later use, because the header is saved as well.

Each news item is considered part of a discussion *thread*. The act of creating *(posting)* a new article on a completely new topic creates a new thread. Newsreaders who want to add their "two cents" to the discussion then make follow-on postings. A follow-on posting creates another article, but tells the news software that it is part of the thread created by the original posting. This allows it to be logically tied to the presentation.

## Using a Newsreader

As we said earlier, we will describe the **nn** newsreader, one of the more popular newsreaders available for UNIX. You can expect other newsreaders to have features that are more or less similar; and, no matter what the commands are, the basic tasks you want to perform (select newsgroups and individual news items, search for different topics) will be identical. Once you understand what you should be able to do, figuring out how to make your personal newsreader do it should be simple.

The **nn** newsreader has two distinct phases (or modes) of operation: the selection phase and the reading phase. In the *selection* phase, you are presented with a menu of news postings in a group you subscribe to and you select the ones you want to read. Assume I went through the laborious newsgroup selection process that we outlined, and ended up subscribing to the single group *rec.music.folk*. When I next give the command **nn**, I will get a menu like this:

```
% nn
Newsgroup: rec.music.folk              Articles: 6 of 6/1
a Mr. Chicago       19  World Cafe
b John Storm         8  >
c Willie Martin      4  >>
d John Bigboote     34  lyric request: HARD TIMES
e Jimmy Gretzky      ?  Jimmy Driftwood
f Jimmy Gretzky      ?  Guitar Strings
  -- 13:16 -- SELECT -- help:? ----All----
```

The format of the listing is pretty simple. There is a title line at the top, telling you what newsgroup you are currently looking at. The rightmost part of the line, beginning **Articles:**, tells you there are six articles you have not seen in this group. The **6/1** says there are six articles you have not seen in all the groups you are subscribed to; there is only one group with unread articles. (Of course, so far you have subscribed to only one group.) At the bottom of the screen, you see a status line. This line tells you the current time, it says that you are now in selection mode, it tells you how to get help (by typing ?), and it states that you are currently looking at the headings for all the unread articles in the newsgroup.

The middle of the listing shows entries for the selectable articles, or news items. Each line has the following format:

```
ID author      size subject
```

The items in each line mean:

*ID*       A letter used to select (or unselect) a particular article for reading. For example, to select the sixth item on the screen, type **f**. If you change your mind, another **f** unselects it. On many terminals, **nn** uses reverse video or more intense lettering to highlight the items that have been selected.

*author*   The name of the person who posted the article. Most news senders include their login name as the name in this field. Some newsreaders allow you to post news with a nom de plume (e.g., Mr. Chicago above). These pseudonyms are frequently used in discussions where anonymity promotes a more complete expression of opinion (as in *alt.sex*).

*size*     The number of lines of text in the article. Some newsreaders fail to provide this information when posting, so you will sometimes see a ? in the size field.

*subject*  The subject of the article, as typed by the submitter. Notice that some subject entries have text, and some only have one or more > characters in that field. The lines that have textual subjects are the original postings for their thread. Lines that have a > are reactions or follow-on postings to the original. Multiple >'s flag these as follow-ons to the follow-ons. In the preceding example, item **b** is a follow-on to the original "World Cafe" posting. Item **c** is a comment on what John Storm said in item **b**.

Pressing the SPACEBAR takes you to the next step in the process. If the status line looks like this:

```
-- 09:37 -- SELECT -- help:? ----Top 6%----
```

it is telling you that there are more articles to be scanned in selection mode; so far, you have only seen 6 percent of the selectable articles in this group. In this case, pressing the SPACEBAR gets you the next menu (the next "page") of unread articles. If you have seen all of the selection menus, pressing the SPACEBAR displays the first article that you have selected. If you have not selected anything, pressing the SPACEBAR moves you to the next newsgroup to which you are subscribed. If you have not subscribed to any more newsgroups, pressing the SPACEBAR exits **nn**. Of course, a ? displays a help menu, and there are many more options.

Often, there will be more than a screenful of news articles to scan—particularly when you have just subscribed to a new newsgroup. To move between screens of articles, use > to move forward a page and < to move backward.

Now, let's assume that you selected Jimmy Gretzky's second posting on Guitar Strings by typing the letter **f**. When you reached the last menu, you press the SPACEBAR. **nn** displays the first item you have selected, one page at a time. Here's Jimmy Gretzky's posting:

```
Jimmy Gretzky: Guitar Strings     Thu, 21 Nov 1991 16:24
I've been following this newsgroup for a long time, to
my knowledge there's never been a discussion of guitar
strings. I have two primary questions:
 1. What's the brand that the good people buy?
 2. How long before a gig should you change
    your strings?
Thanks for any opinions.
-- Jimmy Gretzky    "The old axe man"

-- 13:30 --rec.music.folk-- LAST --help:?--Bot--
```

Now you are in the *reading* mode. Once again, there are a number of different options available; if you type a question mark (?) to get help, you will see the list of options in this mode. You can read the articles you have selected by pressing the SPACEBAR until you have waded through them all. In reading mode, pressing the SPACEBAR takes you to the next page of the article you are reading, or to the next article that you have selected. If you want to move to the previous page of the current article, press BACKSPACE.

If you select multiple items to read, **nn** presents them to you in the order in which they were displayed in the menu, oldest to youngest for each thread. So, if you select an original posting with some follow-up messages, you will see the original first, then the follow-ups. If you get bored with a long item and want to skip to the next one, use the **n** command. After selecting a large number of articles in a thread, you may decide that the whole thread is going nowhere and want to skip the remainder of it. To do so, use the reading mode's **k** command. It skips to the first article you have selected in a different thread.

When you have finished reading all the articles, pressing the SPACEBAR takes you back to selection mode for your next subscribed newsgroup (if there are more groups waiting to be read). If you have finished all the groups, **nn** terminates normally. (Later, we will discuss a few other options.) If you come back later and start **nn** again, you will work through a similar dialog—except that **nn** will display only news items that have arrived since your last newsreading session. This time, you might see a subject line with both a >

and a subject heading. These are follow-on items for a thread whose original message is not displayed because you saw it in a previous session.

When you are in selection mode, you do not have to wade through an entire newsgroup menu before you start to read. The commands **X** and **Z** take you to reading mode immediately and display the first article that you selected. The only difference between the commands is that **X** says you are done selecting; when you are finished reading, you will move on to the next group. **Z** returns to the selection menu for the same group after you have read the articles.

In either reading or selection mode, if you need to quit reading before you have gone through all the groups, type the command **Q**. This command exits **nn** normally, updating the list of news items that have been displayed. When you next start **nn** after issuing a **Q**, you are given the options of starting at the beginning of your group list or continuing where you left off. You do this in response to a question like:

```
Enter clari.biz.market.ny (1 unread)?
```

In this example, *clari.biz.market.ny* is the name of the group you were reading when you quit. Answer **y** to the question, and you are placed back in this group. Answer **n**, and you start at the beginning of the groups you normally read.

## ▦ *The WWW Interface to USENET*

To the uninitiated, **nn** has a learning curve. Commands are not intrinsically obvious, and having help close by is very important. Just as **nn** is easier for experienced UNIX users to learn, WWW browser access to USENET makes it much easier for Web surfers to browse USENET.

### *Netscape Example*

It is likely that many new Internet users have been drawn there by the user-friendly WWW's graphical browsers such as Netscape Navigator. It is also not unreasonable to assume that we may be well into a migration away from the old command-line interface to USENET and toward GUI options like the WWW. We will briefly show how simple it is to use a GUI WWW browser (in this case, it is Netscape for Windows 3.1) to select and reply to an article from the newsgroup *news.newusers.questions*.

The only difficult part may have already been taken care of for you: setting up Netscape Navigator 1.1 to know where the news server is. For the record, this is done by opening up the **Options** menu, selecting **Preferences**, selecting **Mail and News**, and entering the

IP address or domain name of your news server in the **News (NNTP)** box. To access your server, enter **news:*** in the Location box or via the **Open** toolbar button, if visible. As usual, the first time you read news, Netscape has no record of the groups to which you would like to be subscribed. The opening menu, therefore, lists the top hierarchical name for the USENET groups (see Figure 8-6).

Typing **news:*** in the Location box of the Netscape browser asks the server to deliver the newsgroups. Netscape begins by showing you only the largest hierarchies for the newsgroups, in this case *alt, bionet, bit,* etc. Using the mouse to point to a header will bring up that particular hierarchy of newsgroups. Scrolling down and clicking on the *news.* * newsgroups will take you to another level (see Figure 8-7).

Next we find the group called *news.software.readers,* point to it, and click. We are now going to an individual newsgroup, and individual articles may be seen. Note that the browser includes buttons that make it clear what to do if you would like to join in the discussion (Figure 8-8).

This browser shows a selected number of the most recent articles, giving the user the option of going back to earlier articles. The number of articles available is quite finite; you cannot go back to articles that were posted 30 days ago, let alone a year or more.

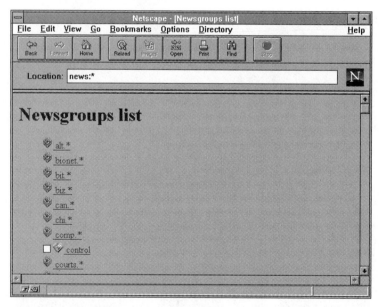

*Figure 8-6    USENET groups via Netscape*

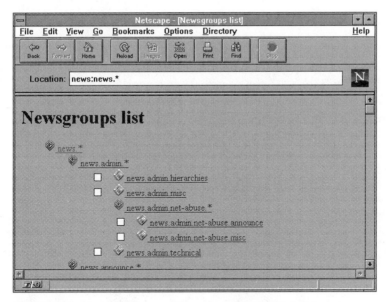

*Figure 8-7*    *Groups in the news hierarchy in USENET via Netscape*

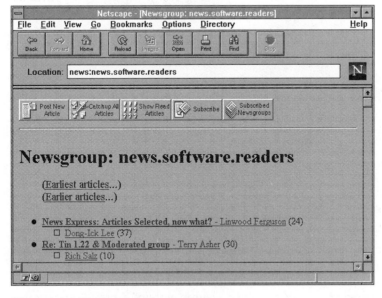

*Figure 8-8*    *The list of articles via Netscape*

## *Steering a Newsreader*

The previous section took you through a typical reading session and showed you some of the turns you might take in the process. Now that you have been introduced to newsreading, let's talk about navigating. As you come back to news time and time again, your biggest problem will be the amount of information that is there for the taking. There is so much information that it is difficult to know where to step without getting caught in the tar pits. How can you move back and forth to read the material that interests you, ignoring material that looks interesting but really is not?

When you are in **nn**'s selection mode, you can:

- Go forward and back between groups
- Go forward and back within the selection menus of a single group
- Go to reading mode
- Quit

When trying to move around in **nn**, or in any newsreader, it is important to think about what mode and group are you in and where you want to go next. Groups are presented in the same order each time you enter **nn**. You will get a feel for when a group will be presented in the normal course of events. If you want to leave the current group and skip forward to the next, type **N**. Type **P** to return to a group that you have previously read or skipped over.

If you want to stay in the same group, you can page back and forth in selection menus with < and >. Once you have selected a few things, you need not page all the way through the menu before reading. We have already mentioned the **Z** and **X** commands that allow you to jump to reading mode directly. Use **Z** if you want to return to the same group after reading what you have already selected. **X** allows you to read, but will finish the group normally and after reading move on to the next group.

Similar options are available in reading mode as well. You can move back and forth between articles with the **n** and **p** commands. You can page forward and back within an article with the SPACEBAR and BACKSPACE. And, even if you have said you never want to return to selection mode for this group again (with an **X**), you can get back there with an equal sign (=).

If you want to jump immediately to a particular group (perhaps a group you are not subscribed to), use the **G** (go to) command. After you type **G**, you will see the prompt:

```
Group or Folder (+./~ %-sneN) ▌
```

Forget about the complicated sequence of letters. Type the name of a newsgroup, followed by ENTER. Alternately, type the name of a file of news articles that you have saved. (The next section describes how to save articles.) In our case, we will jump to the group *rec.music.folk.* Next, we are asked how many articles we want:

```
Number of Articles (uasne)  (a) ▌
```

**u** means all unread articles, and **a** means all articles, whether or not you have read them. You can also type a number, saying how many articles you want to select from; **nn** will pick the most recent. If you just press ENTER without doing anything, you will get the default (in this case, all articles—though it may be different on your system). After you press ENTER, **nn** puts you into the article-selection menu to pick the articles you want to read.

All the commands described here (and more) are listed following our discussion of **nn**.

## Steering Netscape

Netscape allows you to read individual articles by simply pointing and clicking on them. Threads are visually obvious, as follow-up postings are brought to the proximity of the original posting, placed below it, and indented. This process is repeated for replies to the replies, as shown in Figure 8-9. Unlike the older newsreaders, Netscape is taking the postings out of chronological order by grouping them according to subject. This makes following threads quite simple.

## Setting Up nn

Two files govern **nn**'s action when dealing with groups: *.nn/init* and *.newsrc. .nn/init* is used to set configuration variables and to tell **nn** what groups you want to read (and what groups you want to ignore). Use this file to specify which groups you never want to read. The other file, *.newsrc,* keeps track of what groups you are subscribed to and what articles in each group you have read.* Use it to unsubscribe to particular groups that have not been excluded in the *init* file. Let's just start doing it step by step, explaining what is happening along the way.

**1.** If your *home* directory does not contain a subdirectory named *.nn* (you can check with **ls -a .nn**) create one with **mkdir .nn** while you are in your *home* directory (you can get there with a **cd** command with no arguments).

---

*On UNIX systems, just about all newsreaders use the file *.newsrc* to maintain your newsreading history.

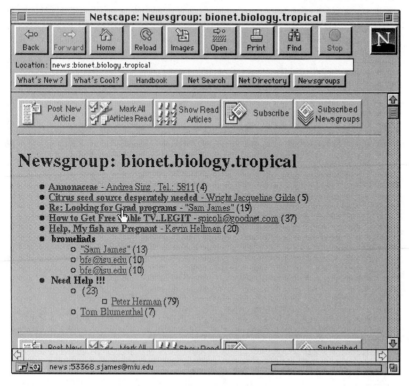

*Figure 8-9    Follow-up USENET articles via Netscape*

**2.** Using the editor of your choice, create a file in the *.nn* directory named *init* (using the **vi** editor, give the command **vi .nn/init**). The contents of the file should look like:

```
sequence
!bionet
!gnu
```

*(List as many groups as required)*

The first line must be the word "sequence." Subsequent lines specify the groups that you never want to subscribe to. In this case, you are excluding any groups starting with *bionet* or *gnu*. You can add any amount of detail to get the job done. For example, if you do not care about any groups about TV that might pop up, you could add the lines:

```
!alt.tv
!rec.arts.tv
```

These would exclude only those portions of the *alt* and *rec* groupings. When you have listed all the groups you do not care about, exit the editor.*

**3.** Issue the **nn** command. When **nn** starts, immediately type **Q**. This quits **nn**, but not before it creates the file *.newsrc*. This file lists all the groups offered by the server you are using.

Edit *.newsrc*. (If you are using **vi**, use the command **vi .newsrc**.) Your display should begin something like:

```
alt.activism:
alt.aquaria:
alt.atheism:
alt.bbs:
alt.callahans:
alt.co-ops:
alt.cobol:
alt.config:
alt.conspiracy:
alt.cosuard:
```

**4.** Issue a "global replace" command that turns all colons (:) into exclamation points (!). This unsubscribes you to everything by changing all colons to exclamation points (a : after the newsgroup name flags the group as subscribed, an ! as unsubscribed). If you are using **vi**, give a **:%s/:/!/** command.

**5.** Find the groups you want to participate in, either by using a search command if you know the group's name (*/name* for **vi** users), or by scrolling through the file (use **CTRL-f** to move down one screen at a time in **vi**). When you find a group you want to subscribe to, change the exclamation point (!) following the name back to a colon (:). By changing the ! to a :, you are flagging that group as subscribed. Repeat as necessary. For **vi** users, position the cursor over the ! and type **r:**.

**6.** Save the file and exit the editing session (in **vi**, the command **ZZ** does both).

You are now subscribed to those groups whose names are followed by a colon and that are not listed in the *.nn /init* file as "do not care" groups.

These instructions are a bit more extensive than is absolutely necessary to do a minimal job. You can easily do steps 1 and 2, cutting the number of groups to around 200; then

---

*How do you know what groups you are not interested in? This is a chicken-and-egg problem; you do not have a newsreader running so that you can use it to tell you what is available. You can make some very broad cuts on the basis of the top-level summaries we have already given, but you might want better control. One way to find out for sure is to ask your news server. Find out the name of the news server your system uses and **telnet** to its nntp port with the command: **telnet your.servers.name nntp**. This command connects you to the server. You should then type the command **list newsgroups**, which will do just that. After you see all the groups fly by, exit by typing **quit**.

use **nn** to unsubscribe to the rest, one at a time. Or you can do steps 3 through 7 to set up your current subscriptions correctly; in this case, you will automatically be subscribed to any new groups that are created, and you will have to get rid of them by hand. Steps 1 and 2 prevent you from subscribing automatically to newly created groups in any of the categories listed in *.nn /init*. In the long run, the complete seven-step procedure does just what you want.

### Selecting Newsgroups with Netscape

As noted above in Figure 8.7, Netscape will display newsgroups as you work your way down from the most broad to the more specific newsgroup names. Once you reach actual newsgroup names (but before selecting an individual newsgroup), you see that Netscape provides check boxes for toggling subscriptions on and off. By selecting a check mark for the box, you are recording a subscription for that newsgroup. Each time you access news via Netscape, pointing and clicking on the Subscribed Newsgroups button (see Figure 8-8) will bring up only those newsgroups to your screen. Similar processing to what we discussed in **nn** is happening in the background when you do this, but there is no need to learn to get around in a UNIX environment.

## ▧ *Reading News*

Now we are through with preliminaries: selecting the newsgroups that you are interested in. Once you are through with this somewhat messy process, you can start the fun part: reading news and creating your own news items.

### Saving News Articles

After reading a news article, you will often want to print it, mail it to someone, or just save it for later. You can save a file while you are in reading mode by entering the **s** command, which appends the current item to the end of a file. In response to an **s**, **nn** suggests a filename that it forms by taking the full name of the newsgroup you are reading, turning the dots into slashes, and interpreting the whole mess as a filename within your *News* directory. This sounds confusing, but in practice it is not bad. If you want to save an article while reading *rec.music.folk*, **nn** generates the path *~/News/rec/ music/folk*—or, equivalently, *+/rec/music/folk*. (~ is a UNIX abbreviation for your *home* directory; + is the newsreader's abbreviation for *~/News*.) This is a great filename for archiving, because it keeps saved entries from the various newsgroups separate in an orderly set of files.

```
Save on (+~|) +rec/music/folk ▮
```

To accept this filename and store the article, press ENTER. If there is already an article in *News/rec/music/folk*, **nn** adds the new article after whatever is already there; you will not lose any old articles. If you would rather use a different name for the file, press BACKSPACE until you erase the portion of the string you want to replace. Because the + represents your *News* directory, we will keep it. But we want a simpler filename: just *guitar*. So we delete *rec/music/folk* and then type our new name after the +:

```
Save on (+~|) +guitar
```

When you are satisfied with the name, press ENTER. In this case, the news item is appended to the file *guitar* in your *News* directory. You can use **nn** to read the articles you have saved by using the **G** (go to) command. When you type **G**, you will see the prompt:

```
Group or Folder (+./~ %=sneN) ▉
```

When you type +, **nn** realizes you want a folder; you will see this:

```
Folder +▉
```

Then type **guitar**, followed by ENTER, and you are done.

It is possible for an administrator to set up **nn** to use different default file-naming schemes. The first time you save an article with **nn**, watch carefully to make sure the filename it picks is what you expect. If it is not, you can change the filename to something else—but it is better to figure out the administrator's naming conventions. Fighting systemwide defaults is always a pain.

### Subscribing and unsubscribing

At the beginning of this chapter, we took you through a relatively laborious procedure for limiting the number of newsgroups that you read. We said that you subscribed to a limited number of groups (out of the many that are available). Just as with a magazine, you can change your subscription status at any time: You can subscribe to new groups and unsubscribe to groups you are currently receiving. Subscribing and unsubscribing in **nn** are done with the **U** command while viewing the group's selection menu. If you are subscribed to the group *alt.callahans,* issuing a **U** will unsubscribe you with the following dialog:

```
Unsubscribe to alt.callahans ?
```

If you answer **y**, **nn** unsubscribes you.

Subscribing presents an obvious problem: If you have not yet subscribed, how do you view the selection menu in the first place? The easiest way to do this is to start a separate **nn** session with some command-line options.*

You can tell **nn** to read a group, even though you are not subscribed to it, by starting it with the command-line option X. Start **nn** with the command:

```
% nn -X group-list
```

If you do this, you will read the specified groups in the normal fashion. For example, to subscribe to the group *alt.callahans,* type the command:

```
% nn -X alt.callahans
```

You will see the selection menu for this group's unread articles. If you now issue the U command, the response will be:

```
Already unsubscribed. Resubscribe to alt.callahans ?
```

Answering with a **y** resubscribes you. If you list groups on the command line, **nn** reads only those groups in this session; you will not see the other groups that you have subscribed to. So you see only *alt.callahans* this time, but the next time you enter normally with **nn**, the newly subscribed group appears in its normal place. **-X** is very useful if you want to browse a group periodically without subscribing to it.

### Killing and auto-selecting items

*Killing* means automatically ignoring some postings within a group, and you will see references to it from time to time in USENET postings. You specify certain criteria; if an article meets the criteria, the newsreader ignores it and you never see it. *Auto-selection* is the opposite of killing. If an article meets the criteria you set, the newsreader automatically selects the article for you when it presents the selection menu. Killing is far more frequently used. This is because judicious use of kill criteria saves you time. There are fewer items to scan, and it takes less time to transmit menus. In this section, we will concentrate on killing. The process for auto-selection is almost identical.

In **nn**, setting kill criteria is done in either mode. You give the newsreader a word or a phrase to search for,† and tell the newsreader whether you want to kill based on the message's contents (as given in the **Subject:** field), or the author. **nn** saves this search

---

*There are other ways. You can also move to unsubscribed groups using the **G** command. This is not an **nn** manual, and using G has more side effects.

†In practice, this can be any string; indeed, it can be a full UNIX "regular expression." If you are not a heavy-duty UNIX user and do not want to learn about regular expressions, just search for words or phrases.

string in one of your startup files. In the future, whenever **nn** creates its lists of interesting articles, it will check each article to see whether or not it matches one of the kill criteria. If it does, the newsreader will ignore the article. (Likewise, if you have specified auto-select criteria, **nn** will automatically select those articles for you.) Let's say you are reading *rec.humor*, and you see this selection menu:

```
Newsgroup: rec.humor              Articles: 671 of 671/1
a willie martin      9  >>>racial
b aaly055            ?  >>>>
c Peter Johnson     39  >
d M K T             30  >>>
e M K T             13  >>>
f Earl Butz         18  >>>
  ...
-- 10:07 -- SELECT -- help:? ----11%----
```

You decide you do not like racial jokes, and you want to suppress their display. Type the command **K**, which is used for both killing and auto-selecting. **nn** returns with:

```
AUTO (k)ill or (s)elect (CR => Kill subject 30 days) ▮
```

At this point, you have three choices. Type **k** to enter a slightly longer dialog about killing the topic; type **s** to enter a similar dialog about auto-selecting the topic; and press ENTER for a "shorthand kill." The shorthand kill uses the subject of a displayed item and remains in effect for 30 days. If you enter a carriage return, **nn** asks:

```
AUTO (k)ill or (s)elect (CR => Kill subject 30 days)
from article: a
```

to which you respond with an **a**, saying "do not let me see any articles with the same subject as article a" for the next 30 days. In this case, you decide the default criteria are not strong enough. If someone posts a new joke with the subject "Racial Joke," you will still see it, because it does not match your kill criterion exactly. You really want to suppress permanently any item with the word "racial" in its subject. To do this, start out with the command **K**, but do not press ENTER; instead, type **k**, and the dialog continues:

```
AUTO (k)ill or (s)elect (CR => Kill subject 30 days) k
AUTO KILL on (s)ubject or (n)ame (s)  s
KILL Subject: (/) racial
KILL in (g)roup 'rec.humor' or in (a)ll groups (g) g
Lifetime of entry in days (p)ermanent  (30) p
CONFIRM KILL Subject perm: racial  y
```

The dialog is fairly self-explanatory, but a few points should be explained. Note that **nn** gives you the option of killing the subject either in this group only or in all groups. Because you may want to read about racial bias in *soc.politics,* you choose to restrict the suppression to the group *rec.humor.*

The newsreader also lets you set the lifetime of the kill: It can be permanent or for a fixed period (by default, 30 days).

Why would anyone would want a non-permanent kill? You may be generally interested in the subject, but you are not interested in the current discussion. For example, you wish to keep up with the WWW and subscribe to *comp.infosystems.www.* An article about "Credit Card Security" appears, but it is not of interest to you. You do not want to ignore articles on WWW security forever; you just want to wait for the current thread to die. Although it is anybody's guess how long a particular discussion will last, a 30-day kill may be appropriate.

Aside from the racial example, there is another situation in which a permanent kill may be preferable to a temporary kill. Some groups have an internal structure. Although the group is not divided into subgroups, the readers of the group have agreed to put certain codes into their subject lines to allow their messages to be categorized easily. For example, the *rec.arts.tv.soaps* group uses codes to indicate which soap opera is being discussed. On the selection menu, it looks like this:

```
Newsgroup: rec.arts.tv.soaps        Articles: 630 of 630/1
a Sherri Lewis      42  >OLTL: Blair-ramblings
b John R. Anderson   ?  >>>>OLTL: Gabrielle's son
c M. T. Czonka      24  >>>
d S. A. Winslow    143  >>>DOOL: Friday 10th of January
e Lisa J. Huff      38  AMC: Terrence Was: The Wedding
f S. A. Winslow     18  >>>DOOL: One Stormy Night Update
g Willie Martin     50  >GH--Faison,etc.
h Willie Martin    126  >GH: More Ramblings
i Liz Wolf           ?  >DOOL : please clear some things up
j Liz Wolf           ?  >>
k Jason Castillo    15  >>
l Liz Wolf           ?  >OLD KL: Question
-- 13:33 -- SELECT -- help:? ----8%----
```

In this example, if the only soap you are interested in discussing is "Days of Our Lives," you could auto-kill all articles that do *not* contain the string "DOOL" in their subject. (If a newsgroup has established conventions like this, someone regularly posts a key showing which flag strings to use.)

## Catching Up

While subscribed to 20 or 30 groups, you go on vacation. You come back to find thousands of articles in those groups waiting for you to scan. When confronted with this daunting task, you may decide that you really *do* need to read all the messages in some of those groups; but for most of them, you would just as soon flush all of the old articles. Most newsreaders provide you with a facility to do this; it is generally called *catching up*. **nn** provides this through the command-line option -a0. To begin catching up, give the command:

```
% nn -a0
```

**nn** then responds:

```
Release 6.4.16,  Kim F. Storm, 1991
Catch-up on 2031 unread articles ?
(auto)matically (i)nteractive  i
  y - mark all articles as read in current group
  n - do not update group
  r - read the group now
  U - unsubscribe to current group
  ? - this message
  q - quit

Update bit.listserv.cdromlan (2)? (ynrU?q)  y
Update comp.dcom.lans (3)? (ynrU?q)  U
Update rec.arts.disney (12)? (ynrU?q)  n
Update rec.music.folk (1)? (ynrU?q)  n
  ...
```

The first question asks whether you want to catch up automatically or interactively. An *automatic* catchup tells **nn** that you want to mark all of the unseen articles, in all groups, as read, so you will not be bothered with them again. It does not do anything to change your subscription status; if you were subscribed to the group before, you are still subscribed, and you will see any future articles that arrive. To do an automatic catchup, type **auto**.

Your other alternative is an *interactive* catchup, for which you type **i**. **nn** starts by telling you the possible responses and then proceeds through the groups you are subscribed to, one at a time. In this case, you choose to update *bit.listserv.cdromlan* (**y**), meaning that it marks all the messages in that group as read, but you remain subscribed to the group. You decided to unsubscribe to the group *comp.dcom.lans* (**U**), so you will never see any messages from it again. You decided not to update the last two groups, meaning that you still want to read the articles that arrived during your vacation (**n**).

The next time we invoke **nn**, you will not see *comp.dcom.lans* at all; you unsubscribed to the group, so **nn** will skip it. You will see the newsgroup *bit.listserv.cdromlan*, but only the new articles that have appeared since the catchup. You will also see *rec.arts.disney* and *rec.music.folk* in full, including the articles that arrived while you were away.

# ■ *Posting Articles*

After reading news for a while, you will be ready to take part in a discussion. There are two basic ways of taking part: adding to an existing discussion thread or starting a new discussion.

## *Adding to an Existing Discussion*

Let's start by adding a follow-up item to an existing discussion thread. This is a bit easier, because all the work of describing the thread (i.e., building the header) is done for you. It is like replying to an electronic mail message. Remember Jimmy Gretzky's question:

```
Jimmy Gretzky: Guitar Strings     Thu, 21 Nov 1991 16:24
I've been following this newsgroup for a long time, to
my knowledge there's never been a discussion of guitar
strings. I have two primary questions:
1. What's the brand that the good people buy?
2. How long before a gig should you change
   your strings?
Thanks for any opinions.
--
Jimmy Gretzky   "The old axe man"
```

You, being a folk guitarist from way back, see this request for comments on guitar strings and wish to respond. So, while viewing this article, you enter **f**, meaning "make a follow-on posting." Note that the **f** has a different meaning now that you are in reading mode. **nn** asks you:

```
Include original article?  n
```

To which you responded no, because nothing would be gained by including the questions. After you are done composing, you have something like this:

```
Newsgroups: rec.music.folk
Subject: Re: Guitar Strings
References: <1991Nov21.162445.17611@yoyodyne.com>

I've been playing acoustic guitar for a long time and
I've found one brand of strings that I think is the
best. I use GHS Bright Bronze, which are the
mellowest-sounding I've ever found.
```

Save the file and exit your editing session normally. At this point, **nn** asks you what you want to do next with the line:

```
a)bort c)c e)dit h)old m)ail r)eedit s)end v)iew w)rite
Action: (post article)
```

which gives you the option of revising your posting (**e**), thinking twice about of posting (**a**), or posting what you just wrote (with ENTER or **s**). You hit ENTER, and your posting is on its way to the world. It will take a while for it to get there, so be patient. (There are other options, obviously, but you can go pretty far without ever using them.)

Some newsgroups are *moderated;* that is, all items in the group are reviewed by a moderator (a *gatekeeper*), who decides which postings are of genuine interest to the rest of the group. A moderated group is thus more like a magazine or journal than a free-for-all discussion. As you might expect, moderated groups have more "quality control," albeit at the cost of spontaneity. Posting to a moderated group is no different than posting to any other group. The news servers know which groups are moderated and who moderates them; your news item will be forwarded to the appropriate moderator automatically.

## Starting a New Discussion

The only difference between a follow-on posting and creating a new thread is that for a new thread, you must supply the information to fill out the header. To begin a new discussion, use the command:

```
:post
```

at any time during an **nn** session. **nn** will ask you what newsgroup you want to post to:

```
POST to group rec.music.folk
```

In this case, you typed the name of the folk music group, *rec.music.folk.* You do not have to be looking at the group, or even subscribed to it. After you type the group's name, **nn** asks you for the subject, keywords, and a summary of the article. These are the items that go in the header to allow searches. Finally, you need to tell the newsreader how far you want your posting disseminated. This exchange looks like this:

```
Subject:  Is Mike Seeger Still Touring?
Keywords:  traditional
Summary:  Wondering if Mike Seeger is still alive
Distribution: (default 'world')
```

The first three lines (Subject, Keywords, and Summary) will be passed from news servers to the newsreaders, allowing them to build selection menus and kill or auto-select your article. Therefore, make it good. It is all the reader has to judge whether your posting is interesting or not. (The actual text of an article is sent from a news server to a newsreader only when someone selects the article for reading. Readers pick which articles they want to read on the basis of the subject, so misleading subject lines can be really annoying.)

The distribution line gives the news system some idea about how far you would like the posting passed. You should treat this as a statement of the minimum coverage required

*Table 8-1    Common Distribution Keywords*

| Keyword | Distribution area |
| --- | --- |
| world | Worldwide distribution (default) |
| att | AT&T |
| can | Canada |
| eunet | European sites |
| na | North America |
| usa | United States |
| IL, NY, FL . . . | The specified state |

for the article. There is no guarantee that it will not be propagated farther than you think. Once you pick a distribution that goes beyond your local server, you are depending on remote servers' configurations to be correct. This is probably too optimistic.

There is no way to find out exactly what distribution lists are available for a server. There is a set of standard distributions that is available on most servers, but they describe only wide areas. They are shown in Table 8-1.

The problem comes with smaller, local distributions whose names are made up by the local server's administrator. So only your administrator can tell you for sure.

This is not quite as hopeless as it sounds. Most of the time, the default for the group is what you want. This is OK, even if it sounds too large. Newsgroup propagation is voluntarily arranged between sites, and most of the time a group of local interest is not sent too far even if you specify "world" as the distribution. The person who runs a neighboring server for the Megabucks Corporation certainly does not want his disk filled up with discussions about the problems with dorm rooms on a remote campus. That server will be set up to ignore the group *hoople.campuslife*.

However, you should restrict distribution if you are trying to contact local people through a worldwide group. What if you wanted to find lunch-hour running partners in your area? One way to approach the problem would be to assume that avid runners would read *rec.running* and post to this group. But *rec.running* is a worldwide group. If you posted a request for jogging partners to this group, you would probably get snide replies like "Sure, meet on the steps of Paddington Station at noon." Quite a jog. What you want to do is post to that group, but use a limited distribution: "campus," "local," "hoople," or whatever your local distribution identifiers are. Similarly, if you are offering an old car for sale, you might want to restrict distribution to your state (unless you are willing to deliver the car): for example, IL, NY, or CA.

One final word of warning about the distribution: You cannot specify a distribution that does not contain your server. For example, you cannot specify a distribution of Florida while sitting on a machine in New York. This is because news is distributed by flooding: It is "poured" into the system by your server to its neighbors, and flows outward. If you specify Florida in a message that is distributed from New York, about the time it gets to New Jersey, machines start saying, "Why did you give this to me?" and throw it away.

After you have specified the distribution, you have completed the header. You then begin an editing session and proceed just as you did when writing a follow-on posting. Write your message, exit your editor, and tell **nn** whether you want to abort, send, or revise your message.

## *Replying via E-mail*

You sometimes want to reply to the submitter of an item privately, through electronic mail. This is useful when the comments you want to make are not of general interest, or should not be widely distributed. To make this easy, **nn** has a mail facility built into it. To invoke it, use the **r** command while reading an item. The mail interface then proceeds much like a follow-on posting. For example, if you were reading the same Jimmy Gretzky item you have been reading throughout this chapter, and you typed an **r**, you would see something like this:

```
Include original article?  n
```

You are then given an editing session (using **vi** or your favorite editor) with a mail header already built:

```
To: gretzky@ux.uiuc.edu
Orig-To: gretzky@ux.uiuc.edu
Subject: Guitar Strings
Newsgroups: rec.music.folk
References: <1991Nov21.233330.1466@ux.uiuc.edu>
Are you the same Jimmy Gretzky who was in the class
of '80 at PS12 in Sheboygan?
```

Again, when you are done, exit from the editor normally. You will return to **nn**, which will ask you:

```
a)bort e)dit h)old m)ail r)eedit s)end v)iew w)rite
Action: (send letter)
```

Of the possible responses, the most useful are to abort sending the message, send the message (pressing ENTER will do this, too), or edit the message again.

## Other Hints and Conventions

Here are some important considerations that are known to most experienced news users:

- Read before you post. Take some time getting to know both the system and the group. If you see any postings marked **FAQ** (Frequently Asked Questions), read them. These postings may be in the group itself, or they may be in the special group *news.answers*. Your question may have already been discussed ad nauseam, and you will look like a novice just asking it again.

- Format your postings nicely. Use a subject that is descriptive. People will choose to read your postings based on the subject. Busy people tend to have less time to read news than they would like, so they choose items that do not appear to be a waste of time. A subject like "Question" will probably be ignored because I would have to be an expert on everything to know I could answer it. Try "Guitar String Question." Never use "gotcha" subjects (e.g., "Subject: Sex," but in the body, "Now that I have your attention, I have a question about insects"). On the other end of the posting, signatures are fine but keep them short.

- Be polite. You asked a question of the network. Someone took their time to answer; a thank-you message back is appreciated. Disagreements are fine, but attacking someone personally for their postings is not good form (although common). This is known in the trade as *flaming*.

- Post and reply appropriately. Post to the smallest distribution that will get the job done. Read the whole thread before responding. If someone asks, "What's the answer?" and someone already said "The answer is 42," you do not add anything by repeating it. Some of this is inevitable because of the delays in news propagation, but avoid contributing to the problem intentionally. If the answer is not of general interest, reply by e-mail.

- Do not automatically include the article to which you are responding. Too many times, articles get longer and longer with each response, because people include all previous discussion. The people who are reading the group chose to read your posting based on the subject. If it is a follow-on posting, they probably have read the initial postings, too (they had the same subject). Please do not make them read it again. If you want to respond point by point, edit the discussion down so only the relevant sentences are included.

- Controversy is fine, but keep it in its place. There are groups designed for pro/con discussions, and there are groups where people of a like mind meet to commiserate. Do not post antigun sentiments on *rec.hunting;* it will not do anything but get you tons of hate e-mail. In any group, flag controversial opinions with *IMHO (In My Humble Opinion),* such as "IMHO, Mossberg makes the best firearms."

■ Be patient; news takes a while to be distributed. When you post something, it goes into a queue on your server; it then needs to be indexed and passed on to the rest of the world. All of this is done by background tasks on the server. So your posting will not appear on your system immediately, and may take a day to get to the rest of the world. Also, do not expect responses immediately, even by e-mail. Some people feel guilty reading *rec.arts.disney* on company time. Therefore, a lot of people read recreational groups only on the weekend.

■ The biggest problem with reading news is that there is so much, and much of it is so interesting. It is easy to be enamored with it. Be selective about which groups you read. It could mean your job, your family, or your college career.

## Summary of nn Commands and Features

The following sections are of interest to you only if you are not using a GUI newsreader such as Newswatcher, WinVN, Netscape, or many others. We are going to summarize the **nn** commands that we have discussed. If you are not using **nn**, these lists may not be of too much value, but take heart; they do provide a "checklist" of worthwhile features.

### Command-line Options

In most of the previous examples, we have assumed that you invoked **nn** with no options. In reality, the general format for invoking **nn** is:

```
% nn options group list
```

If you specify a group list, **nn** examines only those groups listed in this session. The groups you listed are examined only if you are subscribed to them, unless you specify the -X option. If you specify the initial part of a group name in the list, all groups in that hierarchy are examined. For example:

```
% nn -X rec.arts.
```

will show you any groups beginning with *rec.arts.* If you do not specify a group list, all groups you are subscribed to are examined. Options control various aspects of the particular invocation. Some of the more useful ones are:

-a0        Used to catch up on all groups to which you subscribe. (Explained more fully in the "Catching Up" section of this chapter.)

-i              Makes searches of the **n** or **s** command case-sensitive, which means that uppercase letters and lowercase letters are considered different. Normally, case is ignored in matching.

-m              Displays all articles meeting other criteria (specified with other command-line options such as a group list, -s, etc.) on one selection menu, rather than one menu per group. This is useful if you are searching for a particular article and do not know what group it is in. Using -**m** prevents **nn** from marking new items in this session as "seen."

-n*string*       Searches the groups specified in this invocation and selects items whose author name matches the string. (Think of "n" as an abbreviation for "name.") The string may either be a single word, like -**nkrol**, a complete name like "**ed krol**", or a search expression like -**n/**"**ed.**"* to search for all authors beginning with "ed". The search is case-insensitive, but otherwise the name has to match exactly; that is, -**n**"**ed krol**" will not match "Edward Krol".

-s*string*       Searches the groups used in this invocation and selects items whose subject matches the string. The string may either be a single word like -**sgolf**, a phrase like -**s**"**u.s. open golf scores**", or a search expression like -**s/**"**go.***"; the latter searches for articles whose subject contains a word beginning with "go".

-x              Tells **nn** to consider all articles for display, subject to other criteria (e.g., search strings), regardless of whether you have viewed the article previously. Useful when you read an article once and later want to go back and read it again. (Use of -**x** prevents **nn** from marking new items in this session as seen.)

-X              Tells **nn** to consider groups even if you are not subscribed to them. Useful when you are looking for an article in groups to which you are not subscribed.

Here's an example: You remember having seen an interesting posting by John Wadsworth. However, you don't remember the newsgroup it was in, but you do know it was in a newsgroup that you regularly subscribe to. To find it, you can give the command:

```
% nn -x -n"john wadsworth"
```

We used **-x** to search all articles in all newsgroups that we have subscribed to, including articles we have already read. To make an even wider search that includes all articles in all groups, we could have done:

```
% nn -X -n"john wadsworth"
```

Given our example, this wider search is not necessary; in fact, it is a waste of resources. We remember reading the article, so it must be in a newsgroup to which we subscribe. Therefore, **-x** is appropriate. When would you use **-X**? Let's say someone else told you about an interesting article, but she did not remember where it appeared. In this case, **-X** is appropriate. However, you should be judicious in the use of the **-x** and **-X** options. **-x** relaxes the limits on items within groups that are searched. **-X** suppresses limits on what groups are searched. If you use both parameters, the search looks at every news item on the server, which could take a long time. It is better if you can say, "well, I'm sure that article would have appeared in one of the 'talk' groups." Then you can give the command:

```
% nn -X -x -n"john wadsworth" talk.
```

## Some Selection Mode Commands

The following list shows the most important commands available to you while in selection mode. It includes all of the commands that we have covered, and a few that we have not. There are many additional commands that we will not mention; the commands we have listed below are certainly all you need to get going and may be all that you'll ever need.

**lowercase letters**

Select news items; type the ID letter that appears on the left side of the menu. If the news item is already selected, typing its ID letter unselects it.

SPACEBAR

Moves to the next logical step in the process of selecting or reading. If you're reading the selection menu, pressing the SPACEBAR moves you forward to the next menu page, if one exists. If none exists, you move to the first selected item. When you are reading an item, pressing the SPACEBAR moves you to the next page of that item. When there are no more pages, you go to the next item. When there are no more items, you move to the next newsgroup. If there are no more groups, the program terminates.

<      Moves you back one page in the menu.

>      Moves you forward one page in the menu.

| | |
|---|---|
| G | Jump to (go to) another group or a folder of saved news messages. |
| K | Starts the kill dialog to suppress listing of some items (see the section "Killing and auto-selecting items" earlier in this chapter). |
| N | Moves forward to the next group. Any items selected in the group you are leaving remain selected, in case you return to that group. |
| P | Moves backward to the previous group. Any items selected in the group you are leaving remain selected, in case you return to that group. |
| Q | Quits the **nn** session normally. This updates the list of items shown so you won't see articles a second time. |
| S | Saves the articles you have selected in a file. |
| U | Toggles the subscription status of the current newsgroup. If you are currently subscribed, **U** unsubscribes you. If you are currently not a subscriber, it subscribes you. |
| X | Moves to reading mode if anything is selected, or to the next group if not. Marks all items on the menu as having been seen, so you won't see them again. After reading the articles, you won't return to the selection menu. |
| Z | Same as X, except that after reading, you *will* return to this group's selection menu. |

## Some Reading Mode Commands

Here are the most useful commands for reading mode. Again, we have listed all of the commands covered in the text, plus a few more; and again, there are many more commands available, but you may never need them.

| | |
|---|---|
| SPACEBAR | Moves down one page in the article or, if on the last page of an article, to the next article or menu. Note that this is different from the command used to page forward in selection mode. |
| BACKSPACE | Moves up one page in the article. Note that this is different from the command used to page backward in selection mode. |
| = | Switches back from reading mode to selection mode for the current group. |
| C | Cancels this article. It is a way you can retract an article you posted. People will probably see it before you retract it, so you may still catch some grief about it. This can be used only on items you submitted. |

f               Starts a follow-on posting to the current article (see the section, "Adding to an Existing Discussion" earlier in this chapter).

k               Kills the remainder of the current thread. If you select an article and five follow-on articles, then decide you do not care to read them, a **k** skips those articles and any others in the menu for that session.

K               Enters the kill dialog to automatically ignore or select articles (see the section "Killing and auto-selecting items"). Remember the difference between **k** and **K**. Uppercase **K** lets you permanently kill (or auto-select) a group of articles; **k** is used to ignore follow-on articles in the current session that you do not want to bother reading.

n               Stops reading the current article and moves to reading the next selected article.

p               Stops reading the current article and moves to the previously selected article.

r               Replies to the selected item via e-mail (see "Replying via E-mail" earlier in this chapter).

s               Saves the selected item in a file (see "Saving News Articles" earlier in this chapter).

U               Toggles the subscription status of the current newsgroup. If you are currently subscribed, **U** unsubscribes you. If you are not currently a subscriber, it subscribes you (see "Controlling What You Read" in this chapter).

Q               Quits the **nn** session normally. This updates the list of items shown so you will not see the same articles a second time.

## ▦ *A Philosophically Different Newsreader: tin*

There are dozens of newsreaders out there, each doing more-or-less the same job. One reason why so many newsreaders exist is that no one reader suits everyone's habits. For example, you have seen that **nn** maintains a subscription list of groups in which you are really interested. It wants you to scan each subscribed group in a set order. You may quit before you have looked at each group, but when you return you have two options: start at the beginning or start where you left off. What if you have two distinct sets of newsgroups, those to which you must be really responsive (perhaps for work), and those that you read when you have the time (perhaps for recreation)? There are a number of ways you could do this with **nn**, but it would be like pulling teeth. It is not the way the program was meant to be used, so whatever you do, you will be fighting against it.

**tin** is another popular newsreader. It does all the things **nn** does, but has a different philosophy about how to present newsgroups. We are going to introduce you to **tin**, without providing as much detail as we did for **nn**. Because you now know how to use one newsreader, you know what they all can do. If you prefer **tin**'s presentation style, our discussion will get you started. **tin** has a good built-in help facility; to get at it, type **h** at any time.

**nn** divides reading news into two parts: selection and reading. **tin** groups the process into three parts: group selection, thread selection, and reading. When you enter **tin**, you first see a list of all the groups to which you are subscribed:

```
            Group Selection (2585)              h=help

  1   596  alt.1d                     ?
  2   199  alt.3d                     Discussions of 3 dimensi
  3   162  alt.abortion.inequity      Paternal obligations of
  4        alt.abuse-recovery
  5  1384  alt.activism               Activities for activists
  6   291  alt.activism.d             A place to discuss issue
  7   183  alt.adoption               Adopting people.
  8    12  alt.aeffle.und.pferdle     German TV cartoon charac
  9     7  alt.alien.vampire.flonk.flonk.flonk
 10   588  alt.alien.visitors         Space Aliens on Earth!
 11    47  alt.amateur-comp           Discussion and input for
 12        alt.anarchism
 13   490  alt.angst                  Anxiety in the modern wo
 14        alt.angst.xibo.sex         Tightening the screws of
 15    36  alt.appalachian            Appalachian region aware
 16   317  alt.aquaria                The aquarium & related a

<n>=set current to n, TAB=next unread, /=search pattern, c)atchup,
g)oto, j=line down, k=line up, h)elp, m)ove, q)uit, r=toggle all/unread,
s)ubscribe, S)ub pattern, u)nsubscribe, U)nsub pattern, y)ank in/out
```

This is the group selection menu, asking which groups you want to read. Before doing anything else, notice that **tin** lists the most useful commands you can give from this screen at the bottom. As with **nn**, because we just started reading news, we are subscribed to 2,585 groups. This is too many for comfort. But, unlike other readers, **tin** gives you an easy way to prune your subscriptions to a reasonable number. You can unsubscribe to large sets of groups at one time with the **U** (unsubscribe pattern) command. This command allows you to specify a search string including wildcards; it unsubscribes you to any groups that match the string. For example, after you enter **U**, **tin** responds:

```
Enter regex unsubscribe pattern>
```

You then type the wildcard expression **alt\.\***, followed by ENTER to unsubscribe to all the *alt* newsgroups; i.e., all groups containing the string *alt.* in their name.* This single command whittles your subscription list down by a bit more than 700 groups. By repeating the process, you can get the list down to a manageable size quite easily.†

There is one trick that's worth knowing. Let's say that you have unsubscribed all the *alt* groups, but later decide you want to read *alt.aquaria*. It is hard to subscribe to a group (or even to visit it briefly) if it is not on the group selection menu—so how do you get it there? The easiest way is to type **y**, which "yanks" all groups that you have access to onto your menu, whether you have subscribed to them or not. You will see a few thousand groups reappear. Subscribe to the group or groups you want, using the **S** command: type **S**, followed by the group's name *(alt.aquaria)*. You can select some of these unsubscribed groups and read a few articles, just to make sure the group is something you really want. When you have finished updating your subscriptions, type **y** again. The second time you type **y**, all the unsubscribed groups will disappear. Now that you have unsubscribed to groups you never want to see, you can select the newsgroups you want to read in this **tin** session.

The group selection menu has several useful features. For each group, an index number on the left allows you to see that group's article list immediately by entering the index number, followed by ENTER. Next to the index is the number of unread articles in that group. The numbers here are quite large, because we have not read news before. Most groups get only a few postings a day. The group name is shown next. On the right is a short, sometimes meaningful, description of the group.

Now let's read some articles. Basic use of **tin** is deceptively easy. One line on the screen is shown in reverse video; if your terminal does not support reverse video, **tin** uses an arrow instead:

```
          Group Selection (11)                h=help

   1   439  misc.books.technical Discussion of books about technical top
   2        rec.arts.sf.movies   Discussing SF motion pictures.
   3    90  rec.folk-dancing     Folk dances, dancers, and dancing.
   4    73  sci.anthropology     All aspects of studying humankind.
   5   196  sci.classics         Studying classical history, languages,
   6    62  soc.couples          Discussions for couples (cf. soc.single
   7   227  soc.culture.nordic   Discussion about culture up north.
   8    35  misc.kids.computer   The use of computers by children.
   9        fedreg.commerce
  10        sci.bio.ecology      Ecological research.
```

---

*For purists, these are not regular expressions at all; these appear to follow the standard UNIX filename expansion rules. That is, * matches anything; ? matches any single character. So alt\.* matches all subgroups of "*alt*."

†If you want to, you can use the same trick we tried with **nn**: enter **tin** once to let it create your *.newsrc* file and quit immediately. Then edit the *.newsrc* file.

```
11     1  sci.anthropology.paleo

<n>=set current to n, TAB=next unread, /=search pattern, c)atchup,
g)oto, j=line down, k=line up, h)elp, m)ove, q)uit, r=toggle all/unread,
s)ubscribe, S)ub pattern, u)nsubscribe, U)nsub pattern, y)ank in/out
                  *** End of Groups ***
```

On this menu, you move between newsgroups by using the arrow keys on the keyboard. As you would expect, the up arrow moves you to the previous newsgroup; the down arrow moves you to the next. So, if you are positioned on *misc.books.technical,* a down arrow moves you to *rec.arts.sf.movies.* A right arrow accesses whatever is in the current position. If you are on *misc.books.technical,* you can press the right arrow to see the threads of the articles in that group:

```
       misc.books.technical (128T 154A OK OH R)          h=help

 1   +    4 Sale: *Cheap* Unix/dBase/Beginner's/Prog Duc Cheng
 2   + 2  numerical analysis recommendations sought  Craig Levine
 3   +    standard IGES file format                  Oren H. Hershel
 4   +    Bookstores info.                           Antonio Cleopatra
 5   + 3  Anyone know of companies that locate out o S. Slade
 6   +    "The Unicode Standard"                     Rob Warren
 7   +    books in ascii via ftp sought              Wilbur Wright
 8   + 2  >>> Technical Books for sale (X/UNIX/C/C++ S. Slade
 9   + 3  Books on Internet needed                   Andrew Jones
10   + 2  RAID literature                            Betty Brelin
11   +    looking for books on FoxPro ver.2.5 (for D Adrian Hall
12   +    "Scientific C++" wanted, by Guido Buzzi-Fe Calvin Hobbs
13   + 2  books forsale                              Dilbert
14   +    PASCAL BOOKS!!!!  DISCOUNT SALE!!!!         Jian Ng
15   +    books for sale                             Peter Rzewski
16   +    Books forsale                              Willie Martin

<n>=set current to n, TAB=next unread, /=search pattern, ^K)ill/select,
a)uthor search, c)atchup, j=line down, k=line up, K=mark read, l)ist
thread, |=pipe, m)ail, o=print, q)uit, r=toggle all/unread, s)ave, t)ag, w=post
```

This looks a lot like the previous screen, with a reference number on the left. The + tells you that you have not yet read this thread. Some of the threads have a number before the title, showing how many articles are in the thread. Finally, the display shows the thread's subject and the author of the first article. Like **nn, tin** uses the > flag to show that you have missed the beginning of the thread and some responses—for an example, look at article 8.

As on the group selection menu, you navigate with the arrow keys. Pressing the right arrow reads a thread. So if you press the right arrow while article 1 is highlighted, you will see something like this:

```
Fri, 22 Oct 1993 19:43:44  misc.books.technical    Thread 1 of 128
Lines 39 4 Sale: *Cheap* Unix/dBase/Beginner's/Program No responses
dcheng@poi.uhcc.Hawaii.Edu        Duc Cheng at University of Hawaii
SCO Xenix OS Ref. Manual $15
SCO Xenix Develpment Sys. Programmer's Ref. $15
Microsoft Fortran Compiler User Manual $10
Using Norton Backup Manual $6
Using Norton Desktop for Windows Manual $7
Microsoft Win386 Manual Set $5
The Whole Internet, Users Guide and Catalog $10
Quattro Pro Manual Set $18
Lotus Agenda Manual Set $18

A/UX Handbook (422 pages) was $29.95
Excel Macro for the IBM (276pages) was $21.95
Using Clarion Professional Developer (761pg) was $26.95

<n>=set current to n, TAB=next unread, /=search pattern, ^K)ill/select,
a)uthor search, B)ody search, c)atchup, f)ollowup, K=mark read,
|=pipe, m)ail, o=print, q)uit, r)eply mail, s)ave, t)ag, w=post
```

## Following Up and Posting

To post a follow-up message to an existing article, press either **f** or **F** while reading the article to which you want to reply. The only difference between these commands is that **f** copies the text of the original article into your response; **F** does not. In either case, **tin** pops you into the editor of your choice; as with **nn**, it is determined by the EDITOR environment variable. When you exit the editor, **tin** asks:

```
q)uit e)dit p)ost: p
```

If you press ENTER at this point, your article is sent on its way. If you decide to change the article, type **e**; **tin** starts your editor again, letting you modify your article. If you decide that silence is true wisdom, typing **q** gets you out of the mess you created.

Starting a new thread is done with the **w** command. It is similar to **nn**'s **:post** command, but there is one important difference: **:post** asks you where you want your article posted. **tin**'s **w** command posts your new thread to the currently selected group. So, if you type **w** while reading an article in *misc.books.technical,* your new posting will be sent to the group *misc.books.technical.*

The only difference between a follow-up article and a new posting is that you will be asked for a subject when you are making a new posting:

```
post Subject[]>
```

After all, you are starting a new thread of discussion. Enter the subject for your new thread. After providing the subject, you will see the same dialog as before.

One thing to note: **tin** remembers the subject of your most recent post during a session. If you post another note later in the day, you may see something like:

```
post Subject[Unix Book For Sale]>
```

"Unix Book For Sale" was the subject of the last posting you made. If you want to reuse this same subject line, you only have to press ENTER.

## Quitting tin

All of **tin**'s command menus have a **quit** option: just type **q** to quit. Unfortunately, this is a bit misleading. "Quit" does not mean "exit **tin**"; it means "exit the current operation and go to the next higher level." For example, if you are reading an article, you need to type **q** to quit reading and return to the thread menu; then you have to type **q** again to go to the newsgroup selection menu; and **q** a third time to get out of **tin**.

So—what if you want to get out of **tin** easily? There must be an easier way. There is— type **Q**. Whatever you are doing, the **Q** command takes you all the way out.

## Exercises

*Answer the following questions for each USENET interface you will be using (e.g., command-line reader,* **pine***, Lynx WWW text browser, graphical WWW browser). Software for reading news is available at URL* **ftp://ftp.onramp.net/pub/ibm/ NewsReaders** *among others. If you have trouble locating or connecting to an FTP site, try URL* **http://hoohoo.ncsa.uiuc.edu/ftp/intro.html** *for other options.*

**1.** Name five newsgroups that you can use to learn about USENET.

**2.** What is a FAQ?

**3.** Other than your existing news server (whether at school or via a commercial provider), seek two other options for accessing USENET. Explain how you could read news using each alternative. Where did you find this information?

**4.** Answer each of the following for your news provider by printing screen images to show what you did and/or cutting and pasting from the newsreader application into your word processor (be sure to clean up the results to make it easier to show what you did).

In what file are the newsgroup names stored? How do you subscribe to the newsgroup *comp.infosystems.www?* How do you unsubscribe to the same newsgroup? What is a current thread of discussion on *comp.infosystems.www?* Look for an interesting article to read on *comp.internet.net-happenings.* Once you have the item, show how you can do each of the following: e-mail the article to yourself, print out the article, and save the article as a disk file.

**5.** Answer the previous questions for one of the alternative news access points you discovered in exercise 3.

**6.** There often will be items of personal interest to you on newsgroups to which you are not subscribed. It is possible to search USENET for those items. DejaNews is one commercial service (URL: **http://www.dejanews.com**). Stanford Netnews Filtering Service is another alternative (URL: **http://woodstock.stanford.edu:2000/index.html**). Using one of these tools (or both) and another either that you find yourself or that is suggested to you, look for articles on the employment prospects for your professional field. What newsgroup(s) seems to have the most discussion on that topic? How useful is the discussion?

**7.** Your school may have its own local newsgroups that are not available elsewhere, including a group for testing such as *bgsu.test.* If so, name five local newsgroups of interest to you. Is there a group specifically for testing how to post news?

**8.** It is considered very bad netiquette to post a "test" message on any regular newsgroup. You have two options to get around this: First, try to post a message to your local testing newsgroup; second, spend time reading one of the new-users groups you noted in exercise 5 and post your own question about USENET. Using the first option, post a simple message such as a limerick or famous quotation. How can you see if the test posting is there? Remembering that you get the news articles by contacting your news server, why might your successful posting not appear immediately? How can you double-check to see if it was posted properly?

# FINDING FILES

One of the biggest obstacles historically to making full use of the resources available on the Internet has been finding what exists. Anonymous FTP servers sprang up early on, giving users the ability to fetch files from repositories on the network, but the existence of those files was largely communicated by interpersonal networking. This worked while the Internet was a small network used by computer professionals. Now that the Internet provides resources to everyone, the "good old boys" network no longer works. Many new users do not have access to an experienced administrator, and there are so many resources online that not even the best administrator could keep track of them all. You may know that a database or public domain program exists, but finding it is like finding the proverbial needle in the haystack.

Enter *Archie,* a system that works with FTP to allow you to search indexes to locate files that are available on public servers. It is the place you can start if you are searching for programs, data, or text files. Archie indexes more than a thousand servers and millions of files. You use it either to find filenames that contain a certain search string or to suggest files whose description contains a certain word. It returns the actual filenames that meet the search criteria and the name of the servers containing those files. Once you decide which of the files is most likely to meet your needs, you can easily move the file to your computer with anonymous FTP.

First, we will look at how Archie works. We will move to how to use Archie. Like many services on the Internet, Archie can be accessed in multiple ways. It is simplest to use Archie through TELNET, using a public-access client, because you do not need any additional software. From TELNET access, we will go to the other extreme: sending queries to Archie servers through e-mail. E-mail access is useful if you are connected to some other network that provides only e-mail access to the Internet.

Then we will discuss using an Archie client program on your own computer. We will focus on the simple line-oriented client program (**archie**), because you can run it on virtually any kind of computer and any kind of display. The **anarchie** client is one of the best Archie clients around, and includes a built-in FTP client. It uses a graphic display. Finally, you can access Archie through a service we have not talked about yet, named Gopher. We will discuss Gopher access to Archie in chapter 11.

## How Archie Works

The Archie service was developed at McGill University. People who were running servers are asked to register them. The Archie founders ran a program once a month that contacted those servers via **ftp** (Figure 9-1). When the program contacts each server, it builds a directory listing of all the files on that server, using standard **ftp** commands. When you come along some time later and say, "find me a file that contains the string 'Eudora' in its filename," Archie simply scans all the merged directories and sends you the filenames that match your search string, together with the names of the servers where each file is available.

This is the basic service that was created, but limitations appeared. It became obvious that some people choose strange, non-intuitive names for their files, like a filename of the Macintosh e-mail program named Eudora. The Archie developers then asked for people to send information on the major packages they provide. They used this information to create a service called **whatis**, a set of alternative indexing keywords for files on the network that can be used to locate software or data files even if the filename bears no resemblance to its contents. Because this service requires human intervention, it is a lot spottier, but useful nonetheless.

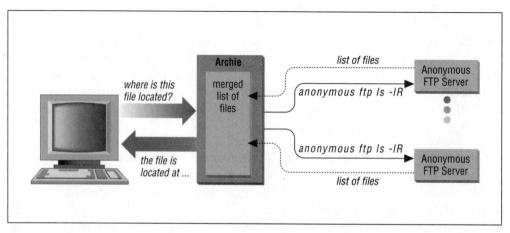

*Figure 9-1   How Archie works*

As Archie's usage grew, the service changed to meet the increased demand. There are many Archie servers scattered across the Internet. Each server builds an index of the FTP archives close to itself, then the servers share the information. This allows the updates to be more timely, without severely loading the network. For the most part, however, you do not care about how the system works. The mechanics are hidden from you; all you need to do is contact any Archie server (they all have the same data) and look up the data you want.

## Contacting Archie

To use Archie, you must choose an Archie server. There are a number of servers, all of which query similar databases. From time to time, differences between Archie servers creep in. They are usually resolved eventually. The Archie developers who took over the service at Bunyip (URL: **http://services.bunyip.com**) are working on ways to solve these problems. If you do not find what you are looking for, you can try another server after you have made sure that everything else is correct (you are doing the right kind of search, you typed the search string correctly, etc.). The differences between servers are very minor. Your concern is to select the server that will answer your queries quickly.

Start the search for a good Archie server with your service provider. If your provider recommends a particular server, try it first. Some providers set up private servers available only to their clientele. As competition increases, service providers are offering more special services like this. If you cannot find the best Archie server from documentation or word of mouth, pick one of the systems listed in the following table.

The "nice" way to pick a server is to choose one that is close to you on the network. This is not easy to do, because you probably do not know exactly where the wires providing your Internet connection go after leaving your campus, home, or office. The best approximation you have is to pick one that is geographically close. Using a server in Australia from the U.S. might be cool, but it is a poor use of slow transoceanic network links. Table 9-1 shows a list of public Archie servers and their general locations.

Archie became a very popular service. It is not unusual for a server to be handling more than 40 requests simultaneously. In order to protect the responsiveness of the service, some servers have limits on the number of concurrent requests that can be handled. If you try to use a server and hit one of these limits, you will get a message like:

```
Due to serious overloading on the archie server,
we have been forced to restrict the number of concurrent
interactive (telnet) sessions to 10.

Connection closed by foreign host.
```

*Table 9-1    Available Archie Servers*

| Name | Suggested Usage Area |
| --- | --- |
| archie.au | Australia |
| archie.edvz.uni-linz.ac.at | Austria |
| archie.univie.ac.at | Austria |
| archie.uqam.ca | Canada |
| archie.funet.fi | Finland |
| archie.th-darmstadt.de | Germany |
| archie.ac.il | Israel |
| archie.unipi.it | Italy |
| archie.wide.ad.jp | Japan |
| archie.kr | Korea |
| archie.sogang.ac.kr | Korea |
| archie.rediris.es | Spain |
| archie.luth.se | Sweden |
| archie.switch.ch | Switzerland |
| archie.ncu.edu.tw | Taiwan |
| archie.doc.ic.ac.uk | United Kingdom |
| archie.unl.edu | USA |
| archie.internic.net | USA |
| archie.rutgers.edu | USA |
| archie.ans.net | USA (for ANS Internet service provider customers) |
| archie.sura.net | USA |

The actual text of the message will vary from server to server, but the intent should be clear. If everyone uses a server close to them, it naturally spreads the load around and minimizes this irritation.

## ■ *Using Archie with TELNET*

After you decide which server is the best one for you to use, the common way to use it is to **telnet** to that hostname. It will come back with a standard (UNIX) login prompt, to which you respond with the login name **archie**:

```
% telnet archie.au
Trying 139.130.4.6...
Connected to archie.au.
```

```
Escape character is '^]'.
      Welcome to Archie.AU (aka plaza.AARNet.EDU.AU)

login:  archie
Last login: Tue Jan 25 21:55:05 from 143.108.1.4
SunOS Release 4.1.3: Wed Oct 20 18:12:43 EST 1993

# Message of the day from the localhost Prospero server:

NOTE: By default this version of archie returns 'au' sites only.

As usual, contact owner-archie@archie.au if you have any problems.

# Bunyip Information Systems, 1993

# Terminal type set to 'vt100 24 80'.
# 'erase' character is '^?'.
# 'search' (type string) has the value 'sub'.
Archie.au>
```

At this point, we are talking to Australia's Archie and can set parameters and make searches. This initial screen gives you a lot of information that will help with your searches. Do not ignore it. According to this screen, Archie thinks you are using a VT100-style terminal, with 24 lines that are 80 characters long; you are doing substring searches, meaning that the characters you search for can occur anywhere in the filename, ignoring case; and you will only find files on Australian computers. You can change any of these parameters, and we will tell you how in a bit. If these conditions are all OK, you can begin searching.

When you are finished searching, you leave Archie with:

```
archie> quit
```

This terminates the TELNET session and returns you to your local computer.

## Searching by Filename

The most common and reliable way to look things up in Archie is to search for likely filenames. It is reliable because you know that the information you find was correct within the past 30 days. If you find a file in the index, you will almost certainly find the same file when you go to fetch it with anonymous FTP. To begin this search, pick a minimal search string that will probably occur in a filename you are looking for. Use the command:

```
archie> prog searchstring
```

to start the search. The search string is interpreted as specified by the "set search" command.

For example, let's say someone suggested you check out the Eudora package to do electronic mail from your Apple Macintosh. You might try:

```
Archie.au> prog Eudora
# Search type: sub, Domain: au.
# Your queue position: 1
# Estimated time for completion: 00:01
```

When you enter a search command, the Archie server puts you in a queue with the rest of the people trying to do searches. It tells you where you are in the queue and estimates how long it will be before it can work on your request. In this case, you are first in the queue and can expect to wait 00:01 (no minutes and one second) to get service. Do not be surprised if it takes a long time to get an answer. Most Archie servers are very heavily loaded.

After the search is complete, the server returns a list of FTP archives and filenames that fit the criteria. Eudora, being a very popular package, is offered by nine servers in Australia alone. An abbreviated listing of this search looks like:

```
Host sunb.ocs.mq.edu.au    (137.111.1.11)
Last updated 11:44 23 Jan 1994

 Location: /Mac/networking
  FILE -r-xr-xr-x 960108 bytes 06:34 28 Oct 1993 eudora-14-manual.hqx
  FILE -r-xr-xr-x 510354 bytes 06:20 28 Oct 1993 eudora-14.hqx
  FILE -r--r--r-- 263976 bytes 01:00 11 Jun 1992 eudora1.3b34.sit.hqx

Host csuvax1.murdoch.edu.au    (134.115.4.1)
Last updated 20:02 24 Jan 1994
 Location: /pub/pc/windows
  DIRECTORY drwxr-xr-x     512 bytes  14:05 11 Nov 1993  eudora

Host ftp.connect.com.au    (192.189.54.17)
Last updated 20:02 24 Jan 1994
 Location: /pub/mac
  DIRECTORY drwxr-xr-x     512 bytes  10:50 22 Nov 1993  eudora

Host ftp.utas.edu.au    (131.217.1.20)
Last updated 19:39 24 Jan 1994
 Location: /pc/win31/mail
  DIRECTORY drwxrwxr-x     512 bytes  22:49  1 Nov 1993  eudora

Host uniwa.uwa.edu.au    (130.95.128.1)
Last updated 11:27 23 Jan 1994
 Location: /pub/mac/freeware
  DIRECTORY drwxrwxr-x     512 bytes  10:22 17 Jan 1994  eudora
```

For each match it finds, Archie tells you the name of the host that offers one or more files that matched the search string. The first host in the example is **sunb.ocs.mq.edu.au**.

Next Archie tells you the directory where the file resides *(/Mac/networking)*, and, finally, it lists the filenames within that directory *(Eudora-14-manual.hqx)*.

Sometimes a search will match a word in a directory path, but no filename in that directory. In that case, the location line gives you the path to the directory that matched the search criterion. Instead of a line beginning with FILE, you will see a line beginning with DIRECTORY, like:

```
Host uniwa.uwa.edu.au    (130.95.128.1)
Last updated 11:27 23 Jan 1994
 Location: /pub/mac/freeware
  DIRECTORY drwxrwxr-x    512 bytes  10:22 17 Jan 1994  eudora
```

This shows that what was found is a directory that might contain something useful (that is what the *d* in *drwxrwxr-x* represents; *rwx* refer to *read, write,* and *execute*—information overload for our purposes here). If you decide that this entry is promising, you will have to use anonymous FTP to find out exactly what it contains.

Because many anonymous FTP servers have the file you want, you now face a new problem: which one to use. This problem is significant, because you find out lots about the files "out there" but you get little or no information to help you decide which file is best to use. Here are a few suggestions:

- If the program runs on several kinds of computers, you have to decide which file contains the version you want. It turns out there are both PC/Windows and Macintosh versions of Eudora. The only help Archie gives you is in the directories and filenames. There are no standards for these names, but most server administrators try to name directories in an intuitive, descriptive way. In this example, you will find that many copies of Eudora reside in some subdirectory called *mac,* which most likely stands for Macintosh. File that reside in directories like *pc, windows,* or *win31* are probably the Windows version of the package. Filename suffixes provide another clue. Certain kinds of compression and file-encoding techniques are common on certain kinds of computers. As noted in chapter 6, *.sit* and *.hqx* are frequently used on Macintoshes. So *Eudora-14.hqx* is probably a Macintosh file.

- Multiple versions of the same software may be available. With some luck, a version number will be encoded in the filename, as in these examples:
  ```
  Eudora-14.hqx
  Eudora1.3b34.sit.hqx
  ```
  If some friends told you about the software, you might ask which version they are running. Otherwise, you might pick the latest version possible, but there are no standards for how version numbers are encoded into the filename. You could guess

that 14 is a later version than 1.3, and you would almost certainly be right.* The directory name is often a clue. If you found directories named */mac/Eudora/old* and */mac/Eudora,* you might presume that the newer software is in the latter directory. Remember that the terms *alpha* and *beta* are used to denote test versions of software. Unless you are willing to accept the risks inherent with using unproved software, avoid these.

■ Pick an official-looking server. (Remember the security discussion from chapter 4, *What's Allowed on the Internet?*) Try to pick a server that is run by someone who should be in the business of delivering software, such as a computer center, network provider, etc.

■ Finally, pick a server that is close. Earlier, we said that you should pick an Archie server that is relatively close to you, to minimize the total network traffic and spread the workload among the different servers. The same logic applies here. To encourage you to use an FTP site that is nearby, some Archie servers (like the one we are using here) tell you only about files within a certain domain—in our example, Australia. It is always possible (and sometimes necessary) to make worldwide searches, but on many servers that is not the default.

■ There is one other important reason to pick an FTP server that is local. If you pick up a file from a server that is not in your country, the file might not be in your native language. If you speak English and grab Eudora from a server in Italy, you might get a surprise: All the menus and prompts have been translated into Italian.

If I were an Australian trying to decide from which of the sites shown in the example to get Eudora, I would probably look in */pub/mac/Eudora* on the **ftp.connect.com.au** server. First, the server is run by **connect.com**, a network service provider in Australia. They have an interest in distributing reliable software to their clients. We do not really know exactly what they have, because the search found only a directory, but it is the first place we would look.

We passed up the obvious choice of **sunb.ocs.mq.edu.au**, because we cannot tell enough about its pedigree. It is probably a Sun workstation in "**ocs**", maybe in the "office of computer science" at some university, but we cannot tell. If we had some knowledge of the site, we might know it was okay to get software there. Lacking that, we would steer clear of it.

---

*In fact, *Eudora-14.hqx* is version 1.4. Files are not always named exactly as you would expect them to be; you may need some creativity to figure out what the names mean.

## Controlling Filename Matching

The discussion of Archie reflects servers running version 3.1 of the Archie software. Some variables (such as **match_path** and **match_domain**) may not exist in earlier versions. The basic search commands and controls will work on any version.

There are other ways to search besides the "substring ignoring case" search we did in the previous section. At any time in a session you can check how the matching is done with the command:

```
archie> show search
# 'search' (type string) has the value 'exact'.
```

Different servers default to different types of searches. Some are case-sensitive, some insensitive. (Some allow full UNIX regular expression searches.) The above server is set to an "exact" match. This means you must match the filename exactly, including case. If you are browsing for software, this probably is not what you want. If you are looking for the package Eudora, you usually want the search to match eudora, Eudora, or EUDORA.

You can change the way your search is conducted with the command:

```
archie> set search type
```

*type* indicates how Archie should conduct your search. It must be one of the following:

**exact**   The search string given must exactly match a filename.

**regex**   The search string is treated as a UNIX regular expression to match filenames.

**sub**   The search string matches any filename that contains it as a substring. The case is ignored when doing the matching. This is probably the most useful search type for general-purpose use.

**subcase**   The search string matches any filename that contains it as a substring. The case of the matching substrings must match as well.

There is no way to specify part of a directory name in the **prog** command that you use to start the search. That is, if you say, **prog Eudora**, Archie will find directories and files named *Eudora*. You may not say **prog pub/Eudora** (*Eudora* in the directory *pub*). In most cases, this is reasonable: The directory structure depends entirely on the FTP server that has the file you want. If you know the directory in which a file resides and the server too, you do not need Archie.

If you really want to look for a file in a specific directory, you can, but it takes two commands. First, you must specify which directories to search. You do this by setting the **match_path** variable with the command:

```
archie> set match_path path-list
```

The *path-list* is a list of strings separated by colons. One of these strings must be found in the directory path. This is always a substring match, ignoring case, regardless of the search type you have chosen. For example, let's say that you are interested in finding a PC version of the Eudora package; software for the Macintosh will not do you any good. Therefore, you would like to restrict your search to directories named *pc* or *win31*. To make this search, give these two commands:

```
archie> set match_path pc:win31
archie> prog Eudora
# Search type: sub, Domain: au, Path: win.
# Your queue position: 8
# Estimated time for completion: 01:14
working... -

Host ftp.utas.edu.au    (131.217.1.20)
Last updated 13:56  2 Feb 1994

    Location: /pc/win31/mail
      DIRECTORY    drwxrwxr-x      512 bytes  22:49  1 Nov 1993  Eudora
```

*. . . (additional matches deleted)*

The first command says that either *pc* or *win31* must occur in the complete directory name; the second command runs the search. Of course, these are not the only directories in which you might find the software; they are only good guesses. If you do not find anything, try a broader search. Remember to give the command **unset match_path** first; the **set match_path** stays in effect until it is changed to something else, or **unset**.

## Controlling a Search Geographically

The newer Archie servers allow you to restrict a search to a particular geographic area—more formally, a particular set of domains. There are a few reasons why you would want to do this:

- In our Australian example, we noted that the server returned information only about files on servers within Australia. We will not consider the possibility that a reader in the U.S. wants to use this server; as we have said, that is impolite. However, an Australian who is looking for something obscure might need to search FTP sites worldwide.

- If you are looking for a popular piece of software, Archie may present you with a huge list of FTP archives, worldwide, where you might find it. Rather than wading through such a huge list, you might want to restrict the search to servers within your area.

- If you are looking for specialty software, you might have ideas about where to find it. For example, if you are looking for a version of Eudora that is been translated into Japanese, you are most likely to find good, up-to-date software by searching the **.jp** domain.

To restrict (or broaden) an Archie search, you use the **set match_domain** command:

```
archie> set match_domain domain-list
```

The *domain-list* is a list of all the domain suffixes you want included in the search. They are listed without a preceding period and are separated by colons. For example, to search for files located in the United States, issue the following command prior to your search:

```
archie> set match_domain us:com:mil:edu:gov
```

Typing this string each time you want to do a search in a particular area could get tedious, but there is a shortcut. Each Archie server may have defined a list of mnemonics for groupings of commonly used domains. You can find out what mnemonics are defined on your particular server using the command **domains**:

```
archie> domains
Domains supported by this server:

africa          Africa          za
anzac           OZ & New Zealand au:nz
asia            Asia            kr:hk:sg:jp:cn:my:tw:in
centralamerica  Central America sv:gt:hn
easteurope      Eastern Europe  bg:hu:pl:cs:ro:si:hr
europe          Europe          westeurope:easteurope
mideast         Middle East     eg:.il:kw:sa
northamerica    North America   usa:ca:mx
scandinavia     Scandinavia     no:dk:se:fi:ee:is
southamerica    South America   ar:bo:br:cl:co:cr:cu:ec:pe:ve
usa             United States   edu:com:mil:gov:us
westeurope      Western Europe  westeurope1:westeurope2
westeurope1                     de:ie:pt:es:uk:at:fr:it:be:nl
westeurope2                     ch:cy:gr:li:lu:tr
world           The world       world1:world2
world1                          europe:scandinavia:northamerica
world2                          southamerica:mideast:africa:anzac:as
```

So, instead of typing **set match_domain us:com:mil:edu:gov**, we could have typed:

```
archie> set match_domain usa
```

Remember, the names you may use are guaranteed to work only on one particular server. Do not use the previous list as a reference; give the **domains** command to see what will work on the server you are using.

## *Searching the Descriptive Index*

Archie also lets you search a descriptive index; this is called a **whatis** search. It searches the so-called "software descriptions database." When administrators place a file in their FTP archives, they may contribute to an index entry for the file to help people find it. The index entry creates a relationship between a filename and a set of keywords. When you do a **whatis** search, your search string is used to examine the keyword list. The search is done with the command:

```
archie> whatis searchstring
```

If the search string matches any of the keywords in the descriptive database, Archie prints the name of the files associated with the keywords. (Searches of the descriptive database are always case-insensitive substring searches, regardless of your search type.) Once you have a filename that sounds appropriate, you must do a filename search to find out where it is located.

Let's say you were looking for a gene sequence map for E. Coli bacteria.* If you do a **prog coli**, Archie would return more than 100 filenames. Most of the matches are obviously not what you want: the broccoli recipes, the horse colic database, etc. There are a few like *colidb* that might be good, but that is all you know. So you decide to try a **whatis** search to get more information:

```
archie>  whatis coli
ECD        Escherichia coli db (M. Kroeger, Giessen)
NGDD       Normalized gene maps for E.coli, S.typh., etc.
                (Y. Abel, Montreal)
```

The file *NGDD* looks like just what the doctor ordered. To find out where it lives, you do a **prog** search, just like you did before:

```
archie> prog NGDD
# Search type: sub, Domain: edu:com:mil:gov:us.
# Your queue position: 2
# Estimated time for completion: 02:40
```

*As this example shows, Archie is not just good for looking up software; it is good for finding all kinds of resources.

```
Host ncbi.nlm.nih.gov   (130.14.20.1)
Last updated 02:23  4 Mar 1992
  Location: /repository
    DIRECTORY rwxrwxr-x    512  Jun 25  1990   NGDD
```

This looks even more promising now. It even comes from a reliable source, the National Institute of Health (**nih.gov**). Notice, however, that what Archie found is not a file called *NGDD,* but a directory by that name. So you do not quite know what you really have. You need to anonymous FTP to **ncbi.nlm.nih.gov** and go to the */repository/NGDD* (**cd repository/NGDD**) directory. Once there, do a **dir** command to see what files are there.

Remember the one caveat: The **prog** index is up-to-date to within 30 days. The **whatis** index is not. Someone can create an entry, and sometime later delete the file. So you may occasionally find something with **whatis** but not be able to locate it with the **prog** command.

As time goes on, the problem with updating the descriptive database has gotten worse. The **whatis** index depends too much on centralized human processing. So much so, that the Archie maintainers have stopped making changes to it. They have designed a new system that allows FTP system administrators to maintain their own information. Unfortunately, this new system is not widely used yet. For now, Archie users are stuck with an index of pretty old information.*

## *Other Archie Commands*

We talked about the **archie** commands that are used regularly. There are a number of other commands that can be useful on occasion. Here is a selection of the other commands you might need:

**bugs**　　　　　　　Displays a list of the current known bugs in the Archie system.

**find**　　　　　　　Synonym for the **prog** command.

**help**　　　　　　　Displays a list much like this one.

**list** *regexp*　　　　Displays a list of anonymous FTP servers that are indexed in the Archie system. If a regular expression is specified, only servers that match the expression are displayed.

---

*This new system is part of the IAFA templates work being done in the IETF. The templates are forms to be filled out by the administrator of each archive and left on the system in a specially named file. They are gathered during the **archie** data acquisition visit to each server, so they would be more up-to-date and maintained by people much closer to the data. It is moving toward standardization, but is not there yet.

**mail** *destination*            Sends the result of the last search to an e-mail address. The destination is optional. If given, it is taken to be an e-mail address to which the search results should be mailed. If no destination is specified, the value of the variable **mailto** is used as the destination.

**manpage**                       Displays the complete reference manual description of the Archie system.

**set** *variable value*          Used to set parameters for controlling your Archie session. The variable name is required (there is a list of variables in the following section). The value is required only if the variable is not a Boolean (on or off) variable. For Boolean variables, **set** *variable* turns the variable on. For other variables, the value is remembered and used appropriately.

**show** *variable*               Displays the value of the specified variable. *variable* is optional. If it is not specified, **archie** displays the value of all variables. **show**, with no variable name, is a good way to get a list of valid variable names or to find out your server's default settings.

**servers**                       Gets a current list of all the known Archie servers.

**unset** *variable*              Turns off a Boolean variable or clears the value of a string variable.

**version**                       Returns the version number of the Archie server you are using.

## Archie Configuration Variables

Here is a partial list of the variables that can be manipulated with the **set**, **unset**, and **show** commands that are not discussed elsewhere in the text:

**mailto** *address*              Sets a default e-mail address; this address is used whenever the **mail** command is given without a parameter.

**match_domain**                  Specifies a list of top-level domains; the FTP server on which any file resides must belong to one of these domains for a match to occur. Explained more fully in the "Controlling Filename Matching" section earlier in this chapter.

**match_path**                    Specifies a list of directory components that must be in the pathname for a match to occur. Explained more fully in the "Controlling Filename Matching" section earlier in this chapter.

| | |
|---|---|
| **maxhits** *number* | Limits the amount of output to *number* entries. (Number must be between 1 and 1,000.) |
| **pager** | XX "pager command:Archie" determines whether the output should stop whenever the screen is full. If **pager** is set, output will be held until you press ENTER when the screen is full. This is a Boolean variable; use **set pager** to turn it on, **unset pager** to turn it off. |
| **sortby** *keyword* | Declares the sort order of the output. For a list of the kinds of sorting available, try **help set sort**. |
| **search** *keyword* | Sets the search type. This is explained more fully in the "Controlling Filename Matching" section earlier in this chapter. |
| **term** *type row col* | Declares that you are using a *type* terminal (e.g., VT100) which has *row* rows on the screen and *col* columns. The type can be any one of the typical terminal abbreviations available in UNIX. *row* and *col* are optional. If they are omitted, the standard size for the declared terminal type is used. |

## ▨ *Using Archie by Electronic Mail*

In addition to logging in to an Archie server directly, you can use Archie via electronic mail. Although it is less convenient than an interactive session, there are two reasons why you might want to use mail. First, you may be forced to: Your network might not allow you to contact Archie via TELNET. This would be the case, for example, if your only connections to the outside world are through UUCP or BITNET. Many of the servers that **archie** indexes provide access through **ftpmail** (see chapter 7, *Electronic Mail*) for those networks that cannot do **ftp**. Second, you may not care to wait around for Archie to do the lookup. If you hear about something great at 4:59 and have to run for the train, send an e-mail query—the answer will be there when you get to work the next morning. The same logic applies if Archie tells you that it is busy or if it is unavailable for some reason.

The commands for using Archie by mail are a subset of those available using **telnet**. You build a message with search commands in it and send it to:

    archie@*server*

where *server* is one of the servers mentioned earlier. Commands must begin in column 1 of a line. You can have as many commands as you like in a message. Any command that cannot be understood is interpreted as **help**. So if you do anything wrong, you get help whether you need it or not. Because interactive responsiveness is not an issue, the arguments all use more powerful search types like **regex**. You can set all of the variables (like **match_path** and **match_domain**) just as you would with the TELNET interface. You can also use any other commands that make sense in the mail environment.

Here is a summary of the most common commands for the e-mail interface:

**path** *email-address*   Tells **archie** to send the responses to *email-address* rather than the address given in the **From:** field of the requesting message. It is useful if you are traversing e-mail gateways and not enough information is conveyed to Archie in the **From:** field for the return trip. If you send requests and never receive an answer, try specifying a very explicit route back to your computer and see if it helps.

**compress**   Causes the output sent to you to be compressed and **uuencod**ed before being sent. It is suggested that you use this option whenever you expect the output to exceed 45K bytes.

**prog** *regexp*   Looks for filenames that match the regular expression.

**help**   Returns a help file for mail **archie**.

**list** *regexp*   Returns a list of all the servers whose names match *regexp*.

**servers**   Returns a list of all the known Archie servers.

**whatis** *keyword*   Returns a list of files that match the keyword argument in the **whatis** database. This can then be used in a subsequent mail message with the **prog** command to look up the location of these files.

**quit**   Causes processing to be terminated and any lines following this command to be ignored. This is useful if you have a signature file that Archie might try to interpret as commands.

For example, let's say you wanted to find an archive for the *sci.geo.meteorology* newsgroup. Of course, because you are interested in meteorology in general, you might also want to go fishing and see if there are any other good meteorology files available. To do this, use your favorite mail program to construct a message like this:

```
% mail archie@archie.rutgers.edu              use any server you like
Subject:                                      no subject necessary
prog meteorology
```

Sometime later, you will receive a message back from the server, containing the results:

```
>From archie-error@dorm.rutgers.edu Sat Apr 11 06:33:30 1992 Received: from
dorm.rutgers.edu by ux1.cso.uiuc.edu with SMTP
Date: Sat, 11 Apr 92 07:32:35 EDT
Message-Id: <9204111132.AA04307@dorm.rutgers.edu>
From: archie@dorm.rutgers.edu
To: Ed Krol <krol@ux1.cso.uiuc.edu>
Subject: archie reply: prog meteorology
Status: R

Sorting by hostname
Search request for 'meteorology'

Host cnam.cnam.fr   (192.33.159.6)
Last updated 02:06  8 Apr 1992
  Location: /pub/Archives/comp.archives/auto
    DIRECTORY rwxr-xr-x  512  Feb  5 21:20   sci.geo.meteorology

Host earth.rs.itd.umich.edu   (141.211.164.153)
Last updated 06:48 10 Apr 1992
  Location: /mac.bin/development/libraries/MacVogl :c4/fonts
    FILE      rw------ 3034  Oct 17 06:55   meteorology

Host rtfm.mit.edu   (18.172.1.27)
Last updated 06:27 26 Mar 1992
  Location: /pub/usenet
    DIRECTORY rwxrwxr-x  512  Feb 19 01:56   sci.geo.meteorology

    ...
```

Well, you found what you were looking for at **cnam.cnam.fr** in France, and at **rtfm.mit.edu** in Massachusetts. You also seem to have come across some Macintosh fonts that might be useful in meteorology at the University of Michigan (**earth.rs.itd.umich.edu**). They could be worth checking.

## ▨ *Archie Using a Client*

The most convenient way to do Archie lookups is with the **archie** command installed on your system. If you have this command available to you, you can do searches with:

```
% archie -modifiers string
```

*string* is the search string, as in all the other **prog** lookups we have discussed previously. The *modifiers* control the type of search. Some of the modifiers available to you are:

-c              Tells **archie** to return files whose names contain the search string. Uppercase and lowercase letters must match exactly.

-e          Tells **archie** to return files whose names match the search string exactly. This is the default.

-r          Tells **archie** that the search string is a UNIX regular expression.

-s          Tells **archie** to return files whose names contain the search string; the case of the letters is ignored.

-l          Tells **archie** to reformat the output so it is suitable for input into another program.

-h*name*    Tells the **archie** client to use the server specified by *name* for the request. With many clients, you can set an environment variable to default this to whatever server you like to use. On UNIX, the variable to set is **ARCHIE_HOST**.

-m*number*  Tells **archie** to return no more than *number* files. If you do not specify this parameter, **archie** returns at most 95 matches.

Any given request can only include one of the -c, -r, or -s modifiers. If -e is used with any of the other search switches, an exact match is tried before doing the more time-consuming search types.

Let's see if we can find the source for the **archie** command for a UNIX workstation, just in case you might want to install it yourself:

```
% archie -s -m5 archie

Host ab20.larc.nasa.gov
  Location: /usenet/comp.sources.amiga/volume89/util
    FILE -rw-rw-r--   5015  Mar 15 1989  archie.1.Z

Host nic.funet.fi
  Location: /pub/archive/comp.sources.amiga/volume89/util
    FILE -rw-rw-r--   4991  Aug  1 1989  archie18.1.Z

Host wolfen.cc.uow.edu.au
  Location: /ab20/usenet/comp.sources.amiga/volume89/util
    FILE -rw-rw-r--   5015  Aug 16 1991  archie.1.Z
    FILE -rw-rw-r--   4979  Aug 16 1991  archie18.1.Z

Host wuarchive.wustl.edu
  Location: /usenet/comp.sources.amiga/volume89/util
    FILE -rw-rw-r--   5054  Mar 16 1989  archie.1.Z
```

This search says: "Search for filenames that contain 'archie', ignoring case (-s); return the first five files you find (-m5)." We found five **archie** clients but they all appear to be for Amiga computers. Because that is not what we are looking for, we will have to issue the search again, making **-m** bigger. I'm sure you get the idea.

## ▦ *Post-processing Archie Output*

Archie's output normally looks like the examples in this chapter. This is fine for human consumption, but occasionally you might want to take Archie's output and use it as input to another program. In this situation, it would be more convenient if all the information about each file were printed on one line, rather than on multiple lines.

Two options give you "one line per file" output formats. They are controlled by the variable **output_format**. Normally, this variable is set to **verbose**, which produces the familiar format. By setting it to **terse**, you get a one line per file output like this:

```
Archie.au> set output_format terse
Archie.au> prog Eudora
# Search type: sub, Domain: au, Path: win31:pc.
# Your queue position: 1
# Estimated time for completion: 02:29
working...

tasman.cc.utas.edu.au  22:49  1 Nov 1993 512 bytes /pc/win31/mail/Eudora
csuvax1.murdoch.edu.au  14:05 11 Nov 1993 512 bytes /pub/pc/windows/Eudora
ftp.utas.edu.au  22:49  1 Nov 1993 512 bytes /pc/win31/mail/Eudora
```

This is our same old search for Eudora for PCs and Windows in Australia. Same files, different format. The output is still fairly readable, particularly the date.

The command **set output_format machine** generates output that can be read easily by a computer, but is not quite so convenient for humans. It gives additional information about file access modes, and displays the file's date in a numeric format. Otherwise, the output is fairly similar to what we saw above:

```
19931101224900Z tasman.cc.utas.edu.au 512 bytes drwxrwxr-x /pc/win31/mail/Eudora
19931111140500Z csuvax1.murdoch.edu.au 512 bytes drwxr-xr-/pub/pc/windows/Eudora
19931101224900Z ftp.utas.edu.au 512 bytes drwxrwxr-x /pc/win31/mail/Eudora
```

If you are using a local **archie** client, use the -l option to get machine-readable output.

## ▦ *Archie Under the Graphical User Interface*

The most user-friendly of Archie clients is **anarchie** for the Macintosh (shareware copy available from URL **ftp://amug.org/pub/peterlewis/anarchie-160.sit.bin**; "160" will change as newer versions are made available). It provides a nice graphical interface to the

Archie service. In addition, it includes a built-in FTP client, so you can use **anarchie** (pronounced "anarchy") to explore directories at FTP sites (a deficiency we have noted with the other clients we have discussed)—and even to retrieve files for you. It comes bundled with more than 50 useful bookmarks, including all of the Info-Mac and University of Michigan archive mirror sites. The program gives you a progress bar and a time estimate to let you know how long a given download will take, and it has a built-in list of Archie servers. Best of all, after an Archie search, you can click on a filename to immediately **ftp** it to your computer.

## ■ *Archie Under the X Window System*

Like **anarchie**, **xarchie** (available via anonymous FTP from **ftp.cs.rochester.edu**) provides a nice graphical interface to the Archie service and includes the built-in FTP client. Starting **xarchie** from the UNIX command line is easy:

```
% xarchie
```

**xarchie** starts by displaying a screen like that shown in Figure 9-2.

Doing a search is easy. Use the **Settings** pull-down menu to change any options (search type, Archie server) as appropriate. Then, position to the **Search Term** box, type the filename you want to search for, and press ENTER. Archie then fills the left column of

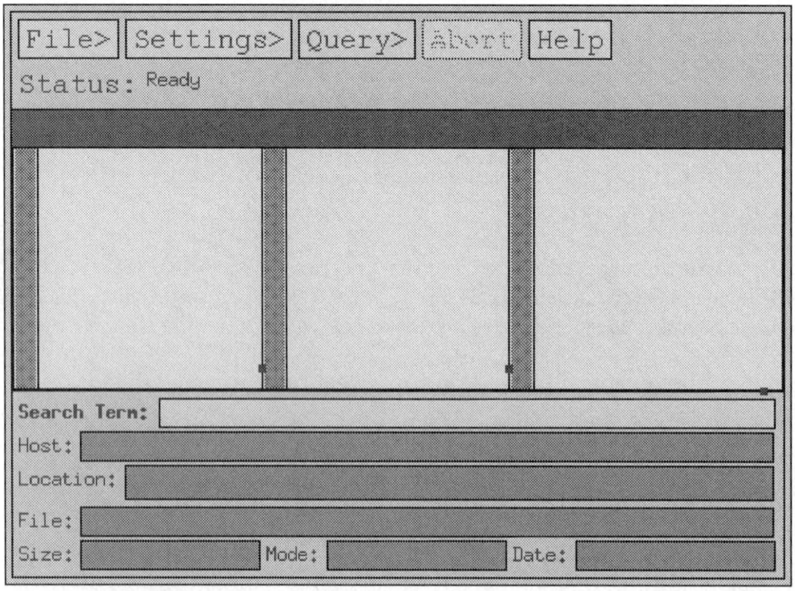

*Figure 9-2    Initial xarchie screen*

the central display with a list of FTP sites that have matches. If Archie found more FTP sites than fit on the display, you can use the scroll bar to the left of the column to move up and down in the list. (The left mouse button scrolls down the list; the right scrolls up.) To find out specifics about the files available at any FTP site, click on that site's name. **xarchie** then displays the directories at that site that have matches in the central column. **xarchie** displays the actual match (directory or file) in the right column. If more than one directory contains matches, the right column is left blank; click on a directory in the center column to see the matches it contains.

Here is how a typical search looks. We will find the PDIAL list, which is a list of Internet service providers. We used the **Settings** pull-down menu to select a case-sensitive substring search (again, probably the most useful kind of search when you are looking for a file). We then typed the name **pdial** in the **Search Term** field, followed by ENTER. After waiting for **xarchie** to do the lookup, we see the screen shown in Figure 9-3.

The leftmost column shows where versions of this file are found. The FTP archive **wais.com** contains a version of our file; the filename *(PDIAL015.txt)* is in the right column, and the directory *(/pub/getting-connected)* is in the center. If the name in any column is too long, you can "stretch" it by dragging the "handle" at the bottom.*

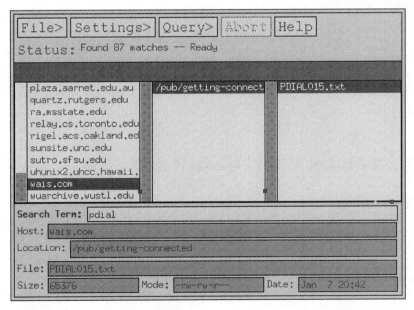

*Figure 9-3　xarchie search results*

---

*Looking up the PDIAL list is a good exercise in what to watch out for when searching the Net. There are many versions out on the Net. Most of them are out-of-date to one extent or another, some by more than a year. Some are tagged with version numbers; others are not.

If several directories at the FTP archive contain matches, **xarchie** lists the directories in the center column and leaves the right column empty; to find the filenames, click on one of the directories.

Here is where having FTP built-in comes in handy. Earlier, we said that Archie searches often match a directory, rather than a file. In that case, you have to **ftp** to the site and look up the directory to find what is in it. However, with **xarchie**, you will see a directory name (rather than a filename) in the right column. Double-click on the directory name; **xarchie** then gets a list of files in the directory and displays the files in the rightmost column.

Whether or not you need to list a directory, you can use **xarchie**'s built-in FTP client to transfer files. Click on the name of the file you want; you can select multiple files by holding down the SHIFT key while clicking. Then go to the **File** pull-down menu. You will see several options. **Open** transfers a text file to your system and displays it in a window. (The window has its own option for saving the file). **Get ftp**s the file to your system, without displaying it, and can be used for any kind of file.

The **Settings** pull-down menu is used to select the search type, the Archie server you want to use, and other features. If you have read the previous discussion, using it should be easy. One note: The **Other** item at the bottom doesn't really mean "other settings"; it is a "form-style" interface to setting Archie options that lets you set several options at once.

One final trick: The central **xarchie** display only has three columns, and sometimes Archie needs more, particularly if it matches a directory name and you ask it to fill in the files within the directory. In this case, you can scroll the main display to the left or right by clicking on the arrows (<<< and >>>) just above the screen.

# ▧ *Using Archie on the World Wide Web*

## *Searching via Interactive Archie Gateway*

Like **anarchie** for the Mac, the Interactive Archie Gateway allows you to use the WWW to accomplish an Archie search. Figure 9-4 shows an example starting from the Interactive Archie Gateway at URL **http://www.bot.astrouw.edu.pl/archie_servers.html** using Netscape as our WWW browser.

From the initial screen, you can select an Archie server from the box cleverly named **Select archie server**. Look for a server in your geographic region. You also can use the normal Archie keys by selecting them with your mouse (see Figure 9-5).

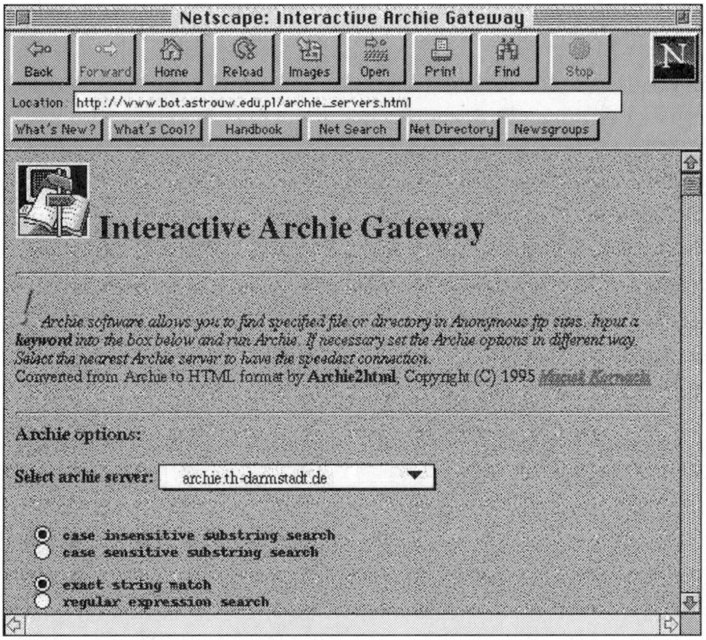

*Figure 9-4    Initial screen from Interactive Archie Gateway*

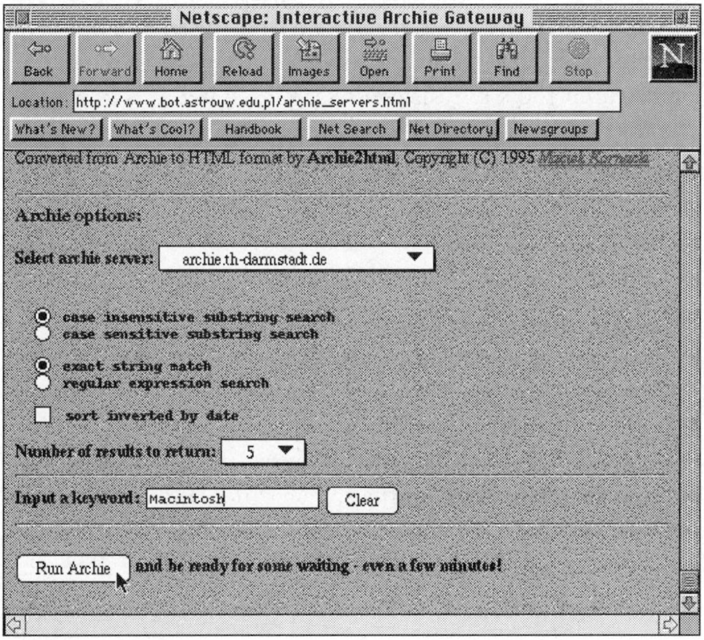

*Figure 9-5    Archie search keys*

Point to the **Input a keyword** box, input a keyword, click, and then enter the search text. In this case, we try the term **Macintosh**. The speed of the search is still limited by that of the chosen Archie server. If it runs more than a few minutes, we may want to try another server. Once the results are displayed on-screen, we can use the hypertext interface of the WWW to select an FTP server with files and/or directories that matched our search for **Macintosh** (Figure 9.6). All we do is use the mouse to point and click on the appropriate server, which is probably in hypertext format.

Scrolling farther down in the results screen, we can see just what we have found. It appears to be a server in Germany (domain name ends with **.de**) with some interesting Macintosh applications directories (Figure 9-7).

Expect more and continually improved WWW and stand-alone GUI interfaces to the Archie search tool. In the short term, knowing the **archie** commands will help make you an Internet research expert.

## Finding Files Using the World Wide Web

Archie still serves an important function on the Internet, but the WWW offers other services for locating information, including files, on the Web. Common search tools include Infoseek, Lycos, SavvySearch, and Yahoo. These are discussed in chapter 13. The remaining drawback of Archie tools is speed. Results remain slow to arrive, a problem far less severe with the new Web tools. It remains a very good idea to master Archie. For the foreseeable future, different search tools use different search databases. No matter which interface you prefer, you may be missing some important and quite relevant items available only in the database of another tool.

## Exercises

*For each of the following exercises, print out your results to show that you were able to find each item. If using a GUI, you can easily cut-and-paste your answers from your online session into a word processor. Seek help locally if you need it.*

**1.** Any Internet search tool will be limited to the database it queries. Just as the Business Periodicals Index is limited to business and related journals, magazines, and newspapers, Archie is limited in its coverage. What files can you expect to find using Archie? What files might be overlooked? If you have trouble answering this question, suggest strategies to seek the answers.

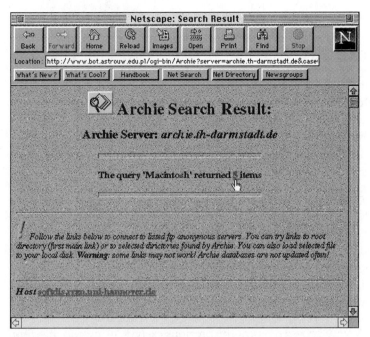

***Figure 9-6*** *Initial search results screen*

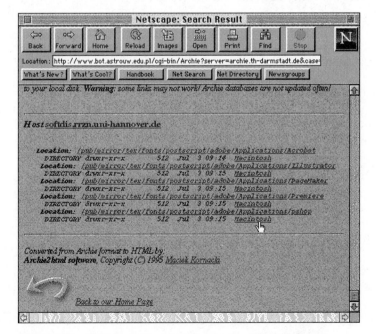

***Figure 9-7*** *FTP servers found via Interactive Archie Gateway*

**2.** Archie databases are located around the world. The closer the server is to you, the less demand you put on the network. Given your location, name the five Archie servers closest to you. Where did you find this answer?

**3.** Let's look for files related to the "national information infrastructure." Using one of the servers discovered, **telnet** to that server and login as **archie**. Begin a search to match the keyword **nii**. Specifically, what will Archie return to you? How can you tell if you have located a file or a directory? If a file, how do you know if it is text or binary? How can you be sure to include both **nii** and **NII** in the same search? What apparently irrelevant matches resulted? How can you peek at a file to see if it is relevant?

**4.** **nni** is only one option for possible matches. Suggest other possible file and/or directory names.

**5.** Use **ftp** to retrieve one of the files. Name three ways you can read the file once you have retrieved it. How might you cite this document in a form that would allow another network user to access it later? Find a style guide that explains how to do this. What is that guide and how did you find it?

**6.** If you have access to a WWW browser, repeat the previous exercise using two different servers offered at Archieplex (URL: **http://pubweb.nexor.co.uk/public/archie/ servers.html**). How do the results compare? How do the results compare to those that you received using **archie** via **telnet**?

**7.** Repeat the search using your e-mail account. Given your experiences in the previous two exercises, why might it be advantageous to use e-mail to perform an Archie search?

**8.** If you have access to the **anarchie** tool locally, repeat the search with it. How do the searches compare? How does **anarchie** compare to Archieplex? Which method do you prefer?

**9.** Complete an Archie search to find software files of interest to you. For example, use **archie** to find locations where compress/uncompress software is available. How can you tell if the file is appropriate for your operating system (e.g., Mac, Windows, Windows 95, etc.)?

**10.** Use **ftp** to access the file, retrieve it, uncompress it if necessary, and execute it.

**11.** Archie may return screens and screens of information. Suggest three ways you can handle a possible deluge of results.

CHAPTER TEN

# FINDING SOMEONE

*Why Isn't There a Single Internet Directory?*
*Finding a User on a Specific System*
*whois*
*The USENET User List*
*X.500 Directory Services*
*Knowbot Information Service*
*Netfind*
*Commercial E-mail Directories*
*The Final Words on E-mail Lookup*

As the phone company can provide a "white pages" telephone directory of its customers, the Internet can, too. The problem is that, just like the phone company, there are multiple phone books for various parts of the Internet. It is easy to find out Willie Martin's phone number if you know he lives in Chicago. If you don't know where he lives or works, it is nearly impossible. The same is true of the Internet. You can probably find someone, but the more you know, the easier it will be.

Attempting to make the service's application obvious, the technical community calls it the white pages, named after the phone book. On the surface, it seems like building a global white-pages service should be easy; after all, we have millions of networked computers. There is no single service, however, for the entire Internet. We will discuss this first, then we will discuss how to look people up.

Discussing how to use the white pages is not as easy as it should be. There are many different kinds of white-pages directories. On top of that, there are usually several different ways to interrogate each kind of directory. For example, one kind of white-pages directory is named *whois*. There is a **whois** command for accessing these directories; you can also make **whois** queries through TELNET, Gopher, WAIS, and the World Wide Web. In this chapter we will focus on the "native" software interfaces to directories, like the **whois** command. We will cover the alternative interfaces (like Gopher) in the chapters on those other services. We do include WWW examples here for learner convenience. Most of the time, these services present white-pages directories as simple index lookups.

# ■ *Why Isn't There a Single Internet Directory?*

There are three reasons why a single, unified Internet user's directory does not exist:

- ■ The ease with which users change location and work habits
- ■ Lack of standards for directories
- ■ Worries about security and privacy

These factors delayed the creation of such a single e-mail directory. Progress is being made now that some of the fundamental problems have been solved, but it is still slow. Let's examine these issues more closely.

## *Mobile Users*

Compare an Internet directory to a telephone directory. If you want a phone, you contact the company, pay them some money, give them some information, get a phone, and they put you in the directory. If you move, you cancel your service, and the company takes you out of the directory. If you stop paying your bill, the company discontinues your service and takes you out of the directory. You have no choice in the matter: Each time you get a new phone, you have to give them information and pay their fees. Under these circumstances, creating and maintaining a directory is easy: The phone company always has all the information it needs.

On the Internet, there is no one group with whom to deal, no one has to collect information, and in most cases no money changes hands. If my workstation is on the network and you want to be on, I can set up an account for you and in five minutes you are an Internet user with all the capabilities of the other hundreds of thousands of users. Since there is no monthly charge for the account, there is no reason to turn your account off if you stop using it. It just sits there looking like the active accounts, waiting to be discovered by someone looking for a name like yours.

This illustrates how difficult it is to keep data accurate, but it is really only the tip of the iceberg. First, many people on the network have multiple accounts. Sometimes they are on co-located computers: Everyone in the office has accounts on each other's workstations. Sometimes, they are widely separated. I may have an account at the San Francisco office so I can work while I am there. In either case, having an account on an Internet-connected machine makes me an Internet user. *It does not mean I will ever use that account again.* If you send an urgent e-mail message to my account at the San Francisco office, I probably will not read it until next year, when I am there for the annual sales meeting. To avoid this, it would be helpful for others to know the last time the account was used, which is possible through tools like **finger** (discussed in the following section).

In order to keep a good directory, someone needs to maintain it; in turn, the maintainer needs the cooperation, even if it is forced, of the user. On the Internet, the first part is easy. The second is almost impossible. Many campuses and corporations maintain internal staff directories. Some of these include electronic access information and some are online. That does not mean the information is up-to-date. Most of the information is gathered when a person is hired, and deleted when he leaves. Updating the information is optional and frequently not done.

## Standards

If everyone creates his or her own version of a service to serve a particular community (say, a university campus), it is difficult for those outside the community to use it. Even if outsiders can get access to the software, you still need one program to access Joe's Directory of Minor League Baseball Players Online, another to access Mary's Directory of Physics Grad Students at the University of Omaha, etc. After an awkward period of confusion, a standard technique emerges and is agreed upon. Anyone who knows the standard can then use the service regardless of where it is located.

A long time ago (by computing standards) the Organization for International Standardization started trying to develop a standard for directory services called X.500 (*Introduction to White Pages Services based on X.500*, August 1994, URL **http:// www.cis.ohio-state.edu/htbin/rfc/rfc1684.html**). There were some non-standard servers already in existence that were built for special groups. As the X.500 standard took longer and longer to complete, more special directory services with their own facilities were built out of need. Now X.500 is a reality, but a lot of the other services are still there working just fine. Almost every campus or corporation has its own local service. The people who use them are reluctant to change for the sake of changing. If it is not broken, why fix it?

## Security and Privacy

When we discussed security, we said that a common way to break into a system was to find a valid username and try common passwords. Since an e-mail address usually contains the recipient's login name, some people think making this information public is a breach of security. It makes it slightly easier for a cracker to break in. Therefore, as a matter of policy, some systems simply refuse to provide any information about users.

The other side of the coin is personal privacy. Some people believe that they should be able to control whether or not their e-mail address and username are publicly accessible. Some countries have very strict personal privacy laws that forbid any personal information being released without express permission. This is not a problem for voluntary systems, where you ask to be included. It arises when you try to include people in directories automatically, without their consent. Most corporations and campuses have e-mail information gathered, but administrative procedures may not be in place to protect the users' privacy. Rather than deal with the administrative problem directly, these organizations solve the problem by refusing to give out any information.

Now that you understand some of the issues, let's look at what directories are available and how to use them. The facilities are not presented in any order of preference; rather, each one has its own place. You have to decide which one will most likely produce results based on whatever information you already know. Again remember, even the best online directory is out of date and gives only approximate information. If you really want to know for sure, gather the information yourself; that is much more accurate. If you need to know Jane Doe's e-mail address, give her a call or look up her business card.

## CSO Directories

CSO-style directories are one of the most prevalent on the Internet. A large number of colleges and universities use them to put their student and staff information online. To use these directories directly, you need a client called **ph** that is occasionally included as part of another package (for example, the mail package Eudora). Most people access CSO directories through Gopher, which does a lot more than white-pages queries. Because they are usually accessed through Gopher, we will defer a detailed discussion of CSO directories until chapter 11. If you cannot wait to check it out, skip ahead to the chapter exercises.

## Finding a User on a Specific System

**finger** is an old and widely used facility that examines the a user's "login file" on a UNIX system. It lets you find out someone's login name (hence the e-mail address) and his or her personal name, given that you know what computer your correspondent uses. **finger** also tells you whether the user you are asking about is currently logged in to the target machine. Although **finger** is closely tied to UNIX, there are clients that allow you to make **finger**-style queries from other types of systems as well.

The general format of the **finger** command is:

```
% finger name@host
```

The *name* is optional and specifies the name you want to look up. The **finger** command goes to the specified host, and returns information on all users whose first or last name matches *name,* or who have chosen *name* as their login ID. *host* is the name of the computer where you want the inquiry to be made. If you are asking about someone on your local system, you can omit *@host;* that is, you do not specify a host, because **finger** will default to searching the computer on which you gave the command.

The mechanics of how the search is done are confusing. The *name* you give must be one of the following:

- An exact match, case-sensitive, for a user's login name. It may help you to remember that UNIX login names are almost always all lowercase.

- An exact match, case-insensitive, for a user's first name, as listed in the system's accounts file (for UNIX users, the so-called GECOS field of */etc/passwd* ).

- An exact match, case-insensitive, for a user's last name, as listed in the accounts file.

In practice, it is not that bad. If you use lowercase letters for everything, you will be fairly safe: You will not inadvertently exclude login names, and you will still find any first and last names that match.

For example, you know that Bruce Klopfenstein uses the computer **bgsuvax.bgsu.edu.** To find his e-mail address, you might try:

```
% finger klopfenstein@bgsuvax.bgsu.edu
Login name: klopfens     (messages off)  In real life: Bruce Klopfenstein
Office: 322WestHall, 372-2138            Home phone: 352-4818
Directory: /home2/itcom/klopfenstein     Shell: /bin/tcsh
On since Sep 21 19:00:22 on ttyqd from opie.bgsu.edu
28 seconds Idle Time
Plan:
This text is entered in a file named .plan  It could be a poem or
anything else I'd like you to see when you finger this account.
```

This query found "klopfenstein" on the machine **bgsuvax.bgsu.edu** with the login of **klopfens** (not "klopfenstein"). There is other information of interest here. If you were looking for a place to send e-mail, you might gather that sending mail to **klopfens@bgsuvax.bgsu.edu** is safe because the account is active at the moment you **finger**ed it.

The **Plan:** display is very interesting. Anything a user enters into a file named *.plan* will be displayed along with the other login information. The file *.project* is treated similarly; if it exists, its contents are displayed at the end of **finger**'s report.*

---

*For this to work, the files must have UNIX "world read permission," and your *home* directory must have world execute permissions.

```
% finger klopfens
Login name: klopfens    (messages off)   In real life: Bruce Klopfenstein
Office: 322WestHall, 372-2138            Home phone: 352-4818
Directory: /home2/itcom/klopfenstein    Shell: /bin/tcsh
On since Sep 21 19:00:22 on ttyqd from opie.bgsu.edu
Project: Bring RTVF into the world of telecommunications.
Plan:

This text is entered in a file named .plan  It could be a poem or
anything else I'd like you to see when you finger this account.
```

**finger** is often used to get a list of the people who are currently using a system. To do this, just omit the login name from your command (remember to put the @ sign before the hostname). The following command uses **finger** to find out who is logged in to the system **uxc.cso.uiuc.edu**:

```
% finger @bgsuvax.bgsu.edu
Login          Name              TTY Idle    When           Office
bblank     Bryan Blank           t2   6d Fri 15:04
root       Charlie               co 9:29 Wed 07:48
hmizoha    Hidetaka Mizohata     p8    9 Thu 17:45
klopfens Bruce Klopfenstein     *qd    3 Thu 19:00   322WestHall 372-2138
```

Notice that the output looks quite different and gives information about the current login, as well as some personal information.

### *finger as a general information server*

**finger**'s ability to display a *.plan* file provides a simple and effective way to distribute small amounts of information. It is often used for this purpose, playing a role as a very simple database server. For example, in the account for **quake@geophys.washington.edu**, someone maintains a listing of recent earthquake information in the *.plan* file. So if you use **finger** to inquire about that login, you get something like this:

```
% finger quake@geophys.washington.edu
Login name: quake                        In real life: Earthquake Information
Directory: /u0/quake                     Shell: /u0/quake/run_quake
Last login Thu Sep 21 15:12 on ttypb from primeg.swc.cc.ca
Mail last read Sun Jul 30 03:37:06 1995
Plan:

The following catalog is is for earthquakes (M>2) in Washington and Oregon
produced by the Pacific Northwest Seismograph Network, a member of the
Council of the National Seismic System.  PNSN support comes from the
US Geological Survey, Department of Energy, and Washington State.
Catalogs for various regions of the country can be obtained by using the program
'finger quake@machine' where the following are machines for different regions.
```

```
gldfs.cr.usgs.gov   (USGS NEIC/NEIS world-wide), andreas.wr.usgs.gov (Northern
Cal.), scec.gps.caltech.edu (Southern Cal.), fm.gi.alaska.edu (Alaska),
seismo.unr.edu (Nevada), mbmgsun.mtech.edu (Montana),
eqinfo.seis.utah.edu (Utah), sisyphus.idbsu.edu (Idaho)
slueas.slu.edu (Central US), tako.wr.usgs.gov (Hawaii),

Additional catalogs and information for the PNSN (as well as other networks)
are available on the World-Wide-Web at URL:'http://www.geophys.washington.edu/'
DATE-TIME is in Universal Time (UTC) which is PST + 8 hours. Magnitudes are
reported as local magnitude (Ml).  QUAL is location quality A-good, D-poor,
Z-from automatic system and may be in error.
 DATE-(UTC)-TIME   LAT(N) LON(W)   DEP  MAG QUAL COMMENTS
 yy/mm/dd hh:mm:ss  deg.   deg.    km   Ml
 95/09/09 03:08:53 47.48N 121.78W  18.2 2.5  A    0.7 km WNW of North Bend
 95/09/09 09:57:43 45.96N 122.61W  18.2 2.0  A   30.3 km  SE of Longview
 95/09/11 08:37:31 45.96N 122.61W  17.6 2.1  B   29.9 km  SE of Longview
 95/09/11 17:42:15 45.96N 122.61W  17.3 2.1  B   30.3 km  SE of Longview
 95/09/12 13:39:19 46.83N 120.70W   0.0 2.3  C   20.6 km  SW of Ellensburg
 95/09/13 14:31:53 45.98N 120.96W   1.2 2.0  D   45.7 km ESE of Mount Adams
 95/09/14 03:18:36 47.93N 122.38W  23.4 2.0  C   15.0 km WSW of Everett
```

If you look through the *Resource Catalog,* you will find a couple of organizations that provide similar information through **finger**.

### When finger fails

**finger** requires that a server be running on the target computer to service the request. If you try to use **finger** on an uncooperative host, you will get a message like this:

```
% finger krol@sonne.cso.uiuc.edu
[sonne.cso.uiuc.edu]
connect: Connection refused
```

In this case, there is nothing you can do. **finger** is simply unavailable on the remote computer. You might complain to the administrator, but it may be that the administrator has decided that running **finger** is a security risk (a point that has been hotly debated on the Net). You must try other means to find the information you require.

## ■ *whois*

**whois** is the name of a particular white-pages directory, a general kind of directory, and an application to access it. The confusion arises because **whois** was the original way of doing Internet directory lookups (on what was at the time the ARPAnet). When you are the only game in town, people are not too accurate with names. You would say, "Gotta run; e-mail me—I'm in **whois**," and everyone would know how to look you up.

The original directory was maintained by the Defense Data Network (DDN) Network Information Center (NIC) and at its peak contained about 70,000 entries. In its prime you were automatically listed in the directory if you had any authority over an IP network or a domain name; in addition, anyone who wanted to be listed could get in the directory simply by filling out a form.

With the ARPAnet's decommissioning, the DDN NIC stopped supporting a global white-pages directory for the Internet. The DDN NIC still exists, but it supports only a directory of people in a restricted part of the Internet call MILNET (used by the U.S. Department of Defense and its contractors). Currently, the Registration Services portion of the InterNIC, the new Internet information provider,* maintains the **whois** directory for nonmilitary network and domain contacts.

This new **whois** directory is a little different from its predecessor. It does not accept random listings from people who want to be included; it is restricted to people with authority over some bit or piece of the Internet. It is restricted because the **whois** technology was never designed to support very large directories (it does not "scale well"). You can still use these two **whois** directories to find someone, but they really help only if you are looking for someone connected with the networking infrastructure.

That is still not the entire story. When the initial database was split up, the DDN NIC wanted only DDN people, and Registration Services of the InterNIC wanted only network and domain contacts. Others fell to yet another party, the Database Services section of the InterNIC, whose task is to begin building the global white-pages directory. They started their task by putting up these old records in yet a *third* directory.†

There are many ways to access these directories. We will discuss the **whois** command and **telnet** access in detail here. You can also get to these directories through the InterNIC's Gopher (URL: **gopher://ds2.internic.net:70/11/.ds**), WAIS (URL: **http://ds.internic.net/cgi-bin/wais.pl**), and World Wide Web (URL: **http://ds.internic.net/ds/dspg01.htmlservers**), and we will discuss these tools in other chapters. To specify a **whois** server directly, consult the list of **whois** servers available from URL **ftp://rtfm.mit.edu/pub/whois/whois-servers.list**.

To use the **whois** command from your system prompt, just type **whois**, followed by the last name of the person you are looking for:

```
% whois klopfenstein
Klopfenstein, Cyndie (CK191)    clk@THEPOWERCO.COM           303-555-0600
Klopfenstein, Jay (JK436)                                    (312)555-1540
```

*There is a longer explanation of what the InterNIC is and how it works at URL **http://ds.internic.net**.

†This directory is really a WAIS database, but it is searchable through the **whois** interface.

```
The InterNIC Registration Services Host contains ONLY Internet Information
(Networks, ASN's, Domains, and POC's).
Please use the whois server at nic.ddn.mil for MILNET Information.
```

What actually can you search for? Individual names are stored as:

```
last name, first name, titles
```

Matches always begin at the beginning of this text, so it is easiest to look up people by last name. If you are hazy about spelling, you can search on a portion of the last name by ending the search string with a period. For example, the search string **kro.** matches all names beginning with the three characters "kro":

```
% whois kro.
Krokeide, Per-Arne (PK117)                      +47-2-800200
Krokoski, Chester (CK124)  OOSCT1G@GW3.ARMY.MIL  (817) 287-3270
Krol, Ed (EK10)
Krol@UXC.CSO.UIUC.EDU   (217) 333-7886
Krolikoski, Stan (SK139)
KROLIKOS@WPAFB.AF.MIL   (507) 253-7200
Kroll, Carol (CK43)         carol@CS.UTEXAS.EDU  (512) 835-6732
<only a portion of the matches>

The InterNIC Registration Services Host contains ONLY Internet Information
(Networks, ASN's, Domains, and POC's).
Please use the whois server at nic.ddn.mil for MILNET Information.
```

If you match more than one item, **whois** gives you a shortened output format, shown above. The funny string in parentheses, like (EK10) for "Krol, Ed", is a unique identifier known as a *handle*. If you have someone's handle, you can get his or her complete record with another **whois** command:

```
% whois \!ek10
```

The exclamation point tells **whois** that you want to look up a person by handle rather than name. When we first looked up Ed Krol, the last line of the **whois** output said something about this directory containing "only Internet information." The **whois** command has the domain name of a server to query built into it. Because the DDN NIC has been around so long, that is the server **whois** will look up. This was a good idea back when the DDN was the only game in town. Unfortunately, it is not such a good idea now that there are many servers around. When the **whois** database was divided, many **whois** clients pointed to the wrong database. All of a sudden, it was not possible to find people anymore.

To get around this problem, the two major **whois** players, **nic.ddn.mil** and **rs.internic.net**, forward requests to each other. Most **whois** commands let you specify an alternate server by using the **-h** option, followed by the server's address. For example, the command below says "look up the handle **ek10** at the InterNIC":

```
% whois -h rs.internic.net \!ek10
```

Be forewarned: Some **whois** clients support the **-h** option, and some do not. This is really too bad, because there are other **whois**-style services around. Some sites who got into the game early standardized on **whois** for their online phone books. You can access any of these special servers by issuing the **whois** command with a special hostname, as in the previous example.*

So far, we have mentioned searching only two of the three major **whois** directories. How do you get at the third? This time, we will point **whois** at **ds.internic.net**:

```
% whois -h ds.internic.net krol
```

The server at **ds.internic.net** automatically searches all three directories in sequence. Because this server accesses all three databases, it is the best one to use for most requests (unless you know you are looking for someone involved with network management).

You can also access the Registration Services **whois** using **telnet**. Start by **telnet**ing to the **ds.internic.net** address.† When you get there, give **whois** as a login name, and start making queries. For example:

```
% telnet internic.net
Trying... Connected to INTERNIC.NET.

SunOS UNIX 4.1 (rs1) (ttyq6)

***************************************************************************
* -- InterNIC Registration Services Center  --
*
* For wais, type:               WAIS <search string> <return>
* For the *original* whois type: WHOIS [search string] <return>
* For referral whois type:      RWHOIS [search string] <return>
*
* For user assistance call (703) 742-4777
# Questions/Updates on the whois database to HOSTMASTER@internic.net
* Please report system problems to ACTION@internic.net
***************************************************************************
Please be advised that use constitutes consent to monitoring
(Elec Comm Priv Act, 18 USC 2701-2711)

6/1/94
```

---

*There are lists of **whois** servers available. See URL **ftp://rtfm.mit.edu/pub/whois/whois-servers.list**.

†Not every **whois** server allows TELNET access.

```
We are offering an experimental distributed whois service called referral
whois (RWhois). To find out more, look for RWhois documents, a sample
client and server under:
gopher: (rs.internic.net) InterNIC Registration Services ->
        InterNIC Registration Archives -> pub -> rwhois
        anonymous ftp: (rs.internic.net) /pub/rwhois
Cmdinter Ver 1.3 Thu Sep 21 20:51:26 1995 EST
[vt220] InterNIC > whois
Connecting to the rs Database . . . . . .
Connected to the rs Database
InterNIC WHOIS Version: 1.0 Thu, 21 Sep 95 20:52:01

Whois: krol
Krol, Ed (EK10)                    e-krol@UIUC.EDU
        (217) 333-7886 (FAX) 217-244-7089
Whois: [vt220] InterNIC >
Thu Sep 21 20:54:05 1995 EST

Connection closed by Foreign Host
%
```

When you are done, you need to send two **CTRL-D** characters: one to end the **whois** session and one to close the connection to the InterNIC.

The **whois** database contains more than just people. There are several other kinds of entries. This is important for two reasons. First, if you make broad searches, you will probably see some odd stuff returned. Second, you may occasionally need other kinds of information. After the information about users, the most useful data in the **whois** database concerns network and domain ownership. Let's try to find some information about the networks at the University of Illinois. This time, let's do it by e-mail. First, construct a message like the one below, and send it to **mailserv@internic.net**, using your favorite e-mail program:

```
% mail mailserv@internic.net
Subject:
whois University of Illinois

.
```

In about a day, you will get a response containing an answer to the request. It will look something like this:

```
>From mailserv@internic.net Tue Mar  1 07:34:59 1994
Date: Tue, 1 Mar 94 06:17:58 EST
From: mailserv@internic.net (Mail Server)
To: krol@uxh.cso.uiuc.edu
Subject: Re: whois university of illinois
```

```
University of Illinois (ILLINOIS-DOM)                          ILLINOIS.NET
University of Illinois (NET-NCSA-K12-NET) NCSA-K12-NET          192.17.6.0
University of Illinois (NET-UI-ISDN-NET) UI-ISDN-NET            192.17.7.0
University of Illinois (NET-UIUC-CAMPUS-B) UIUC-CAMPUS-B       128.174.0.0
University of Illinois (NET-UIUC-NCSA) UIUC-NCSA              130.126.0.0
University of Illinois (ASN-UIUC) UIUC                                  38
University of Illinois (GARCON) VIXEN.CSO.UIUC.EDU           128.174.5.58
University of Illinois (UIUC)   A.CS.UIUC.EDU               128.174.252.1

<output truncated for space considerations>
```

Our query was about the University of Illinois. But you can use the same technique to inquire about people, domains, and other networks.

## ■ *The USENET User List*

MIT maintains a list of the names and e-mail addresses of everyone who posts USENET news. This list is generated by automatically extracting names and addresses from all the news postings that pass through MIT—which includes just about all of the official and alternative newsgroups described in chapter 8, *Network News*. The extraction itself is fairly simple. Most news messages contain a line like the following:

```
From: krol@ux1.cso.uiuc.edu (Ed Krol)
```

A newsreader uses this information to tell you that someone named Ed Krol posted the message. MIT's address service uses this line to infer that the e-mail address **krol@ux1.cso.uiuc.edu** will probably work if you want to contact Ed Krol.

To use this service, send an e-mail message to **mail-server@rtfm.mit.edu**. The body of the message should look like:

**send usenet-addresses/**search-string

search-string is the name that you are interested in finding. The search-string can be only one word without spaces. Matches will not occur on a partial word. So you can't use "kro" to find "krol." For example, to look up "Ed Krol" using the USENET address database, send a message like this:

```
% mail mail-server@rtfm.mit.edu
Subject:
send usenet-addresses/krol
.
```

Sometime later, you will receive a response:

```
From daemon@bloom-picayune.MIT.EDU Mon Feb 28 09:52:54 1994
Date: Mon, 28 Feb 1994 10:41:09 -0500
```

```
From: mail-server@BLOOM-PICAYUNE.MIT.EDU
To: Ed Krol <krol@uxh.cso.uiuc.edu>
Subject: mail-server: "send usenet-addresses/krol"
Reply-To: mail-server@BLOOM-PICAYUNE.MIT.EDU
Precedence: junk
X-Problems-To: owner-mail-server@rtfm.mit.edu


----cut here----
        krol <krol@TISLINK.TIS.ANL.GOV> (Apr 21 93)
Ed Krol <krol@UX1.CSO.UIUC.EDU> (Aug 3 93)
Melanie.Krol@f152.n321.z1.fidonet.org (Melanie Krol)     (Aug 26 93)
Ed Krol <e-krol@UIUC.EDU>        (Dec 5 93)
e-krol@uiuc.edu (Ed Krol)        (Jan 8 94)
krol@ux1.cso.uiuc.edu (Ed Krol) (Jan 8 94)
Ed Krol <krol@ux1.cso.uiuc.edu> (Oct 15 93)
meajjk@ercx44.Skferc.Nl (Jan Jitze Krol)        (Apr 21 93)
        Rosemary Krol <B42603BC@ANLCV1.BITNET>  (Apr 11 93)
Andrzej Krol <genda@LILY.ICS.AGH.EDU.PL>        (Aug 3 93)
genda@galaxy.uci.agh.edu.pl (Andrzej Krol)      (Feb 11 93)
krol@Mari.Unit.NO (Kristian Olsen)      (Mar 11 93)
```

Notice that the search found multiple Krols, and a few possible e-mail addresses for Ed Krol. You have to figure out, or guess, which address is most likely to reach the person you are looking for.

If your search request fails to locate anyone, the response will look like this:

```
From daemon@bloom-picayune.MIT.EDU Mon Feb 28 09:49:36 1994
Date: Mon, 28 Feb 1994 10:24:25 -0500
From: mail-server@BLOOM-PICAYUNE.MIT.EDU
To: Ed Krol <krol@uxh.cso.uiuc.edu>
Subject: mail-server: "send usenet-addresses/ekrol"
Reply-To: mail-server@BLOOM-PICAYUNE.MIT.EDU
Precedence: junk
X-Problems-To: owner-mail-server@rtfm.mit.edu

----cut here----
No matches for "ekrol".
----cut here----
```

This service has a few minor limitations. First, it does not know about people who do not post news at all, or who post only to local newsgroups, or who post with restricted distribution that does not include the MIT campus.

Somewhat more important, this service depends on information in the **From:** field of news postings. Many users use pseudonyms when they are posting messages. So if Ed Krol has his newsreader configured to post with an alias like "Mr. Hockey," you will not find "Ed Krol" in this directory. If you happen to know that Ed's alias is "Hockey," you could look this up, instead.

# ◼ *X.500 Directory Services*

None of the services we have mentioned so far "scale well." That is, **whois**-style directories work just fine for 70,000 entries, but would fail horribly if asked to list millions of users. As is often the case, the Internet is the victim of its own success; when **whois** was planned, no one thought that the database would ever have 70,000 entries, to say nothing of the millions of Internet users who are not listed.

At the beginning of this chapter, we mentioned the X.500 directory service, adopted by the Organization for International Standardization (ISO). Unlike **whois**, X.500 does scale well (meaning that it is useful regardless of system size). In fact, it is the only currently available technology which does, so it has been chosen for the global online Internet directory that the InterNIC is building. Unfortunately, although it solves the scaling problem, it creates another: The standard offering is very cumbersome to use directly. We will start by talking a bit about the philosophy of X.500, then move on to looking at how to do a search with a public client.

## Native X.500

Let's go back to our first analogy: the phone company. If you were looking up Willie Martin in Chicago, you could start at one end of a shelf of phone books and look at each one sequentially, but it would take all day. Instead, you would find the U.S. section of the shelf, within that find the Illinois section, then find the Chicago directory, and finally look up Willie. This is known as a *tree structure*. Figure 10-1 shows how to model a collection of phone books as a tree.

If you want to find a person, you start at the top and pick the most likely path. When you finally get to the node at the bottom, which has the directory information, you can look up Willie. The path from the top of the tree to the bottom should identify a particular Willie:

```
World, US, IL, Chicago, Willie Martin
```

This points to your Willie, not the one in Grovers Mill.

X.500 views "the white-pages problem" as a library of telephone books. Each participating group is responsible for its own directory, just as Ameritech is responsible for the Chicago phone book. Figure 10-2 shows the tree structure for the X.500 directory service. The structure is very similar to our phone book model, though the labels for each level are different. The levels shown are fairly static. At the organization level, each organization has responsibility for its own lower structure. This is analogous to the set of phone books for Illinois, where any changes to the books, or to their structure, are made by Ameritech.

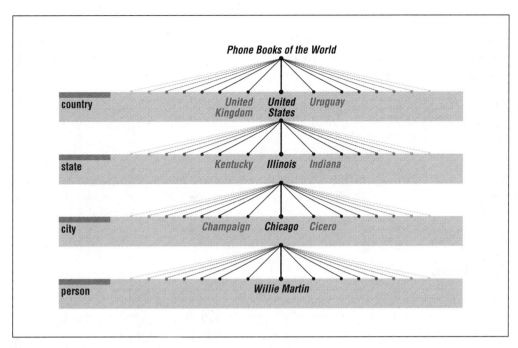

***Figure 10-1*** *Phone book structure*

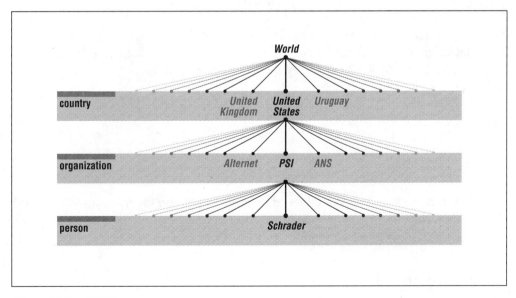

***Figure 10-2*** *X.500 tree structure*

Therefore, with the X.500 service, once you know the right organization, you can probably find the name you want without trouble. If you like, you can poke around and find out about the organization's internal structure, but you do not need to. Limiting your search to the organization will suffice for doing queries.

How does this work? If I were searching for my buddy Bill Schrader, who works for Performance Systems International, I would type something like:

```
c=US@o=PerformanceSystemsInternational@cn=Schrader
```

As you can see, direct X.500 has a fairly complex syntax. You might not have considered **whois** terribly "friendly," but X.500 is less friendly. To be fair, X.500 was designed to be used by computers, rather than people. And, as we know, computers are not bothered by complexity.

### X.500 access

The ISO usually decides that standard terminology is not good enough to describe what they do, so they always develop their own language. X.500 clients are known as Directory User Agents (DUA). To do a white-pages search, you need to get the DUA you are using to contact a Directory Server Agent (DSA), which actually does the search for you. If you are lucky enough to have a DUA on your local computer, you can use it to do queries. If you do not, you need to get at a public DUA somehow.

There are several ways to contact public DUAs: Gopher, WWW, and TELNET all work. We will concentrate on TELNET access using the client at **ds.internic.net**. The InterNIC's DUA breaks down the X.500 directory structure into four levels:

- Person
- Department
- Organization
- Country

How does this work in practice? **telnet** to **ds.internic.net** and log in with the password **x500**. It looks like this:

```
% telnet ds.internic.net
Trying...
Connected to ds.internic.net.
Escape character is '^]'.
              InterNIC Directory and Database Services
```

Welcome to InterNIC Directory and Database Services provided by AT&T.
These services are partially supported through a cooperative agreement
with the National Science Foundation.

First time users may login as guest with no password to receive help.

Your comments and suggestions for improvement are welcome, and can be
mailed to admin@ds.internic.net.

AT&T MAKES NO WARRANTY OR GUARANTEE, OR PROMISE, EXPRESS OR IMPLIED,
CONCERNING THE CONTENT OR ACCURACY OF THE DIRECTORY ENTRIES AND
DATABASE FILES STORED AND MAINTAINED BY AT&T. AT&T EXPRESSLY
DISCLAIMS AND EXCLUDES ALL EXPRESS WARRANTIES AND IMPLIED WARRANTIES
OF MERCHANTABILITY AND FITNESS FOR A PARTICULAR PURPOSE.

```
        ********************************************************
        DSO will be rebooted every Monday morning between 8:00AM and 8:30AM
                    Please use DS1 or DS2 during this period.
        ********************************************************
```

SunOS UNIX (ds)

login: x500
Last login: Fri Sep 22 13:36:45 from bgsuvax.bgsu.edu
SunOS Release 4.1.3 (DS) #3: Tue Feb 8 10:52:45 EST 1994

```
*****************************************************************************
                Welcome to the InterNIC Directory and Database Server.
*****************************************************************************
```

Welcome to the InterNIC X.500 Directory Service

Connecting to the Directory - wait just a moment please ...
You can use this directory service to look up telephone numbers and electronic
mail addresses of people and organisations participating in the Pilot
Directory Service.

Select the mode you would like:

S Simple queries - if you know the name of the organization you want to search
  (this is how the interface always used to behave)

P Power Search - to search many organizations simultaneously

Y Yellow Pages - power searching but allows user to search for an entry
  based on criteria other than the entry name

U Enter search string in form of User-Friendly Name - e.g,
  p barker, ucl, uk

```
I Brief instructions explaining the program modes and how to use the program

? The help facility - usage and topics

Q To quit the program

Enter option: Enter option: S                    For this example, we select S.
?          for HELP with the current question you are being asked
??         for HELP on HELP
q          to quit the Directory Service (confirmation asked unless at the
           request for a person's name)
Control-C  abandon current query or entry of current query

Simp
Person's name, q to quit, * to list people, ? for help
:-
Department name, * to list depts, ? for help
:-
Organization name, * to list orgs, ? for help
:- p*
Country name, <CR> to search 'United States of America', * to list countries, ?
for help
:-
United States

Got the following matches.  Please select one from the list
by typing the number corresponding to the entry you want.
United States
     1 Pace University
     2 Pacific Northwest Laboratory
     3 Performance Systems International
     4 Portland State University
     5 Princeton University
     6 Princeton University Plasma Physics Laboratory
     7 United States Postal Service
Organization name, * to list orgs, ? for help
:-
```

Once you give the login name **x500**, you are logged in without a password, and the search software is available to you. We select option **S** for "Simple queries."

Let's say you want to look up your old friend Bill Schrader again. You remember he changed jobs and now works for the firm "Performance something or other." How do you find him? First, you need to find the organization's exact name. Let's look at all the organizations that start with the letter "p". This can be done by responding to the first two questions (person's name and department name) by pressing ENTER, and typing **p\*** when you are asked for the organization:

```
Enter option: Enter option: S
?          for HELP with the current question you are being asked
??         for HELP on HELP
q          to quit the Directory Service (confirmation asked unless at the
           request for a person's name)
Control-C  abandon current query or entry of current query

Simp
Person's name, q to quit, * to list people, ? for help
:-
Department name, * to list depts, ? for help
:-
Organization name, * to list orgs, ? for help
:- p*                                        Here is where we enter p*
Country name, <CR> to search 'United States of America', * to list countries, ?
for help
:-
United States
```

The **p\*** says: "find all the entries starting with 'p' of type *organization*." Note the use of the \* as a wildcard to match any string of zero or more characters. The result of this search is:

```
Got the following matches.  Please select one from the list
by typing the number corresponding to the entry you want.

United States
    1 Pace University
    2 Pacific Northwest Laboratory
    3 Performance Systems International
    4 Portland State University
    5 Princeton University
    6 Princeton University Plasma Physics Laboratory
    7 United States Postal Service
Organization name, * to list orgs, ? for help
:-
```

Number three looks like a good candidate for Bill's employer. Let's display it by responding to the following query with a **3**:

```
:- 3
United States
  Performance Systems International
    postalAddress        PSI Inc.
                         Reston International Center
                         11800 Sunrise Valley Drive
                         Suite 1100
                         Reston, VA 22091
```

```
                           US
                           PSI Inc.
                           5201 Great American Parkway
                           Suite 3106
                           Santa Clara, CA 95054
                           US
                           PSI Inc.
                           165 Jordan Road
                           Troy, NY 12180
                           US
         telephoneNumber   1-703-620-6651 (Corporate Offices)
                           +1 800-836-0400 (Operations)
                           +1 800-82PSI82 (Sales)
                           +1 518-283-8860 (Troy Office)
                           +1 408-562-6222 (Santa Clara Office)
         fax               +1 703-620-4586
    SPACE for next screen, q to quit pager; or the number of the entry:
```

The search was successful. Now let's try to look up Bill:

```
    Person's name, q to quit, * to list people, ? for help
    :-  schrader
    Department name, * to list depts, <CR> to search all depts, ? for help
    :-                                          press ENTER
    Organisation name, <CR> to search 'Performance Systems International',
            * to list orgs, ? for help
    :-                                          press ENTER
    Country name, <CR> to search 'United States of America', * to list countries, ?
    for help
    :-                                          press ENTER
```

Notice that Performance Systems International became the "default organization" for this search because we displayed it in the previous search. So here we just had to press ENTER at the Organization prompt, rather than retype the name. Here is the successful result:

```
    United States of America
      Performance Systems International
        Reston
          William Schrader
            postalAddress         PSI Inc.
                                  Reston International Center
                                  11800 Sunrise Valley Drive
                                  Suite 1100
                                  Reston, VA 22091
                                  USA
            telephoneNumber       +1 703-620-6651 x310
            fax                   +1 703-620-4586
            electronic mail       wls@psi.com
```

```
Person's name, q to quit, <CR> for 'schrader', * to list people, ? for help
:-  q
If you have any comments, or have had any difficulties while using this
service, or if you would like further information, please contact:
  InterNIC Directory Services Help
  email:          admin@ds.internic.net
Connection closed by foreign host.
```

The quit command, **q**, tells the client that you are finished. This ends the session and logs you out, returning you to the system from which you started.

Remember that X.500 is a decentralized database. Every participating organization is responsible for its own server. Sometimes a server may be unavailable. If this occurs you will get the message:

```
The search for 'schrader' has failed, probably because a Directory
server is temporarily unavailable.

In the meantime, displaying organization details.
For information on people, try again a little later.
```

This means that the server that is responsible for the organization "Performance Systems International" was unavailable; you had better try other means to find the name. You might try the same query a few hours later, on the chance that PSI's server is only temporarily out of commission.

## ■ *Knowbot Information Service*

The *Knowbot Information Service (KIS)* is an experimental white-pages meta-server. That is, it does not itself hold any white-pages data. Instead, it knows about other servers and allows you to query them all through one set of commands. You say "find krol," and it contacts **whois** servers, X.500 servers, **finger** servers, and so on. You do not have to think about what tool to use; Knowbot does that for you.

On the surface, this sounds so nice that you are probably wondering why we bothered talking about the other servers. For two reasons: First, Knowbots are actually an area of research that far exceeds just white-pages services. (They are discussed more generally in chapter 14, *Other Applications*.) KIS is one of the first Knowbot applications. Because the area is so new, any part of it may change or become unavailable for a time. We did not want you to be left high and dry should this occur.

The second reason is that the Knowbot "ease of use" philosophy is currently somewhat constrained by practicality. KIS could easily be made to access every host on the Internet when looking for a person, but the search would take days. Therefore, you do not really escape the basic phone book problem: You need to know something about how to search before you can search effectively. A Knowbot can use **finger**, but only if you tell it on what host to inquire. It can use X.500, but only if you tell it an organization. In short, you have to know enough about these services to use them through KIS, but why bother? It is far easier to inquire with **finger** directly than to have a Knowbot do the search for you.

Nevertheless, Knowbots are useful, because they know how to access some unusual directories. One such service is the MCImail directory, which contains information about users of MCI mailboxes. Another unusual directory is the RIPE directory, which contains the names and addresses of Internet networking people in Europe. Let's see how it works.

KIS can be used with **telnet**. You **telnet** to port 185 of **info.cnri.reston.va.us**. On UNIX, you'd use the command:

```
% telnet info.cnri.reston.va.us 185
```

You will be asked to add your e-mail address to the KIS "guestbook"; if you want to be private, you can ignore this. The easiest way to use KIS is to type the name you want to find at the prompt. For example, let's look up "krol" again, this time using KIS:

```
% telnet info.cnri.reston.va.us
Trying 132.151.1.15...
Connected to info.cnri.reston.va.us.
Escape character is '^]'.

              Knowbot Information Service
KIS Client (V2.0).    Copyright CNRI 1990.    All Rights Reserved.

The KIS system is undergoing some changes.
Type 'news' at the prompt for more information
Type 'help' for a quick reference to commands.

Backspace characters are '^H' or DEL

Please enter your email address in our guest book...
(Your email address?) > krol@ux1.cso.uiuc.edu

> krol
Connected to KIS server (V1.0). Copyright CNRI 1990. All Rights Reserved.

Trying whois at ds.internic.net...

The ds.internic.net whois server is being queried:

No match for "KROL"

The rs.internic.net whois server is being queried:
```

```
Krol, Ed (EK10)          Krol@UXC.CSO.UIUC.EDU
   University of Illinois
   Computing and Communications Service Office
   195 DCL
   1304 West Springfield Avenue
   Urbana, IL 61801-4399
   (217) 333-7886

<This goes on to match a number of other krols in various directories>
> quit
```

You can make as many requests as you like in this fashion. When you are done, type **quit** to exit.

If your request had not been serviced at the NIC, the Knowbot would have gone ahead and tried a number of other places. Unless you tell it otherwise, it will try, by default, the following directories:

- DDN NIC and InterNIC **whois** servers
- MCImail
- RIPE

KIS knows how to search in many more places, including most of the places we have visited in this chapter and some we have not. You can get a list of all the directories it knows about with the command **services**:

```
> services
nic
mcimail
ripe
latin-america-nic
x500
finger
nwhois
quipu-country
quipu-org
>
```

If you want one of these listed directories used in the search, such as the combined Latin-American directories, add it with the **service** command:

```
> service latin-america-nic
```

When you are done, you can exit by typing **quit**.

# ◾ *Netfind*

Netfind is a useful but intrusive way to find people. Rather than a white-pages directory, it is more like a private investigator. You tell Netfind to find someone, give it some idea about where to look, and it searches that general geographical area for you. On the surface this sounds great, but it should be employed only in the most desperate cases. It is not an extremely efficient use of your time, nor of the computer resources on the Net; and, like a private investigator, it is intrusive.

Netfind does its work in two phases. In the first phase, it takes the list of "hints" you gave and locates every domain in that geographical area. If the list is small enough, it then uses a variety of means, like **finger**, to interrogate each machine in the area. If there are too many domains, Netfind shows you the list and asks you to pick a likely few, then does its **finger**ing within your selected domains. Already you might see the problem. If you do not know where someone is, you might not know enough to pick likely domains. Because of the dynamic nature of Netfind's search procedures, and variations in Internet availability, different results can be obtained for the same search on different occasions.

The most common way to do a Netfind search is to **telnet** to a Netfind server; alternatively, you can use Netfind through an integrated package like Gopher. As before, we will concentrate on TELNET access here. To start, pick a server from Table 10-1 and **telnet** to it.

Once there, you enter a search string something like this:

```
name key key
```

*name* is usually the person's last name, and the *key*s are keywords ("hints") used to constrain the search to an area. In all of the search strings you give, case is ignored. The keys can be city and state names (if you know them) or domain names (separated by spaces rather than periods). For example, let's look for "krol" at a university in Illinois:

```
krol university illinois                              look at universities in Illinois
```

Netfind says the search is too broad, and it returns a list of hundreds of domains where it would be happy to look, some of which are:

```
cs.uiuc.edu (computer science department, university of illinois, urbana-champaign)
csl.uiuc.edu (university of illinois, urbana-champaign)
cso.uiuc.edu (computing services office, university of illinois, urbana-champaign)
cso.niu.edu (northern illinois university, dekalb, illinois)
csrd.uiuc.edu (university of illinois, urbana-champaign)
```

*Table 10-1　Public Netfind Access Sites\**

| Host | Country |
|------|---------|
| archie.au | Australia |
| bruno.cs.colorado.edu | USA |
| dino.conicit.ve | Venezuela |
| ds.internic.net | USA |
| eis.calstate.edu | USA |
| hto-e.usc.edu | USA |
| krnic.net | Korea |
| lincoln.technet.sg | Singapore |
| malloco.ing.puc.cl | Chile |
| monolith.cc.ic.ac.uk | Great Britain |
| mudhoney.micro.umn.edu | USA |
| netfind.anu.edu.au | Australia |
| netfind.ee.mcgill.ca | Canada |
| netfind.if.usp.br | Brazil |
| netfind.oc.com | USA |
| netfind.vslib.cz | Czech Republic |
| nic.uakom.sk | Slovakia |
| redmont.cis.uab.edu | USA |

\*See URL http://www.earn.net/gnrt/netfind.html.

The search is too broad because it will look at the University of Illinois, Urbana; the University of Illinois, Chicago; Illinois State University; and so on. If you really wanted to narrow the search, you could do Urbana, but there are still hundreds of domains at the University of Illinois, Urbana. The search becomes productive only if you know that this guy works for the Computing Services Office (**cso**):

```
Please form a more specific query.
Enter person and keys (blank to exit) --> krol illinois university cso
( 0) check_name: checking domain cso.uiuc.edu.  Level = 0
( 1) check_name: checking domain cso.niu.edu.  Level = 0
MAIL FOR Ed Krol IS FORWARDED TO krol@ux1.cso.uiuc.edu

NOTE:   this is a domain mail forwarding arrangement - so mail intended
        for "krol" should be addressed to "krol@cso.uiuc.edu"
        rather than "krol@ux1.cso.uiuc.edu".
```

```
( 0) check_name: checking host ux1.cso.uiuc.edu.  Level = 0
The domain 'cso.niu.edu' does not run its own name servers,
        and there is no aliased domain IP address/CNAME/MX record for
        this domain -> Skipping domain search phase for this domain.
SYSTEM: ux1.cso.uiuc.edu
        Login name: ajzxmvk                    In real life: Marge Krol
        Directory: /mnt/courtesy/ajzxmvk       Shell: /bin/csh
        Last login Thu Jan 20 17:06 on ttysk from goofy.aiss.uiuc.
        No Plan.

        Login name: krol                       In real life: Ed Krol
        Directory: /cso/staff/krol             Shell: /bin/csh
        On since Feb 28 08:15:46 on ttyph from maced
```

If you know that much about "krol," you can look directly in the University of Illinois' online white-pages server and be sure, rather than **finger**ing every machine at the campus.

The bottom line is that if you have any clue about someone's whereabouts, it is probably better to use a few of the online white-pages servers than Netfind. If the last you heard, Willie Martin was a computer programmer at an Illinois university, it would probably be faster to try every online phone book in Illinois looking for "martin, wil*" than to use Netfind. If you look in a white-pages directory for "martin, wil*" and it doesn't find anyone, you can be reasonably sure he is not there and move on to another directory. With Netfind, you never know. You might look for Willie in an Illinois university, and it would return hundreds of departmental domain names, most of which hire programmers. You can waste a long time searching and come up empty.

Even if you know someone's whereabouts, there is no guarantee that Netfind will work. Let's say that you know that Willie is a chemist at the University of Illinois. There is no reason, however, to believe that you will find him by searching the Chemistry Department. There is a good chance you will, but he may pick up his mail at a computer with a domain of **cso**. Netfind works best when you can make good educated guesses about where people are located; and those guesses are often really hard to make.

## ■ *Commercial E-mail Directories*

It is becoming easier to find the account name for someone using a commercial online account, such as with a company like America Online, CompuServe, The Microsoft Network, or Prodigy.

A commercial organization, Four11 (URL: **http://www.Four11.com**), offers a service that maintains a growing, central database of e-mail and address information. It is based

Chapter 10 — Finding Someone

on voluntary participation and an expanded, fee-based service. It may be a while before it becomes comprehensive enough to warrant the fee payment.

Commercial online services have their own e-mail directories that allow their users to find one another. As full Internet access is completed, online directories can be expected. If you have the username for a particular service, here is a reminder of syntax conventions for the "big three" online services:

For America Online:

> *user*`@aol.com`

For Prodigy:

> *user*`@prodigy.com`

For CompuServe:

> *nnnnn.nnn*`@compuserve.com`

In the CompuServe example, *nnnnn.nnn* refers to the CompuServe account ID, but do note that the Internet e-mail address uses a period instead of the CompuServe login sequence that uses a comma.

## ▣ *The Final Words on E-mail Lookup*

Human intervention can be missed as perhaps the most obvious solution to finding someone's e-mail address. If you have a person's e-mail domain name, you can try to reach a human "postmaster" by using the address **postmaster** *@domain.name* to send a query about a user address. Responses will vary by the person who reads the postmaster's mail. Some will be more cooperative than others (who might be reasonably uncooperative if it is clear that no effort was made to find the person's e-mail address). In general, this approach ought to be reserved for near emergencies.

If you were to find the address of a friend or colleague, there are a number of ways you might pursue it. You can check for a listing in your own address book, you can look for an old business card, or perhaps you can find an old piece of correspondence. If all else fails, there is a good chance you can find a phone number using directory assistance of the town in which he lives or from the organization at which he works or goes to school. An easily missed point in finding e-mail addresses is this: In many cases, you may be just as well off calling the person whose e-mail address you need. This can be the fastest and most foolproof method available to you (at least until more comprehensive and user-friendly e-mail address directories are introduced).

# ■ *Exercises*

*For each of the following exercises, print out your results to show that you were able to find each item. If using a GUI, you can easily cut-and-paste your answers from your online session into a word processor. Seek help locally if you need it.*

Any e-mail search tool will be limited to the database it queries. If this sounds familiar, it should, because no matter how sophisticated the tool, it is the database that will give a successful result. Test the utility of the various e-mail address tools by seeking the e-mail address for a friend at your school, one at another school, and a public figure such as a politician. If you need a suggestion, you can always try an unusual name like Ed Krol or Bruce Klopfenstein. In the first exercises, compare *each* e-mail address database on at least three criteria you select for those tools. Here are some example criteria:

- size of the database
- response time of the search
- precision of the search (how many "hits" include names other than that for which you are searching)
- search keys available
- ability to modify the search based on results
- natural language interface

You may try URL **gopher://ds.internic.net/11/.ds/.whitepages** to access some of these tools. Another possibility is URL **http://sunsite.unc.edu/~masha.**

1. finger

2. InterNIC

3. Netfind

4. whois

5. X.500

6. A commercial service (use one of the following if necessary)

    LookUP! (URL: **http://www.lookup.com**)

    Four11 (URL: **http://www.four11.com**)

7. Of all the sites you tried, which one will you try first from now on to find an e-mail address?

**8.** What interface does your local system provide for seeking e-mail addresses?

**9.** If you know the name of a site where someone (whose real name you know) has an e-mail account, suggest three ways you can use that site to discover that person's e-mail address.

**10.** How can you find the e-mail address of someone at a commercial online service such as America Online, CompuServe, eWorld, The Microsoft Network, or Prodigy?

**11.** What are some advantages and disadvantages of your registering your own e-mail address in Internet directories?

# CHAPTER ELEVEN

# TUNNELING THROUGH THE INTERNET: GOPHER

*The Internet Gopher*
*Finding Internet Resources*
*Using Bookmarks*
*Gopher Development*
*A Last Word*

I n the past few chapters, we have talked about tools that allow you to do particular tasks: find people, documents, software, or data. The next three chapters introduce you to some tools that can do much more. They try to be "friendly" and help you to search a variety of online resources. To understand what each of these tools does, consider your local public library. It is convenient and it has a collection of books and periodicals on its shelves. It also belongs (most likely) to a system of cooperating libraries. The library in the next town belongs to the same system, and there are both overlapping and unique materials in each. If your library does not have something, the neighboring library will honor your library privileges. You do not even need to visit the other library in person. You talk to your local librarian, arrange an interlibrary loan, and the materials you need are shipped from the next town to you.

This chapter discusses Gopher, a remarkable menu-driven tool that lets you prowl through the Internet by selecting resources from menu choices. If you want to use one of the resources that Gopher presents, it helps you access it. This is like helping you browse the remote library's card catalog and automatically sending the material you want. It does not really matter where the library is located, so long as it is part of the Gopher system. To veteran Internet users, the introduction of Gopher seemed like we had reached Net Nirvana. Gopher clients provide gateways to other information systems (World Wide Web, WAIS, Archie, **whois**) and to network services (TELNET, FTP). Gopher is often the most convenient way to navigate in an FTP directory and to download files, especially if you have a text-only interface to the WWW (i.e., no Windows or Macintosh). In a nutshell, Gopher pulled various Internet resources together in a menu-driven environment.

In the next chapter, we will look at the Wide Area Information Service (WAIS). This service helps you search indexed material. You can search for particular words or phrases; it gives you a list of online files that contain those words. WAIS is like walking into a library with a quote ("These are the times that try men's souls"), and having the library automatically check out everything that contains the quote.

In chapter 13, *The World Wide Web and Netscape Navigator,* we will discuss the newest arrival from the Internet's toolshop. The World Wide Web promises to replace all other individual interfaces between the user and the networked information on the Web. On the surface, the Web looks like a variation on Gopher: It is another menu-based service that helps you access different resources. The Web is based on a much more flexible "hypertext" model that allows cross-references, or links, among related resources. Some of these related resources may also be different media. It allows pictures, text, and audio to all appear as one image. Unlike Gopher, the Web is a "read/write" resource (at least potentially). It really offers a different paradigm for working: If you have a Web server and a hypertext editor, it will support all kinds of collaboration and joint authorship. The number of Web servers on the Internet has grown exponentially since 1993. It is still a chore to create hypertext, because hypertext editors are scarce; but the potential here makes the World Wide Web one of the most interesting new tools on the Internet.

Gopher really is more difficult to describe than it is to use. To understand its utility, read this chapter while online at a Gopher server. Remember that you cannot do anything to harm the Gopher server. It simply waits for your information requests and it will answer them.

## The Internet Gopher

*Gopher,* or more accurately, "the Internet Gopher," allows you to browse for resources using menus. When you find something you like, you can read or access it through Gopher *without having to worry about* domain names, IP addresses, changing programs, and the like. For example, if you want to access the online library catalog at the University of California, rather than looking up the address and **telnet**ing to it, you find an entry in a Gopher menu and select it. Gopher then "goes for" it.*

The huge advantage of Gopher is not just that you do *not* have to look up the address or name of the resources, or that you do *not* have to use several commands to get what you want. The real cleverness is that it lets you browse through the Internet's resources, regardless of their type, just as you might browse through your local library, with books, filmstrips, and phonograph records on the same subject grouped together.

---

*Although this use of the word "gopher" seems to fit nicely, it is not how the name came into being. The menu-based system for navigating the Internet was developed at the University of Minnesota, whose nickname is the Golden Gophers.

Let's say you are interested in information about the American West: history, climatological data, mineralogy, and so on. You can use Gopher to wander around the Internet, looking for data. By looking through a menu of "online catalogs" or "libraries" (the exact menu item will vary, depending on your server), you see that the University of California library catalog is available, and you know that its collection of Western Americana is very strong; so you access the catalog and try to look up relevant books. (You may even be able to use Gopher to arrange interlibrary loans through the online catalog, if the library permits it.) A search of FTP archives finds some data about the relationship between drought cycles and snow pack, which is interesting; looking further, you might find some meteorological statistics from the time of the Gold Rush. Yes, you still need to know what you are looking for, and a little bit about where the resource might be located, but Gopher makes the search less painful.

To think about how to use Gopher, it is best to return to our well-worn library metaphor. Think of the pre-Gopher Internet as a set of public libraries *without* card catalogs and librarians. To find something, you have to wander aimlessly until you stumble on something interesting. This kind of library is not very useful, unless you already know in great detail what you want to find and where you are likely to find it. A Gopher server is like hiring a librarian, who creates a card-catalog subject index. You can find something by thumbing through the subject list, then showing the card to the librarian and asking, "Could you help me get this, please?" If you do not find it in one library, you can electronically walk to the next and check there.

Unfortunately, Gopher services usually did not hire highly trained librarians. There is no standard subject list, like the Library of Congress Subject Headings, used on most Gophers to organize things. The people who maintain each server took their best shot at organizing the world, or at least their piece of it. It is the same state we would be in if one library had things filed under a subject called "Folklore, American," and another had the same works under "Funny Old Stories." Each server may be organized differently, but the Gopher interface itself will work the same.

Gopher does not allow you to access anything that would not be available by other means. There are no specially formatted "Gopher resources" out there for you to access, in the sense that there are FTP archives or white-pages directories.*

Once you find something you want, Gopher will also help you. Gopher uses whatever application (**telnet**, **ftp**, white pages, etc.) is needed to get a particular item in which you are interested and does it for you. Each resource is handled differently, but they are all handled in an intuitive manner, consistent with the feel of the Gopher client you are using.

---

*Some files might be available only through Gopher, but that is strictly a security issue. If you access those files through Gopher, they actually come to you via FTP.

If you have followed the discussion so far, you should realize that it really does not matter what Gopher server you contact first. Your home server determines only the first menu you see. The other menus all come from whatever server is appropriate at that point. Each server, like each library, has a unique collection.* Popular files, such as collections of frequently asked questions, may be in several places. Obscure collections of data might be found only through a single server. If you do not find what you want at your initial library, you can search elsewhere. When you find what you like, get it by

---

### Where Gopher Was Born

The name "Gopher" is an interesting pun. It started out as a distributed campus information service at the University of Minnesota, home of the "Golden Gophers." Because its primary function is to "go for" information, the name "Gopher" was coined and stuck.

The service was designed so that each piece of a bureaucracy could have control over its own server and data. That is, the school administration could have a computer in the administration building that could deliver information on "administrivia." The athletic department could have a sports-schedule server in its offices. Each academic department could provide a server with a class schedule; and so on. There can be as many servers as there are groups who want to provide them.

Gopher's developers then created a special application that could guide students to the information, with no training required. To do this, they organized the system by topic so that it looks like one large database, rather than hundreds of smaller databases. It can access files in FTP archives, phone numbers from white-pages servers, and library catalogs and other databases with special-purpose (TELNET-based) servers. Only Gopher knows where the data really is and how to access it, and that there are multiple servers providing it.

It did not take much effort to see that if this could work for a bunch of servers in various departments, it could work for servers all over the world. All it took was the Internet to connect them all together. In the space of about four years, the Gopher system has gone from one site to more than 1,300 sites.

---

*In reality, the collection might be housed elsewhere, but that is the beauty of Gopher. It does not matter where the collection is; it will be retrieved automatically should you request it.

interlibrary loan. With libraries, this can take a while; with Gopher, getting material from somewhere else is instantaneous.

Finally, the system is smart enough to enforce licensing restrictions. Some software or resources (e.g., online newspapers) may be licensed for use only within a particular city or campus. You may access a remote Gopher server, but it may prevent you from accessing a particular resource because you are not local. This is annoying, but inability to enforce licensing has been a major stumbling block in the delivery of online information. If a university has a contract with a database provider to make certain information available to that campus community, it is paid for based upon those users. Gopher helps the university by limiting access to local users.

## Finding a Gopher Client

To access the Gopher system, you need a **gopher** client program. The special client software must be installed on a computer that is on the Internet. There is free **gopher** client software for just about any computer you might have (UNIX, Macintosh, IBM/ PC, X Windows, VAX/VMS, VM/CMS, etc.).

Each client has the "look and feel" of the system it runs on. If you are an IBM/PC user, the PC version will work just like other PC applications. The Macintosh version will look like a hypercard stack with buttons to push. The X Windows version also has a point-and-click interface. Almost anything that you can do with one **gopher** client you can do with another. It may be easier if you have a mouse, but it works just fine without one. Ultimately, the choice of a client is not important; find one that suits your taste. You can get the software you need from the anonymous FTP site URL **ftp:// boombox.micro.umn.edu**, in the directory *pub/gopher.* You can also use Archie to find other sources for the client software (and a good way to practice).

Whichever client you decide to install, it will be preconfigured with the Internet address of a home server. Because all servers are public, it does not really matter where it points initially. You can start the client, get a menu, and use **gopher**. When you have some experience, you can decide which Gopher server you want to be your home and change the configuration accordingly.*

We start by using the nongraphical version of **gopher**. It is worth learning. First, you do not need a mouse or a super graphics monitor. Second, when you are starting off with **gopher**, you are more likely to access the client on a "public" client computer somewhere, rather than set up a new client on your own system. If you use **telnet** (or a dial-up

---

*How you change the configuration varies from client to client. Check the documentation that comes with the client you have installed. If you are using this on campus, everything has already been set up for you.

*Table 11-1    Public Gopher Access Sites*

| Address | Location |
| --- | --- |
| (Log in as **gopher** unless indicated otherwise.) | |
| info.anu.edu.au | Australia (login: **info**) |
| tolten.puc.cl | Columbia |
| ecnet.ec | Ecuador |
| gopher.ebone.net | Europe |
| gan.ncc.go.jp | Japan |
| gopher.chalmers.se | Sweden |
| gopher.sunet.se | Sweden |
| consultant.micro.umn.edu | USA |
| gopher.msu.edu | USA |
| ux1.cso.uiuc.edu | USA |
| panda.uiowa.edu | USA* (login: **panda**) |

*panda.uiowa.edu uses a different line-oriented Gopher client (called **panda**) than the one we discuss. It works just fine, but you may need to check out the help facility to use it.

modem) to access a Gopher server on a remote system, you are most likely to see the UNIX text-only client.

If you want to try **gopher** at one of the public Gopher sites, pick one from Table 11-1 that is geographically close to you. **telnet** to the computer name shown and log in using the corresponding login name. It will automatically start **gopher** for you when you log in.

Public-access Gophers are fine for getting the flavor of the Gopher system, but you will be severely hampered in certain areas. Any use that either (1) leaves the Gopher system, such as accessing TELNET resources, (2) requires disk space, such as saving files you find, or (3) e-mails the results will be prohibited. If you want to do these things, you must access a client on a computer on which you have your own account (which is likely the case on campus).

## How Gopher Works

When you first start up a **gopher** client, it contacts its home server and asks for its main menu. The server sends the menu and some hidden information to your client. The hidden information tells your client what each item on the menu represents (e.g., a text file, a directory, a host, a white-pages server, etc.), the IP address of a server for that item, a port number to use, and a directory path to a file. The IP address could be the home server itself, if that is where the resource resides; it could just as easily be another server somewhere else. It does not matter; when you pick a menu item, the client does the same thing. Your client saves its current position (in case you want to return) and contacts the new server. Then the process repeats itself.

Eventually, you will choose a resource rather than a menu. Your **gopher** client will choose an appropriate utility for dealing with the resource you select, whatever it is. If it is a file, the client **ftps** it for you. If the resource is a login resource (i.e., a system you can log in to), it creates a TELNET session. If it is a collection indexed by Archie or WAIS, Gopher uses Archie or WAIS to find out what is relevant. The **gopher** client you are using allows you to speak to it in a screen-oriented, menu-driven fashion. It takes what you say and turns it into real commands for the appropriate application. So, if you are in Gopher, you never have to type an **ftp get** command.

## ■ *Finding Internet Resources*

Getting started is easy. To start a **gopher** client on a text-only system like UNIX, type the command:

```
% gopher
```

or **telnet** to one of the public-access clients. Whatever client you use, and whatever Gopher server it connects to, your first menu will look something like this (which comes from URL **telnet://consultant.micro.umn.edu**):

```
            Internet Gopher Information Client v2.1.3

               Home Gopher server: gopher.tc.umn.edu

    -->  1.  Information About Gopher/
         2.  Computer Information/
         3.  Discussion Groups/
         4.  Fun & Games/
         5.  Internet file server (ftp) sites/
         6.  Libraries/
```

```
   7.  News/
   8.  Other Gopher and Information Servers/
   9.  Phone Books/
  10.  Search Gopher Titles at the University of Minnesota <?>
  11.  Search lots of places at the University of Minnesota <?>
  12.  University of Minnesota Campus Information/

Press ? for Help, q to Quit
```

Note that **gopher** is accessible via a WWW browser like Netscape. This same site is shown via Netscape in Figure 11-1. As usual, the difference between the WWW and the text-based version is that you can use the mouse to navigate from point to point on the Web version, whereas you enter menu numbers manually in the text-based version.

If your initial server resides at the University of Minnesota, you may find items in the menu about Minnesota campus events. If you use the University of Illinois, you will find items of interest to its students. In addition to these local-interest categories, though, you will always find a few topics of general interest. For example, note items 6, online library catalogs; 7, news (which has a link to current weather and forecasts on the next page); and 8, software and data sources. You will also find a way to reach other servers (items 10 and 11), and are likely to find some introductory information (item 1). Usually it will be pretty obvious what an item is from the menu entry. If it is not, try accessing it and see if it looks interesting.

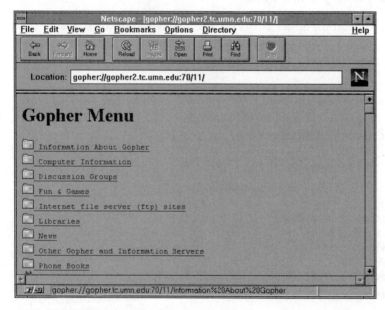

*Figure 11-1    Search results shown via Netscape*

**gopher** keeps track of several different types of entities. The most important are directories and text files; we will see the others later. All clients use some kind of flag to show you what kind of entity any menu item represents. The client we are using puts a slash at the end of a line to denote a directory.* A directory is really equivalent to another menu. That is, if you select a directory and access it, you will see another menu—this time, one that is more specific to your topic. (Selecting item 8 gives you a menu of other Gopher servers.)

With this Gopher implementation, you move between menu items by typing the line number you want, or by using the arrow keys to move up and down the screen. As you move around the menu, the arrow on the left will show you which item is selected. If you are interested in libraries, you would move the cursor (i.e., the arrow) to number 6.

Notice that the line has a slash (/) on the end of it. This indicates that it is a directory; expect another menu when you access it. When you want to access this directory, or any other resource you have selected, press ENTER or RIGHT ARROW. In this case, your screen changes to:

```
        Internet Gopher Information Client v2.1.3

          MINITEX Library Information Network

  --> 1.  About The MINITEX Gopher
      2.  MINITEX Programs and Services/
      3.  MINITEX Messenger/
      4.  MINITEX VERONICA Service/
      5.  MINITEX Training Sessions, Workshops and Events/
      6.  Internet and Bitnet Addresses for MINITEX Participants/
      7.  Other Gophers and Information Servers/
      8.  Feedback about the MINITEX Gopher/
      9.  Committees and Task Forces/
      10. Internet Guides/
      11. What's New on the 'Net/

      12. Search Menu Items in the MINITEX Gopher <?>

  Press ? for Help, q to Quit                       Page: 1/1
```

You can do several other things besides selecting a menu item. Sometimes a menu will not fit onto a single screen. The **Page** item in the lower-right corner shows you how much material there is and where you are. (This example happens to be page 1 of 1.) To move between pages, press the < key to move backward and > to move forward. Sometimes you may find yourself in a menu with many pages, perhaps more than 20. An easy way

---

*Fancier clients (such as Macintosh or X clients) will most likely use an icon.

to search for things with a menu is with the **/** command. In response to this command, **gopher** asks:

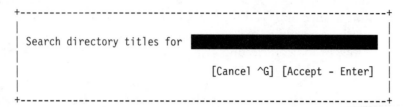

```
+--------------------------------------------------------------+
|                                                              |
| Search directory titles for  ██████████████████████         |
|                                                              |
|                               [Cancel ^G]  [Accept - Enter]  |
|                                                              |
+--------------------------------------------------------------+
```

You type the string you are searching for and then press ENTER. Gopher positions the cursor at the next menu item that contains that string. If Gopher cannot find the string you are looking for, you will get a message saying "Search failed."

If you find yourself somewhere you did not want to be, or if you decide that you are done with a topic, you can move up to where you came from by pressing the **u** key. If you did this now, you would move back up to the main menu. If you really get lost, you can get back to your main menu anytime by pressing **m**. Finally, when you are done with **gopher**, press the **q** (quit) key to exit. This is all it takes to use **gopher**.

## *Looking at Text Files*

The first menu we looked at showed us only directories. This second menu (Libraries) also shows directories (/). We need to continue searching before we get to entries that end in periods rather than slashes. These are text files. To read a text file, access it just like you accessed a directory: Select it and press ENTER or the RIGHT ARROW key.

For example, let's try another Gopher server, Academe This Week, available via **gopher** to **chronicle.merit.edu** (URL: **gopher://chronicle.merit.edu**). Here's what it looks like when you connect:

```
                Internet Gopher Information Client v2.1.3
                Home Gopher server: chronicle.merit.edu

    --> 1.  NEW in "ACADEME THIS WEEK"
        2.  "ACADEME TODAY": a new on-line service for Chronicle subscribers/
        3.  A GUIDE to The Chronicle of Higher Education, September 29, 1995/
        4.  INFORMATION TECHNOLOGY in Academe/
        5.  -- News of Information Technology
        6.  -- Information provided by Lotus Development Corporation/
        7.  FINANCES AND PERSONAL PLANNING in Academe/
        8.  -- News of Finances and Personal Planning
        9.  -- Information provided by TIAA-CREF/
```

```
10. -- Information provided by VALIC/
11. -- Information provided by Fidelity Investments/
12. NOTABLE INTERNET RESOURCES in Academe/
13. BEST-SELLING BOOKS in Academe: a new list
14. EVENTS AND DEADLINES in Academe/
15. 1995 FACTS AND FIGURES on U.S. higher education/
16. JOBS in and out of Academe: more than 610 openings/
17. INFORMATION about The Chronicle's publications/
18. ABOUT "ACADEME THIS WEEK": search tips and more/

Press ? for Help, q to Quit                              Page: 1/1Press
```

Let's say you want to peek at the BEST-SELLING BOOKS in Academe. Type **13**, which is the line number, and press ENTER. The carriage return moves the selection arrow to line 13 and accesses the document; you will see something like this on your screen:

```
BEST-SELLING BOOKS in Academe: a new list (2k)                      39%
+----------------------------------------------------------------------+

   WHAT THEY'RE READING ON COLLEGE CAMPUSES

   Best-selling books in college bookstores,
   compiled by The Chronicle of Higher Education

                                              Previous
                                              Survey
                                              --------
      1. THE STONE DIARIES, by Carol Shields .........   5
      2. THE ALIENIST, by Caleb Carr ................    1
      3. INSOMNIA, by Stephen King ...................    -
      4. CHICKEN SOUP FOR THE SOUL, compiled by
         Jack Canfield and Mark Victor Hansen ........    -
      5. THE BODY FARM, by Patricia Cornwell .........    -
      6. THE HOT ZONE, by Richard Preston ...........    2
      7. MEMNOCH THE DEVIL, by Anne Rice ............    3
      8. DEBT OF HONOR, by Tom Clancy ...............    4
      9. POLITICALLY CORRECT BEDTIME STORIES,
+----------------------------------------------------------------------+
```

[PageDown: d] [Pageup: b] [Help: ?] [Exit: q] [Find: /] [Download: D] Network

Pressing the SPACEBAR advances you to the next screen of text. Clients that are more window-oriented use a scroll bar to page back and forth. When you get to the end of the text (by pressing the SPACEBAR) or quit (by pressing **q**), **gopher** asks what you want to do next:

```
Press <RETURN> to continue, <m> to mail, <s> to save: ▮
```

Press ENTER if you want to return to the menu from which you selected this item. If you want a copy of the document you are looking at, you can get one either by e-mail or as a file.*

You can e-mail a copy of the file to yourself (or anyone else) by pressing **m**. You will see a prompt like this:

```
Mail document to: ▮
```

Then type your e-mail address:

```
Mail document to: klopfens@bgsuvax.bgsu.edu
```

followed by ENTER. Eventually, you will receive the document as an e-mail message; you can use your favorite e-mail program to read it and save it, just like any other message.

You also can save a copy of the item in your file space on the computer running the **gopher** client. This might not be of much use if you are using a public client, because you will not have any file space on the client's computer. If you ran the client on a computer that allows you to create files, you can wander the world, collecting souvenirs as you go. When you get home, you can admire your collection. To save a file, press **s**. **gopher** asks:

```
Enter save filename: ▮
```

Type the filename you want for the saved article. **gopher** saves the article in the current directory (the one that was in effect when the **gopher** client started). It does not matter what Gopher server you happen to be using or where the data resides: **gopher** knows how to move the file to the computer that is running your client.

In the next few sections, we will visit a few other menus. These should give you a feel for how to navigate through Gopher and what kinds of information you are likely to find.

## Moving to Other Servers

By poking around with **gopher** on your home server, you might find 80 percent of everything you ever wanted to find. Now you need to find the other 20 percent. You can do this by poking around on other servers. **gopher**'s main menu will usually have an entry that looks something like:

```
--> 8.  Other Gopher and Information Servers/
```

---

*Mail and save are disabled if you are using a public-access Gopher.

The wording may change from server to server. Sometimes it may be one level down in menus, underneath Other Services or something like that. It may be hidden, but it is always there.

Moving from one server to another is no different from any other search: You look through menus and pick a resource. So, after picking the Other Gophers entry, you may have to go through a few screens to find one you want. Some servers break them up alphabetically, according to the server's name:

```
1.  Gopher Servers (A-G)/
2.  Gopher Servers (G-T)/
3.  Gopher Servers (U-Z)/
```

Some break them up by geographical area, usually by continent. Move around until you find an entry you want to try:

```
--> 1.  CICNET gopher server/
    2.  CONCERT Network -- Research Triangle Park, NC, USA/
    3.  Cornell Information Technologies Gopher/
    4.  Cornell Law School/
```

Notice that other servers are flagged as directories: Their menu entries end in a slash. If you think about it, this makes sense—if you access any of these servers, you get a menu of services. It is not important that the services are provided by another server.

From the preceding list, you might be able to gather that some servers are general, like the one we have been using. Some, like the server at the Cornell Law School (number 4), have a particular focus. On a focused server, you might not find any of the specific items we have seen so far, such as the list of top-selling books or a general directory of white-pages services. *You will always find a way to move to other Gophers.* If your interests lie in the area of one of these special servers, you might consider making it your home base; the Cornell Law School server would be an obvious choice if you are specifically interested in legal questions. It can place much of the information you need for day-to-day existence at your fingertips, and someone else maintains it for you.

If you already have a particular server in mind, there is an easier way to get to it than going through a chain of Gopher menus. You can point your **gopher** client at a particular server by putting the server's Internet name on the command line. Let's say you want to access the Cornell Law School **gopher, fatty.law.cornell.edu**. To do so, just add the Internet address to your **gopher** command (URL **gopher://fatty.law.cornell.edu** will take you to the same gopher site via the WWW):

```
% gopher fatty.law.cornell.edu
```

You will start with Cornell Law School's main menu; you do not have to track down the server. Given the rate at which Gophers multiply, this is a more effective way to get started; it is how we list Gopher resources in the *Resource Catalog.* If you are using a public Gopher client, you do not have this luxury; you will have to hunt down your Gopher servers through a chain of menus. That is one good reason for getting your own client.

## Index Searches

Let's say that you are a biologist and are looking for strains of Drosophila (fruit flies) for a particular experiment. You go to the Indiana University Biology Archive (**gopher ftp.bio.indiana.edu** or URL **gopher://ftp.bio.indiana.edu**), and see an item called Flybase. After selecting that item and poking around a little more, you get to a menu called Stocks. That menu is cluttered with "questionable" items:

```
               Internet Gopher Information Client v2.1.3
                             Stocks

      -->  1.  Search Stock-center stocks (gopher+ form)/ <??>
           2.  Search Stock-center stocks (gopher-) <?>
           3.  Search stocks from various labs <?>
           4.  Search species stocks (gopher+ form)/ <??>
           5.  Search species stocks (gopher-) <?>
           6.  HELP.doc  [17Aug95, 6kb]
           7.  labs/
           8.  stock-centers/
           9.  stock-order  [ 7Sep95, 2kb] <??>
          10.  stocks.doc  [ 5Dec94, 5kb]

      Press ? for Help, q to Quit, u to go up a menu        Page: 1/1
```

The symbol <?> refers to a type of entry that we have not seen yet. These are *indexed directory* resources. In a normal Gopher directory (/), you select the directory and see a menu of everything in it. An index is similar. When you select an item that ends with <?>, you get an opportunity to do a *keyword search* through a database. First, you will be asked for a search string; **gopher** then searches for items that match your string and presents you with a special menu containing only the items it found rather than a complete list of the directory's contents. For your experiment, you need a strain of Drosophila with purple eyes. So, after finding the Stocks menu, you select resource 1, Search stocks at Bloomington, USA. Then you see this display on-screen:

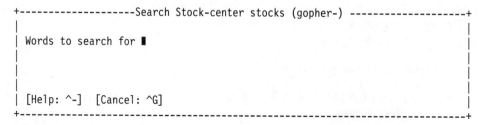

```
+-------------------Search Stock-center stocks (gopher-) -------------------+
|                                                                           |
| Words to search for █                                                     |
|                                                                           |
|                                                                           |
|                                                                           |
| [Help: ^-]  [Cancel: ^G]                                                  |
+---------------------------------------------------------------------------+
```

Now you can type keywords. If you have previously performed a search, **gopher** will remember the keywords you used last time and show them on-screen. This makes it easier to repeat your search if you do not get what you want the first time. If you want entirely different keywords, just BACKSPACE over your old keywords and start again.

In our case, we want to find out about Drosophila with purple eyes, so we type the keyword **purple**, followed by ENTER.

```
Words to search for: purple
```

When you press ENTER, **gopher** searches the index and builds a custom directory menu that contains only items matching your search criterion. In this case, you will see a new menu that contains only items that match the keyword **purple**:

```
              Internet Gopher Information Client v2.1.3
              Search Stock-center stocks (gopher-) : purple
    --> 1.  B-#2520   D. mauritiana  pr-3[1]
        2.  B-#3583   D. simulans  pur[1] osp-3[1]
        3.  B-#3584   D. simulans  pur[1] e[1]
        4.  B-#3592   D. sechellia  pur[1]


Press ? for Help, q to Quit, u to go up a menu                   Page: 1/1
```

This menu is no different from the other menus. You are looking at a list of files (the entries end in periods). Therefore, selecting item 1 just displays the file:

```
B-#2520   D. mauritiana  pr-3[1]  (Ok)                                    100%
+----------------------------------------------------------------------------+
>>>
B-#2520   D. mauritiana  pr-3[1]
Breakpoints:
Chromosome(s) affected: 3               Date added: 5/01/90
Donor: Jerry Coyne  Donor's source:
Comments: purple eye
Center: Bloomington Drosophila Stock Center  Contact: matthewk@indiana.edu
+----------------------------------------------------------------------------+

[PageDown: d] [Pageup: b] [Help: ?] [Exit: q] [Find: /] [Download: D]
```

Indexed searches are a great feature, but there are some tricks. The Gopher interface is very general and, as with anything very general, there are several causes for confusion. First, you have no idea what kind of computer or software is really doing the search. Gopher can do searches through Archie servers, WAIS servers, and others. Each of these servers has its own search rules and interprets keywords differently. Some, like Archie, let you search only for a single word. Some servers accept strings of keywords, but the meanings of these keywords may change as you move from index to index. For example, consider the string:

```
clinton and gore
```

Does this mean that for the search to match, the item must contain the words "clinton", "and", and "gore"? Or is the "and" a directive telling the server to find entries that contain the word "clinton" and the word "gore"? You do not know, and you cannot tell beforehand.

Another problem is that Gopher tends to reduce the search capabilities of different servers to the intersection of their features. You get to use the features they all have in common, not the best of any one. For example, you can access WAIS servers through Gopher. WAIS searches are extremely powerful, much more sophisticated than anything we have discussed in the book so far. If you use a WAIS server through Gopher, much of its power is lost, because you cannot use all its facilities with Gopher's simple line-oriented keyword interface.

You may also find that the resources that are most useful to index also tend to have licensing restrictions. Most of the time, you are able to see a database listed, but you are not allowed to use it. For example, the University of Minnesota's Gopher server has wire service news feeds listed as, in this case, option 19:

```
               Internet Gopher Information Client v2.1.3
                                 News

  --> 19. Wire Service News (Reuters/AP/UPI) U of Minnesota Only/
```

If you try to access it, you get:

```
+----------------------Gopher Transmission Error------------------------+
|                                                                       |
|  1 University of Minnesota Gopher Team <gopher@boombox.micro.umn.edu> |
|  Sorry Dude, we don't allow off-site access to this server            |
|                                                                       |
|                                           [Cancel: ^G] [OK: Enter]    |
+-----------------------------------------------------------------------+
```

This is because the license that allows the University of Minnesota to have the news feeds online forbids them from distributing it off-campus. Gopher knows where you are coming from and enforces this restriction.

With a little experience, you will hardly notice the differences in how searches work. Here are a couple of hints to help you through:

■  Gopher searches are always case-insensitive; uppercase and lowercase letters are considered the same.

- When you approach a new index, keep the search simple. If you want articles containing "clinton" and "gore", just look for "gore". He is likely to appear in fewer articles, hence the resulting menu will be shorter. If your search is too broad, the menu will just be longer.

- If you use a particular resource regularly, take five minutes to experiment. Find an article and read it. Jot down a few terms from the article. Try a few searches with multiple keywords, including some with "and", "or", and "not" between them. See what happens; are words like "and" considered part of the search string, or are they keywords? Remember that the rules change from resource to resource; that is, two different resources that you access from the same Gopher server may behave differently.

- If you move from Gopher server to Gopher server, the way a search is conducted for a similarly named resource may vary. If you always use a resource from the same Gopher server, the search semantics will remain the same.

- There is no obvious way to cancel a search once you have started. If you react instinctively by pressing CTRL-C, you will cancel the **gopher** client. The best you can do is let it complete and give you a bizarre collection of menu items.

## Searching Menus

We see that it is fairly easy to move around in one Gopher server and to move from Gopher server to Gopher server. This points to a problem: How do you find the item you want among the tens of thousands of Gopher menus available? Until two people at the University of Nevada at Reno built the Gopher equivalent to Archie, there was no way to know. With tongue firmly in cheek, they named their Archie-like facility "Veronica," after the comic-book character.

### Basic Veronica

Veronica acquires its data exactly like Archie does: It visits Gopher servers worldwide and traverses their menus, remembers what is there, and builds a combined index of Gopher menus. The good news about Veronica is that you know how to use it already. It appears to be just another index search. You select it just like any other search menu item. It asks you for words to search for and builds you a custom menu. The menu items are items from all the Gophers worldwide that contain the words for which you are looking.

To access Veronica, you may **gopher** to **veronica.scs.unr.edu** and continue with menu choice:

```
Search ALL of Gopherspace (5000+ gophers) using Veronica/
```

(or you can go to URL **gopher://veronica.scs.unr.edu:70/11/veronica**). You may also look around on any Gopher server for a menu item like this:

```
Search titles in Gopherspace using Veronica <?>
```

Select this item; your next menu will look something like this:

```
                  Internet Gopher Information Client v2.1.3
            Search ALL of Gopherspace (5000+ gophers) using Veronica

  --> 1.  How to Compose veronica Queries - June 23, 1994
      2.  Frequently-Asked Questions (FAQ) about veronica - January 13, 1995
      3.  More veronica: Software, Index-Control Protocol, HTML Pages/

          Simplified veronica chooses server - pick a search type:
      6.  Simplified veronica: Find Gopher MENUS only <?>
      7.  Simplified veronica: find ALL gopher types <?>

      9.  Find GOPHER DIRECTORIES by Title word(s) (via UNINETT..of Bergen) <?>
      10. Find GOPHER DIRECTORIES by Title word(s) (via NYSERNet   ) <?>
      11. Find GOPHER DIRECTORIES by Title word(s) (via PSINet) <?>
      12. Find GOPHER DIRECTORIES by Title word(s) (via University of Koe.. <?>
      13. Find GOPHER DIRECTORIES by Title word(s) (via U. Nac. Autonoma .. <?>
      14. Search GopherSpace by Title word(s) (via UNINETT/U. of Bergen) <?>
      15. Search GopherSpace by Title word(s) (via NYSERNet   ) <?>
      16. Search GopherSpace by Title word(s) (via PSINet) <?>
      17. Search GopherSpace by Title word(s) (via University of Koeln) <?>
      18. Search GopherSpace by Title word(s) (via U. Nac. Autonoma de MX.. <?>

  Press ? for Help, q to Quit, u to go up a menu                    Page: 1/1
```

The first thing to notice is that there are several menu entries, associated with several different Veronica servers. The number of servers varies from place to place and from time to time. Some Gopher servers are smart enough to know when a Veronica server is unusable, and delete unusable servers from their menus dynamically. Others leave them all there and let you try and fail.

There are many servers, because they are heavily used; one server could not handle the searches for the whole Internet. How do you know which one to use? There is no way to know beforehand which is the best. They all contain the same data, but you cannot tell which are busy and which are not. As with Archie, start by trying a server that is close to you; if that does not work, try one slightly farther away, until you reach one that responds. When you select a Veronica server, Gopher asks you for your search words. Healthcare is a major political topic, and you would like to follow the debate. You are interested in finding a place where you can drop in occasionally and find out what is new. You start by typing your search term:

```
+----------------Search gopherspace at University of Cologne----------------+
|                                                                           |
| Words to search for                                                       |
|                                                                           |
| healthcare                                                                |
|                                                                           |
| [Help: ^-]   [Cancel: ^G]                                                 |
+---------------------------------------------------------------------------+
```

At this point, you can cancel the search by typing CTRL-G; you will return to the previous menu. To proceed with the search, press ENTER. If all goes well, you will be rewarded with a menu of items related to healthcare. You may see a screen like this:

```
            Internet Gopher Information Client v2.1.3
       Simplified veronica: find ALL gopher types: healthcare

-->  1.  Wait... trying another server
     2.  Wait... trying another server
     3.  Wait... trying another server
     4.  Wait... trying another server
     5.  Wait... trying another server
         6.  *** All of the veronica servers are busy - try again soon ***
```

Like Archie, Veronica suffers from its own success. It is not unusual to find that the servers are too busy. If this happens, try another server or try the server later. Gopher remembers your search string, so you will not have to enter it time and time again. The following result came from:

```
            Internet Gopher Information Client 2.0 pl11

       Search GopherSpace by Title word(s) (via PSINet): healthcare

-->  1.  05.. 1995 Computers in Healthcare Education Symposium Call for Papers
     2.  (NR-94-02-09)  New Center for Healthcare Technologies Gains First D..
     3.  healthcare-reform-group
     4.  Baxter Healthcare Corp:IT and Competitive necessity.
     5.  Baxter Healthcare
     6.  Healthcare Employment Opportunities/
     7.  Healthcare Management and Reform/
     8.  Healthcare Management and Reform/
     9.  womancare - healthcare for women, by women
    10.  Conference on Healthcare for the Poor and Uninsured: Preventative H..
    11.  Healthcare Informatics Conference/NI
    12.  Clinton Healthcare Plan/
    13.  healthcare-plan/
    14.  Cutler: Release of Healthcare Task Force Documents  8/17/94
    15.  with Letter Writers on Healthcare  5/9/94
    16.  Re: GOPHER> BlueCross..Shield of Alabama Healthcare Information (fwd)
```

```
17. GOPHER> BlueCross/Shield of Alabama Healthcare Information (fwd)
18. PREFERRED_FAMILY_HEALTHCARE,_INC._-_1
```

```
Press ? for Help, q to Quit, u to go up a menu              Page: 1/12
```

This search gave you 12 pages, which might be more than you may have wished.

If you occasionally want to find out what is new on a particular topic, you would rather find a few collections of information than a long list of scattered resources. This means searching for a *directory*, rather than for individual resources. That is why the Veronica menu contained items like the following:

```
--> 7.  Search Gopher Directory Titles at University of Cologne <?>
```

The first search we did found any item that matched our keywords; this item searches only for directories (which are, by definitions, collections of things). The actual mechanics of the search are exactly the same in either case: Veronica asks you what to search for; you enter a string followed by ENTER. If we did our healthcare search, looking only for directory titles, we would get a more reasonable number in response:

```
                  Internet Gopher Information Client v2.1.3

     Search Gopher Directory Titles at University of Cologne: healthcare

  -->  1.  COLUMBIA HEALTHCARE CORP/
       2.  alt-healthcare.software/
       3.  Scholarships For Healthcare Related Disciplines/
       4.  whitehouse-healthcare.archive   Whitehouse materials relating to h../
       5.  alternative-healthcare/
       6.  whitehouse-healthcare.archive   Whitehouse materials relating to h../
       7.  HEALTHCARE SERVICES GROUP INC/
       8.  Healthcare (Medical/Paramedical/Pharmaceutical)/
       9.  Healthcare Management and Reform/
      10.  U S HEALTHCARE INC/
      11.  alt-healthcare.software/
      12.  Government Healthcare Institutions/
      13.  If you caabout quality healthcare, PLEASE READ! (Threaded)/
      14.  PHP HEALTHCARE CORP/
      15.  Healthcare Center/
      16.  HORIZON HEALTHCARE CORP/
      17.  *NEW* What Every Healthcare Provider Needs to K... (Kenkel)/
      18.  Home Healthcare Nurse: The Professional Journal... (Caserta)/

  Press ? for Help, q to Quit, u to go up a menu              Page: 1/4
```

That results in a shorter list. Now you simply begin browsing to see what you can find.

Of course you can initiate a Veronica search using the WWW as well. Figure 11-2 shows the results of a search on healthcare using another Veronica server.

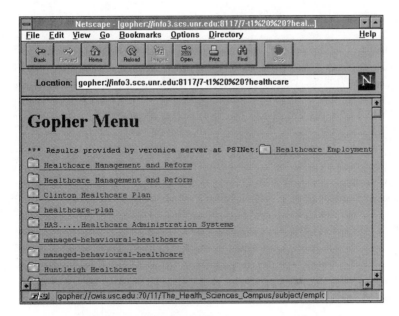

*Figure 11-2    Results of Veronica search*

### Advanced Veronica

When we talked about index searches earlier, we noted that you do not know what kind of software is actually doing the search for you. You could not try sophisticated search strings unless you had inside knowledge of the index server. Veronica servers allow limited Boolean and substring searches.

Boolean searches allow you to use the words "and", "or", and "not", together with parentheses, to allow you better control of the search. For example, if you were interested in healthcare as it relates to women or families, you could have used the search string:

```
healthcare and (women or family)
```

This string is interpreted as a mathematical expression; "healthcare and" applies to all the items within the parentheses. The meaning of this expression is: Return any items that contain both of the words "healthcare" and "women" or both of the words "healthcare" and "family". The result would be:

```
              Internet Gopher Information Client v2.1.3

   Search gopherspace at University of Cologne: healthcare and women or family

   --> 1.  I97  SLU  5741 FAMILY INTERACTION UNDER STRESS
       2.    Association of Family Women; Newsletters, 1975-1979
       3.  FAMILY REUNION LEGISLATIONS. THANKS TO MI MI SR. FOR INVITING ME TO
```

```
 4.  Newell, Peter Family papers: Peter Newell: Visual Materials
 5.  Family /
 6.  Trust Fund:  School, Family, and Community Partnerships in High Sch..
 7.  df940803.jpg   The Human Cannonball Family <Picture>
 8.  EPSY 482   Section: 201 , Sem-Marriage & Family
 9.  family-issues
10.  Work and Family Programs
11.  Gallagher, Hugh F., Jr., family papers
12.  Diffusion Multisystemic Family
13.  The British Columbia Task Force on Family Violence - Backgrounder
14.  Family Law
15.  FEMALE-HEADED FAMILY IN SOCIAL AND ECONOMIC CONTEXT: RACIA.. <PC Bin>
16.  Human Development and Family Studies <McHale>
17.  Bill 45: Child, Youth and Family Advocacy Act (61k)
18.  Student Family Residences


Press ? for Help, q to Quit, u to go up a menu                    Page: 1/12
```

As a shorthand, the "and" is assumed between any two adjacent words, unless there is another directive present. That is, searching for "healthcare and women" is the same as "healthcare women". Why type it if you do not need it?

If you think carefully about the search we just did, you will realize that it might exclude some entries we would like see because they contain "woman" (or even "womyn") rather than "women". To handle situations like this, use the partial-word character *. In our current search, "wom*" takes care of most possibilities in addition to finding articles about the care of wombats. The * may be used only at the end of a word.

Finally, our fishing expedition also landed a lot of information about Student Family Residences, an item about dwelling units for rent. We could have excluded it with the Boolean "not". So, we can further refine our search to:

```
healthcare and (wom* or family) not Residences
```

We want healthcare and some word starting with "wom", or healthcare and family, but if the menu item has "Residences" anywhere in it, ignore it.

Another method for accomplishing this may be requested by a server that does not use parentheses. You may find an explanation like this:

```
Parentheses are not allowed here. (explanation) (Ok)                      82%


+--------------------------------------------------------------------------+
Explanation of the message "Parentheses are not allowed here"
This veronica server does not accept parentheses ().
You can avoid parentheses in most cases if you use the fact that the
evaluation is from left to right.
```

```
Instead of...                    use...
(a and b) or c                   a and b or c
(a or b) and                     a or b and c
(a and (not b)) and c            a not b and c
a and (b or c)                   b or c and a
a or (b and c)                   b and c or a
a not (b or c)                   a not b not c
(a and b) or (c and d)           2 queries for "a and b"
                                 and for "c and d"
Parentheses are not allowed here because the search method is simpler
without parentheses and parentheses were used in only 0.5% of the queries.
+----------------------------------------------------------------------+

[PageDown: d] [Pageup: b] [Help: ?] [Exit: q] [Find: /] [Download: D]
```

The translation for "healthcare (wom* or family) not Residence" is "healthcare and wom* or family not Residence".

## Jughead

We have explored two kinds of searches in Gopher, an index search of a particular database and an index search of the whole Gopher community. We mentioned earlier the idea that each department of a university could have its own Gopher server: one for administration, one for athletics, etc. All of these servers were part of one community. Using Veronica, there is no way to say, "Search only at the University of Minnesota's Gophers"; that is what Jughead is for.

Jughead is an indexing facility that indexes a particular set of Gopher servers. You will rarely see the name Jughead. Rather, you will see another kind of index search in a Gopher menu (usually a site's main menu), like this:

```
5. Search Gopher Menus at the University of Minnesota <?>
```

For you, it is just another index search. The underlying technology is Jughead, but you use it just like you would use any other index item.

## White-pages Servers

In chapter 10, *Finding Someone,* we discussed white-pages services, which are essentially electronic phone books. However, we omitted one important group of more than 300 phone book servers: those available through Gopher. White-pages services are offered through Gopher in two ways: as normal index searches, and as CSO name servers.* If

---

*So named because they were developed from the CSnet name server code at the Computing Services Office of the University of Illinois, Urbana.

you find a menu item on a Gopher server called something like "Phone books" and follow it down through a bunch of geographic areas, you will eventually get to lists of white-pages servers for different groups of people. On that list, you might see the following entries:

```
    142. Penn State University <CSO>
-->143. Performance Systems International <?>
```

The items flagged <CSO> are CSO-style servers, and the ones labeled <?> are Gopher index servers.

## Gopher index white-pages searches

White-pages directories offered through the Gopher index facility work just like you would expect them to. You select the directory you want to use, it gives you a familiar dialog box, you fill in your search term, and Gopher looks up the name. For example, let's pick the Performance Systems International server and look up "Bill Schrader":

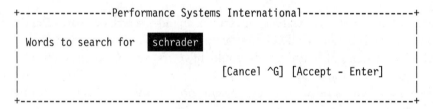

You type in the name and press ENTER. Gopher looks up the name and returns some information about it in a menu item named **Raw Search Results**. If you select that menu item (often it is the only one), you will see:

```
William Schrader (1)                        wls@psi.com
  President
  Chief Executive Officer
  PSI Inc.
    Reston International Center
    11800 Sunrise Valley Drive
    Suite 1100
    Reston, VA 22091
    USA Telephone: +1 703-620-6651 x310
    FAX:        +1 703-620-4586 Locality:     Reston, Virginia ...
```

In principle, these searches are easy. The catch is that you can never be too sure of what you are allowed to search for. Some of these places have indexed the whole text of their internal directory, some have indexed only names, and some are somewhere in between. Keep it simple and search only for first and last names.

## *CSO directory searches*

When CSO directories were first developed, you needed a special client program to look up names. The software for this client is not widely available; if you are not at a site that has a CSO name server, you probably do not have access to it. (That is why we did not cover it in chapter 10.) However, Gopher knows how to perform CSO name-server lookups; so, once you are comfortable with Gopher, you can access these online directories too.

Let's go to the main menu of the Gopher server at the University of Illinois.

```
              Internet Gopher Information Client v2.1.3

             University of Illinois at Urbana-Champaign

    --> 1.  Welcome to the University of Illinois at Urbana-Champaign Gopher
        2.  Campus Announcements (last updated 9/28/95)/
        3.  What's New?/
        4.  Information about Gopher/
        5.  Keyword Search of UIUC Gopher Menus <?>
        6.  Univ. of Illinois at Urbana-Champaign Campus Information/
        7.  Champaign-Urbana & Regional Information/
        8.  Computer Documentation, Software, and Information/
        9.  Libraries and Reference Information/
        10. Publications (U of I Press, Newspapers, Newsletters, etc.) & Weath../
        11. Other Gopher and Information Servers/
        12. Phone Books (ph)/
        13. Internet File Server (ftp) Sites/
        14. Disability Information and Resources/


    Press ? for Help, q to Quit, u to go up a menu            Page: 1/1
```

Item 12 on this menu is labeled **Phone Books**. If you select this item, you will see something like "Phone books at other institutions". If you select this, you will see another menu, dividing all possible phone books into geographical menus. Eventually, you will wind your way down to something like this:

```
              Internet Gopher Information Client v2.1.3

                          North America

    --> 1.  Albert Einstein College of Medicine <CSO>
        2.  Algonquin College of Applied Arts and Technology, Nepean, Ont.. <CSO>
        3.  American Mathematical Society Combined Membership List <?>
        4.  American University, Washington DC <CSO>
        5.  Arizona State University <?>
        6.  Auburn University <?>
        7.  Bates College <CSO>
```

```
 8.  Baylor College of Medicine <CSO>
 9.  Beth Israel Hospital (Harvard Univ.) <CSO>
10.  Board of Governors Universities (Illinois) <CSO>
11.  Boston University <CSO>
12.  Bowling Green State University <CSO>
13.  Bradley University <CSO>
14.  Brigham Young University <CSO>
15.  Brookhaven National Laboratory <CSO>
16.  Brown University <CSO>
17.  Bucknell University <CSO>
18.  Bull HN Information Systems <?>

Press ? for Help, q to Quit, u to go up a menu            Page: 1/19
```

The <CSO> suffix at the end of a line tells you it represents CSO-style white-pages servers. The entries are generally large universities, where CSO servers are most popular. If you access one of these items, just like you accessed the file we used in the previous example, you can look things up in the selected directory.

For example, let's say that you accessed the server for the University of Illinois by pressing ENTER. Now you get a new menu for entering search criteria:

```
+-------------------University of Illinois Urbana-Champaign-------------------+
|                                                                            |
| name                                                                       |
| alias                                                                      |
| email                                                                      |
| curriculum                                                                 |
| phone                                                                      |
| office_phone                                                               |
| fax                                                                        |
| address                                                                    |
| office_address                                                             |
| office_location                                                            |
| nickname                                                                   |
| department                                                                 |
| title                                                                      |
| hours                                                                      |
| project                                                                    |
| other                                                                      |
| www                                                                        |
| callsign                                                                   |
| pager                                                                      |
|                                                                            |
| [Help: ^-]  [Cancel: ^G]                                                   |
+----------------------------------------------------------------------------+
```

The cursor is originally positioned on the **name** field. You can type the words you want to search for there. If you want to constrain the search with any of the other fields, you can press TAB to move down the screen to the relevant field and add what is necessary. Do not press ENTER until you have filled in everything you want; ENTER starts the search.

CSO's search rules make sense, but they are a little different from what you might be used to. Each word in the name is taken as an item, with wildcard characters allowed.* The words in the search string must all be found in the target for the target to match. Substrings do not automatically match. If you met Ed Krol at a conference and tried to look up "Ed Krol" when you wanted to reach him, you would likely have trouble. "Ed" would not match "Edward" or "Edwin", and his first name is not "Ed". Therefore, it is usually safer to search for wildcarded first names like "Ed*". Order and case are not important. That is:

```
name      Ed* Krol ▉
```

would match "Edward M Krol", because both "Ed" followed by any characters and "Krol" were in that name. Similarly,

```
name      Krol Ed* ▉
```

would also work. You needn't match every word in an entry, like the middle initial "M". After entering either of these strings, press ENTER to start the search. When it is finished, you will see:

```
University of Illinois Urbana-Champaign (Ok)                        100%

+------------------------------------------------------------------------+
---------------------------------------------------------------
          alias: e-krol
           name: krol edward m
          email: krol@ux1.cso.uiuc.edu
          phone: (217) 333-7886
        address: 1121 dcl, MC 256
              : 1304 w springfield
              : urbana, il 61801
     department: ccso - computing
          title: asst director
            www: http://ux1.cso.uiuc.edu/~krol/
+------------------------------------------------------------------------+

[PageDown: d] [Pageup: b] [Help: ?] [Exit: q] [Find: /] [Download: D]
```

---

*For review: * matches any sequence of characters. [*list*] matches any single character between the brackets (e.g., [abc] matches a, b, or c). CSO name servers do not honor UNIX regular expressions or the ? wildcard character.

As with the text file that we retrieved earlier, you can either continue (i.e., look up another address), save this output in a file, or mail it to yourself.

One quirk of CSO-style servers is that they index only entries based on some fields in an item. Your search must be based on the person's name, phone number, or e-mail address. You can use any fields, however, to further constrain a search. For example, let's say you got a note saying "Please call L Ward at 244-0681." You do not recognize the name; after playing telephone tag for a while, you decide to try e-mail. So you do a lookup on "L* Ward":

```
    name      L* Ward ▮
```

The result is:

```
    query name=L* Ward
    Too many entries to print.
```

The search was too broad, and the server is refusing to print all the matching entries (you are usually limited to about 20). You can further constrain the search by adding the telephone number. You will be rewarded with a single matching entry (see the exercises at the end of the chapter).

## FTP Through Gopher

Now that you know about Gopher and indexes, you can use Gopher as an alternative interface for FTP. Gopher's FTP features currently allow you to move files from anonymous FTP servers to the computer running your **gopher** client (or your own computer if properly configured).

Let's return to Gopher's main menu at the University of Minnesota:

```
              Internet Gopher Information Client 2.0 p111

                          University of Minnesota

     -->  1.   Information About Gopher/
          2.   Computer Information/
          3.   Discussion Groups/
          4.   Fun & Games/
          5.   Internet file server (ftp) sites/
          6.   Libraries/
          7.   News/
          8.   Other Gopher and Information Servers/
          9.   Phone Books/
```

```
        10. Search Gopher Titles at the University of Minnesota <?>
        11. Search lots of places at the University of Minnesota  <?>
        12. University of Minnesota Campus Information/
```
*(blank lines deleted)*
```
   Press ? for Help, q to Quit, u to go up a menu              Page: 1/1
```

Choice 5 is Internet file server, so we press **5** and ENTER:

```
        Internet Gopher Information Client 2.0 pl11

              Internet file server (ftp) sites

  -->  1.  About FTP Searches
       2.  InterNIC: Internet Network Information Center/
       3.  Popular FTP Sites via Gopher/
       4.  Query a specific ftp host <?>
       5.  Search FTP sites with Archie (gopher+ version)/
       6.  Search FTP sites with Archie (non-gopher+ version)/
       7.  UnStuffIt <HQX>
```
*(blank lines deleted)*
```
   Press ? for Help, q to Quit, u to go up a menu              Page: 1/1
```

Choice 3 is Popular FTP sites via Gopher, so now we press **3** and ENTER:

```
        Internet Gopher Information Client 2.0 pl11

              Popular FTP Sites via Gopher

  -->  1.  Boombox - Home of Gopher and POPmail/
       2.  Case Western Reserve University FREENET/
       3.  Indiana University Mac Gopher Client App (beta)/
       4.  Indiana Windows Archive/
       5.  Interest Group Lists/
       6.  Internet Resource Guide (tar.Z files)/
       7.  Latest Disinfectant (ftp.acns.nwu.edu)/
       8.  Lyrics/
       9.  NCSA - Home of NCSA Telnet/
       10. National Science Foundation Gopher (STIS)/
       11. Newton Archives at Johns Hopkins University (bnnrc-srv.med.jhu.edu../
       12. OCF Document Archives/
       13. OSS-IS Info Archives (slow)/
       14. Read Me First
       15. SUMEX-AIM Archives - (Includes Info-Mac: a large collection of Mac../
       16. Scholarly Communications Project of Virginia Tech/
       17. Software Archives at MERIT (University of Michigan)/
       18. Sonata NeXT software archive (sonata.cc.purdue.edu)/

   Press ? for Help, q to Quit, u to go up a menu              Page: 1/2
```

Choice 10 is the National Science Foundation:

```
               Internet Gopher Information Client 2.0 pl11

                  National Science Foundation Gopher (STIS)

  -->  1.  About this Gopher
       2.  About STIS/
       3.  Search NSF Award Abstracts <?>
       4.  Instructions for "Search NSF Award Abstracts"
       5.  Search NSF Publications <?>
       6.  Instructions for "Search NSF Publications"
       7.  Phone Books and Directories/
       8.  NSF Publications/
       9.  NSB - National Science Board/
      10.  Office of the Director/
      11.  OIG  - Office of the Inspector General/
      12.  BIO  - Dir. for Biological Sciences/
      13.  CISE - Dir. for Computer and Information Science and Engineering/
      14.  EHR  - Dir. for Education and Human Resources/
      15.  ENG  - Dir. for Engineering/
      16.  GEO  - Dir. for Geosciences/
      17.  MPS  - Dir. for Math and Physical Sciences/
      18.  SBE  - Dir. for Social, Behavioral and Economic Sciences/


  Press ? for Help, q to Quit, u to go up a menu            Page: 1/2
```

Choice 18 takes us to the Social, Behavioral and Economic Sciences area.

```
               Internet Gopher Information Client 2.0 pl11

            SBE  - Dir. for Social, Behavioral and Economic Sciences

  -->  1.  International Documents/
       2.  Letters/
       3.  Program Guidelines/
```

Choice 2 now reveals documents available to us including binary word-processor documents:

```
               Internet Gopher Information Client 2.0 pl11

                         International Documents

  -->  1.  int94004   - INT94-004 - Japanese Government Science and
       2.  int94005   - INT94-005(a)    Measures for Promoting Japan's Ocean
       3.  int9403    - INT9403 Japan's Polar Research
       4.  int9403.doc - INT9403 Japan's Polar Research <PC Bin>
       5.  int95002   - INT 95-002 - Current Status of Programs to Support Am..
       6.  int95004   - INT 95-004 - 1994 Survey of Research and Development ..
       7.  int95009 (29.9K) INT 95-009 - Association of Scientific Societies o..
```

```
 8.  int95009.doc (59.0K) INT 95-009 - Association of Scientifi.. <PC Bin>
 9.  int95010 (12.9K) INT 95-010 - Internet Access to Japanese S&T Infor..
10.  int95010.doc (22.5K) INT 95-010 - Internet Access to Japan.. <PC Bin>
11.  int95011 (47.6K) INT 95-011 - Jjapan's Basic Plans for Promoting R&..
12.  int95011.doc (84.0K) INT 95-011 - Jjapan's Basic Plans for.. <PC Bin>
13.  int95012 (10.1K) INT 95-012 - Japanese Engineers - Profile and Envi..
14.  int95012.doc (35.0K) INT 95-012 - Japanese Engineers - Pro.. <PC Bin>
15.  int95013 (7.3K) INT 95-013 - Foreign Students in Japan
16.  int95013.doc (28.5K) INT 95-013 - Foreign Students in Japa.. <PC Bin>
17.  int95014 (6.7K) INT 95-014 - NISTEP Workshop on Regional S&T
18.  int95014.doc (38.5K) INT 95-014 - NISTEP Workshop on Regio.. <PC Bin>

Press ? for Help, q to Quit, u to go up a menu                Page: 1/2
```

By selecting choice 10, Gopher is now ready to send us a file automatically using **ftp**:

```
int95010.doc (22.5K) INT 95-010 - Internet Access to Japanese S&T Information+
|                                                                            |
| Save in file:                                                              |
|                                                                            |
|  int95010_doc_-22.5K-_INT_95-010_-_Internet_Access_to_Jap                  |
|                                                                            |
|               [Cancel: ^G] [Erase: ^U] [Accept: Enter]                     |
+----------------------------------------------------------------------------+
```

By pressing ENTER ([Accept: Enter]), the Microsoft Word document will be delivered to our local directory. We do not have to include any FTP commands. Gopher takes care of that for us. The final step is getting the file from that account to our local machine, which, of course, you probably have mastered by now.

## Using Gopher to Search for FTP Files

The NSF site also allows searching. Returning to the NSF (STIS) menu above. Choice 3 invites a search of the server:

```
--> 3.  Search NSF Award Abstracts <?>
```

Let's see what NSF has to offer in the area of telecommunications by pressing **3**, ENTER, and typing **telecommunications**:

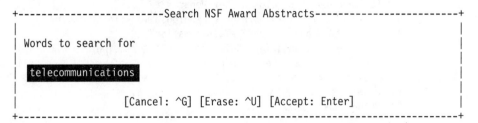

```
+------------------------Search NSF Award Abstracts------------------------+
|                                                                          |
| Words to search for                                                      |
|                                                                          |
|  telecommunications                                                      |
|                                                                          |
|               [Cancel: ^G] [Erase: ^U] [Accept: Enter]                   |
+--------------------------------------------------------------------------+
```

The response includes 12 pages of items:

```
Internet Gopher Information Client 2.0 pl11

Search NSF Award Abstracts: telecommunications

  --> 1.  [a8814169] Sixteenth Annual Telecommunications Policy Research Conf..
       2.  [a9152161] Development of an Analog..Technical Institute - Sweetwater
       3.  [a9354116] Native American Telecommunications Forum
       4.  [a9119792] Computer Science and Telecommunications Board Core Suppo..
       5.  [a8910336] Core Support of the Board on Telecommunications and Comp..
       6.  [a9351476] Computer and Information Sciences Undergraduate Laborato..
       7.  [a9215376] U.S.-China Cooperative Research on Trade and Telecommuni..
       8.  [a9416164] Indirect Effects on the Performance of Telecommunication..
       9.  [a9454703] Project Smart: A Systemic Model for Advancing Restructur..
      10.  [a9526593] Seed Funding for Institute for Computer and Telecommunic..
      11.  [a9216229] Japan STA Program: State Management of Competition in Ja..
      12.  [a9422295] Renewal of Core Support for the Computer Science and Tel..
      13.  [a8811111] Engineering Research Center for Telecommunications
      14.  [a8421402] Engineering Research Center for Telecommunications
      15.  [a9206148] Searching for Good Call Admission Policies in Telecommun..
      16.  [a8952357] Telecommunications Technology Instrumentation Project
      17.  [a9460615] Adaptive Signal Processing Techniques for Hands-Free Tel..
      18.  [a9319677] Telecommunication and Information Infrastructure Policy:..


Press ? for Help, q to Quit, u to go up a menu                    Page: 1/12
```

We can retrieve any of them by selecting the appropriate number and pressing ENTER. Notice that it is not obvious if these are text or binary (word-processor) files. A quick check will reveal which is the case.

Let's return to Gopher's main menu at the University of Illinois:

```
Internet Gopher Information Client v2.1.3

University of Illinois at Urbana-Champaign

  --> 1.  Welcome to the University of Illinois at Urbana-Champaign Gopher
       2.  Campus Announcements (last updated 9/28/95)/
       3.  What's New?/
       4.  Information about Gopher/
       5.  Keyword Search of UIUC Gopher Menus <?>
       6.  Univ. of Illinois at Urbana-Champaign Campus Information/
       7.  Champaign-Urbana & Regional Information/
       8.  Computer Documentation, Software, and Information/
       9.  Libraries and Reference Information/
      10.  Publications (U of I Press, Newspapers, Newsletters, etc.) & Weath../
      11.  Other Gopher and Information Servers/
      12.  Phone Books (ph)/
```

```
            13. Internet File Server (ftp) Sites/
            14. Disability Information and Resources/

Press ? for Help, q to Quit, u to go up a menu          Page: 1/1
```

You see an item labeled Internet File Server (item 13). The name may change from server to server, but you should be able to recognize which item we mean. Once you have selected this item, you will see one of two types of menus; which menu you will see depends on how your Gopher server works with FTP sites. Some servers use FTP directly, in which case you will see an alphabetic list of sites, annotated with their holdings (items 11, 12, 13, etc., below):

```
             Internet Gopher Information Client v2.1.3

                  Internet File Server (ftp) Sites

        1.  About this directory
        2.  About Anonymous FTP
        3.  Search of Most FTP sites (archie) <?>
        4.  Keyword Search of Entries in FTP Menus <?>
        5.  FTP.CSO: University of Illinois CCSO's Main FTP Server/
        6.  FTP.NCSA: University of Illinois NCSA's Main FTP Server/
        7.  Boombox at Minnesota, Home of the Gopher and POPmail/
        8.  Type in the ftp site name for direct access <?>
        9.  Wuarchive.wustl.edu   Just about everything .../
        10. Popular FTP Sites via Gopher/
        11. FTP sites that start with 'a'/
        12. b/
  -->   13. c/
        14. d/
        15. e/
        16. f/
        17. g/
        18. h/

Press ? for Help, q to Quit, u to go up a menu          Page: 1/2
```

If you see a menu like this, you will have to search through a series of menus to find the server and file you want. In this case, let's try to reach one of the most popular servers on the Internet, choice 9:

```
             Internet Gopher Information Client 2.0 pl11

             Wuarchive.wustl.edu   Just about everything ...

        1.  README
        2.  README.NFS
        3.  bin/
        4.  decus/
```

```
  -->  5.  doc/
       6.  edu/
       7.  etc/
       8.  graphics/
       9.  info/
      10.  languages/
      11.  mirrors/
      12.  multimedia/
      13.  packages/
      14.  private/
      15.  pub/
      16.  systems/
      17.  usenet/
      18.  vendor/


Press ? for Help, q to Quit, u to go up a menu              Page: 1/1
```

Choice 5, doc/, should include documents of some kind.

```
             Internet Gopher Information Client 2.0 pl11

                               doc

  -->  1.  EFF/
       2.  bible/
       3.  coombspapers/
       4.  graphic-formats/
       5.  ietf/
       6.  internet-drafts/
       7.  internet-info/
       8.  mailing-lists/
       9.  minsky/
      10.  misc/
      11.  network-reading-list/
      12.  noctools/
      13.  nsfnet/
      14.  nsfnet-stats/
      15.  org/
      16.  publications/
      17.  rfc/
      18.  std/


Press ? for Help, q to Quit, u to go up a menu              Page: 1/2
```

Now let's try item 7, a directory called *internet-info:*

```
          Internet Gopher Information Client 2.0 p111

                          internet-info

  -->    1.   INDEX.resources
         2.   bibliography.txt
         3.   cruise.dos/
         4.   cruise.mac/
         5.   cwis.ps
         6.   hitchhikers.guide
         7.   libs.ps
         8.   resource-guide/
         9.   user.profiles/
        10.   zen-1.0/


  Press ? for Help, q to Quit, u to go up a menu          Page: 1/1
```

Internet Cruise is a very nice Internet tutorial from the Merit network in Michigan. We can choose a Macintosh or DOS version. Let's take a look at the Macintosh directory:

```
          Internet Gopher Information Client 2.0 p111

                           cruise.mac

  -->    1.   INDEX.cruise.mac
         2.   merit.cruise2.mac.hqx <HQX>
         3.   merit.cruise2.mac.readme

  Press ? for Help, q to Quit, u to go up a menu          Page: 1/1
```

We can download the software now by selecting item 2:

```
+---------------------------merit.cruise2.mac.hqx-----------------------------+
|                                                                            |
|  Save in file:                                                             |
|                                                                            |
|   merit_cruise2_mac.hqx                                                    |
|                                                                            |
|                  [Cancel: ^G] [Erase: ^U] [Accept: Enter]                  |
|                                                                            |
+----------------------------------------------------------------------------+
```

What is interesting about this process is that the machine you are receiving the file from may not belong to the Gopher system at all; it can be just an anonymous FTP server somewhere.

Of course, the process we just described really is not all that convenient. Gopher makes the search a little more convenient, but you still have to know (or at least have an idea) which server has the data you want. That is where the other kind of FTP menu comes in. Some Gopher servers use Archie to look up FTP resources. This builds an indexed resource, accessible by menu, of the entire world's supply of anonymous FTP servers. If the Gopher server you are using is using one of these, you will see a menu like this:

```
    FTP Sites

--> 1.  Read Me First
    2.  Exact Word FTP Search <?>
    3.  Partial Word FTP Search <?>
    4.  University of Minnesota - Gopher, POPMail/
    ...
```

We are no longer looking at "raw" directories, as in the previous example; we are looking at indexed directories, accessed via Archie. That is, rather than traversing a series of menus to find a server, you can use a Gopher-style indexed-directory search to find the file you want. You are actually using Archie but, as you would expect, Gopher hides the details of Archie from you. You can perform two kinds of searches, corresponding to two of Archie's search types: You can perform exact string matches (item 2) or Archie substring searches (item 3).

Do not be surprised if you see both interfaces: an Archie-like indexed directory, plus an alphabetical list of FTP servers. Archie's resource list is probably more reliable, but both are useful in their own way. The indexed list is obviously appropriate if you are looking for information about a particular topic and do not know where to find it. The alphabetical list may be easier if you already know where the data is (you do not have to try constructing an appropriate search), or if you have heard that the FTP server at **hoople.usnd.edu** has some great stuff and you would like to check it out.

Gopher works just fine for text (ASCII) files, but binary files are more troublesome. To handle a binary file appropriately, **gopher** must be able to guess the file's type, based on extensions to the name (e.g., *.tar.Z, .hqx,* etc.). If it finds a file it recognizes as binary, **gopher** flags it for you with the **<BIN>** suffix. There is a lot of development in this area; the way **gopher** handles these files may vary from client to client. For example, the Macintosh client may work perfectly with binary files and unpack them if they end with the extension *.hqx.* All of this has been changing toward making the entire process appear transparent to you, the user. The key really is "If at first you don't succeed, try, try again."

Even if your **gopher** client refuses to handle binary files (or if it tries, but does something unreasonable), it still is not useless. The equal sign (=) command shows, technically, what **gopher** is doing. Once you select a resource and press =, you will see something like this:

```
Type=9
Name=Technology Innovation Strategy of the US EPA (WordPerfect)
Path=9/Initiatives/TechInitiative/tecstrat_wp
Host=gopher.epa.gov
Port=70
URL: gopher://gopher.epa.gov:70/99/Initiatives/TechInitiative/tecstrat_wp
+----------------------------------------------------------------------------+

[PageDown: <SPACE>] [Help: ?] [Return to Menu: u]
```

The important thing here is **Path**. It tells you exactly where the resource is located. Even if **gopher** cannot transfer the file for you, you still know that the hostname is **gopher.epa.gov**. You can use anonymous FTP to access this host, **cd** to *pub/drought,* and retrieve any files you want with your FTP client. Once you have the file, you would do whatever decoding is necessary to make it usable.

The = command gives you Gopher's internal information on any kind of resource; what you do with that information varies by resource type. If it is a TELNET resource, you will have to use **telnet** to access it; if it is a file, you will need to use FTP, etc. If it is a Gopher resource, you can be guaranteed access only with **gopher**. You can always try anonymous FTP to the same machine name, but it might not work.

## Using TELNET Through Gopher

Gopher can connect you to resources using **telnet** as an interface. You do this in the same fashion as every other resource: Walk through the menus, and then select a resource that interests you. For example, while browsing through a menu under the title Libraries, you notice the resource below:

```
--> 23. University of California MELVYL <TEL>
```

This is an online, TELNET-style interface to the University of California's card catalog. The marker <TEL> at the end of the entry tells you that this is a TELNET resource. When you select a TELNET resource, **gopher** gives you a warning and a help screen:*

---

*This facility is very different in the Macintosh Hypercard Gopher.

```
+----------University of California (MELVYL)-------------+
|                                                        |
|   Warning!!!!!, you are about to leave the Internet    |
|   Gopher program and connect to another host. If       |
|   you get stuck press the control key and the          |
|   ^ key, and then type q.                              |
|                                                        |
|   Connecting to melvyl.ucop.edu, port 23 using telnet. |
|                                                        |
|                                                        |
|                                                        |
|                         [Cancel: ^G] [OK: Enter]       |
|                                                        |
+--------------------------------------------------------+
```

**gopher** gives you this warning because it loses control of your session once **telnet** starts; it regains control when **telnet** finishes. If you get hung up somewhere in TELNET, you are on your own. Pressing CTRL-] (Control–right bracket) is the common way to get to **telnet**'s command mode.*

Depending on the resource, the warning screen may have some hints about how to use it. For example:

```
Use login "Guest"
```

   *or*

```
When you get connected do a "DIAL VTAM"
```

In other cases, you are on your own. You may need to contact the site to arrange an account. Just because you are getting there through **gopher** does not mean you bypass security.

Now that you have read the warnings, press ENTER to get connected to the resource:

```
Trying...

Connected to MELVYL.UCOP.EDU.
DLA LINE 72 (TELNET) 10:28:00 09/30/95   (MELVYL.UCOP.EDU)
Please Enter Your Terminal Type Code or Type ? for a List of Codes.
TERMINAL?
```

When you are done and log out, you will return to **gopher** and to the menu where you selected the resource.

---

*If you are using **telnet** to access a public Gopher client, remember the cautions about escape characters when running multiple TELNET sessions. Note that public Gopher servers usually will not allow you to access a TELNET resource. To get to TELNET resources, you need to run a client either from your own computer or from an account of your own. Chapter 5, *Remote Login,* describes TELNET in detail.

# ▨ *Using Bookmarks*

Once you are comfortable moving around in **gopher**, you will not have to have wait long to experience one of its frustrations: the tedium of getting to somewhere through a long series of menus. You start at your main menu, pick other Gophers, pick USA, North Carolina, NCSU Library Gopher, Library without Walls. You did all of this just so you can look at the resource you really wanted to use. This is not so bad when you are simply browsing to find out what is interesting; but what if you find a resource and you cannot remember how you found it?

The solution to this problem is the **gopher** bookmark. *Bookmarks* are available in almost all clients; they let you mark a particular place, so that **gopher** can return to it later—possibly in another session.

What if you do Veronica searches regularly? Rather than search through menus to find the Veronica items, you might to place a bookmark on the directory where Veronica searches live. Creating a bookmark is a two-step process. First, position to the menu item you want to remember:

```
--> 45. Information Organization - by Subject (Library of Congress)/
```

That accomplished, create the bookmark with the **a** command. Pressing **a** yields a dialog box:

```
+--------Information Organization - by Subject (Library of Congress)---------+
|                                                                            |
| Name for this bookmark:                                                    |
|                                                                            |
|  Information Organization - by Subject (Library of Congress)               |
|                                                                            |
|                 [Cancel: ^G] [Erase: ^U] [Accept: Enter]                   |
+----------------------------------------------------------------------------+
```

It is asking you to give the bookmark a name so you can recognize it later. It suggests using the item's menu string as a name. If that is OK with you, press ENTER and you are done. If you want to give the bookmark some other name, BACKSPACE over the suggested name and type whatever you like. Press ENTER when you are finished.

You now have a bookmark. You can do a search now, move somewhere else, or quit. It does not matter what you do because you can always jump back to this directory. You do this with the **v** command, which brings up a menu of all the bookmarks you have set:

```
Internet Gopher Information Client 2.0 pl11

                            Bookmarks
```

```
  -->  1.  10.20.94_BA_Praises_FCC_on_VDT_Rulings
       2.  Information Organization - by Subject (Library of Congress)/
```

To jump straight to the Library of Congress directory, just select it like any other menu item.

Sometime in the future, you might want to get rid of a bookmark. You may not need the resource anymore, or the resource may have disappeared or moved. (The Internet in general, and Gopherspace in particular, is constantly in flux.) To delete a bookmark, go to the Bookmarks menu (with a **v**), select the bookmark you want to delete, and press **d**.

Bookmarks are especially useful after Veronica searches. You might get back a bunch of articles you think are really great. You haven't a clue where they live. You might figure it out with an =, but why bother? Simply set a bookmark on the articles you want to remember and you are done.

A variation of the bookmark command remembers how you got to a particular menu, rather than an item within the menu itself. This is the **A** command. On the surface, this appears to be a two-keystroke shortcut: I can use **A** to mark the previous (or parent) menu, rather than using **u** to move to the previous menu, and **a** to set a bookmark. There is one obvious reason for doing this. Often you get to a directory that looks interesting, but you do not know that it really contains what you want until you look at some of the items within it. Now, when you are looking at those items, you can note that this entire directory is something worth remembering, and type **A**.

The real beauty of **A** is not as a shortcut. It allows you to remember searches. That is, if you type **A** after performing a search, **gopher** remembers the search menu and the search string you used. Let's say you want to save our previous Veronica search for articles related to women's healthcare. By the time we finished refining the search, it was pretty complicated—healthcare (wom\* or family) not Residence—and not something you would want to type every week when you check for new articles. To save the search itself: Make the Veronica search, check to see that it found the resources you want, and type **A**. That saves the search as a bookmark. In the future, when you select the bookmark, **gopher** will rerun your search, rather than just deliver the articles you already know about. It is an easy way to check periodically for new resources. Bookmarks can be used only to remember your position in the Gopher system. If you leave Gopher to access something through TELNET, you can place a bookmark on the actual <TEL> resource, but you cannot place one within the resource. For example, you can place a bookmark to get you to:

```
  23.  University of California MELVYL <TEL>
```

When you enter this resource, you will get the warning message noted previously. Among other things, this message means that **gopher** can no longer keep track of where you are. If it cannot do that, it cannot set a bookmark. For example, you cannot remember a particular menu or resource within MELVYL.

### Pointing to Another Server

Earlier, we said that every Gopher client is configured with a default server that it contacts when it starts, and that you can specify an alternate server on the command line as follows:

    % **gopher** *server-name*

There are two reasons you might want to go directly to a server. The first is to connect quickly. If you know that the information you want is offered by one particular server, you can go there directly, rather than hunt through a number of menus. With thousands of servers out there, finding the one you want on a menu can be tedious.

Second, there will be times when your main menu server is unavailable. The solution is to try another Gopher server, such as:

    % gopher gopher.internic.net

How do you find server names like **gopher.internic.net**? The easiest way is browse around the Other Gopher and Information Servers menu. When you find a particularly well-stocked server, use the = command and scribble down its name.

## Gopher Development

Because the Gopher service is still under development, the features that are available are changing. Client programs for other types of computers are being developed by volunteers. Also, as they are developed, some may have different features. Some clients may omit certain features; others may have strange implementations of some features. So be forewarned: If you expect some surprises, you will be able to deal with them without too much trouble.

Every day, people are learning more and more about how to put various kinds of resources up on the network. In some respects, that is adding to the chaotic nature of the Net. However, it is also driving the development of new servers and indexing tools to make the Net more usable and friendly. It also means that your favorite Gopher server will be somewhat different every time you visit it.

### *Other Gopher Clients*

In this chapter we have discussed a simple line-oriented **gopher** client for UNIX. That was an obvious choice, because it is what you will see if you stick your toe in the water by **telnet**ing to a public Gopher client. However, there are many other clients available: **xgopher** for the X Window System, TurboGopher for the Macintosh (quite highly regarded), and several clients for Windows. The best Gopher client is ironically not a Gopher client at all. It is any of the WWW browsers available in UNIX, Windows, and Macintosh versions. We explore this in chapter 13.

## ◼ *A Last Word*

We hope we have given you some idea of what is available through Gopher, which is almost everything. One thing that we cannot give you is a better sense of how Gopher is organized: for example, where to look if you are an archaeologist, or a communications student, or a software developer, or a Dante scholar. Gopher may help guide you to the resources, but you still have to know your resources fairly well. In a traditional library, there is no substitute for browsing through the stacks and seeing what looks interesting. The same is true for Gopher: There is no substitute for exploring. Not only will you become familiar with the various commands, you will also find out where the good stuff is. And you will probably find some useful services that you did not know existed.

## ◼ *Exercises*

*Print out your responses to each of the following items. Seek help locally if you need it.*

**1.** Do you have access to Gopher via both a graphical user interface *and* a text-only interface? What GUI Gopher clients are available (e.g., TurboGopher, WinGopher)?

**2.** Locate your local Gopher server. Compare your server to that of the "mother of all Gophers" located via **gopher gopher.micro.umn.edu** (or URL **gopher:// gopher.micro.umn.edu**).

**3.** Locate and list 10 Gopher servers of interest to you personally, academically, or professionally.

**4.** How can you access Veronica? List five advantages and disadvantages of using Veronica.

**5.** Try to find each of the following items available via Gopher. What is the **gopher** address for each service's server? How did you find it?

- AskERIC
- Clearinghouse for Subject-Oriented Internet Resource Guides
- Careers and Occupations
- Your local weather forecast
- TurboGopher
- WinGopher

**6.** Using Gopher's CSO phone book server, look up "L Ward" at the University of Illinois with the phone number of 244-0681. What information do you get from this exercise? If you were placed in charge of Gopher privacy issues, what concerns might you have about making information available electronically? What, if any, differences are there between similar information being printed in paper directories locally versus access to the information being made globally via Gopher?

**7.** Use **gopher** to try to find the e-mail address and phone number of someone you know at another university or organization. Explain succinctly but precisely how you do this.

**8.** What resources are located at the Apple Gopher server(s)? the IBM Gopher server(s)? the Microsoft Gopher server(s)?

**9.** Compare Gopher to Archie. What do you see as the relative advantages and disadvantages of each?

**10.** Using the Gopher search tool of your choice, find a document related to global warming (or another topic chosen by your instructor). Demonstrate three ways that you can have a copy of that document in your possession for future reference.

**11.** You can save resources (e.g., paper and/or disk space) by saving only the **gopher** address of the document you just found. Explain succinctly but completely how you would do this on your local system.

**12.** Gopher now includes links to USENET news. Is this access available at your location?

# SEARCHING INDEXED DATABASES: WAIS

Wide Area Information Service (WAIS, pronounced "wayz") is another of the Internet's services. It is great for searching through indexed material and finding articles based on what they contain. That is, WAIS lets you search through Internet archives looking for articles containing groups of words. Whereas Gopher is a browsing tool, WAIS is for direct searches.

WAIS is probably *not* one of the Internet's more popular tools, particularly among inexperienced users. Its application is not readily apparent, and early, command-line versions are not very user-friendly. Nevertheless, WAIS is a unique tool that merits attention by anyone interested in becoming an Internet expert, including, we hope, you.

In *WAIS—A New Vision for Publishing* by Michael Robin (URL: **http://www.wais.com/ newhomepages/mt-apr-94.html**), Brewster Kahle, founder of WAIS, Inc., compares WAIS to Gopher and the World Wide Web. If you think of the Web as a large network book, then Gopher, with its hierarchical browsing approach, is the table of contents. The World Wide Web is hypertext pages that allow users to click from one page to another, and from author to author. WAIS is index in the back of the book, where you turn when you know what you want.

WAIS is really a tool for working with collections of data, or *databases.* To many people, databases connote a file full of numbers or, once you have seen a little of what WAIS can do, a set of articles about some topic. That is too narrow a view. WAIS can deal with much more; the format of the information presented does not matter much. It does not really look at the data in the process of a search—it looks at an index. If you or someone else takes the trouble to build an index, WAIS can select information and present it to you regardless of its format.

It is most common to see indexes for various kinds of text (articles and so on), but you can build an index for anything. For example, someone could build an index from descriptions of great works of art; the data tied to the index could be the works of art themselves stored in some standard graphical format (e.g., GIF). You could then search for "gothic", and up would pop Grant Wood's painting *American Gothic.* There are many such indexes built from data that is available elsewhere (such as **whois** and Archie indexes). Some of them are useful and some are not, but you can search them and frequently come up with what you want.

The "official" terminology used to discuss WAIS is obtuse. The database language is overly abstract and prevents you from seeing what WAIS can do. Think of WAIS databases as private libraries devoted to a particular topic: for example, a library of architectural building standards and codes. Because this is an easier way to view things, that is how we will talk about them for the rest of the chapter.

Like Gopher, WAIS allows you to find and access resources on the network without regard for where they reside. In Gopher, you find resources by looking through a sequence of menus until you find something appropriate. WAIS does the same thing, but it does the searching for you. You tell it what you want; it tries to find the material you need. A WAIS command is essentially: "find me items about this in that library." WAIS then looks at all the documents in the library (or libraries) you gave it and tells you which documents are most likely to contain what you want. If you like, WAIS then displays the documents for you.

There are more than 500 free WAIS libraries on the network now. Because they are maintained by volunteer effort and donated computer time, coverage tends to be spotty. For topics where there are many willing volunteers, coverage is good: As you would expect, there are many libraries for computer science, networking, and molecular biology. Some literature libraries exist, such as Project Gutenberg's collection and various religious texts. Coverage in the social sciences has been lacking, but this inevitably has started to change. Libraries are always being added. There is a way to ask: "Is there a library for this topic?" You can easily check whether or not WAIS has any resources that are relevant for your research needs.

Some commercial information products, such as the Dow Jones Information Service, provide their product through a WAIS interface. You pay a fee to use services like this. Once you have arranged for payment, these services are no different than the free network WAIS services.

We will introduce you to WAIS by discussing how it works. There are some good and bad points about how WAIS does its job. It takes practice to get WAIS to do what you want; you have to ask it the right questions. Understanding how to construct these questions is easier if you know what WAIS does with them. Once that is behind us, we can do some searches. Finally, you can use WAIS to build and search private libraries, and we will touch on that briefly.

## ■ *How WAIS Works*

WAIS is a distributed text-searching system based on a standard named Z39.50 (URL: **http://lcweb.loc.gov/z3950/agency**).* The standard describes a way for one computer to ask another to do searches for it. WAIS is one of the first systems based upon this draft standard. At this point, it is also the most common.

To make a document available through a WAIS server, someone must create an index for that server to use in the search. For textual information, every word in the document is usually indexed. When you request a search from a WAIS client, it contacts the servers that handle the libraries you suggested. It asks each server, in turn, to search its index for a set of words. The server then sends you a list of documents that may be appropriate and a "score" telling how appropriate it thinks each one is. The scores are normalized so that the document that best matches your search criterion is given a score of 1,000; others get proportionally less.

If you say, "Find me documents that contain 'clinton and gore,'" WAIS looks in the index and counts how many times each document contains the word "clinton", the word "and", and the word "gore". The sum of these counts, weighted slightly by what the word is, is converted to a score for a document. After all the libraries have been searched, WAIS gives you the titles of the documents that received the highest scores. There is a limit to the number of documents it reports (usually between 15 and 50, depending on which client you use). You can then pick which documents to view, and WAIS will display them for you.

You should see a problem already. How many times can you conceive of selecting a document because it contained the word "and"? You might have thought that "and" meant the logical *and* operation in WAIS. In fact, *there are no special words in WAIS; every word counts in the ranking.* A document that contains 1,000 matches for "and" but no matches for "clinton" or "gore" might just have the best score; or, more likely, a score high enough to place it in the top 10. Remember that WAIS is still a relatively new

---

*Z39.50 is a draft ANSI standard for requesting bibliographic information. It has been under development for a long time within the library and computing communities.

facility, and improvements are continually added. As the software matures, some of these problems will be resolved.

A second problem that may not be as obvious is that WAIS lacks "contextual sensitivity." You could ask WAIS to find articles containing the words "problem children", but it would also be just as happy with an item containing the sentence, "The children had a problem; they'd lost their lunch money." You cannot tell WAIS that the words must occur in a certain order, and you cannot provide any information about the context in which they occur.

Finally, once a search has taken you astray, you cannot tell WAIS to exclude any "wrong turns" or portions of a source. That is, you cannot give a command like, "Find articles with the words 'problem children', but throw out articles that contain references to lunch." There is also no way to ask, "What's been added to this source since last year?" This makes it hard to do searches repeatedly in a changing source. If your source is an index of papers from a journal, there is no way to say, "Look for the articles that have been published since the last time I checked."

Even with these flaws, you will find that WAIS is one of the most useful lookup tools on the Internet. And it is possible that future versions of WAIS will solve these problems. WAIS has one really unique feature going for it: *relevance feedback*. Some clients allow you to find articles that are similar to the articles you have already found. Let's say your search for "problem children" turned up an article titled "Educational Problems in Gifted Children," in addition to the spurious lunch-money article. "Educational Problems . . ." happens to be exactly what you are looking for. Relevance feedback allows you to take some text from that article and have WAIS extract good words from it to use in future searches. These searches can be done either within the same source or in a different source.

## ▓ *Getting Access*

Accessing WAIS is analogous to Gopher. In order to use it, you need a computer running a WAIS client program. You can install the client program on your own workstation, or you can access a computer that already has the client installed and run it there. As usual, your campus network most likely has a WAIS client available to you.

As is the case with Gopher, there are WAIS clients for most standard operating systems and computers: Macintosh, DOS, X Windows, NeXT, UNIX, and so on. In other sections of the book, we have often included command-line versions of Internet tools, and there is a UNIX line-oriented interface called **swais**. The problem is that explaining how to do WAIS searches using **swais** is quite confusing. You have to give many commands and additional keystrokes just to set up the search, and it is not clear what is happening. It is much easier to visualize what is happening with a graphical client, such as **xwais**, which runs under the X Windows system. So, in the next section, we will first do a few examples with the X client. When you know what is happening, we will show you how to use the line-oriented client (**wais** or **swais**) too.

The line-oriented client is important because it is available at a number of public-access sites around the Internet. As with Gopher, you can **telnet** to a particular computer and log in with a special ID, such as **wais**, and do some simple searches. You can also do WAIS searches through Gopher and the World Wide Web (which we will discuss in chapter 13). Most Gopher servers have a line like this on the main menu:

```
9.  Other Gopher and Information Servers/
```

If you select this item, the next menu will have an entry:

```
6.  WAIS Based Information/
```

This item lets you use the Gopher index interface to search any WAIS source for which there is no charge. The only thing you cannot do with this facility is search multiple sources at one time.

You might want to use one of these public servers the first time to try things out. If you decide you want to use it regularly, get yourself a better client (like Gopher, WAIS clients are getting better all the time). They are all available for free from various places. You can use **archie** to find them. Look for something called *freeWAIS*.* As with the other software we have discussed in this book, the choice of a WAIS client is often a matter of personal taste.

## *Formulating a WAIS Search*

Now that we are through the preliminaries, let's get started. You need to make a leap of faith and forget how you would normally work with computer databases. When many users try WAIS for the first time, they ask the question, "What libraries of documents are available?" This is the wrong approach. People are used to relying on the computer for some tasks and their brain for the others. The brain is usually responsible for scanning lists to look for interesting items. In order to use WAIS most effectively, you must trust WAIS and let it do the scanning for you.

---

*Two FTP archives where you can find this software are **ftp.cnidr.org** in the U.S. and **nic.funet.fi** in Europe. Although the development of WAIS was done by Thinking Machines, Apple, Dow Jones, and accounting firm KPMG Pete Marwick, most of the current work on the free software *(freeWAIS)* is coordinated by the Clearinghouse for Networked Information Discovery and Retrieval (CNIDR).

*Figure 12-1    xwais main window*

WAIS tools have not diffused as quickly as other Internet tools. We will include the X Windows version of WAIS here, which has led the way for development of Windows and Macintosh interfaces to WAIS.

When you start the WAIS client for X Windows, **xwais**, the first thing you will see is the main window, which appears in Figure 12-1. WAIS clients maintain two libraries: a library of questions and a library of sources.* This window shows both. The **Questions** section at the top contains identifiers for queries you may want to make again. If you want to see what is new in a particular field every month, you can reexecute the search in its original form, or modify it and issue it again. Here we see one saved question, named *child-sources.*

The **Sources** section, just below the **Questions** section, is for source library maintenance. It shows a "scrollable" list of libraries that your client knows how to locate and search.

---

*These libraries are stored in directories named *wais-questions* and *wais-sources* in your *home* directory for the account you use to run this client.

The **Questions** and **Sources** sections each have three buttons:

**New**         Creates a new question or source window.

**Open**        Displays an existing question or a source that you have selected by clicking on it. The **Open** button is used to change and reexecute a question, or to change source entries.

**Delete**      Deletes an existing question or a source that you have selected.

Toward the bottom of the window, there are two buttons. The **Help** button gets you help if you click on it. **Quit** terminates **xwais**.

### Finding a library

There is a list of public WAIS libraries, but that list is a WAIS library itself. If you know about one library, the *directory-of-servers,* you have got it all. But instead of reading the list of libraries yourself, you should start your search by asking WAIS: "What library do I look in for 'gifted children'?" To start the process, click the **New** button. This displays another window, with a template for asking a question.

Let's compose a search. Before starting, we will give you a clue. "Gifted children" is much too narrow a term; if you look for libraries that are appropriate for "gifted children," you are not likely to find any. This makes sense, if you think about traditional (books and paper) libraries: There are probably very few libraries in the world with "gifted children" in their name. If you had an index of important special collections, you would probably find a few that contained the words "gifted children". If you restricted your search to these libraries, you would miss many libraries with excellent social science collections, some of which may be more useful than the special-purpose libraries. WAIS is no different. The right way to find an appropriate library is to use really broad terms. Think about what kind of people would be concerned about gifted children. You might think of social workers, educators, or parents. Because adding more terms to a search in WAIS makes it easier to match, try to search the *directory-of-servers* with your relevant terms:

```
social work
education
parenting
```

Type the keywords into the **Tell me about** window, as shown in Figure 12-2.

After you have filled in the relevant terms, click on the **Add Source** button. This displays a pull-down menu of all the libraries listed in your client's library of sources, shown in Figure 12-3.

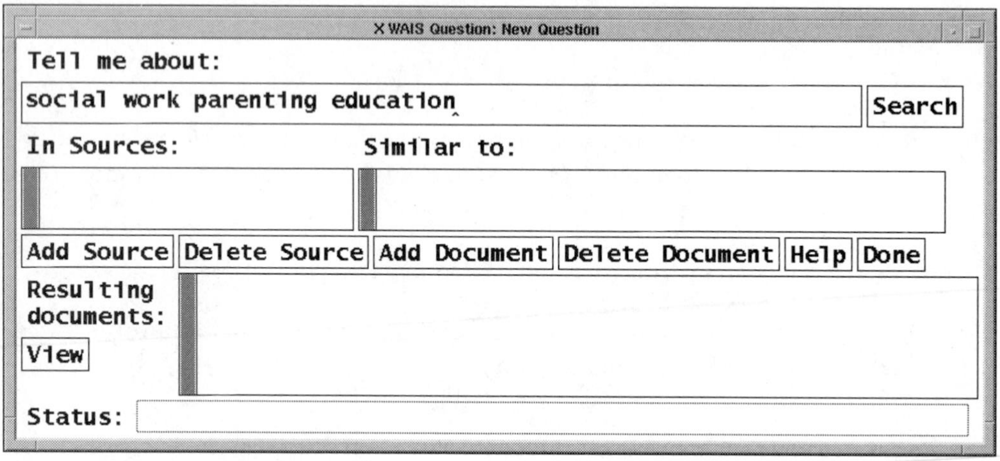

*Figure 12-2    directory-of-servers query*

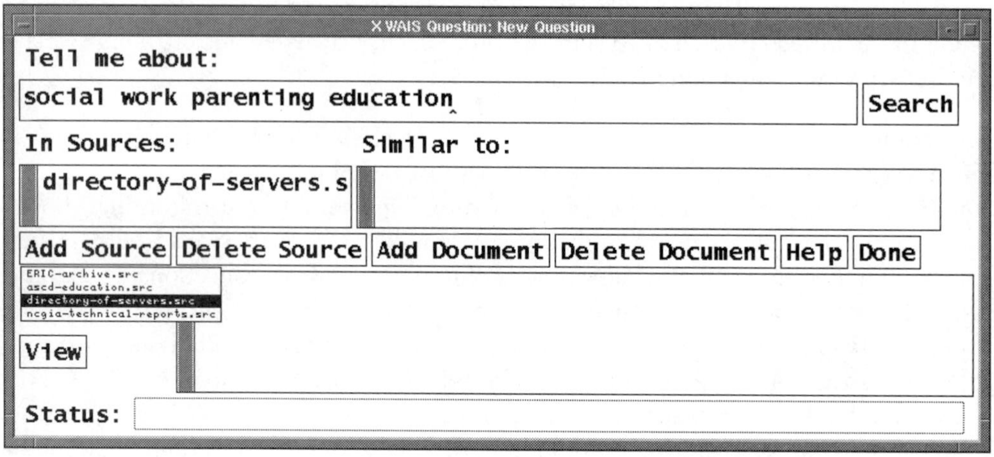

*Figure 12-3    Selecting a source*

Move the arrow to the *directory-of-servers,* which appears in reverse video, and release the button; the *directory-of-servers* will appear in the **In Sources** box. Now you are ready to run your query by pushing the **Search** button.

If you did things correctly, WAIS will fill in the **Resulting documents** section of the window, as shown in Figure 12-4.

Look at the first result:

```
1000   986 ascd-education.src /proj/wais/wais-sources
```

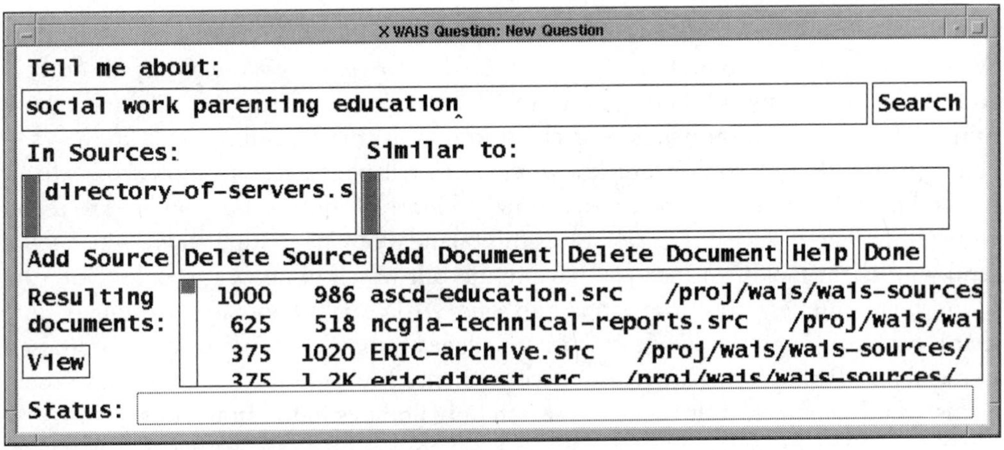

*Figure 12-4   Results of directory search*

The 1000 is its score; this score indicates that it fit your search criteria better than any other source, not that it was a perfect match—but you are more likely to find interesting articles here than anywhere else. The size is listed next: 986 characters.* The name of the index, *ascd-education.src*, sounds promising. When you make your next search, looking for actual articles (rather than promising libraries), you will select *ascd-education.src* in the **Add Source** menu and add it to your search list, **In Sources**. At the end of the line, you see the filename of this source. You can ignore this for now.

If you scroll down the list of prospective sources, you will find their scores fall off significantly after the top four. So, you decide to draw the pass/fail line there and use the top four for the real search:

```
ascd-education.src
ncgia-technical-reports.src
ERIC-archives.src
eric-digest.src
```

Now that you have successfully searched for something, it is really tempting to click the **Done** button and get rid of the search window, but you will need this information again. The *directory-of-servers* is like the Yellow Pages telephone directory. It tells you what telephone numbers to call for different services, but it does not call them for you. The *directory-of-servers* likewise tells you where to look to find what you want. You will need to take the sources you just found, and use them in the next search. Leave the window on-screen, and you will not have to write the names of those four libraries on a piece of paper to use them.

---

*This is the size of the item you found. In this case, it is the size of the server descriptor. The 986 characters have nothing to do with the size or completeness of the *ascd-education* library itself.

It is time to think about what we just accomplished. There are obvious questions that WAIS users ask at this point. First: "How do the *directory-of-servers,* the library of sources, and the **In Sources** area of the screen relate?" To make sense of this, you need to keep in mind what you know and what your client knows. In the beginning, you know what you want to ask, but you do not know where to tell your client to look. Your client knows how to look in all the servers listed in its library of sources, but you have to tell it which ones. The *directory-of-servers* solves this quandary by suggesting where you should send your client looking. Once you have found out which libraries are useful, you can fill in the **In Sources** part of a question and send WAIS off.* On occasion, you may find that a search through the *directory-of-servers* suggests libraries that your client does not know about. Perhaps they are new and your client's source library does not have their entries yet (remember, your client can search only libraries found in its sources library). For now, let's assume that any source suggested to you by the *directory-of-servers* is in your client's library of sources.

The second question is simply, "Why do we bother?" Why do we not just tell WAIS to "look everywhere"? There are several reasons. First, selecting sources is one way to narrow the search. If you ask WAIS to look up items about "cars," you could get articles on toys, automobiles, and Computer Aided Registration Systems (CARS). Selecting some suitable libraries, such as *automobile-repair-records,* focuses your search.† Wading through hundreds of articles to decide which are relevant is a waste of your time, and finding relevance is what WAIS is supposed to do. Second, searching everywhere could take a long time. You do not go to the library and start at one end of the shelves, looking at every title to find something of interest. You know automobile repair starts at 629.28, so you find that section and browse only that section.

### Asking your question

Now that we have these questions out of the way, let's get back to behavior problems: How do we compose an appropriate question? The real search is similar to the directory search with which we started. Go to the main menu and click the **New** button in the question area. Now you have a new question menu; fill in some relevant keywords:

```
behavior problems in gifted children
```

Fill in the sources section. That is, you fill in the "phone numbers" you found previously from the "Yellow Pages." You do this as before, with the pull-down menu under **Add Source,** but you need to do it four times, once for each source. Now you

---

*You may also find that searching the *directory-of-servers* leads you to another directory of servers: for example, *JANUS-dir-of-servers* (a good place to look for legal and UN-related resources). This is fine. Just add the new directory to your source list and ask a general question again.

†I used this for illustration; I do not think this library exists—yet.

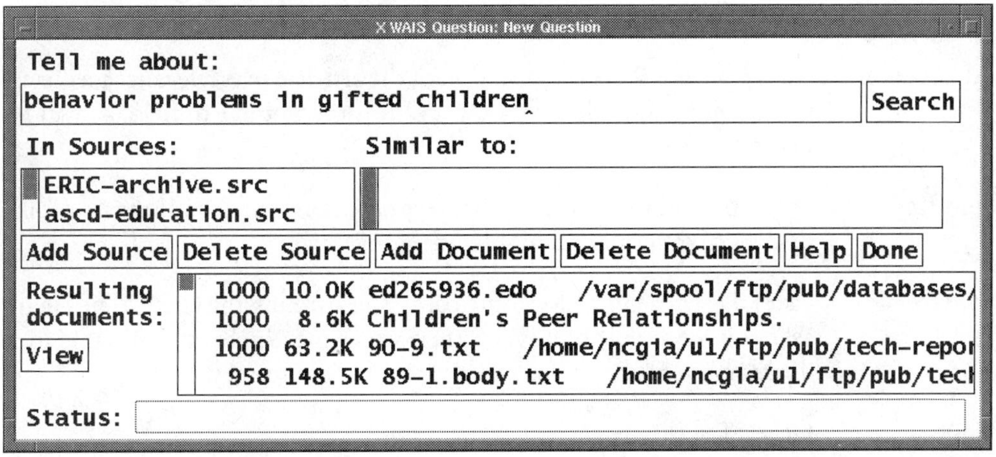

```
┌─────────────────────────── X WAIS Question: New Question ───────────────────────────┐
│ Tell me about:                                                                        │
│ ┌──────────────────────────────────────────────────────────────────┐  ┌──────────┐  │
│ │ behavior problems in gifted children                              │  │ Search   │  │
│ └──────────────────────────────────────────────────────────────────┘  └──────────┘  │
│ In Sources:                      Similar to:                                          │
│ ┌──────────────────────────────┐ ┌──────────────────────────────────┐                │
│ ║ ERIC-archive.src             │ │                                  │                │
│ │   ascd-education.src         │ │                                  │                │
│ └──────────────────────────────┘ └──────────────────────────────────┘                │
│ ┌────────────┐┌──────────────┐┌──────────────┐┌───────────────┐┌────┐┌────┐          │
│ │ Add Source ││ Delete Source││ Add Document ││ Delete Document││Help││Done│          │
│ └────────────┘└──────────────┘└──────────────┘└───────────────┘└────┘└────┘          │
│ Resulting   ║  1000 10.0K ed265936.edo    /var/spool/ftp/pub/databases/              │
│ documents:  │  1000  8.6K Children's Peer Relationships.                              │
│ ┌────────┐  │  1000 63.2K 90-9.txt    /home/ncgia/ul/ftp/pub/tech-repor              │
│ │ View   │  │   958 148.5K 89-1.body.txt    /home/ncgia/ul/ftp/pub/tec               │
│ └────────┘                                                                            │
│ Status: ┌─────────────────────────────────────────────────────────────────┐          │
│         └─────────────────────────────────────────────────────────────────┘          │
└───────────────────────────────────────────────────────────────────────────────────────┘
```

*Figure 12-5    Result of behavior problems search*

are ready. You click the **Search** button, and off you go. Soon the results return, as shown in Figure 12-5.

Now you have what you wanted: a set of articles that sound interesting. (If you want to see more of the titles, you can expand the window horizontally.) The item's size field tells you the size (in bytes) of what will be fetched. If you click on **Children's Peer Relationships** and click on **View**, WAIS will fetch the article (8.6K characters worth) for you and will display it in another window. This is shown in Figure 12-6.

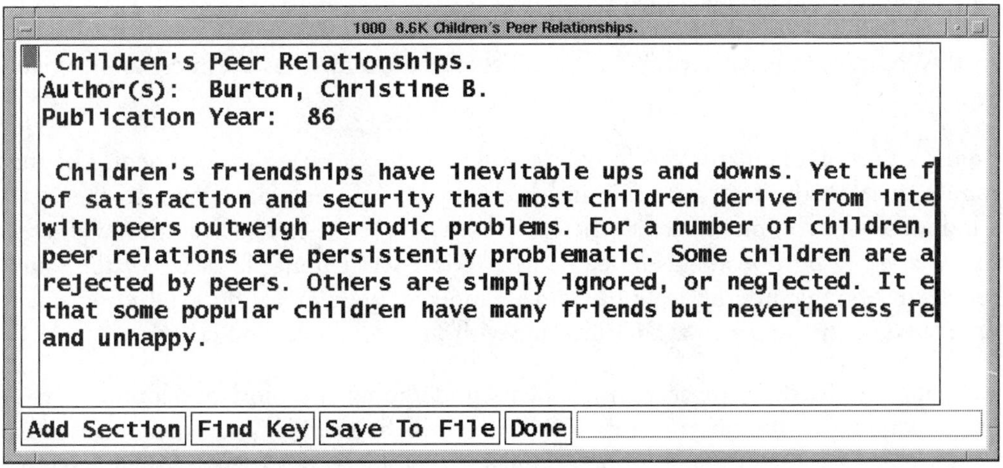

```
┌─────────────────────── 1000 8.6K Children's Peer Relationships. ───────────────────────┐
│ ║ Children's Peer Relationships.                                                        │
│ │ Author(s):   Burton, Christine B.                                                     │
│ │ Publication Year:  86                                                                 │
│ │                                                                                        │
│ │  Children's friendships have inevitable ups and downs. Yet the f                      │
│ │ of satisfaction and security that most children derive from inte                      │
│ │ with peers outweigh periodic problems. For a number of children,                      │
│ │ peer relations are persistently problematic. Some children are a                      │
│ │ rejected by peers. Others are simply ignored, or neglected. It e                      │
│ │ that some popular children have many friends but nevertheless fe                      │
│ │ and unhappy.                                                                          │
│ │                                                                                        │
│ ┌─────────────┐┌──────────┐┌─────────────┐┌──────┐┌──────────────────────────────┐     │
│ │ Add Section ││ Find Key ││ Save To File││ Done ││                              │     │
│ └─────────────┘└──────────┘└─────────────┘└──────┘└──────────────────────────────┘     │
└─────────────────────────────────────────────────────────────────────────────────────────┘
```

*Figure 12-6    Article you retrieved*

This screen lets you do four things, in addition to reading the article:

**Add Section**   Adds a previously selected section of the article to the relevance feedback section of the question window. (This is the **Similar to** field, shown in Figure 12-5.)

**Find Key**   Skips forward in the text to the next occurrence of a word that was one of the search terms and highlights it.

**Save to File**   Saves the article in a file on the computer running the client. The client asks you for a filename. WAIS then stores the article by that name in a directory, *wais-documents,* under your *home* directory.

**Done**   Gets rid of the article and the window.

Finally, with your problem solved, you can push the **Done** button on the question window. WAIS will ask you if you want to save the question. If you do, you need to provide a filename. After saving a question, it will appear in your "question library." Next time you want to ask the same question, just select it from the **Questions** section of the main window and click on the **Open** button.

## Refining a Search

Relevance feedback lets you use the results of a search to further refine the search. You do this by selecting items, either whole or in part, that you have already found and moving them to the **Similar to** area of the question window. If you want to use the whole article, you select the article in the question window and click on **Add Document**. The result of this action is shown in Figure 12-7.

In this example, you selected "Children's Peer Relationships" as the most appropriate article to use.

To use a portion of an article as feedback, you must be viewing the document. Use the mouse to select the text you want and click on the **Add Section** button in the view window. When you move back to the question window, the feedback section will refer to the selected portions of the document. You can select multiple pieces of the same article, or of different articles, in the same manner. When you are done selecting, click on **Search** to try the search again, this time with the added selection criteria.

Relevance feedback is the section of clients undergoing the most development. If a client is going to die on you, this is where it will happen. If your client runs into trouble, check whether a newer one is available (e.g. CNIDR's freeWAIS has versions 0.03, 0.04, and 0.05).

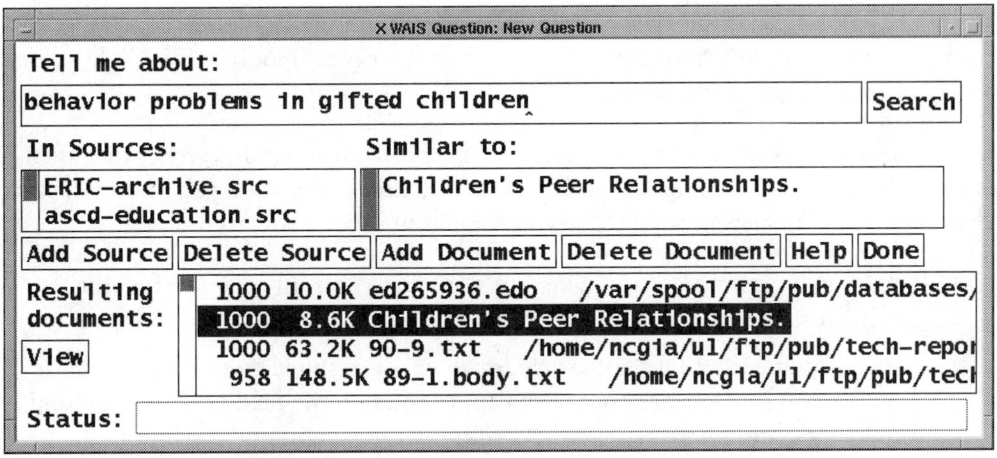

```
 X WAIS Question: New Question
Tell me about:
behavior problems in gifted children                    Search
In Sources:              Similar to:
  ERIC-archive.src         Children's Peer Relationships.
  ascd-education.src
Add Source Delete Source Add Document Delete Document Help Done
Resulting    1000 10.0K ed265936.edo   /var/spool/ftp/pub/databases,
documents:   1000  8.6K Children's Peer Relationships.
View         1000 63.2K 90-9.txt       /home/ncgia/ul/ftp/pub/tech-repor
             958 148.5K 89-1.body.txt  /home/ncgia/ul/ftp/pub/tech
Status:
```

*Figure 12-7    Feedback search setup*

From start to finish, there are a lot of steps. A summary of how to go about searching is in order:

1.  Select the *directory-of-servers*.

2.  Ask a general question of the *directory-of-servers* to find any libraries that are relevant to your topic. Do this as often as you need, to find good libraries.

3.  Select the libraries that look interesting.

4.  Ask a specific question to find the articles (or other items) that you are searching for.

5.  If you are not satisfied with the results, refine your search (possibly using relevance feedback) to get a new set of articles.

As we have said, formulating good WAIS searches can be tricky. With some practice, though, you will get the hang of it.

## When Searches Do Not Go as Planned

Sometimes your searches will not retrieve what you want; you may get articles that are unrelated or you might find nothing at all. There are two possible solutions: You can try to find more appropriate keywords or the other sources. That is one reason why most WAIS clients let you save your questions. Some questions are hard to construct. Once you have one that works, you may not want to let it go. Even if you do not want to ask the same question next time, you may find it easier to modify an old search than to start from scratch. It is not unusual to do a search many times, modifying it slightly each time until you get what you want.

Of course, saving your searches does not solve the problem at hand: searches that are not effective in the first place. The only real solution is to keep trying until you find something that does work. However, we can give you some hints about how to proceed:

- If the search results are reasonable, but not what you really want, refine the search, either by adding keywords yourself or using relevance feedback.

- View an apparently irrelevant article to see why it resulted from your search. It may give you some ideas about terms appropriate to the field you are searching. You will not find many matches for "God" in the Koran, but you will find "Allah". WAIS does not automatically try synonyms. This technique might also turn up some variant spellings ("behavior" versus "behaviour") or relevant synonyms (such as "Llah").

- If WAIS does not find anything and if you are confident of the sources, try a simple search first, for which you are sure there will be some articles. Look at the results; this may give you some clues about the best words to search for.

- If you keep getting irrelevant articles, try to limit the number of sources you use. The problem is that a highly rated source can, on occasion, provide a lot of irrelevant articles. So you have got to find out which source is providing the irrelevancies and eliminate it from your search. Unfortunately, not all WAIS clients tell you which source a particular document came from. You might be able to guess by checking whether the article's filename corresponds to the source's name. (This will not always help, but it is worth trying.) It you need to, you can delete a source and try the search again. If it is better, leave it out. If it is worse, put it back and delete another.

## ▓ *Public WAIS Clients*

Using the line-oriented public client **swais** is not particularly hard. (Remember, **swais** is not really different. It is just a particular WAIS client, which is used when you are using a line-mode terminal.) Just like Gopher, it may be available on the computer you normally use. If it is, you should be able to access it just by entering **swais**. For the sake of the discussion, I will assume that you are using a public client. So, the first thing you must do is pick a likely prospect out of the Public WAIS Servers table (Table 12-1) and **telnet** to it.

*Table 12-1    Public WAIS Servers*

| Name | Login | Location |
|------|-------|----------|
| info.funet.fi | wais | Europe |
| swais.cwis.uci.edus | wais | Western U.S.* |
| cnidr.org | demo | Eastern U.S. |
| sunsite.unc.edus | wais | Eastern U.S. |
| quake.think.com | wais | Eastern U.S. |

*This server has a limited number of databases, mostly of interest only to University of California, Irvine, students and staff. It can still be used to practice and investigate **swais**.

When you are connected, use the login shown, and you will automatically be placed in **swais**. For example:

```
% telnet quake.think.com

Trying 192.31.181.1...

Connected to quake.think.com.
Escape character is '^]'.
SunOS UNIX (quake)
login: wais
Welcome to swais.
Please type user identifier (i.e. user@host):  krol@ux1.cso.uiuc.edu
TERM = (unknown)  vt100
Starting swais (this may take a little while)...
```

What happens next will vary significantly from place to place. When the number of WAIS databases was small, each of these public clients would have all known databases in its available-source list. Now that there are hundreds of WAIS libraries, if they were all in the source list, it would be around 25 pages of sources to wade through.

Because you have no storage to build a personal set of interesting sources, and working with all the databases at once is unwieldy, many of these public clients start with a single source: the *directory-of-servers*. Even if you know exactly which source you want to use, you must still search the *directory-of-servers* to find it.

This search retrieves the database's descriptor records. You then add the descriptors to the list of sources available in your current session and select them to do your real search. If the client you use gives you the whole list of sources at this point, you may skip the first search of the *directory-of-servers*—provided that you already know which sources you want. Just find them (in the 25-page listing) and select them. (It still might be easier to go through the *directory-of-servers.*)

Let's say that you would like to find an interesting fish dish to make for dinner tonight. After connecting to **quake.think.com** and logging in, you are greeted with this basic **swais** screen:

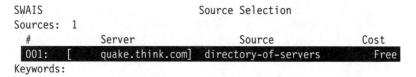

```
SWAIS                          Source Selection
Sources: 1
   #          Server              Source            Cost
 001:    [    quake.think.com]  directory-of-servers      Free
Keywords:

<space> selects, w for keywords, arrows move, <return> searches, q quits, or ?
```

You have at your disposal one source, the *directory-of-servers*. First, select that source as the one you want to use. (You do not have much choice; it is either this or nothing.) To select a source, move down to the line on which it is listed, either by using your arrow keys or typing the source's number, followed by ENTER. Once you have yourself positioned, press the SPACEBAR to select the source. Because there is only one source available to you, you should only need to press the SPACEBAR. An asterisk appears in the display to flag the *directory-of-servers* as a selected source:

```
 001:   *  [    quake.think.com]  directory-of-servers     Free
```

Once you have chosen a source, you need to enter the keywords you want to search for. Pressing **w** signals that you want to enter keywords; the client positions the cursor near the bottom left of the screen, and prompts you:

```
Keywords: ethnic cooking
```

You type the words you are interested in, separated by spaces. We're looking for some interesting fish recipes, so we will start with "ethnic cooking". Why not just start with "fish"? At this point, we are still looking for cookbooks in our electronic card catalog; we are not yet looking for recipes. Once we find some cookbooks, we will do a more specific search.

After typing the search string, press ENTER; that starts the actual search. When the search is completed, it will return a screen similar to this, showing the results:

```
SWAIS                          Search Results
Items: 8
   #    Score    Source              Title                 Lines
 001:  [1000]  (directory-of-se)  ANU-Aboriginal-Studies        73
 002:  [1000]  (directory-of-se)  ANU-CanbAnthropology-Index    86
 003:  [1000]  (directory-of-se)  ANU-SSDA-Australian-Census   106
 004:  [1000]  (directory-of-se)  ANU-SSDA-Australian-Opinion  114
 005:  [1000]  (directory-of-se)  ANU-SSDA-Australian-Studies  126
 006:  [1000]  (directory-of-se)  ANU-Thai-Yunnan               83
 007:  [1000]  (directory-of-se)  recipes                       15
 008:  [1000]  (directory-of-se)  usenet-cookbook               21
```

```
<space> selects, arrows move, w for keywords, s for sources, ? for help
```

This is really interesting (and an explanation as to why the novice may shy away from WAIS). You found eight sources; they all get a score of 1000. Some of them are mighty odd. This is a good illustration of how WAIS works. You were looking for the words "ethnic" and "cooking". The ANU resources are sociological sources that matched the single word "ethnic". Sources 7 and 8 matched the single word "cooking". Because each source matched one word, they were all given the same score.

Now that you know what sources to use, you need to add them to the list of sources available to you. Select each source that looks interesting, either by using the arrow keys or typing its number and pressing ENTER. When you have positioned the cursor, type the **u** command (use this source). This will cause the bottom-left line to say things like "Initializing connection . . ." followed by "Adding source . . .", but will not change the display you are looking at. In this example, you would issue two **u** commands, one while positioned at line 7 and one at line 8 (type 7 ENTER **u** 8 ENTER **u**).

To see the effect of what you have done, issue the **s** command to view sources. Its output will now look something like this:

```
SWAIS                           Source Selection
Sources:  3

   #            Server                   Source              Cost
001: * [      quake.think.com]  directory-of-servers         Free
002:   [      wais.oit.unc.edu] recipes                      Free
003:   [ cmns-moon.think.com]   usenet-cookbook              Free
Keywords: ethnic cooking

<space> selects, w for keywords, arrows move, <return> searches, q quits, or ?
```

Notice that you now have three possible sources to search, but you still have the *directory-of-servers* selected (remember the asterisk). If you were to search for a recipe now, you would search only the *directory-of-servers*—not what you had in mind. You must do two things: First get rid of the current selected sources, then select the sources you want. This is easily done. Press = to deselect all current sources. It will get rid of all the asterisks in the display. Next, select the sources you want just as you selected *directory-of-servers* initially: Move to lines 2 and 3 and press the SPACEBAR.

You have finally set up the environment for doing the search you originally wanted. You need to change keywords, so you type **w** again. Surprise: It positioned you after the keywords, "ethnic cooking", that you entered earlier. You need to clear these out by typing **CTRL-U**. After clearing the keyword list, list the ingredients you are looking for in the recipe:

```
Keywords:  garlic fish rice onion
```

Pressing ENTER signals the end of keyword entry and starts the search. Let's see what you caught:

```
SWAIS                 Search Results                    Items: 40

   #    Score   Source          Title              Lines
 001:   [1000] (cmns-moon.think) · SARDINE-FRY(M)  USENET Cookbook    47
 002:   [1000] (       recipes)  gidh@buckn Re: COLLECTION  LONG I 936
 003:   [ 946] (       recipes)  arielle@ta Re: Appetizers (Long) 1591
 004:   [ 946] (       recipes)  arielle@ta Re: Appetizers        1590
 005:   [ 931] (cmns-moon.think) RICE-BEAN-BAKE     USENET Cookbook 61
 006:   [ 931] (cmns-moon.think) CURRIED-RICE       USENET Cookbook 67
 007:   [ 924] (cmns-moon.think) CABBAGE-SALAD(SL)  USENET Cookbook 45
 008:   [ 917] (cmns-moon.think) TARAMOSALATA-1(A)  USENET Cookbook 61
 009:   [ 917] (cmns-moon.think) HOT-FANNY-1(S)     USENET Cookbook 64
 010:   [ 910] (cmns-moon.think) TORTILLA-SOUP(SPV) USENET Cookbook 74
 011:   [ 910] (cmns-moon.think) STROGANOFF-1(M)    USENET Cookbook 56
 012:   [ 889] (cmns-moon.think) PONCIT(M)          USENET Cookbook 54
 013:   [ 889] (cmns-moon.think) PEANUT-SAUCE-1(M)  USENET Cookbook 62
 014:   [ 889] (cmns-moon.think) CUBAN-BEANS(MV)    USENET Cookbook 67
 015:   [ 882] (cmns-moon.think) BLACK-EYE-RICE(B)  USENET Cookbook 57
 016:   [ 882] (cmns-moon.think) AFRICAN-STEW(MV)   USENET Cookbook 56
 017:   [ 869] (cmns-moon.think) PICADILLO(M)       USENET Cookbook 92
 018:   [ 862] (cmns-moon.think) CHICKEN-WINE(M)    USENET Cookbook 52

 <space> selects, arrows move, w for keywords, s for sources, ? for help
```

You can view any one of these items by selecting it, as before, and pressing the SPACEBAR. Notice that a lot of these items do not have much to do with fish; next time, you might be better off with a more restrictive search. The first item, SARDINE-FRY, looks appetizing. It is highlighted, so it is already selected; just press the SPACEBAR to see the recipe:

```
SARDINE-FRY(M)               USENET Cookbook            SARDINE-
FRY(M)

SLOPPY SARDINES
     SARDINE-FRY - Sardines with garlic and tomato. A quick and easy meal for
     two people. This is a recipe conjured up by my friend, Carole Senior.

INGREDIENTS (serves 2)
     2          cans of sardines
     1          small onion chopped
     1/2        green pepper, chopped
     6 oz       tomatoes (1 small can)
     1/2        garlic clove, crushed
     pinch      salt and pepper
```

```
2 Tbsp    cooking oil
1 cup     uncooked white rice
2 cups    water
```

PROCEDURE
   (1)  Heat the oil in a small frying pan.
   (2)  At the same time place the water, rice and a pinch of salt
        into a small saucepan and simmer for 15 minutes.
   (3)  Place the chopped onion and pepper in the frying pan and
        cook until the onion becomes soft.
   (4)  Add the tomatoes, garlic, sardines, salt and pepper to the
        frying pan and cook for 10 to 15 minutes, stirring occasionally.
   (5)  Serve over the rice.

RATING
   Difficulty: easy. Time: 5 minutes preparation, 15 minutes cooking.
   Precision: measure the rice.

CONTRIBUTOR
   Andy Cheese, Department of Computer Science, University of Nottingham, UK
   abc@uk.ac.nott.cs   mcvax!ukc!nott.cs!abc

The USENET Cookbook. Copyright 1991 USENET Community Trust.

Permission to copy without fee all or part of this material is granted
provided that the copies are not made or distributed for direct commercial
advantage, the USENET copyright notice, title, and publication date
appear, and notice is given that copying is by permission of the USENET
Community Trust.

That is all. If you want to get your own copy of the message, type **q** to get back to the list of recipes; then type **m** to mail the recipe to yourself. You will be prompted for your e-mail address. When you are done with **swais**, type **q** to exit the program.

We have now demonstrated all the commands that you need to use the **swais** client, but there are a few more that might make your life a bit easier:

*/string*        Search for a particular string in the results.

S            Save an article in a file. (This does not work on public WAIS clients.)

r            Use an article for "relevance feedback."


# ◼ *Adding Sources*

When we composed the question before about "behavior problems in gifted children," we first looked up some interesting source libraries in the *directory-of-servers*. We then used the **Add Source** pop-up menu to add these to the source list for our "real" question. Now it is time to ask: How does a source get onto the **Add Source** menu?

In our example, we assumed that the WAIS client already knows about all the sources— at least, all that were interesting to you. This is normally a good assumption. However, you will occasionally find sources that your WAIS client does not already know about. These sources may show up in the *directory-of-servers,* and therefore may appear in searches through the directory, but you will not find them on the **Add Source** menu. (It is also possible to discover sources that are not even listed in the *directory-of-servers;* we will describe that situation later.)

Remember that the *directory-of-servers* is like the phone book's Yellow Pages; likewise, the **Add Source** menu is like a set of "speed-dial" buttons on your telephone. If you look up your favorite pizzeria in the Yellow Pages, you will find it listed there; but you could just press the speed-dial button on your phone (you probably programmed it last year). However, if you want to try a new pizzeria, you will have to look it up in the Yellow Pages *and* program it into your phone.

To see why this analogy is relevant, think about what the *directory-of-servers* is. It is just another library (or database). The actual information is not on your client, but on a server in some remote part of the world (probably Cambridge, Massachusetts, where Thinking Machines, one of the WAIS developers, is located). You can make WAIS searches on that server and dig up any information that it knows about. People often create new WAIS libraries, tell the people at Thinking Machines (who maintain the *directory-of-servers*), and these new sources appear there. Your client does not know anything about these new sources, any more than your phone automatically knows about every number in the Yellow Pages. You find a new library in the library of servers and you would like to use it; but your local client does not even know the name of the system on which to find it. This information is available, but it is all in Cambridge.* How do you tell your WAIS client about the new library?

This is called "saving," or "adding," a source. It is really quite easy. Most WAIS clients let you copy a source entry directly. In fact, if you have used the public **swais** client, you have already done this. When you used the **u** command to "use" a source, you actually were telling **swais** to add the source you selected to the sources library. With the public client, you get a source library scratch space when you start; it is destroyed when you leave.

---

*We can explain why WAIS is so confusing. If you had to think in detail about what information was where, and who knew what, everything would be clear. After all, if someone told you, "There is a great new FTP archive about gerontology," you would know that you do not have enough information to use the archive; you would immediately ask, "Where?" But WAIS really gives you the illusion that all the data is available locally. You still have to ask "where" (or get WAIS to ask "where") but it almost seems like you should not have to.

It is just as easy to do this in **xwais**, if not easier. Let's say your question to the *directory-of-servers* about social work accidentally turned up a strange source called *beer.src* with a fairly low score. This probably is not relevant, but you think it is interesting; it might contain recipes for home-brew, or something else you would like. You ignored it when you were looking up articles about behavior problems in gifted children, but now you want to see if you can find a new recipe for lager. So you pop up a new question window and start searching the **Add Source** menu. Surprise! *beer.src* does not show up. With the X client, go to the menu where you searched the *directory-of-servers* for relevant libraries— i.e., the question in which you discovered this new library. Click on *beer.src*, and then "view" the library. You will see a new window with a description of the library. This window will have a button labeled **Save**. If you click on that button, your client will save the source automatically; you do not need to type anything.

Now you can go back to your new question. This time, when you search through the **Add Source** menu, you will see *beer.src*. Your client now knows about it; you have added it to the "speed-dialing" library. Add it to your search list, just like any other source.

## New Sources Not Found in the directory-of-servers

Most of the time, you will discover new sources through the *directory-of-servers*. However, on occasion you will find one through other means. You might be prowling through a newsgroup and see a message like this:

```
I just created a new and most wonderful source:

(:source
    :version  3
    :ip-name "nic.sura.net"
    :tcp-port 210
    :database-name "/export/software/nic/wais/databases/ERIC-archive"
    :cost 0.00
    :cost-unit :free
    :maintainer "info@sura.net"
    :description "ERIC (Educational Resources Information Center)
Digests

Information provided by EDUCOM

ERIC Digests are:

- short reports (1,000 - 1,500 words) on one or two pages, on topics
  of prime current interest in education.

- targeted specifically for teachers and administrators, and other
  practitioners, but generally useful to the broad educational community.
```

```
- designed to provide an overview of information on a given topic,
  plus references to items providing more detailed information.

- produced by the 16 subject-specialized ERIC Clearinghouses, and reviewed
  by experts and content specialists in the field.

- funded by the Office of Educational Research and Improvement (OERI),
  of the U.S. Department of Education (ED).

Created with WAIS Release 8 b4 on Apr 10 13:02:45 1992 by
lidl@nic.sura.net
")
```

Most of this message (everything following the first line) is a standard WAIS descriptor
for the source. To tell your client about this source, go to the **Sources** section of the main
menu. Click on the **New** button. After you push that button, **xwais** puts up a blank
template for you to fill in the information necessary to add a source.* If you were to fill
in the template given for the "ERIC-archive" source shown in the previous example, it
would look like Figure 12-8. Retyping the source by hand may be painful, but if you are
using a window system, you should have a copy/paste mechanism to move large chunks
of text automatically.

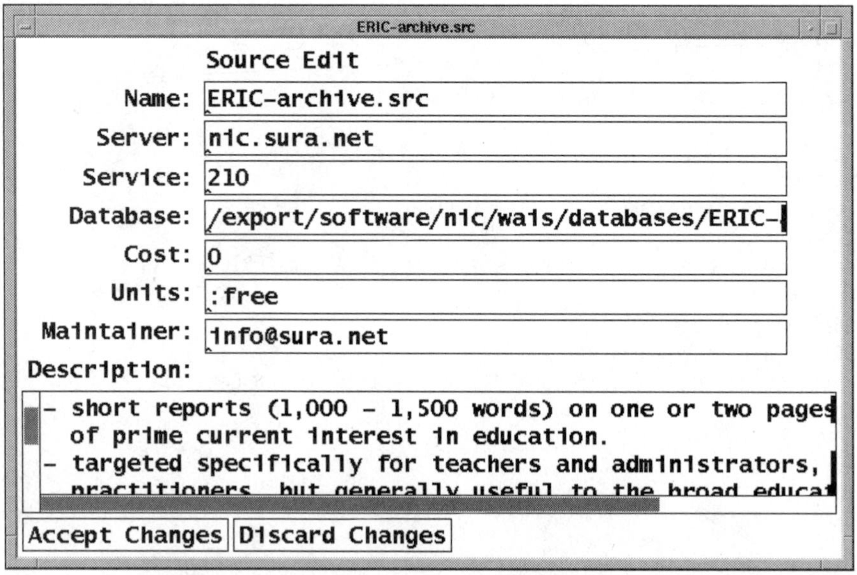

*Figure 12-8    Source maintenance window*

---

*Before copying the source descriptor by hand, though, it might save you some work to search the *directory-of-servers* to see
whether or not it has been added "officially" to the list. Anyone who creates a new library is supposed to tell Thinking
Machines. This does not always happen, but it is worth checking.

When you are done adding or changing an entry for a source, you can either save your changes or throw them away by using the **Accept Changes** or **Discard Changes** button at the bottom of the window.

## Building Your Own Sources

The software archives that provide WAIS clients also provide programs and documentation for creating your own sources and offering your own servers. One of these, **waisindex**, takes a set of files and builds an index from them. It knows about various forms of data: normal text, various text formatters (e.g., LaTeX), mail folder format, etc. These formats are shown in Table 12-2.

*Table 12-2    waisindex Input Formats*

| Name | Description |
| --- | --- |
| *text* | Simple text files |
| *bibtex* | BibTeX/LaTeX format |
| *bio* | Biology abstract format |
| *cmapp* | CM applications from Hypercard |
| *dash* | Entries separated by a row of dashes |
| *dvi* | *dvi* format |
| *emacsinfo* | GNU documentation system |
| *first_line* | First line of file is headline |
| *gif* | *gif* files, indexes only the filename |
| irg | Internet *Resource Catalog* |
| *mail_digest* | Standard Internet mail digest format |
| *mail_or_rmail* | mail or rmail or both |
| *medline* | MEDLINE format |
| *mh_bboard* | MH bulletin board format |
| *netnews* | Net news format |
| *nhyp* | Hypertext format, Polytechnic of Central London |
| *one_line* | Each line is a document |
| *para* | Paragraphs separated by blank lines |
| *pict* | *pict* files, indexes only the filename |
| *ps* | PostScript format |
| *refer* | **refer** format |
| *rn* | Net news saved by the **rn** newsreader |
| *server* | Server structures for the *directory-of-servers* |
| *tiff* | *tiff* files, indexes only the filename |

If you want to build a WAIS index for the e-mail you receive, you can. It is really beyond the scope of this book to tell you how to do this. Many people find that once they learn WAIS, it is a valuable tool for searching many other things. If you would like to experiment, look for **waisindex** via Archie. It is also part of the distribution package for UNIX WAIS servers, available by anonymous FTP to **think.com** in the directory *wais*.

## ▦ *A Macintosh WAIS Client*

The following three screen images show a sample WAIS client for the Macintosh that is similar to the X Windows examples displayed earlier. It is called MACWAIS (URL: **http://www.qub.ac.uk/sigweb/mac-comms-utils.html**) and is available for downloading from URL **ftp://nic.switch.ch/mirror/wais/clients/macintosh/einet/macwais1.29.sea.hqx**. Once launched (and assuming it is already properly installed on the Macintosh), the opening window invites you to **Tell Me** what your search terms are. Figure 12-9 shows the opening screen with the search keys "future world wide web" included in the **Tell Me** box.

Once you have inserted your search keywords, click on the **Ask** button. This will query the *directory-of-servers* and return results, as shown in Figure 12-10.

One of the results looks interesting to you. You point at the database **ANU-SocSci-WWW-Gopher-News-L.src**. This result is displayed in Figure 12-11.

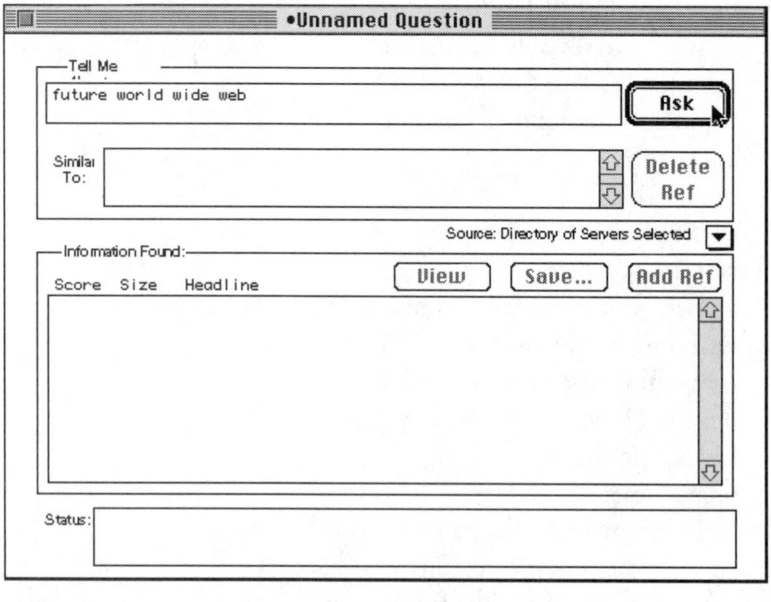

*Figure 12-9    Macintosh WAIS main window*

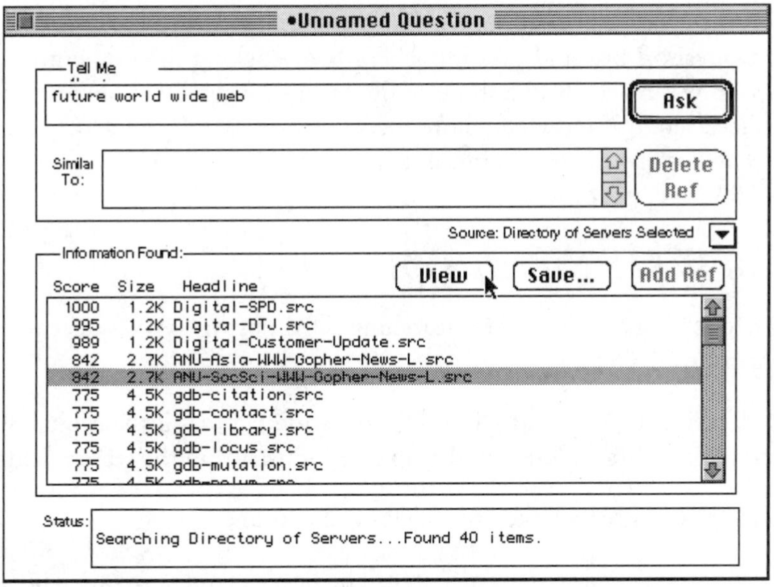

*Figure 12-10   Results of search*

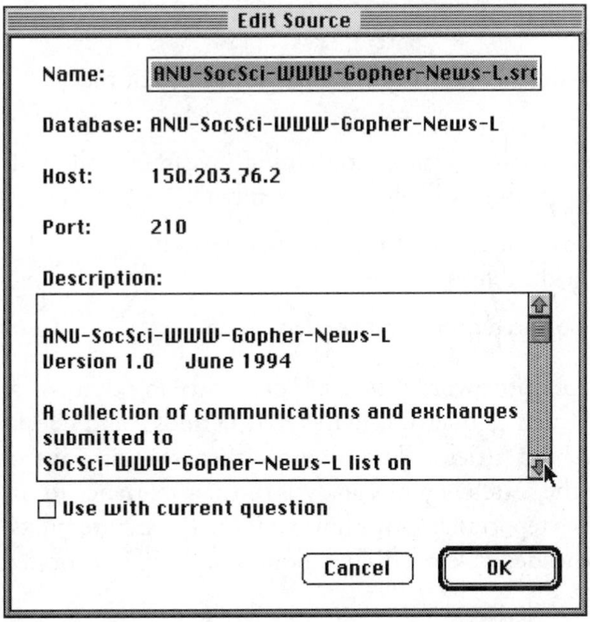

*Figure 12-11   Selection of database*

You may now proceed with your original query on "future world wide web" by checking the **Use with current question** box and pressing ENTER or clicking the **OK** button. This will continue your WAIS search like those outlined previously. Development of these WAIS tools will accelerate if and when more users demand it and/or one or more of these tools are "discovered" by a significant number of users.

## ◼ *Summary of WAIS Search Tips*

WAIS, Inc., offers the following concise tips for searching (URL: **http://www.wais.com/ newhomepages/srchtips.html**):

1. To search a WAIS database, type a word ("Feast"), a question ("What is the capital of the United Kingdom?"), or a phrase ("crisis in the finance industry") in the search field.

2. Click on **Search**, and a list of titles linked to articles will appear.

Boolean operators may be used in either type of search. The Boolean operators are "and", "or", "not", and "adj". Here are some examples of their use:

- **Kohl and ECU** finds articles containing both words.
- **Oil or Petroleum** finds articles containing either word.
- **Election not California** finds articles containing the first word but not the second.
- **Weather adj Boston adj November** finds articles containing "Weather" followed immediately by "Boston", followed immediately by "November".
- **Simpson and (law or legal)** finds articles containing the first term in combination with the second or third term.

We recommend that search queries be entered in lowercase letters.

The WAIS search engine ignores common words such as "do" and "in" (known as *stopwords*), along with punctuation (such as question marks and periods), and checks the remaining words against its index of articles. The program then returns a list of articles that are ranked according to the search engine's analysis of their relevance to the query. The end of the list also contains a report that shows how your query was interpreted by the search engine. Further details headed "Detailed Tips about Searching" are located at the URL noted previously.

WAIS, Veronica, and even **whois** may seem too complicated to the user who does not want to study the tools in order to use them properly. To become an Internet expert before now, you really had no option but to do just that. The answer to complicated Internet tools would be a user-friendly interface that directs the user where he or she wants to go. It would use the established tools of the Internet but in a format that made them accessible to the new user. Understand this, and you already have a good idea as to why graphical user interfaces to the World Wide Web have finally positioned online communication to take its place in the changing media habits of people around the world. That is the subject of chapter 13.

## ▓ *Exercises*

*Print out your responses to each of the following items. Seek help locally if you need it.*

You can access WAIS using Gopher to connect to this site: **gopher-gw.micro.umn.edu** (URL: **gopher://gopher-gw.micro.umn.edu**). WAISGATE (try URL **http:// www.wais.com/waisgate-announce.html**) allows WAIS searching via a WWW browser.

**1.** Do you have access to WAIS via both a graphical user interface *and* a text-only interface? What GUI WAIS clients are available to you?

**2.** Find five WAIS servers using any search tools available to you (e.g., Veronica).

**3.** Locate your local WAIS server. Compare your server to the commercial WAIS, Inc., service (URL: **http://www.wais.com/directory-of-servers.html**). How do the interfaces compare? Which is easier for you to use and why?

**4.** Using your local WAIS server and that of WAIS, Inc., try a search on "competition between cable television and telephone." How do the results compare? Is there overlap? Which gets faster results?

**5.** Given the results from exercise 4, revise and resubmit the search with different search terms.

**6.** Demonstrate three ways that you can have the results of a WAIS search in your possession for future reference.

**7.** Repeat exercises 4 and 5 using a search combination of professional or academic interest to you.

**8.** Compare WAIS to Gopher. What do you see as the relative advantages and disadvantages of each?

**9.** Compare WAIS to Archie. What do you see as the relative advantages and disadvantages of each?

**10.** You can save WAIS searches with bookmarks. Explain succinctly but completely how you would do this on your local system.

**11.** Repeat one of your previous searches by starting at URL **http://www.ub2.lu.se/ auto_new/UDC.html**. Once again, how does this site compare to others you tried?

CHAPTER THIRTEEN

# THE WORLD WIDE WEB AND NETSCAPE NAVIGATOR

*What Is Hypertext?*
*Getting Started: The URL*
*A Text-Based Browser: Lynx*
*Navigating the Web with Netscape Navigator*
*Selected WWW Search Tools*
*The Future of the WWW*

T wo major barriers to widespread adoption of the various resources on the Internet existed into the early 1990s. Its intimidating UNIX environment and predominant use by those with an interest in the computer and telecommunications fields conspired against the Internet's becoming accessible to a wider audience both inside and out of academe. That changed dramatically with the birth of the World Wide Web (WWW), followed quickly by the invention of graphical "browsers" for using the Web, such as Mosaic from the National Center for Supercomputing Applications (NCSA). In this chapter we will summarize the tools available for use on the WWW including the very popular Netscape Navigator WWW browser.*

We focus on Netscape Navigator because not only is it the most popular browser overall (for current browser use statistics, see URLs **http://www.cen.uiuc.edu/~ejk/bryl.html** and/or **http://www.yahoo.com/Computers/World_Wide_Web/Browsers/ Browser_Usage_Statistics**), it dominates use in academic settings. There is no guarantee that Netscape Navigator will retain this lofty position, but it is reasonable to assume both that it will remain one of the top browsers for the foreseeable future and that competitive browsers will look something like the market leader. WWW browsers have common characteristics. If you master Netscape Navigator, chances are you will be in a

---

*As an Internet expert, you will need to keep up with current events in the "browser market." In less than a year, sales of Web browsers soared from almost zero to $50 million, according to Forrester Research. By the year 2000, Forrester estimates annual sales will be around $250 million. These growth numbers are tempered by a short product life cycle that can lead to obsolescence in a brief period of time (e.g., six months). Constant innovation and price-reduction pressures combine to make this a very competitive business environment and one that is quite difficult to predict (see *Information Week,* October 23, 1995, p.81, as cited in the 22 October 1995 edition of Edupage at URL **http://www.educom.edu/edupage.old/ edupage.95/edupage-10.23.95**). This environment may or may not play to Netscape's favor as one of the first kids on the block as well as one that is well financed.

position to master other browsers. In fact, competitors will be smart to follow Netscape Navigator's lead, because they will need to win over existing users.* Before we get to browsing the Web, some background information will be helpful.

## What Is Hypertext?

The term "hypertext" was coined by Ted Nelson in 1965 (for a time line of the history of hypertext, see URL **http://epics.aps.anl.gov/demo/guide/www.guide.app.a.html**). The earliest electronic model of such a system was proposed in a historically significant and prophetic 1945 article by Vannevar Bush, "As We May Think," published in the July issue of *The Atlantic*. As noted by David Hirmes in the 0.9 version of *hypertext.faq* (URL: **http://www.eit.com/reports/ht93/hypertext.faq.txt**):

> By 1945, Bush had realized that an era of information was approaching. He commented: "The summation of human experience is being expanded at a prodigious rate, [but] the means we use for threading through the consequent maze to the momentarily important item is the same as was used in the days of square-rigged ships."
>
> Bush wrote of a "memex," a conceptual machine that could store vast amounts of information, in which a user had the ability to create information "trails": links of related text and illustrations. This trail could then be stored and used for future reference. Bush believed that using this associative method of information gathering was not only practical in its own right, but was closer to the way the mind ordered information.

Putting Bush's and Nelson's ideas into action, Tim Berners-Lee of CERN, the European Particle Physics Laboratory, proposed the actual World Wide Web project in 1989 (URL: **http://www.w3.org/hypertext/WWW/People/Berners-Lee-Bio.html**).

Hypertext is known today to be a method of electronically linking documents. A hypertext footnote in an electronic document can be a link to the electronic source of that document (whether in another file on your local computer or one connected to the Internet). These links to other documents may be text, graphics, audio, or video (see URL **http://abbott.ccm.emr.ca/guide/graphics/hypertext.gif**). For the sake of illustration, assume that your library has a hypertext card catalog. If you pull up the card for a particular book, it might look like this:

```
AUTHOR       Kellerman, Henry.
TITLE        Sleep disorders insomnia and narcolepsy / by Henry Kellerman.
```

---

*Experience has shown that once Netscape offers a final version upgrade, users adopt the new version quickly. To keep up with new versions, you can always go to Netscape's own online handbook at URL **http://home.netscape.com/eng/mozilla/2.0/handbook**, where 2.0 will be replaced by the version number that you are using (so long as it is recent or current; old versions of the handbook will not be kept online indefinitely). Wadsworth Publishing will also keep updated WWW information at the book's WWW home page, URL **http://www.thomson.com/wadsworth.html**.

```
PUBLISH INFO      New York : Brunner/Mazel, c1981.
DESCRIPT'N        xiv, 228 p. : ill. ; 23 cm.
NOTE              Bibliography: p. 211-20.
SUBJECTS          Insomnia.
                  Narcolepsy.
NLM NO            WM 188 K29s 1981.
                  WM 188 K29s 1981.
OCLC #            7694052.
ISBN              0876302649.
```

If the capitalized fields like SUBJECTS are links, you can make a link to Insomnia and Narcolepsy. If you choose AUTHOR, you might end up in a hypertext database of Who's Who in sleep-disorder research and find out where Henry Kellerman was trained. Once you have reached another database (the Who's Who in sleep-disorder research database), you might find other authors and their works. You may have begun another hypertext search through more and more references of interest to your research project.

The amount of hypertext on the Net has exploded in the past few years. Many museum exhibitions, magazines, and other hypertext presentations are available, including America Online's Global Network Navigator (GNN, URL **http://www.gnn.com**). The big problem used to be a scarcity of tools to build the linked structure. Most of the hypertext documents available early on were painstakingly built by hand. Hypertext editors are now available, including extensions for popular word processing software (URL: **http://www.w3.org/hypertext/WWW/Tools/Filters.html**).

In this chapter we will start the browser discussion using a simple line-oriented browser, Lynx. A public-access Lynx client is available by **telnet**ing to **ukanaix.cc.ukans.edu**. You may also find that some Internet service providers offer Lynx browsers to their clients.*

## ■ *The World Wide Web*

You might say the WWW is infatuated with itself. There are a multitude of guides and tutorials on the Web that cover its history and how to get started. Kevin Hughes is responsible for one of the best-known online histories of the Web, and his *Guide to Cyberspace* can be found at URL **http://www.eit.com/web/www.guide**. Rather than duplicate those many fine efforts, we simply highlight the subject here. You will be asked to follow up on this in the chapter exercises.

As recounted by Kevin Hughes, the World Wide Web began in March 1989, when Tim Berners-Lee of the European Particle Physics Laboratory (known as CERN, a collective

---

*The software is available via anonymous FTP from URL **ftp://ftp2.cc.ukans.edu** in the directory *pub/lynx*.

of European high-energy physics researchers) proposed the project to be used as a means of transporting research and ideas effectively throughout the organization. Effective communications was a goal of CERN for many years, as its members were located in a number of countries. The initial project proposal outlined a simple system of using networked hypertext to transmit documents and communicate among members in the high-energy physics community. By the end of 1990, the first piece of Web software was introduced on a NeXT workstation. It had the capability to view and transmit hypertext documents to other Internet users, and came with the capability to edit hypertext documents on-screen. The new medium was officially baptized via a demonstration given to the Hypertext '91 conference.

We now know the World Wide Web as the hypertext-based information service on the Internet. Although early development took place at CERN, the Web quickly became an information organizational tool applicable to all forms of data. To try the Web via text-only medium, **telnet** to **telnet.w3.org**. This will automatically drop you into a public-access client *browser*, a program that takes you around the WWW. If you wish to view a remote file (that is, a file residing on some computer system other than the one upon which you are running a browser like Lynx) without first viewing a local file, you must identify that file by using its *Uniform Resource Locator (URL)*, which is discussed later in this chapter. When you use a Web browser and follow a link, what really happens is that a file is returned to you locally by the remote computer (called a server and, more specifically in this case, a WWW server).

Here is what you might see:

```
                    THE WORLD WIDE WEB

    This is just one of many access points to the web, the universe of
    information available over networks. To follow references, just type the
    number then hit the return (enter) key.

    The features you have by connecting to this telnet server are very primitive
    compared to the features you have when you run a W3 "client" program on your
    own computer. If you possibly can, please pick up a client for your
    platform to reduce the load on this service and experience the web in its
    full splendor.

    For more information, select by number:

        A list of available W3 client programs[1]

        Everything about the W3 project[2]

    1-3, Up, <RETURN> for more, Quit, or Help:
```

By entering choice 3, you will see the following information on-screen:*

```
                       Overview of the Web
WWW[1]

               GENERAL OVERVIEW OF THE WEB

There is no "top" to the World-Wide Web. You can look at it from many points
of view. Here are some places to start.

Virtual Library by Subject[2]
                       The Virtual Library organizes information by subject
                       matter.

List of servers[3]     All registered HTTP servers by country

by Service Type[4]     The Web includes data accessible by many other
                       protocols. The lists by access protocol may help if
                       you know what kind of service you are looking for.

If you find a useful starting point for you personally, you can configure
your WWW browser to start there by default.

1-5, Back, Up, <RETURN> for more, Quit, or Help:
```

This is a line-oriented browser (a hypertext reader) that will work with a traditional terminal. More precisely, a browser is any program for reading hypertext. Several other browsers are available; if you decide to install your own (and that is highly recommended if you want to use the Web frequently), you can choose between the line-oriented browser and several browsers for your desktop computer (see URL **http://www.w3.org/hypertext/ WWW/Tools/Overview.html**). The key difference between the popular graphic browsers and the text-only browsers (e.g., Lynx) is that the text browsers are fast because they ignore images.

Many WWW browsers are available. As of this writing, the most advanced widely used browser is Netscape Navigator. It works on various platforms from Mac and Windows

---

*In the rather unlikely event that your local host does not have its own WWW client but does provide outgoing TELNET service, you can use **telnet** to connect to a public WWW client (browser). You might need to use a slightly different syntax or pull down a menu or click a button to start TELNET and select the host:

```
telnet fatty.law.cornell.edu
Login: www
          This is the WWW service provided by the Legal Information
          Institute, Cornell Law School, Ithaca, NY.  We provide

          a line-mode browser (Lynx) for using the World-Wide Web.
```

The result is very much like **gopher**. We discuss a line-oriented WWW browser, Lynx, later in this chapter. Unless you are satisfied with this TELNET option, you should seek a WWW browser locally. A very good source for WWW browsers is NCSA's anonymous FTP archive **ftp.ncsa.uiuc.edu** at URL **ftp://ftp.ncsa.uiuc.edu**.

to UNIX. Netscape Navigator is so popular that as of the end of 1995 it was setting the standards for all WWW browsers. Most estimates showed that at least 70 percent of "browsing" near the end of 1995 was done via the Netscape Navigator browser (see URLs **http://www.tisco.com/browsers.shtml** and **http://www.galcit.caltech.edu/~ta/ browsers/browser.shtml**; links to various statistics on browser use may be found at URL **http://www.cen.uiuc.edu/~ejk/bryl.html**).

## ▧ *Getting Started: The URL*

What is WWW about? It is an attempt to organize and link all the information on the Internet as a set of hypertext documents. This certainly may include whatever local information you want. Users traverse the network by moving from one source to another via links. Documents are identified by their WWW address: the Uniform Resource Locator (URL). We have identified many such sources throughout this book by referencing their URLs.

Within the URL of a source, the first portion is the name of the interface, or *scheme* (hypertext, **gopher**, **ftp**, etc.), separated from the rest of the object by a colon. The remainder of the URL follows the colon in a format depending on the scheme. Those schemes that refer to Internet protocols start with a double slash, //, to indicate their presence, and continue until the following slash, / (although in practice the ending slash is often not used). For example, sources available via the hypertext transfer protocol are identified with a URL that begins with the identifier **http**, and those available via the file transfer protocol are identified with one that begins with **ftp**. As you know from previous chapters in this book, URLs take the general form:

    protocol://host/path/filename

where *protocol* identifies the communications protocol used by the server that will provide the file, *host* is the Internet address of the computer system on which the server is running, and *path* and *filename* identify the directory path and file of interest. One of the many exciting aspects of the WWW is that it allows the use of various Internet protocols. Here are some sample URLs that show this:

> HTTP (hypertext transfer protocol)
> > **http://www.w3.org**
>
> Gopher
> > **gopher://gopher.micro.umn.edu/11/**
>
> FTP (file transfer protocol)
> > **ftp://ftp.apple.com**

WAIS (Wide Area Information Service protocol)
  **wais://cnidr.org/directory-of-servers**

TELNET
  **telnet://spacelink.msfc.nasa.gov**

USENET news
  **news:comp.dcom.telecom**

These URLs are identical regardless of WWW browser. The URL often takes us to a home page.

### What Is a Home Page?

A *home page* is an HTML document on the WWW. As noted by D. C. Denison (URL: **http://www.ora.com/gnn/netizens/fieldguide.html**):

> A personal home page occupies a unique niche on the World Wide Web: it represents the Web at its most basic and at its most eccentric. We can lay the blame for this multiple personality disorder on evolution. Because from simple text-based roots in CERN, the WWW home page has rapidly grown into a flexible self-publishing tool: it can now serve as anything from a conservative, professional-looking front door on the Net, to a medium of personal expression that intersects with autobiography, e-zines ["electronic magazines"], and science fiction.

You have to start somewhere on the WWW, and that somewhere is probably someone's home page. Browsers are what we use to access and display files on the Web (see the sidebar "Evolution of a Home Page" later in this chapter).

## A Text-Based Browser: Lynx

*Lynx* is a very popular text-only WWW browser. Information about Lynx may be accessed via URL **http://kufacts.cc.ukans.edu/about_lynx/about_lynx.html**. To execute Lynx from the command line, type **lynx** followed by the URL of the file you are trying to retrieve. If you need help launching Lynx, seek help locally. For example, using Lynx, enter the following command to reach the WWW Consortium at URL **http:// www.w3.org**:

```
lynx http://www.w3.org
```

You should see a screen like the following:

```
                              The World Wide Web Consortium (W3C) (p1 of 9)
                         WWW THE WORLD WIDE WEB
          * Web Specifications and Development Areas
          * Web Software
          * The Web Community
          * About the World Wide Web Consortium
     -------------------------------------------------------------------------
     ------
     News and Updates
                    + W3C Workshop on Style Sheets: 6-7 November 1995 in Paris,
                      France NEW!
                    + W3C Working Draft: The HTML3 Table Model
                    + W3C Announces Platform for Internet Content Selection (PICS)
                    + Fourth International World Wide Web Conference: 11-14
                      December 1995
                    + News and Updates Archive

     -- press space for next page --
       Arrow keys: Up and Down to move. Right to follow a link; Left to go back.
     H)elp O)ptions P)rint G)o M)ain screen Q)uit /=search [delete]=history list
```

This is the World Wide Web Consortium's current home page. Your home page is the hypertext document you see when you first enter the Web. Depending on the browser you are using, hypertext links are highlighted in some way (e.g., underlined or reversed text). To follow any link, just move to the text with your cursor and press ENTER. Note that the mouse may be of use only on your local screen; a text-based browser may not recognize your use of the mouse. On a graphical browser, the links are highlighted (color, a different font, underlined, etc.); to follow a link, click on the word with your mouse.

Let's return to the WWW browser, Lynx, and see what happens when we select one of the links. If you move your cursor to highlight **Web Specifications and Development Areas** (visible on the next screen), here is what you see next:

```
                              The World Wide Web Consortium (W3C) (p3 of 9)
          Web Specifications and Development Areas

          W3C Tech Reports
                 Technical reports and draft specifications released by the W3C.

          HTTP   All available information on Hypertext Transfer Protocol (HTTP)
                 and related protocols.

          HTML   The hypertext markup language, including style sheets.
```

```
    Content Selection
            W3C's Platform for Internet Content Selection (PICS) is an
            effort to enable content labeling & rating for the Web.

    Security
            Resources relating to security on the World Wide Web.

    Collaboration
            Resources and examples relating to interaction on the World
            Wide Web through structured discussion, shared annotation and

-- press space for next page --
  Arrow keys: Up and Down to move. Right to follow a link; Left to go back.
  H)elp O)ptions P)rint G)o M)ain screen Q)uit /=search [delete]=history list
```

Note that the title of this page is visible at the top of the screen. If you want to see where you are, press the equal sign (=) on your keyboard, and something like the following appears (depending on the version being used):

```
            YOU HAVE REACHED THE INFORMATION PAGE

File that you are currently viewing

    Linkname:  The World Wide Web Consortium (W3C)
         URL:  http://www.w3.org/#Specifications
    Owner(s):  None
        size:  178 lines
   Lynx mode:  normal

Link that you currently have selected

    Linkname:  W3C Tech Reports
    Filename:  http://www.w3.org/TR/
```

This page shows you the URL of the page you are on (the file that you are currently viewing) and the link on which your cursor resides (the link that you have currently selected). This is only one of the options available from Lynx. Returning to the previous screen by pressing any key, note that help items appear at the bottom of the screen. Once again, these items will vary according to the version of Lynx and the operating system you are using. The Print command (**P**) is even more useful than it might appear. This can allow you to print, e-mail, or save the document currently on-screen. As is the case with **gopher**, you can create bookmarks to keep track of sites and return to them by using the **V** for the View Bookmark command. Here is a summary of the Lynx commands:

**H)elp**                   As it implies, Help takes you to a menu of Lynx commands. Rather than accessing them locally, it obtains them by going to URL **http://kufacts.cc.ukans.edu/lynx_help/ lynx_help_main.html.**

| | |
|---|---|
| **O)ptions** | This command allows you to personalize Lynx by choosing options for your personal use. These include (among others) an editor, bookmark filename, your preferred e-mail address, and your level of Lynx knowledge (novice, intermediate, or advanced). |
| **P)rint** | You may save the on-screen file as a local file, mail it to yourself, scroll it on-screen (which allows you to capture it in your terminal buffer), print it on a printer, or specify your own Print command. |
| **G)o** | This choice allows you to enter a URL directly and "go" to it. |
| **M)ain screen** | This takes you back to the home page that is the default for your Lynx system. |
| **Q)uit** | This will exit Lynx after prompting you for confirmation. |
| **/=search** | The slash key allows you to search through the file that is displayed on-screen. |
| **[delete]=history list** | Pressing the DELETE key (which depends on your local PC or terminal) will show you a list of the sites you have visited in the current session. |

This table is not all inclusive. Lynx keystroke commands (see URL **http://kufacts.cc.ukans.edu/lynx_help/keystroke_commands237/keystroke_help.html**) offer still more options that reveal the powerful nature of the Lynx browser.

Any of these hypertext pages can be changed, we hope for the better, at any time. It is important to realize that the home page, the index of Virtual Library, and everything else that's available is not built in to your browser. They are just hypertext documents that can be modified at will. Some screens are not even documents in the traditional sense (i.e., files that exist on some system's disk); they are generated "on the fly" by gateways between the Web and other services. Therefore, do not be surprised if you see text that does not match our sample screens. The Web is constantly changing, and that is part of its beauty.

## ■ *The Web Versus Gopher*

Although many, many documents are made available specifically for WWW browsers, the Web was designed to incorporate existing Internet services like Gopher. With a text-only browser such as Lynx, the WWW may seem less than revolutionary when compared,

# Evolution of a Home Page

The rapid diffusion of the World Wide Web in 1994 was a seemingly unprecedented event in media history. A perceptual switch from seeing the Internet as a mainly computer network to the new vision of the WWW as a communications medium served as a catalyst for interest in new applications. Because of their historical involvement with the Internet, universities quickly established *home pages* on the WWW. The evolution of such a home page gives a historically compressed glimpse of how quickly the tools of the WWW trade changed over a short period of time. Let's take Bowling Green State University (BGSU) as an example.

## Dabbling on the WWW

John Hasley, a UNIX expert at BGSU, taught himself HTML and created the first BGSU home page in the summer of 1993. The page contained information that was displayed on more than one screen, and the university seal was the only graphic included (see Figure 13-A). The page was very exciting to the few users who knew about it at the time. The hypertext link to an image of a BGSU

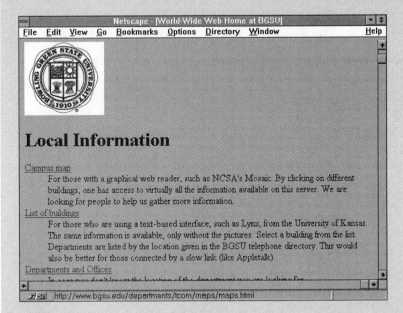

*Figure 13-A    Initial BGSU home page*

campus map was particularly amazing. To those used to seeing little more than text files on the Internet, this was an incredible sight.

As the WWW became familiar to more people on campus and home pages began to spring up online around the world, it did not take BGSU long to realize that it would need to perfect its home page to portray a positive image among its colleagues in cyberspace. A decision was made in November 1994 to put further development of the home page in the hands of media and public relations experts rather than leave it with the experts in campus computing. This decision may have been made hundreds of times at various organizations as they learned about the communication potential of the WWW.

## *The Home Page as Electronic Brochure*

### *Development of the Web Design at BGSU*

At the start of this phase of the BGSU Web project, a team from the university community identified the audiences for the home page as:

- Prospective students and their parents
- Current BGSU students and their parents
- Faculty, staff, and administrators
- The university community, to include the residents of Bowling Green and surrounding communities
- Internet surfers

New attention was given to content and layout, and the results are shown in Figure 13-B. This version of the home page was introduced on March 31, 1995. While the page was being redesigned, rules were devised for what was most appropriate for display on the university's Web pages. Because this new medium allowed potential authorship to anyone in the university community, concerns were raised about the need to balance university goals against potential conflicts with free-speech issues. Other universities were queried for their ideas as the local experience was being played out on campus after campus across the country and beyond.

The revised home page included links to many other university home pages, and various departments on campus began to create their own pages (see Figure 13-C). This new design included orange boxes and accompanying photos of campus buildings. In order to have some continuity among university pages, guidelines

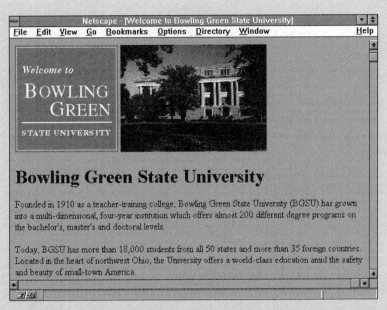

*Figure 13-B    First redesigned BGSU home page*

*Figure 13-C    Redesigned BGSU home page (continued)*

were developed for page authors. As shown in Figures 13-B and 13-C, the more visually striking home page still spilled over more than the initial screen. It had not been initially obvious that it was better to confine one idea per screen (pioneers in videotex learned this nearly 15 years earlier).

This design was too cumbersome to maintain, and so it did not last long. Members of the team (who completed this work in addition to all their existing duties) had to customize an orange box for every department and office and find matching photos that were also unique from other photos on the site. WWW technology had also marched past this simple outline style for home pages, and team members wanted to put their best foot forward for the university.

### *The Mature Welcome Page*

While efforts to refine rules and communication goals for the site continued (see URL **http://www.bgsu.edu/explorer/styleGuide/guidelines-overview.html**), faculty in the School of Art were enlisted to apply their graphical expertise to the home page. *Imagemaps* were introduced that allowed the user to point at an area of an image and go to a hypermedia link related to that area. Designers realized that one key to home page appeal is to constantly update information, so a "Special feature" is added regularly to the first screen of the home page (see Figure 13-D).

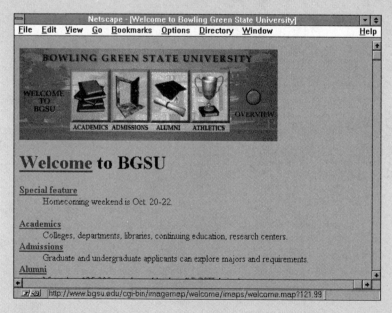

**Figure 13-D**    *Final 1995 version of the BGSU home page*

As the project evolved, the team determined the need for a separation between the needs of the internal and the external audiences. To meet the needs of the internal audiences, a page for navigating the BGSU site and WWW was created (the BGSU Explorer, URL **http://www.bgsu.edu/explorer**). This allowed the team to reexamine the audience of the BGSU home (or welcome) page. Because the message was now aimed almost exclusively off campus, the primary demographic segment became prospective students. By this time (five months into the project), mail to the "webmaster"* was being evaluated to provide additional input to the redesign of the welcome page. A good portion of the mail was from alumni, many writing through commercial online services. They were asking to contact other alumni and/or their Web pages, requesting information on athletic events, and inquiring about a "photographic tour of campus," which was an unlinked, undeveloped topic on the welcome page. Reflecting on the university's specific marketing emphases, cumulative response to the earlier Web pages, and its own convictions, the audience was redefined as:

- Prospective students (and their parents)
- Alumni
- Other "friends" of the university, including residents of Bowling Green and surrounding communities in northwest Ohio
- Internet surfers

In conjunction with the designer (Mark Marcin, an assistant professor of computer art), the Web design team decided to limit the number of topics in the newly designed imagemap on the welcome page. After ranking all possible welcome page topics for importance to the audiences, the four icons of the imagemap became **Academics**, **Admissions**, **Alumni**, and **Athletics**. This first one addresses the university's primary mission.

The icons (books, open door, mortarboard, and award cup) are images that were newly created for the BGSU Web site. The background photos are "ghosted" images that change for every major area and for the generic header designed to be used on pages that do not link directly from one of the four major areas. Inset buttons were designed that return the user to the welcome page or take the user to the overview, a specially designed program that indexes all titles of the BGSU Web site.

---

*A webmaster is an e-mail alias that Net surfers can use to send feedback about the home page for which the alias was created. The address is usually **webmaster@***domain.name*.

Along with with the design of the imagemap, the welcome page's other topics were being determined. Every entity at the university was assigned to an area that might become a welcome page topic. There were two goals for this process: to limit the number of welcome page topics to eight or fewer and to make it as simple as possible for the user to find his or her next choice. Areas and departments were assigned and realigned until the current list of topics led to every possible choice the user could make.

The "final" version of the university home page was unveiled on August 28, 1995. It includes imagemaps that allow viewers to point and click at a screen image button to follow a link to the next document. The page is sure to continue its evolutionary design path, but the frenetic pace of WWW home page creation that began in 1994 may never quite be duplicated. The university made its first plunge into the inevitable multimedia future by adding QuickTime videos with audio from a news piece produced by a commercial television station in nearby Toledo. Given the long interconnection between the Internet and the academic community, universities will continue to keep pace with media breakthroughs as they occur on the Net.

The first piece of interactive programming on the BGSU home page was a calendar of events. This tool allows customized delivery of information to the individual user. Members of the campus can input events for display via the Web server. This ability puts an exclamation point on how the WWW is putting control of content into the hands of users rather than restricting it to producers (as has been the case throughout the history of mediated communication).

for example, to Gopher. While there are similarities, the Web via text browser and Gopher differ in several ways.

First, the Web is based on hypertext documents and is structured by links between pages of hypertext. There are no limiting Web rules about which documents can be pointed to and, in fact, a WWW link can point to anything that the creator finds interesting. A WWW text about chemistry might point to a periodic table entry for lithium, which might in turn point to some other articles discussing the properties of lithium, which might point to an FTP server containing spectral data for various lithium compounds.

Graphical browsers such as Netscape Navigator and its ancestor Mosaic add another dimension: Documents can contain illustrations and sound.

Gopher is just not as flexible. Its presentation is based on individual resources and servers. When you are looking at an FTP resource, this may not make much of a difference. In either case, you will see a list of files. Yet Gopher knows nothing about what is inside of files; it has no concept of a link between something interesting on one server and something related somewhere else. By nature, Gopher menus allow only short descriptions; the Web's hypertext model provides as much (or as little) description as required for each item. Although some Gopher clients can understand pictures and sound, they cannot integrate pictures or sound with other kinds of data.

Second, the Web does a much better job of providing a uniform interface to different kinds of services. Providing a uniform interface is also one of Gopher's goals; but the hypertext model allows the Web to go much further. What does this mean in practice? For one thing, there are really only two Web commands: follow a link (that we have already demonstrated) and perform a search (that we will examine in detail in the next section). No matter what kind of resource you are using, these two commands are all you need. With Gopher, the interface tends to change according to the resource you're using.

Simple as the Web is, it is still flexible. For example, the Web allows you to read USENET news. If you read any news, you have probably noticed that each posting contains references to other messages. A client restructures news postings as hypertext, turning these cross-references into links: So you can easily move between original postings, follow-ups, and cross-references, just by selecting links. Graphical Web browsers have recently exploited this natural Web application. Gopher has no way of organizing news articles; they are just there.

Finally, the Web eliminates the barrier between your data and "public data." If you set up a WWW server and an appropriate hypertext editor, you can integrate your own personal notes into the Web. (Your notes, of course, remain private, but they can have links to public documents.) Ten years ago, a few dozen boxes full of index cards was de rigueur for anyone writing a dissertation or an academic book. With the Web, a few hypertext documents make all that obsolete. Rather than copying a quote and sticking it into an index box, you can just create a link from a notes file to the document you are quoting. Editing your own hypertext files is beyond the bounds of this book, but it is an important topic and something that should become easier in the future. (Today, browsers are pretty much read-only tools; in the future, though, browsers and editors will be integrated.)

The best way to see the difference between Gopher and the Web is to look at some real hypertext documents. If you are using the simple Lynx browser, probably the easiest way to familiarize yourself with hypertext is to spend some time reading the World Wide Web documentation. To get to the online documentation, start the Lynx browser and then give the command **H** for the help manual. This is highly recommended; even if you do not care about the documentation itself, it is a good way to see what is possible. If you are using Netscape Navigator or Mosaic, you can go a lot further. Try looking at any of the sites listed in the *Resource Catalog* or at the book site (URL: **http:// www.thomson.com/wadsworth.html**).

## ■ *Navigating the Web with www*

Most readers should skip this section. Lynx is the most popular text-oriented browser. In case you are one of the few who must use it, however, here is an overview of the browser called **www**. To start the line-oriented browser, use one of these commands:

```
%   telnet info.cern.ch                      to use the public browser at CERN

%   www                                      to use a local client
```

The CERN browser is fine for experimentation, but if you are going to use the Web heavily, you should get your own. Whichever you do, you will see a home page; at the bottom of the home page (and every other page you read), you will see a line like this:

```
1-7, Back, Up, <RETURN> for more, Quit, or Help:
```

These lines summarize some of the commands that are available for moving from one document to another. They're the most useful. Most simply: typing a number selects a document; **Back** returns you to the previous document; **Up** moves to the previous page of the current document; pressing ENTER takes you to the next page of the current document; **Quit** exits the Web; and **Help** shows you a help screen.

These simple commands are not really enough. If you reach a dead end, you may not want to type **Back** 30 times before returning to some recognizable point. Therefore, there are a number of navigational shortcuts:

**home**          Moves you to the home page, which is the page you saw upon entering the Web. If you use an off-the-shelf browser, it may well be the introductory page from CERN.

**recall**        The **recall** command is the equivalent of the **gopher** bookmark. It lets you return to any of the documents you have already visited. This is a much more convenient way of navigating than simply crawling back and forth. By itself, **recall** lists the documents you have already visited, with numbers:

```
Back, Up, Quit, or Help:  recall
Documents you have visited:-
R  1)   in Welcome to CERN
R  2)   in User Guide for the WWW Line Mode Browser
R  3)   Commands -- /LineMode
R  4)   in Welcome to CERN
R  5)   in Academic information
R  6)   in Commercial data available through WWW-WAIS
R  7)   abstracts index
R  8)   in batch (in abstracts)
R  9)   Document
```

To return to any of these documents, give the command **recall**, followed by the document's number. In this example, **recall** 7 takes you back to the abstracts index. To save typing, you can abbreviate the command to **R 7**.

**next**  Goes to the next article in a list of articles. Or, more precisely, follows the next link. Let's say that I'm looking at a hypertext article about shale. I see something interesting, so I follow a link to another article—say, the seventh. The **next** command takes me to the next link from my previous article (in this case, the eighth link from the original article about shale). This command comes in handy if you want to read the responses to a posted news message in order.

**previous**  Goes to the previous article in a list of articles; similar to **next**.

**top**  Moves to the beginning (first screen) of the current document.

**bottom**  Moves to the end (last screen) of the current document.

There is more to surfing than moving around; you may want to print a document or save your own copy of it. So there are a few more commands:

**print**  Prints the current document. (Your administrator may need to fiddle with things to make it work properly.) This command is meaningful only if you're running your own browser. Obviously, if you're using a public browser, like the one at CERN, printing a document somewhere in Switzerland is not going to help much.

**> *filename***  Saves the current document in the local file *filename*. Available only on UNIX systems. Again, it is meaningful only if you're running your own browser.

>> *filename*   Appends the current document to the local file *filename*. Available only on
              UNIX systems.

| **unix-command**

              "Pipes" the document into the given UNIX command. For example, you
              might pipe a large document (like the cross-reference index to the CIA
              World Fact Book) into a UNIX **grep** command to eliminate entries you
              do not want. Available only on UNIX systems.

Commands  such as **next**, **up**, and so on can be abbreviated; you need to type only
enough letters to distinguish the commands from others. In most cases, the first letter is
sufficient. If you do not enjoy **www**, abandon it and head for the world of graphical user
interface browsers.

## Navigating the Web with Netscape Navigator

*Mosaic* originally was designed as a World Wide Web graphical user interface browser at
the University of Illinois's National Center for Supercomputing Applications (NCSA).
It presented the first widely available multimedia interface to the Internet. It does more
than present hypertext with links into other documents; it is a *hypermedia* tool, which
means that it can handle audio, pictures, and even video (moving pictures). It simplifies
the interface to different Internet tools. There are times when specialized tools do a
better job—but if you could install only one piece of network navigating software on
your system, Mosaic would be the one to choose. Mosaic requires a direct connection to
the Internet; you cannot run it if you are only dialing into a timesharing account. Mosaic
will be painfully slow unless you have at least a 14,400-baud modem.

### Netscape Navigator 2.0b

Now we will discuss *Netscape Navigator,* a commercial descendent of the Mosaic browser.
In fact, Marc Andreessen, a University of Illinois graduate student who headed the Mosaic
development there, is one of the founders of Netscape (originally called Mosaic
Communications). There are versions for the X Windows, Microsoft Windows, and
Macintosh platforms. All the versions are available via URL **http://home.netscape.com/
comprod/mirror/index.html**. Directions for uncompression and installation are included
for each platform.

For most purposes, the UNIX, Windows, and Mac versions of Netscape Navigator are
identical. Some details differ from one version to another, but the point-and-click user
interface, and even the menus, are largely the same.

## Getting Started

Starting Netscape Navigator is very simple once you find the Netscape icon on your system's desktop. Unless you change it, you will begin at the Netscape home page (URL **http://home.netscape.com**). See Figure 13-1.

Let's start with a tour of the screen. The line across the very top shows the title of the page where you are located (technically, this actually is the last file you retrieved); in this case, it is "Welcome to Netscape." Just below are the familiar Windows menu choices (e.g., **File**, **Edit**, etc.). When you move the mouse pointer to one of these menus and hold down the left button, you will get a list of choices. Move the pointer to the choice you want and release the button. If you have used GUI computers much, we should not have to say much more about menus. For your information, the **Exit** command (to get out of Netscape Navigator) is located at the bottom of the **File** menu. On the far right side, you will see a **Help** menu. You can view all of this documentation through the online handbook. We will return to other menu items later in this chapter.

At the right side of the screen is a scroll bar that you can use for looking at documents that are longer than one page. Click at the bottom of the scroll bar to move farther down (i.e., toward the end); click at the top to move up. If the document is too wide, Netscape Navigator also puts a scroll bar at the bottom of the screen. Scrolling left and

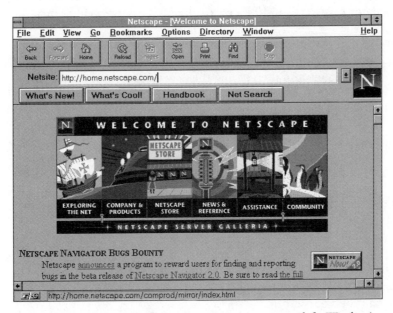

*Figure 13-1   Netscape Navigator home page (Netscape 2.0b for Windows)*

right is not convenient; it is easier to resize the screen so it is wide enough to display the whole document.

Underneath the Netscape Navigator 2.0b menus, you see the toolbar. Its choices are as follows:

**Back**        This button returns you to the previously accessed link/document.

**Forward**     This button works only after you have begun browsing. It will take you forward one link from your current location (assuming you have backtracked to some extent).

**Home**        This button returns you to your designated home page.

**Reload**      **Reload** makes a new request to the server from which you last retrieved a document. This is useful for rapidly updated information (e.g., sports scores) and/or to reload a document that did not load completely or otherwise properly on the previous attempt (e.g., a busy server).

**Images**      This option allows you to toggle image viewing, allowing images to be loaded and viewed on-screen if you have turned this option off via the **Options, Auto Load Images** menu sequence. The option to turn images off can save time in downloading information, and is wise only when the images are not necessary (and/or a particular server is especially slow).

**Open**        Like the **Go** command in Lynx, **Open** allows you to enter a URL into a window created when this button is selected. Using your mouse to point to the Netsite text box and then typing the new URL gives the same result.

**Print**       This button allows you to print the on-screen document on your terminal's printer.

**Find**        As in a word processor program, **Find** searches for text in the current document.

**Stop**        **Stop** breaks the link from your client machine to the server you are currently trying to reach.

You can hide these buttons by selecting the **Show Toolbar** command of the **Options** menu, as shown in Figure 13-2. Simply pointing to the item with your mouse button pressed down then releasing it will turn the toggle off. This can be handy if you want to see more of the home page on your screen.

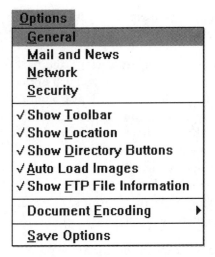

*Figure 13-2    Options menu of Netscape Navigator 2.0b*

Rather than explain every item on the Netscape Navigator window, we will discuss certain items as they apply to various tasks in browsing the Web. Obviously, you need to take some time to familiarize yourself with the available Navigator options. Remember, too, that you may access the Netscape Navigator handbook by selecting **Help** from the menu bar.

Like all Web browsers, Netscape Navigator starts by finding a home page somewhere on the Internet (as set up in one of the browser's options). Unless your browser has been specially configured, you will see Netscape Communication Corporation's default home page. You can create your own or point to any of the thousands of home pages scattered across the Net. Two options may be especially attractive depending on your Web use. One is to set the home page to a WWW search tool such as SavvySearch that allows you to begin your Netscape session by starting there. Another is to choose a daily news site of some kind, so that each time you launch Netscape you see that news source. Once you have chosen your home page reference site, you can set it up via the **Options** menu by choosing **General**, and then **Appearance**.

The home page consists of illustrations and text. Underlined and/or highlighted text is linked to another document (or perhaps another spot in the current document); if you click on that text with the left mouse button, Netscape Navigator downloads and displays the new document, including any graphics. For example, if you click on the phrase "Exploring the Net" (see Figure 13-1), Netscape displays a document about the Web: a brief explanation, plus additional links to more-detailed explanations. Thus, in addition to providing a nice user interface and multimedia support, Netscape Navigator presents you with several online catalogs and other demonstrations.

If you follow a link and then decide that it is not what you wanted, click on the **Back** button to return to the previous page. When you see the old page again, you will notice that the link you selected looks different—it is probably a different color. This is a notice that you have already followed that link. It does not mean that you cannot look at the same link again; you certainly can. It just indicates that you have been there before. After you have spent some time browsing the Net, you will start seeing "already visited" links on pages you cannot remember visiting. Netscape Navigator will keep track of previously visited sites (no matter what path you took to reach them) for 30 days; this time period can be reset to whatever value you choose via the **Options**, **General**, **Appearance**, **Followed Links Expire After [30] Days** menu sequence.

Other good browsing starting points are listed on the Netscape Navigator home page or via the **What's New!** or **What's Cool!** toolbar buttons. These items, which have changed as versions of Netscape Navigator are updated, are highlighted along with accompanying directory buttons. Each takes you on a Netscape link:

What's New!   As the name implies, this is a selected list of new WWW home pages that is updated frequently. It is not comprehensive (that would be virtually impossible), but attempts are made to highlight the more interesting new sites.

What's Cool!   This is an arbitrary list of newer sites that also have some Web "sex appeal."

Handbook   This takes you to the same documents as the **Help** menu.

Net Search   Netscape offers links to some of the best WWW search tools via this button. This area has changed relatively infrequently, as established tools such as Infoseek and Lycos have remained among the best available.

We will use several WWW search tools to further demonstrate how the Netscape Navigator works. The searches we conducted cannot be duplicated precisely by you because the databases covered by the search tools are constantly changing. Although we encourage you to conduct these or other searches, too, do not be surprised that your results do not match those reported here.

## ■ *Selected WWW Search Tools*

As an academic user of the Internet, you are about to reach WWW nirvana. Just as Archie and WAIS allow searching on the Internet, there are a growing number of different search tools available for the WWW. We will briefly discuss a few of the more popular and well-established ones. Those of us who were used to finding information on the Internet before the WWW took center stage cannot help but be impressed by the ease with which these new search tools can be used.* Like the Internet tools before them, however, WWW search tools will discover items only within the domain of their own searches: the database(s) they cover.

Although it would be difficult to select any one search engine as the overall best, there are some evaluation criteria than can be used for making your own choices. One easily overlooked fact is that the search is only as good as the database searched by the tool. Other criteria besides content includes interface, searching options (Boolean, adjacency of terms, scoring, etc.), output, and performance (see "World Wide Web searching tools—an evaluation," by Ian R. Winship in UK library magazine, *VINE* (99), 1995, pp. 49–54 or URL **http://www.bubl.bath.ac.uk/BUBL/IWinship.html**). Speed of performance can be a leading factor in user satisfaction.†

## *Lycos (URL http://www.lycos.com)*

One of the first WWW search tools available, *Lycos* (the first five letters of the Latin name for "Wolf Spider") was developed at Carnegie Mellon University in 1994. The Lycos robot searches the Web every day, indexing new pages, and then updates the database weekly. About 8 million URLs (HTTP files, Gopher files, and FTP files), more than 90 percent of all that exist, reportedly had been cataloged by 1995. Lycos is now an incorporated entity and has a goal of cataloging nearly all of them. The Microsoft Network (MSN), an online subscription-based service, is one of several licensees of the Lycos technology. In addition to all those who can use Lycos over the Internet for free, MSN subscribers reportedly will also have access to Lycos.

Lycos offers you a form as soon as you connect to its server. The Lycos home page also allows you the opportunity to add a home page to its database. This is one way to help others find your home page once you have one. Lycos takes it a step further by allowing you to remove it later. (These links are visible as buttons on the Lycos home page, as shown in Figure 13-3.)

---

*As of this writing, a shakeout of WWW search tools appears to be imminent.

†Excite (URL **http://www.excite.com/Handbook/HowToSearch.html3**) offers some wise tips about searching in general that we emphasize for your own searches:

- Use selective words to refine your search (e.g., "Cleveland Indians" rather than "baseball team").

- Be as specific as you can by adding words that uniquely refer to the object of your search. If you want certain words in your search phrase to be given extra consideration, you may repeat them. For example, you might use the search phrase "MCI's strategy for Internet access MCI MCI" to emphasize that it is *MCI's* strategy you are interested in. If there are multiple accepted spellings for a certain word, you can include each in your search. If there happens to be a common misspelling of a keyword, you probably should try using it.

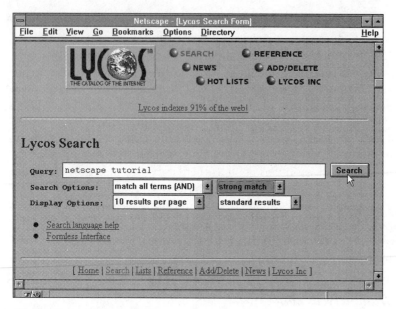

*Figure 13-3   Lycos search form*

As a sample search project, we will try to find online examples of Netscape Navigator tutorials.* Although we could search using the Lycos default settings, we will select our own options instead. As shown in Figure 13-3, we have entered "netscape tutorial" as our search words, we are asking that Lycos find both words in its search, we want a strong match with this search, and we ask that Lycos return 10 results per retrieval, and that they be displayed in the search engine's standard format.

By pressing the **Search** button, we tell Lycos to execute the search of its proprietary database of WWW sites. In earlier days, Lycos was subject to slow responses due to very heavy use. This situation had been resolved by the time Lycos was incorporated in 1995. Our search results are reported rapidly. We also are offered a new search window that immediately allows us to further refine the search if needed. "netscape tutorial" is a relatively specific search (as opposed to "Internet help," for example), so we can scroll down the page using Netscape Navigator's vertical scroll bar to see the results reported by Lycos that are in categories like this:

```
URL     The uniform resource locator
Title   The Title field
Outline The first 200 characters in header fields
```

---

*The number of tutorials on a multitude of topics continues to grow on the WWW. These resources are an exciting example of the education and training potential of the Web.

```
Keys    The 100 most statistically salient words contained in the document
Excerpt The smaller of the first 20 lines or 20% of the document
Desc    Up to 16 lines of "hyperlink" or "anchor" text from other pages with
        links to this document.
```

On the day of this actual search, we found that there were 90,220 documents matching at least one of our search terms. Given our optional settings, Lycos returned only the first four documents matching "netscape tutorial", and here is our first result:

```
1) Netscape Tutorial [1.0000, 2 of 2 terms, adj 1.0]
Abstract: Netscape Tutorial A step-by-step tutorial on how to use one of the
finest World Wide Web Browsers available The software industry offers a number
of World Wide Web browsers. Netscape is one of those W...
http://w3.ag.uiuc.edu/AIM/Discovery/Net/www/netscape/index.html (2k)
```

The top score when there is a direct match of search terms by definition is 1.0000, and Lycos reports this. Other "hits" are reported by their score, and this is determined by a combination of factors related to search term occurrence in the discovered items (e.g., how far into the document they appear; hits in the title or first paragraph are scored higher).

It so happens that the resulting home page found by Lycos is, in fact, a very nice Netscape tutorial. There were three references to it in its database. A completely different second tutorial also was found via this Lycos search. Links to the documents are available on-screen, so we can go directly to each to check it out. By using the **Back** toolbar button on the Netscape Navigator screen, we can immediately return to the results of our search. Should we spend a few minutes exploring a number of additional links, we can return to the Lycos results using the **Go** menu shown in Figure 13-4.

We can create a permanent electronic bookmark for any of these links by going to it and then choosing the **Add bookmark** option from Netscape Navigator's **Bookmarks** menu. The difference between **Go** and adding a bookmark is that the bookmark stays until we delete it, whereas **Go** is only a temporary buffer that is tracking our electronic footsteps.

Look back at the Lycos search results once again. Why did our effort net only four hits? Recall that we set the Lycos search option to "strong match," which limited our results. By returning this to "loose match," the acceptable score is lowered to 0.1 from 0.9, and we then find 29 hits. "netscape tutorial" no longer looks for the two words to be adjacent, and our results include items for which we were not seeking. This is often serendipitous. Just as you may find an interesting book on the library shelf next to the one you set off into the stacks to retrieve, Lycos may find some very useful sources that do not quite match the original search criteria.

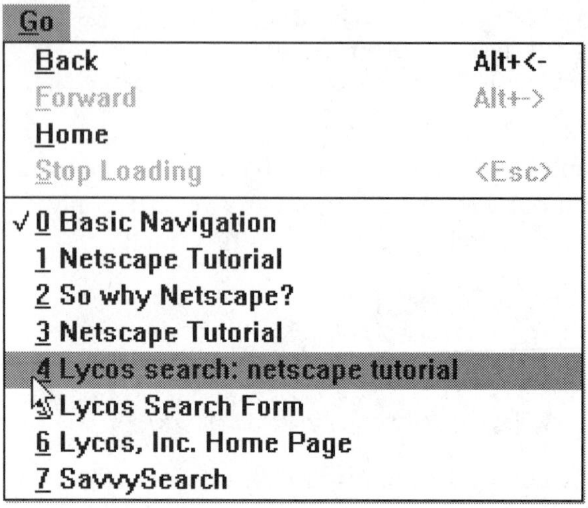

```
Go
 Back                        Alt+<-
 Forward                     Alt+->
 Home
 Stop Loading                <Esc>
 √ 0 Basic Navigation
   1 Netscape Tutorial
   2 So why Netscape?
   3 Netscape Tutorial
   4 Lycos search: netscape tutorial
   5 Lycos Search Form
   6 Lycos, Inc. Home Page
   7 SavvySearch
```

*Figure 13-4    The Go menu will take you directly to a site
you visited in the current session*

Lycos has added a directory of Web categories to its home page. This new addition allows Lycos users to look up general categories of Web sites like the famous Yahoo directory originally created at Stanford. The inclusion of this directory option comes at a time when WWW search tool formats seem to be converging.

## Infoseek (URL http://www2.infoseek.com)

*Infoseek* is a commercial search tool that was easy to locate with the Netscape Navigator by hitting its **Net Search** button; Infoseek has been one of the search choices. It grew in popularity quickly, in part, because it was at one time so much faster than the more established Lycos tool. Infoseek initially allowed only 10 "free" results, with additional results coming only to those who chose to subscribe to the service. A decision was made to increase this to 100 hits while refining the subscription offer to additional databases including, for example, USENET news.

When the Infoseek form has been retrieved and displayed for us on our Netscape Navigator screen, we once again enter "netscape tutorial" as our search terms at the appropriate place on the form. Remember that not only will the interface differ, but Infoseek is not using the Lycos database. Our results are expected to be different, although some overlap in results will certainly not be surprising. Indeed, the results returned from Infoseek are similar to those from Lycos; even the format of the results is not dramatically different. Infoseek displays an abstract of the listed documents and offers a link directly to each. As of this writing, Infoseek does not give a score for its search results. Here is the first item we got:

```
Titles: 1 through 10 of 100
Netscape Tutorial
        A step-by-step tutorial on how to use . one of the finest World Wide Web
        Browsers available . The software industry offers a number of World Wide
        Web browsers. Netscape is one of those World Wide Web browsers. Why does
        the ...
        --- http://w3.ag.uiuc.edu/AIM/Discovery/Net/www/netscape/index.html (1K)
```

Although the similarity between the format of this result and that of Lycos reported above is obvious at this time, remember that the masters of these Web sites are constantly tinkering with them. Indeed, "your mileage may vary."

## *The Infoseek "not" option*

Simple as it is, Infoseek allows you to exclude keywords as well as include them. In the world of Boolean searching, this is known as the "not" option. Infoseek allows you to exclude a search term by placing the minus sign (–) before it.

In the case of our Netscape tutorial search, there is one hit that is returned in multiple forms. This is the Netscape tutorial we found at URL **http://w3.ag.uiuc.edu** authored by Scott Wennerdahl. Because we are well aware of this site (and it is returned many times), we choose to eliminate this from another search. This is accomplished by inserting the following text on the Infoseek search form:

```
Netscape tutorial -Wennerdahl
```

By executing this search, our results change considerably. We are left with a wider variety of tutorials without the repetitious Wennerdahl item. Eliminating keywords can be an extremely valuable way of honing your search. Another way you can refine an Infoseek search is to use the plus sign (+) to force the inclusion of a search word. You might wish to do this, for example, in the case of matching two or more common words in one query.

Experience is without doubt the best teacher here, but begin with the most obvious keywords, then use the + or – options to improve your results. Another useful option from Infoseek is using quotation marks to keep two search words (such as "netscape tutorial") together; "netscape tutorial" will seek only instances in which those words are adjacent to one another. For still more hints, see the Infoseek tips at URL **http:// www2.infoseek.com/doc/help/Tips.html**.

## Excite (URL http://www.excite.com)

Excite is a newer search engine on the WWW. Because of its lack of a track record, it is difficult to determine how successful this site will be. Excite does add different twists to the search process that may be harbingers of what's to come, so we examine it here as an example of what is already possible on the Web. Excite's Netsearch includes yet another proprietary database, and please remember that there is no easy way to determine from outside these services how the databases themselves compare. Two early and obvious examples of Excite's uniqueness are its inclusion of these databases: the previous two weeks of USENET news and what it calls "classified ads" (actually, it is a subset of USENET groups known to be groups with classified advertising posted there).

Excite also differentiates between keyword searching and concept searching. Whereas keywords track down all the documents containing the words in your search phrase, concept-based searching tries to find what you *mean* instead of just what you say. "Grouping by Confidence" is the default mode for viewing Excite results; the response to your subject search is a list of those items that best match your request, rank ordered by how well they match it.

We start with a concept-based search using the "netscape tutorial" terms. Excite returns findings that differ from Lycos and Infoseek:

```
        Scores with a red icon show confidence in the match between the document
and your search.
        Search for similar documents by clicking on the red or black icons next to
each score.
Documents 1 to 10 (of 40) found by matching keyword prefixes and concept-based
associations:
    83%
        Netscape/Mosaic Tutorials
        Summary: Tutorial on form creation with examples of form servers that
        send mail based on submissions. PERL: Perl This package contains a group
        of useful PERL routines to decode forms.
```

The URLs of the results are not displayed but can be seen at the bottom of the Netscape Navigator window by pointing to the link with your mouse. Because the URL is not displayed, you cannot cut and paste it from this Excite result to another application. The percentage reported is a measure of Excite's calculated confidence score for the resulting item, and this score is valuable in relative terms versus the other resulting items in the search. The results of this search did not include many tutorials on how to use Netscape Navigator. Instead, various tutorials are listed.

Now let's repeat this search from Excite by switching from the default search words describing a concept to the keywords option. There is a button that allows this change on the Excite search page. In this particular case, the search results are identical. Whether this is a result of the simple two-word search or some other limitation of Excite is unknown (and no response from Excite to an e-mail query about this was forthcoming).

## *Ranking Web sites*

Excite also allows searching of a separate database for reviewed Web sites. This option may portend a trend in WWW use. Simply finding a site may be far less desirable than finding sites that have already been critiqued in some form. NetReviews points you to Web sites and USENET groups rather than to particular Web pages and USENET articles. NetReviews organizes the Web sites and USENET groups into categories of sites and newsgroups. All the sites and newsgroups about education, for example, are grouped together. NetReviews also describes sites with professionally written reviews. This additional element is a good example of "value added" for this particular search tool.

To execute a search of Excite's NetReviews database, we click on it and are once again presented with the choice of the default concept search or the keyword search. Going with the concept search, the results differ considerably from both the Lycos and Infoseek results (*differ* does not necessarily mean *better*) and from the original Excite search as well. Our first hit is one we did not notice in any of our searches up to this point, and it is one of a total of only 23 hits (reflecting the more limited size of the database of reviewed sites):

```
Documents 1 to 10 (of 23) found by matching keyword prefixes:
    79%
            Wade's WWW Tutorials
            Topic: /Computing/Authoring/HTML/Basic_HTML/
            Review: Chock-full of examples and including such relatively recent
            topics as tables and fill-out forms, this is a top-shelf tutorial from a
            first-year grad student at MIT. While this lesson does not go into
            Netscapisms, it offers links to a companion tutorial on the subject,
            as well as other helpful spots for furthering one's web education.
```

Once again, the URL is not included in the result, but there are new Topic and Review fields that are unique to NetReviews. This result also is not a Netscape tutorial, but the directory style Topic and the original review are two helpful ways to look through the other hits to find the closest match to our intended search.

## *SavvySearch (URL http://www.cs.colostate.edu/~dreiling/ smartform.html)*

SavvySearch is a meta-search tool, designed to send a user's information query to several different Internet search engines in real time (i.e., a parallel search). SavvySearch offers the advantage of a one-stop location and common user interface for querying many diverse databases, then comparing and summarizing the results.

As of this writing, SavvySearch does not use any query language (e.g., Boolean searches). The only query term operator is white space, which is interpreted as an "and" (i.e., "netscape and tutorial") whenever possible. If you really need the effect of an "or", you will need to perform multiple searches. A future version is in the works that will accommodate some standard Boolean operators. The information categories (WWW, news, software, etc.) are used by SavvySearch to determine which three to five servers will provide the most relevant information. Note that there is not a one-to-one correspondence between these broad categories and search engines, but rather a matrix of weights that guide the decision. As a "new kid on the block," it is especially reasonable to assume that SavvySearch will look different over time.

SavvySearch queries other search tools on the Web (see Figure 13-5), including, Lycos, Web Crawler, NIKOS, Archie, Infoseek, Webster, Roget's Thesaurus, Harvest, EINet Galaxy, Yahoo, DejaNews, and the Internet Movie Database. SavvySearch matches these databases to the choices made in the Expert Options dialog box.

We will try our "netscape tutorial" search on SavvySearch by selecting **WWW Resources**, **Reference**, and **Academic**, because these would seem to hold the most promise. SavvySearch is slower than other existing search tools, because it is dependent upon those other tools to complete its search. The results (Figure 13-6) are displayed following a varying "quote of the moment," a new one of which appears while SavvySearch is completing its task. Presumably, this amusing distraction may disappear as the task is completed more quickly in the future.

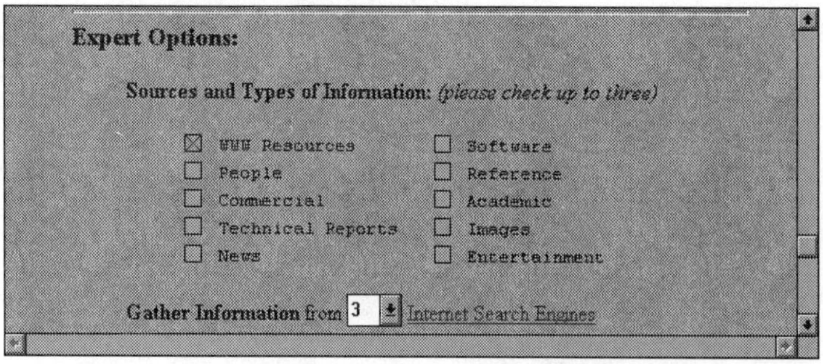

*Figure 13-5    SavvySearch sources and types of information*

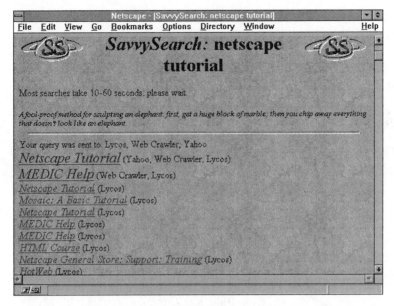

*Figure 13-6    SavvySearch results screen*

SavvySearch displays the source of the hit in parentheses, with duplicated results emphasized by a larger font. Because the results actually come from Lycos and Infoseek, among others, the results are not very different from our previous search attempts. SavvySearch may represent another step in the evolution of WWW search tools and, like the Web itself, epitomizes this very fluid point in the Web's history.

## WWW Directories

Beyond the tools that actively allow database surfing are the more simple WWW *directories*. These indexes of Web content are arranged by categories. A search engine works best when you are not sure what you are looking for, but directories are there when you simply need to look up some information.

### Global Network Navigator (URL http://www.gnn.com)

The Global Network Navigator (GNN) (see URL **http://www-e1c.gnn.com/gnn/wel/ GNNhistory/index.html**) has superseded its famous Whole Internet Catalog (URL: **http://www.gnn.com/gnn/wic/index.html**), the latter of which was put online initially in 1992. The online catalog is intended as a WWW version of the printed catalog that appears at the end of this textbook. The current GNN was acquired by service provider America Online in June 1995, and the cliché that nothing here has remained the same certainly fits.

It is fair to say that if you want to stay current with the WWW, go to the GNN home page. Not only will you find the constantly updated Whole Internet Catalog, an online-only magazine called Web Review (URL: **http://www.gnn.com/gnn/wr/index.html**), and still more original material, but you are sure to see information about and applications of the latest WWW technology at this site.

### Yahoo (URL http://www.yahoo.com)

Created by graduate students at Stanford in 1994, "Yahoo" stands for "Yet Another Hierarchical Officious Oracle." As one of the first and most comprehensive categorical directories of WWW sites, Yahoo quickly became one of the most popular of all sites on the Web. Here's a sample of the broad categories available from Yahoo:

| | |
|---|---|
| Arts | Literature, Photography, Architecture, . . . |
| Business and Economy [Xtra!] | Directory, Investments, Classifieds, . . . |
| Computers and Internet | Internet, WWW, Software, Multimedia, . . . |
| Education | Universities, K-12, Courses, . . . |
| Entertainment [Xtra!] | TV, Movies, Music, Magazines, Books, . . . |
| Government | Politics [Xtra!], Agencies, Law, Military, . . . |
| Health | Medicine, Drugs, Diseases, Fitness, . . . |
| News [Xtra!] | World [Xtra!], Daily, Current Events, . . . |
| Recreation | Sports [Xtra!], Games, Travel, Autos, . . . |
| Reference | Libraries, Dictionaries, Phone Numbers, . . . |
| Regional | Countries, Regions, U.S. States, . . . |
| Science | CS, Biology, Astronomy, Engineering, . . . |
| Social Science | History, Philosophy, Linguistics, . . . |
| Society and Culture | People, Environment, Religion, . . . |

Yahoo has also added its own search interface toolbar that allows you to search for entries in its catalog. Inserting "netscape tutorial" returns the following results:

```
Yahoo Search Results
3 matches were found containing all of the substrings (netscape, tutorial).
Computers and Internet:Internet:Beginner's Guides
     Netscape Tutorial
Computers and Internet:Software:Data Formats:HTML:Guides and Tutorials
     Wade's HTML Tutorial - Info and examples of page setup, text, images,
```

```
links, imagemaps,
      mailto, and Netscape extensions.
Computers and Internet:Software:Protocols:Winsock
      FAQ - Winsock - Connecting with Windows: What software you need, how it
works,
      tutorials. Winsock stacks (Trumpet, etc.), Winsock apps (Netscape, etc.).
```

The objects of the search are both the Yahoo category and the matched search result indented below. Both are hypertext links, meaning you could go to the appropriate Yahoo category (e.g., "Computers and Internet:Internet:Beginner's Guides") or the matched item ("Netscape Tutorial", which in this case is actually a link to Scott Wennerdahl's work once again). For the moment, the addition of a search tool is welcomed because the directory has become so large. If it is an open-ended search you want, however, that is not the purpose for which Yahoo was intended.

## Searching Through a Document

Some documents that you retrieve from the WWW may be long ones. There might be some that seem like mismatches from a search that you have just completed. You can search through the item retrieved into your Netscape Navigator window by pointing and clicking on the **Find** toolbar button. You are presented with a dialog box (Figure 13-7) in which you can enter a search term *for the document on your screen*. This is *not* a search of the WWW, as you quickly will learn through practice.

Click on **Up** if you want to search upward in the document from the point where you are; click on **Match Case** if you want to limit the text search by making it case-sensitive. Type your search word or phrase into the **Find What** text box, and click on the **Find Next** button. Netscape Navigator then finds the text string within the current displayed document and highlights it.

## Saving and Printing Files

Remember that documents displayed via Netscape Navigator are representations of files that have been retrieved through the WWW. They have been stored temporarily for you locally, and you can now manipulate that information. To save it as a file, you would

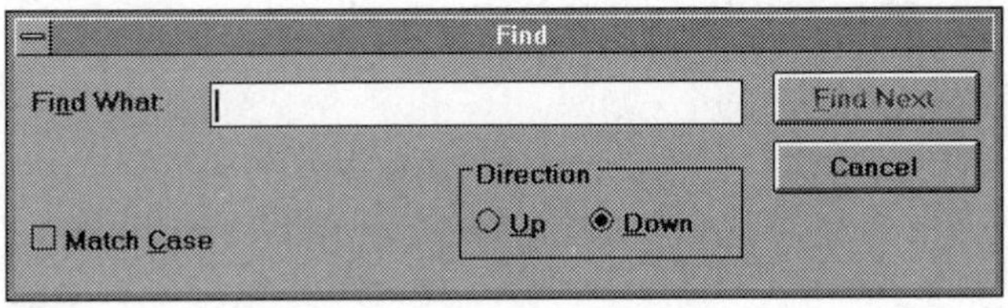

*Figure 13-7   Search through current document window*

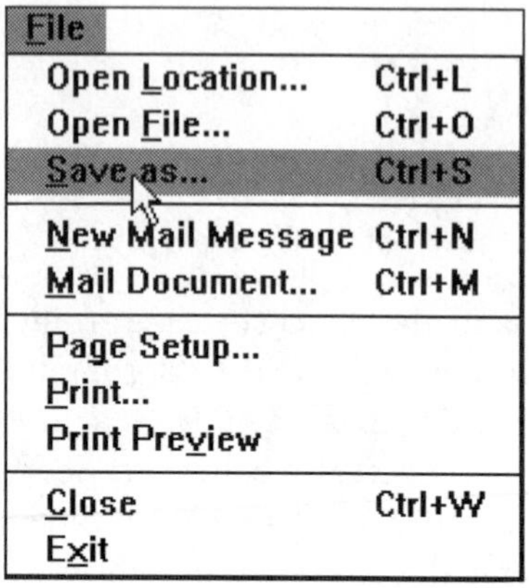

```
┌─────────────────────────────────────┐
│ File                                │
├─────────────────────────────────────┤
│ Open Location...        Ctrl+L       │
│ Open File...            Ctrl+O       │
│ Save as...              Ctrl+S       │
│                                      │
│ New Mail Message        Ctrl+N       │
│ Mail Document...        Ctrl+M       │
│                                      │
│ Page Setup...                        │
│ Print...                             │
│ Print Preview                        │
│                                      │
│ Close                   Ctrl+W       │
│ Exit                                 │
└─────────────────────────────────────┘
```

*Figure 13-8    Netscape Navigator File menu options*

choose the **Save As** option from the **File** menu. The options of the **File** menu are shown in Figure 13-8 and are summarized as follows:

**Open Location**        This will take you to any URL you enter.

**Open File**            This will read a local file into the Netscape Navigator. If you are preparing your own home page, for example, you can test it this way by opening your HTML file here.

**Save as**              This will save the current document you are viewing in Netscape as a local file. If you are looking at an HTML file, the HTML code can be saved by choosing the **Source (*.htm)** option of the **Save file as type** box in the Save As dialog box.

**New Mail Message**     You can create an original e-mail message here and also forward an attachment (e.g., a local file).

**Mail Document**        This is the same as **New Mail Message** except that it automatically inserts the current document URL to your new message.

**Page Setup**           This works with your printer to set up the manner in which you want to print the document being displayed.

**Print**                This will print the file currently being displayed. Although you may be looking at the first screen of a 30-page document, you can print all or as many pages as you wish (see Figure 13-9).

**Print Preview**        This option will show you how the document will look when printed.

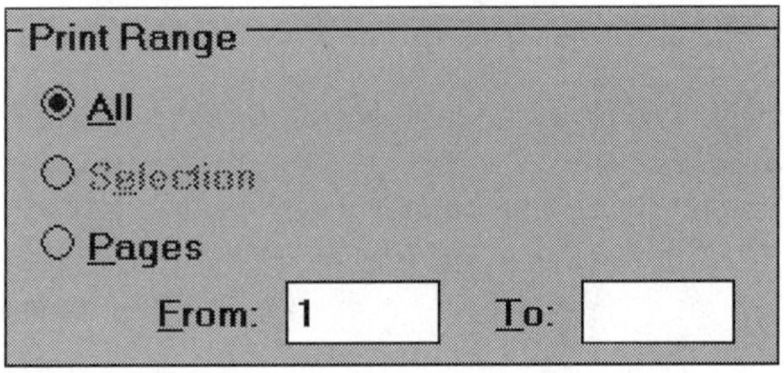

*Figure 13-9*   *Page-range options in the Print dialog box*

| | |
|---|---|
| **Close** | This closes the current Netscape Navigator window but does not exit the program. |
| **Exit** | This exits the Netscape Navigator program without saving where you are. |

After opening the **File** menu and choosing **Save as**, you are presented with the Save As dialog box. You then have to specify a filename. The **Drives** list box shows the directory from which you started Netscape Navigator. Move the mouse to this box and, if appropriate, edit the path shown; if the directory shown is OK, just type a filename in the **File name** text box. This is analogous to selecting a folder on the Macintosh or in Windows 95. If you do not include a filename, Netscape Navigator will use the name of the file employed at its origination site. When you are ready to save the file, click on the **OK** button. If you change your mind, click on **Cancel**.

Printing the document is also simple. When you select the **Print** option of the **File** menu, you will see the Print dialog box, part of which is shown in Figure 13.9 (depending on your local system). This is no different from any Windows or Macintosh application, although the Windows and Mac Print dialog boxes may differ somewhat from each other.

The **Print** command will follow your instructions from choosing from a possible selection of connected printers to limiting the number of pages you print. Once again, if this causes you trouble, seek local experts to help make sure everything is configured properly.

## Selecting a Default Netscape Navigator Home Page

Only as an example, let's make the search site Infoseek the home page for our Netscape Navigator browser. To do this, select the **Options** menu followed by **General** (see Figure 13-10). Then select **Appearance**, **Start with**, then **Home Page Location**. Enter the URL for Infoseek in that spot and press ENTER. Now, each time you click on the

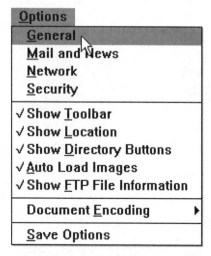

*Figure 13-10   Selecting the General
option from the Options menu*

Home button on Netscape Navigator, you will go to the Infoseek home page. Once you find a site from which you might often wish to launch your Web surfing sessions, make that your home page. As mentioned earlier, an oft updated news source might also be a good choice for your default home page.

## Advanced Navigation

Once you can move around, save files, and know where to find some interesting things, you are most of the way there. WWW browsers like Netscape Navigator do a lot to make Internet navigation easier for you. In this section we will describe three special features:

- How to use bookmarks
- How to work with multiple windows
- How to use the **Go** menu as a history window

### Using Bookmarks

When you start using Netscape Navigator, you will spend time clicking on items and following links around the world. You will soon find that some documents are particularly interesting to you, whether it is the GNN home page or the Library of Congress (URL: **http://lcweb.loc.gov**). There is no need to find yourself trying to relocate something you already found. Veteran Web surfers can tell you the frustration of trying to return to an interesting site after they've forgotten where it is.

To solve this problem, Netscape Navigator provides bookmarks (which are analogous to *hotlists* on some browsers). A *bookmark* is similar to a Gopher bookmark—it is a permanent list of document URLs and titles that you find interesting and can access with a single menu selection. Once you have found an interesting document, adding it to your bookmark list is easy. Just go to the **Bookmarks** menu and select **Add Bookmark**, as shown in Figure 13-11. The URL and document title are saved to your current bookmark file, and it is possible (although probably unnecessarily risky for a new user) to create more than one bookmark file.

When Netscape Navigator is installed for the first time, it comes with a list of general bookmarks that are certainly worth exploring. To see your list of bookmarks, select **Bookmarks, Go to Bookmarks,** and they are displayed in file/folder format, as shown in Figure 13-12). If you wish to delete a bookmark, here is your chance: Point to the bookmark you wish to delete, select **Edit,** and then **Delete.**

*Figure 13-11    Adding a bookmark*

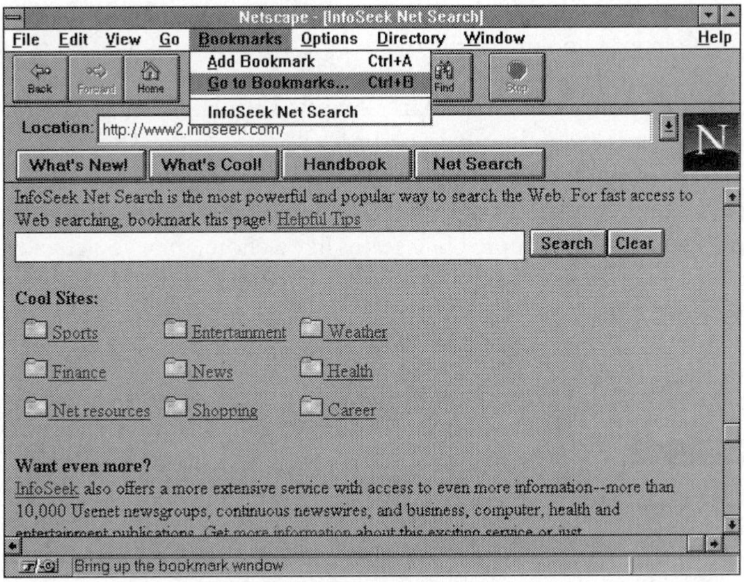

*Figure 13-12    Displaying the list of bookmarks*

This process you may have found to be relatively easy. It has been my experience, however, that the Netscape Navigator's bookmark function has been its most unwieldy tool and the one most in need of continual improvement. We will not spend undue time here on bookmarks on the assumption that the developers will continue to strive toward significant improvements in the manipulation of bookmarks.

To see where your current bookmark file is, open the **Options** menu, select **General**, and then **Bookmarks**. You should now see a dialog box displaying the name of the bookmark file and the directory in which it resides. The defaults are *bookmark.htm(l)* in the Netscape directory or folder (DOS cannot handle *.html* as an extension, so DOS HTML files are limited to the extension *.htm*). If you want to create an entirely new bookmark file, type the filename you wish, including *.htm* for DOS or *.html* for non-DOS machines. This will set up an initially blank bookmark file.

## Inserting Bookmarks and Headers

Can you imagine teaching someone to ride a bike by simply talking them through it? The description may not even make sense to the new rider. It is much better to show the pupil the bike and explain what to do next while he is actually on the bike. In the same way, these directions will not make much sense unless you are sitting at your screen and following along.

Depending on the version and copy of Netscape Navigator that you are using, there may or may not be bookmarks already included with your browser. To see if this is true, point to the **Bookmarks** menu and select **Go to Bookmarks** (see Figure 13-12). In our case, we are starting with an empty bookmark file (see Figure 13-13).

There may be folder called *Personal Bookmarks* that is empty. Let's begin by putting a reference to the Whole Internet Catalog in our bookmark file (see Figure 13-14). You can find the catalog by doing an appropriate search or by simply clicking on the Netscape Navigator **Open** button and entering the following URL text: **http://gnn.com/gnn/wic/index.html** (if typing this relatively simple URL seems like a chore, then you already know one benefit of using bookmarks: Once a bookmark is recorded, you can access it by simply pointing to it and clicking).

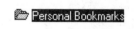

*Figure 13-13    Netscape Navigater new bookmark.htm file*

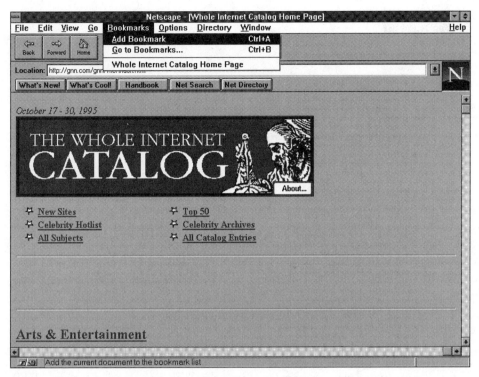

*Figure 13-14    Adding a bookmark to the bookmark.htm file*

You can now point to **Bookmarks**, and the title of the document ("Whole Internet Catalog Home Page") will appear in the bookmarks list box. If you select **Go to Bookmarks**, you will see that the bookmark was entered in your current (and to this point, only) folder (possibly named *Personal Bookmarks* by default). Note that we did not enter the bookmark URL directly into the *bookmark.htm(l)* file ourselves. The software did this for us and with good reason. Netscape Navigator will track sites in our bookmark file for us, adding the updated date of our last visit to that site. (This is one reason why it is not a good idea to try to edit the *bookmark.htm(l)* file unless you *really* know what you are doing.) Versions of Netscape Navigator more current than 2.0b also will allow us to sort our bookmarks by date and perhaps other options. As a user of this or any browser, you should not be inhibited from making suggestions for improvements to the software developer.

Eventually, you might want to take your bookmarks everywhere you go (e.g., if you do not have your own computer and have to use a public computer running Netscape Navigator). If so, you may save them to a floppy disk by issuing the familiar **File**, **Save as** command sequence after you have selected **Go to Bookmarks** (see Figure 13-15).

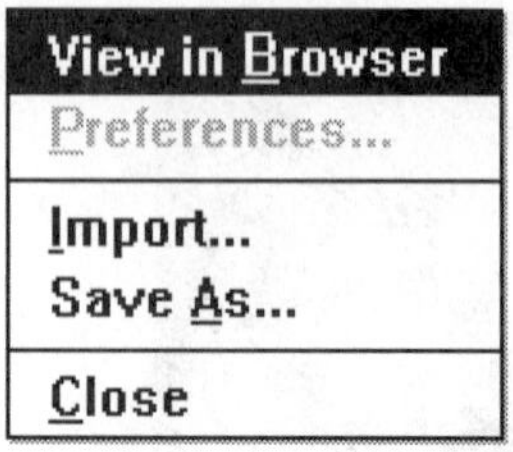

| View in Browser |
| Preferences... |
| Import... |
| Save As... |
| Close |

*Figure 13-15    Netscape Navigater bookmark file options*

Let's add another handy site to our nascent bookmark file: Yahoo. Once again, we have to find its URL or enter it directly into the dialog box invoked by clicking on the **Open** button. The starting point for Yahoo is URL **http://www.yahoo.com**. Once again, it is quickly added to our *bookmark.htm* file by choosing **Bookmarks** then **Add Bookmark**. As it turns out, there are many subcategories listed at Yahoo that we may be interested in. For example, there are subdirectories (with their own URLs) such as "FTP sites" and "Searching the Web" to name just two. So long as there is a unique URL, we can add another bookmark for it. Because we are heavy into **ftp**ing and searching the Web, let's go to each of those individual pages and add two more bookmarks by following the same directions.

Now when we **Go to Bookmarks**, we have four items listed: Whole Internet Catalog Home Page, Yahoo home page, Yahoo Searching the Web page, and the Yahoo FTP Sites page. This brings up another logical bookmark application: *folders*. Why not put all the Yahoo sites in a new Yahoo folder? To do this, we return to the Netscape Bookmarks window (invoked by **Bookmarks, Go to Bookmarks**). Once there we will choose the menu option **Item** followed by **Insert Header**. A new dialog box appears that allows us to enter a name and description for our new folder (see Figure 13-16). We enter a name

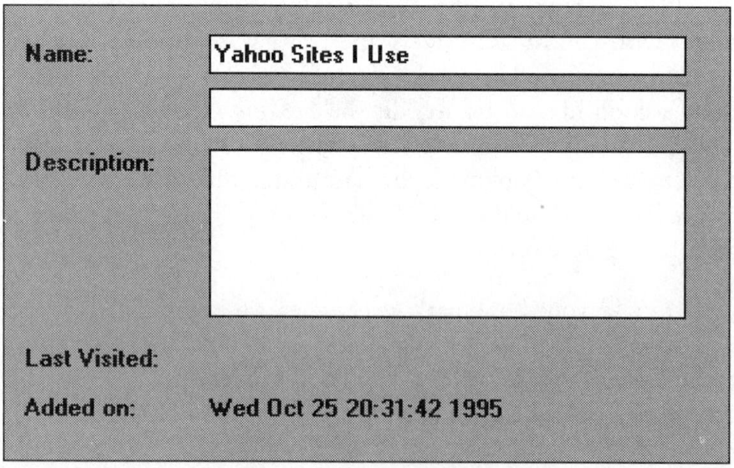

| Name: | Yahoo Sites I Use |
| Description: | |
| Last Visited: | |
| Added on: | Wed Oct 25 20:31:42 1995 |

*Figure 13-16    Creating a bookmark folder*

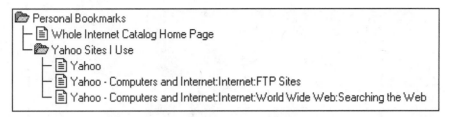

*Figure 13-17*   *The Netscape Navigator bookmark folder*

like "Yahoo Sites I Use" (a somewhat bad folder name choice; it is better to use something that will most easily remind you of what is in this directory).

Once the folder is created, you can use the mouse to drag the desired bookmarks into the new folder. In this case, all three Yahoo bookmarks can be dragged into the Yahoo folder. The results are shown in Figure 13-17.

Once you have begun collecting bookmarks and placing them into folders, your Bookmarks window will be affected. Without folders, going to the Bookmarks window results in the entire list of bookmarks being displayed on-screen. This may be fine if your number of bookmarks remains relatively small; but once your bookmark collection begins to grow, the utility of grouping them into folders becomes more and more apparent.

As a heavy Web surfer, *I* have quite a collection of bookmarks (and they are waiting for a rainy day on which I can organize them better). Some of them are in folders such as "Research Tools", as shown in Figure 13-18. Note that the list of bookmarks shows

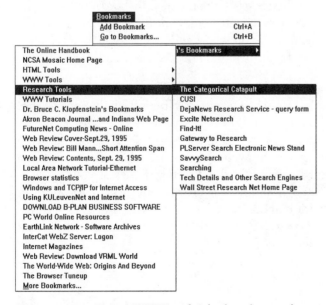

*Figure 13-18*   *Veteran WWW surfer's bookmark conundrum*

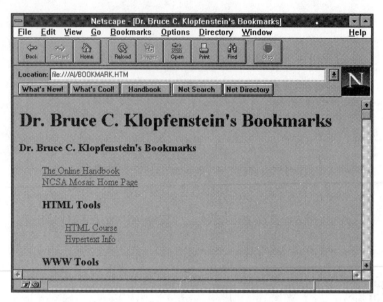

*Figure 13-19    Reading a bookmark file into Netscape Navigator*

"orphan" bookmarks (e.g., not in a named folder) and that the Research Tools folder has been opened to reveal its contents in a new menu immediately to its right.

There are a few other tricks that you may use with bookmarks. You may load them into the Netscape Navigator browser window using either **Bookmarks**, **Go to Bookmarks**; or **File**, **View**; or **File**, **Open File**, then entering the name of your bookmark file. The former does not require that you know where your bookmark file is saved whereas the latter do. If nothing else, viewing them in the browser window gives you an alternative view of your bookmarks. Items within folders will be indented (see Figure 13-19).

As more research resources are made available via the WWW, you may create separate bookmark files for each project. Let's say you begin a research project on the convergence of media technologies (print, broadcasting, and film). Remembering to *always* back up your work on *separate* disks (including floppy backups for hard drive files), you begin the project by looking for research sites on the Web related to the topic. You can create a file called *bookmark.htm(l)* on your floppy or in the directory/folder of your research project using your text-only editor (e.g., SimpleText on Macintosh or *notepad.exe* on Windows/DOS). The file begins with no bookmarks, and once you issue the Netscape Navigator menu sequence **Options**, **General**, **Bookmarks** to point to this new bookmark file, you begin the information-gathering task.

## *Window History*

Like the Lynx browser, Netscape Navigator keeps track of the documents you have seen and lets you move back to your previous selections (see Figure 13-20). At the simplest level, you can use the **Back** button to move to the previous document. Once you have moved back, you can then move forward again by using the **Forward** button. (Moving forward is inoperable until you at least have moved from your opening home page to another location.)

You can also get a window history via Netscape Navigator's **Window** menu. When you select the **History** option, you will see a lists of every document you've looked at with this window. (As you will see in the following section, you can have several windows; each window has its own history.) The document you're currently looking at will be highlighted. To view any document in the list, double-click on it with the mouse. You may also copy any item (URL) from this history list directly to the bookmark file by selecting it and then choosing **Add Bookmark** from the **Bookmarks** menu.

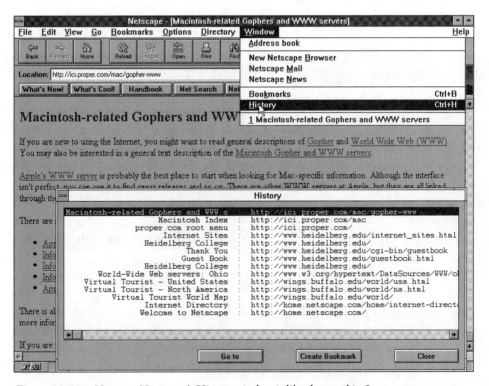

***Figure 13-20*** *Netscape Navigator's History window is like that used in Lynx*

## *Working with Multiple Windows*

You can create multiple Netscape Navigator windows; Figure 13-21 shows two search home pages on-screen simultaneously. This allows you to view more than one document at a time or perform more than one Web task at a time (e.g., viewing a site in one window while waiting for the completion of a search in another). This multitasking application of Netscape Navigator is indicative of a trend in desktop computing and one reason why larger monitors are coming into higher demand (i.e., so the various documents are visible on one screen). Also note the "broken glass" icon in Figure 13-21; this indicates that a graphic did not download and display properly. Pressing the **Reload** button will usually correct this, refreshing the screen and replacing the icon with the graphic.

Issuing the **Window, New Netscape Browser** menu sequence will launch another Netscape Navigator window by showing your default home page. To return to having only one Navigator window open, choose **Close** from the **File** menu (**File, Exit** will shut down your application completely).

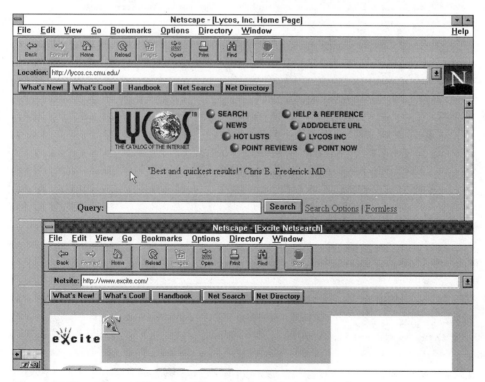

*Figure 13-21    Lycos and Excite in different Netscape Navigator windows*

*Figure 13-22    An example three-paned home page using Netscape Navigator 2.0b*

Another advance in HTML allows multiple, independently controlled windows from one home page. An example is shown in Figure 13-22. Although not easily displayed via this static depiction, a user may scroll through the windows on the left and right side of this window while the image at the top of the screen stays in place. It remains to be seen how popular this more complicated rendition of a home page becomes.

## Working with Other Services

Web clients such as Lynx and Netscape Navigator are not limited to hypertext documents. Many WWW documents, the Whole Internet Catalog being a prime example, consist largely of links to more prosaic services: Gopher servers, FTP servers, TELNET servers, and so on. In this section we will touch on how other services behave when you access them through the Web. It is actually quite simple; for most services, the Web presents a very clean, friendly interface.

### Searchable indexes

As you travel through the Web, you will find many searchable indexes. Searchable indexes present many different kinds of resources: Veronica searches, WAIS searches, CSO phone book lookups, and so on. The same WWW user interface is used for all searches, no matter what their type. In many cases, you need not even know what kind of search you are making. *If you take the time to understand how to use these other tools, this understanding is what will make you the Internet expert that is in such great demand right now.*

If you are using the Lynx browser, the slash key (/) is the search command. It is analogous to the **Find** button in Netscape Navigator. You certainly may use Lynx to access any of the WWW search engines reviewed previously, but you will not see anything but text; graphics (or imagemaps) are not seen. For example, to reach Infoseek using Lynx, launch Lynx, press **G** for **go**, and enter the URL **http://www2.infoseek.com**.

### Gopher and FTP servers

The World Wide Web is a great way to access FTP and Gopher servers; you will find these sites frequently in various resource lists and indexes. For the most part, using them should be fairly self-explanatory, but there are a few extras that are limited to the WWW.

Web browsers use the same interface for both Gopher and FTP services. For example, Lynx presents an FTP or Gopher directory just as easily as a WWW home page menu. You get a list of items; items (whether files or directories) may be accessed via a text link. To select any item, position the cursor on it and press ENTER; if it is a text file, Lynx displays the file for you to read. (If it is a binary file, you will be asked what to do next, such as download the file). If you select a directory, Lynx displays the directory.

Netscape Navigator is substantially more sophisticated. Once again, you retrieve a list of files that you can select. Each filename has an icon next to it, telling you something about the file's contents. Figure 13-23 shows a typical screen. Table 13-1 shows the icons you will see (some of these are shown in Figure 13-23).

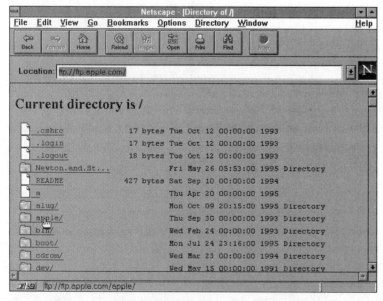

*Figure 13-23   Netscape Navigator viewing an FTP archive*

*Table 13-1   Common Netscape Navigator Icons*

| File type | Icon |
| --- | --- |
| Directory | File folder |
| Text file | Sheet of paper with writing |
| Compressed text file | Sheet of paper with writing |
| Binary file | Sheet of paper with zeros and ones |
| Image | Sheet of paper with a square, sphere, and triangle |
| Misread image | Broken sheet of paper with a square, sphere, and triangle (looks like broken glass) |
| Movie | Film strip |
| Audio | Musical notes |
| Phone books | Binoculars |
| Veronica searches | Binoculars |
| Searchable indexes | Binoculars |

If you select a directory, Netscape Navigator displays the items in the directory as if it were a Gopher client. If you select a file, Netscape does what it can to display the file. Unlike Lynx, Netscape Navigator will seek to match applications to nontext (i.e., binary) files. In particular:

- If it is a text file, it displays the file on-screen. Use the **Save As** command to save it.

- If it is a compressed text file, it uncompresses the file and displays it. For example, Netscape for Windows recognizes zip files as ones that can be uncompressed with *unzip.exe.* Again, use the **Save As** command to save the file.

If it is a picture, a movie, or an audio file, it is downloaded and played if the appropriate application is accessible. If not, Netscape Navigator displays a pop up window asking what you would like to do (launch the proper application, save the file, or cancel the transfer).

Any browser is not flawless; it can be confused (particularly by files with two or more extensions, such as *foo.tar.gz*), and there are things it does not recognize. It does make a good, and usually useful, attempt to do something intelligent with binary files.

If you have followed this discussion, you are probably already asking: How do I save picture, audio, and video files? By default, Netscape Navigator doesn't; it plays the file, and then it is gone. If you've just downloaded a 5MB audio file and would like to listen to it more than once, you might find this frustrating. To save files that Netscape Navigator normally plays, go to the **Options** menu and select the **Load to Local Disk** option. When this option is in effect, Netscape Navigator will not display pictures, movies, or sounds. Instead, it displays the **Save As** dialog box, allowing you to save the file.

When you access an FTP server, Web clients automatically insert a **Parent Directory** link at the head of the directory list. This makes it easier to navigate around the server's file system; clicking on this icon is equivalent to **cd ..** or **cdup**. One particularly nice feature for FTP users is that Netscape Navigator handles the mechanics of anonymous FTP for you; it logs in automatically. However, there are a few limitations worth noting:

- Web clients don't handle groups of files—it is strictly one file at a time. There's no equivalent to **mget**. If you habitually collect lots of stuff, **ftp** might work better.

- There's no equivalent to the **put** command; the Web is strictly for downloading files.

- It is not possible to find out how large a file is before downloading it. So you can suddenly find that you have transferred 2 megabytes, and you have no idea how much more is to come.

Now, a few notes about Gopher servers. An inherent limitation of Gopher, no matter whether you are using a Gopher client or a Web client, is that there's no concept of a parent menu; hence, there's no equivalent to the **Parent Directory** icon. To move back "up" a tree, you have to use the **Back** button or the **Window, History** command sequence. If you are using Netscape Navigator, you could also add bookmarks to note particularly interesting menus.

Gopher's Veronica searches are presented as searchable indexes; they are identical to other searches that you find.

### Using TELNET servers

Accessing a TELNET server is more or less what you would expect; on UNIX, Netscape Navigator creates a new window with a TELNET session running in it. On a Macintosh or Windows system, it will do something equivalent.

If you select a TELNET resource while using the line-oriented browser, you will temporarily "drop out" of the Web and start a **telnet** session. When you end the **telnet** session, you will return to the Web. For security reasons, you can't access TELNET resources from a public browser (like the one at *info.cern.ch*). If you try, you will see a message telling you that TELNET access is not allowed. Get your own browser and try again.

### Using WAIS servers

There are many WAIS resources available through the World Wide Web. As you might expect, WAIS resources appear as searchable indexes. For example, the CIA World Fact Book is available via URL **http://wais.wais.com/wais-dbs/world-factbook.html** to search a database (in this case, a WAIS database). Try out its form as an example of the WAIS-WWW interface.

## ■ *Reading Network News*

There are a few documents with links to newsgroups. If you find one of these, you can use your Web browser as a newsreader. To save the suspense and trouble of looking, you can find an entry into the newsgroup world by looking at "Data Sources By Service," which is in the "Starting Points for Internet Exploration" document in the *Resource Catalog*. If you do not want to search for them, The World Wide Web Consortium lists some newsgroups at URL **http://www.w3.org/hypertext/DataSources/News/Groups/ Overview.html**. Once you get to this page, you will see a list of "top-level" newsgroups: *rec, comp, alt,* and so on. Select the top-level group you want; when you see the next page, select an interesting newsgroup within that category. If all goes well (i.e., the news server is correctly configured in your Netscape Navigator), you will see a list of articles that are available in the group.

To read news, you must either have a news server (an NNTP [Network News Transfer Protocol] server) running on your local system, or you must access one somewhere else on the network. If you get an error message when attempting to read news, it means either you do not have access to a news server or, if you do, your server may not be receiving that particular newsgroup. As always, if you have any trouble with this, ask your local system administrator.*

### *Netscape Navigator and USENET News*

Let's take a brief, graphical tour of USENET using Netscape Navigator. The interfaces in versions 1.1 and 2.0 differ, and you need to be on the lookout for constant upgrades. You will also be able to read your e-mail using Netscape Navigator in a format similar to that used for news. Remember to head for the Netscape Handbook via the Navigator **Help** menu to look for the inevitable updates. The logic behind newsgroup displays should remain more predictable.

---

*Reading news is becoming much more integrated into the Web. WWW newsreading includes some features that you will not find elsewhere: for example, cross-references to other articles are rendered as links to those articles. This makes it easy to go from any article to its predecessors. Older WWW browser newsreaders were missing some features. You could not reply or post articles, the browsers did not have a concept of "subscribing" or "unsubscribing," they did not keep track of articles you have read, and so on. If your current browser has these limitations, it is time to upgrade to a newer version. Netscape Navigator reads news in its versions 1.1 and 2.0b, but the way articles are displayed is quite different.

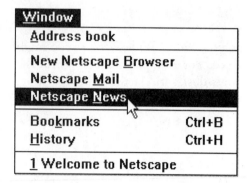

*Figure 13-24    Connecting to USENET via Netscape Navigator*

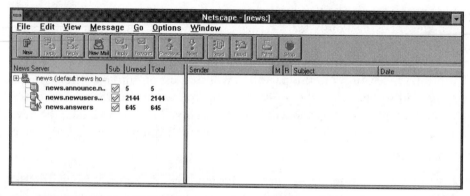

*Figure 13-25    The first USENET screen via Netscape Navigator*

To access newsgroups, open the Navigator **Window** menu and select **Netscape News** (it is not news about Netscape, but rather the link to USENET), as shown in Figure 13-24.

By accessing this option, you will see a list of the newsgroups to which you are subscribed. In our example, this initially includes the three groups shown in Figure 13-25.

To open a subscribed newsgroup, click on that newsgroup's name or its news icon, and the articles appear in a new window on the right, as shown in Figure 13-26. To read an article, click on it, and it will appear on the bottom portion of the screen (Figure 13-27).

Recall from chapter 8 that the specific newsgroups accessible vary from site to site (and Internet service provider to Internet service provider). Figure 13-28 shows you some of the groups available at Bowling Green State University, including local groups under the *bgsu.* heirarchy.

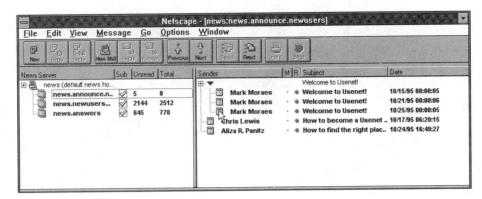

*Figure 13-26    Opening a newsgroup*

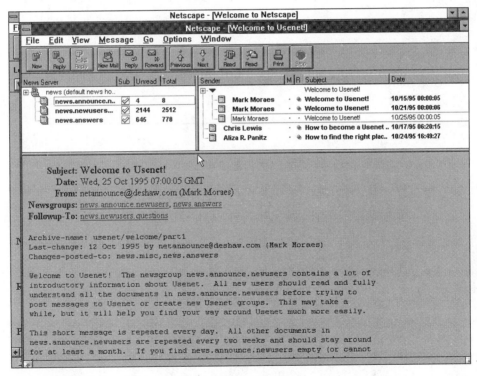

*Figure 13-27    Netscape Navigator's newsgroup window panes*

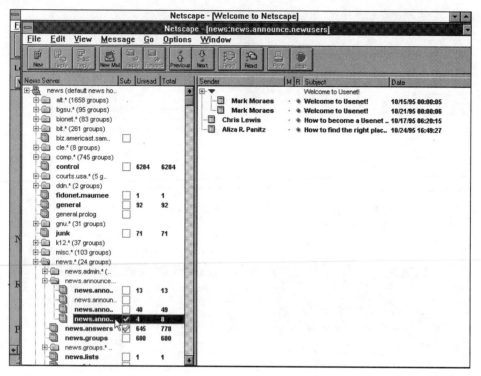

*Figure 13-28    Listing all newsgroups*

If you look carefully at Figure 13-27, you can see the mouse pointer at the conjunction of the three window panes: the list of subscribed newsgroups, the opened newsgroup, and the selected article. By pressing the mouse button at this position, you can change the relative size of all three windows, a big change with version 2.0 of Netscape Navigator (that is not limited to viewing newsgroups). You may also change the size of each individual window by dragging its edge (which is nothing new to Windows and Macintosh veterans).

To post a message (or compose an e-mail message), select the **Message** menu at the top of your USENET screen. There are a number of logical choices: **Post News**, **Post Reply**, and others including composing e-mail. To post a message to a newsgroup, select **Message** and then **Post News** (see Figure 13-29).

To write an e-mail message, click on the **New Mail** button or the choose **New Mail Message** from the **Message** menu, as shown in Figure 13-30.

Another dialog box appears that lets you easily post news or compose and send a message to another person. You cannot post articles or send mail, however, until you have filled

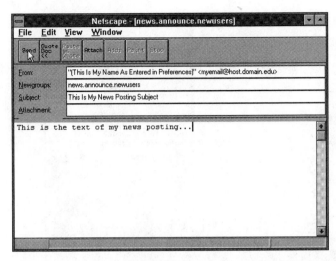

*Figure 13-29   Posting a USENET message using Netscape Navigator*

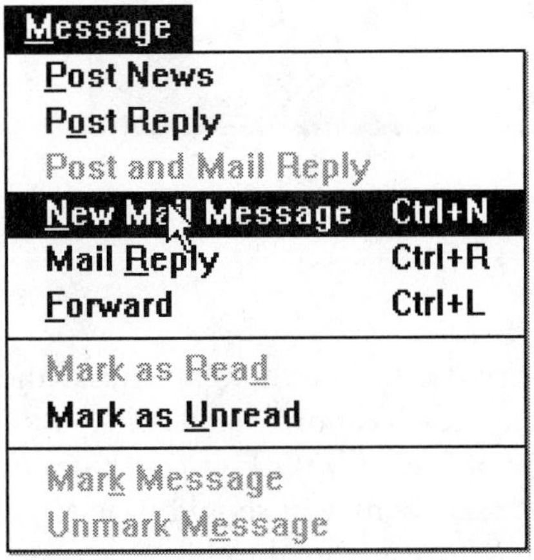

*Figure 13-30   Preparing to compose an e-mail message on Netscape Navigator*

in your name and e-mail address via the **Options, Preferences** menu sequence on the original Netscape Navigator window. In our example (Figure 13-31), we made something up in the Preferences window that then appears in the Message Composition dialog box.

Note that posting a message to a newsgroup and composing e-mail are quite similar on Netscape Navigator 2.0b.

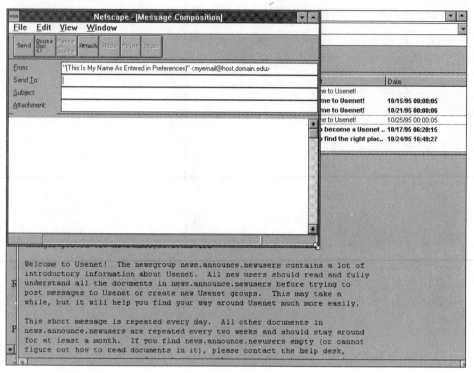

*Figure 13-31    Composing an e-mail message*

## Going Outside the Web

Although the World Wide Web spreads farther every day, it does *not* encompass the entire Internet. There remain resources that you cannot reach simply by following links. Many library databases remain outside the purview of the WWW. This continues to change. The previous edition of *The Whole Internet* asked why you should have to go through three or four menus to find an FTP server. Whereas it used to be easier to go directly to the FTP server, FTP itself is incorporated into the WWW.

Before we can go to an arbitrary resource on the Net using a World Wide Web browser, we have to answer two questions:

- How do you do it? (What's the command?)
- How do you name the resource you want?

The first question is mechanical and fairly simple. Netscape Navigator and Lynx have commands for finding resources directly. The second simply involves uncovering the resource URL. That is where the search engines and WWW directories come in. Because URLs are standardized, they are the same for all Web browsers and other tools.

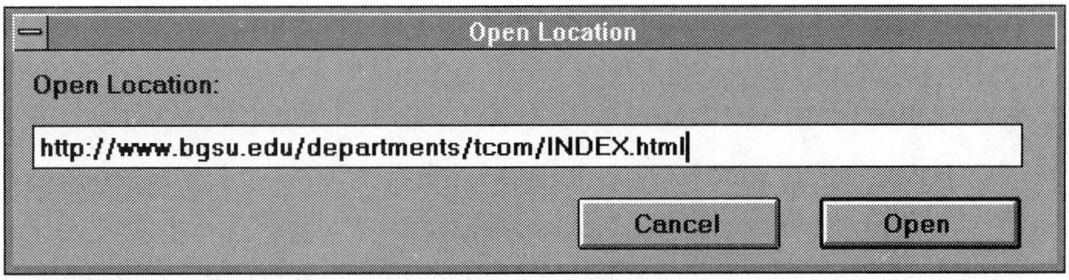

**Figure 13-32**   *Opening a resource*

## Opening Other Resources

If you're using Lynx, just type **G** for the **go** command, followed by the URL of the resource in which you are interested. For example, to jump directly to the University of Minnesota's Gopher server, type the URL **gopher://gopher.tc.umn.edu.**

With Netscape Navigator, click on the **Open** button (there is also an **Open Location** option in the **File** menu—it does the same thing). When you click on **Open**, you will see the menu shown in Figure 13-32.

Type the URL of the resource you want into the editing window. Clicking on the **Clear** button erases the window; clicking on the **Open** button tells Netscape Navigator to access the resource and display it appropriately.

### Uniform Resource Locators

Let's review how to construct a URL. Here's a brief and simplified synopsis.

For FTP resources, a URL has the format:

```
file://internet-name/remote-path
```

where *internet-name* is the name of the server you want to access, and *remote-path* is the file you want. For Macintosh users, remember that directories are analogous to folders. If you don't specify the *remote-path,* the browser shows you the FTP server's root menu— that is, the directory you'd see when you log in. If you specify a directory, the browser shows you that directory; you can then use point-and-click navigation to find the file you want. And if you specify a file, the browser gets the file for you, without any further navigation. (Line-oriented browsers like **www** may have trouble if you specify a binary file.) For example, to get the file *ls-lR.Z* from **ftp.uu.net**, use the URL **file://ftp.uu.net/ ls-lR.Z.** To get UUNET's root directory, use the URL **file://ftp.uu.net.**

Netscape Navigator assumes that FTP servers are "well behaved"—that is, that they behave like UNIX FTP servers, which are a de facto standard. In particular, they need to accept an anonymous login. That's usually the case, but you may run into trouble with servers that require **ftp** or something else as the anonymous login name. Using a more general form of the URL can help:

```
file://username@internet-name/remote-path
```

For example, to access the server **foo.bar.edu** that requires the login name **ftp**, use the URL **file://ftp@foo.bar.edu**. You may still have trouble with servers that break the rules in other ways; IBM mainframes are most likely to be tricky. If you can't make things work, get out the old-fashioned FTP client we discussed in chapter 6.

This syntax also allows you to specify a password following the username; use a colon to separate the two. As you might guess, you can use this feature to **ftp** to a private account. However, your password will be visible as you type it; furthermore, Netscape Navigator has the additional disadvantage of showing your password in the URL field at the top of its display. For this reason, we do not recommend using a Web browser for private **ftp**.

For TELNET resources, a URL has the format:

```
telnet://internet-name:port
```

The *internet-name* is the name of the host you want to access. The *port* is optional; you need it only if the TELNET server you want uses a non-standard port.

For Gopher resources, a URL has the format:

```
gopher://internet-name:port
```

Again, *internet-name* is the name of the host you want to access; *port* is needed only if the Gopher server uses a non-standard port. For example, to **telnet** to the MTV Gopher server, use the URL **gopher://mtv.com**.

It is worth noting that Gopher URLs are really much more complicated; what I've shown above is about all that's useful to a human. There is no good way to specify a particular directory on a Gopher server, unless you're a computer.

For network news, a URL for a newsgroup has the format:

```
news:newsgroup-name
```

For example, to read the newsgroup *alt.3d,* use the URL **news:alt.3d**. There is currently no way to specify a news server, though this may be possible in the future. On UNIX systems, the environment variable NNTPSERVER specifies your news server.

For hypertext resources, a URL for a hypertext page has the format:

```
http://internet-name/remote-path
```

The *internet-name* is the name of the server, and *remote-path* is the pathname for the file you want to read. It is assumed to be an HTML file and can contain links to embedded pictures and other documents.

By the way, do you find the process of constructing a URL laborious and confusing? There's a solution. Once you've constructed the URL and visited the item you want, just add it to your hotlist!

## Setting Up Your Own Home Page

When your browser starts, it presents you with a default home page. As already explained, you are not stuck with the home page it gives you by default (it needs to start somewhere). You can select other home pages around the Net. There are many reasons to select a different home page:

- You may find another home page that's more to your liking; for example, you might like starting with ORA's Whole Internet Catalog or CERN's virtual library. Or you might prefer some specialized subject index that's appropriate for your interests.

- The server that provides the default home page for your browser may be overloaded—and therefore inconvenient, or even impossible, to use. You can find another home page, or (when the server is not badly loaded) make your own copy of its home page.

- If you want to learn HTML, the markup language in which World Wide Web documents are written, you can download a home page from somewhere else, and customize it—i.e., add your own favorite resources.

There are many ways to pick your own home page. You may very well wish to make *The Whole Internet: Academic Edition* at URL **http://www.thomson.com/wadsworth.html** your home page at least for starting out. This can be done with both Netscape Navigator and Lynx. Look to the Wadsworth home page for important links on how to *author* your own home page. There are a multitude of wonderful tutorials available on the Web to help you with this. Wadsworth has links to the best ones.

## Multimedia Files

If you stumble across an audio or video link, there usually are directions on the page with the multimedia file(s) that tell you what to do. Simply put, Netscape Navigator must recognize the file application and launch a player on your local system. These "helper" programs must be available on your system along with Netscape Navigator. Thus, if you click on an audio link and nothing happens, you might need an audio player installed. Common players are available from URL **ftp://ftp.ncsa.uiuc.edu.** Once

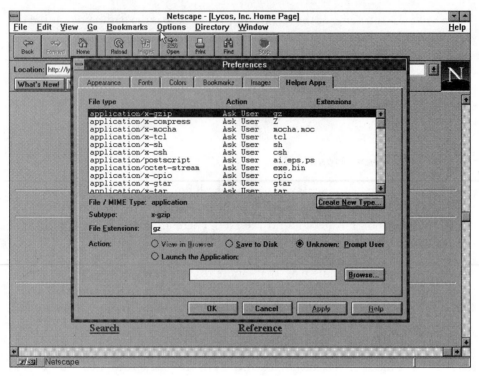

**Figure 13-33**    *Application preferences in Netscape Navigator*

installed properly on your local system, you need to tell Netscape Navigator how to: (1) recognize the file by its extension or type, and (2) associate that type with the player you have installed. Both of these are accomplished by issuing the **Options**, **General** menu sequence and then choosing **Helper Applications** (see Figure 13-33).

# Hints for Netscape Navigator Users

We have covered most of what you need to use Netscape Navigator and Lynx effectively. However, since Netscape Navigator is the ultimate power tool, a few formal hints are in order. You would probably figure out most of these yourself, but we can get you pointed in the right direction.

## Canceling

If you get tired of waiting to retrieve a document, or if you decide you have made a mistake, you can cancel most operations by clicking on the Netscape Navigator **Stop** button in the upper-right corner of the screen. **CTRL-C** will interrupt a request on Lynx.

## Minimizing Delays While Loading Images

If you are using Netscape Navigator over a medium-speed link (e.g., between 9,600 and 19,600 baud), you will find that it takes a fair amount of time to load graphics. For many documents, that is not a problem; for example, GNN includes many graphics, but it is organized in relatively short chunks, so waiting for them to "come down the line" is not burdensome. However, there are documents that contain so many graphics that you easily can spend several minutes (that seem like hours) waiting. The worst offenders in this regard have tended to be the exhibitions and museums.

To eliminate the time it takes to load the pictures, open the Netscape **Options** menu, choose **General**, then **Images**. Among the image choices, you will find **Display Images After Loading**. The reason this is often a good choice is that text loads quickly and images do not. If you send a request to a server, it responds, but nothing is appearing on your screen; it is amazing how often you can hit the **Stop** button and see the page's text just fine and discover that only the graphics did not load. More often than not, the images are not critical. Consider this option highly recommended.

## Getting the Big Picture—or the Big Sound

Often, pictures are miniatures of a larger image. In these cases, the picture itself is a link, and probably has some kind of noticeable outline. When you click on a picture, Netscape Navigator transfers the full-sized image and displays it on your screen. (Remember, though: A full-sized figure can be as large as a megabyte and may take a very long time to transfer, unless you have a high-speed network connection).

The same is true with sound and video icons. When you click on a sound or video icon, Netscape Navigator transfers the file and renders it appropriately by launching related application software that can "play" the sound or motion picture files. Be aware, though, that sound and video require even more data than pictures. RealAudio is discussed elsewhere in the book, and it is a real breakthrough because it plays an audio file *while it is downloading*. This circumvents the problem of time lost to a large downloading process. Watch Hollywood studios and even the television networks for breakthroughs in video download/display. They have the resources and the incentives to polish RealAudio-like applications for video. It is virtually inevitable (no pun intended).

You may need some external software to view large pictures, listen to sound files, or watch movies. For Netscape Navigator, the programs differ by platform (e.g., Windows versus Macintosh). There have been many developments here in the past year, so we are tracking them for you on our WWW site. You can also take a look at this Hong Kong site: URL **http://www.cuhk.hk:80/rthk/helper.html.**

## When Things Go Wrong

If Netscape Navigator tells you that the information server you want could not be accessed, you can click the **Reload** button to tell it to try again. Obviously, if a server is not responding, trying again won't help; your best bet is to try later. It can help if the problem is on your end: If your connection to the Internet is congested or momentarily flaky, a retry might be all you need to set things right.

## Working with the Netscape Cache

Maybe you wondered how Netscape Navigator knows how to display links you've already visited differently from links you have not. Netscape Navigator keeps track of your global history in a folder/directory called *cache* with filenames only vaguely related to the original filename. You can access these cache files directly, but that really is not their intent. They are temporary files of the information you have accessed recently on the Web, and Netscape Navigator ingeniously saves you time by returning to existing files in your system's storage (e.g., its hard drive) rather than wait for all that information to reload when you return to the original site.

A problem with this solution occurs when you return to a time-sensitive home page. In an obvious example, ESPN's sportszone (URL: **http://espnet.sportszone.com**) produces real-time updates of sporting results as they happen. If you understand how Netscape Navigator uses its cache, you know what problem is coming. In your normal browsing, you may return to ESPN. Thinking it is doing you a favor, Netscape checks its cache, sees that you have been there before, and calls out the previously viewed information. Unfortunately, you must hit the Reload button to contact the ESPN server and get another feed that will include the new scores.

Obviously, the cache will grow over time and could eventually become extremely large—possibly filling up your file system (or even causing your system administrator some grief). If you start detecting some illogical errors (such as repeated failure to find URL files that you know exist), try manually clearing your cache. This is possible by issuing the **Options, Network, Memory and/or Disk cache clear** menu sequence. As you will see, you can also limit the size of each cache. If Netscape is allowed to use too much of your system memory, your other applications will be crippled.

## Making Your Own Links

Netscape Navigator's bookmarks allow you to link public documents (and even FTP directories) to your own notes; your notes can also contain links to other documents.

## Creating Hypertext Documents

You can create your own WWW documents by editing them with a traditional text-only editor such as *notepad.exe* for Windows or SimpleText for Macs. This is how most of the original documents on the Web were created. Look at all the stuff you need to enter just to get the beginning of a possible GNN home page:

```
<HEAD> <TITLE> GNN Home Page </TITLE> <ISINDEX> <BODY> <H1>GNN Home Page </H1>
<P> The Global Network Navigator (GNN), an Internet-based Information Center, is
a production of O'Reilly & Associates, Inc. and an application of the World Wide
Web. <P>
```

You would really like a tool that helps you to add all the extra Hypertext Markup Language (HTML) commands without having to memorize and type all of them. There are two ways of doing this: with a special editor or with a conversion package. In another dramatic development from the previous edition of this book, HTML editors are available in droves. You can access many of them from "W3 and HTMLTools" at URL **http://www.w3.org/hypertext/WWW/Tools/Overview.html**. Currently, not all HTML editors allow WYSIWYG HTML composition (what you see is what you get—something we take for granted with modern word processors on Windows or Macintosh). Once again, you cannot afford to be bashful. Ask locally what editors people are finding most useful, get a copy, and see what you think. There are plenty of vegetables out there, but personal preferences will vary.

The most dynamic area of HTML generation is in creating programs to convert other, more common, rich text formats into HTML. For example, you can convert WordPerfect or Microsoft Word documents with different fonts and styles into HTML easily. The documents will look the same, and you can add links to other documents. Utilities for Microsoft Word 6.0 for Windows were available by 1995, as is also true for WordPerfect 5.1 for DOS. The list at URL **http://www.w3.org/hypertext/WWW/Tools/Overview.html** is a bit overwhelming now, another reason to borrow from your local colleagues' expertise in trying any out.

The trend is clear. The days of entering arcane HTML commands are numbered. Netscape Navigator Gold 2.0, for example, claims to include everything in Navigator as well as the WYSIWYG HTML editor that lets users write scripts, build tables, and split the screen into multiple, scrollable windows. It includes the ability to place permanent features on the screen, such as a stock ticker or a button bar that remains in place when moving to the next page. The latter ability is welcomed by commercial sponsors of Web sites.

# ▨ *The Future of the WWW*

In the first and second editions, we ended with a discussion of where the Web is going. Here is a recap, taking into account events of the past year and a half. At this point, the World Wide Web has become the most important information delivery system on the Internet. It has been immensely successful, and continues to be so, in large part because of Netscape Navigator and Mosaic, which have encouraged people of all kinds—not just physicists—to build hypertext documents. The existing online services—America Online, Prodigy and particularly CompuServe—were slow to move into the WWW. Now each has its own proprietary Web browser, even as The Microsoft Network was launched in August 1995 and AT&T announces aggressive Internet plans. If the WWW was "wowing" us before, the amazement should continue as these large players finally lumber into the Internet and WWW worlds. The WWW may or may not be big enough for all these players, so it is reasonable to expect a shakeout in the coming years, certainly, if not months following publication of this book.

The pace of technological change is accelerating. This means that predicting the future is more difficult and perhaps less meaningful and appropriate than it may have been in the past. Rather than try to forecast what tomorrow can bring, a better approach may be to isolate some general trends.

## *Other Kinds of Documents*

When we first wrote about the Web, we said that it consisted mostly of textual documents and that there was a significant need for browsers that could make intelligent decisions about processing different kinds of files. We have witnessed tremendous progress in this area. Netscape Navigator and other browsers will continue to incorporate the ability to process different file types correctly, and we are nearly there now.

## *Multimedia Is Inevitable*

Other than being known for its ability to transfer software files via **ftp**, the Internet was relegated to a mainly text-only and e-mail tool for much of its history. Sending an individual graphic image used to be a bandwidth-consuming task. The combination of improved compression techniques and an increase in new communication channels is allowing for the continued development of multimedia on the WWW. Expect increasing media fidelity (in audio, video, and virtual reality). To track the latest trends, watch the home pages of movie studios and consumer electronics companies. When you realize that the telephone, broadcasting, and cable television industries do not yet have a presence on the Web, you will have some sense that we may not have seen anything yet.

## *Virtual Reality*

Much as hypermedia languished as a tool of computer, Macintosh, and information science gurus until the WWW was invented, virtual reality (VR) has never lived up to the extreme hype that surrounded it in the early 1990s. VRML (Virtual Reality Modeling Language) may well change all that. Expect to see considerable activity in this area in the next year, and it will not take long to find out if it is a credible addition to the WWW community or just another gasp for air from a technology in search of a solution. (Certainly, VR has its specific applications in training, medicine, and interaction with hazardous materials, but there is little doubt few of us have walked into our VR-designed new kitchens or any of hundreds of such applications predicted a few short years ago.)

## *Human Interface*

You need not be a computer guru to understand that making the interface between human and computer transparent has surrounded much of the innovation in computing, particularly in the past 10 years. Voice recognition and speech synthesis both may be nearly economically viable for inclusion in WWW applications. These technologies have been under development for years, and the WWW may add the final economic and technological boosts necessary to bring them into mainstream applications.

Christmas 1995 brought a new video game product on the market: one that purports to react to the player's thoughts as recorded by a static finger attachment while the player urges the game on by thinking about his ensuing moves. Remember, this is a consumer electronics device, not a top-secret and expensive military simulator. Whether this particular product succeeds or fails, advancing technology for simpler interfaces that may be applied to the Web is another clear trend. It will also become easier for browsers to handle all manner of WWW file formats. Heed this trend: The more transparent this aspect of Web browsing becomes, the faster the diffusion of WWW applications on the Web will be.

Natural-language searching of the Web is already possible, and the future promises to bring innovations that continue to improve on this. As search engines "learn" more about our interests, we will find more precise matches between what is out there and that limited portion of it that we wish to access. The reason for very serious concern here is that we may need to access information that we may not really want to have.

In the future (i.e., after simple hypertext editors are available), special-purpose editors designed for collaborative work may be developed. This is clearly an exciting research topic; although there are some ideas, no one yet knows exactly what such an editor would be like.

## How to Stay Current

The URL for *The Whole Internet, Academic Edition* is **http://www.thomson.com/ wadsworth.html**, and you should include it as a bookmark if not your default browser home page. It has links to various WWW sources that update current developments on the Internet and WWW. The Whole Internet Catalog, Global Network Navigator, and Web Review are three examples we have already given. Mecklerweb (URL: **http:// www.mecklerweb.com**) and CMP Publications' Techweb (URL: **http:// www.techweb.com**) are two more sites with a wealth of current information on Web developments.

Among the other links you will find at the Wadsworth site, the following are of particular interest:

> **http://info.cern.ch/hypertext/WWW/Tools/Filters.html**
>      HTML filters

> **http://siva.cshl.org/~boutell/www_faq.html**
>      WWW FAQ

> **http://www.eit.com/web/www.guide**
>      A guide to cyberspace

> **http://info.cern.ch/hypertext/WWW/MarkUp/HTML.html**
>      Hypertext Markup Language (HTML)

> **http://curia.ucc.ie/info/net/htmldoc.html**
>      How to write HTML files

How lucky we are, and how appropriate it is, that information about the Web in this textbook may be updated at any time on its related WWW site. Never have outside sources been more important to supplementing a physical textbook.

## Exercises

The WWW is a dynamic place. As a subject of current awareness, it is quite clearly a moving target, and this chapter may be the most directly affected. Our WWW site for *The Whole Internet: Academic Edition* is linked from URL **http://www.thomson.com/ wadsworth.html**. If there are substantial changes in any of the WWW items used in these chapter exercises (e.g., changes in search engines), they will be noted at the book site. You may also notify Bruce Klopfenstein of any need for updates by sending e-mail to him at **klopfens@bgnet.bgsu.edu**.

*Unless your instructor tells you differently, print out your responses to the following exercises. Seek help locally if you need it. Help for graphical user interface (GUI) browsers like Netscape will be available from that browser whether via a built-in local help utility resident with the software or (quite likely) via a Web page associated with the browser. Using Lynx, for example, you will find that help appears when you press* **H**. *Lynx help is also available from these sources:*

- *URL* **http://kuhttp.cc.ukans.edu/lynx_help/Lynx_users_guide.html**
- *University tutorials such as this one at the University of Massachusetts: URL* **http://www.umassd.edu/Help/LynxDemo/lynx1.html**

*If you have a print screen function that allows you to print your screen and/or save it as a file, use it as appropriate to show your instructor how you did the exercises.*

**1.** Do you have access to the WWW via both a graphical user interface like Netscape Navigator *and* a text-only interface (Lynx)? What GUI WWW browsers are available to you? Given a choice, suggest three reasons why someone might choose to use Lynx rather than Netscape Navigator. That is, what advantages does a text-only browser like Lynx have over a GUI one like Netscape Navigator? Do you think text browsers will still exist in five years?

**2.** In just two or three paragraphs, summarize the historical highlights of the WWW. Limit yourself to documents only from the current WWW site of its birthplace, the European Laboratory for Particle Physics: URL **http://www.cern.ch**. The purpose of this exercise is for you to browse one Web site and learn something about Web history by doing so.

**3.** As an object of study, the World Wide Web is clearly a moving target. Suggest a search strategy to locate sites on the Web that will allow you to do this (i.e., find sites that present current WWW news and developments). What keywords do you want included? What concepts might you wish to include? What is the difference between a keyword search and a concept search? (*Hint:* Visit Excite at URL **http://www.excite.com**.)

**4.** Use Lycos to find five tutorials on how to create a WWW home page. Explain what you used as search terms and what you did to refine the search if necessary, then list each site (with title, URL, and brief description). Repeat this exercise by looking for five tutorials on HTML (Hypertext Markup Language).

**5.** Use Yahoo to find five directory names where Yahoo has referenced WWW image sites (i.e., sites with digitized images). What, if anything, do the different Yahoo directory names have in common?

**6.** Use Infoseek to find 10 online periodicals related to the WWW. Explain what you used as search terms and what you did to refine the search if necessary. Then, by simply cutting and pasting text as appropriate, list each site (with title, URL, and brief description). How can you use Infoseek to specify a search for a weekly periodical that covers the WWW but does not include the word "Internet" in its title?

**7.** For the previous Infoseek search, create a directory in your Netscape Navigator bookmark file called *WWW Periodicals.* Place your top five choices into the file and explain how you did this. Print screen images to accompany your explanation.

**8.** Use SavvySearch to conduct and report the results of three separate searches (five results each) for WWW sites of interest to you (1) personally, (2) academically, and (3) professionally. Contrast how you used the SavvySearch interface for each search. What **Sources** and **Types of Information** did you choose for each and why?

**9.** Name a topic of interest to you about which you would like to check for current conversations on USENET. Using a USENET news search tool (e.g., Excite or DejaNews), find articles on that topic. In the context of the search tool (as opposed to a commentary on USENET itself), explain why the tool succeeded or failed to find what you were looking for. If this is a new USENET search tool, how did you find it?

**10.** Find and visit a site that displays *very* timely information (such as current sports scores) from events as they are happening (e.g., ESPN at URL **http:// espnet.sportszone.com**). How is the information updated? Can you find a site that updates its information on your screen *without* your having to press the **Reload** button?

**11.** Using any search engine *other than those used in previous exercises,* locate a VRML (Virtual Reality Modeling Language) site. Find a player (e.g., a software program) that will allow you to view a VRML file. Explain the steps you followed to find the site and the player. Explain how to use this program with your Netscape (or other GUI) browser to view the file.

**12.** How are WWW resources limited? For example, what documents are you *missing* when you do an online WWW search?

**13.** Personalized electronic newspapers can use the WWW to produce a publication unique to each of us according to what we state are our interests. What do you see as the positive and negative consequences of this new application of the Web? You may wish to relate your answer to differences in editorial decision making at *The New York Times* versus that made at a supermarket tabloid.

**14.** As a user of the WWW, you may give up information about yourself both voluntarily (by choice) and involuntarily. Explain this using specific examples. If necessary, do a search to see what is being written on the subjects of privacy and marketing on the WWW.

**15.** If the inauguration of the WWW was text and graphics, the future of the Web is multimedia. This means WWW browsers must be able to decipher miscellaneous files (e.g., audio, video, animation, and graphics) in a variety of formats. Go to the WWW Viewer Test Page at URL **http://www-dsed.llnl.gov/documents/WWWtest.html** and note which examples your copy of Netscape Navigator can display properly (without any intervention by you, the user) and which ones it cannot.

**16.** What can you do if Netscape Navigator's helper applications do not open a file properly? Explain briefly how you can modify Netscape Navigator to handle such a file. Suggest an alternative way to handle such a file on your local system (e.g., if it is a video file that could not be played, what can you do to try to play the video properly?).

**17.** Movie studios, Internet service providers, and consumer electronics companies are among the industries who are most likely to show off the latest in WWW technologies and applications. Find five advanced WWW sites from these or other industry groups, and explain how they appear to be pushing the envelope in Web technology.

**18.** WAISGATE is the WAIS, Inc., interface between the World Wide Web and databases searchable via WAIS software. Go to URL **http://www.wais.com** and repeat one of your earlier searches from the previous exercises by inserting your search keywords in the box provided. How does this WAIS tool compare with the other WWW search tools you have tried? What do you like and dislike about it? How do your results compare? When might you prefer to use WAIS?

# OTHER APPLICATIONS

We have covered all of the standard, system-independent, and useful software that an expert Internet user needs to access the tools of the network. There are many other Internet facilities that do not fit these categories. Some of them are useful but system-specific (i.e., they can be used only among UNIX systems). Some are useful to system administrators and software developers, but not to a general-purpose user. Some are new and have not made it to the Internet's mainstream. And some never will. Notwithstanding these problems, no book on the Internet could be complete without introducing a few such applications.

This chapter is a brief introduction to some of the "miscellaneous" applications that you will find on the Net. The facilities discussed are treated unevenly. We have eliminated some of the UNIX references on the assumption that today's new Internet users are not likely to be using UNIX directly via the old command-line interface. Some facilities are really useful to normal network users and are discussed in detail. In these cases, we have given only a brief, conceptual explanation—enough so that you will know what exists and what to ask for.

## ■ *X Windows*

The X Windows system is not a network application in itself. It is a special way of delivering network applications. It is an industry-standard means of displaying graphical information and reading information from graphics and keyboard devices.

To understand what the X Windows system does, you need to understand the problem it solves. One long-standing problem with computer graphics was that every graphic display is different. To drive a Tektronix graphics terminal, for example, you need completely different commands than to drive a Hewlett-Packard display. A third graphics display would be different again.* If you bought a fancy program to display car crash simulations, you might have to buy a special graphics display to run it; this would probably be a different display than the one you used to do stress analysis; and so on. Each program might know about only a few of the many output devices available.

Some developers at MIT did some thinking about this problem and suggested the following approach. What if:

- we designed, not as hardware but as a set of software facilities, a mythical graphics device with all the bells and whistles you might want

- programs wrote software to drive this mythical device, not particular hardware

- software was written for each workstation to translate mythical terminal commands into actual commands to drive their particular display

Then any software that could drive the mythical terminal could be used on any computer that simulated the mythical terminal. The mythical terminal was dubbed an X-terminal.

It turns out that describing, programming, and setting up a computer for the X Windows environment, as the system is called, is not easy. But, luckily for you, using it is a snap. Each application you use under X has the same look, feel, and features. So once you learn the X Windows system, you can easily figure out how to use any application that runs under it. You have a standard set of buttons and menus available to you, regardless of what you are doing.

To use X, you need a suitable display, mouse, and software for your workstation. All the necessary pieces are available to make almost any computer work in the X environment. As we said before, you may need some help getting set up to use X, but once you start, you should feel comfortable pretty quickly.† Most of the time, you use the same commands you always did, except that some of them are preceded with an "x", like **xgopher** or **xwais**.

To get a feel for the X Windows system, think of a typical personal computer. It has a monitor, a mouse, a keyboard, and a main computational unit. What if, rather than wiring them all directly together, you connected the monitor, mouse, and keyboard as a

---

*The same actually is true of normal terminals, such as a VT100. However, normal terminals are "more or less" the same; they differ mostly in their advanced features. Certainly all character-based terminals take the same approach: You send them characters, they display them on-screen. With graphics terminals, there is really no common ground. Each manufacturer's terminal is completely different from everyone else's. As a result, software to support all the different types would be unmaintainable.

†O'Reilly & Associates publishes the definitive set of X manuals, should you really get into it.

group to the computer via the Internet; then they would no longer have to be colocated. We will call the monitor-mouse-keyboard package an *X terminal.* There are products called X terminals that are exactly like this—but keep in mind that the X terminal can be an independent computer in its own right.

So far so good, but now let's make the model a bit more complex. What if you sat at your X terminal and ran **telnet** on your computer, now in another location. You might log on to a computer somewhere else on the Internet, say **yoyodyne.com**, and once there, run another program. With traditional terminals, data would be sent from **yoyodyne.com** to your computer and then forwarded to your terminal. With X, the data can be sent directly to your X terminal, with no forwarding.

Because **yoyodyne.com** communicates with your computer by knowing its IP address (or domain name), and your computer communicates with your X terminal group by knowing its IP address, there is no reason why the X application on **yoyodyne.com** cannot send data directly to your X terminal. To do this, the X application needs to know the IP address and some other information about the display you want it to use. With UNIX, this is normally conveyed to the application through the environment variable DISPLAY, which is set by the X system software when you begin your X session. The problem is that some TELNET clients do not pass this variable to the remote system when you log in.* To get around this problem, make sure you set the DISPLAY variable appropriately on the computer running the application.

For example, assume you normally use **ux1.cso.uiuc.edu** for all your computing with X. You decide to try **xwais**, but find it does not have the client installed. So you **telnet** to **wais.uiuc.edu**. When you fire up **xwais**, you get the message:

```
Error: Can't Open Display
```

To solve this problem, you need only to set your DISPLAY variable. The problem is: what to set it to? The easy way to find out is to print it on your original system before you do the **telnet**:

```
% printenv DISPLAY
ibmxtrm1.cso.uiuc.edu:0.0
% telnet yoyodyne.com
```

Once TELNET has established a connection, and you have logged in to the remote system, you need to give a **setenv** command to set DISPLAY properly. Just set it to the same value you got above:

```
% setenv DISPLAY ibmxtrm1.cso.uiuc.edu:0.0
```

---

*Because TELNET predates the X system, the ability to do this was added later, as a standardized extension. Not all vendors have embraced this standard.

One more "gotcha" you may need to deal with is authorization. An oddity of X is that an application may put a window on any terminal it has the address for, regardless of who owns that terminal. This could lead to a lot of obnoxious behavior, so most system administrators prevent their system from receiving X displays from strange places. Most of the time this is fine; there is rarely a good reason for commandeering a display somewhere else on the network. However, occasionally you want to use a service, but happen to find yourself at a strange X terminal or workstation and you get an authorization failure. For example, let's say you are at the workstation **theotormon.beulah.com** and you cannot get an application to work right. You are sure that it works back on your own system, **rintrah.blake.com**—so you would like to log in to your own system, run the application there, but display it across the Internet on **theotormon**. Using a remote display across the Internet is often very slow, but X lets you do it—and there are times (like this) when it is necessary.

The problem is convincing **theotormon** to let **rintrah.blake.com** use its display. This is done with the **xhost** command, followed by the name of the computer that will be running the application. Log in to **theotormon** and give the command:

```
% xhost +rintrah.blake.com
```

Then **telnet** (or whatever) to **rintrah.blake.com**, set the DISPLAY variable, and start the application. If you worry about such things, you can give the command **xhost -rintrah.blake.com** when you are finished; that will prevent an unauthorized user on **rintrah** from grabbing **theotormon**'s display without permission.

## Disk and File Sharing

Up to this point we have talked about copying a file from a remote system in order to use it—or putting that file back onto the remote system to make it available to someone else. But it is possible to do better. The next logical step is to use the file where it is. That is, why can't you just use the network to make a disk somewhere else on the network appear to be part of your computer's hardware? Then you could access it just like any other disk, without needing special commands. You might not even know, or care, where the file was physically located. If it is on your local system, that's fine; if not, it still "looks like" it is on the local system.

As you might expect, there are a few ways of doing this. Just as with e-mail, there are two basic approaches: those that grew up in the Internet community and those that grew up in the LAN/microcomputer community. The basic functionality of these approaches is identical. Depending on what type of computer you are using, your computer sees a disk file structure like */remote /...* (UNIX), a D: disk (DOS), or an icon (Macintosh) for another disk. The differences lie in the software required.

The Internet approach is the network filesystem, *NFS*. It was championed by Sun Microsystems and is a UNIX-oriented approach. If you are using a UNIX workstation, you probably have the necessary software already. For most other systems, NFS implementations are available for an extra cost. It requires careful cooperation among the managers of all the systems sharing disks. As a result, NFS can be hard to set up when the systems can't be tailored easily to fit the NFS environment. The biggest advantage of NFS is that it was based on the Internet protocols from the beginning. As a result, you can use it to access disks anywhere that the Internet reaches (provided, of course, that the necessary arrangements have been made in advance). The drawback is that performance can be very slow: It is limited by the rate at which you can move data across the Net.*

Approaches that have grown out of the LAN/microcomputer community are based on so-called "LAN operating systems" such as Novell NetWare or Microsoft LANmanager. These products were designed for file sharing within a local area network. The competitive pressures of the marketplace made the manufacturers design for access speed. The speed issue forced them to use proprietary network protocols optimized for a particular hardware and software platform. They were not designed for generality: They were stripped bare to work fast. Because LAN operating systems were designed for the small-business market, the designers did not consider UNIX worthy of support. And they did not use the Internet's TCP/IP protocols, so they were inherently limited to a local network.

Over time, these two camps have grown together. Some third-party vendors now provide NFS support for non-UNIX computers and gateways to support NFS in other environments, such as Appletalk. Coming from the other direction, many LAN operating-system suppliers have enhanced their products to use TCP/IP, hence the Internet, as a transport medium. Some have also begun to offer NFS support.

In either case, it is nice to know that these facilities exist as a tool to solve certain problems. However, before you can use any of them, a system administrator will have to make the necessary arrangements. So if you think you need these facilities, give your local administrator a call. It is beyond the scope of this book to tell you which approach is best and how to install it.

## ▓ *Time Services*

Computers have had built-in clocks since the early days of computing, mainly to help figure out what happened when something went wrong: Did event A happen before

---

*A newer alternative to NFS—namely the "Andrew Filesystem," also called AFS and sometimes called DFS—will solve some of these problems. AFS has been in use in some research environments for a while, but solid commercial products are now on the market.

event B, or after it? What if you start two jobs: one to create a file and one to use it, in that order. The second job fails because the file was not found. To see what happened, you check the log to see whether the second job ran faster than the first, and tried to use the file before it was created.

Before networking, time synchronization did not matter much. Whenever you needed to compare two times, the times that you were comparing were all taken from the same clock. It did not really matter if that clock was inaccurate; it would still tell you that event A took place before event B. With the advent of networks, the same problems existed, but you needed to compare events that happened on different computers. Each computer's clock was set by a half-asleep myopic operator, who typed in the time from the wall clock when the system booted. Needless to say, there was a lot of error entering this data. So, the times on various computers were never quite the same. Did event A occur before B? You never really knew, particularly if the times were close.

In order to get around this problem, a program called **timed** was developed for UNIX. **timed** just runs in the background and watches clocks. It contacts other **timed** programs running on other computers on the same local network and compares their clocks. Each computer adjusts its clock slowly until the whole network reaches some average network time. From then on, **timed** continues monitoring to make sure the clocks stay synchronized, making slight modifications if needed.

This was good as far as it went. The next problem was: How do you synchronize clocks on computers that are widely separated? How do you keep a computer in California synchronized with a computer in Massachusetts? This problem is much harder: You have to account for the time the synchronizing messages take to reach their destination, including (if you really need accuracy) the time it takes for an electrical signal to travel down a wire at the speed of light. To handle this case, a more advanced service was developed: the network time protocol, or NTP. NTP uses time servers at various points on the Internet. These time servers are all synchronized to something called Coordinated Universal Time, which they get through a variety of means such as listening to time synchronization broadcasts from the U.S. Naval Observatory, and make the time available to computers that need it. This is a really hard problem, considering that the network distributing the information has variable delays. So a lot of fancy computations are done to derive some statistically reasonable time to the requesting computer.

These are neat things, but in reality, using them may be beyond your control. In order to set up either **timed** or NTP, you need to be a system administrator. For NTP, you also need to find a willing time server. If you feel you are in need of these services, you might ask your network service provider for the best time sources on their portion of the Internet.

(It is possible to buy the necessary hardware and software to become your own time server, but this costs thousands of dollars.)

## Faxing over the Internet

These days everyone seems to have access to a facsimile (fax) machine. To use one, you need a communications medium. Because the Internet is a communications medium, you would assume that the technologies should merge: It should be easy to send fax transmissions over the Internet. Well, the technologies are indeed merging, but certainly not as smoothly nor as quickly as you would anticipate. The reason for this is most likely a "not invented here" phenomenon. The people who developed fax are making money hand over fist, because it works fine over phone lines. They aren't primarily computer networking people, and they're perfectly happy sending fax transmissions over the phone. On the other hand, computer people have viewed fax as a lesser service, because the documents are not machine-readable, merely machine-transferable and -displayable. That is, you cannot fax a document to a computer and then edit it with a text editor. What's there is not text, but a picture of the page. It is only those of us who might find the facility useful who are tugging at the coat tails of the manufacturers saying, "Pardon me, but can you make fax work over the Internet?"

As stated, the technologies have merged to a limited extent. You can take a file (either a text file, or a file in any number of standard display formats) and send it via a modem to a fax machine. Likewise, you can receive a fax and have it placed in a file, where you can examine it with a display program. All the software you need is available commercially. If you poke around, you should be able to find the necessary software on the Net for free. (Try getting the file *pub/systems/fax-3.2.1.tar.Z* from the anonymous FTP server **transit.ai.mit.edu**.) There are a number of sites (often college campuses) that have local e-mail–to–fax gateways; these gateways are often restricted to the site's local users.

In 1993 a group of people got together and tried an experiment to provide Internet fax services on a wider basis. They recognized that the ability to send faxes over the Internet means that you could transfer the "fax" file by whatever means to another system across the Internet. Then you could view it or refax it to its destination by placing a local phone call, saving long-distance charges. If sites were already paying for Internet services, why not make it more useful?

This group has solicited sites in various geographical areas to act as fax gateways. If you volunteer, you allow a system on your site to receive faxes from anywhere in the world via the Internet, and then you relay these fax transmissions by phone to fax machines in your local calling area.

To send a fax via this service, you have to create a really strange e-mail address that contains the destination fax machine's phone number. For example, say you wanted to send a fax to Ed Krol, whose fax phone number is 1-217-555-1234.* You would send an e-mail to the following address:

```
remote.printer.Ed_Krol/1120_DCL@12175551234.iddd.tpc.int
```

The mailbox (the part to the left of the @) always starts with **remote.printer**. After **remote.printer**, you can put some text that will be printed on the fax's cover sheet. To get things through the e-mail system, where spaces in names are forbidden, use an underscore ( _ ) in place of a space, and a slash (/) to signal a new line. So the address above puts the following text on the cover sheet:

```
Ed Krol
1120 DCL
```

This address format is relatively new; if you have trouble getting it to work, try using an address like this one:

```
remote.printer.Ed_Krol/1120_DCL@4.3.2.1.5.5.5.7.1.2.1.tpc.int
```

Note that the phone number is listed in the host part of the domain name in reverse order.

No matter what the address looks like, the body of the mail message is just a normal e-mail message. The text of this message is printed on the recipient's fax machine. If you are using a MIME-compliant mailer (discussed in chapter 7, *Electronic Mail*), you can also include images in various standard formats.

International faxes are no different, except that the phone numbers are longer. If you send an international fax through the Internet, omit the international access code but leave the country code on the phone number.

If all this sounds too good to be true, it sort of is. The area covered by volunteer gateways is constantly growing, but there is no guarantee that the area you want to reach is covered. And, like any volunteer service, it can be unreliable. If one of the relaying systems crashes while its owner is at work or on vacation, there is no staff to rush out and get it fixed. The best way stay on top of Internet faxing is to send e-mail to **tpc-faq@town.hall.org** to receive the documentation. (The message itself can be null; all they care about is your e-mail address.) You can also send e-mail to **tpc-coverage@town.hall.org** to receive a list of the areas currently covered. If you would like to volunteer to serve as a gateway in your local area, the document will tell you how.

---

*Do not send faxes here; I just made this number up!

# Conversations with Others: IRC and WWW Chatting

Several facilities allow you to "connect" to someone at another Internet site and type messages back and forth. These facilities are generically called **talk** (for two-way conversations) or **chat** (for group discussions). Of course, communications are what you make of them. **talk**s and **chat**s can be business-oriented, helping you win the Nobel prize. Or someone may be giving you grief because your team lost the big playoff game. They can be used either way, so it is hard to condemn or restrict their use.

## Internet Relay Chat

The Internet is sometimes described as "an anarchy that works." If that's true, then Internet Relay Chat, or *IRC,* is a microcosm of it. The model for a **chat** has always been a cocktail party, where people gather into groups and talk about whatever interests them; IRC is a really big party. There are usually many simultaneous users worldwide, and more than 15,000 connections a day.

Granted that this is an anarchy, still—what allows you to accomplish anything at all? With many simultaneous users, what's the difference between an IRC and shouting at a friend at the other side of a basketball stadium? **chat**s work because you aren't on line chatting away simultaneously with everyone in the world. **chat**s are divided into small groups called *channels.* There can be any number of channels in the IRC, and any number of people within a channel. Some channels exist all the time, like **#hottub** (a channel modeled after a hot tub at a ski resort), where anyone can talk to anyone else about anything at any time. And some channels come and go as the need arises.

Each channel has at least one operator, and possibly more, who is responsible for managing the channel. The first person in a channel is the first operator. He or she can then give away operator privileges to others, who can then give it away to others, etc. That's about all there is for law and order on the IRC.

Like most of the applications we've discussed in this book, you can get at the IRC in two ways. You can use **telnet** to contact a public client running on some other system; or you can have your own client on your local computer. In the case of IRC, using a public client isn't a very good option. They exist, but they are very dynamic: They come and go all the time and are very hard to keep track of. Therefore, it is really better to have your own client. The best way to find out where to get client software and public-access clients is to read the newsgroup *alt.irc.* That will also provide an introduction to the IRC culture, if you do not already belong to it.

The hardest part about using IRC is getting started. IRCs do have a culture all their own. Let's throw caution to the wind, flash our ID to the bouncer at the door, and walk in:

```
% irc TWI
```

Getting in is pretty easy; it's like a campus bar. You type the name of your client (usually called **irc**), and a nickname (in this example, "TWI"). From now on you are known in the IRC world by that nickname, or, like the campus bar, your fake ID. Your client then contacts an IRC server somewhere in the world, and you're in:

```
*** Welcome to the Internet Relay Network TWI
*** If you have not already done so, please read the new user information with
+/HELP NEWUSER
*** Your host is irc.uiuc.edu, running version 2.8.16
*** This server was created Tue Mar 1 1994 at 15: 39:50 CST
*** umodes available oiws, channel modes available biklmnopstv
*** There are 1605 users and 763 invisible on 100 servers
*** There are 80 operators online
*** 819 channels have been formed
*** This server has 139 clients and 14 servers connected
*** Message of the Day:
***
*** The University of Illinois at Urbana IRC Server.
***
*** The NO BOTs server.
***
*** Fetch a list of IRC Servers by anon ftp from h.ece.uiuc.edu
***
*** End of Message-of-the-Day
*** Mode change "+i" for user TWI by TWI
-service.de- * This Nickname is already used frequently by another
person.
+Please try to avoid confusion and choose another one.
[1] 05:05 TWI (+i) * type /help for help
```

As you can see, there is a bit of a jargon problem here, but I'll try to translate some of the highlights of this introductory screen.

- First, this screen suggests that you issue the command **/help newuser** if you are just starting out. All IRC commands start with a slash; that's what differentiates them from the stuff you are typing to others on your channel.

- There are 1,605 people currently using IRC worldwide, with 80 operators controlling 819 channels.

- You are connected to a server running at the University of Illinois, Urbana. It does not matter which server you connect to; IRC is a distributed system, so messages you type are relayed to other servers, and from there to the users connected to those other servers.

- This particular server does not allow "Bots" (IRC slang for software robots) to take part in conversations on channels. Bots have been known to take over a channel by continuous jabbering. This is often done maliciously. (I told you this was an anarchy.)

- Finally, the server says that someone has already chosen my nickname and that I should pick another. There is a central registry where people may register their nicknames, but you really should be involved with IRC for a while before you go that far, so I'll leave you on your own for this fine point.

To pick another name I give the command:

```
/nick newname
```

To request the nickname "maddog," I give the command:

```
/nick maddog
```

At this point, it is a good time to give the commands:

```
/help newuser
/help intro
/help etiquette
```

They will tell you about all the commands you need to know, and how to fit into the IRC culture. Just to give you a feel for what an IRC session is like, we will continue with maddog's exploits.

First, since you are new to the game, you might give the **/list** command to list the channels that are active. That might be a bad idea; you would get a list of 800 channels, which wouldn't really be manageable. To get a more reasonable number, give a command like this:

```
/list -min 10
                                                  a bunch of lines deleted here
*** #malaysia  18    Steal Someone's Nick And Get Excited!
*** #warung    37    Hari Raya Menjelang..Hehehe
*** #Talk      21    *** Topic for #talk: *** Topic for #talk:
+#talk
*** #Unix      21    I await the wisdom of the Internet.
*** #Twilight_ 35    How do you go from 170 clients to 114 in 2
+minutes? (a lot of K: lines)
```

```
*** #amiga      39      we all wonder _why_ cyclone lives anyway
*** #hkfans     10      Welcome to the arena.
*** #indo       22      #medan is under our control...
*** #thailand   16      }=- Welcome to land of smiles -={
*** #chat       22      The Pseudo-Friendly Channel (tm)

[1] 08:12 maddog (+i) * type /help for help
```

The names of the channels are listed, followed by the number of people currently active, followed by an optional (and sometimes useless) description of the channel. The lines with a + in column 1 are continuations of the previous line; many IRC clients use this convention.

Well, let's join the **#talk** channel and see what's happening:

**/join #talk**

A message is sent to everyone else on the channel, telling them that maddog has joined the channel, and your screen lights up with the following. (Remember, you have just walked in on multiple ongoing conversations; unless you frequent the channel, listen for a while before butting in.)

```
*** Topic for #talk: *** Topic for #talk: *** Topic for #talk: *** Topic for
+#talk
*** Users on #Talk: maddog Molok Jordan @KEWL_KAT @Tango ILikeFish alpha-S
+claudio @JABBAH @DasBot @SnuffBot panda ella Lw Styng OverNet jevans @YaZoO
+o662 @Ekim dHitMan Keimaster @PikerBot
<KEWL_KAT> can you see why it didn't work? MOLOK!!!!
<panda> molok...
<claudio> all: i must bid you, adieu.
<KEWL_KAT> oops
<alpha-S> claudio exits???
<KEWL_KAT> I needed an enter in there =]
<Lw> heheh Yaz: good way to test the new Feature.. :)
*** Cybrarian (bubtb@alf.uib.no) has joined channel #talk
<YaZoO> lw :d
* panda jumps in front of alpha's car.. *crunch*
<claudio> au revoir mes amis
*** Molok has left channel #talk
<Cybrarian> Hi ppl
*** cob (sin_aarr@ask.gih.no) has joined channel #talk
<ILikeFish> panda : Well, let me know!  I need to go to to offy later, so I'll
+have a look too.

[1] 08:17 maddog (+i) on #talk (+nt) * type /help for help
```

At this point, anything you type will be sent to everyone in the channel unless it is preceded by a slash (in which case, it is interpreted as a command). Anything you type is preceded by your nickname. So if Maddog types "hi all", everyone sees:

```
<maddog>hi all
```

As you can see, the normal chatting channels are free-for-alls, demanding a lot of attention. They're really pretty useless. Most people who are really into IRCs do not frequent these; most of the time, they "channel shop" until they find a place where they feel at home. Then they come back repeatedly, developing a set of friends who know their nickname.

When you are done with one channel and want to leave, you can do so with:

```
/leave #talk

*** maddog has left channel #talk
```

When you get enough of IRC, you may leave it with **/quit**.

IRC is not just a place for college undergraduates to waste time until they flunk out. There are channels used by kids, and channels used by professionals. It is not all that different from getting together with coworkers for a beer after work to gossip about the job. People do the same thing through IRC. If they wanted to, a group of microbiologists could create a channel called **#bacteria** and chat about the day's happenings and discoveries.

Finally, I feel I need to give you some warnings. First, IRC can be addicting. Some people get so into their electronic community that they ignore their real-life responsibilities. Many people who get enamored with IRC know little else about computers, and think they know a lot about their IRC friends. Well, they may not know all that much. All they really know is their friends' nickname and a signon, which might be fraudulent. There have been many cases in which people have gotten into trouble by following the advice of some IRC buddy. In one case I know of, someone was complaining about how slow IRC was, and someone else said, "I have a file that can make it go faster; do you want it?" The file was a *.rhosts* file that allowed the second user access to the first user's account without knowing his password.

All this is not to say that you should avoid IRCs. If that's what interests you, go ahead and try. Just be careful; do not do anything that might get you in trouble, or cause trouble for someone else.

## *WWW Chatting*

As is the case with other existing Internet services, World Wide Web applications to those tools are being developed. An example is the Internet Roundtable Society's WebChat™ service (URL: **http://www.irsociety.com/webchat.html**). This site adds not only the WWW interface to chatting, but allows users to include their own photos or other images along with their name (see Figure 14-1).

According to its authors, WebChat is a real-time, fully multimedia chatting application for the Web. Users can quickly incorporate images, video and audio clips, and "hotlinks" into their chat. It works with any standard browser, requiring no special software from Web visitors. Not only can users talk to other individuals, but they can also join special forums with guests from authors to politicians in a computer-mediated analog to talk radio.

Figure 14-2 shows the opening screen from one of the available forums, the Internet Roundtable. In this case, author Guy Kawasaki was interviewed online, and observers were able to join in.

As shown in Figure 14-3, users are invited to choose image "handles" (like the old CB radio handles) from their picture library. In the case of the pictured forum, the images of the guest and interviewers are positioned next to their comments.

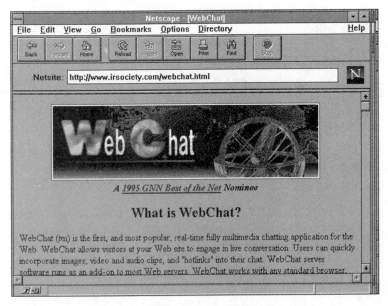

*Figure 14-1    Internet Roundtable Society's WebChat home page*

*Figure 14-2    Internet Roundtable forum opening screen*

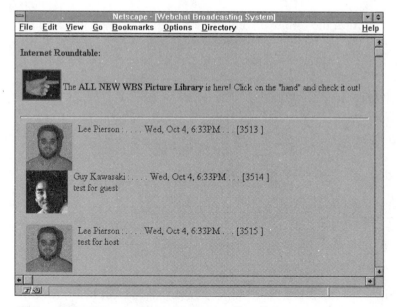

*Figure 14-3    Users are able to choose image "handles"*

This site seems typical of the transition we have been seeing in recent years from the text-only origins of the Internet to the multimedia future of the WWW. On another level, this also demonstrates the potential for "microbroadcasting" on the Web. Specialized topics and very small audiences (in the context of traditional broadcasting) will be completely viable on the Web.

## Talking

The UNIX **talk** program used to be the most common application used for direct communication with others. To use **talk**, two people must agree to communicate with each other. The process starts when one person calls the other, using **talk** to set up the communications link. Let's say that Stimpy on **cat.nick.org** wants to talk to Ren on **chihuahua.edu**. He starts by issuing the command:

```
% talk Ren@chihuahua.edu
```

If Ren is logged in, a message like this will appear on his screen:

```
Message from Talk_Daemon@chihuahua.edu at 13:15 ...
talk: connection requested by Stimpy@cat.nick.org.
talk: respond with:  talk Stimpy@cat.nick.org
```

Just in case Ren doesn't notice, the terminal will beep a few times. If Ren wants to talk back, he must issue the command **talk Stimpy@cat.nick.org**. When he does this, a connection is made and the screen clears. The screen is then divided in half horizontally. Anything Stimpy types to Ren is displayed on the top half of his screen, and the bottom half of Ren's screen, and vice versa. In this example, Stimpy's screen would look like this:

```
[Connection established]
Happy, Happy, Joy, Joy



    _____

What is it, man!


```

Stimpy typed everything that appears above the line; Ren's replies appear below the line. It is a little hard to describe how this works, but you will get used to it fairly quickly once you try.

**talk** displays everything you type, one character at a time, as you type it. You cannot edit something before you send it off as you can with e-mail. **talk** does not even wait until you finish typing the line. If you are a bad typist, the other person can see how slowly you type, and every mistake you BACKSPACE over (which often is not necessary). As with e-mail, discretion is advised. Antagonistic comments still appear for an instant, even though they are erased.

**talk** pages (the message and the bell) can be irritating: for example, you may not want one appearing suddenly on your screen when you are proofreading the final copy of a report. This is easily prevented. The command:

```
% mesg n
```

disables incoming **talk** conversations. You can still call other people, and they can connect to a call you make. The only thing that is affected is your ability to receive **talk** messages initiated by someone else. This remains in effect until you log off or give the command:

```
% mesg y
```

If you are not participating, the requesting person will get the message:

```
[Your party is refusing messages]
```

Some programs, such as text formatters, may put your session into **mesg n** mode for you. They do this so their output is not disrupted by random **talk** messages. When they finish, they return you to the state you were in before you invoked them.

There is no way for a caller to know if your refusal is temporary or permanent. If you try to contact someone and see that he's refusing messages, you can only try again later, send electronic mail, or make a phone call.

Some **talk** programs are incompatible. You may get a "Connection requested" message, but when you try to connect, your **talk** program never realizes you were trying to connect to that person. The problem is that older versions of **talk** tend to send characters out in a manner that is specific to a particular vendor's hardware. The only thing you can do is look for a program called **ntalk**, which works exactly like **talk**, or **ytalk** (explained in the following section).

## Chats

**chat**s are generalizations of **talk**, wherein multiple people converse at once. Some of them are extensions of the **talk** program we just discussed, and some are like an electronic cocktail party, except without drinks. Groups gather to converse about various subjects. You can feel free to wander from group to group and take part as you like. Sometimes you might feel the need for a private conversation with someone in the discussion—i.e., drop out of the **chat** and revert temporarily to a two-person **talk**. All this is possible within the framework of **chat** facilities.

### ytalk

ytalk is a newer **talk** client.* It allows you to have conversations with people using **talk**, **ntalk**, or **ytalk**. It gets around all of the incompatibility problems of the previous two and also allows you to have multiple conversations simultaneously. **ytalk** works just like **talk**: To strike up a conversation, give a command like this:

```
% ytalk person@machine
```

and the screen separates into "to" and "from" halves, just like before.

You can also accept other conversations, or list multiple names on the **ytalk** command line. As you get connected, the screen subdivides again and again until there is no room left. If everyone in a conversation is using **ytalk**, everything you type appears on everyone's terminal, and vice versa. If you are talking to someone who is using a more traditional **talk** program, he or she will see only a private conversation with you, even if you have other connections open.

**ytalk** is very new and still under development. It was available for normal character-oriented terminals, with the developers promising an X version. The only documentation right now is a *README* file which comes with the software.

## ■ *The Uncategorizable: MUDs*

Multi-User Dungeons *(MUDs)* were created around 1980 as a network-accessible version of the *Dungeons and Dragons* adventure game. In the beginning that's exactly what it was. You could create a character and wander through the dungeon, meeting other characters, fighting various foes, and accumulating treasures and experience. They've changed a lot since then: There are still the original adventure-style games, but there are also MUDs that are more oriented toward conversation, toward teaching, and even toward various kinds of experimentation. The thread that holds MUDs together is that they are all games in which people interact with their surroundings.

Note that I said "games"—plural. Unlike most of the other software discussed in this book, MUDs are very hard to categorize. There are perhaps a half-dozen basic categories (MUD, MUSH, tinyMUD, MUSE, MOO, etc.) and many variations within each category. Each kind of MUD has its own client and server software, but they all support the same general type of game. A MUD and a MUSH might both describe a *Star Trek* sort of world, but what you can do will be different. Have I muddied this up enough?

---

*****ytalk** is not very readily available, but it is being talked about more and more on the Net. You might want to bring it up with your system administrator, or find it using Archie and install it on your personal system. Right now it exists only for UNIX.

Basically, there are two things that determine what any MUD will look like: the software it is running on, and the database that describes the world. A MUSH looks a lot like another MUSH in basic characteristics, but the world defined might be drastically different.

By now, it is probably completely unclear what exactly MUDs are. Certainly, the majority of them are still dungeon or combat games of some form. However, consider what it takes to build one of these dungeon games, and you will realize that there are other possibilities. You build a world complete with a variety of objects, and manipulate those objects with commands like "take axe", "look book", etc. It takes very little to turn a fantasy world into a poor person's virtual reality. What if there were a MUD designed for teaching chemistry? If you give the commands "pour water into beaker" and "pour acid into beaker" in that order, it is OK; if you give the commands in the other order, you get a message like:

```
The mixture foams and gets very hot, cracking the beaker.
Concentrated sulfuric acid splashes in your face!
```

It is arguably better to learn this way than by playing around with real chemicals. So, in addition to their role as diversions, some MUDs have found a home in education. There isn't a chemistry lab MUD that I know of, yet. I used it as an example, because it shows fairly well what you might do with a MUD's facilities. Currently, most of the educational MUDs I know about are in the social sciences, computer science, or humanities. One such MUD is a model of a society: It has its own newspaper, a bar, a town hall, etc. There are some MOO-style MUDs used as conferencing tools in molecular biology and genetics. If interest and discussion is any measure, many more MUDs for research and education will be springing up in the near future.

Some of the games even let players of sufficient experience modify the game. In the dungeon games, you might be allowed to "dig" a new section of tunnel. In the chemistry MUD, you might be able to define a new experiment. Changing things usually means you need to learn a bit of programming in some language; it might be the C programming language, or some language specific to your MUD. Do not even think about modifying a game until you have *a lot* of experience!

There are two basic problems with MUDs. First, you need to find one that matches your interests. Then you need to figure out how to use the MUD once you find it. So, how do you get started in MUDing? Start with the FAQ posted to the newsgroup *rec.games.mud.announce*. The first part gives you a general introduction to MUDs. The second part tells you, in general, which software is used for what kind of MUD. For example, if you are into combat, you might look for DIKU sites (DIKU is a particular class of MUD, which tends to be used for the traditional slaughter-and-pillage games).

If not, you might look at tinyMUSHs. There is not always an exact correlation between the type of software that's used and the type of game that's played, but it's a start.

Once you have read the FAQ, you can look at the MUD newsgroups:

```
rec.games.mud.announce
rec.games.mud.diku
rec.games.mud.misc
rec.games.mud.tiny
```

This is where you will see announcements about MUD software, ongoing games, and so on. Even if the first MUD you learn is not destined to be your eventual home, it will be fairly painless to make the transition to other MUDs of the same class (i.e., other MUDs using the same software). And—even if you are not enamored of the first MUD you play—you will find out about others from the adventurers you meet while playing.

Now, how do you do all of this? Well, it is possible to play a MUD with nothing but **telnet**; all you need to do is **telnet** to a special port on the MUD server. However, that's a pretty painful way to play; you are much better off with a client on your local system. Again, there are many clients, and they're all slightly different; the best way to find out about them is to read the FAQ on MUDs, which is posted to the above groups. Good luck!

## ▨ *Games*

The Internet gives you many ways to waste time, both yours and the network's. Some people read recreational newsgroups. Others talk to other people or play games. There is fairly wide disagreement by system administrators about the validity of these uses. For this reason, I do not want to encourage you. But if I didn't tell you about them, you would find out they exist on your own.

Computer games have been around for ages. In fact, the UNIX operating system was invented in order to play a game called Space Travel.* However, the past few years have spawned a number of person-to-person games played via the computer. These range from traditional games, such as Chess and Go,† to real-time simulation games. The traditional games are not really a problem on the network, since they consume few resources. The others, however, have the ability to consume both computers and networks.

In real-time simulation games, each player is the commander of something (like the starship *Enterprise,* a tank, or an F16 fighter). The players all take part in a simulated battle, complete with cockpit displays and visual effects. These games were really designed

---

*Maurice J. Bach, *The Design of the UNIX Operating System* (Prentice Hall: 1986), page 2.

†Check out "Recreation" in the *Resource Catalog.*

to be played over LANs because of their high-speed communication requirements. They require more speed than most intercampus Internet connections provide. As a result, if you play these games over the Internet, two things will happen:

- You will get other network users (and maybe some administrators) mad at you, because you are dragging down the network's performance.

- You will lose. You are at a competitive disadvantage because the speed with which you can react to threats is limited by your link to the Internet's speed.

Play if you must, but be discreet and considerate. There is no inalienable right to play games on the Internet, and put yourself in the shoes of someone waiting to use your machine to finish that class project due the next day.

## ▓ *Audio and Video*

It is either trivial or very hard to send audio or video over the Internet, depending on how you look at it. If you want to send only a snippet of voice, a song, or a short video, it is easy. All these things are just files: rather large files, but nonetheless just files. For example, Carl Malamud produces an Internet radio show called *Internet Talk Radio*. He tapes interviews with well-known people within the networking community. He then places the digitally encoded interviews on a number of anonymous FTP servers. If you want to hear what the "Geek of the Week" said, you can download one of these files with FTP (or a higher-level tool like Mosaic) and play it through your workstation. These are large files (15 megabytes), but they're still just files: You download them and play them at your leisure.

Most recent workstations and PCs either have the equipment and software needed to create your own audio or video files, or make it available as an option. Once you have captured the audio or video, you can mail it to your friends using a MIME-compliant mailer, or put it in an FTP archive. The files are large, but that's just an inconvenient detail.

The hard thing about audio and video is doing it in "real time."* That is, it is very difficult to have a phone or video conference over the Internet. The problem is that the Internet was not really designed to do this. To understand, think about the telephone. When you dial a phone number, you are essentially renting a phone line all the way from your house to whomever you are calling. It is yours and you are paying for it whether you are talking or not. No one else can use it so long as you have it reserved.†

---

*Technically, these are known as *isochronous applications*. They require a steady stream of equally spaced information.

†That is no longer quite true. However, if you are a stickler for accuracy, you do not have to think back too far to get to a time when it was true.

The Internet gets its cost advantage over traditional telephone service by sharing telephone lines. If data networking required placing a long-distance phone call every time a computer wanted to use a resource elsewhere, it would be prohibitively expensive—much more expensive than the network of high-speed leased lines that is currently in place. The problem with sharing resources is that things can get busy. When a network like the Internet gets busy, data just moves more slowly. There is no such thing as a busy signal. If you are **ftp**ing a file or using a TELNET server somewhere, that's exactly what you want. But real-time applications cannot deal with slowdowns. A video playback application needs some number of frames per second, regardless of what else is happening in the world. You would be very annoyed if your networked video conference suddenly went into slow motion (to say nothing of the technical problems this would cause).

Today, real-time video and audio work on the Internet only because the paths they take are not busy. It is generally accepted that if many people tried to do live audio or video, the Internet would get real slow, real fast. There is, however, a lot of research on two topics, resource reservation and multicasting, to try to expand the usability of the Internet to these areas.

*Resource reservation* is just what it sounds like: allowing someone to pay for a dedicated piece of the Internet for a while. You might be doing a video conference with someone and would like to tell your service provider, "I'd be willing to pay five dollars per minute for a guaranteed television channel between here and Stanford."

*Multicasting* involves using wisely the lines you have. Imagine doing a three-way video conference with sites in London, Washington, D.C., and New York. The obvious way to set up the conference would be to open three channels, one between each site. There are two problems with this. One is that as the number of sites goes up, the number of channels goes up faster. The second is that some channels are more expensive than others. It would be much more cost-effective for London to open one channel to the U.S. and have the channel duplicated once it crossed the ocean. One of the copies would be sent to Washington, D.C., and one to New York, thereby saving a transoceanic channel. The work to support audio and video is being done by the Internet Engineering Task Force.

## RealAudio and CU-SeeMe

Progressive Networks' RealAudio Sound created a breakthrough on the Internet by allowing "real time" (listen while you download) audio listening on the Net. The compression techniques necessary to do this are mind-boggling, but the progress in this area was predictable given the interest and efforts to accomplish it. Parallel efforts are taking place in video, although the challenges for compression video and audio together are all the more daunting. Downloading RealAudio is simple. If you have a multimedia personal computer, RealAudio then allows you to listen to an audio file in its *".ra"* format during the download process. URL **http://www.realaudio.com** is the RealAudio home page.

Reed Hundt is the Clinton administration's chair of the Federal Communications Commission. He gave a speech to the National Press Club on July 27, 1995, concerning children and television (URL: **http://town.hall.org/Archives/radio/IMS/Club/ 950727_club_00_ITH.html**). According to its proponents, key features of the RealAudio player are:

- Full control of RealAudio streams much like a VCR, with start, stop, and pause options

- Ability to instantly jump to any part of an audio program, much like a CD player

- Enables users to insert bookmarks and hotlist entries into Web browsers to allow for direct access to the RealAudio home page and other sites of interest

- CU-SeeMe

CU-SeeMe (URL: **http://cu-seeme.cornell.edu**) is an Internet videoconferencing program (under copyright of Cornell and its collaborators), available to anyone with a Macintosh or Windows. It is now being developed jointly by White Pine Software and Cornell, with White Pine as master licensee of the CU-SeeMe technology. With CU-SeeMe, you can create a videoconference with another site located anywhere in the world. By use of a reflector, multiple parties/locations are able to participate in a CU-SeeMe conference, each from his or her own desktop computer (see Figure 14-4). A number of universities and nonprofit and private organizations, led by Cornell University, have formed the CU-SeeMe Consortium to support further innovation, development, and dissemination of CU-SeeMe (URL: **http://cu-seeme.cornell.edu/ConsortBrief.html**).

*Figure 14-4   Video Images from CU-SeeMe*

To use CU-SeeMe, there are separate hardware and software requirements. Hardware requirements include computer video processors, an inexpensive video camera, and a microphone. Load the software on your machine and connect to someone else who is already up and running. (This is like the early days of the telephone when you could only call someone else who also had a phone). The Cornell reflector is a good place to begin. To understand what all the icons and menu choices mean, look over the "Getting Started" guide compiled by M. Sattler and Jher (URL: **http://www.indstate.edu/msattler/ sci-tech/comp/CU-SeeMe/how-to.html**). Video images over CU-SeeMe are transmitted in black-and-white at a slower frame rate than full-motion video to reduce demand on the network. As the availability of ISDN lines and ATM switches becomes more commonplace, performance and quality will improve greatly.

NASA-TV uses CU-SeeMe to broadcast daily with space shuttle transmissions, astronaut interviews, control room activity, and more. Students in classrooms around the country are experimenting with the technology—from a special "Computers in School" elementary-grade program in Arlington, Virginia, to college-level instruction at the University of Massachusetts. The entertainment world has experimented with live-over-the-Internet performances, ranging from rock concerts to comedy club acts (URL: **http:// /www.wpine.com/press.html**).

For an example of QuickTime Video technology, see URL: **http://www.cnn.com**.

## ■ *Robotic Librarians*

We talked about Knowbots in chapter 10, *Finding Someone,* as a white-pages server. This is only a minor use of the Knowbot concept. The model for Knowbots is a reference librarian. You do not go into a library and ask: "I need to know this. Could you look it up in that book?" If you knew where to look it up, you could do it yourself. (Besides, this is what WAIS does.) You ask only, "I need to know this." The reference librarian is trained to know how to find it. "Robotify" this model and you have a Knowbot.

Knowbots are generally thought of as software worms that crawl from source to source, looking for answers to your question. As a Knowbot looks, it may discover more sources. If it does, it checks the new sources too. When it has exhausted all sources, it comes crawling home with whatever it found.

Clearly, this is a very futuristic view of the information retrieval problem. It is probably an idea whose time has not quite come. There are pilot projects and research in the area, but the fields of networking, computing, and information science are not quite ready to support them. Perhaps they will be by the fourth edition of this book.

## ▦ *Exercises*

*Print out your responses to each of the following items. Seek help locally if you need it.*

*If you need to, download RealAudio (URL:* **http://www.realaudio.com***), which allows you to listen to a .ra file.*

**1.** The Telecommunications Radio Project produces an award-winning radio series, *The Communications Revolution,* an example of which is the program "Vanishing Privacy in the Information Age" from July 1994 (URL: **http://town.hall.org/Archives/radio/IMS/ CommRev**). Using this file as an example, explain precisely but succinctly how to download the files and play them using RealAudio.

**2.** Find five "Internet Radio" sources from the RealAudio home page (URL: **http:// town.hall.org/radio**) that are of interest to you personally, professionally, and/or academically. List them and/or five corresponding *.ra* audio files.

**3.** Here is an example of a radio newscast available for RealAudio; see if you can get it to play:

**http://www.radio.cbc.ca/radio/programs/news/wr8.html**

If not, what seems to be missing from your machine? Here is another option:

**http://www.npr.org/news.ram**

List five sources for RealAudio *(.ra)* files. Find a real-time radio station broadcasting on the Internet using RealAudio.

**4.** The clear trend on the Internet is toward multimedia. What do you see as the possibilities for using resources other than text-only files for research purposes? How might this affect education, both K–12 and college? What social obstacles might slow the adoption and use of multimedia in education?

If you need it, download QuickTime (URL: **http://quicktime.apple.com**), which allows you to view QuickTime movies. Specific directions for downloading are included at the Web site.

**5.** Find five QuickTime sources from the QuickTime home page (URL: **http:// quicktime.apple.com/archive/index.html**). Save one *(be careful of file size)* to a diskette to show your instructor. Describe the movie briefly. What problems did you encounter, if any, when trying to view the file? How did you (try to) solve them?

**6.** It is easy to find entertainment-oriented **chat** channels. For this exercise, identify one IRC channel and one WebChat (or similar WWW **chat** service) channel of professional and/or academic interest to you. Explain precisely yet succinctly how a new user could reach each channel and participate in the discussion. To show your abilities, cut and paste enough screen information to show that you were able to join each channel. Finally, what was the topic of discussion at the time you joined? Is there an archive of either of these **chat** channels? What are the implications of this for your participation in the **chat** channel?

**7.** Multimedia is the next step in the evolution of the WWW as evidenced by the exercises you just completed. Name three other recent applications available on the WWW that may serve to accelerate this process.

**8.** Dr. David J. Farber gave the keynote speech for the SIGCOMM 95 Award (URL: **http://www.realaudio.com/contentp/rabest/farber.html**). This address on the convergence of the computer and communications industries, which includes predictions on technological changes over the next 50 years, is available via RealAudio. How does the availability of this speech impact the way you might do research on the future of computing? If you are used to studying while the radio or television in on, do you think that the availability of this new resource will make your research tasks more or less efficient?

# CHAPTER FIFTEEN

# DEALING WITH PROBLEMS

*The Ground Rules*
*Gather Baseline Information*
*The Battle Plan*
*Talking to Operations Personnel*
*Dealing with Coaxial Ethernets*
*Token Ring Notes*

Y ou will on occasion run into difficulties in your travels on the Net. This is predictable, and even though you should not have to be an Internet guru to use the Net, you may need others' help from time to time. The key is for you to be as much help as possible in diagnosing the problem you encounter. Ideally, you will jot down the time and the things you were doing when you encountered the difficulty. Other problems may not require anyone else's intervention. For example, you will eventually walk up to your workstation and type:

```
% telnet ux1.cso.uiuc.edu
Trying 128.174.5.59...
```

You wait and wait until finally after a few minutes it prints:

```
telnet: Unable to connect to remote host: Connection timed out
```

Now what?

You don't have to be an ace network technician to deal with this situation, but you do need some guidance about managing in the face of adversity. First, we will talk about what usually happens, then what you need to know to attack a problem. After that, we will give you a reasonable approach to deal with common network problems. It is not an exhaustive guide. We could easily construct scenarios that would lead you astray with this approach, but they would not be common in real life. Finally, some hints are given about how to deal with some common LANs.

It is likely that your school has some mechanism in place to handle problems. Fullerton College has an example, *Fullerton College Internet Troubleshooting procedure,* at URL **http:/**

**/www.fullcoll.edu/fc/ic/net_srvc/inetprob.htm**. This chapter is intended to help you understand the source of some common problems, but solutions will also depend upon your local situation. If you want to seek out additional information beyond what you find locally, there is always help on the Net (see the exercises at the end of the chapter for some help in that direction).

## The Ground Rules

When you are thinking about what is wrong with the network, there are two rules to keep in mind:

1. The cheaper the component, the more likely it will fail and the less likely it will be noticed by someone who is able to fix it

2. You need to know what's right before you can figure out what's wrong

What do these rules mean? The Internet is frequently described as an amorphous cloud, as in Figure 15-1.

Think about this cloud in the context of rule 1. As you move away from your workstation, you know less and less about what happens to your packets; you enter the cloud. As you get closer to the cloud, components get more expensive. Inside the cloud are many expensive computers and telephone lines. If one of them fails, a lot of people could be affected: A campus or even an entire country could be disconnected. So the cloud is monitored continuously and built as redundantly as possible. If something goes wrong, technicians notice and take corrective action immediately.

On the other extreme, you are probably sitting at a $5,000 workstation, talking to a network over a $150 Ethernet interface connected to a $5 piece of cable running across the floor. If something happens to these, no one except you will notice. In between, an

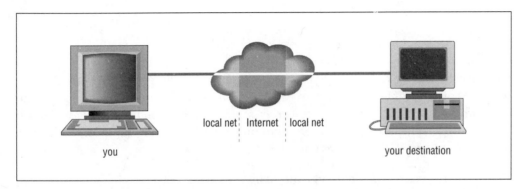

*Figure 15-1    The Internet cloud*

area of reduced visibility, there will be a campus or corporate network connecting you to the Internet cloud. It is medium-priced, fairly well protected, and frequently monitored during business hours.

Most unexpected network outages occur fairly close to the ends: either around your computer or the one you are trying to reach. It may be in your computer or between your computer and the wall, but the closer you get to the cloud, the less likely the problem is to occur. This does not mean that problems are always your fault. There is a destination computer sitting just as far from the cloud as you are, somewhere else in the world. The problem is just as likely to be on the other end. And, on rare occasions, there are problems in the cloud itself. But that should be your last assumption, not your first.

When something goes wrong, your major goal is not fixing the problem. If you can, great, but more often than not, the problem will be something you cannot control. Although you are close to the point of failure, much of the time fixing it will be beyond your means. Even if you happen to be a skilled technician, a daunting problem may be a function of failure probabilities, how things are built, and who has spare parts. Even if the problem occurs in your building, it could be in a locked network closet. This is where the cloud starts: wherever the network gets beyond your control. Your goal is finding out when you can expect it to be fixed. Do you sit in your office at midnight banging on the ENTER key, or do you go home and watch David Letterman? If it's 10 P.M. and you deduce that the problem is a bad cable, you can go home; the guy who has the key to the supply cabinet will not be back until morning. If you learn that you are accessing a service that is temporarily offline until 11 P.M., you might stick around and play some network game.

Even if you cannot fix the problem, you can help by narrowing down the area to be searched by others. When a technician is handed a stack of trouble tickets with equal priorities, it is natural to work on the most specific problem first. What would you do if someone handed you some assignments, one of which said, "It doesn't work," and another stating, "Bad Ethernet cable—needs new one"? You could go to the second assignment and fix the problem in five minutes, making someone happy. The other might be just as easy, or it might take hours—you just don't know. If you attack them in the opposite order, both users could be unhappy for a long time. The problem gets even worse if there are multiple technicians responsible for different pieces of your connection (e.g., one does PC Ethernet cards, another does cables)—you have to call the right one. The moral is simple but vital: *Even if you cannot fix the problem, the more you know, the better the service you will get.*

Now we start getting into rule 2. You need to learn a little about your network and your network neighbors while the network is running correctly. When things go wrong, a few simple tests will show you what has changed. You do not need anything special for these tests. You already have the tools you need: a **telnet** program and your eyes.

## ■ *Gather Baseline Information*

To do any reasonable amount of network troubleshooting, you need to push the cloud back a bit. You need some information on your local connection to the network and the router that connects you to the rest of the Internet. If you push back the cloud, every network in the world looks something like Figure 15-2.

The technology may change from place to place. The physical wiring might be thin coax Ethernet, phone wire Ethernet, Token Ring, or something else. In any case, a wire connects your computer to something else. You need to find out a little about the "something elses": who is responsible for them and how fast they respond. So right now, go shopping for the following items:

- The IP address of your computer and another computer on the same LAN (there may not be any others)

- The IP address of the router closest to your computer that is responsible for connecting you to something larger (the router in Figure 15-2)

- A list of who to call, by hour of the day and day of the week, when something goes wrong with your LAN (item 1) and your closest gateway (item 2); these are not necessarily the same person

- The state of the status lights on any networking equipment you have access to

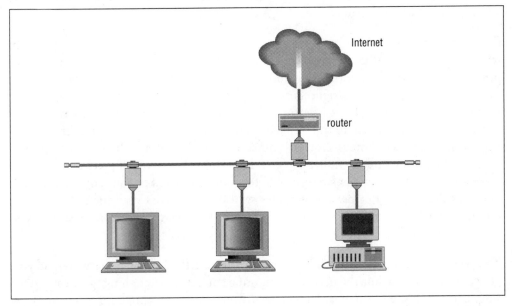

*Figure 15-2   Network schematic*

These points are just guidelines. What is appropriate varies from connection to connection. For small sites or dial-up users, there may not be any other IP addresses, and there might not be anyone local to call: just you and your service provider. For really large sites, the network infrastructure may be complicated, but so is the support structure. The heartening thing is that the more complex your network is, the more local help you are likely to find. In a really large network, "who to call" is probably a single phone number, answered 24 hours per day, seven days a week. In almost every case, the information required is quite manageable, but you need to modify the shopping list based on how your connection is made.

Do not underestimate the importance of items 1 and 2: the numeric Internet address of your system, a neighbor's, and the closest router. Elsewhere, we have always used computer names to contact things, rather than IP addresses. Troubleshooting is the exception to this rule. In order to use a name to make contact, your computer may automatically seek out a Domain Name Server to convert the name to an address. This requires a healthy network. If your net is in sad shape, it will not be able to do this; the tests you run using a name will be meaningless. An IP address is immediately usable, so it eliminates one source of error. You can test this at a DNS lookup site such as URL **http:// union.ncsa.uiuc.edu/HyperNews/get/hypernews/71.html**.

## The Battle Plan

Let's get back to the task at hand. You walked into your office to work on the big project at 10 P.M. and you cannot connect to the Federal Information Exchange. Your first question should be "Do I have time to fiddle with the problem?" If the project is really important, you might not want to waste an hour worrying about a network problem. It might be better to try using a colleague's computer in the next office. If his connection works, you can get your work done. You also have a clue to the problem: Something is wrong with your computer or its connection to the network.

Let's say your buddy's office is locked and you have to get the report out tomorrow. So it is time to look at the problem. Throughout this discussion, we need to assume that your connection has been working and just quit. It is beyond the scope of this book to tell you how to configure your system for the first time. Your service provider or corporate/ campus network group should help you with this.

### Know the Hours of Operation

The computers that provide network resources range from PCs to gigantic mainframes. Most of these, along with the network control computers, require some kind of periodic maintenance. Most sites schedule maintenance during odd hours, such as 2 A.M. on Saturday, when the network load is usually light. However, scheduled "down time" varies from resource to resource. If you use a resource regularly, you should try to find out what its hours are supposed to be. You may save yourself a midnight attempt to access a resource that is not available anyway. Also, remember that the Internet is worldwide. Friday during business hours in the United States is Saturday at 2 A.M. in Japan.

If you are trying sources randomly, you will not be aware of the site's schedule. If you try in the middle of the night, you run a greater risk of finding a computer out of service. The computer may be down for scheduled maintenance, or it may have crashed and no one is around to bring it back up. Remember, many resources are volunteer efforts. If the last volunteer locks up the office and goes home at 5:00, it could be the next morning before someone can restart a crashed application.

## *Read the Error Message*

When some people get an error message, they become so flustered that they see only:

```
ERROR  - glitzfrick framus gobbledegook
```

Relax, read the error carefully, and write it down. You need to write it down so that you have the exact text of the message if you have to report it to someone. Nothing is more frustrating, for the network technician and the network victim, than a message like, "It said 'error something something something'."

Before you start calling out the troops, you might be able to fix your own problem. Even if you do not understand the whole message, you should be able to pick out a couple of words to help you along. Several words and phrases crop up regularly: "unknown," "unreachable," "refused," "not responding," and "timed out." Let's try to deal with each of these, mapping them into some telephone-call scenarios.

*unknown*              You called directory assistance and asked for Willie Martin's phone number. The operator responded, "I'm sorry; there is no listing for Willie Martin." This problem usually shows up when your computer tries to convert a name into an IP address. You told the computer to call **ux1.cso.uiuc.edu**. It tried to find the address, but was told that the computer did not exist. Either you specified the name incorrectly (e.g., spelled it wrong) or the computer could not convert it. This might be because your computer does not use the Domain Name System, but rather the old system in which all names are looked up in a file (under UNIX, */etc/hosts*).* There could also be a problem

---

*UNIX systems will probably have an */etc/hosts,* with one or two entries in it, even if they are using the Domain Name System. So, if you find */etc/hosts* but there are only two entries, do not conclude that you are not using DNS. You are almost certainly wrong. For that matter, even if you find a huge host table, you still cannot conclude that you are not using DNS— that table might be left over from the "olden days."

with the Domain Name System. This is almost certainly something you cannot handle; get on the phone. In a pinch, if someone can tell you the IP address you need, you can use it and bypass this problem.

*unreachable*      You dialed the number and get the message, "I'm sorry; the number you have reached is out of service." This is a real network problem. A portion of the network is down. The network is telling you, "I know where you want to go, but you cannot get there from here." If this happens, there is nothing you can do: Call for help.

*refused*      You tried to make a person-to-person call and got the correct number, but the person you want is not there. The computer at the far end needs to accept connections for a particular service (e.g., TELNET). Your computer successfully contacted the destination computer and asked to make the connection to a service, but the destination said no. There are several possible reasons for this. The computer may be running but not available for user access. This is frequently the case during maintenance periods or while doing filesystem dumps. It's also possible that the service has been canceled: i.e., the system's manager has decided not to provide it. For example, you might hear that a great game is available if you **telnet** to **game.edu** at port 5,000. When you try this, you get a "connection refused" message. This probably means that the computer's owner decided not to allow game playing anymore.

*timed out*      This may mean that you called and no one answered, or that you were put on hold indefinitely. When TCP sends messages to a remote computer, through whatever application you are using, the local TCP process expects responses in a reasonable length of time. This is usually a few minutes. If it does not get one, it gives up and sends you this message. It usually means that the destination computer or a piece of the network is dead. This can happen in the middle of an ongoing conversation. Try again in about 10 minutes. This is long enough for most systems to recover from a crash automatically, if they are going to. If it still does not work, investigate further. (You would get this message if the network cable suddenly fell off your computer.)

*not responding*      This is very similar to a "timed out" message, but the conversation is happening with UDP rather than TCP. (Different applications use different protocols. From your point of view, it should not matter.) It does mean that packets were sent to the remote site and nothing came back. As with the "timed out" message, try again in about 10 minutes. If it still does not work, investigate further. (Again, you'd get this message if the network cable suddenly fell off your computer.)

## Did You Change Anything?

If you have ever used a computer, or helped others use computers, the following dialog should come as no surprise:

"It stopped working."

"Did you change anything?"

"No, it was working yesterday and then it just stopped."

"You are sure?"

"Well, I did change the screen color in my configuration file, but that would not affect it."

If it worked yesterday and does not work today, something has changed. It may be your computer, it may be the network, it may be the destination. Changes you have made are the easiest to undo but the hardest to acknowledge as a problem. People change things on their computers because they are trying to accomplish something. If I tell you that your changes caused some problem, you will probably think that I'm trying to impede progress. But in many cases, your recent changes probably did cause the problem. If you have changed anything, a file or some hardware "thing," and your network connection has not worked right since, do not consider it unrelated, even if the relationship appears remote. Before looking anywhere else, try to undo the change. You only have to go back to your old version of config.sys (or whatever the file might be). You did copy *config.sys* to *config.bak* before you made the change, didn't you?

A good rule of thumb is to assume that the problem is at your end of the connection before you suspect problems at the other end. Make sure your end is working correctly before looking elsewhere. "Why?" you ask? "Didn't you say that the problem is equally likely to be at the far end?" Yes, that is true. But think about this: The far end is as likely to be in Japan as in Chicago, and almost certainly is not close to you. Before making a long-distance phone call to Japan, make sure that the problem's not on your end.

## Try a Different Destination

Because you did not change anything, you need to find out what has changed. First, try accessing a different destination. You do not even have to leave your seat. Look in the *Resource Catalog* and pick any destination that allows TELNET access; then **telnet** to it. If you get through, the problem is probably at the first destination you tried to reach. A successful **telnet** to any remote destination tells you that your system is working and that the network as a whole is working. If you are desperate to use that resource, you can call them up and ask them what the story is. Or you could just call it a night. In any case, your network connection is working just fine. Once the "remote end" gets its act together, you should be able to reach it.

Just to be comprehensive, I'll repeat a tip I gave earlier. If you get a message with a phrase like "host unknown" in it, your computer is having trouble looking up the Internet address of the remote system you want. Make sure you spelled the name correctly. Then see if you can find the (numeric) Internet address of the remote system. Using the numeric address should solve your problem.

## Try Your Neighbor's System

Because you are still reading, I assume that did not fix it. Earlier, I suggested that you go to your buddy's office and try again. If you can get to whatever resource you want, you know two things:

- You can work until the office's owner shows up in the morning
- The problem is most likely with your workstation—it certainly is not with the resource you want to access, or the network

If you cannot reach the resource you want, your local network or (in rare circumstances) the Internet itself is in trouble. Eventually, you will need to call someone and ask for help. But there are still a few things to check.

## Try to Reach a Local System

On the shopping list, we told you to get the IP address of another computer on the same local network. Here is where you use that information. Try to **telnet** to that machine. You should see its login prompt:

```
% telnet 192.33.44.56
Trying 192.33.44.56
Connected to 192.33.44.56
Escape character is '^]'.

login:
```

If you get this far, you have proven that your system is probably working. If you can reach local systems but not remote systems, the problem is most likely somewhere on your local net—very likely a router or some other piece of hardware that connects your network to the rest of the Internet. If you know a lot about how your local net is structured, you can make lots of experiments and maybe even pinpoint the trouble spot. However, that is not really your job. It's time to start making phone calls.

## *Look Around Your Office*

Now, assume that the finger of Murphy's Law is pointing directly at you—or your computer. It's time to start looking around your office. In World War II, the problem was "gremlins." They caused bombs not to explode, engines to stop, etc.—all for unknown causes. For the network, the problem is usually people: custodians, office mates, you. It is amazing how many network problems are caused by damage to that $5 piece of wire between your computer and the wall. Custodians knock it out with a broom, or you roll over it a hundred times with a chair wheel and cut it. If you find something obviously wrong (for example, thick Ethernet transceiver cables* on the back of a computer have a tendency to fall off), fix it (or get someone to fix it).

***Caution:*** If you are on a coaxial cable Ethernet (a round cable running to your computer, not a flat one) do not do anything until you read the section on "Dealing with Coaxial Ethernets" later in this chapter.

If you have access to any networking equipment, look at it. Do the lights look normal? Are they on at all? If none of the lights are on, check the power to the unit. If they are on but abnormal, there is probably nothing you can do except note the colors of the lights and call someone for help.

There is one situation where you might be able to help yourself out. Are you on a *10baseT* Ethernet† or a Token Ring LAN? These are probably the most common types of local area networks on the Internet these days, so the odds are pretty good that you fit into this category. For both kinds of network, each computer plugs into a separate port in a box called a "multiport repeater" (if you are on an Ethernet) or "media access unit" (MAU, for a Token Ring). Each port usually has a status light next to a plug. Locate the plug next to your computer's connection.‡ Is the light next to the cable from your computer red or off, and are the lights next to the other cables green? If so, try moving your plug to a vacant port. Did the new port's light turn green when you plugged in your cable, or did it remain red or dark? If it is now green, leave it there and try your computer again. You may have been plugged into a bad port and have bypassed the problem. If the new light turns red or remains unlit, it means there is something wrong with the wire to your computer, or the interface card in it. Unless there is something

---

*A 15-pin connector, explained more fully later in this chapter in "Dealing with Coaxial Ethernets."

†This is an Ethernet that uses normal telephone wiring and modular phone jacks, like the ones your home telephone uses to plug into the wall. They are also referred to as Ethernet on *UTP,* unshielded twisted-pair.

‡If you cannot find your computer's connection, call it a day (or a night). Wiring closets are often messy places. If the cables are not clearly labeled, or if there is not an up-to-date map telling you what each cable is, do not touch anything. This also would assume that you properly have access to the network equipment. In many cases it's locked away to prevent random people (i.e., you) from moving wires. If you do take it upon yourself to move some wires, be sure to tell the person responsible for the network what you did, so he can get the port fixed and update any documentation necessary.

obviously wrong, like a loose cable, it's hopeless to proceed without some other test equipment. (If you are on a Token Ring LAN, there is a section on Token Ring hints later in this chapter.)

## Check Your Local Connection

If you cannot get through to any remote destination but you can connect to computers in your local group, the problem is somewhere between your computer and the router that connects your group of computers to the Internet. "Group" is a pretty fuzzy term. You may be in a group by yourself, particularly if you connect using a dial-up, SLIP, or PPP connection. Your group may be a large number of computers sharing a local network and connected to an on-site router; at the extreme, your group may be a whole campus or corporate network.

Now, you have to figure out whether the problem is within your area (your LAN or computer), or somewhere farther away and out of your control. In this case, what you should do depends on how you are connected to the Net. Dial-up connections, in which you get network services by logging in to some "directly connected" computer over a modem, are significantly different from "direct connections." With SLIP or PPP, you have the worst of both worlds: You have to use the dial-up debugging techniques until the connection gets made and then deal with problems as if you had a dedicated connection. This is because these protocols set up temporary IP protocol connections between your computer and the service providers, just as if you had a dedicated connection.

### Dial-up connections

Once again, by "dial-up connections" we mean that you dial into another computer over a phone line, log in to it as a regular user, and use that computer's network services. What happens if you cannot log in to the remote computer? The problem is clearly not with the Internet, because you have not gotten anywhere close to it.

Again, most problems fall into a few common categories. Although the symptoms and remedies listed below are not exhaustive, they should take care of most situations:

*Phone does not dial*

> There is a problem in either your terminal emulator software, or between your computer and the modem. Your terminal emulator and modem are speaking different speeds or using different data formats. Check that out. It could also be that the location of the modem is not what your software thinks it is. (PCs have two communications ports, called COM1 and COM2; you have to pick the one your modem is plugged into. A similar

thing happens on Macintoshes with the "phone" or "printer" plug. For that matter, most UNIX systems have two or more terminal connectors on the back.) Other possibilities are that your telephone line is dead, or the phone cable is not plugged into the modem or the wall, or the modem is not plugged into the computer. Even if you know that everything is wired correctly, checking never hurts. Also: Find the phone jack where your modem plugs into the wall. Try plugging a regular telephone into the jack. Do you get a dial tone? If not, call the phone company.

### Ring, no answer

Check the number you dialed. Was it correct? If you dialed correctly and the remote system does not answer, the remote system may be down or its modem may be bad. Check the published hours of operation to make sure it should be up. If it should be working, try the same phone number a few times. Better yet, if you have any alternate numbers, try them. If you have two phone lines available, try dialing the number with a phone on the line that does not have the modem. While it is ringing, dial with your modem phone and see if it gets through. (Sometimes if there are multiple phone lines through one number, one bad line will always answer the call. If you keep it busy with another phone, your modem call might get to a good one.) Even if you get through eventually, call your service provider and report the problem so it can be fixed.

### Answer, then nothing

Here is one common scenario: The modem dials correctly, the remote system answers, the modems whistle a few tones at each other, and you get the message "Connected" (or its equivalent) on your screen. Then nothing happens; everything goes dead. This usually points to a problem with your service provider's gear. Either the provider's modem is bad, or the port on the computer it is connected to is bad. Either way, the only thing you can do is call in and report it. You might try again a few times. If you have an alternate number, try it. Getting a different modem to answer might bypass the problem.

There is one other possibility. There are certain modems that do not like to talk to each other, particularly if they are made by different manufacturers. We are assuming, however, that you are troubleshooting a connection that has worked for you in the past. Unless you have just bought a new modem, incompatible modems probably are not the problem.

### *LAN, PPP, or SLIP connections*

If you are directly on some kind of local network, or if you connect to a service provider using PPP or SLIP, your situation is somewhat different.* Try to **telnet** to the closest router that services you. This address was on the shopping list at the beginning of the chapter. If the router responds at all, your computer and connection are OK. The problem is in the "cloud"; it must be solved by whoever worries about the router and the network that it's connected to. This could be your service provider, the networking staff for your campus or corporation, or (if you have a large in-building network) someone in your department.

Note that we said, "If the router responds at all." You might see a login prompt, or just the message "Connection refused." Both of these are equally good responses. You do not know how to log in to the router, or the router may not be interested in letting anyone log in—who cares? To get either of these messages, you had to traverse your local network connection and get to something bigger. It is not your problem. Call the appropriate person and report it.

### *Some Consolation*

It may sound like there is not much you can do. In some senses, that is true. Think of your washer, dryer, or VCR. If they break, you can make sure all the plugs and hoses are tight, or maybe pull out a jammed cassette. There are a few things you can attempt. Much of the time, however, there is nothing you can do but call up the expert and talk about the problem knowledgeably. As we said earlier, even if you cannot solve the problem yourself, the more information you can gather, the better service you will get.

## ■ *Talking to Operations Personnel*

Whenever pilots talk on the radio to air traffic controllers, they are taught that every message should say:

- Who you are
- Where you are
- What you want to do

These same guidelines apply to calling network operators. First, they need to know who you are—otherwise, they cannot ask you for more information, or tell you that they've

---

*Although we do not present it here, it is probably a very good idea for you to take some time to learn about SLIP and/or PPP. Various tutorials are available online, and this is the object of one of the chapter exercises. You will be in a better position for reporting problems if you have at least some knowledge of these important protocols.

solved the problem. "Where you are" (the name of your computer and possibly its IP address) and "what you want to do" (the name of the remote computer and the service you want to get) allow operators to figure out the path your communications should take. This is the essential data necessary to diagnose and solve a problem. It is the bare minimum required, however. In addition, keep in mind why you have called the network operators. If you have followed our short procedure above, remember what you have done, why you did it, and what the results were. Why are you convinced that the problem is not on your desktop? The answer to this question contains very important clues about the nature of the problem.

The operator you call should be the one operating the network closest to you. Your local network operators are the only ones who monitor connections to your campus or building. It is not like calling up the president of GM to get some action on your car. In the network world, a national operator knows only about his network's connection to regional networks. Once he or she determines that the NSFnet, or NREN, or whatever is not at fault, he will call the regional network responsible for your connection. In turn, the regional network will call your campus or corporate networking center. Very likely, they will then call you. Save yourself some time: Start at the bottom.

## ■ *Dealing with Coaxial Ethernets*

Traditional coaxial cable Ethernets are special because, in many cases, fiddling with the wiring can break the network for other working computers. An Ethernet that uses coaxial cable has two parts: the bus and a number of taps (shown in Figure 15-3). The *bus* is the cable that snakes from computer to computer. There are two kinds of cable: "thick" and "thin." In thick Ethernets, the cable is about ⅜ inch in diameter, and yellow or orange with black marks every 2 meters. Thin Ethernets usually use gray, white, or black cable

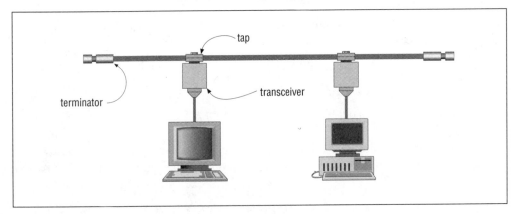

*Figure 15-3    Typical thick Ethernet*

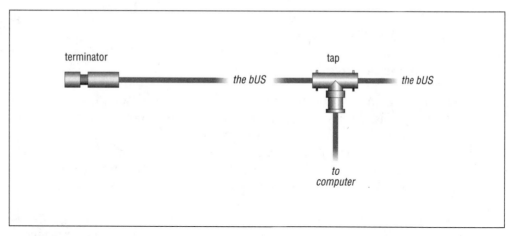

**Figure 15-4**   *Thin Ethernet—tap and terminator*

⅓ inch in diameter. Each end of the bus must have a special "cap" called a *terminator*. Between the two terminators may be a number of taps. A *tap* is where one computer connects to the network. For thick Ethernets, a tap is built in the *transceiver*, a little box a bit bigger than a pack of cigarettes hanging off the cable. This box allows your computer to connect to the Ethernet. A transceiver or *AUI* cable runs between it and your computer. For thin Ethernets, a tap looks like a "T" made of metal tubing, shown in Figure 15-4. It's usually located on the back of your computer. In this case, there is still a transceiver, but it is built into your computer.

If your computer has only a transceiver cable port, it might have an external transceiver next to the cable, just like a thick Ethernet would have.

Why do you care so much about the parts of an Ethernet? Whatever you do, the bus must always remain "electrically intact." This means that there must be an unbroken connection from one end (one terminator) to the other. If the bus is broken for any reason, it stops working for everyone connected to it.* So, by improperly disconnecting the Ethernet cable in your office, you can easily make enemies out of friends. Two rules for dealing with Ethernets will get you through most situations:

- You can do anything to the connection from your Ethernet tap to your computer without affecting other people
- If you need to break the bus for repairs, warn others and make it quick

---

*You might think that the network would still work, although in pieces: two computers should still be able to communicate if they are both on the same side of the break. Sorry, it's not that simple.

The first rule is pretty straightforward. If you need to disconnect your computer from the network, leave the "T" in the cable, and disconnect the vertical part of the "T" from the computer (shown as "to computer" in Figure 15-4). On thick Ethernets, leave the tap and transceiver in the cable, but disconnect the transceiver cable.

The second rule is a bit harder. You must recognize that there are times when it's necessary to do things to the bus. If it is damaged or cut and everyone is down, it is not an issue. It's down and you are doing everyone a service by fixing it. If it's working for everyone but you, you have a problem. This is quite common if a thick Ethernet transceiver dies. Fixing your connection could take everyone off the air. In this case you have two choices: Do it when they are not around or do it so fast they hardly notice.

Because most protocols, like TCP, are designed to deal with communication glitches of short duration, you can break an Ethernet for 10 seconds or so without permanently impacting people's work. Whatever they are doing will stop momentarily, but that is it. If you break their connection for too long, first they will notice the lack of response, then later (usually over a minute) TCP will time out.

*Note:* Whether or not you should touch the cable at all depends on your environment. On some networks, the policy might be "no one but a cable technician or network administrator touches the wiring." Abide by your local rules.

## ■ *Token Ring Notes*

If you are on a Token Ring net, here are a few pointers. First: Some MAUs do not have status lights. On these, you have no help figuring out if your port is bad or not. If you are desperate, you might just try plugging your computer into a vacant port.

Second: If you move the plug on a MAU, you may need to reboot your computer before you try again. (On some systems, you only may need to restart the Internet software.) The software has to perform a special "ring insertion" to become active on the network. A ring insertion happens only once, when the software first starts running. Your system will not automatically notice that it is back on the network and try to insert itself again. So if you change the cabling, you need to force a ring insertion before you can be active on the network. This may be possible within your TCP/IP software package. If you cannot figure out how to do it gracefully, a reboot always works.

In any case, try to leave the network in the same configuration that you found it (with perhaps some bad cables replaced and now in working order).

## ▓ *Exercises*

*Print out your responses for each of the following items. Seek help locally if you need it.*

**1.** What computer help services does your campus make available to you? Is there a telephone and/or electronic mail hotline for your questions?

**2.** Does your local computer services office have a standard form for reporting problems? Does it appear to be tedious? Why might it need to be?

**3.** Are/were there recurrent technical problems over the length of this course? If so, have the proper technicians been informed? How will you personally deal with these problems after the class is over?

**4.** If you really want to know more about any of the problems discussed in this chapter, there are tutorials available to you on the Web. Using your favorite search engine, scan the Net for matches between "tutorial" and each of the following:

- modem
- Ethernet
- LAN (local area network)
- ISP (Internet service provider)
- SLIP or PPP

Find at least one source that is accessible to you (that is, fits your interests and especially your personal computer experience or lack of same).

**5.** "Troubleshooting" is a descriptive term that fits what you are doing when you try to solve a problem, including one on the Net. Using your favorite search engine, scan the Net for matches between "troubleshooting" and each of the following. Find at least one source that is accessible to you.

- modem
- Ethernet
- LAN (local area network)
- ISP (Internet service provider)
- SLIP or PPP

**6.** If you have Net access via an Internet service provider, what technical support do they offer? Is there toll-free 24-hour telephone access? If so, can you get through for help? Is lack of technical support enough reason to switch providers?

# Resources on the Internet

*Stalking the Wild Resource*
*A Few Special Resources*
*How We Did It*
*Using the Catalog*

Up to this point, I've given you a lot of "how to" advice. Now it's time to discuss "to what?" There are lots of resources out there—but there's no official list. Anyone who has an Internet connection can put a new resource online at any moment without telling anyone—and they do. So the trick is finding out what's available. First, we'll discuss how to use the tools we've covered to find resources. Next, we'll talk about a few resources we know about that we think are pretty special. One of these, the Global Network Navigator (GNN), is the basis for the *Resource Catalog* in this book. We'll talk about how the *Resource Catalog* in GNN was created and how it eventually ends up in this book. Finally, we'll introduce the format and use of the *Catalog*. In the J.C. Penny catalog, this section would be called "How to Order." Then you'll be ready to start shopping in the *Catalog* itself.

Remember, the Internet is dynamic. The half-life of an Internet resource is about four years.* Translated into practical terms, this means that given any index of network resources, in the next year about a quarter of them will change in such a way that the index's information about them is unusable. That's as true of the *Resource Catalog* in this book as it is for any (and every) other resource list out there. The moral of the story is that resource lists are nice, but they aren't the final word. They are always partly out of date; and they're always missing the latest and greatest things on the Net.

---

*It's probably not a coincidence that this is also the average time a student, whether undergraduate or graduate, remains at the same institution.

Another problem is that quality of network resources varies greatly. Although resource lists try to focus on the "best" resources they can find, it's certainly true that beauty is in the eye of the beholder. To become truly fluent in using the Net, you must learn how to find your own truffles amid the muck.

## Stalking the Wild Resource

In chapter 12 I drew some analogies between the Internet and a library without a card catalog. It's time to start thinking about that again. You may be without an official card catalog, but you are not without tools. The major tools at your disposal are your friends, network news and mailing lists, and the Archie, Gopher, WAIS, and World Wide Web services. Let's look at how each of these may be used to find the resource of your dreams.

### Friends

Your friends are your friends because you have interests in common with them. In addition to your regular friends, you will make a set of network friends through e-mail. These friends may be looking for the same things you are; or even if their interests differ, they may be aware of resources that you want. In the real world, a friend who knows you are into female mystery writers might tell you, "Sara Paretsky has a new book out": He knows you are interested and will appreciate the tip. In the network world, a friend who knows you are interested in agriculture resources might send you a message saying, "Have you seen Not Just Cows, the Internet ag resources guide?" He, being a pencil collector, would love to hear from you if you found a complete pencil-pricing database. Life on the network is not all that different from "real life."

### Network News and Mailing Lists

Network news and mailing lists are resources themselves. Newsgroups are shown in the catalog by topic. Lists of mailing lists are compiled and are listed under Network Information. These resources are also gateways to other resources. If you are interested in pencil collecting and follow the *rec.pencil-collecting* group (or a mailing list—same facilities, but different technology) for a while, one of three things will happen. First, someone might post a news item announcing a great find, like "Pencil Collecting Database Found." Second, these great finds will probably be collected into a group of frequently asked questions (FAQs). FAQs are posted to the newsgroup or to *news.answers* periodically (usually monthly).* By reading the FAQs, you can instantly be brought up-to-date on whatever the newsgroup is discussing.

---

*FAQs have been archived, so they are available when you want them via **ftp**. See the "USENET Periodic Posting Archives" (under Network News) in the *Catalog* for their location.

If you don't find what you want in a FAQ, you can "go fishing" for an answer. Write a posting to the pencil-collecting newsgroup (or mailing list) asking, "Does anyone have a database of current pencil prices?" It is easy to cast out and see what you can catch.

## Archie

Archie (discussed in chapter 9) is primarily a service for locating files by name. It makes a slight attempt to allow searches by topic, but this facility is limited and dated. However, in reality Archie is more general-purpose than this description implies. People who maintain anonymous FTP servers try to name things logically. Frequently, they use the structure of a filesystem to help organize: Related files are stored in the same directory, which will probably have a useful name. In these cases, Archie doesn't tell you exactly what you want to know, but gives you an idea of where you might look. For example, to locate pencil-collecting information, you might try the following command:

```
% archie -s pencil

Host blandsworth.usnd.edu
    Location: /pub
        DIRECTORY drwxr-xr-x    512  May 17 05:19   pencils
```

You didn't search for a particular topic, you searched for a file starting with "pencil". What Archie found was not a file, but a directory named */pub/pencils,* on the computer **blandsworth.usnd.edu.**

At this point, you don't know if there is anything useful to you on that computer or not. But—let's face it—how many people would create a directory named *pencils* for numerical analysis software? Not many. There's a good chance that this directory will contain something to do with pencils—maybe not exactly what you're looking for, but probably something interesting. All you need to do is **ftp** to **blandsworth.usnd.edu,** log in as **anonymous, cd pub/pencils,** and do a **dir.** Poke around a bit. It may contain good stuff, and it may not. It is a reasonable place to start.

## Gopher

Gopher (chapter 11) can be used to access other resource finders such as Archie and WAIS. It can also be used by itself; Gopher menus are themselves pointers to resources. When looking for resources with Gopher, there are two particularly useful ways to start hunting: read the list of all the Gopher servers in the world, or start searching for particular menus with Veronica.

There are getting to be more and more specialized Gopher servers around. Someone sees the power Gopher could bring to a community, so he or she builds a Gopher server tailored to that community. The person responsible for the server is on the lookout for more information sources in the area of interest. If you can find a Gopher server that has a collection you like, you can stay up-to-date by dropping into that server every now and then. To find a server that appears to have similar leanings to your own, just start from any server; find the list of "other Gopher servers"; and page through it. There are lots of them but, if you are lucky and patient, you might find the University of Minnesota Pencil Collection Gopher. That might be pushing it a bit, but there are already specialized Gopher servers for soil science, history of science, bird watching, and law. Pencil collecting can't be far behind.

If you can't find a specialized server to your liking, use Veronica to search for a couple of keywords that are relevant to your quest. Remember that if you find an interesting resource through a Gopher server, you can either continue to use that resource through Gopher (set a bookmark to come back again easily), or you can ask Gopher how to access the resource directly.* If Gopher accesses the resource through TELNET, you can just start **telnet** manually and skip the Gopher menus.

## WAIS

The *directory-of-servers* makes it easy to find any WAIS service (chapter 12). Some of the servers are actually indexes into other services. For example, the whole of the Archie database or the archives of many newsgroups can be searched through WAIS. This allows you to use the extended search capabilities of WAIS to look for things you might want.

### The World Wide Web

The World Wide Web (chapter 13) is also a great way to hunt for useful resources. Not only does it have resources of its own, but it allows you to use all the other search services. There are several subject-oriented menus, such as CERN's "Virtual Library," and Yanoff's list of "Special Internet Connections." Resource lists like these are maintained by volunteers and are improving with time.

Make sure you check out lists of home pages when you find them. Lists of home pages are roughly equivalent to lists of Gopher servers. If you manage to find a home page with an interesting title, such as the "Pencil Institute of America Home Page," remember its URL or add it to your client's hotlist. Some Web clients come preconfigured with lists of good home pages in a pull-down menu.

---

*If you're using the ASCII ("curses") **gopher** client, use the = command.

# ■ *A Few Special Resources*

We tried to be selective in choosing resources for our *Catalog;* we definitely didn't list every file that's available, or every site that has collections of files. It seems to have worked out very well, if we do say so ourselves. There are a few resources that are so exciting or important that we thought we would highlight them here.

## *The InterNIC*

For a long time, no one has had the responsibility for providing network information services for the whole Internet. There have been any number of NICs (Network Information Centers). Each has had a particular constituency; for example, the NYSERnet NIC would provide network information for customers of NYSERnet (an Internet service provider). So many global projects, like a unified white-pages directory, were never done. Everyone knew that these projects were good ideas, but no one was willing to step forward and volunteer—particularly if it was a big, unending job. The InterNIC, particularly funded by the National Science Foundation, was formed to solve this problem. In the parlance of sports advertising, it is the official information provider of the Internet. InterNIC services are available to the entire Internet community, including users outside the U.S. Other NICs in the U.S. and abroad are working in cooperation with the InterNIC, and new NICs are being formed, such as the Asia-Pacific NIC (APNIC) and the Agriculture NIC (AgNIC).

The InterNIC has three parts:

- ■ Registration Services
- ■ Database Services
- ■ Information Services

Each of these components is run by a different company with its own charter; but together they are providing a unified, useful service.

### *Registration Services*

The InterNIC's Registration Services are responsible for assigning network addresses and top-level domain names. Important as this service is, it's not something you're likely to need, unless you're setting up a network at a new site—and even then, it's more common for your Internet service provider to deal with registration and related issues.

You might find Registration Services information useful if you need to get information about some remote domain or network. For example, the big boss comes down and says, "Find out if we can do e-mail with Tunisia." The InterNIC might be able to tell you who to contact to find out more about computer networking in Tunisia; in particular, they would probably be able to put you in touch with their Tunisian counterparts (i.e., whatever organization is responsible for network registration and coordination).

### Database Services

The Database Services component of the InterNIC has the task of creating databases in service to the Internet community. A big part of that is to coordinate the creation of a global white-pages directory. We showed you how to use the beginnings of this in chapter 10, *Finding Someone*. This means that the traditional problem of finding someone on the Internet may be solved sometime soon.

The Database Services people are also trying to create an Internet equivalent to the "yellow pages." That is, they'd like to have a directory of services that's sorted by the service type, rather than alphabetically by name. Services could get a small listing for free, or they could pay something for a big listing, complete with pictures. It's not quite there yet, but will probably happen.

### Information Services

The Information Services component of the InterNIC disseminates a wealth of information about the Internet by a variety of means (see Table 1). They are a reference desk where you can call, fax, or e-mail questions. They run Gopher, WAIS, World Wide Web, and anonymous FTP servers to give free public access to this information. The Web server offered by the InterNIC includes an indexing service that allows easy searches for documents by topic and level of expertise. Much of it is user-oriented; it includes lists of resources, lists of network providers (including international providers), training courses, books, statistics, and archives of articles about the Internet. A lot of this information is available on a CD-ROM product called NICLink, intended for novice users and Internet trainers.

The InterNIC is known as the NIC of first and last resort. This means that they accept questions directly from users who are having trouble, but they are also a resource for other NICs to use when they encounter a question that stumps them.

## U.S. Government Resources

The U.S. government (like many governments worldwide) issues tremendous amounts of information on just about every topic imaginable, ranging from economic statistics to hints on home maintenance. In the past, a lot of this information has been hard to

*Table 1*   *Accessing The InterNIC*

| Method | Address |
|---|---|
| E-mail | info@internic.net |
| TELNET | internic.net |
| FTP | ftp.internic.net |
| Archie | archie.internic.net |
| Gopher | gopher.internic.net |
| World Wide Web | http://www.internic.net |
| Telephone | (800) 444-4345, (619) 455-4600 |
| Fax | (619) 455-4640 |

get. Often, it has been very expensive; and even if it hasn't been expensive, it's been hard to find.

One of the Clinton administration's goals is to release as much of this information as possible through the Internet. One of the biggest conduits for releasing information is the Extension Service of the U.S. Department of Agriculture (**esusda.gov**), partnering with universities in every state and territory across the nation. Don't let the name fool you; it isn't just soybeans and hog bellies. How about:

- Distance education (education at remote locations, through correspondence, video, etc.)
- Problems of large cities
- Ethnic diversity
- Children and families
- Sustainable agriculture
- Economics of communities
- NAFTA accord
- National Performance Review
- National Health Care Reform Report
- National Water Quality Information Database
- National Family Life Database
- International Food and Nutrition Database
- White House press reports

There's a lot more; these are a few of the highlights. Some of these resources are listed in the *Resource Catalog,* but what's there is expanding all the time. If you are interested in information like this, your best bet is to get a catalog right from the source.

Most of these resources are provided by Almanac servers, which are like list servers. (How to use them is explained in chapter 7). There are any number of servers, each of which has its own collection of information. To get detailed information about how to use Almanac servers, send the one-line e-mail message **send guide** to **almanac@esusda.gov**. For a catalog of what's available on any one server, send the one-line message **send catalog** to that server; for example, to find out what's available at the Extension Service's own server, send this message to **almanac@esusda.gov**. For an overall list of known servers, some hints on getting started, and a general survey of topics covered by Almanac servers, send the one-line message **send ces-docs explore-inet** to **almanac@esusda.gov**.

Here's a short—and, no doubt, already incomplete—list of Almanac servers.

*Table 2   Almanac Servers*

| *Location* | *Internet Address* |
| --- | --- |
| Americans Communicating Electronically | **almanac@ace.esusda.gov** |
| Auburn University | **almanac@acenet.auburn.edu** |
| Cornell University | **almanac@cce.cornell.edu** |
| Extension Service—USDA | **almanac@esusda.gov** |
| National Ag Library | **almanac@cyfer.esusda.gov** |
| North Carolina State University | **almanac@ces.ncsu.edu** |
| Oregon State University | **almanac@oes.orst.edu** |
| Purdue University | **almanac@ecn.purdue.edu** |
| University of California | **almanac@silo.ucdavis.edu** |
| University of Missouri | **almanac@ext.missouri.edu** |
| University of Wisconsin | **almanac@joe.uwex.edu** |
|  | **almanac@wisplan.uwex.edu** |

## *The Global Network Navigator*

The Global Network Navigator (GNN) is one of the first attempts to commercialize the World Wide Web technology. You might think of GNN as an online magazine, but it's probably better to think of it as an information service. Its news stories and features include links to the services being described, so you can think of it as a kind of "information interface" to the Net. The GNN editorial staff does the "Net surfing" for people who don't have the time or experience to do it themselves, researching special-interest areas of the Net, providing reviews of Internet resources, adding interesting editorial content, and clustering all this additional information around links to other Internet services.

GNN is a great place to start exploring the Net, especially if you have a direct (TCP/IP) connection.* In addition to the news magazine, GNN includes an expanded online version of the *Whole Internet Catalog* included at the back of this book. Instead of typing a command to access the service being described, you can just click on a hypertext link to reach it. The online version of the *Catalog* is updated regularly; you can check in at any time to find new resources. It's also a good way to track down resources that have changed or been reorganized since the last edition of the *Catalog*.

GNN also includes "interest centers" that try to group all significant Internet services in a particular category, together with pointers to related commercial services. There is currently a travel center; other interest centers are being developed. The travel center includes travel book reviews and links to all the travel-related newsgroups, Gophers, FTP archives, and Web sites, plus a syndicated World Travel Watch column that describes trouble spots around the world, access to an up-to-date currency conversion program, dispatches and photos from travel writers, and advertising from travel publishers.

Advertising? On the Internet? Of course. Many commercial sites are now offering Gopher catalogs, or in some cases even Web servers, providing access to their information. This is non-intrusive advertising—making information available for people who want it. GNN goes one step further. Its developers argue that once the novelty factor has worn off, just throwing up a Gopher catalog won't do more than serve the customers you already have. In order to bring in new people, you need to create added value for specific audiences. Once people are visiting a travel center, links to travel-related catalogs and commercial services are providing an information service for the reader, rather than an additional nuisance.

The GNN Marketplace is another important innovation. The Marketplace contains pointers to various advertising documents—like an online version of the Yellow Pages. Unlike most advertising, GNN's advertisements are not thrust upon you; it's up to you to decide when (and whether) to read them. So, if you just had a huge lunch and are feeling fat, you can pop into the NordicTrack listing and see what you should be doing rather than eating.

---

*Chapter 1 and Appendix A explain different types of Internet connections; Appendix A also discusses how to get an Internet connection.

## *Domain Name Lookup*

Throughout this book, we've talked in terms of these nice, memorable "domain names." Maybe you don't find them memorable, but they're certainly nicer than the alternative: addresses like 143.209.24.92. In chapter 3, we described the Domain Name System, which translates names into addresses.

Unfortunately, there are a few sites that don't have access to the Domain Name System. This is a problem that really should be remedied by a system administrator or a service provider—but when things are broken, sometimes you don't have the option of waiting until they're fixed. If you're in this situation, take heart: There is a way out! There are a few services for looking up numeric addresses "by hand"; once you've done that, you can use the numeric address instead of the name. None of the tools we've discussed (except for e-mail) care which you use—even the Web browsers! Just substitute a numeric address for the Internet name in the URL, and you can use it.

So—what are these magic resources? The easiest one to use is a **telnet** service run by the SWITCH (Swiss Academic and Research Network). Just **telnet** to the address **130.59.1.40**, log in as **lookup**, and enter the name you want to convert to an address. For example, you'd get an address for the FTP archive **ftp.uu.net** (an important source for software of all sorts) like this:

```
% telnet 130.59.1.40
login: lookup

SWITCH Internet Domain Name Service

Enter the full domain name or HELP:  ftp.uu.net

Non-authoritative answer:

Name: ftp.uu.net
Address: 192.48.96.9
```

You can type **help** to get a help screen. However, there isn't much help to give; you know just about all there is to know about this service.

Once you have the address, you can then use it in an **ftp** command:

```
% ftp 192.48.96.9
```

It's not convenient, but it works.

You can also get Internet addresses via electronic mail. The name server you use depends on where you are; it is best to use the server closest to you. In the U.S., use the address

**resolve@cs.widener.edu** and include the message **site** *internet-name.* Outside the U.S., use the address **dns@grasp.insa-lyon.fr** and include the message **ip** *internet-name.* For example, to find out the address of **ftp.uu.net**, send the message **ip ftp.uu.net** to **dns@grasp.insa-lyon.fr**; equivalently, send the message **site ftp.uu.net** to **resolve@cs.widener.edu**. You'll get a message back looking like this:

```
Return-Path: <dns-request@grasp.insa-lyon.fr>
Date: Tue, 1 Mar 1994 20:17:33 GMT
From: dns@grasp.insa-lyon.fr (Mail Name Server)
Subject: Reply to your queries

you> ip ftp.uu.net

Official hostname: ftp.uu.net
Registered address(es):
        192.48.96.9
```

You may wonder why you can use an e-mail address like **dns-request@grasp.insa-lyon.fr**, when you can't use other Internet addresses. Unlike the other services, electronic mail is a "store and forward" service. Your own computer doesn't necessarily need to look up domain names; it can send the mail on to a "smarter" computer that knows how to interrogate the Domain Name System. So you can often use e-mail addresses even when you can't use domain names.

## ◼ *How We Did It*

How did we create our *Resource Catalog?* What techniques did we use? We did all of the following:

- We listened to newsgroups and mailing lists looking for interesting announcements.

- We used what we learned to find other lists and used their information.

- We looked for sparse areas in the *Catalog* and used Archie to perform subject searches (e.g., **archie -s music**). With that information, we then looked at the anonymous FTP servers to see if there was anything interesting in them.

- We visited a number of Gopher servers and tried to list any unique services we found.

- We included a summary of the most useful WAIS services from the *directory-of-servers.*

- We were happy to hear about neat resources other people have used, found, or created. If you find a new one, mail us at **wic@ora.com**, and we'll take a look.

## What Is a Resource?

What we included as a resource varies from subject to subject. There are subjects, like the Internet itself and computer science, where thousands of important files are scattered throughout the Internet, almost randomly. We chose not to include such resources; anyone can find these with Gopher or WAIS. There are other groups for which the sole motivation to be on the Internet might be to access one particular file; we tried to include these. In general, we included the most unique and interesting things we could find. Within each subject, resources were "graded on the curve." There was no absolute measure for what we considered interesting.

We biased our choices in favor of resources that anyone could use, or that could be used on the spur of the moment from the network. A prime example of this would be computational resources. We didn't list the NSF supercomputer centers, even though they were one of the prime reasons why the network became ubiquitous. Anyone who wants to do heavy-duty research computing can request time on a supercomputer, but they are not for everyone to use. If you are a valid user, each center will supply you with lots of documentation about how to use it. You can't just decide "I think I'll play on a Cray today."

On the other hand, there are a few sites that offer free UNIX computing. That is, anyone can **telnet** to them and run selected programs. With the emphasis on "anyone," we included such resources.

Finally, we tried to be broad rather than deep. In one respect, this book is an argument about why you should use the Internet. And the simplest argument for using the Net is that there are loads of resources interesting to all sorts of people, not just "geeks with pocket protectors." To prove this, we've tried to hit as many different and diverse topics as possible. If we've succeeded, even Internet veterans should be surprised at what we've found.

## Accuracy and Permissions

We verified that every listed resource was working and available at some time when we were gathering information. That doesn't mean that these resources are still available, or that the usage information is still the same. There were times when the access information changed in the two weeks between the time we discovered the resource and the time we actually tried it. If we could figure out how to use a resource, we included it; if not, we chucked it.

For this reason, we included references to other resource directories and guides. They have the advantage of being online, hence easily updatable. This doesn't mean they actually are updated frequently. There's really no way to tell whether any online database is more or less up-to-date than this *Catalog.* Online indexes are usually maintained by volunteer effort; you never know how much effort the volunteer has to expend.

*Remember:* A resource that is publicly accessible isn't necessarily a public resource. This caused me a bit of trouble. If I stumbled upon a good resource, how could I decide if it was intended to be public? The rule of thumb I used was that a public resource had to fall into one of these categories:

- Commonly known within the community (e.g., frequently mentioned and discussed in newsgroups)
- Listed in other resource guides or catalogs
- Easily found with public index utilities (e.g., Gopher, WAIS)

We ran across a few resources that didn't fall into these categories, were subject to restrictions, or seemed "dangerous" to the offerer. In these cases, we asked the owner if he or she would like to see the resource listed. Usually the answer was yes. If the answer was no, the resources are still available on the Internet, but you aren't hearing about them from me.

## Using the Catalog

We tried to group the resources into the areas where they belonged, but then what do we know?* After a description of the resource, we tell you how to access the resource. We'll show you what kind of a resource is listed (FTP, TELNET, WAIS, Gopher, or World Wide Web), followed by the site's Internet address, followed by any other information you need: how to log in, what directory to **cd** to, what port to use (if it's non-standard). The command itself isn't that important; its main purpose is to tell you what kind of a service you're using. Use whatever command you have available that knows how to access that kind of service; use your FTP client to access an FTP resource, a Gopher client to access a Gopher resource, and so on.

The descriptions for WAIS, Gopher, and World Wide Web servers get a little more complicated. For WAIS servers, Internet addresses are irrelevant. Instead, we show the name of the WAIS database that you have to look up. This database should be in the list of databases your WAIS client knows about. If it isn't, you can find it in the master WAIS database, *directory-of-servers.src.*

---

*I'm not the only one who doesn't know about this. Cataloging of online resources is a really hot area of research in the library science community.

For Gopher servers, the *Catalog* shows which server to connect to, followed by the menu items to select. For the Flybase Gopher server (which contains information about fruit flies), the *Catalog* shows the following entry:

> *gopher ftp.bio.indiana.edu/Flybase*

This means to point your Gopher client at the server **ftp.bio.indiana.edu**, and then select the "Flybase" item from its root menu. To get to this server, you can either put its address on the command line, or search through a menu of Gopher servers until you find it.

A typical World Wide Web entry looks like this:

> *www http://www.nr.no/ordbok*

This resource is an online dictionary of Norwegian (listed under "Norway" in the "International Interest" section of the *Resource Catalog*). To access this resource, just type the command **www http://www.nr.no/ordbok**. If you're using a public **www** client, give the command **go http://www.nr.no/ordbok**. That's a lot of typing—and this is a short URL. Unfortunately, there's really no other way to describe a Web resource.

Of course, you may not be using a program that's exactly equivalent to the one we list. Don't let that bother you. There are many World Wide Web clients besides **www**. You may be using Lynx, a version of Mosaic, or any of a number of other browsers. Don't let that confuse you; they should all work the same way. Similarly, if you're using **xgopher** or the Mac's TurboGopher, or another Gopher client, use the client you have—don't be confused because we list a different program name in the *Catalog*.

Remember that the Internet is always changing. Servers get reorganized, so the resources that are already there move around. If you can't find something, look around a bit; the server that provides the information may have undergone some "housecleaning," and you'll find what you want elsewhere.

# AERONAUTICS & ASTRONAUTICS

**Newsgroups:**
sci.space, sci.astro,
sci.aeronautics

## NASA News

A short listing of current happenings at NASA. If you're interested in the space program, this is a great way to stay up-to-date. On a typical day, you'd find out about expected launches or (perhaps) progress on a Space Shuttle mission.

**Access via:**
*finger nasanews@space.mit.edu*

## NASA Spacelink

Entries about the history, current state, and future of NASA and space flight, provided by the NASA Marshall Space Flight Center. Also, some classroom materials and information on space technology transfer. This is a particularly valuable resource for educators.

**Access via:**
*telnet spacelink.msfc.nasa.gov;* login *newuser;* password *newuser*

**Information:**
Telephone: (205) 544-6531

## Shuttle and Satellite Images

The following FTP sites make available photographs and other images taken from the Space Shuttle, Magellan and Viking missions, and other good stuff. The data formats vary; check any *README* files, or other descriptive files that are available.

**Access via:**
*telnet sanddunes.scd.ucar.edu*
(E-mail: kelley@sanddunes.scd.ucar.edu for login, password, and manual.)

*ftp sseop.jsc.nasa.gov;* login *anonymous*
(Space Shuttle images.)

*ftp explorer.arc.nasa.gov;* login *anonymous;* cd *pub/SPACE/GIF*

(Images are in GIF and JPEG directories; lots of other information about all aspects of the U.S. space program in other directories. A gigantic archive.)

## Space FAQs

Have you ever thought about becoming an astronaut? Here's where to find out what's required. Fifteen lists of "Frequently Asked Questions" are available. The lists are on topics ranging from "Astronomical Mnemonics" to "Orbital and Planetary Launch Services"—including "How to Become an Astronaut." Other files include a report on tidal bulges, information on interpreting satellite weather photos, and databases on constellations and nearby stars.

Other subdirectories under *pub/SPACE* contain detailed reports about individual space missions.

**Access via:**
*ftp explorer.arc.nasa.gov;* cd *pub/SPACE/FAQ*

## SpaceMet

A bulletin board system for exchanging information about space exploration from the view of science educators. Has information on past, current, and future NASA plans. Also contains information on curriculum planning. There is a section on events and meetings, but it is pretty local to the Northeastern U.S.

**Access via:**
*telnet spacemet.phast.umass.edu*

# AGRICULTURE

**Newsgroups:**
alt.agriculture.[fruit, misc], misc.rural

**See also:** Forestry; Gardening; and Horticulture.

## Advanced Technology Information Network

Any farmer knows that farming isn't a "mom and pop" business anymore; it's high-tech, and it's important to keep up with the latest developments. This resource, and the others in this group, will help you stay up-to-date. A fairly complete agricultural information service offers market, news, events, weather, job listing, and safety information. Offered by the California Agricultural Technology Institute, so there is a "West Coast" bias to the information. Also contains information on trade, exports, and biotechnology.

**Access via:**
*telnet caticsuf.csufresno.edu;* login *super*

## Commodity Market Reports

Commodity reports compiled by the U.S. Department of Agriculture Market News Service. Twelve hundred reports covering the U.S., updated daily.

**Access via:**
WAIS *agricultural-market-news.src*

**Information:**
E-mail: wais@oes.orst.edu

## Not Just Cows

A guide to resources on the Internet and BITNET in agriculture and related subjects. Compiled by Wilfred (Bill) Drew.

**Access via:**
*ftp ftp.sura.net;* login *anonymous;* cd *pub/nic;* get *agricultural.list*

**Information:**
E-mail: drewwe@snymorva.bitnet

## PEN Pages

A complete information server concerning all aspects of rural life. Sections on commodity prices, family farm life, seniors on the farm, news, and nutrition. Also, provides various announcements by the USDA including its CITExtension newsletter. Service provided by the Pennsylvania State University, so some information may be specific to that region.

**Access via:**
*telnet psupen.psu.edu;* login your two-letter state abbreviation

## U.C. Davis Extension 4-H Project Catalog

Intended to help members of the 4-H youth project get started in areas ranging from bee-keeping to "poultry science," these files are available in PostScript and WordPerfect 5.1 formats.

**Access via:**
*gopher gopher.ucdavis.edu/The Campus/ U.C. Cooperative Extension/4h-youth*

*ftp ftp.ucdavis.edu;* login *anonymous;* cd *pub/extension/4h-youth*

## USDA Extension Service Gopher

A "master gopher" for the U.S. Department of Agriculture's activities and extension service. This includes information about the extension service, policies of the USDA and extension

*Excerpt from* **PEN Pages**, *7/14/92:*

ADAPTING HOMES FOR ELDERLY

Since most information about a person's surroundings comes through eyesight, reduced vision problems related to aging are often compounded by the interior design of a home. The yellowing of the eye's lens produces less contrast between objects and makes it harder to see colors in the blue-violet range. Using warm colors in the red and yellow range are more comfortable for elderly persons. The use of contrasting colors helps to make distinctions and judgements easier for elderly persons. For example, the use of contrasting colors can separate the floor from the baseboard. Also, using floor coverings that are different in color and texture could help an elderly person identify danger areas such as stairways.

Source: Sarah Drummond, Assistant Extension Specialist, Oklahoma
------------------------------------
Editor: J. Van Horn, Ph.D., CFLE, Professor, Rural Sociology Dept. of Ag. Economics and Rural Sociology, Penn State May 1992 PENpages Number 085072114
------------------------------------
Keywords: AGRICULTURAL-EC-RUR-SOC, ELDERLY, HOME, HOUSING, MAPP, NEWS, SAFETY, VANHORN-JAMES

service, educational (and other) projects of the extension service, disaster relief information, and many pointers to other government resources. The "About the Extension Service" file (on their main menu) is a helpful guide to the service they offer.

**Access via:**
*gopher esusda.gov*

A gopher server for CYFERnet, the Children Youth Family Education Research Network. The primary focus of this service is the support of child, youth, and family development. There are pointers to resources on education, nutrition, the 4-H, etc. One interesting section of this server is ACE (Americans Communicating Electronically), a project for providing wider access to government information.

**Access via:**
*gopher cyfer.esusda.gov*

## USDA Research Results

Summaries of recent research results from the USDA's agricultural and economic research services. Updated at least bimonthly.

**Access via:**
WAIS *usda-rrdb.src*

**Information:**
E-mail: wais@esusda.gov

# *ANTHROPOLOGY*

**Newsgroup:**
sci.anthropology

## Aboriginal Studies

A collection of records from the Aboriginal Studies Electronic Data Archive at the Australian Institute of Aboriginal Studies and the Australian National University.

**Access via:**
WAIS *ANU-Aboriginal-Studies.src*

## Coombspapers Social Sciences Research Data Bank

An extensive archive of research information on the study of humans and their cultures. It is heavily laden with bibliographies, abstracts, books by Australian National University authors, and conference papers, rather like your library's old Vertical File, but you may be able to find more valuable information here, too.

**Access via:**
*ftp coombs.anu.edu.au; login anonymous; cd coombspapers*

## Rice Anthropology Gopher

Mostly a set of pointers to other anthropology resources; nothing local as of November 1993.

**Access via:**
*gopher riceinfo.rice.edu/Information by Subject Area/Anthropology and Culture*

## Thai Yunnan Project

Annotated bibliography and research notes collection of the Thai-Yunnan Project, Dept. of Anthropology, Australian National University, GPO Box 4, Canberra ACT 2601. Lots of data on ethnic groups of southeast Asia, including languages, religions, customs, etc.

**Access via:**
WAIS *ANU-Thai-Yunnan.src*

**Information:**
Telephone: +61 6 249-9262
E-mail: gew400@coombs.anu.edu.au

# ARCHAEOLOGY

**Newsgroup:**
sci.archaeology

**See also:** Classical Languages & Literature

## Ancient Near East—Cambridge

This site for Ancient Near East studies specializes in Egyptological material, and encourages scholarly contributions. Also contains a notice of an e-mail list for the discussion of the Ancient Near East.

**Access via:**
*ftp newton.newton.cam.ac.uk; login anonymous; cd pub/ancient*

**Information:**
E-mail: Helen Strudwick (H.M.Strudwick@newton.cam.ac.uk) or Nigel Strudwick (ncs3@cus.cam.ac.uk)

## Classics & Mediterranean Archaeology (U Mich)

A resource sponsored by the Department of Classical Studies, University of Michigan; many of the items pointed to here are to be found in this *Catalog*. See in particular the Pylos Regional Archaeological Project's 1993 *Preliminary Report*, a good example of the use of the Net for scholarly publication.

**Access via:**
*www http://rome.classics.lsa.umich.edu/welcome.html*

## Dead Seas Scrolls Exhibition

An online version of the Library of Congress's exhibition titled "Scrolls from the Dead Sea: The Ancient Library of Qumran and Modern Scholarship." The exhibition covers the Jewish and Christian context of the scrolls and the Qumran community that deposited them, and includes images not only of selected pieces of the scrolls, but of other archaeological artifacts, such as pottery and coins.

Both FTP and WWW interfaces are available:

**Access via:**
*ftp ftp.loc.gov;* login *anonymous;*
cd *pub/exhibit.images/deadsea.scrolls.
exhibit*

*www http://sunsite.unc.edu/expo/
deadsea.scrolls.exhibit/intro.html*

## New World Archaeology

ArchNet, at the University of Connecticut Dept. of Anthropology, covers archaeology in the Northeastern U.S. The home page also offers links to other archaeology sites.

**Access via:**
*www http://spirit.lib.uconn.edu/HTML/
archnet.html*

*gopher spirit.lib.uconn.edu/Academic
Subjects and Services/Information by Subject
Area (at Rice University)/Anthropology and
Culture/ArchNet - Archaeological Data at
UConn*

## Oriental Institute

The FTP server of the Oriental Institute of the University of Chicago hosts announcements and the newsletter of the Archaeological Institute of America, the archives of the Ancient Near East e-mail discussion list, announcements and the newsletter of the American Schools of Oriental Research, information about the Oriental Institute, its publications and holdings, along with some miscellaneous items of interest, and other research on the Ancient Near East. Encourages scholarly contributions.

**Access via:**
*ftp oi.uchicago.edu;* login *anonymous;*
cd *pub*

# ASTRONOMY

**Newsgroups:**
sci.[astro, astro.fits, astro.hubble, astro.planetarium]

## American Astronomical Society

Original material here is confined to information on the Society, meeting schedules, meeting abstracts, a staff directory and the AAS Job Register.

**Access via:**
*www http://blackhole.aas.org/
AAS-homepage.html*

## Astronomical Databases

This FTP site includes several databases of astronomical objects, including the Yale Bright Star catalog, the Saguaro Astronomy Club databases, and an asteroid database. Some IBM PC software for using these databases is also available.

**Access via:**
*ftp pomona.claremont.edu;* login *anonymous;*
cd *yale_bsc.dir*

## Astronomical Internet Resources

A hypertext roundup of worldwide Internet resources on astronomy and space, classed by method of access (WWW, Gopher, WAIS, FTP).

**Access via:**
*www http://stsci.edu/net-resources.html*

## Astronomy at University of Massachusetts, Amherst

Both technical tools and astronomical images are available at this expanding site.

**Access via:**
*www http://donald.phast.umass.edu/
umasshome.html*

## Centre de Donnés Astronomiques de Strasbourg

The Strasbourg Astronomical Data Center (CDS) is dedicated to the collection and worldwide distribution of astronomical data, and is located at the Observatoire de Strasbourg. The CDS hosts the SIMBAD astronomical database, a world reference database for the identification of astronomical objects, and other information and pointers of interest to stargazers.

**Access via:**
*www http://cdsweb.u-strasbg.fr/CDS.html*

## Conservatoire National des Arts et Metiers (Images)

A bilingual French and English astronomy site, specializing in pictures. *README* files in all subdirectories give size and description of each image, and images added within the past 15 days are listed in *READMENEW.* The FTP interface gives access to additional lists of images.

**Access via:**
*www http://web.cnam.fr/astro.english.html* (In English.)

*www http://web.cnam.fr/astro.french.html* (In French.)

*ftp ftp.cnam.fr;* login *anonymous;* cd *pub/Astro*

## Lunar and Planetary Institute Information

Information about NASA's Lunar and Planetary Institute and its services. It includes a bibliographic database and allows access to an electronic journal, "The Lunar & Planetary Information Bulletin." There is also a service called IRPS, which is the "Image Retrieval and Processing System." It is possible to order and (with the appropriate software) display digital images of the

planets. Primarily of use to researchers in lunar or planetary studies.

**Access via:**
*telnet lpi.jsc.nasa.gov;* login *lpi*

## NASA/IPAC Extragalactic Database

The NED contains information about over 200,000 astronomical objects, as well as abstracts and bibliographies of astronomical publications.

**Access via:**
*telnet denver.ipac.caltech.edu;* login *ned*

## NASA Langley Research Center

A WWW home page for this part of NASA. A link to "Other Government Labs" is interesting, too.

**Access via:**
*www http://mosaic.larc.nasa.gov/larc.html*

## NASA Information Services via WWW

Gives access to all the NASA Center home pages.

**Access via:**
*www http://hypatia.gsfc.nasa.gov/ NASA_homepage.html*

## National Space Science Data Center

The interface to many NASA data catalogs and centers. This system allows you to connect to facilities such as the Astronomical Data Center, access the CANOPUS newsletter, and get data from and about various satellite sensors.

**Access via:**
*telnet nssdca.gsfc.nasa.gov;* login *nodis*

### Project STELAR (Study of Electronic Literature for Astronomical Research)

A comprehensive home page for NASA's Goddard Space Flight Center's WWW server, highlighting the National Space Science Data Center's Project STELAR. Project STELAR itself is a pilot study of technical and practical issues in electronic access to astronomical literature; links are provided to relevant government and nongovernment resources too.

**Access via:**

*www http://hypatia.gsfc.nasa.gov/ STELAR_homepage.html*

### Space Images at Arizona

Maintained by the University of Arizona chapter of SEDS (Students for the Exploration and Development of Space), this site contains a considerable collection of images, along with other astronomical information.

**Access via:**

*ftp seds.lpl.arizona.edu; login anonymous; cd pub*

*gopher bozo.lpl.arizona.edu/ ANONYMOUS FTP*

### Space Remote Sensing Center

The Institute for Technology Development/ Space Remote Sensing Center, at NASA's Stennis Space Center in Mississippi, is a not-for-profit organization dedicated to the development and commercialization of remote sensing. It is also the North American Application Development Center for the pricey French SPOT Image Corporation. The contents are mostly data processing programs; there are also a few low-quality satellite images of the 1993 flood in the Midwest.

**Access via:**

*www http://ma.itd.com:8000/welcome.html*

*ftp pa.itd.com; login anonymous; cd pub*

### Space Telescope Science Institute

Information about the Hubble Space Telescope and the Space Telescope Science Institute. Includes instrument reports, ample data, grant information, FAQ lists, long- and short-range plans, software, etc.

**Access via:**

*www http://stsci.edu/top.html*

*gopher stsci.edu*

*ftp stsci.edu; login anonymous*

## AVIATION

**Newsgroup:**
rec.aviation

### Aeronautics Archives

A group of aviation archives. Among other things, these archives include rec.aviation postings, aircraft specifications, FAQs, and reviews of flight simulation software.

**Access via:**

WAIS *aeronautics.src*

*ftp rascal.ics.utexas.edu; login anonymous; cd misc/av*

### DUAT

Pilot flight services via the Internet. It provides pilots with weather briefings and flight planning services. You must be a pilot (or a student pilot) to use this resource.

**Access via:**
*telnet duat.gtefsd.com*

*telnet duats.gtefsd.com*
(For students.)

# BIOLOGY

**Newsgroups:**
sci.bio.[ecology, ethology, evolution, herp, technology], bionet.[cellbiol, general, molbio]

## Biology Overview

The revolution in biotechnology has provided a tremendous increase in the amount of information biologists are able to obtain about genetics and molecular biology. A worldwide increase in funding for genome research (the study of the information contained within the chromosomes of an organism), has caused the amount of new information to double yearly.

This increasing volume of information has created problems because the ability to distribute this genome information via traditional paper methods has been impossible for several years. The creation of the Internet protocols WAIS, Gopher, and WWW caused an explosion of biological information freely available on the Internet. Entries in this section represent Internet resources that specialize in information on one particular species, provide a specific type of information on all organisms, or distribute collections of general information. Most of these resources are Gopher servers, but many sites are rushing to convert their services into WWW.

## Arabidopsis Information

*Arabidopsis Thaliana* is a small, rather unimpressive flowering plant used as a model system for research on plant biology. The Arabidopsis Research Companion supplies a Gopher interface to a WAIS database of the information in the Arabidopsis Thaliana Database. Highlights include known DNA sequences, genes, straines, and research literature citations; but there's much more available.

**Access via:**
*gopher weeds.mgh.harvard.edu/Arabidopsis Information (thale cress)*

## Australian National University Bioinformatics Hypermedia Service: Biodiversity, Taxonomy, and Conservation

Plant biodiversity and conservation, including Australian and regional biodiversity information.

**Access via:**
*www http://life.anu.edu.au/biodiversity.html*

## Australian National University Bioinformatics Hypermedia Service: Molecular Biology

A directory of links to molecular biology databases, bibliographies, and other information.

**Access via:**
*www http://life.anu.edu.au/molbio.html*

## Biodiversity and Biological Collections Gopher

Run by Harvard University's Herbarium, "this Gopher contains information of interest to systematists and other biologists of the organismic kind." It also has information on Museum, Herbarium, and Arboretum collection catalogs, Biodiversity information resources, and other directories, publications, and software.

**Access via:**
*gopher huh.harvard.edu*

## Flybase

Information about Drosophila (fruit flies, to the uninitiated). The Gopher server has lots of other information for and about fly genetics. The entry for "stocks" is a searchable catalog of different genetic traits, and where to find flies with those traits. This is also an excellent site for pointers to other biology Gophers, software related to biology, news, and other material of interest.

**Access via:**
*gopher fly.bio.indiana.edu/Flybase*

## EMBNET Bioinformation Resources

EMBnet (European Molecular Biology Network) is a computer network for European molecular biology and biotechnology researchers. To date this multinational collaboration has focused on DNA and protein sequence databases as well as analysis software.

**Access via:**
*www http://shamrock.csc.fi/htbin/ imagerect/bank?64,314*

## GenBank & SwissProt

GenBank contains all published nucleic acid sequences. SwissProt, a European protein sequence database maintained by Amos Bairoch (Geneva) and the EMBL Data Library (Heidelberg), contains all published protein sequences. Searches of these databases may be based on accession number, description, locus name, keywords, source, organism, author, and title of journal article.

**Access via:**
*gopher ftp.bio.indiana.edu/Genbank-Sequences*

## Geneva University Hospital Molecular Biology Server

This server is also known as the ExPASy Molecular Biology Server and is located in Geneva. ExPASy is focused on the analysis of protein and nucleic acid sequences. Links are provided to a variety of sequence databases: SWISS-PROT, SWISS-2DPAGE, PROSITE, REBASE, EMBL, and OMIN, via Gopher, WAIS, and WWW.

**Access via:**
*www http://expasy.hcuge.ch*

## GrainGenes, the Triticeae Genome Gopher

The GrainGenes Project is one of several genome database efforts funded by the United States Department of Agriculture and the National Agricultural Library. GrainGenes contains information on the genetics, biology, pathology, and seed resources of a variety of commercially important grain species, including wheat, barley, and oats. This information is provided as images, WAIS indexes, and text files.

**Access via:**
*gopher greengenes.cit.cornell.edu*

## Johns Hopkins Bioinformatics Web Server

This creative WWW server provides a collection of interconnected protein sequence, structure, and enzyme function databases. These protein databases also include links to other information such as bibliographic citations from MEDLINE and pictures of three-dimensional crystal structures from the Brookhaven structural database (PDB). Electronic publications for biology include the *Primer on Molecular Genetics*, genomic information databases such as the Mouse Locus Catalog (with a fetching portrait of its subject), and links to other resources.

**Access via:**
*www http://www.gdb.org/hopkins.html*

## Indiana Molecular Biology Archives

An extensive collection of information on genetics and molecular biology, including the GenBank collection of nucleic acid sequences.

**Access via:**
*gopher fly.bio.indiana.edu/ Molecular-Biology/Archive*

*www http://fly.bio.indiana.edu*

## Maize Genome Database Gopher

The Maize Genome Database Project is one of several genome database efforts funded by the United States Department of Agriculture and the National Agricultural Library. The Maize Genome Gopher provides access via WAIS indexes to information derived from the relational database MaizeDB, maintained by Prof. Ed Coe and his colleagues at the University of Missouri. MaizeDB includes a wealth of information on Maize including scientific literature, genetic maps, Maize researchers worldwide, and a catalog of available seed lines. The Gopher also provides access to the Maize Newsletter via text files or a WAIS index.

**Access via:**
*gopher teosinte.agron.missouri.edu*

## Molecular Biology Sites

These links lead to a comprehensive Gopher site at Stanford that includes pointers to other Molecular Biology WWW, FTP, and Gopher sites.

**Access via:**
*gopher genome-gopher.stanford.edu/FTP Archives for Molecular Biology*
(Pointers to other sites.)

*gopher genome-gopher.stanford.edu/Global Biological Information Servers by Topic*
(Overview by topic.)

## Molecular Biology WAIS Databases

These WAIS databases are relevant to the subject of Molecular Biology.

**Access via:**
WAIS *biosci.src*
(All messages posted to the BioSci electronic conferences, on a variety of biological research topics.)

WAIS *biology-journal-contents.src*
(A collection of bibliographic references from several journals made available to the BioSci

system; updated weekly, Mondays 3 A.M. to 6 A.M. PST, and unavailable during this period.)

WAIS *prosite.src*
(PROSITE is a collection of protein sequence patterns that are characteristic of a particular function or type of protein. Included is a short descriptive summary of the patterns' significance as well as appropriate references to the literature.)

WAIS *REBASE-enzyme.src*
(Keywords are strings of amino acids, such as CCCGGG.)

WAIS *REBASE_help.src*

WAIS *REBASE_news.src*

WAIS *REBASE_references.src*

## National Genetic Resources Program Gopher

The NGRP Gopher server provides germplasm information about plants, animals, microbes, and insects within the National Genetic Resources Program of the U.S. Department of Agriculture's Agricultural Research Service (ARS). Links to the following topics are provided, along with links to other Gophers: National Plant Germplasm System (NPGS); National Animal Germplasm (including aquatics); National Microbial Germplasm; National Insect Genetic Resources; Plant Genome Database Gophers.

**Access via:**
*gopher gopher.ars-grin.gov*

## Pacific Rim Biodiversity Catalog

A catalog of the taxonomic, geographic, and temporal composition of the Pacific Rim zoological and paleontological holdings of scores of natural history institutions around the world. The catalog is searchable using keywords from a list provided. The project is a venture of the University of California Berkeley Museum of Paleontology and the Pacific Rim Research Program.

**Access via:**
*www http://ucmp1.berkeley.edu/ pacrim.html*

## TAXACOM FTP Server

An information service for systematic biology. Data includes back issues of the journal Flora Online; Beanbag, a newsletter for legume researchers; Taxonomic standards; and many other resources for taxonomists. The README.TAX file serves as a table of contents.

**Access via:**
*ftp huh.harvard.edu;* login *anonymous;* cd *pub*

# BOTANY

## Botany at Georgia

The Botany Department at the University of Georgia maintains this WWW site, including departmental information, overviews of work currently being done on problems extending from molecular genetic regulatory mechanisms to the ecology of acid rain, and a Greenhouse Tour (takes some time to load).

**Access via:**
*www http://dogwood.botany.uga.edu*

# BUSINESS

**Newsgroups:**
biz.*, comp.newprod, misc.jobs.[offered, wanted]

**See also:** Economics

## EDGAR

EDGAR is database of filings with the U.S. Securities and Exchange Commission (SEC). The file *full-index/company.idx* is an index (by company) of the files available.

**Access via:**
*ftp town.hall.org;* login *anonymous;* cd *edgar*

## NASDAQ Financial Executive Journal

An electronic version of a quarterly sent free of charge to NASDAQ National Market company Chief Financial Officers and by subscription to others. As of January 1994 there were three issues available of this joint project of the Legal Information Institute at Cornell Law School and the NASDAQ Stock Market.

**Access via:**
*www http://www.law.cornell.edu/nasdaq/ nasdtoc.html*

## North American Free Trade Agreement

NAFTA is complex; this resource provides an indexed view of the agreement and various ancillary documents. There is also currently an electronic conference on NAFTA sponsored by MexNET ("The Mexico Business Network"), for which a $25 registration fee is charged. For information on this conference send e-mail to john.peake@mexnet.org.

**Access via:**
*gopher wiretap.spies.com/North American Free Trade Agreement*

## Online Career Center

A resource for people who are recruiting employees or looking for jobs. It includes its own job listings and résumés, plus excerpts from other sources of job listings. There is also general corporate information, plus information about professional organizations, outplacement, and "employment events." You may post your résumé in their database by mailing it (in ASCII form) to the address below; the message's "Subject:" line is the résumé's title.

**Access via:**
*gopher garnet.msen.com/The Online Career Center*

**Information:**
E-mail: occ-resumes@msen.com; occ-info@mail.msen.com

## University of Minnesota Management Archive

Working papers, teaching materials, conference announcements, and the like, on the subject of business management. The archives of discussion lists sponsored by the Academy of Management are maintained here, too.

**Access via:**
*gopher chimera.sph.umn.edu*

## U.S. Commerce Business Daily

A demo issue of the Commerce Business Daily. The entire publication is available by subscription.

**Access via:**
*gopher gopher.counterpoint.com/ Counterpoint Publishing/United States Commerce Business Daily*

## Stock Market Summary

A summary of the activity of the world's stock markets, including the New York Stock Exchange. This is part of the demo information of a2i, and while very cumbersome to get to, it is at least updated daily.

After logging in as "guest", select "n" ("NEW SCREEN-ORIENTED GUEST MENU"), specify your terminal type, select item 13 ("Current system information"), and finally select item 6 ("Market report").

**Access via:**
*telnet a2i.rahul.net;* login *guest*

## Vienna Stock Exchange

Price and volume information for the Vienna Stock Exchange, covering the past day's trading and extending back a couple of months.

**Access via:**
*telnet fiivs01.tu-graz.ac.at;* login *boerse*

# CHEMISTRY

**Newsgroups:**
sci.[chem, engr.chem, chem.organomet]

**See also:** Molecular Biology

## American Chemical Society Gopher

Appears to cover journals and books published by the American Chemical Society, including a searchable index of ACS publications.

**Access via:**
*gopher infx.infor.com*

## Periodic Table of Elements

What else can you say?

**Access via:**
*gopher gopher.tc.umn.edu/Libraries/ Reference Works/Periodic Table of Elements*

## Molecular Graphics Software

Contains various pieces of the raster3D application for molecular graphics, including several previewers.

**Access via:**
*ftp stanzi.bchem.washington.edu;* login *anonymous;* cd *pub/raster3d*

## Sheffield Chemistry Server

Run by the Department of Chemistry at the University of Sheffield, this site offers a periodic table database, interactive isotope pattern calculator, and more.

**Access via:**
*www http://mac043025.shef.ac.uk/ chemistry/chemistry-home.html*

# CLASSICAL LANGUAGES & LITERATURE

**Newsgroup:**
sci.classics

**See also:** Archaeology; Literature

## Bryn Mawr Classical Review

Mostly a review journal of Greek and Latin classics, this database also includes public interest articles on the classics.

**Access via:**
WAIS *bryn-mawr-classical-review.src*

*gopher orion.lib.Virginia.EDU/Alphabetic Organization/Bryn Mawr Classical Review*

## Electronic Antiquity: Communicating the Classics

An Australian electronic journal inspired by the Bryn Mawr Classical Review and carrying academic articles on Greek and Roman Antiquity. The editors have maintained a monthly schedule since June 1993. There are both Gopher and FTP interfaces.

Please try to connect during off hours in Tasmania (Britain is more or less 10 hours behind Tasmanian time; California, 18 hours; Japan, 2 hours).

**Access via:**
*gopher info.utas.edu.au/Publications/ Electronic Antiquity: Communicating The Classics*

*ftp ftp.utas.edu.au; login anonymous; cd departments/classics/antiquity*

## Gesamtverzeichnis der griechischen Papyrusurkunden Aegyptens

This is an index of dated Greek papyri from Egypt, arranged by century. The contents of the documents are not included, but standard papyrological abbreviations point to the printed literature. Entries span the dates 331 B.C.– A.D. 835.

**Access via:**
*gopher sun3.urz.uni-heidelberg.de/ Fakultaeten und Institute/Institut fuer Papyrologie*

## Project Libellus (Classics)

Classical texts formatted in the TEX typesetting language, with the TEX files necessary to format them if you have TEX on your system, and TEX-to-ASCII conversion programs. Works by Caesar, Catullus, Livy, and Virgil are available, along with at least one commentary.

**Access via:**
*ftp ftp.u.washington.edu; login anonymous; cd public/libellus*

## Tables of Contents of Journals of Interest to Classicists

An extensive volunteer project to abstract the tables of contents of scholarly journals. You can search for the author or title of articles by topic (Archaeology, or Religion and Near Eastern Studies) but apparently not by field, although the files are marked up in such a way as to support such searching.

**Access via:**
*gopher gopher.lib.Virginia.EDU/Alphabetic Organization/TOCS-IN: Tables of Contents of journals of interest to classicists*

# COMPUTING

**Newsgroups:**

comp.admin, comp.sys.[3b1, acorn, alliant, amiga.*, apollo, apple2, atari.*, att, cbm, cdc, concurrent, dec, encore, handhelds, hp48, hp, ibm.pc.*, ibm.ps2.*, intel, isis, laptops, m6809, m68k, m88k, mac.*, mentor, mips, misc, ncr, newton, next.*, northstar, novell, nsc, palmtops, pen, powerpc, prime, proteon, pyramid, ridge, sequent, sgi, sun.*, super, tahoe, tandy, ti, transputer, unisys, xerox, zenith], comp.[ai, arch, cog-eng, compilers, compression, databases, dcom, editors, graphics, human-factors, lang, lsi, multimedia, music, parallel, programming, protocols, realtime, research, robotics, security, simulation, specification, terminals, theory, windows]

**See also:** Internet

## CERT

CERT, the Computer Emergency Response Team, is a federally funded group charged with dealing with computer and network security problems. Their server has papers about security concerns, tools to evaluate security, and an archive of alerts about current break-in attempts.

**Access via:**
ftp *cert.sei.cmu.edu;* login *anonymous;* cd *pub*

## CERT Security Advisories

Security has become a really hot topic in the past five years. Whether you're trying to protect your system from bright high school "crackers" or professional spies, it's certainly something you should keep informed about. CERT, the Computer Emergency Response Team, is a national focal point for security-related problems. When the CERT finds a security-related problem, it issues warnings to various mail lists. This is an indexed archive of those warnings. All system administrators should be aware of this archive!

To receive advisories as they are issued, send e-mail to cert@cert.sei.cmu.edu.

**Access via:**
WAIS *cert-advisories.src*

## Communications of the ACM

An experimental server offering the Communications of the ACM, from April 1989 to April 1992. It is unclear whether this will be offered in the future.

**Access via:**
WAIS *cacm.src*

## Comprehensive TEX Archive Network

Contains tools, fonts, graphics, etc., for use with the TEX typesetting system, as well as the TEX software itself for various computers. The computer typesetting system, TEX, is the subject of CTAN, the Comprehensive TEX Archive Network.

**Access via:**
ftp *ftp.shsu.edu;* login *anonymous;* cd *tex-archive/*

## Compression and Archival Software Summary

A table listing available software, by type of computer, to do and undo archiving and compression. For example: If you use an IBM PC running MS-DOS, and you want to read a UNIX compressed file, what software do you need? Where would you get the software? The more you use the Internet, the more this table will help you.

**Access via:**
ftp *ftp.cso.uiuc.edu;* login *anonymous;* cd *doc/pcnet;* get *compression*

*Excerpt from* **Computer Ethics Archive**, *7/1/85:*

COMPUTER CRIME AND UNLAWFUL
COMPUTER ACCESS

According to Section 21-3755 of
the Kansas Criminal Code, which
went into effect July 1, 1985,
computer crime is:

a) Willfully and without authorization gaining or attempting to
gain access to and damaging,
modifying, altering, destroying,
copying, disclosing, or taking
possession of a computer,
computer system, computer
network, or any other property;

b) using a computer, computer
system, computer network, or any
other property for the purpose
of devising or executing a scheme
or artifice with the intent to
defraud or for the purpose of
obtaining money, property, services, or any other thing of
value by means of false or fraudulent pretense or representation; or

c) willfully exceeding the limits
of authorization and damaging,
modifying, altering, destroying,
copying, disclosing, or taking
possession of a computer,
computer system, computer
network, or any other property.

## Computational Science Education Project

Electronic teaching materials for advanced
undergraduates and beginning graduate
students in computational sciences and
engineering, from Vanderbilt University.

**Access via:**
*www http://csep1.phy.ornl.gov/csep.html*

## Computer Ethics

Contains the computing ethics policies of over
thirty universities. It also includes a bibliography, the BITNET abuse policy, and relevant
laws covering computer crime from Canada
and several states in the U.S.

**Access via:**
*ftp ariel.unm.edu;* login *anonymous;* cd *ethics*

## Computer Science Archive Sites

This is a list of 210 sites that provide
collections of computer science technical
reports through anonymous FTP. This list is
regularly posted to the news group
comp.doc.techreports.

**Access via:**
WAIS *cs-techreport-archives.src*

## Computer Science Paper Bibliography

The file is a list of journal articles from many
computer journals. You can either get the
entire list via FTP, or use WAIS to search for
interesting articles.

**Access via:** *ftp cayuga.cs.rochester.edu;*
login *anonymous;* cd *pub;* get *papers.1st*

## Computer Science Tech Reports

A collection of technical reports, abstracts,
and papers in the field of Computer Science.

**Access via:**
WAIS *cs-techreport-abstracts.src*

WAIS *cs-techreport-archives.src*

**Information:**
E-mail: farrell@coral.cs.jcs.edu.au

## Cryptography for Computers

The subject of cryptography grows more important to computing and the Internet with every passing day. Here are the leading resources we've located.

CipherText is newsletter in ASCII, new in November 1993, covering current cryptographic issues.

**Access via:**
ftp *rsa.com;* login *anonymous;*
cd *pub/ciphertext*

These sites offer a wide selection of documents and software pertaining to cryptography.

**Access via:**
ftp *scss3.cl.msu.edu;* login *anonymous;*
cd *pub/crypt*

ftp *black.ox.ac.uk;* login *anonymous;*
cd *DOCS/security*

ftp *ripem.msu.edu;* login *anonymous;*
cd *pub/crypt*

ftp *ftp.dsi.unimi.it;* login *anonymous;*
cd *pub/security*

## Free Software Foundation

The Free Software Foundation (FSF) is an organization devoted to the creation and dissemination of software that is free from licensing fees or restrictions. Software is distributed under the terms of the "General Public License," which also provides a good summary of the Foundation's goals and principles. The FSF has developed the GNU Emacs editor, in addition to replacements for many UNIX utilities and many other tools. A complete UNIX-like operating system (HURD) is in the works. FSF software is available from many places; the archive listed here is probably the most complete and up-to-date. In addition to the software itself, a number of position papers for the FSF are available. To read the GPL, look at the files whose names begin with *COPYING*.

**Access via:**
ftp *prep.ai.mit.edu;* login *anonymous;*
cd *pub/gnu*

## High Performance Computing and Communications

The National Coordination Office for HPCC provides Internet users with access to material about the Federal HPPC Program.

**Access via:**
www *http://www.hpcc.gov*

## Information System for Advanced Academic Computing

An information service for IBM customers to promote the use of their high-end computers in research and education.

**Access via:**
telnet *isaac.engr.washington.edu*
(Must apply for an account; can take a few weeks.)

**Information:**
E-mail: isaac@isaac.engr.washington.edu

## INRIA Bibliography

The library catalog of the Institut National de la Recherche en Informatique et en Automatique (INRIA). The institute's mission is to provide for the management and knowledge transfer of scientific and technological information. The database, which is updated nightly, contains thousands of research reports, Ph.D. dissertations, and conference proceedings, along with hundreds of periodical subscriptions and videos. Keywords and catalogs are maintained in English and French.

**Access via:**
www *http://zenon.inria.fr:8003*

WAIS *bibs-zenon-inria-fr.src*

**Information:**
E-mail: doc@sophia.inria.fr

## The Jargon File

This is a computing jargon dictionary. It was the basis for the book *The New Hacker's Dictionary.*

**Access via:**
*www http://web.cnam.fr/bin.html/ By_Searchable_Index* (Hypertext version.)

WAIS *jargon.src*

## League for Programming Freedom

The League for Programming Freedom is an organization that opposes software patents and interface copyrights. They maintain an archive of position papers and legal information about important test cases.

**Access via:**
*ftp prep.ai.mit.edu;* login *anonymous;* cd *pub/lpf*

**Information:**
E-mail: lpf@uunet.uu.net

## Multimedia

A substantial list of pointers to multimedia software, resources, and demos on the Internet.

**Access via:**
*www http://cui_www.unige.ch/OSG/ MultimediaInfo*

## Neural Networking Collection

A collection of literature, bibliographies, and indexes for the study of neural networks.

**Access via:**
WAIS *neuroprose.src*

*ftp archive.cis.ohio-state.edu;*

login *anonymous;* cd *pub/neuroprose*

---

*Excerpt from* **The Jargon File**, *3/16/94*

**kluge**
/klooj/ [from the German 'klug', clever] 1. n. A Rube Goldberg (or Heath Robinson) device, whether in hardware or software. (A long-ago "Datamation" article by Jackson Granholme said: "An ill-assorted collection of poorly matching parts, forming a distressing whole.")

**snarf**
/snarf/ vt 1. To grab, esp. to grab a large document or file for the purpose of using it with or without the author's permission. See also BLT

**wetware**
/wet'weir/ [prob. from the novels of Rudy Rucker] n
1. The human nervous system, as opposed to computer hardware or software.
2. Human beings (programmers, operators, administrators) attached to a computer system, as opposed to the system's hardware or software. See liveware, meatware.

## NeXT.FAQ

A set of frequently asked questions about NeXT computers, dealing with hardware, software, specialized jargon, and configurations.

**Access via:**
WAIS *NeXT.FAQ.src*

**Information:**
E-mail: akers@next2.oit.unc.edu

## Non-Latin Character Sets

Here we've gathered some resources that deal with fonts and character sets for languages that do not use the Latin alphabet.

**Access via:**
*ftp rama.poly.edu;* login *anonymous;*
cd *pub/reader*
(For Arabic script — Arabic, Persian, Urdu, etc.)

*ftp ifcss.org;* login *anonymous;*
cd *archive/act-info;* get *act.faq*
(For Chinese.)

*ftp ftp.uwtc.washington.edu;*
login *anonymous;* cd *pub/Japanese*
(For Japanese.)

*ftp mimsy.umd.edu;* login *anonymous;*
cd *pub/cyrillic*
(For Russian.)

## PC Magazine

Utility programs for IBM PC–compatibles, from PC Magazine, published by Ziff Davis.

This is just one of many places where this resource is available. Find others with "archie pcmag".

**Access via:**
*ftp ftp.wustl.edu;* login *anonymous;*
cd *systems/ibmpc/msdos/pcmag*

## Public UNIX Access

A few sites on the Internet are "freeish" public UNIX servers. The number of concurrent users is limited. On some servers, priority is given to "patrons" who make donations to keep the service alive.

**Access via:**
*telnet nyx.cs.du.edu;* login *new*

## Repository of Machine Learning Databases and Domain Theories

The repository contains documented datasets and domain theories to evaluate machine learning algorithms in various areas. Some of the areas available are materials science, games, medicine, mechanical analysis, pattern recognition, and economics.

**Access via:**
*ftp ics.uci.edu;* login *anonymous;*
cd *pub/machine-learning-databases*

**Information:**
E-mail: ml-repository@ics.uci.edu

## San Diego Supercomputer Documentation

Primarily designed as a service to their own users; a lot of the information is not relevant to the average person. However, it is a free place to look at Cray documentation. If you want to find out what it's like to use a supercomputer, you can look here.

**Access via:**
WAIS *San_Diego_Super_Computer_Center_Docs.src*

## SGML (Standard Generalized Markup Language)

SGML is a standard document markup language, increasingly used for marking up documents for interchange and for use with multiple document processing tools. The following sites all mirror each other to some degree.

**Access via:**
WAIS *SGML.src*

One of the best SGML information archives is maintained by the International SGML Users Group at the University of Oslo.

**Access via:**
*ftp ftp.ifi.uio.no;* login *anonymous;*
cd *pub/SGML;* get *FAQ.0.0*
(A must for novice SGMLers.)

At Exeter, the SGML Project maintains a site that includes the archive of the Text Encoding Initiative (TEI), a major SGML effort aimed at representing historical literature, among other things.

**Access via:**

*ftp sgml1.ex.ac.uk; login anonymous; cd tei*

Documents produced by the SGML Users' Group's (SGML-UG) Special Interest Group on Hypertext and Multimedia (SIGhyper) may be searched by WAIS.

**Access via:**

WAIS *SIGHyper.src*

The University of Virginia Rare Book School maintains a set of documents explaining SGML and how to use it. There is also a very substantial archive of historical texts marked up in SGML, with plain text versions, and in some cases images of the documents. Access to texts restricted to University of Virginia users—which is frustrating because this would otherwise be the most significant collection of electronic text available.

**Access via:**

*gopher orion.lib.Virginia.EDU/Electronic Text Center*

## Supernet

A bulletin board system for people doing supercomputing. General areas of postings include a research register, job bank, supercomputing journal review, and software.

**Access via:**

*telnet supernet.ans.net; login hpcwire*

## UNIX Booklist

A compilation of UNIX and C book titles, along with pertinent information for locating them (including ISBN, publisher, and ordering information where available). Also includes short reviews and summaries of book contents. Maintained by Mitch Wright in his spare time. He encourages contributions and corrections.

**Access via:**

*ftp ftp.rahul.net; login anonymous; cd pub/mitch/YABL; get yabl*

**Information:**

E-mail: Mitch@yahoo.cirrus.com

## UUNET FTP Archives

One of the largest archives of free source code and USENET news available. The file *ls-lR.Z* is a compressed master list of everything that's available. You can also search the UUNET archives using WAIS.

**Access via:**

*ftp ftp.uu.net; login anonymous*

## WAIS Software Search Sources

An extension of Archie, searchable through WAIS, using some of the same techniques as Netfind. Make sure you read the WAIS source file listed below to understand how to search it.

**Access via:**

WAIS *dynamic-archie.src*

# COOKING

**Newsgroups:**

rec.food.[cooking, drink, recipes, restaurants, sourdough, veg], rec.crafts.brewing

## Beer & Brewing

Spencer's Beer Page is a general-purpose all-around collection of resources on beer, ale, and brewing, from "kegging" to "wort chillers." It's maintained by Spencer W. Thomas, at the University of Michigan.

### Access via:

*www http://guraldi.itn.med.umich.edu/Beer*

This library contains a good collection of beer recipes and other information. Lots of information for home brewers, including software, recipe books, and archives of the Homebrew mailing list. Send subscription requests to homebrew-request.

### Access via:

*ftp mthvax.cs.miami.edu;* login *anonymous;* cd *homebrew*

Or search the relevant WAIS database:

### Access via:

WAIS *homebrew.src*

## Fat-Free FAQ

The "FAQ" is actually a directory of information about fat-free cooking; there is also a fat-free/vegetarian recipe archive.

### Access via:

*ftp rahul.net;* login *anonymous;* cd *pub/artemis/fatfree/FAQ* (FAQ.)

*ftp ftp.halcyon.com;* login *anonymous;* cd *pub/recipes* (Recipe archive.)

## Info and Softserver

A general information server at the University of Stuttgart. Has a collection of recipes and a cookbook online. Instructions are presented in German. Recipes are in both German and English.

### Access via:

*telnet rusmv1.rus.uni-stuttgart.de/cookbook;* login *info*

## Recipe Archives

Recipe archives are proliferating; the largest are those containing recipes that have passed through the rec.food.cooking and rec.food.recipes newsgroups.

### Access via:

WAIS *recipes.src*
(A set of recipes searchable by keyword and contents.)

WAIS *usenet-cookbook.src*

*ftp gatekeeper.dec.com;* login *anonymous;* cd *pub/recipes* (Organized by title.)

*www http://www.vuw.ac.nz/non-local/ recipes-archive/recipe-archive.html* (Archives of the rec.food.recipes newsgroup, and the rec.food.cooking FAQ.)

## Sourdough

Over half a dozen FAQs, on starters, bread, and sauerkraut.

### Access via:

*ftp microlib.cc.utexas.edu;* login *anonymous;* cd *pub/sourdough*

# ECONOMICS

**Newsgroup:**
sci.econ

**See also:** Business

## Economics Overview

There are many useful resources for economists and business users in general on the Internet. A comprehensive overview of many of these resources, "Resources for Economists on the Internet," by William L. Goffe, can be found at the Sam Houston State Gopher, and in other locations, too.

Among the best repositories of information (all of which have their own entries in this *Catalog*) are the U.S. Department of Commerce's Economic Bulletin Board, which lists a huge amount of current and historic U.S. macroeconomic data; the Rice Economics Gopher; and the Washington University Economics Working Paper Archive. These services are specifically designed to serve the needs of economists.

## Cliometric Society

Contains searchable indexes of the membership lists of the Cliometric Society and the Economic History Association, along with the Cliometric Society's Newsletter and abstracts from ASSA meetings.

**Access via:**
*gopher nextsrv.cas.muohio.edu/Cliometric Society*

## Economic Bulletin Board

Resources and pointers for both domestic and international trade.

**Access via:**
*gopher una.hh.lib.umich.edu/ebb*

## Economic Data

Among tools for economists, much macroeconomic data is available in Clopper Almon's EconData package at the University of Maryland, which, when linked with its analysis and display package, is an especially useful tool for users of personal computers.

**Access via:**
*gopher info.umd.edu/Educational Resources/ Economic Data*

## Rice Economics Gopher

A compendium of Gopherable economics resources, updated weekly. Contains information from the 1990 census, lots of news about Asia and the Pacific Rim, plus access to several other resources covering economics and business. The latter group includes a TELNET-based bulletin board run by the U.S. commerce department. Also contains the electronic journal "Internet Business Journal: Commercial Opportunities in the Networking Age."

**Access via:**
*gopher chico.rice.edu/Information by Subject Area/Economics and Business*

## Sam Houston State University Economics Gopher

This site displays an extensive array of economics resources, including many pointers to resources at other sites. It is maintained by the Network Access Initiative sponsored by the university's Department of Economics and Business Analysis. The site is organized and maintained by George D. Greenwade. Among the highlights is a particularly well organized and extensive bibliography of resources, written by Bill Goffe, "Resources for Economists on the Internet."

**Access via:**
*gopher niord.shsu.edu/Economics (SHSU Network Access Initiative Project)*

## University of Manchester NetEc Gopher

A major source of economics papers in two parts: BibEc, an ASCII bibliography, and WoPEc, a collection of working papers in compressed PostScript format.

**Access via:**
*gopher uts.mcc.ac.uk/Economics—NetEc*

## University of Michigan Economics Gopher

Includes bibliographies, data sets, and a section on the "Economics of the Internet."

**Access via:**
*gopher alfred.econ.lsa.umich.edu*

## Washington University Economics Working Paper Archive

An extensive archive of economics working papers, catalogued by subject matter. Abstracts are available in ASCII, and most other papers are in TEX or PostScript. Both Gopher and WWW interfaces are available.

**Access via:**
*gopher econwpa.wustl.edu*

*www http://econwpa.wustl.edu/ Welcome.html*

# EDUCATION

**Newsgroups:**
k12.ed.[art, business, comp.literacy, health-pe, life-skills, math, music, science, soc-studies, special, tag, tech] and k12.lang.[art, deutsch-eng, esp-eng, francais, russian]

## Academe This Week

Excerpts from the Chronicle of Higher Education, the weekly tabloid that covers all aspects of the college and university business.

**Access via:**
*gopher chronicle.merit.edu*

## Educator's Guide to E-mail Lists

A quite long collection of e-mail lists that may be of interest to teachers.

**Access via:**
*ftp nic.umass.edu; login anonymous; cd pub/ednet; get educatrs.lst*

## ERIC Digests Archive

Short reports of 1,500 words or fewer, of interest to teachers, administrators, and others in the field of education. The reports are typically overviews of information on a given topic. Reports were produced by the ERIC Clearinghouses, funded by the U.S. Department of Education.

**Access via:**
WAIS *eric-archives.src*

WAIS *eric-digests.src*

WAIS *AskERIC-Helpsheets.src*

WAIS *AskERIC-infoguides.src*

WAIS-*AskERIC-Lesson-Plans.src*

WAIS *AskERIC-Minisearches.src*

WAIS *AskERIC-Questions.src*

## Federal Information Exchange

 An information liaison between various government agencies and the higher education community. Provides timely information on federal education and research programs, scholarships and fellowships, surplus equipment, funding opportunities, and general information.

**Access via:**
*telnet fedix.fie.com; login new*

## International Centre for Distance Learning

This database concentrates on "distance learning": correspondence courses, courses offered via television or audiotape, and other forms of "remote education." The database includes descriptions of "distance-learning" programs, and secondary literature about distance learning. The courses cover all academic disciplines (humanities, arts, sciences, engineering, agriculture, medicine, social sciences), all educational levels (from primary to post-graduate), and are taken from all parts of the world. This is normally a "for-pay" resource; the file *icdlinfo* describes how to register for an account. As of early 1994, this was being offered free, with a disclaimer that it may not remain so.

**Access via:**
*telnet acsvax.open.ac.uk;* login *ICDL;* give country name without spaces as account code; password *AAA*

*telnet acsvax.open.ac.uk;* login *ICDL* (For icdlinfo file.)

**Information:**
E-mail: n.ismail@vax.acs.open.ac.uk (comments on database); E-mail: l.r.a.melton@vax.acs.open.ac.uk (enquiries)

Telephone: +44.908.653537

## Minority Online Information Service

Information about Black and Hispanic colleges and universities. Includes information on faculty, academic programs, degrees granted, and specialties. Part of the Federal Information Exchange.

**Access via:**
*telnet fedix.fie.com;* login *new*

## National Center on Adult Literacy (NCAL)

NCAL's Gopher includes information on literacy programs in the U.S. and abroad.

**Access via:**
*gopher litserver.literacy.upenn.edu*

## Software and Aids for Teaching of Mathematics

A collection of software to aid in the teaching of mathematics at the college and university levels. Also includes newsletters, reprints, and other material of interest in the area. Most of the software is for IBM PC compatibles. Other computers may be supported in the future.

**Access via:**
*ftp archives.math.utk.edu;* login *anonymous*

**Information:**
E-mail: husch@math.utk.edu

## SpaceMet

**See:** Aeronautics and Astronautics.

## Teacher*Pages

A resource provided by Penn State University for educators at all levels. Information is available for many different school levels, academic areas, and subject areas.

**Access via:**
*telnet psupen.psu.edu;* login your two-letter state abbreviation

## U.S. Department of Education Gopher

New in November 1993, this Gopher provides information about the Department of Education's programs and staff, along with announcements, press releases, and pointers to other resources.

**Access via:**
*gopher gopher.ed.gov*

# ELECTRONIC MAGAZINES

**Newsgroups:**
alt.[authorware, etext, motherjones, wired, zines], rec.mag

## Electronic Magazines Overview

Hundreds of electronic publications have been started in the past few years. Some of these are still in production; the static hulks of others litter many an Internet site.

Most are in ASCII text format, although a few are in proprietary or system-specific formats (i.e., Macintosh HyperCard). Distribution methods include e-mail, USENET, FTP, Gopher, and World Wide Web.

## The CICNet Electronic Journal Project

Intended to be a comprehensive archive of electronic journals and other publications. Possibly out of date; the index was last updated in July 1993.

**Access via:**
gopher *gopher.cic.net/Electronic Serials*

## e-zine-list

A directory of electronically accessible 'zines, often personal and esoteric. Updated monthly.

**Access via:**
ftp *ftp.netcom.com;* login *anonymous;*
cd *pub/johnl/zines;* get *e-zine-list*
(In ASCII.)

www *file://ftp.netcom.com/pub/johnl/*
*zines/e-zine-list.html*
(In HTML.)

## Electric Eclectic

A multimedia Internet journal based on the MIME standard. The Eclectic is envisioned as a "meta-journal" or collection of "virtual magazines" on various topics, including literature, art, philosophy, current events, music, and almost anything else imaginable.

**Information:**
E-mail: ee-subscribe@eit.com
E-mail: ee-submit@eit.com
E-mail: ee-discuss-request@eit.com
E-mail: ee-volunteer@eit.com

## Fine Art Forum

Fine Art Forum is a monthly magazine of arts announcements from persons and organizations in the U.S. and Europe. Although the magazine itself is still only ASCII text, a WWW front end has been added, with pictures of the artists and their works, and links to other arts resources on the Net.

**Access via:**
www *http://www.msstate.edu/*
*Fineart_Online/home.html*

gopher *gopher.msstate.edu/Resources*
*Maintained at MsState University/FineArt*
*Forum Online*

ftp *ftp.msstate.edu;* login *anonymous;*
cd *pub/archives/fineart_online*

## GRIST Online

A monthly, text-only magazine of poetry. Also has a few essays, letters to the editor, and calendars and announcements of readings, shows, and workshops. GRIST was originally published in print in the 1960s and has been revived for the electronic medium (although print editions are still available).

**Access via:**
gopher *etext.archive.umich.edu/Poetry/Grist*

ftp *etext.archive.umich.edu;*
login *anonymous;* cd *pub/Poetry/Grist*

## International Teletimes

A monthly general-interest publication from Vancouver, Canada. Themes of past issues include history, the environment, and human rights. Regular departments feature a photography gallery and cuisine from around the world.

**Access via:**
www *http://www.wimsey.com/*
*teletimes.root/teletimes_home_page.html*

## Mother Jones Magazine

Still carrying the torch of "progressive" politics, but now in hypertext.

**Access via:**
*www http://www.mojones.com*

## Quanta Magazine

The science fiction and fantasy magazine Quanta, in ASCII and PostScript formats.

**Access via:**
*gopher gopher.cic.net/Electronic Serials/ Alphabetic List/Q/Quanta*

*ftp export.acs.cmu.edu; login anonymous; cd pub/quanta*

*ftp catless.newcastle.ac.uk; login anonymous; cd pub/Quanta*

## The University of Michigan Electronic Text Archive

A large and current archive of 'zines and other publications. The definitive source for current publications.

**Access via:**
*gopher etext.archive.umich.edu*

## Whole Earth 'Lectronic Magazine

An electronic journal consisting mostly of fiction and book reviews. The server on which it sits contains areas on art, communications, cyberpunk, the Grateful Dead, the military and its practices, and issues of the Whole Earth Review (successor to the Whole Earth Catalog). This magazine is published by the WELL (Whole Earth 'Lectronic Link), which was one of the early efforts at creating an electronic community, and was also spawned by the Whole Earth Catalog.

**Access via:**
*gopher gopher.well.sf.ca.us/Whole Earth Review, the Magazine*

# ENGINEERING

**Newsgroups:**
sci.engr, sci.engr.[chem, biomed, civil, control, manufacturing, mech]

## Cornell Theory Center Server

The Cornell Theory Center is one of four National Advanced Scientific Computing Centers supported by the National Science Foundation, and this is its home page. The site supports serious computer software and documentation only.

**Access via:**
*www http://www.tc.cornell.edu/ctc.html*

# ENVIRONMENTAL STUDIES

**Newsgroups:**
sci.[environment, bio.ecology], talk.environment

## BSIM Simulation Package

The Habitat Ecology Division of the Bedford Institute of Oceanography developed this simulation package, which is designed to help develop ecosystem models.

**Access via:**
*gopher biome.bio.ns.ca/BSIM simulation package*

*ftp biome.bio.dfo.ca; login anonymous; cd pub/bsim*

## Carbon Dioxide Information Analysis Center

CDIAC is part of Oak Ridge National Laboratory. It provides information to researchers, policymakers, and educators about atmostpheric changes and climate change (in particular, "global warming"). Contains both data and scientific papers in this area. In addition to information about carbon dioxide levels, there is also information about CFCs (chlorinated fluorocarbons) and other gases. Sponsored by the U.S. Department of Energy.

**Access via:**
*ftp cdiac.esd.ornl.gov; login anonymous; cd pub*

## CIESIN Global Change Information Gateway

The Consortium for International Earth Science Information Network (CIESIN) provides information from the Socioeconomic Data and Application Center (SEDAC), CIESIN's gateway to the NASA Earth Observation System Data and Information System (EOSDIS), and the Global Change Research Information Office (GCRIO), CIESIN's gateway to the U.S. Global Change Research Program.

**Access via:**
*gopher gopher.ciesin.org*

## Environmental Protection Agency Library

A catalog to the holdings of the EPA's national library. The database has subsections for material on hazardous waste, lake management and protection, and chemical agents. The library includes EPA reports and many other kinds of documents. Includes abstracts.

**Access via:**
*telnet epaibm.rtpnc.epa.gov; select PUBLIC*

## Environmental Safety & Health Information Center

The Environmental Safety & Health Information Center (ESHIC) contains Department of Energy information relating to the environment.

**Access via:**
WAIS *eshic.src*

## ERIN (Environmental Resources Information Network)

A World Wide Web cover page that collects information and newsletters about ecology-related programs, projects, and issues, primarily in Australia.

**Access via:**
*www http://kaos.erin.gov.au/erin.html*

## Gopherable Environmental Studies Resources Index

A comprehensive index of Gopherable environmental resources.

**Access via:**
*gopher gopher.unr.edu/Selected Information Resources by Discipline/Environmental Studies Resources*

## Oak Ridge National Laboratory (Environmental Science Division)

The Oak Ridge National Laboratory, now run by Martin Marietta Energy Systems for the U.S. Department of Energy, is emphasizing its environmental concerns:

"Whose 'backyard' should we store hazardous wastes in? What would restore public confidence in nuclear power? What's the best way to encourage investments in energy efficiency? Over the past two decades, ORNL has developed social science theory and tools to tackle energy and environmental problems such as these. By teaming social scientists with physical scientists, analyses are conducted that reflect the complexity of real-world choices."

**Access via:**
*www http://jupiter.esd.ornl.gov*

## Pesticides

An agricultural extension bulletin written by Sue Snider and Mark Graustein. This bulletin explains what a pesticide is, the laws that regulate pesticides, and their uses, benefits, and detriments.

**Access via:**
*gopher bluehen.ags.udel.edu/Search AGINFO/Pesticides*

## United Nations Rio Conference Agenda

**See:** Law, Columbia Online Legal Resources (JANUS)

## Water Quality Education Materials

A set of educational materials on U.S. water quality assessment, maintenance, and improvement, provided by the Cooperative Extension System.

**Access via:**
WAIS *water-quality.src*

# FORESTRY

## Dendrome: Forest Tree Genome Mapping Database

Dendrome is a collection of specialized forest tree genome databases being developed by the Institute of Forest Genetics under the auspices of the National Agricultural Library.

**Access via:**
*gopher s27w007.pswfs.gov*

## Social Sciences in Forestry

An annotated bibliography of the Forestry Library at the University of Minnesota, College of Natural Resources. The bibliography covers many areas of forestry, including the history, legislation, taxation, social and communal forestry, and agroforestry.

**Access via:**
*gopher minerva.forestry.umn.edu/Social Sciences in Forestry Bibliography*

## Trees

Various kinds of information about trees, including care and maintenance, planting, selection, and signs and symptoms of tree problems, thanks to the University of Delaware Agricultural Extension Service.

**Access via:**
*gopher bluehen.ags.udel.edu/Info by type of publication/Fact Sheets/Ornamental Horticulture*

# FREE-NETS

## Free-Net Overview

Free-Nets are grassroots efforts to provide networking services to an urban community, with access either at public libraries or by dialing in. It's also possible to access Free-Nets through the Internet. Free-Nets are usually organized around a model town that you "walk" through. You can stop at the "courthouse and government center" and discuss local issues with the mayor. Or you can stop by the "medical arts building" and discuss health issues with a health professional. Aside from discussions, there are usually bulletin boards, electronic mail, and other information services.

There are real hidden gem resources on some Free-Nets. These are indexed separately. Anyone can use a Free-Net as a guest, but guest privileges are limited; for example, you can't use e-mail and a few other things. You can get further privileges by registering; registration is usually free to people within a certain district, and available at nominal charge to those outside. When you log in as a guest, you'll probably see a message telling you how to get registration information.

Free-Net software is menu-driven and designed for ease of use. So give them a try. If you think you'd like to organize a Free-Net for your town, contact Dr. T. M. Grundner at *tmg@nptn.org*.

## Buffalo Free-Net

Contains information about Western New York.

**Access via:**
*telnet freenet.buffalo.edu;* login *freeport*

## CapAccess: The National Capital Area Public Access Network

A Free-Net for the Washington, D.C., metropolitan area. Concentrates on K-12 education, health and social services, library services, and government.

**Access via:**
*telnet cap.gwu.edu;* login *guest;* password *visitor*

## Cleveland Free-Net

The original Free-Net and still the hub of Free-Net development. Very heavily used, and therefore hard to log in to.

**Access via:**
*telnet freenet-in-a.cwru.edu*

## Columbia Online Information Network

Community, education, and local government information for the Columbia, Missouri, area.

**Access via:**
*telnet bigcat.missouri.edu;* login *guest*

## Denver Free-Net

Fairly strong on the fine arts.

**Access via:**
*telnet freenet.hsc.colorado.edu;* login *guest*

## Erlangen-Nuernberg Free-Net

A Free-Net located in Germany, with topics including the European Community, film and video, education, and recreation. Menus are in German and English.

**Access via:**
*telnet freenet-a.fim.uni-erlangen.de;* login *gast*

## Heartland Free-Net

A Free-Net centered in Peoria, Illinois. Contains information about recreation and jobs in the State of Illinois. Check the "home and garden center" for information about gardening.

**Access via:**
*telnet heartland.bradley.edu;* login *bbguest*

## Lorain County Free-Net

A Free-Net centered in Elyria, Ohio. Pen pals, even some games.

**Access via:**
*telnet freenet.lorain.oberlin.edu;* login *guest*

## National Capital Free-Net (Canada)

Some French-language menus; Canadian resources; Canadian politics.

**Access via:**
*telnet freenet.carleton.ca;* login *guest*

## Tallahassee Free-Net

This Florida Free-Net includes information on business, religion, disabilities, and gardening.

**Access via:**
*telnet freenet.fsu.edu;* login *visitor*

## Victoria (British Columbia) Free-Net

Contains sections on the environment and medicine.

**Access via:**
*telnet freenet.victoria.bc.ca;* login *guest*

## Youngstown Free-Net

A Free-Net centered in Youngstown, Ohio. Very strong health section (see "hospital"), veterinarian (see "animal hospital"), and human services.

**Access via:**
*telnet yfn.ysu.edu;* login *visitor*

# GARDENING

**Newsgroup:**
rec.gardens

## The Gardener's Assistant

A shareware program for the personal computer (IBM PC) that assists one in planning and planting a garden. You feed it a bunch of information, and it tells you what type of plants to grow, when to plant, and how to care for them. Registration information is available.

**Access via:**
*ftp wuarchive.wustl.edu;*
cd *systems/ibmpc/msdos/database;*
get *gardener.zip*

## Master Gardener Information

This Gopher server (run by the Texas Agricultural Extension Service) offers information on fruits and nuts, flowering plants, annual and perennial ornamental trees and shrubs, turf grasses, and vegetables.

**Access via:**
*gopher gopher.tamu.edu/Texas A&M Gophers/Texas Agricultural Extension Service Gopher (Linux)/Master Gardener Information*

## University of Missouri Horticulture Guides

Scores of articles, covering topics from "Armillaria root rot in fruit orchards" to "Vegetable harvest and storage." The emphasis is on the Missouri perspective, but much of the information is valuable wherever you garden.

**Access via:**
*gopher bigcat.missouri.edu/Reference and Information Center/University of Missouri Horticulture Guides*

# GEOGRAPHY

## CIA World Map

The CIA map database. The directory includes a map drawing program.

**Access via:**
*ftp ftp.cs.toronto.edu;* login *anonymous;*
cd *doc/geography/CIA_World_Map*

## Geographic Information Server

An interface to data supplied by the U.S. Geodetic Survey and the U.S. Postal Service. Make requests by name (Sebastopol, or

Sebastopol, CA); the server returns latitude, longitude, population, zip code, elevation, etc.

Not all of this information is correct (zip code for Sebastopol, for example)!

**Access via:**
*www http://sipb.mit.edu:8001/geo*

*telnet martini.eecs.umich.edu 3000*

# GEOLOGY

**Newsgroup:**
sci.geo.geology

## Computer Oriented Geological Society (COGS)

The archives of the Computer Oriented Geological Society's bulletin board service. It contains lots of interesting material, including application forms for membership in the society. One file that's particularly worth having is *internet.resources.earth.sci*. This is a detailed list of many resources available, including many data archives, digitized maps, bibliographies, and online publications. There's also a lot of software available, for disciplines such as Geophysics, Geochemistry, Hydrology, Mineralogy, Mining, oil exploration, etc. Landsat images are also available.

**Access via:**
*ftp csn.org;* login *anonymous;*
cd *COGS*

**Information:**
E-mail: cogs@flint.mines.colorado.edu

Telephone: (303) 751-8553

## Earthquake Information

Information about recent earthquakes. Location, magnitude, and accuracy are given for each event.

**Access via:**
*finger quake@geophys.washington.edu*

## Global Land Information System

GLIS is an interactive system supported by the U.S. Geological Survey, apparently providing access to or ordering information for all public computerized geographical information maintained by the USGS. It allows you to browse as a "guest" user, but you must register to obtain full functionality.

**Access via:**
*telnet glis.cr.usgs.gov;* press RETURN;
type *GUEST*

## USGS Geological Fault Maps

A digital database of geological faults, covering the United States. Includes software to draw maps from the faults. The raw data isn't in any standard format (it appears to be latitude/longitude pairs), so you'll need the mapping software.

**Access via:**
*ftp alum.wr.usgs.gov;* login *anonymous;*
cd *pub/map*

## USGS Weekly Seismicity Reports

Weekly reports of seismic activity (earthquakes, volcanos, etc.) and maps for Northern California, the U.S., and the world.

The weekmap.dos file is in ASCII format.

**Access via:**
*ftp garlock.wr.usgs.gov;* login *anonymous;*
cd *pub/WEEKREPS/*
(Including maps in GIF format.)

## USGS Information

A service provided by the United States Geological Survey; information about the survey, resources they provide, software, and other services related to geology, hydrology, and cartography. Organized by topic, it includes audio and animated material as well as text and pictures.

**Access via:**
*www http://info.er.usgs.gov*

# GOVERNMENT, U.N. & INTERNATIONAL

## International Treaties

The text of scores of treaties, both ratified and proposed.

**Access via:**
*ftp wiretap.spies.com;* login *anonymous;*
cd *Gov/Treaties/Hague*
(For information on the Hague Conventions.)

*ftp wiretap.spies.com;* login *anonymous;*
cd *Gov/Treaties/Geneva*
(For information on the Geneva Conventions.)

*ftp wiretap.spies.com;* login *anonymous;*
cd *Gov/Treaties/League*
(For information on protocols related to the League of Nations.)

*ftp wiretap.spies.com;* login *anonymous;*
cd *Gov/Treaties/Sea*
(For information on the U.N. Convention on the Law of the Sea, not yet in force.)

*ftp wiretap.spies.com;* login *anonymous;*
cd *Gov/Treaties/Treaties*
(For information on many other treaties.)

## NATO

Press releases, speeches by the Secretary General, a Fact Sheet, and electronic versions of the NATO Handbook and the NATO Review, all in ASCII.

Under "Allied" are press releases relating to current NATO operations, such as air flights over Bosnia.

**Access via:**
*ftp info.umd.edu;* login *anonymous;*
cd *info/Government/US/NATO*

## United Nations Gopher

The U.N.'s very own Gopher, offering information on the United Nations, what it is and what it does, communications information pertaining to the U.N., and notably the World Health Organization Gopher.

**Access via:**
*gopher nywork1.undp.org*

## World Constitutions

Over a dozen constitutions and similar documents from countries and would-be countries around the world.

**Access via:**
*ftp wiretap.spies.com;* login *anonymous;*
cd *Gov/World*

# GOVERNMENT, U.S.

## Americans with Disabilities Act Regulations

The Americans with Disabilities Act reaches into many aspects of life. This resource includes not only the text of regulations, subdivided by federal agency, but also a wealth of supporting information and pointers to off-line resources.

**Access via:**
*ftp info.umd.edu;* login *anonymous;*
cd *inforM/Educational_Resources/
United_States/Government/NationalIssues/
ADARegulation*

## Budget 1993

Summary of the budget as proposed by the president on April 8, 1993, subdivided by subject. The file modestly titled "totals-million" gives the big picture.

**Access via:**
*ftp info.umd.edu; login anonymous;*
*cd inforM/Educational_Resources/*
*United_States/Government/NationalIssues/*
*Budget-93*

## Budget 1994

The proposed 1994 budget is available in several compressed forms and by section. You can select: Budget authority and Federal programs by agency; Federal programs by agency and account; Outlays by agency; Totals.

**Access via:**
*ftp sunsite.unc.edu; login anonymous;*
*cd pub/academic/political-science*

## Census 1990

A two-page summary of census results is available for each state.

**Access via:**
*ftp info.umd.edu; login anonymous;*
*cd inforM/Educational_Resources/*
*United_States/Government/NationalIssues/*
*Census-90*

## Congress Overview

A Democratic view of the Congress. Oddly, it also includes information on communicating with the Cabinet and other parts of the executive branch. There are biographical blurbs on Democrats (but no one else), and special files on women in the House and Senate.

**Access via:**
*ftp info.umd.edu; login anonymous;*
*cd info/Government/US/Congress*

## Copyright Information

The Library of Congress's information on works registered for copyright since 1978, including books, serials, films, music, maps, sound recordings, software, multimedia kits, drawings, posters, and sculpture.

**Access via:**
*telnet locis.loc.gov*

A Gopher interface is available through MARVEL.

**Access via:**
*gopher marvel.loc.gov/Copyright*

## FDA Electronic Bulletin Board

**See** Medicine.

## Federal Legislation

Access to information about federal legislation.

**Access via:**
*telnet locis.loc.gov*

## Federal Register

The Federal Register, categorized by agency, date of issue of regulation, and category, from July 1990. Published not by the government but by Counterpoint Publishing and the Internet Company. Full access is available only to subscribers (something to write your representative about!), and anything not typeset electronically is missing.

**Access via:**
*gopher gopher.counterpoint.com 2002*

## Government Accounting Office

GAO reports on scores of topics.

**Access via:**
*ftp info.umd.edu; login anonymous;*
cd *inforM/Educational_Resources/*
*United_States/Government/NationalIssues/*
*GAO*

## Library of Congress Services

More than just an online library catalog.
LOCIS, the TELNET interface, is pokey, but
MARVEL, the Gopher interface, is easy to use
and has a lot of interesting material.

MARVEL is the Library of Congress's Machine-
Assisted Realization of the Virtual Electronic
Library, which combines the information
available at and about the Library of
Congress with other Internet resources. It aims
to serve the staff of the Library of Congress,
the U.S. Congress, and constituents
throughout the world. Most files are plain
ASCII text.

**Access via:**
*telnet locis.loc.gov*

*gopher marvel.loc.gov*

## National Archives

The National Archive's Center for Electronic
Records provides a historical repository for
significant electronic records collected by the
federal government. Although the records are
not available through the Internet, inquiries
can be made through the e-mail address
noted in the *national.archives* file, which
includes a write-up.

**Access via:**
*ftp ftp.msstate.edu; login anonymous;*
cd *pub/docs/history/USA/databases;* get
*national.archives*

**Information:**
E-mail: tif@nihcu.bitnet

Telephone: (202) 501-5579

## National Information Infrastructure Proposal

The highly touted but rather vague proposal
to network the country, released by the U.S.
government in September, 1993, in a
hypertext version. To avoid the large graphics
on the title page, you can go directly to the
text of the proposal.

**See also:** Law, Columbia Online Legal
Resources (JANUS)

**Access via:**
*www http://sunsite.unc.edu/nii/NII-Table-of-*
*Contents.html*
(To start at the cover page.)

*www http://sunsite.unc.edu/nii/NII-Agenda-*
*for-Action.html*
(For the text of the proposal.)

*ftp sunsite.unc.edu; login anonymous;*
cd *pub/academic/political-science/internet-*
*related/National-Information-Infrastructure*

*gopher sunsite.unc.edu/What's New on*
*SunSITE/National Information Infrastructure*
*Information*

## National Performance Review

A hypertext version of Vice President Gore's
proposal for "reinventing government,"
prepared by the Office for Information
Technology at the University of North
Carolina.

**Access via:**
*www http://sunsite.unc.edu/npr/nptoc.html*

*ftp sunsite.unc.edu; login anonymous;*
cd *pub/academic/political-science/*
*National_Performance_Review*

*gopher sunsite.unc.edu/What's New on*
*SunSITE/National Performance Review*
*(Reinventing Government)*

*WAIS National-performace-Review.src*

## National Referral Center

The National Referral Center Resources File (NRCM) provides more than 12,000 descriptions of organizations qualified and willing to answer questions and provide information on many topics in science, technology, and the social sciences. This file, updated weekly, is based on a national inventory program begun in 1962. Each description in the file lists the name of the organization, mailing address, location, telephone number, areas of interest, holdings (special collections, databases, etc.), publications, and information services. Additional information is often provided on an organization.

### Access via:
*telnet locis.loc.gov;* Select *5. Organizations*

## NSF Awards

This is a subset of the STIS service. It consists of the abstracts of the awards made by NSF since 1990.

### Access via:
WAIS *nsf-awards.src*

## NSF Publications

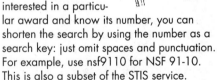

Publications of the National Science Foundation. They can be searched. However, if you are interested in a particular award and know its number, you can shorten the search by using the number as a search key: just omit spaces and punctuation. For example, use nsf9110 for NSF 91-10. This is also a subset of the STIS service.

### Access via:
WAIS *nsf-pubs.src*

## Science and Technology Information Service

STIS provides information about programs sponsored by the National Science Foundation. The NSF Bulletin, Guide to Programs, program announcements, press releases, and a listing of awards are available.

### Access via:
*gopher stis.nsf.gov*

*telnet stis.nsf.gov;* login *public*

## Social Security Administration

Lots of documents about Social Security, as you'd expect. You'll find listings of social security publications, speeches and testimony by members of the Social Security Commission, press releases, etc. However, the archive certainly isn't limited to Social Security information; there are a lot of other government documents, along with random collections of information, such as an archive of news postings on carpal tunnel syndrome. Because there is so much information, of so many types, you should look at the *index* file before going anywhere else. (Skip the first part, which talks about the Administration's internal e-mail system.)

### Access via:
*ftp soaf1.ssa.gov;* login *anonymous;* cd *pub*

## Supreme Court Rulings

**See:** Law

## White House Overview

The FAQ file contains information on signing up for daily electronic publications (press releases), searching and retrieving speeches and press releases, and sending e-mail to the White House.

### Access via:
*ftp info.umd.edu;* login *anonymous;*
cd *info/Government/US/WhiteHouse*

# HISTORY & CIVILIZATION

**Newsgroups:**
soc.history, sci.classics

**See also:** Literature; Classical Languages & Literature; History of Science

## Bryn Mawr Medieval Review

A sister publication of the Bryn Mawr Classical Review; the first issue went out in late 1993.

**Access via:**
*gopher orion.lib.Virginia.EDU/Electronic Journals/Bryn Mawr Medieval Review*

## EXPO: WWW Exhibit Organization

EXPO is the central point for a number of hypertext versions of exhibitions, including Library of Congress exhibitions, which are also listed individually in this *Catalog*. Much of the work behind EXPO has been done by Frans van Hoesel. For a quick look at EXPO's contents, see the "EXPO Overview" document.

**Access via:**
*www http://sunsite.unc.edu/expo/ticket_office.html*

*www http://sunsite.unc.edu/expo/expo/overview.html*

## Middle East Studies Association

The Middle East Studies Association, a professional organization for scholars of the Middle East and related areas, maintains this site for certain parts of its Bulletin and other relevant information.

**Access via:**
*gopher vmsgopher.cua.edu/The Catholic University of America Gopher service/Special Resources/Middle East Studies Association Bulletin*

## Mississippi State History Archives

This is an FTP site that contains many resources related to the study of history. It includes the National Council of History's Education newsletter (in the directory newsletters, files beginning with *NCHE*), materials on the Vietnam War, various bibliographies, and other material. Aside from the material on Vietnam and the NCHE newsletter, there doesn't appear to be any particular theme to what's available: there's material on medieval studies, French socialism, Andrew Jackson, the Native American movement, and other topics scattered around. If you're a historian, it's worth 10 minutes of your time to see what's available here.

**Access via:**
*ftp ftp.msstate.edu; login anonymous; cd docs/history*

## Soviet Archives

The Library of Congress has an exhibit of materials from the newly opened Soviet archives. There is information about life under the Soviet system, Chernobyl, the Cold War, the Cuban Missile Crisis, and many other topics. Anyone interested in understanding recent history should know about this archive.

Both FTP and WWW interfaces are available:

**Access via:**
*ftp ftp.loc.gov; login anonymous; cd pub/exhibit.images/russian.archive.exhibit*

*www http://sunsite.unc.edu/expo/soviet.exhibit/soviet.archive.html*

## U.S. Historical Documents

A selection of documents and secondary material relating to major events in U.S. history, such as the Mayflower Compact and the WWII Japanese Instrument of Surrender.

**Access via:**
*ftp wiretap.spies.com; login anonymous; cd Gov/US-History*

As part of Project Gutenberg:

**Access via:**
*gopher spinaltap.micro.umn.edu/Gutenberg/
Historical Documents*

The following resource also includes important U.S. historical documents, such as selections from the Federalist Papers.

**Access via:**
*ftp ftp.eff.org;* login *anonymous;*
cd *pub/academic/civics*

## 1492 Exhibition

An online version of the Library of Congress's 1992 exhibition titled "1492: An Ongoing Voyage," which concentrates on the New World and the Mediterranean world.

Both FTP and WWW interfaces are available:

**Access via:**
*ftp ftp.loc.gov;* login *anonymous;*
cd *pub/exhibit.images/1492.exhibit*

*www http://sunsite.unc.edu/expo/
1492.exhibit/Intro.html*

# HISTORY OF ART

**Newsgroups:**
alt.architecture, rec.arts.fine

## Architecture, etc.

ArchiGopher advertises itself as a server dedicated to the dissemination of architectural knowledge but actually covers more than that. There are links to a small archive of Kandinsky paintings; a small sample of drawings of Andrea Palladio's architectural projects, a collection of CAD computer models, and other possibly interesting items.

**Access via:**
*gopher libra.arch.umich.edu*

Included for some reason in the History of Science Gopher at Johns Hopkins University is

a set of photographs of French "architectural projects," which include fanciful design projects and sculpture.

**Access via:**
*gopher gopher.hs.jhu.edu/—>...Images/
Architecture*

## Art History in Australia

The first resource below leads to a copy of the hypertext set of text and images, including a tutorial for learning about the history of prints and sample images from objects in the Australian National Gallery's collection, constructed by Michael Greenhalgh.

The second leads to Prof. Greenhalgh's expanded art history server at the Australian National University, which contains a good deal more material.

**Access via:**
*www http://www.ncsa.uiuc.edu/SDG/
Experimental/anu-art-history/home.html*

*www http://rubens.anu.edu.au*

## Black Artists at the National Museum of American Art

Half a dozen images by black artists, from the collection of the National Museum of American Art, along with a text file explaining the holdings of the museum in this area (more than 1,500 works of art in a variety of media, from portraiture of the early Republic to contemporary artists).

**Access via:**
*gopher gopher.upenn.edu/PennInfo via the
Gopher —>Penninfo Gateway/PennInfo/
Interdisciplinary Programs/African Studies*

## Bodleian Library MSS

Announced as an experimental server, this Gopher site contains images of some of the many illustrated manuscripts in the collection of Oxford's most famous library.

**Access via:**
gopher rsl.ox.ac.uk/Bodleian Libraries (inc. Radcliffe Science Library)

## Japanese Art

Here's a directory of GIFs of prints in the Ukiyo-e style (seventeenth to nineteenth centuries).

**Access via:**
ftp ftp.uwtc.washington.edu;
login *anonymous;*
cd *pub/Japanese/Pictures/Ukiyo-e*

## Krannert Art Museum

A hypertext home page for the Krannert Art Museum (University of Illinois at Urbana-Champaign), including a Guide containing sample images of objects in the collection, each with commentary. The Guide is rather oddly divided into these sections: Sculpture, American and European painting, Twentieth-century art, [East and South] Asian art, Medieval and Near Eastern art.

Although no author is mentioned, a glance at the exhibition calendar shows Eunice Maguire to be the principal curator.

**Access via:**
www http://www.ncsa.uiuc.edu/
General/UIUC/KrannertArtMuseum/
KrannertArtHome.html

## A Roman Palace in ex-Yugoslavia

An experiment in online art history presentation technique, this exhibit was constructed by Michael Greenhalgh, Department of Art History, Australian National University.

"Split—or Spalato—is one of the most extraordinary places of the later Roman world, being no less than the palace which the Emperor Diocletian began building in A.D. 293 in readiness for his retirement from politics in 305. On the Dalmatian coast, adjacent to the Roman city of Salonae, it takes the dual form of a legionary camp similar to those still to be seen on the frontiers of Syria (appropriately so, for Diocletian was of necessity a military emperor) but also, with its splendid loggias, of an Italian house."

EXPO also offers a version of this material.

**Access via:**
www http://www.ncsa.uiuc.edu/SDG/
Experimental/split/split1.html

www http://sunsite.unc.edu/expo/
palace.exhibit/intro.html (EXPO.)

## Vatican Library MSS Exhibit

Images and text from a recent exhibition at the Library of Congress, including manuscripts from the Vatican Library in all areas of historical interest. Images are in JPEG compression format and are *large*. A hypertext version is available through EXPO at the University of North Carolina.

**Access via:**
ftp ftp.loc.gov; login *anonymous;*
cd *pub/exhibit.images/vatican.exhibit*
(Text in ASCII.)

www http://sunsite.unc.edu/expo/
vatican.exhibit/Vatican.exhibit.html
(Hypertext version, courtesy EXPO.)

# HISTORY OF SCIENCE

## History of Science Server

An attempt to collect and catalog the writings and papers of respected scientists in a single place.

**Access via:**
gopher gopher.hs.jhu.edu

## HOST: An Electronic Bulletin for the History and Philosophy of Science and Technology

Published by the Institute for the History and Philosophy of Science, Toronto, this is a serious academic journal, dealing with the history of science from antiquity to the present, and includes book reviews and pointers to Internet resources. HOST is scheduled to appear semiannually, in Spring/Summer and Fall/Winter.

**Access via:**
*gopher miles.library.arizona.edu/Resources By Discipline/History/History and Philosophy of Science and Technology*

# HOBBIES

**Newsgroups:**
alt.[aquaria, magic, sewing], rec.[antiques, aquaria, collecting, crafts.brewing, crafts.misc, crafts.textiles, folk-dancing, gambling, gardens, guns, juggling, models.railroad, models.rc, models.rockets, photo, radio.amateur.misc, radio.amateur.packet, radio.amateur.policy, radio.cb, railroad, roller-coaster, woodworking]

## Ceramics Gopher

An experimental database of glazes, part of a project of the GlazeBase Working Group of the National Council for Education in the Ceramic Arts (NCECA). Includes information on and archives of a mailing list called ClayArt, articles on ceramics, a list of ceramics suppliers, GlazeBase (glaze database), and a material database.

**Access via:**
*gopher gopher.sdsu.edu/SDSU Campus Topics/Departmental Information/Art Department/The Ceramics Gopher*

## Ham Radio

The national ham (amateur) radio call sign index allows you to look up hams by call sign, name, or area.

**Access via:**
*www http://www.mit.edu:8001/callsign*

*telnet callsign.cs.buffalo.edu 2000*

*www http://www.mcc.ac.uk/OtherPages/ AmateurRadio.html*

This resource contains information on newsgroups related to amateur radio, excerpts from FCC rules, an FAQ, pointers to other sites, and a license exam quiz server.

**Access via:**
*www http://www.acs.ncsu.edu/HamRadio*

## Hockey Cards Mailing List Archive

A mailing list dedicated to hockey card collectors. People to trade with and checklists are available. Subscribe with hockey-request@yahoo.cirrus.com.

**Access via:**
*ftp ftp.rahul.net;* login *anonymous;* cd *pub/mitch/hockey*

**Information:**
E-mail: mitch@cirrus.com

## Horticultural Engineering Newsletter

Issues of the publication are available. Contains information on greenhouses, seeds, and other technical information about horticulture techniques. Accessed through the PEN Pages (see Agriculture).

**Access via:**
*telnet psupen.psu.edu;* login *your two-letter state abbreviation*

## Tango

History of the tango, lyrics, notations, biographies, you name it; if it's about the tango, it may very well be here.

**Access via:**
*www http://litsun.epfl.ch/tango/ welcome.html*

# INTEREST GROUPS

**Newsgroups:**
soc.[answers, bi, college, couples, culture, feminism, men, motss, penpals, politics, religion, rights, roots, singles, veterans, women], talk.*

## Columbia Index to Hispanic Legislation

Data provided by the Library of Congress to Columbia Law School concerning Hispanic-oriented legislation.

**Access via:**
WAIS *columbia-spanish-law-catalog.src*

**Information:**
E-mail: willem@lawmail.law.columbia.edu

## Deaf Gopher

This Gopher at Michigan State University contains information about services for the deaf in Michigan, as well as "Deaf Alert," a collection of files containing information on the deaf in history and culture.

**Access via:**
*gopher burrow.cl.msu.edu/Information for the MSU Community/MSU College & Departmental Information/Deaf-Gopher*

## Hispanic Interest

UCLA sponsors a Chicano-LatinoNet Gopher, with a WAIS index, lists of conferences, scholarships, and the like; there is also a directory with links to libraries containing material of Chicano-Latino interest.

**Access via:**
*gopher latino.sscnet.ucla.edu*

## Feminism Information

Archive of information on feminism drawn from or related to the newsgroup soc.feminism, not including archives of that newsgroup.

**Access via:**
*ftp rtfm.mit.edu;* login *anonymous;* cd *pub/usenet/news.answers/feminism*

## Queer Resources Directory

A good resource for the gay, lesbian, and bisexual community. Has sections concerned with AIDS, facts and treatments; contact information for various support and activist groups; bibliography of publications of interest to the community; civil rights; and domestic partnerships. Also, has portions of the GLAAD Newsletter online.

**Access via:**
*www file://vector.casti.com/pub/QRD/ .html/QRD-home-page.html* (WWW interface.)

*gopher vector.casti.com/Queer Resources*

*ftp vector.casti.com;* login *anonymous;* cd *QRD*

**Information:**
E-mail: QRDstaff@vector.casti.com

# INTERNATIONAL INTEREST

**Newsgroup:**
soc.culture.*

## Algeria

A rather small archive, including travel information and contact information for the

Algerian government and Algerian universities (all in English).

**Access via:**
ftp *ftp.cse.psu.edu;* login *anonymous;*
cd *pub/mbarki/information/algeria*

## Australia

Information compiled about computing, networking, and libraries in Australia.

**Access via:**
WAIS *aarnet-resource-guide.src*

A short hypertext "Guide to Australia," relying heavily on the Australian National University's Biodiversity server.

**Access via:**
www *http://life.anu.edu.au/education/
australia.html*

## Brazil

This server is run by the Rede Nacional de Pesquisa (National Research Network), which is apparently based in Rio de Janeiro. The information is in Portuguese.

**Access via:**
www *http://www.rnp.br*

## Chinese Community Information Center

 This resource is run by the International Federation of Chinese Students and Scholars, that is, overseas Chinese, not the Chinese government. It offers information on immigration and tax law, Chinese studies, computing with Chinese characters, and related topics, and has a picture archive. There are both WWW and FTP interfaces.

**Access via:**
www *http://ifcss.org:8001/index.html*

ftp *ifcss.org;* login *anonymous*

gopher *ifcss.org*

## Esperanto

Offers a course in Esperanto, a synthetic language invented by L. L. Zamenhof, a Pole, in 1887. The home page is in Dutch, but an English version is offered, too.

**Access via:**
www *http://utis179.cs.utwente.nl:8001/
esperanto/hyperkursus/oficej.html*

## Europe

A home page for Europe, maintained in Portugal but including links to country-specific home pages in other countries.

**Access via:**
www *http://s700.uminho.pt/europa.html*

## France & French Language

Le petit coin des francophones et autres grenouilles is a collection of pointers to French resources (in France and in French, both) of all types. This should be your first stop in exploring the French parts of the Internet.

**Access via:**
www *http://cuisg13.unige.ch:8100/
franco.html*

## Germany

A small archive of information about Germany, Germans, and German culture. There is material in both German and English.

**Access via:**
ftp *rascal.ics.utexas.edu;* login *anonymous;*
cd *misc/germans*

## Holland

A menu of information about Dutch Internet resources, including universities and libraries. This link is to the English version; there's a Dutch version, too.

**Access via:**
*gopher rugcis.rug.nl/Informatiediensten buiten RUG/Nederland*

## Iran

A good collection of information and software relating to Iran and the Persian language. The *Iran_Lib* directory contains subdirectories including pictures (*/Images/GIF*), sounds, software for Persian, and much else.

**Access via:**
*ftp tehran.stanford.edu;* login *anonymous*

*www http://tehran.stanford.edu*

## Israel

The largest directory of information on Judaism, Hebrew, and Israel that we've found is in New York.

**Access via:**
*ftp nysernet.org;* login *anonymous;* cd *israel*

## Japan Information

A multimedia site for information on Japan (want to hear the Japanese national anthem?). The link below leads to an English document that includes information on how to display the corresponding Japanese version.

**Access via:**
*www http://www.ntt.jp/japan*

## Lebanon

This commodious archive is a volunteer effort, established by Bertha Choueiry "as a repository of cultural material in the form of text, graphics and sounds pertaining to Lebanon and the Middle East, . . . [without] political,

religious, sectarian or ethnic affiliations." It includes everything from a list of Lebanese restaurants in London to GIFs of Lebanese musicians; there is also some material on Arabia and other parts of the Levant.

**Access via:**
*ftp liasun3.epfl.ch;* login *anonymous;* cd *users/choueiry*

Barre Ludvigsen has collected pointers to this and other Net resources relating to Lebanon.

**Access via:**
*www http://www.ludvigsen.dhhalden.no/ webdoc/levant_servers.html*

## Latin American Network Information Center

This Gopher is managed by the Institute of Latin American Studies (ILAS) at the University of Texas at Austin to provide Latin American users with access to information services worldwide and to provide Latin Americanists around the world with access to information on and from Latin America.

**Access via:**
*gopher lanic.utexas.edu*

## Mexico

Established in 1993, this Gopher is intended for both academic and commercial use.

**Access via:**
*gopher telecom.mty.itesm.mx*

## New Zealand Information

A hypertext home page for New Zealand, with pointers to the Wellington City Council Gopher and the Victoria University at Wellington home page. Includes information on the Maori language, New

Zealand food, and the tuatara, a carnivorous reptile that has three eyes when young (it must be true—we read it on the Internet!).

**Access via:**
*www http://www.cs.cmu.edu:8001/Web/People/mjw/NZ/MainPage.html*

## Norway

The Norwegian Televerkets Forskningsinstitutt has opened this WWW site, serving also the University of Oslo. Information is in Norwegian. There is a hypertext presentation of the Telemuseum Meny that includes pictures (small) and movies, among other items.

**Access via:**
*www http://www.nta.no/uninett/norweb.html*

There's a Norwegian online dictionary at another site in Norway, run by Norsk Regnesentral.

**Access via:**
*www http://www.nr.no/ordbok*

## Polish Journals

Collections of news analysis, press reviews, and humor from or about Poland and the Polish community abroad. The journal is in Polish.

**Access via:**
*gopher gopher.cic.net/Electronic Serials/Alphabetic List/P/Pigulki*

If you're interested in Polish studies, also check out the Donosy journal. The journal is in Polish.

**Access via:**
*gopher gopher.cic.net/Electronic Serials/Alphabetic List/D/Donosy*

## Portugal

Basic information, along with a clickable map that takes a long time to load.

**Access via:**
*www http://s700.uminho.pt/Portugal/portugal.html*

## The Project for American & French Research of the Treasury of the French Language

Also known as ARTFL, this is a searchable database of nearly 2,000 texts, ranging from classic works of French literature to various kinds of nonfiction prose and technical writing. The eighteenth, nineteenth, and twentieth centuries are about equally represented, with a smaller selection of seventeenth-century texts as well as some medieval and Renaissance texts. Genres include novels, verse, journalism, essays, correspondence, and treatises. Subjects include literary criticism, biology, history, economics, and philosophy. In most cases, standard scholarly editions were used in converting the text into machine-readable form, and the data include page references to these editions.

Users access the database through the PhiloLogic system, "an easy-to-use full-text retrieval package."

This WWW site also includes pointers to other French-language resources.

**Access via:**
*www http://tuna.uchicago.edu/ARTFL.html*

## Russian

A collection of information and humor about Russia and the former Soviet Union, along with software (mostly fonts) for supporting the Cyrillic alphabet.

**Access via:**
*ftp mimsy.umd.edu;* login *anonymous;* cd *pub/cyrillic*

## Turkey

Middle East Technical University, near Ankara, sponsors this WWW site, which provides information about the university and pointers to other resources in and relating to Turkey. Much of the information at this site is in Turkish.

**Access via:**
*www http://www.metu.edu.tr*

# INTERNET INFORMATION & RESOURCE DIRECTORIES

## Acceptable Use Policies

Acceptable use policies for many networks. These define what kinds of network traffic are permitted on a particular network.

**Access via:**
*ftp nis.nsf.net;* login *anonymous;* cd *acceptable.use.policies*

## Anonymous FTP Sites

A very long list of sites that allow anonymous FTP, formatted in ASCII.

**Access via:**
*ftp ftp.ucsc.edu;* login *anonymous;* cd *public;* get *ftpsites*

## Archie Request Form

A neat forms-based WWW gateway to a multitude of Archie servers; makes Archie really easy. Be careful not to overdo it!

**Access via:**
*www http://hoohoo.ncsa.uiuc.edu/ archie.html*

## BITNET and EARN Information

Everything you could want to know about BITNET and its European counterpart, EARN.

**Access via:**
*ftp lilac.berkeley.edu;* login *anonymous;* cd *netinfo/bitnet*

## Computers, Freedom, and Privacy

The proceedings of an ACM conference on these topics.

**Access via:**
WAIS *computers-freedom-and-privacy.src*

Computer usage policies, archives of old discussions, bibliographies.

WAIS *comp-acad-freedom.src*

**Information:**
E-mail: archivist@archive.orst.edu

## December's Guide to Internet Resources

A lengthy list of pointers to information describing the Internet, computer networks, and issues related to computer-mediated communication, compiled by John December and updated regularly. Topics include the technical, social, cognitive, and psychological aspects of the Net.

The guide is available in plain ASCII, HTML (for WWW), and other formats.

**Access via:**
*ftp ftp.rpi.edu;* login *anonymous;* cd *pub/communications*

## Directory of WAIS Servers

This is a list of all known servers for the WAIS system, offered as a WAIS database. The directory of servers is usually the first database you'll search when you start a WAIS search; it's where you'll find the databases that are relevant to the topic you're researching.

**Access via:**
WAIS *directory-of-servers.src*

WAIS *au-directory-of-servers.src* ("Backup" copy, located in Australia; may have more info about Australian resources.)

## Domain Name Lookup

Resources to turn domain names like wuarchive.wustl.edu into a numeric address. These are particularly useful if you find yourself on a computer that doesn't participate in the domain name system.

**Access via:**
*telnet 130.59.1.40; login lookup*

**Information:**
E-mail: resolve@cs.widener.edu; send message "site" followed by site name
E-mail: dns@grasp.insa-lyon.fr; send message "ip" followed by site name

## Fidonet Node List

This is, essentially, a list of Fidonet addresses. Given the name of a person or organization on Fidonet, you can look up the relevant Fidonet node name, then convert the node name into an Internet address, as described in chapter 7, *Electronic Mail.*

**Access via:**
WAIS *fidonet-nodelist.src*

**Information:**
E-mail:
David.Dodell@f15.n114.z1.fidonet.org

## Gophers Worldwide

Some Gopher servers, with especially complete lists of international Gopher servers.

**Access via:**
*gopher gopher.micro.umn.edu/Other Gopher and Information Servers*
(Indexed by continent and country.)

*gopher gopher.rediris.es/Otros Gopher - Other Gophers/Otros servidores de Informacion - Other Gopher and Information Servers*

*gopher sunic.sunet.se/Infoservers in European Countries*

*gopher sunic.sunet.se/Other Gopher and Information Servers*

## HYTELNET

HYTELNET is a menu-driven version of TELNET. It offers much of the functionality of Gopher's TELNET interface. This is an index of all the servers it knows about. You can use it to find library catalogs, bulletin boards, campus information servers, and other TELNET sites.

**Access via:**
WAIS *hytelnet.src*

## IETF Documents

The IETF is the voluntary engineering group for the Internet. It produces various working group and planning reports. This service contains the text of those reports.

**Access via:**
WAIS *ietf-documents.src*

WAIS *ietf-docs.src*

WAIS *netinfo.src*

WAIS *netinfo-docs.src*

## IETF Drafts

Whereas "IETF Documents" contains the official documents that have been received by the group, this resource contains the documents under construction. This is where you look if you want to find out where the Internet is heading.

**Access via:**
ftp *ds.internic.net;* login *anonymous;*
cd *internet-drafts*

WAIS *internic-internet-drafts.src*

WAIS *ripe-internet-drafts.src*

## Internet Services

A voluntarily compiled list of Internet services, commonly referred to as the "Yanoff list." It gives a short description of each service and access.

**Access via:**
ftp *csd4.csd.uwm.edu;* login *anonymous;*
cd *pub/inet.services.txt*

gopher *csd4.csd.uwm.edu/Remote Information Services/Special Internet Connections*

**Information:**
E-mail: yanoff@csd4.csd.uwm.edu

## Internet Information Search

Many of the standard help texts and guides, such as the Hitchhikers Guide to the Internet,

Zen and the Art of the Internet, Netiquette, and others are indexed and contained here.

**Access via:**
WAIS *internet_info.src*

## Internet Mail Guide

A detailed description of how to address electronic mail so that it will get from any network to any other network. This list includes lots of very small networks, special interest networks, and corporate networks, in addition to well-known networks such as MCI and CompuServe. Updated monthly.

**Access via:**
ftp *csd4.csd.uwm.edu;* login *anonymous;*
cd *pub;* get *internetwork-mail-guide*

## InterNIC Information Services

The InterNIC is the Internet's master information service. This resource includes gateways to major white-pages services (X.500, whois, and netfind), plus lists of known FTP archives, Gopher servers, and pointers to other resources.

**Access via:**
gopher *is.internic.net*

## List of Lists, Listservers & Newsgroups

A compilation of news and mailing lists, both on BITNET and the Internet. There is a lot of overlap among the sources, so if you search you will likely find something multiple times. Most valuable as a "master list" of all known electronic mail discussion groups.

**Access via:**
ftp *ftp.sura.net;* cd/*pub/nic;* get *interest-groups.txt*

(**WARNING:** This is a very long file.)

A long ASCII file, in alphabetical order, of listservers, written by Diane K. Kovacs.

**Access via:**
ftp *class.org;* login *anonymous;* cd *class;* get *kovacs_library_listservers*

Another large collection of mailing lists, maintained by Stephanie da Silva. For those with World Wide Web browsers, this is the most useable of all the lists of lists.

**Access via;**
*www http://www.ii.uib.no/~magnus/ paml.html*

## Matrix News

 Matrix News is a newsletter of the Matrix Information and Directory Services, Inc. The topics concern current and future network applications. Articles are copyrighted, but may be used freely with attribution. They may not be sold. Complete use of information can be found by searching for copyright.

**Access via:**
WAIS *matrix_news.src*

**Information:**
E-mail: mids@tic.com

## Network Information Online

This service, formerly called NICOLAS, is now represented in the Godard Space Flight Center's Gopher site. The subdirectories contain much information on using the Internet (see in particular "Networking").

**Access via:**
*gopher gopher.gsfc.nasa.gov*

## National Institute of Standards & Technology Gopher

The National Institute of Standards & Technology (NIST) deals with a wide range of

topics; this Gopher is concerned with computers and networking.

**Access via:**
*gopher gopher-server.nist.gov*

## NNSC Internet Resource Guide

The NSF Network Service Center asks people offering a service on the Internet to submit a description of the service. These are collected in this database.

**Access via:**
*gopher ocf.berkeley.edu/OCF On-line Help/ The Outside World*

## NorthWestNet User Services Internet Resource Guide

A book much like this one, which contains information on network use and resources available. Files are in PostScript and some are compressed.

**Access via:**
*ftp ftphost.nwnet.net;* login *anonymous;* cd *user-docs/nusirg*

## RFC (Request for Comments)

RFCs are the documents that define the Internet. They talk about how it works, how to use it, and where it is going. Most RFCs are fairly technical. There are over 1,200 RFCs. An index is in file *rfc-index.txt.* Some RFCs are distributed in text, and some in PostScript. The text documents have names of the form *rfcnnnn.txt.* PostScript RFCs are in files named *rfcnnnn.ps.* In either case, *nnnn* is the number of the RFC you want. Many computers archive only partial sets. The sources listed here are "official" servers with complete sets.

For more information on fetching RFCs, send an e-mail message like:

mail rfc-info@isi.edu

Subject: getting rfcs

help: ways_to_get_rfcs

### Access via:

WAIS *rfc.src*
(A search aid to the index of RFCs.)

*ftp ftp.internic.net;* login *anonymous;* cd *rfc*

*ftp nic.ddn.mil;* login *anonymous;* cd *rfc*

*ftp nis.nsf.net;* login *anonymous;* cd *internet/ documents/rfc*
(A VM/CMS server—filenames are different.)

*ftp ftp.jvnc.net;* login *anonymous;* cd *rfc*

*ftp wuarchive.wustl.edu;* login *anonymous;* cd *doc/rfc*

*ftp src.doc.ic.ac.uk;* login *anonymous;* cd *rfc*

*gopher gopher.internic.net/Internic Information/Internet Information/All About Request for Comments/RFCs Directory*

### Information:
E-mail mailserv@ds.internic.net. The message body should contain any of:

document-by-name rfcnnnn (for plain text file)
file/ftp/rfc/rfcnnnn.txt (for a plain text file)
file/ftp/rfc/rfcnnnn.ps (for a PostScript file)

## Zen and the Art of the Internet

This is the well-received booklet by Brendan Kehoe about using the Internet. It is a good introduction to the topic, told in a readable fashion. The work is available in several formats.

### Access via:
*ftp ftp.cs.widener.edu;* login *anonymous;* cd *pub/zen*

# INTERNET ORGANIZATIONS

### Newsgroups:
news.[announce.important, announce.newusers, newusers.questions, answers, groups, future, lists, software.readers, sysadmin, misc]

## Electronic Frontier Foundation

The EFF exists to promote existing academic and personal freedoms in the new worldwide computer society. It fights against such things as network censorship and for such things as freely available information. Included on this server is information about the foundation (in the EFF directory), the Computer and Academic Freedom Archives, and many electronic journals and magazines, such as Effector, Athene, and DragonZine.

### Access via:
WAIS *eff-documents.src*

WAIS *eff-talk.src*

*ftp ftp.eff.org;* login *anonymous;* cd/pub/EFF

## Internet Society

The Internet Society is an international professional organization established to encourage the evolution, standardization, and dissemination of techniques and technologies that allow diverse information systems to communicate. The Society publishes newsletters, organizes conferences, and manages e-mail distribution lists to educate a worldwide community about the global network of networks known as the Internet, which links more than 4 million users and 1 million computers. The Society sponsors the Internet Architecture Board and its Internet Engineering and Research Task Forces, and maintains liaisons with other international organizations and standards bodies as part of its effort to assist in the evolution and growth of the critically important infrastructure represented by the Internet.

### Access via:
*ftp cnri.reston.va.us;* login *anonymous;* cd *isoc*

### Information:
E-mail: isoc@nri.reston.va.us

Telephone: (703) 620-8990

## INTERNET SERVICES

**Newsgroups:**
news.[announce.important,
announce.newusers, newusers.questions,
answers, groups, future, lists,
software.readers, sysadmin, misc]

## Internet Service Providers

Listings, variously organized, of organizations
that provide commercial and noncommercial
access to the Internet, drawn from the book
*Internet: Getting Started.*

**Access via:**
*ftp nis.nsf.net;* login *anonymous;*
cd *internet/providers*

## Prototype WAIS FTP Server

Sort of "Archie meets FTP," with a WAIS
interface. Here is the description from the
directory of servers:

"This server searches README files throughout the entire FTP directory tree. When an
interesting file is found, it should be used as a
relevance feedback document. When the
search is re-done, the user will get a listing of
the FTP directory in which the README file
resides. The user can then retrieve files from
that directory. Text files are returned as type
TEXT, all other files are returned as type FTP."

**Access via:**
WAIS *quake.think.com-ftp.src*

## LAW

**Newsgroup:**
misc.legal

## Columbia Online Legal Resources (JANUS)

A specialized WAIS server and public access
client for the legal community. Databases
available include the Columbia law catalog,

the Law of the Seas, legal employers (index
of U.S. and overseas firms), U.S. Supreme
Court decisions, and U.S. court clerkship
requirements. Also includes the Agenda of
the United Nations Rio Conference (on the
environment), other databases about the
U.N., and WAIS-searchable sources for the
National Information Infrastructure and
National Performance Review proposals.

**Access via;**
*telnet lawnet.law.columbia.edu;* login *lawnet;*
select *"Project JANUS"*

WAIS *JANUS-dir-of-servers.src*

*www http://www.janus.columbia.edu*

**Information:**
E-mail: willem@futureinfo.com

## Declaration of Independence

The most subversive document in the history of
the world, in ASCII (signers' names omitted).

**Access via:**
*ftp ftp.eff.org;* login *anonymous;*
cd *pub/academic/civics;* get *dec_of_ind*

## Cornell Legal Information Institute

The leading Internet site for law, part of the
Cornell Law School. Gopher and WWW
interfaces exist.

The Gopher interface
includes an index of
legal academia, an
archive of the "law-lib"
mailing list, the
"teknoids" mailing list
(which has lots of
articles about computer
applications used in
law), and other services
of interest.

The WWW interface
includes directories
dealing with the U.S.
Copyright Act, the U.S.

Patent Act, the U.S. Lanham Act (trademarks), and the Nasdaq Financial Executive Journal; the site is expanding actively.

**Access via:**
gopher fatty.law.cornell.edu

www http://www.law.cornell.edu/
lii.table.html

## Corporation for Research and Educational Networking (CREN)

CREN is the corporation that runs BITNET. It has asked its attorneys to research their liability in using the network to access foreign countries. These files are specific to BITNET, but are probably applicable to the Internet as well.

mail listserv@bitnic.bitnet; body of message should contain 3 lines:

get legal commerce

get legal gtda

get legal counsel

## Indiana University Law School

This server includes two legal journals (Global Legal Studies and Federal Communications Law), information on feminist law resources, plus pointers to other legal resources on the Internet.

**Access via:**
www http://www.law.indiana.edu/law/
lawsch.html

## Supreme Court Rulings

Project HERMES is a project to make the Supreme Court's opinions and rulings publicly available via the Internet. Opinions and decisions since the 1989 term are available. It helps to know the number of the document you are looking for.

**See also:** Columbia Online Legal Resource (JANUS)

**Access via:**
ftp ftp.cwru.edu; login anonymous; cd hermes

ftp info.umd.edu; login anonymous;
cd info/Government/US/SupremeCt

## Sydney University Law School FTP Archive

Contains an interesting collection of various U.S. laws. The laws are both state and federal. Organized both by state and topic.

**Access via:**
ftp sulaw.law.su.oz.au; login anonymous;
cd pub/law

## U.S. Constitution

The text of the Constitution in full or divided by article and amendment.

**Access via:**
ftp info.umd.edu; login anonymous;
cd info/Government/US/Constitution

## Washington and Lee Law Library

A mixed collection of legal data. Text of some laws can be found, along with some information on conferences and meetings.

**Access via:**
ftp liberty.uc.wlu.edu; login anonymous;
cd pub/lawlib

# LITERATURE

**Newsgroups:**
rec.arts[books, sf, theatre, poems, prose]

**See also:** Classical Languages & Literature

## L'Association des Bibliophiles Universels

ABU is a library of public domain French literature, with pointers to other resources. The group was founded in April 1993 to develop and promote "numerical techniques enabling the free manipulation of information, the use of these techniques for the diffusion of the research work of members of the society and public domain information."

**Access via:**
*www http://www.cnam.fr/ABU/principal/ABU.v2.html*

## Chinese Literature

This resource offers novels, poetry, and classics of Chinese literature, in Chinese characters. These are the archives of the alt.chinese.text newsgroup. If you want to learn how to ftp or read Chinese files, send a message to ftp-info@ifcss.org, or get the *act/chinese-text-faq* file.

**Access via:**
*ftp ifcss.org;* login *anonymous;* cd *act/archive*

*gopher ifcss.org/act/archive*

## CURIA Irish Manuscript Project

Also known as the *Thesaurus Linguarum Hiberniae,* this project is dedicated to collecting and generating machine-readable copies of Irish manuscript texts from A.D. 600 to 1600, some of which may be browsed online.

**Access via:**
*www http://curia.ucc.ie/curia/menu.html*

## Dante Project

Contains reviews of Dante's *Divine Comedy* by various historical authors. A useful service for Dante scholars, but the user interface is very confusing.

**Access via:**
*telnet lib.dartmouth.edu;* connect *dante*

## Dracula

Bram Stoker's 1897 horror novel, lightly hypertexted.

**Access via:**
*www http://www.cs.cmu.edu:8001/Web/People/rgs/drac-table.html*

## Indexes of Online Books

Hypertext indexes of books available online, recently updated.

**Access via:**
*www http://www.cs.cmu.edu:8001/Web/bookauthors.html*
(Indexed by author.)

*www http://www.cs.cmu.edu:8001/Web/booktitles.html*
(Indexed by title.)

## Internet Wiretap Book Collection

A rather large collection of electronic texts, including religious texts, fiction, nonfiction, and electronic texts available from other sources.

**Access via:**

*gopher wiretap.spies.COM/Wiretap Online Library*

## Lewis Carroll

Slightly hypertexted versions of Project Gutenberg's original electronic versions of *Alice's Adventures in Wonderland* and *Alice Through the Looking Glass*. Easier to read than ASCII.

**Access via:**

*www http://cs.indiana.edu/metastuff/ dir.html*

## Online Book Initiative

Electronic texts by many authors, from Emily Brontë to Karl Marx, along with electronic journals, excerpts from newsgroups, and pointers to other sources of electronic texts and other Internet resources. A major resource for literature—and all texts are freely redistributable.

The FTP interface provides a long menu, not well organized (a good point at which to use your browser's search facility). The Gopher interface includes links to the OBI FAQ, an explanatory file, and a long but properly alphabetized menu of the same contents.

**Access via:**

*ftp world.std.com; login anonymous; cd obi*

*gopher world.std.com/OBI The Online Book Initiative/*

## Online Books FAQ

One of the best hypertext directories of electronic books available through the Internet, along with other pertinent information.

**Access via:**

*www http://cs.indiana.edu/metastuff/ bookfaq.html*

## Poetry

A collection of poems by Emily Brontë, Burns, Byron, T. S. Eliot, Frost, Yeats, and others. The WAIS index *poetry.src*, which is a different resource, provides the poems of Shakespeare, Yeats, Elizabeth Sawyer, and others.

**Access via:**

*gopher ocf.berkeley.edu/OCF On-line Library/Poetry*

*WAIS poetry.src*

---

*Excerpt from* **Shakespeare**, *3/20/94,* *(http://the-tech.mit.edu/Shakespeare.html )*

```
HAMLET
Now I am alone.
O, what a rogue and peasant slave
  am I!
Is it not monstrous that this
  player here,
But in a fiction, in a dream of
  passion,
Could force his soul so to his
  own conceit
That from her working all his
  visage wann'd,
Tears in his eyes, distraction
  in's aspect,
A broken voice, and his whole
  function suiting
With forms to his conceit? and
  all for nothing!
For Hecuba!
What's Hecuba to him, or he to
  Hecuba,
That he should weep for her?
  What would he do,
Had he the motive and the cue for
  passion
That I have? He would drown the
  stage with tears
And cleave the general ear with
  horrid speech,
Make mad the guilty and appal
  the free,
Confound the ignorant, and amaze
  indeed
The very faculties of eyes and
  ears.
```

## Project Gutenberg

Project Gutenberg is an ambitious nonprofit and volunteer effort to get as much literature as possible into machine-readable form. Their holdings include the works of Shakespeare, lots of Lewis Carroll, *Moby Dick,* and a rapidly growing number of classic texts, speeches, and reference materials. Manuscripts are in text only, with no special formatting. Filenames vary from server to server, but usually will have a mnemonic name followed by a version number (e.g. *alice28.txt*). The higher the version number, the more verification of the electronic text has been done. Since the text takes up a lot of disk space, some servers don't store the entire archive, and some compress the texts. Newsletters of the society, an index, and a *README* file are available on the mrcnext.cso.uiuc.edu source.

### Access via:

*www http://med-amsa.bu.edu/Gutenberg/ Welcome.html*
(A WWW interface to the mrcnext.cso.uiuc.edu files.)

*gopher gopher.tc.umn.edu/Libraries/ Electronic Books*

*ftp mrcnext.cso.uiuc.edu;* login *anonymous;* cd *etext*

### Information:

E-mail: hart@vmd.cso.uiuc.edu

## Project Runeberg (Scandinavian Literature)

A Project Gutenberg for Scandinavian languages, complete with support for Scandinavian character sets.

### Access via:

*gopher gopher.lysator.liu.se/Projects...Project Runeberg, Scandinavian e-texts*

*ftp ftp.lysator.liu.se;* login *anonymous;* cd *pub/runeberg*

*www http://www.lysator.liu.se/ runeberg.html*

## Science Fiction Newsgroup Archive

The archives of rec.arts.sf.reviews. The archives are available in "raw form," through anonymous FTP. The *README* file explains how the archive is organized. You can also search the archive through WAIS. This is another great place to look for spontaneous reviews or discussions of science fiction.

### Access via:

WAIS *sf-reviews.src*

## Shakespeare

A complete corpus of Shakespeare online, in ASCII.

In England, ftp to the Imperial College, London:

### Access via:

*ftp src.doc.ic.ac.uk;* login *anonymous;* cd *pub/literary/authors/shakespeare*

In the U.S., gopher to the University of Minnesota:

**Access via:**
*gopher joeboy.micro.umn.edu/Ebooks/By Title/Complete Works of Shakespeare*

All of Shakespeare's plays, lightly hypertexted but with built-in links to a glossary:

**Access via:**
*www http://the-tech.mit.edu/ Shakespeare.html*

## MATHEMATICS

**Newsgroups:**
sci.[math, math.num-analysis, math.stat, math.symbolic, math.research], k12.ed.math

### Centre International de Rencontres Mathematiques Bibliography

The bibliography of the CIRM in Marseille. Index words are in French.

**Access via:**
WAIS *cirm-books.src.src*

WAIS *cirm-papers.src*

**Information:**
E-mail: rolland@cirm.univ-mrs.fr

### e-MATH

e-MATH is an Internet node that provides mathematicians with an expanding list of services that can be accessed electronically. e-MATH is intended as an electronic clearinghouse for timely professional and research information in the mathematical sciences. Some of the current services are the AMS (American Mathematical Society) membership database, employment opportunities, publication ordering, author lists, meeting notices, and a directory of journals and newsletters.

**Access via:**
*telnet e-math.ams.com;* login *e-math;* password *e-math*

**Information:**
E-mail: support@e-math.ams.com

### Fractals

Both static and animated (MPEG) fractal images are available from Rennes University, France. Note that MPEG files are long and take some time to retrieve.

**Access via:**
*www http://www.cnam.fr/fractals.html*

## MEDICINE

**Newsgroups:**
sci.med, sci.med.[aids, dentistry, physics, pharmacy, nutrition, occupational, psychobiology, telemedicine]

**See:**
Agriculture—PEN Pages

### Alcoholism Research Database

A database of articles and other information related to alcoholism and other forms of substance abuse.

**Access via:**
*telnet lib.dartmouth.edu*

**Information:**
Once you're in, type "Select file cork"

### AIDS Information

The National Institute of Allergy and Infectious Disease maintains a special section of its Gopher for AIDS information.

**Access via:**
*gopher odie.niaid.nih.gov/AIDS Related Information*

Here's an online newsletter on the treatment of AIDS.

**Access via:**
*gopher gopher.cic.net/Electronic Serials/ Alphabetic List/A/AIDS News Service*

## CancerNet (NCI International Cancer Information Center)

The National Cancer Institute's Gopher and WWW server, with information for physicians and patients both.

**Access via:**
*www http://biomed.nus.sg/Cancer/ welcome.html*

*gopher biomed.nus.sg/NUS-NCI CancerNet Gopher*

## Cholesterol

An explanation of what cholesterol is, where it comes from, and how it affects the body.

**Access via:**
*gopher bluehen.ags.udel.edu/Cooperative Extension/Cooperative Extension Bulletins/ Food, Health and Nutrition/Cholesterol*

## Clinical Alerts

Clinical Alerts are distributed by the National Institutes of Health and the National Library of Medicine for the purpose of getting important findings out to health professionals as quickly as possible.

**Access via:**
*gopher uicvm.uic.edu/The Library/Clinical Alerts*

## Conversational Hypertext

A "natural language information system." We don't know if this is more interesting as an example of a hypertext application or as a source of information. At any rate, information on AIDS and epilepsy is currently

available, along with the Canadian Department of Communications.

**Access via:**
*telnet debra.dgbt.doc.ca 3000*

## Family Medicine Discussion Archives

A growing collection of material relating to family medicine, including archived mailings from the FAM-MED listserv. These are discussions about uses of computers and networking to help in the teaching and practice of family medicine. Also included are pointers to other relevant Internet resources.

**Access via:**
*ftp ftp.gac.edu; login anonymous; cd pub/fam-med*

## FDA Electronic Bulletin Board

A bulletin board containing information on FDA (Food and Drug Administration) actions, congressional testimony, news releases, consumer information, AIDS, and veterinary medicine. You can use this database to find out, for example, what drugs have been approved recently.

**Access via:**
*telnet fdabbs.fda.gov; login bbs*

## Great Beginnings

A newsletter on the care and feeding of infants and young toddlers. It includes information about parental expectations, typical behavior, home-made toys, language games, and so on.

**Access via:**
*gopher bluehen.ags.udel.edu/Information By Topic/Families/Great Beginnings Newsletters*

## Handicap News BBS Archive

A collection of information and sources for and about the disabled. The archive includes legal and medical data in addition to information about social services.

**Access via:**
*ftp handicap.shel.isc-br.com;* login *anonymous*

*ftp handicap.shel.isc-br.com;*
login *anonymous;* cd *pub*

## Internet/BITNET Health Science Resources

A very large file of e-mail discussion lists, USENET newsgroups, Free-Nets, and other Internet resources relating to health and medicine, compiled by Lee Hancock of the University of Kansas Medical Center.

**Access via:**
*ftp ftp.sura.net;* login *anonymous;* cd *pub/nic;* get *medical.resources.9-93*

## MEDLINE

The MEDLINE database contains article citations and abstracts, indexed from over 4,000 journals in medicine and related health sciences. Some university libraries, especially medical school libraries, provide access to MEDLINE; however, access is normally limited to students, faculty, and staff. We've listed several libraries that provide MEDLINE. If you don't have ties to one of these institutions, check with your local library.

**Access via:**
*telnet melvyl.ucop.edu*

*telnet lib.dartmouth.edu*

*telnet library.umdnj.edu;* login *LIBRARY*

*telnet utmem1.utmem.edu;* login *HARVEY*

## National Health Security Plan

The proposal formally announced in September 1993 by President Clinton to overhaul the practice of medicine and medical insurance in the U.S., in a hypertext version.

**Access via:**
*www http://sunsite.unc.edu/nhs/NHS-T-o-C*

## National Institute of Allergy and Infectious Disease Gopher

Notable for its AIDS directory, but includes much administrative information also.

**Access via:**
*gopher gopher.niaid.nih.gov*

## National Institutes of Health (NIH)

This is the former Gopher server, with a WWW front end now available, too. The site includes information on and links to biomedical data, activities and grants of the NIH, and the NIH Library (via TELNET).

**Access via:**
*www http://www.nih.gov*

*gopher gopher.nh.gov*

## National Library of Medicine

The National Library of Medicine (NLM) holds over 4.5 million records, including books, journals, reports, manuscripts, and audiovisual items, and offers online information on a variety of medical topics.

**Access via:**
*www http://www.nlm.nih.gov*

*telnet etnet.nlm.nih.govi;* login *etnet*

## Palo Alto Medical Foundation

A symposium on managed health care: Is it capable of maintaining quality while reducing costs? It includes representatives from the government, business, industry, and academia. A very interesting set of presentations.

**Access via:**
*www http://www.service.com/PAMF/ home.html*

## World Health Organization

A Gopher service offering information on the WHO's major health programs, as well as press releases, e-mail/phone contacts, and general information about the organization.

**Access via:**
*gopher gopher.who.ch*

The WHO's FTP site offers some of the same information, particularly under the directories "programme" and "subject", but is less easy to navigate.

**Access via:**
*ftp ftp.who.ch;* login *anonymous*

## *Miscellaneous*

### Genealogy

Genealogical information of all types, including database programs, lists of genealogical societies, and newsletters, as well as cemetery information. There is also information on the National Genealogical Society and a list of tips for beginners.

**Access via:**
*ftp ftp.cac.psu.edu;* login *anonymous;* cd *genealogy*

*Note:* All files that are not programs have a *.zip* extension.

## Wedding Planner

Weddings are complicated affairs, particularly if you want to observe all the proper protocols. This resource may help you: it's a shareware Wedding Planner program for a personal computer.

**Access via:**
*ftp wuarchive.wustl.edu;* cd */systems/ibmpc/ msdos/database;* get *wedplan.zip*

## *Movies*

**Newsgroups:**
rec.arts.[animation, cinema, movies]

### Film Database

An indexed database of synopses, cast lists, etc., for over 6,500 films. All films were released prior to 1986.

**Access via:**
*gopher info.mcc.ac.uk/Miscellaneous items/ Film database*

### Hypertext Movie Database Browser

New in August 1993, this interface promises eventually to provide sound and video clips.

**Access via:**
*www http://www.cm.cf.ac.uk/Movies/moviequery.html*

### USENET Movie Review Archive

An archive of movie reviews that have appeared in the news group rec.arts.movies organized by year and month; can be rather slow.

**Access via:**
*gopher ashpool.micro.umn.edu/fun/Movies*

## *Music*

**Newsgroups:**
alt.[emusic, exotic-music], k12.ed.music, rec.music.[afro-latin, a-cappela, beatles, bluenote, cd, celtic, christian, classical, compose, country, dementia, dylan, early, folk, funky, gaffa, gdead, indian, industrial, info, makers, marketplace, misc, newage, reggae, reviews, synth, video]

### Acoustic Guitar Digest

An electronic magazine for the acoustic guitar enthusiast.

**Access via:**
*www http://www.acns.nwu.edu/guitar*

*ftp casbah.acns.nwu.edu;* login *anonymous;* cd *pub/acoustic-guitar*

### Banjo Tablature Archive

Includes original and transcribed tablature for the five-string banjo; all styles are represented, from bluegrass to jazz and classical.

**Access via:**
*www http://www.vuw.ac.nz/who/Nathan.Torkington/banjo/tab/home.html*

### The Bottom Line Archive (Bass)

An electronic magazine for acoustic and electric bass enthusiasts. Contains music and equipment reviews, lots of good information from other bass players, and our favorite picture of Carol Kaye, grandmother of all electric bassists.

**Access via:**
*www http://syy.oulu.fi/tbl.html*

*ftp ftp.uwp.edu;* login *anonymous;* cd *pub/music/lists/bass*

### Digital Tradition Folk Song Database

Allows users to search for and display lyrics, and can even provide audio of the song tunes for some systems.

**Access via:**
*www http://web2.xerox.com/digitrad*

*ftp parcftp.xerox.com;* login *anonymous;* cd *pub/music/digital_tradition*

### Ethnomusicology Research Digest

Serious information about tools and techniques for recording music in the real world, formatted in ASCII.

**Access via:**
*gopher gopher.cic.net/Electronic Serials/Alphabetic List/E/Ethnomusicology Research Digest*

### Folk Music

Sources for folk music lyrics, discographies, clubs, and so on.

**Access via:**
*ftp nysernet.org;* login *anonymous;* cd *folk_music*

## Guitar Chords and Tablature

Guitar tablature and chords for songs of many popular artists from current to old, electric to acoustic. Entries are submitted by the people on the Net who have worked out the tab or chords. Submissions copied from books are not allowed. Organized by artist/group.

**Access via:**
*ftp ftp.nevada.edu;* login *anonymous;*
cd *pub/guitar*

## Indian Classical Music

A database of Indian CDs. Coverage is best for Hindustani music, but it also includes some Karnatic CDs. Try searching for Shankar to get a flavor for what is there.

**Access via:**
WAIS *indian-classical-music.src*

## MIDI Information

MIDI (Musical Instrument Digital Interface) is a common interface for computer-assisted music. The NetJam resource at Berkeley is meant to stimulate musical collaboration through organized exchange of MIDI and other related information. The WAIS database points to archives of technical documents and discussions about MIDI.

**Access via:**
*ftp xcf.berkeley.edu;* login *anonymous;*
cd *pub/misc/netjam*
(NetJam.)

WAIS *midi.src*

## MTV.COM

Adam Curry's mtv.com site offers information on pop music, interviews with musicians, and even some short videos. Choose your method of connection!

**Access via:**
*gopher mtv.com*

*ftp mtv.com;* login *anonymous*

*www http://mtv.com*

## University of Wisconsin-Parkside Music Archive

A general source for many types of music information, both recorded and home-made. Items include information on building classical CD collections, lyrics, guitar chords, and pictures of artists.

**Access via:**
*ftp ftp.uwp.edu;* login *anonymous;*
cd *pub/music*

## WNUR-FM Jazz Information Server

A hypertext resource on jazz, including discographies, lists of jazz music stores, hotlines, clubs, radio stations, and pictures of jazz musicians. This Web site is maintained by the staff of WNUR-FM of Evanston, Illinois.

**Access via:**
*www http://www.acns.nwu.edu/jazz*

# OCEANOGRAPHY

### Bedford Institute of Oceanography

Existing for the purpose of exchanging scientific data and programs with other marine scientists, the Habitat Ecology Division of the Bedford Institute of Oceanography developed the BSIM simulation and has files of the Uniforum Atlantic minutes. This server also has information on fishery science.

**Access via:**

*gopher biome.bio.dfo.ca*

*ftp biome.bio.dfo.ca;* login *anonymous*

## OCEANIC (Ocean Information Center)

The Ocean Information Center Bulletin Board provided by the University of Delaware. Has very technical and organizational material about various oceanographic experiments, field trials, and meetings.

**Access via:**

*telnet delocn.udel.edu;* login *info*

## USGS, Branch of Atlantic Marine Geology

Located in Woods Hole, Mass. Contains abstracts and preprints of several geological journals, marine geology data sets, and information about what goes on in Woods Hole.

**Access via:**

*gopher bramble.er.usgs.gov*

# PALEONTOLOGY

**Newsgroup:**
sci.archaeology

## Honolulu Community College Dinosaur Exhibit

A fun, well-designed tour of the permanent dinosaur exhibit at Honolulu Community College, complete with photographs, illustrations, movies, and even audio narration. The exhibits themselves are actually replicas from the originals at the American Museum of Natural History in New York City.

**Access via:**

*www http://www.hcc.hawaii.edu/dinos/ dinos.1.html*

## U.C. Berkeley Museum of Paleontology Gopher

Includes information on the U.C. Berkeley Museum of Paleontology and its holdings. This is an obvious resource if you're interested in fossils, but it has a lot of resources for other naturalists. The library of images includes a large collection of shark pictures, plus pictures of animals, plants, birds, and a library of animal sounds (including whale sounds).

**Access via:**

*gopher ucmp1.berkeley.edu*

### U.C. Berkeley Museum of Paleontology Public Exhibits

The Museum's own WWW site features exhibits on Fossil Life, Sharks of the California Coast, and the Palaeontological Institute of Russia. The Fossil Life exhibition is also accessible through EXPO.

**Access via:**
*www http://ucmp1.berkeley.edu/ welcome.html*
(At Berkeley, all exhibits.)

*www http://sunsite.unc.edu/expo/ paleo.exhibit/paleo.html*
(EXPO, Fossil Life only.)

### Paleontological Society Gopher

A Gopher server providing skeletal information about the Kentucky Paleontological Society. Contains information about the Society, notices of meetings and conferences, job postings, grant availability, book notices, etc.

**Access via:**
*gopher uicvm.uic.edu/The Researcher/ Paleontology/Paleontological Society*

### Palynology & Palaeoclimatology (ANU Bioinformatics Hypermedia Service)

Mainly links to Australian National University or other Internet resources relating to the Quaternary period (that's the past two million years or so). Palynology is the study of pollen.

**Access via:**
*www http://life.anu.edu.au/ landscape_ecology/pollen.html*

# PETS

**Newsgroups:**
rec.pets, rec.pets.[birds, cats, dogs, herp]

**See:**
Free-Nets—Youngstown Free-Net; Medicine & Health—FDA Electronic Bulletin Board

### AVES: Bird-Related Information

An archive of images of birds, with very basic information about various species, keyed to the images. Also includes sounds. Some of the images are of only moderate quality.

**Access via:**
*gopher vitruvius.cecer.army.mil*

### Llamas

A small directory including information about organizations of llama enthusiasts, a *Llama.FAQ* file, and some small black-and-white images.

**Access via:**
*gopher gopher.hs.jhu.edu/—>...Images/ Miscellaneous/Llamas*

### Pet FAQs

News group FAQs, mostly about dogs, but there are also FAQs on aquariums and fleas.

**Access via:**
*ftp quartz.rutgers.edu; login anonymous; cd pub/pets*

# PHILOSOPHY

**Newsgroup:**
sci.philosophy

## American Philosophical Association Gopher

Serious information on serious subjects. Contains addresses, information on upcoming events, grants, fellowships and academic positions, bibliographies, and calls for papers.

**Access via:**
*gopher apa.oxy.edu*

# PHYSICS

**Newsgroups:**
sci.physics.[accelerators, fusion, particle, research], sci.space

## High Energy Physics (CERN)

Physics resources are a bit hard to come by, on the Internet: Physicists have their own network, called HEPnet, which uses a different set of protocols. However, the World Wide Web provides access to many resources through a gateway—which you'd expect, since it was spawned at CERN, the European high-energy physics laboratory. WWW currently provides access to information from CERN, DESY (a German physics lab), NIKHEF (Dutch physics center), SLAC (Stanford Linear Accelerator), and Fermilab.

**Access via:**
*www http://info.cern.ch/hypertext/ DataSources/bySubject/Physics/HEP.html*

## Los Alamos Physics Information Service

Both nuclear and particle physics are represented on these Gopher and WWW servers, which are maintained by the Los Alamos National Laboratory (LANL). Primarily devoted to preprints on nuclear and high-energy physics. Abstracts and the papers themselves are available, as well as text searching of abstracts, authors, and titles.

**Access via:**
*www http://mentor.lanl.gov/Welcome.html*

## Nonlinear Dynamics Archive

Contains reprints of papers, abstracts, software, and other material related to nonlinear dynamics. Apparently organized according to the institution that the software or paper came from, so you'll need to look at the *README* file to figure out what's available.

**Access via:**
*ftp lyapunov.ucsd.edu;* login *anonymous;* cd *pub*

**Information:**
E-mail: mbk@inls1.ucsd.edu (Matt Kennel)

## Physics News

News and information related to physics, including links to other science news resources and updates on congressional action on science funding.

**Access via:**
*www http://www.het.brown.edu/news/ index.html*

# POLITICS & POLITICAL ACTIVISM

**Newsgroups:**
alt.activism, misc.activism.progressive, soc.politics

## Congressional Contact Information

Contains the names, addresses and phone numbers of members of Congress. It can be searched by name, city, state, or zip code.

**Access via:**
WAIS *US-Congress-Phone-Fax.src*

## Environmental Activism Server

What's your favorite cause? This server carries information on all sorts of causes, ranging from "Agran for President '92," to "Earth First!" to the Gulf War, to U.S.-Japan trade. It also includes lists of government telephone numbers, articles, and judicial decisions on the environmental movement.

**Access via:**
*ftp pencil.cs.missouri.edu;* login *anonymous;* cd *pub/map*

## Political Contact Information

Addresses, telephone and fax numbers, and other contact information for government and media people, mixed with historical documents.

**Access via:**
*ftp ftp.eff.org;* login *anonymous;* cd *pub/academic/civics*

## Presidential Election 1992

History is written by the victors, so this resource largely reflects the Democratic Party's view of the election, and a subdirectory is devoted to the "Year of the Woman." There is a subdirectory titled "Republican," though.

The "IssueBriefs" subdirectory includes positions by both parties. There is no trace anywhere of Ross Perot.

**Access via:**
*ftp info.umd.edu;* login *anonymous;* cd *info/Government/US/Election92*

## Privacy Forum

The Internet Privacy Forum is a moderated digest for the discussion and analysis of issues relating to the general topic of privacy.

**Access via:**
*gopher vortex.com/\*\*\* PRIVACY Forum \*\*\**

## Ross Perot

Ross' book *United We Stand,* broken up into chapters formatted in ASCII.

**Access via:**
*gopher joeboy.micro.umn.edu/EBooks/ By Title/United We Stand*

# PSYCHOLOGY

**Newsgroup:**
sci.psychology

## Princeton Psychology Archive

A large repository, apparently mostly for the American Psychological Association's electronic journal *Psycoloquy.*

**Access via:**
*ftp princeton.edu;* login *anonymous;* cd *pub/harnad*

## Psycoloquy

An online academic journal about psychology, published by the American Psychological Association.

**Access via:**
*www http://info.cern.ch./hypertext/ DataSources/bySubject/Psychology/ Psycoloquy.html*

# RECREATION

**Newsgroups:**
alt.[aquaria, magic, sewing], rec.[antiques, aquaria, collecting, crafts.brewing, crafts.misc, crafts.textiles, folk-dancing, gambling, gardens, guns, juggling, models.railroad, models.rc, models.rockets, photo, radio.amateur.misc, radio.amateur.packet, radio.amateur.policy, radio.cb, railroad, roller-coaster, woodworking]

## Biking Information (Norway)

A program called Bike Manager, instructions for making your own brake booster, and the "Great Trail of Strength Report" for 1991 through 1993 can be found here.

**Access via:**
*ftp ugle.unit.no;* login *anonymous;*
cd *local/biking*

## Chess

The FTP site listed below contains a lot of material, including chess programs for various computer platforms and a FAQ.

At Assumption College there is a server that allows you to meet and play chess with other people. If you prefer, you can just "watch." Players must register with the server, allowing them to save games and participate in a rating system.

**Access via:**
*ftp remus.ucs.uoknor.edu;* login *anonymous;*
cd *pub/chess*

*telnet eve.assumption.edu*

## Internet Go Server

A computer that allows you to meet other people and play "go" with them. Watching and kibitzing on other games is allowed.

**Access via:**
*telnet hellspark.wharton.upenn.edu 6969;*
login *guest*

## Juggling FTP Archives

A set of resources for the juggling enthusiast. Has such resources as Jugglers World Newsletter, lists of vendors, festivals, and clubs. Also, some information on the International Jugglers Association.

**Access via:**
*ftp cogsci.indiana.edu;* login *anonymous;*
cd *pub/juggling*

**Information:**
E-mail: moocow@piggy.cogsci.indiana.edu

## Martial Arts

A martial arts archive in Israel includes information on several of the martial arts, including "Stretching."

**Access via:**
*www http://archie.ac.il:8001/papers/rma/rma.html*

More specifically, here are lists of known Aikido dojos by continent. Affiliation is flagged in the list as well. Other information includes listings of events, books, and videos.

**Access via:**
*ftp cs.ucsd.edu;* login *anonymous;*
cd *pub/aikido*

Additional Aikido information may also be found in this Gopher resource:

**Access via:**
*gopher somalia.earth.nwu.edu/Aikido Resources*

 ## Scuba Diving Information

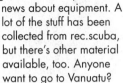

Lots of information about scuba diving, including reviews of different places to go, condition reports, and news about equipment. A lot of the stuff has been collected from rec.scuba, but there's other material available, too. Anyone want to go to Vanuatu?

**Access via:**
*ftp ames.arc.nasa.gov;* login *anonymous;*
cd *pub/SCUBA*

**Information:**
E-mail: yee@ames.arc.nasa.gov

## Skiing FAQ

A list of frequently asked questions about skiing, as well as ski information for Utah, Idaho, and Wyoming. The Utah information is the most complete.

**Access via:**
*ftp ski.utah.edu;* login *anonymous;* cd *skiing*

## Skydiving

Includes pictures, a FAQ, the archive of rec.skydiving, and pointers to other skydiving resources on the Internet.

"If piloting an airplane is flying, then piloting a boat is swimming. To get the full experience, you have to get out into the element."

**Access via:**
*www http://www.cis.ufl.edu/skydive*

## Simulated Conversations

The Conversational Hypertext server offers some simulated conversations, some of which are similar in flavor to fantasy games. They are a big improvment over the time-honored (but rather worn) psychoanalysis simulations.

**Access via:**
*telnet debra.doc.ca*

## Windsurfing

You want to windsurf in Corpus Christi, TX, or down the Columbia River Gorge? How about information on windsurfing shops and launch sites in the San Francisco Bay Area? This, along with phone numbers for various wind reporting stations, windsurfing bitmaps, and hot topics of discussion are located here.

**Access via:**
*ftp lemming.uvm.edu;* login *anonymous;* cd *rec.windsurfing*

# REFERENCE

## Acronym Dictionary

A searchable Gopher index of 6,000 acronyms.

**Access via:**
*www http://curia.ucc.ie/info/net/ acronyms/acro.html*

## CIA World Factbook

The CIA maintains a dossier on every country in the world. This is the 1993 version of that dossier, describing 249 nations. Each entry contains information about population, economic condition, trade, conflicts, and politics. There's lots of stuff you won't find here—such as the number of nuclear warheads aimed at the Pentagon. But you will find lots of basic information about almost any country you can think of.

**Access via:**
WAIS *world-factbook93.src*

## Online Dictionary

An online English dictionary; type the word, you get the definition.

**Access via:**
*telnet chem.ucsd.edu;* login *webster*

## Reader's Guide to Periodical Literature

Yes, that old workhorse, the *Reader's Guide to Periodical Literature,* is available on the Internet. In case you've forgotten, it's a topic-oriented index to virtually all general-interest magazines published in the U.S.: *Time, Popular Mechanics,* etc. You can search it electronically by author, title, subject, keyword, and so on.

**Access via:**
*telnet lib.uwstout.edu;* login *library*

## Roget's Thesaurus

**See:** Literature—Project Gutenberg

## Zipcode Guide 1991

A list of postal zipcodes for the U.S. from 1991. The format is:

00401:Pleasantville, NY

00501:Holtsville, NY

**Access via:**
WAIS *zipcodes.src*

# RELIGION & BELIEF

**Newsgroups:**
soc.religion.[bahai, christian, christian.bible-study, eastern, islam, quaker], alt.atheism, alt.atheism.moderated, alt.hindu, alt.religion, talk.religion

## ANU Asian Religions Bibliography

A collection (450 K) of bibliographic references to selected (mainly Buddhist) Asian religions. From documents deposited with the Coombspapers Social Sciences Research Data Bank, Research Schools of Social Sciences and Pacific Studies, Australian National University, GPO Box 4, Canberra ACT 2601.

**Access via:**
WAIS *ANU-Asian-Religions.src*

**Information:**
E-mail: wais@coombs.anu.edu.au

Telephone: +61 6 249-4600

## Astrology

This astrology resource resides under the Southern Cross, in Australia. It includes lessons, a bibliography, and lists of resources about astrology, in addition to newsgroup archives and relevant software.

**Access via:**
*ftp hilbert.maths.utas.edu.au;*
login *anonymous;* cd *pub/astrology*

## Atheism

Mostly composed of material from alt.atheism and alt.atheism.moderated, including FAQs.

**Access via:**
*ftp ftp.mantis.co.uk;* login *anonymous;*
cd *pub/alt.atheism*

## Bible

A complete King James Bible, with cross references and lexicon.

**Access via:**
WAIS *bible.src*
(Available 9 A.M.–9 P.M. EST.)

The King James Bible in compressed format for the PC or the Mac.

**Access via:**

*ftp wuarchive.wustl.edu; login anonymous; cd doc/bible*
The Bible can be found in many languages (English, Finnish, German, Greek, Hebrew, Latin, Swahili, Turkish) in Finland.

**Access via:**

*ftp nic.funet.fi; login anonymous; cd pub/doc/bible/texts*

The Bible in two English translations, plus Greek (including the Septuagint) and Latin, all keyword searchable. Also includes material on the Church Fathers. Even if you're not interested in biblical studies, this resource shows you how good a well-constructed server can be. This site also has information on Islam and Mormon, and many other electronic texts. (Access to some electronic texts is limited to the campus.)

**Access via:**

*gopher ccat.sas.upenn.edu/CCAT Text Archives and Related Material from Elsewhere/Religion/Biblical*

## Book of Mormon

The Book of Mormon, searchable through WAIS; also available through Project Gutenberg in text form.

**See also:** Literature—Project Gutenberg

**Access via:**

WAIS *Book_of_Mormon.src*

## Catholicism

A Gopher resource at American University provides a rich mine of material on Catholicism, including recent Papal encyclicals.

**Access via:**

*gopher auvm.american.edu/Catholic Files*

John Ockerbloom maintains a fine set of pointers to "Catholic Resources on the Net."

**Access via:**

*www http://www.cs.cmu.edu:8001/Web/ People/spok/catholic.html*

## Coptic Christianity

Copt Net is a group serving the emigrant Coptic (Egyptian) Orthodox. The FTP archive includes contents of the group's newsletter, articles on the Coptic church, a directory of Coptic churches worldwide outside Egypt, a GIF archive of religious images, the King James Bible, texts of hymns, a selection of lections, and more.

**Access via:**

*ftp pharos.bu.edu; login anonymous; cd CN*

Ecumenical efforts to heal the schism that developed in A.D. 451 at the Council of Chalcedon are discussed from the Coptic point of view in a long article, "Recent Efforts for Unity Between the Two Families of the Orthodox Church."

**Access via:**

*gopher wiretap.Spies.COM/Wiretap Online Library/Articles/Religion and Philosophy/ orthodox.cop*

## Electric Mystic's Guide to the Internet

A rather long and thorough bibliography of Internet resources on religion (not just mysticism), by Michael Strangelove. It's available in various but nonhypertext formats; you'll have to retrieve the document in parts, whichever format you prefer. Many of the resources are at the Australian National University.

In the same directory as Strangelove's guide, there are other bibliographies on religion, referring to Internet and print sources.

**Access via:**
*ftp panda1.uottawa.ca;* login *anonymous;* cd *pub/religion*

## Hinduism

Archives of *Hindu Digest,* an electronic publication distributed on the newsgroup alt.hindu.

**Access via:**
*gopher gopher.cic.net/Electronic Serials/ Alphabetic List/H/Hindu Digest*

## Islam

The Qur'an is available in English translation via Gopher and WAIS.

**Access via:**
*WAIS Quran.src*

*gopher latif.com/The Quran* (In English only.)

*gopher cs1.presby.edu/Religion Resources/ Quran (Koran) - full text*

A large archive is maintained by the American Arab Scientific Society, Boston Chapter; despite the nonsectarian name of this group, the archive is largely of interest to Muslims, including information on sightings of the hilal, prayer timing software, and a list of bookstores that sell books on Islam or the Middle East, or books in Arabic or Persian.

**Access via:**
*ftp cs.bu.edu;* login *anonymous;* cd *amass*

A new "Guide to Islamic Resources on the Internet."

**Access via:**
*ftp aql.gatech.edu;* login *anonymous;* cd *pub/NetInfo/Documents;* get *Guide_to_Islamic_Resources_on_ The_Internet.gz*

*ftp ftp.netcom.com;* login *anonymous;* cd *pub/amcgee/african/islam/ cybermuslim.guide*

An evangelistic group called the Organization for New Muslims maintains a collection of resources mainly useful to American Muslims, including some of those cited above.

**Access via:**
*gopher latif.com*

## Jainism

An Indian religion dating from the sixth century B.C. and related to Hinduism. This resource offers explanatory material, bibliography, and documents comparing Jainism with certain other religions.

**Access via:**
*gopher wiretap.Spies.COM/Wiretap Online Library/Religion/Jainism*

## Judaism

The largest directory of information on Judaism, Hebrew, and Israel that we've found is in New York.

**Access via:**
*ftp nysernet.org;* login *anonymous;* cd *israel*

## Mystical & Occult

These resources were collected on Friday the thirteenth before moonrise. Novices will have to grope around a bit; initiates may be able to divine which directories are the ones they seek.

**Access via:**
*ftp quartz.rutgers.edu;* login *anonymous;* cd *pub/occult*

*ftp ftp.netcom.com; login anonymous; cd pub/alamut/mageguide*

*ftp slopoke.mlb.semi.harris.com; login anonymous; cd pub/magick*

## Presbyterianism

The *Westminster Confession of Faith* is available in ASCII.

**Access via:**
*gopher cs1.presby.edu/Religion Resources/ Westminster Confession of Faith*

## Religious Studies Publication Journal

This journal is designed to facilitate the dissemination of religious studies publications and resource information.

**Access via:**
*gopher gopher.usak.ca/Library/ E—Journals/ Humanities & Social Sciences/Religious Studies Publications Journal - CONTENTS*

## Satanism Enthusiasts

Archives of a newsletter called *The Watcher: New Zealand Voice of the Left Hand Path,* which is an occult print and electronic publication. These people appear to be having a lot of fun with their religious opinions.

**Access via:**
*gopher gopher.cic.net/Electronic Serials/ Alphabetic List/W/watcher*

## Urantia Book

An anonymous spiritualist and Christian revelation, ca. 1920–35, actually written by Wilfred C. Kellogg (d. 1956) and edited by William Samuel Sadler (1875–1969), both former Seventh Day Adventists, and published in 1955. Kellogg was an informally adopted son of the founder of the corn flake company.

This archive contains an index, in several formats, and commentary.

**Access via:**
*ftp wuarchive.wustl.edu; login anonymous; cd pub/urantia; get ubpapers.txt*

## *TECHNOLOGY*

**Newsgroups:**
sci.engr, sci.engr.[chem, biomed, civil, control, manufacturing, mech]

## NASA Mid-Continent Technology Transfer Center

As part of the National Technology Transfer Network, six Regional Technology Transfer Centers were established in 1991 by the United States government and NASA. The 14-state mid-continent region is served by the Mid-Continent Technology Transfer Center (MCTTC). The 14 states in the region are: Arkansas, Colorado, Iowa, Kansas, Missouri, Montana, Nebraska, New Mexico, North Dakota, Oklahoma, South Dakota, Texas, Utah, and Wyoming.

The mission of the Mid-Continent Technology Transfer Center is to serve the national interest by providing business, engineering, scientific, information, and educational services for the mid-continent region enabling public and private enterprises to acquire, develop, and apply technologies from or with NASA, federal laboratories, and other sources to expand the use of technology, promote commercialization, and improve competitiveness.

This is a good site for reaching other technology-related Gopher servers.

**Access via:**
*gopher technology.com*

# TELEVISION

**Newsgroups:**
alt.fan.*, alt.tv.*, rec.arts.*, rec.music.*, rec.arts.startrek

## Monty Python

A large collection of Monty Python sketches.

**Access via:**
*gopher ocf.berkeley.edu/OCF On-line Library/Monty_Python*

## Satellite TV

Pointers to useful information on the Net relating to satellite TV and radio, assembled by Jay Novello.

**Access via:**
*www http://itre.uncecs.edu/misc/sat.html*

## The Simpsons Archive

Everything you wanted to know about the Simpsons. Play dates, credits, bibliographies, episode summaries, etc.

**Access via:**
*ftp ftp.cs.widener.edu;* login *anonymous;* cd *pub/simpsons*

# TRAVEL

**Newsgroups:**
rec.travel, rec.travel.[air, marketplace]

**See also:** International Interest

## SPIRES Guide to Restaurants

A database of restaurant information, searchable by name, cuisine, city, state, and average price per meal. Listings are thin: Only two restaurants are listed for Los Angeles, for example.

**Access via:**
*gopher isumvs.iastate.edu/Serendipity/ Restaurants: SPIRES Guide to Restaurants*

## State Department Travel Advisories

These advisories from the U.S. State Department warn about some of the areas in which travel is dangerous. If you like to travel to out-of-the-way places, this resource is invaluable!

St. Olaf College in Northfield, Minnesota, is the Internet and BITNET distribution point for this information and has made it part of their WWW and Gopher sites; the FTP directory maintained by the University of Maryland mirrors the same information.

**Access via:**
*www http://www.stolaf.edu/network/ travel-advisories.html*

*gopher gopher.stolaf.edu/Internet Resources/ US-State-Department-Travel-Advisories*

*ftp info.umd.edu;* login *anonymous;* cd *inforM/Educational_Resources/United States/ Government/TravelAdvisories*

## Travel Information Library

Includes information about travel modalities, destinations, and the like, along with pointers to other travel information resources; much of the contents seems to be derived from the newsgroup rec.travel.

**Access via:**
*ftp ftp.cc.umanitoba.ca;* login *anonymous;* cd *rec-travel/README.html*

*www ftp://ftp.cc.umanitoba.ca/rec.travel/ README.html*

## Virtual Tourist

Connections to tourist guides for a number of locations, including Australia, Japan, New Zealand, many European countries, and many points in the United States. The Japanese tourist guide contains a number of maps, several audio files (including the national anthem), plus weather information, cultural information, etc.

**Access via:**
*www http://wings.buffalo.edu/world*

## GNN Travelers' Tales Resource Center

O'Reilly's own online travel center, with articles on using the Internet to prepare for a trip, travel information for destinations around the world, pointers to other travel resources, and a marketplace.

**Access via:**
*www http://nearnet.gnn.com/mkt/travel/ center.html*

# USENET NEWS

**Newsgroups:**
news.answers, news.newusers.questions, news.software, news.groups

## All the FAQs

"Frequently Asked Questions" files for all newsgroups are archived at rtfm.mit.edu. An index file lists every file in the directory with full title and a list of newsgroups, which may be useful for searching. There is also a "periodic-postings" directory containing files that discuss other helpful files posted periodically to newsgroups.

**Access via:**
*ftp rtfm.mit.edu;* login *anonymous;* cd *pub/usenet/news.answers*

## News Posting Service via E-mail

These servers allow you to post to USENET newsgroups even if you aren't part of the USENET system. Use dashes in the groupname rather than periods: for example, rec-music-folk rather than rec.music.folk. Remember to include your e-mail address in your posting so you can get replies.

**Information:**
E-mail: groupname@cs.utexas.edu, or
E-mail: groupname@pws.bull.com

## USENET Software: History and Sources

A frequently updated list and comparison of news reading software. A good place to start if you are unhappy with the newsreader you are currently using and want to see what alternatives are available.

**Access via:**
*ftp rtfm.mit.edu;* login *anonymous;* cd *pub/usenet/news.answers/usenet- software;* get *part1*

## USENET Periodic Posting Archives

A repository of the periodic informational postings of the newsgroups. There is a directory corresponding to each newsgroup name. The directory contains all regular postings to the newsgroups (including FAQ lists), as well as many other "general interest" postings that have sprung out of the newsgroups.

**Access via:**
*ftp rtfm.mit.edu;* login *anonymous;* cd *pub/usenet-by-group*

## What is USENET?

A long explanation for what the USENET news system is, how it is managed, and how it got to be the way it is.

**Access via:**
*ftp rtfm.mit.edu; cd pub/usenet-by group/ news.answers/what_is_usenet?; get part1*

# WEATHER & METEOROLOGY

**Newsgroup:**
sci.geo.meteorology

## Australian National University (ANU); Bioinformatics Hypermedia Service: Weather

Satellite images, forecasts, and links to other weather resources. Best used for weather information you can't find closer to your own site.

**Access via:**
*www http://life.anu.edu.au/weather.html*

## Minnesota Climatology Working Group

The University of Minnesota Climatology Working Group exists to provide climatological information to public agencies in the State of Minnesota. Information such as insect degree days (an important piece of information for campers!), crop degree days, and almost any type of climatological information pertaining to Minnesota that you'd want to know.

**Access via:**
*gopher gopher.soils.umn.edu/MN Climatology Working Group*

## NCAR Data Support Section Server

The National Center for Atmospheric Research has a wide variety of data and programs available to aid meteorological research. Some of these are available for free through this server. Some are offline, but can be "mounted" (i.e., placed online

for temporary access) for a fee. And some are so big they can only be ordered on tape.

**Access via:**
*www http://www.ucar.edu/metapage.html*

*ftp ncardata.ucar.edu; login anonymous; cd pub/weather*

## Network Sources for Meteorology and Weather

A regularly updated compilation by Ilana Stern of the National Center for Atmospheric Research, describing weather and meteorological data sources for the Internet, as well as on CD-ROM and tape.

**Access via:**
*www http://www.cis.ohio-state.edu/ hypertext/faq/usenet/weather/top.html*

*ftp rtfm.mit.edu; login anonymous; cd pub/usenet/news.answers/weather/data*

## Weather Maps

Many sites make various different collections of weather maps available. The data available and their formats vary, so you'll have to look carefully at what you find. It's important to look at any *README* files, or other descriptions, that are in these archives.

**Access via:**
*ftp unidata.ucar.edu; login anonymous; cd images*
(Weather radar maps, GOES HUGO images.)

ftp *aurelie.soest.hawaii.edu;*
login *anonymous;* cd *pub/avhrr/images*
(Sea surface temperature data for Hawaii and
vicinity.)

## Weather Underground

What's the weather in Butte, Montana? This is
where to find out; it's one of the most interesting (and, if you're a skier, useful) services
on the Internet. The Weather Underground
provides a menu-driven server giving current
weather information and forecasts for noncommercial use. The weather reports are
taken from the National Weather Service;
reports are available for the entire United
States and Canada. As we said, ski
conditions are available in the winter. Several
weather advisories and earthquake reports
are also available.

**Access via:**
WAIS *weather.src*

telnet *madlab.sprl.umich.edu 3000*

# WHITE PAGES

## Knowbot Information Service

The Knowbot Information Service is a "white
pages" service that will search for a name
through a large number of Internet databases.
It's a great way to look up friends and
acquaintances. It's not yet as convenient as it
might be, but Knowbots are among the
newest and most advanced services on the
Internet; it's worth knowing about them.

**Access via:**
telnet *info.cnri.reston.va.us185;* enter *e-mail
address*

## Knowbot Information
## Service Documentation

Documentation describing the philosophy and
use of the Knowbot Information white-pages

service. Files are available in PostScript and
ASCII format.

**Access via:**
ftp *nri.reston.va.us;* login *anonymous;*
cd *rdroms*

## List of Internet Whois Servers

Lists of all of the known whois-style white-
pages servers on the Internet, and related
information.

**Access via:**
ftp *rtfm.mit.edu;* login *anonymous;*
cd *pub/whois*

**Information:**
E-mail: mhpower@athena.mit.edu

## Netfind

A very persistent program that searches a
variety of databases to help you find
someone. Not very easy to use, but it may be
easier than looking through several different
white pages servers to find someone.

**Access via:**
telnet *bruno.cs.colorado.edu;* login *netfind*

telnet *archie.au;* login *netfind*

telnet *dino.conicit.ve;* login *netfind*

telnet *ds.internic.net;* login *netfind*

telnet *mudhoney.micro.umn.edu;* login *netfind*

telnet *netfind.oc.com;* login *netfind*

## PSI White Pages Pilot Project:
## User's Handbook

In PostScript format; many files.

**Access via:**
ftp *ftp.psi.com;* login *anonymous;* cd *wp/ps*

## USENET Addresses

This contains a list of all people who have posted to USENET newsgroups passing through MIT. This is an excellent way to find out a reasonably up-to-date address for many users of the Net.

For information by e-mail, send mail to mail-server@pit-manager.mit.edu; place "help" in the message body.

The filenames begin with *addresses*, one for each month back into 1992 and for occasional months before that. They are very large.

### Access via:

*ftp rtfm.mit.edu;* login *anonymous;*
cd *pub/usenet-addresses/lists*

# GETTING CONNECTED TO THE INTERNET

*Grades of Service*
*Service Providers*

No matter who you are, you get access to the Internet via a service provider. Service providers sell several different kinds of service, each with its own advantages and disadvantages. As with buying a car, you have to decide what features you want and how much you're willing to pay, and then go comparison-shopping.

But before you even read the list of providers, there's one thing you should do. In chapter 1, *What This Book Is About,* we said that many, many people have access to the Internet and don't know it. Are you one of these? Find out. If your company or school is on the Internet, it almost certainly has better service than you can afford as an individual.

In other words, you may already have an Internet connection available to you. You don't need to go out and find a service provider, you don't need to pay any extra bills; you just need to use what you already have. If you're a student at a four-year college or university, you can assume that your school is on the Internet, and you can probably get access as a student. Many junior colleges and a growing number of secondary schools are on the Net. Go to your computer center or computer science department and ask around. Ask a number of places before giving up—many times the only people who are aware of the Internet are those people who actually use it. If you're no longer part of academia, the problem is a little more difficult.

How do you find out if your company has Internet access? Anyone who is responsible for managing computer systems or taking care of your corporate network should be able to tell you. If most of your computer systems run UNIX, there's a good chance that you're on the Internet or at least can exchange e-mail and USENET news with the Internet. For historical reasons, if your computers are mostly running DOS, you probably aren't connected to the Internet—but there's no reason you couldn't be. Don't hesitate to dig some; if you're in marketing or accounting, you may not be aware of the nice Internet connection that the research or engineering group has been keeping to itself. If your company has a connection but it's not in your department, your job is to ask why. Write a proposal and get it into next year's budget. Do whatever is necessary. If the resource already exists, it won't cost your company much more to give it to you. And even if your company doesn't have a connection, it's still the best place to start. Find some other people who need Internet access, figure out how to justify it economically, and make a proposal.

If your company doesn't have a connection and you're not a student, there are still two ways of coming by Internet access inexpensively. The first thing to do is check out the public library. Some libraries offer a service called a Free-Net. It is a community-based information and e-mail system that allows Internet access. You can either use the Free-Net from the library or dial in to it. Although only a few libraries provide this service at the moment, the number is growing.

The second is to become a student. Find out whether or not your community college has an Internet connection. If it does, sign up for a course or two. At many community colleges, it is cheaper to take a course than it would be to arrange Internet services with a service provider as an individual. Learn basket weaving, and you can have something to do when you go crazy because the network is down. Once you are enrolled, ask for Internet access. There's a need for a public archive of significant basket designs—isn't there?

## Grades of Service

Well, you're still reading. So you probably didn't find any "free" Internet access points. Or, perhaps, someone said, "Sounds like a good idea. Why don't you do some research about what it will cost?" As we said, there are many different ways of connecting to the Internet. So, before you start your research, here's a summary of some types of connections that are available.

### Dedicated Internet Access

Corporations and large institutions that want Internet access should look into dedicated network access. This gives you complete access to all of the Internet's facilities. A service provider leases a dedicated telephone line at a speed of your choosing (the faster the line speed, the more it costs), and places a special routing computer at your location. That router is responsible for taking communications from your site destined for somewhere else and sending them on their way (and vice versa). This is all quite expensive, running at least $2,000 initially and several thousand dollars a year in monthly fees. However, once you've set up the connection, you can let as many computers as you like connect to the Internet—perhaps one computer in every classroom in your high school. To do so, you need only to place the computers on a local area network, along with the router.

Dedicated access offers the most flexible connection. Each computer is a full-fledged Internet member, capable of performing any network function. If there is some really neat new application you want to try, you just need to load the software and give it a whirl. However, since a dedicated connection is costly, it is most appropriate for a group setting, and impractical for home users.

Dedicated Internet access usually requires some support structure for your local network. The service provider will help you in the beginning, but once you get running, he is only responsible for the router and the phone line. What happens on your local network is your business. If you are responsible for the care and feeding of the LAN, this book won't be enough. The Nutshell Handbook *TCP/IP Network Administration,* by Craig Hunt, will help you to set up and run your local network. A class or two wouldn't hurt. And keep this book in mind; you may want to give it to users who keep bothering you with simple questions.

## SLIP and PPP

In the past few years, some less expensive techniques for "almost-dedicated access" have appeared. These are called SLIP and PPP; they are versions of the Internet software that run over normal phone lines, using standard high-speed modems. You may have to buy the SLIP or PPP software and a more expensive modem, but you won't have the very high connection costs.* You don't even have to use a "dedicated" phone line; you can use SLIP or PPP to dial in to your network when you want access, leaving the phone line free for other use when you don't need it. The real advantage of SLIP or PPP is that it allows a full-fledged connection to the Internet. You're not using someone else's system as an "access point" to the Net; you're on the Net yourself.

SLIP and PPP are very appropriate for connecting a home computer to a larger local network, which is in turn connected to the Internet. For example, you might use SLIP to connect your home computer to your company or campus network; then your home computer will have full Internet access, just as if it were on your company's Ethernet. SLIP and PPP are also appropriate for connecting a home computer (or perhaps a very small local network) to a service provider, who can give you full Internet access. They

---

*By high-speed, we mean at least 9,600 baud. A V.32bis or V.42bis modem is ideal. You could probably make SLIP work with a cheaper 2,400-baud modem, but it would be painful. In any case, your service provider will be able to make recommendations about what to buy. Some service providers even sell modems; that's a good way to avoid problems. You will usually get a good price, and if you run into trouble, your provider can't tell you, "Your modem isn't a type we support."

aren't appropriate for connecting a medium-sized or large network to the Internet; they can't talk fast enough to support many users at once. So if you have a medium or large network (or if you might have one in a few years), it's best to look into "real" dedicated access.

SLIP is a moderate-cost option: It provides very good service and isn't terribly expensive— but you'd wish it were cheaper. A service provider, such as UUNET or PSI, would typically charge something like $250 per month for unlimited SLIP or PPP service; alternatively, there may be a lower monthly charge, with an additional hourly fee. You also have to worry about the telephone bill. Many service providers provide 800 numbers or local access numbers in major urban areas to minimize this cost.

Installing SLIP or PPP, configuring them, and getting them running are not covered in this book. See the Nutshell Handbook *TCP/IP Network Administration* for more information about them. If you use Microsoft Windows, look into O'Reilly & Associates's "Internet in a Box" product; it's a nicely packaged Internet kit that includes newsreaders, mailers, Web browsers, and support for PPP.

## ISDN Access

ISDN stands for "Integrated Services Digital Network." In essence, it means using a digital telephone line between your home or office and the telephone company's switching office (or "central office"). This might sound like a new technology, but it actually isn't. Although it's only now coming into common use in the United States, ISDN has been widely used in Europe for a number of years. ISDN access can be either dial-up (intermittent access, as needed), or dedicated (a permanent connection to the Internet).

The big advantage of ISDN is that it provides very high-speed access at relatively low cost. One ISDN channel includes two 56KB or 64KB digital channels (depending on the implementation your phone company uses). With access speeds like this, multimedia services really zip! You won't have to wait 10 minutes to download someone's graphics-filled WWW home page.

Pricing is a big variable. It is almost certainly a lot less than a traditional dedicated line of the same speed would have cost a few years ago. Typical ISDN line charges are in the $20 to $50 per month range. Rates depend entirely on how the service is tariffed with the local public utilities commission. You may be able to save some money by using your ISDN line for your regular phone service, in addition to Internet access, but be careful. You can't use regular phones over an ISDN line, and ISDN phones cost hundreds of dollars. And, sometimes, ISDN voice calls are billed at business rates, so your cost per call might be higher.

The disadvantage of ISDN that its availability in the United States is spotty. If you're in a big city, there's a good change you can get it; if you're in a suburb, you probably can't; if you're in a rural area, forget it. You may need to spend a week trying to find the one person at your local phone company who knows what ISDN is (and getting past the two hundred who don't and try to sell you something else).

Since there hasn't been a lot of ISDN service around, many Internet providers don't have the equipment to handle incoming ISDN calls. ISDN equipment used to be pretty scarce, but it is getting cheaper and more available as demand increases. You may need to shop around to find service, but you should eventually find it.

## Dial-up Access

What if you can't afford dedicated access and you don't want to experiment with SLIP or PPP? Is there any easy way to get network access? Yes—just get a timesharing account on a computer that already has dedicated access. Then use your home computer to log in to this remote system, and do your surfing there. Timesharing access is almost (but not quite) as good as having your own connection, and it's considerably easier to set up. Your computer doesn't actually become part of the Internet; it's just accessing a service computer that's permanently connected to the network. Many organizations provide this kind of service. Since you are sharing the connection with others, the cost of these services is greatly reduced (typically around $10 to $40 per month—possibly with some additional per-hour access fee). The cheapest rates apply if you contract for "off peak" service only (i.e., nights and weekends). If you can find a Free-Net in your area, it will be even more economical; as the name implies, the service is free.

This type of connection has its pros and cons. On the good side, you probably have all the hardware and software you need (i.e., a modem and a terminal emulation package). Even if you have to buy them, you can come by them for less than $200. On the bad side, you can do only what the service provider allows. You may not be able to use all the services that the Internet has. There is probably no way to load a random nifty software application and use it; you have to appeal to the provider to add that service. Some access providers may limit the amount of disk space you can use. And again, you're responsible for phone bills, though (as we said above) some providers have 800 numbers or local access numbers.

By the way, it's worth mentioning one new kind of dial-up service. PSI (one of the major service providers) is distributing a free software package called PSIlink. It allows a PC running DOS to connect to their system and use the Internet's electronic mail, bulletin board, and file transfer services. They've managed to hide most of the problems that dial-up access entails; the files you want are automatically transferred to your home system, for example. The cost of this service is roughly $30 per month. The drawback is that you're limited to what one service provider gives you. As you might expect, the software that companies like PSI give away won't work with their competitors' systems. If this strikes you as a fair trade, look into it.

## UUCP Access

We'll mention, in passing, a subclass of dial-up access. All UNIX systems support a set of services called UUCP, which transfer data over standard phone lines. If you find a cooperating service provider (like UUNET, an employer, or a friend), you can arrange to use UUCP to pick up Internet mail and USENET news. Your system uses UUCP to dial in to a remote system at regular intervals and transfer news and mail back home. You can therefore read your mail on your own system, rather than someone else's. You can't do much more than read mail and news, since you're really not connected to the Internet at all. Your computer just dials up an Internet computer periodically and transfers files.

UUCP is common, and (if you have UNIX and a modem) you won't need to spend anything on software or equipment. Any UNIX system has all the software you need. And it's easy to find someone to give you a UUCP connection for free, or at least cheap. If all you want is electronic mail on your home system, it will do the job. Setting up UUCP is not trivial, but not terribly difficult, either. See the Nutshell Handbooks *Managing UUCP and USENET* and *Using UUCP and USENET* for more information.

## Access via Other Networks

Most networking services, such as BITNET and CompuServe, have set up gateways that allow you to exchange electronic mail with systems on the Internet. Some have set up gateways that let you read the Internet's bulletin boards (USENET news). And there are a few services scattered around that let you request a file via an e-mail message; such services fetch the file and mail it to you automatically. This isn't as good as getting the file directly, but it works.

This may be all you need. But it's definitely not an Internet connection; you have access to only a few services. What you can do is fairly limited; there's a lot more out there waiting for you.

There is another way you might use other networks to get to the Internet. If you are using one of the "UNIX for the masses" services, such as the Well, to provide you with Internet dial-up services, you usually have to pay for your own long-distance calls to the host computer. It might be more economical to use other networks, like CompuServe, to get from your home to the Internet computer. Then you can get to wherever on the Internet you like.

## Telephone Connections

Whatever alternative you choose, you're going to have some kind of telephone connection—whether it's a very expensive T3 line or a standard voice line. Here's a summary of the most common service grades:

*Table A-1*    *Telephone Line Options*

| Service Grade | Speed | Notes |
|---|---|---|
| Standard voice line | 0 to 28.8KB | No extra cost; SLIP or dial-up connections |
| ISDN | 56 to 128KB | Digital phone line; availability spotty; dedicated or dial-up |
| Leased line | 56 to 64KB | Small dedicated link to a service provider |
| T1 | 1.544MB | Dedicated link with heavy use |
| T2 | 6MB | Not commonly used in networking |
| T3 | 45MB | Major networking artery for a large corporation or university |

# ■ Service Providers

Internet service providers are participating in a competitive market. For any given kind of service, there are usually several providers available—and several different price structures. In the following tables, we've listed as many service providers as we could find. There are probably others. I can't tell you which ones are better than others; like the evolution of species, each has its own niche in the market. As you investigate, you'll certainly find different trade-offs you can make: quality of service versus price; initial cost versus monthly cost; 800-number access versus long-distance phone charges; and so on. However, I can give you some hints about how to shop.

## POPs and 800 Numbers

One of the largest expenses in getting an Internet connection may be your phone bill. Service providers have come up with two approaches to this problem. One is to install 800 numbers that you can dial "for free." The other is to install local access numbers (called points of presence, or POPs) in major metropolitan areas. Providers such as PSI and Netcom take the POP approach; AlterNet takes the 800-number approach. (These options are irrelevant to leased-line connections, which are negotiated separately with your phone company.)

Both approaches have obvious advantages and disadvantages. Dialing into a service provider can get very expensive if it isn't a local call. The 800 number seems to be cheaper, but—realize that someone still has to pay the bill, and that's going to be you. The provider may be able to get a better "bulk rate" for 800 service than you can for regular long-distance calls, but the difference won't be that substantial. You can expect service providers with 800 access to charge significantly higher monthly fees, or to have some kind of surcharge based on your connection time. Make sure to take that into account when doing a cost comparison. Estimate the amount of time you're going to spend on the Net,* figure out how much this would cost in long-distance charges to a provider, and compare that with the charges for the equivalent 800-number service.

Getting access through a local POP is ideal—if you can find one. You'll have only local phone calls to deal with. Even if your Internet time rivals the time your teenage kid sister spends on the phone, there won't be any extra charges to surprise you. However, that's only an option if there really is a local POP. If you live just one town outside of a provider's local calling area, tough. (And if you live out in the sticks, good luck!)

You should also consider how you will use your connection. If you are a traveling salesman driving from small town to small town, 800 service will probably be better, because you can call it from anywhere. If you travel between large cities, any national or international service provider with POPs will work, too. There will be a POP in every reasonable-sized city (populations above about 500,000, it appears). If you are looking for a cheap connection only to be used from home, you might check out the rash of local service providers. (In this case, you might try joining one of the "Internet Coops" that are starting up—particularly if you have some technical skills.)

## There's No Such Thing as a Cheap Lunch

Since the first edition of this book, service providers have sprouted like weeds. And still there aren't enough of them. It's becoming clear, though, that there are wide differences in the quality of service that the providers offer. Some hold your hand while you get started, answer your questions, fix things quickly when they break, and so on. Others don't. That's not surprising—auto dealers, insurance agencies, and other businesses are the same. Most Internet service providers are extremely helpful. Their biggest problem is that, as a rule, they're too busy. But there are some service providers who will pocket your check and walk away. Some careful shopping will keep you out of trouble.

Here's one particular aspect of service you should think about. Lately, we've seen some very low-priced offers for true Internet connectivity (i.e., SLIP or PPP connections) in the range for $20 per month for unlimited access. That's certainly a good deal. If it really works—which it may. But it may not.

---

*Be careful not to underestimate; networking often becomes addicting.

What's the problem? I suspect that these service providers are working on a "health club" model. For every person who buys a health club membership and works out faithfully, there are four or five who buy memberships and show up once or twice. If all the members worked out three times a week, the health club couldn't stay in business without drastically raising its prices and alienating its members . . . in which case, it would go out of business anyway. The same thing may be going on here. To offer unlimited access with very low monthly fees, the service provider must have a huge number of users and a relatively small number of phone lines and modems. The more users are sharing a limited bank of phones, the more likely you are to get a busy signal when you try to dial in. $20 per month is not a good price if all you're buying is a busy signal.

Keep in mind, though, that you might not have this problem. Nobody really knows how the service provider business will shake out. And getting people who use the Net for an hour every other month to subsidize your networking habit is great; but there's the risk that more people will actually make use of the service than you (and the service provider) are counting on. Just keep your eyes open and realize that there may be some drawbacks to offers that sound too good to be true.

## Internet Coops

One exciting development in the service provider arena has been the development of Internet cooperatives: groups of individuals and companies who buy a high-speed dedicated line from another service provider and then share it. As a result, the members get better service for less money than they could afford individually. Coops range from a few individuals sharing a PPP connection to elaborate arrangements for sharing leased T1 lines.

Since labor for running the coop (system administration, network administration, dealing with service providers and phone companies, billing) is often donated, members with technical skills are particularly valuable. You're particularly valuable if you have any technical expertise. Don't count yourself out if you're not a UNIX guru; other kinds of expertise are needed, too. Someone with a solid telecommunications background, or someone who can help support clients using Windows, would be very valuable to most coops. For that matter, few coops would sneer at a lawyer who could file incorporation papers or an accountant who could prepare financial statements.

A few of the providers we've listed are cooperatives. The more important question, though, is whether a cooperative is forming in your area—and there's no way we can tell you about that. Talk to your friends who are interested in the Internet; listen for rumors and investigate them. If you have access to USENET news, watch the newsgroups *alt.internet.access.wanted* and *alt.internet.services*. The first group consists mostly of people trying to find out how to get Internet access in a particular area. Don't just listen; get things started yourself by asking, "Does anyone know how to get an Internet connection in Fargo, North Dakota?" You may find out about an active service provider in your neighborhood, a coop that's forming in your area, or other people who would like access with whom you can form a coop of your own.

## Regional Versus National

Service providers within the U.S. and Canada tend to group themselves into two categories: national and regional. National providers market their services to anyone in their nation. Regional providers have staked out an area of the country and market their services only within that area. Of course, once you're connected to the Internet, you have access to the entire world. So the difference between national and regional providers depends on what you like. Regional providers would claim that they give better ("more personal" service) and that they can adapt more quickly to their clients' needs. (One regional provider helps its clients do teleconferencing, for example.) National providers would counter that claim by saying that they can bring more resources to bear to solve a particular client's problems.

International providers (providers that offer Internet connections in more than one country) are more difficult to categorize. One would assume that the national providers are ones who do international connections, too. This is true, but a number of regionals also do this. Many U.S. regional providers got dragged into providing international connections early in the Internet game, before most of the national providers existed, and they still have them today. So, if you are looking to connect from another country, you need to look at both regional/national and international provider tables.

Who you call depends on how and where you want to connect. How you should connect depends on the size of your connection. If you are an individual or really small business, you will probably be looking for providers of dial-up or SLIP/PPP services. Medium to large businesses should look to SLIP/PPP or dedicated services. Here are a few guidelines to help you in looking for a provider:

- If you want to connect a single site in one country to the Internet, or if you want to connect several sites in the same geographical area to the Internet, call either regional or national providers that offer suitable services. For example, if you want to connect several offices in New England to the Internet, you can contact either Northeast regional providers or national providers. Obviously, if you're interested in connecting only one site to the Internet, regional and national providers can serve you equally well; your choice will be based on price and the services available.

- If you want to connect several widely distributed sites within the same country to the Internet (e.g., offices in Washington, D.C., Los Angles, and Chicago), talk to suitable national providers. If you try to do this with regional providers, you will probably end up dealing with multiple contracts, operations centers, etc. It's probably not worth the effort.

- If you want to connect sites in the U.S. and sites in other countries to the Internet (e.g., offices in Washington, D.C., and London), talk to either a national provider or a regional provider with international connections on the coast closest to where you want to reach. It may be very hard to deal with a foreign bureaucracy; an experienced provider who is currently serving the country in question is valuable.

- If you are a lone researcher outside of the U.S., would like an Internet connection for yourself or your institution, and don't know where to start, try contacting:

Robert D. Collet
Principal Investigator
NSFnet International Connections Manager (ICM)
Program Manager, SprintLink
Sprint Communications Company
Government Systems Division—Mail Stop: VAHRNA611
13221 Woodland Park Road
Herndon, Virginia, 22071 USA
Tel: +1-703-904-2230
Fax: +1-703-904-2119
Pager: +1-800-SKY-PAGE   PIN: 45469
e-mail: rcollet@icm1.icp.net, rcollet@sprint.com, or
     PN=ROBERT.D.COLLET/O=US.SPRINT/ADMD=TELEMAIL/C=US/@sprint.com

He is the person responsible for international connections for the NSFnet portion of the Internet.

In Europe, you might also try:

RIPE NCC
Kruislaan 409
NL-1098 SJ
Amsterdam
The Netherlands
Tel: +31 20 592 5065
e-mail: ncc@ripe.net

## The Providers Themselves

The following table is of providers offering regional service within the U.S. and Canada, followed by a table of providers offering international service. But first, we'll tell you how to get your own information. You can find an extensive list of providers from Collosus, Inc., at **http://thelist.com**. Another excellent resource is ATrueStory; send an e-mail message reading **MY AREA CODE** - *your area code,* to **zahner@aimnet.com** and you'll receive a list of providers in your area. Also watch the newsgroups *alt.internet.services* and *alt.internet.access.wanted* to find out about Internet access opportunities.

The following tables are by no means exhaustive, and you should check all providers for your state/province, as a provider's POPs may extend beyond the metropolitan area in which it's listed. Most providers listed offer both individual/residential services and business services, but a number specialize in one or the other; shop around to find the best offer. All providers listed support PPP or SLIP connections. An asterisk (*) indicates providers who also offer dedicated connections at T1 or higher levels, making good choices for LAN connections or other multiuser networks. Inclusion in the list is not an endorsement of the service.

*Table A-2    Regional and National Service Providers: U.S. and Canada*

| State/City/Providers | E-mail | Telephone |
|---|---|---|
| ALABAMA | | |
| *Birmingham* | | |
| Cheney Communications Company* | info@cheney.net | (800) CHENEY-1 |
| The Matrix | webmaster@the-matrix.com | (205) 251-9347 |
| SouthEast Information Systems | myoung@secis.com | (205) 678-9945 |
| Viper Computer Systems, Inc.* | vipersys@viper.net | (205) 978-9850 |
| *Mobile* | | |
| Mobile Area Free-Net | info@maf.mobile.al.us | (334) 405-4600 |
| WSNetwork Communications Services* | info@wsnet.com | (334) 263-5505 |
| ALASKA | | |
| *All points* | | |
| Corcom, Inc. | support@corcom.com | (907) 563-1191 |
| ImagiNET, Inc. | coppick@imagi.net | (907) 455-9638 |
| Internet Alaska* | info@alaska.net | (907) 562-4638 |
| MicroNet Communications | info@lasertone.com | (907) 333-8663 |
| PolarNet | help@polarnet.fnsb.ak.us | (907) 457-4929 |

| State/City/Providers | E-mail | Telephone |
|---|---|---|
| **ALBERTA** | | |
| *Calgary* | | |
| AlphaCom Business Center | quint@alphacom.com | (403) 245-4512 |
| Debug Computer Services | root@debug.cuc.ab.ca | (403) 248-5798 |
| Nucleus Information Service | markm@nucleus.com | (403) 541-9470 |
| OA Internet Inc.* | info@oanet.com | (403) 430-0811 |
| *Edmonton* | | |
| Alberta SuperNet, Inc. | info@supernet.ab.ca | (403) 441-3663 |
| CCINet | info@ccinet.ab.ca | (403) 450-6787 |
| **ARIZONA** | | |
| *Phoenix/Mesa* | | |
| Crossroads Communications* | info@xroads.com | (602) 813-9040 |
| Evergreen Internet* | evergreen@enet.net | (602) 926-4500 |
| GetNet International, Inc.* | info@getnet.com | (602) 943-3119 |
| Internet Access | bang@neta.com | (602) 820-4000 |
| Internet Direct, Inc.* | info@indirect.com | (602) 274-0100 |
| NETWEST Communications, Inc. | webmaster@netwest.com | (602) 948-5052 |
| Primenet* | info@primenet.com | (602) 395-1010 |
| Systems Solutions Inc.* | webmaster@syspac.com | (602) 955-5566 |
| *Tucson* | | |
| ACES Research* | sales@aces.com | (520) 322-6500 |
| Internet Direct, Inc.* | info@indirect.com | (520) 324-0100 |
| Opus One* | info@opus1.com | (520) 324-0494 |
| **ARKANSAS** | | |
| *All points* | | |
| Axess Providers* | info@axs.net | (501) 225-6901 |
| Information Galore! | info@elvis.infogo.com | (501) 862-0777 |
| IntelliNet, LLC* | info@intellinet.com | (800) 290-7677 |
| world lynx | ivars@cei.net | (501) 562-8297 |
| YourNET | newuser@yournet.com | (501) 988-9432 |
| **BRITISH COLUMBIA** | | |
| *Vancouver* | | |
| auroraNET, Inc.* | sales@aurora.net | (604) 294-4357 x101 |
| Cyberstore Systems, Inc.* | info@cyberstore.net | (604) 482-3400 |
| Helix Internet* | info@helix.net | (604) 689-8544 |
| ICE Online | info@iceonline.com | (604) 298-4346 |
| Internet Direct | sales@direct.ca | (604) 691-1600 |
| MIND LINK! Communication Corporation* | info@mindlink.net | (604) 668-5000 |

| State/City/Providers | E-mail | Telephone |
|---|---|---|
| Wimsey Information Services Inc.* | info@wimsey.com | (604) 257-1111 |
| *All other points* | | |
| A&W Internet Inc.* | info@awinc.com | (604) 763-1176 |
| Fairview Technology Centre Ltd. | bwklatt@ftcnet.com | (604) 498-4316 |
| Island Net, AMT Solutions Group, Inc. | mark@islandnet.com | (604) 383-0096 |
| NETinterior ComputerLinks, Ltd. | info@netinterior.com | (604) 851-9700 |
| Okanagan Internet Junction* | info@junction.net | (604) 549-1036 |
| Sunshine Net, Inc. | admin@sunshine.net | (604) 886-4120 |
| UNIServe Online* | info@uniserve.com | (604) 856-6281 |
| Whistler Networks* | webmaster@whistler.net | (604) 932-0606 |

## CALIFORNIA

*Bakersfield*

| | | |
|---|---|---|
| Kern Internet Services | support@kern.com | (805) 397-4513 |
| Lightspeed Net | hostmaster@lightspeed.net | (805) 324-4291 |

*Fresno*

| | | |
|---|---|---|
| Cybergate Internet Services | info@cybergate.com | (209) 486-GATE |
| InfoNet Communications* | johnb@icinet.net | (209) 446-2360 |
| ValleyNet Communications* | info@valleynet.com | (209) 486-VNET |

*Los Angeles*

| | | |
|---|---|---|
| Artnet Communications | info@artnet.net | (310) 659-0122 |
| Cogent Software, Inc.* | info@cogsoft.com | (818) 585-2788 |
| DigiLink Network Services | info@digilink.net | (310) 542-7421 |
| DirectNet* | sales@directnet.com | (213) 383-3144 |
| EarthLink Network | info@earthlink.net | (213) 644-9500 |
| Flamingo Communications Inc. | sales@fcom.com | (310) 532-3533 |
| LA Free-Net | info@lafn.org | (310) 724-8713 |
| LA Internet | info@lainet.com | (310) 442-4670 |
| Lightside, Inc.* | info@lightside.net | (818) 858-9261 |
| The Loop Internet Switch Co. | info@loop.com | (213) 465-1311 |
| PacificNet* | info@pacificnet.net | (818) 717-9500 |
| ValNet | info@val.net | (818) 506-5757 |

*Oakland*

| | | |
|---|---|---|
| Beckemeyer Development* | info@bdt.com | (510) 530-9637 |
| Community ConneXion | info@c2.org | (510) 601-9777 |
| Direct Network Access (DNAI) | info@dnai.com | (510) 649-6110 |
| Idiom Consulting | info@idiom.com | (510) 644-0441 |
| LanMinds, Inc. | info@lanminds.com | (510) 843-6389 |
| Norcov Research | info@norcov.com | (510) 559-9645 |
| Surf Communications, Inc. | info@expressway.com | (800) 499-1517 |

| State/City/Providers | E-mail | Telephone |
| --- | --- | --- |
| *Orange County* | | |
| Delta Internet Services* | sales@delta.net | (714) 778-0370 |
| *Riverside/San Bernardino* | | |
| EmpireNet | support@empirenet.com | (909) 787-4969 |
| PE.net | info@pe.net | (909) 320-7800 |
| *Sacramento/Yolo* | | |
| CalWeb Communications* | info@calweb.com | (916) 641-WEB0 |
| Coastal Web Online | info@cwo.com | (916) 552-7922 |
| mother.com, Inc.* | info@mother.com | (916) 757-8070 |
| NSNet* | sales@ns.net | (916) 856-1530 |
| ProMedia | info@promedia.net | (916) 853-5520 |
| QuikNet* | sales@quiknet.com | (916) 773-0917 |
| Sacramento Network Access, Inc.* | ghall@sna.com | (916) 565-4500 |
| *San Diego* | | |
| American Digital Network | info@adnc.com | (619) 576-4272 |
| ConnectNet | sales@connectnet.com | (619) 450-0254 |
| CTSNet* | info@cts.com | (619) 637-3637 |
| Data Transfer Group | info@thegroup.net | (619) 220-8601 |
| ElectriCiti | info@electriciti.com | (619) 338-9000 |
| SuperSales Internet | wjnorris@supersales.com | (619) 220-2125 |
| ZNet* | info@znet.com | (619) 755-7772 |
| *San Francisco* | | |
| Connex Communications | admin@connex.com | (415) 386-7734 |
| CreativeNet | info@creative.net | (415) 495-1811 x14 |
| Hooked | info@hooked.net | (415) 343-1233 |
| The Little Garden/TLGnet* | info@tlg.net | (415) 487-1902 |
| QuakeNet Internet Services* | info@quake.net | (415) 655-6607 |
| Sirius Connections | info@sirius.com | (415) 284-4700 |
| SlipNET* | info@slip.net | (415) 281-3196 |
| Televolve, Inc. | televolve@sfo.com | (415) 867-7712 |
| *San Jose/Palo Alto* | | |
| Ablecom | support@ablecom.net | (408) 280-1000 |
| Aimnet Infomation Services* | info@aimnet.com | (408) 257-0900 |
| Bay Area Internet Solutions* | info@bayarea.net | (408) 447-8690 |
| InterNex Tiara* | info@internex.net | (408) 496-5466 |
| InterServe Communications, Inc.* | info@interserve.com | (415) 328-4333 |
| Internet Public Access Corporation* | info@ipac.net | (408) 532-1000 |
| ISP Networks* | info@isp.net | (408) 653-0100 |
| MediaCity | info@mediacity.com | (415) 321-6800 |
| NETCOM On-Line Communication Services | info@netcom.com | (408) 983-5950 |

| State/City/Providers | E-mail | Telephone |
| --- | --- | --- |
| NetGate Communications* | info@netgate.net | (408) 565-9601 |
| Silicon Valley Public Access Link | support@svpal.org | (408) 448-3071 |
| West Coast Online* | info@wco.com | (800) 926-4683 |
| *Ventura* | | |
| FishNet Internet Services of Ventura | daveh@fishnet.net | (805) 650-1844 |
| Internet Access of Ventura County | info@vcnet.com | (805) 383-3500 |
| RAIN | rain@rain.org | (805) 650-5354 |
| Silicon Beach Communications* | info@silcom.com | (805) 730-7740 |
| WestNet Communications, Inc. | info@west.net | (805) 892-2133 |
| **COLORADO** | | |
| *Denver/Boulder/Greeley* | | |
| Colorado Internet Cooperative Association* | info@coop.net | (303) 443-3786 |
| Colorado SuperNet, Inc.* | info@csn.net | (303) 296-8202 |
| Computer Systems Design Company* | support@csd.net | (303) 443-0808 |
| DASH* | custserv@dash.com | (303) 674-9784 |
| @denver.net | info@denver.net | (303) 973-7757 |
| EnvisioNet | info@envisionet.net | (303) 770-2408 |
| Indra's Net, Inc. | info@indra.com | (303) 546-9151 |
| *Colorado (southeast)* | | |
| Internet Express* | service@usa.net | (800) 592-1240 |
| OldColo Company | dave@oldcolo.com | (719) 636-2040 |
| Rocky Mountain Internet, Inc.* | info@rmii.com | (800) 900-RMII |
| **CONNECTICUT** | | |
| *Hartford* | | |
| imagine.com* | postmaster@imagine.com | (860) 293-3900 |
| MiraCom* | sales@miracle.net | (860) 523-5677 |
| NETPLEX* | info@ntplx.net | (860) 233-1111 |
| North American Internet Company* | info@nai.net | (800) 952-INET |
| *New Haven/Meriden* | | |
| CallNet Information Services | info@callnet.com | (203) 389-7130 |
| PCNet | info@pcnet.com | (203) 250-7397 |
| **DELAWARE** | | |
| *All points* | | |
| Business Data Systems, Inc.* | info@bdsnet.com | (302) 674-2840 |
| DCANet* | info@dca.net | (302) 654-1019 |
| iNET Communications* | info@inetcom.net | (302) 454-1780 |
| Internet Delaware | delnet@mail.delnet.com | (302) 737-1001 |
| The Magnetic Page | info@magpage.com | (302) 651-9753 |
| SSNet, Inc.* | info@ssnet.com | (302) 378-1386 |

| State/City/Providers | E-mail | Telephone |
|---|---|---|
| **DISTRICT OF COLUMBIA** | | |
| *All points* | | |
| Capital Area Internet Service* | info@cais.com | (703) 448-4470 |
| ClarkNet* | info@clark.net | (410) 254-3900 |
| CrossLink | sales@crosslink.net | (703) 642-1120 x175 |
| digitalNATION | lori@csgi.com | (703) 642-2800 |
| Internet Access Group, Inc. | info@iagi.net | (301) 652-0484 |
| Internet Interstate | info@intr.net | (301) 652-4468 |
| NetRail, Inc.* | info@netrail.net | (703) 524-4800 |
| RadixNet* | info@radix.net | (301) 567-9831 |
| USNet* | info@us.net | (301) 572-5926 |
| Virginia Internet Services | info@vais.net | (703) 913-0823 |
| World Web Limited* | info@worldweb.net | (703) 838-2000 |
| **FLORIDA** | | |
| *Jacksonville* | | |
| First Coast Online | schuyler@moe.fcol.com | (904) 279-0009 |
| Jacksonville Internet Services, Inc. | info@jax-inter.net | (904) 296-1201 |
| Jax Gateway to the World* | sales@jax.gttw.com | (904) 730-7692 |
| Southeast Network Services, Inc.* | sysop@jaxnet.com | (904) 260-6064 |
| *Miami/Fort Lauderdale* | | |
| Acquired Knowledge Systems, Inc. | info@aksi.net | (954) 525-2574 |
| BridgeNet, LC | access@bridge.net | (305) 374-3031 |
| Compass.Net | jason@compass.net | (954) 733-2556 |
| CyberGate* | sales@gate.net | (954) 428-4283 |
| Internet Gateway Connections* | info@igc.net | (954) 430-3030 |
| Neptune.com | mario@neptune.com | (305) 597-8226 |
| NetPoint Communications, Inc.* | info@netpoint.net | (305) 891-1955 |
| Paradise Communications | sales-info@paradise.net | (305) 598-4426 |
| SatelNet Communications | info@satelnet.org | (954) 321-5660 |
| Shadow Information Services, Inc. | admin@shadow.net | (305) 594-3450 |
| World Information Network | info@winnet.net | (305) 535-3090 |
| *Orlando* | | |
| AccNet* | info@acc.net | (407) 834-2222 |
| Global DataLink, Inc. | info@gdi4.gdi.net | (407) 841-3690 |
| GS-Link Systems Inc. | info@gslink.net | (407) 671-8682 |
| Infinite Space Systems Corporation | info@ispace.com | (407) 850-2404 |
| Internet Access Group* | sales@iag.net | (407) 786-1145 |
| MagicNet, Inc.* | info@magicnet.net | (407) 657-2202 |
| Onet, Inc. | info@onetinc.com | (407) 291-7000 |
| Online Orlando Internet Services | support@oo.com | (407) 647-7559 |
| Sundial Internet Services | info@sundial.net | (407) 438-6710 |

| State/City/Providers | E-mail | Telephone |
|---|---|---|
| World Ramp Inc. | info@worldramp.net | (407) 740-5987 |
| *Tampa/St. Petersburg/Clearwater* | | |
| Bay-A-Net* | info@bayanet.com | (813) 988-7772 |
| Centurion Technology, Inc. | info@tpa.cent.com | (813) 538 1919 |
| CFTnet* | info@cftnet.com | (813) 980 1317 |
| Intelligence Network Online, Inc.* | info@intnet.net | (813) 442-0114 |
| InterAccess | info@interaccess.com | (813) 254-9435 |
| InterNet Integration, Inc. | info@icubed.net | (813) 633-9555 |
| OpenNet* | info@opennet.com | (813) 446-6558 |
| PacketWorks, Inc. | info@packet.net | (813) 446-8826 |
| *West Palm Beach/Boca Raton* | | |
| The EmiNet Domain* | info@emi.net | (407) 731-0222 |
| Magg Information Services, Inc.* | help@magg.net | (407) 642-9841 |
| Netline Communications, Inc. | info@netline.net | (800) 638-0023 |
| StarDate Communications | info@stardate.com | (407) 683-3235 |

## GEORGIA
*Atlanta*

| | | |
|---|---|---|
| America Net (nta) | info@america.net | (770) 751-9425 |
| CyberNet Communications | sfeingold@atlwin.com | (770) 518-5711 |
| Digital Service Consultants | john@dscga.com | (770) 455-9022 |
| Intergate, Inc.* | info@intergate.net | (770) 429-9599 |
| Internet Atlanta* | info@atlanta.com | (770) 410-9000 |
| Internet Services of Atlanta (ISA) | info@is.net | (770) 662-1616 |
| Lambda.Net Information Services | info@lambda.net | (770) 441-0265 |
| Lyceum Internet Services | info@lyceum.com | (404) 248-1733 |
| Mindspring* | info@mindspring.com | (800) 719-4332 |
| Navigator Communications | sales@nav.com | (770) 441-4007 |
| NetDepot, Inc.* | info@netdepot.com | (770) 434-5595 |
| Random Access, Inc.* | marius@randomc.com | (770) 804-1190 |

*Georgia (north)*

| | | |
|---|---|---|
| Internet CSRA | info@csra.net | (706) 724-1509 |
| Znet* | info@znet.augusta.ga.us | (706) 722-2175 |

*Georgia (south)*

| | | |
|---|---|---|
| Homenet Communications, Inc. | info@hom.net | (912) 329-8638 |

## HAWAII
*All points*

| | | |
|---|---|---|
| 1Source* | info@1source.com | (808) 293-0733 |
| Data Plus Systems | hostmaster@dps.net | (808) 678-8989 |
| Flex Information Network | postmaster@aloha.com | (808) 732-8849 |

| State/City/Providers | E-mail | Telephone |
|---|---|---|
| Hawaii OnLine(HOL)* | info@aloha.net | (800) 207-1880 |
| HulaNet | hulagirl@hula.net | (808) 524-7717 |
| Interlink Hawaii | sales@ilhawaii.net | (808) 334-4000 |
| Inter-Pacific Networks* | sysman@interpac.net | (808) 935-5550 |
| LavaNet | info@lava.net | (808) 545-5282 |
| Maui Global Communications Co.* | info@maui.net | (808) 875-2535 |
| Pacific Information eXchange (PixiNet)* | info@pixi.com | (808) 596-7494 |

## IDAHO
### All points

| | | |
|---|---|---|
| Micron Internet Services* | info@micron.net | (208) 368-5400 |
| NICOH Net | info@nicoh.com | (208) 233-5802 |
| SRVnet, Inc.* | nlp@srv.net | (208) 524-6237 |

## ILLINOIS
### Chicago/Gary/Kenosha

| | | |
|---|---|---|
| American Information Systems* | info@ais.net | (312) 255-8500 |
| CINnet* | sales@cin.net | (708) 310-1188 |
| Crown.Net Inc. | info@crown.net | (219) 762-1431 |
| InterAccess | info@interaccess.com | (708) 498-2542 |
| Interactive Network Systems | info@insnet.com | (312) 881-3039 |
| Macro Computer Solutions, Inc.* | rate-request@mcs.net | (312) 248-8649 |
| Millenia Services | sales@miint.net | (312) 341-0192 |
| NetWave | info@maui.netwave.net | (800) 961-WAVE |
| OnRamp, Ltd. | info@theramp.net | (708) 222-6666 |
| Ripco Communications, Inc. | info@ripco.com | (312) 665-0065 |
| StarNet, Inc. | info@starnetinc.com | (708) 382-0099 |
| Sun Valley SoftWare, Ltd.* | ken@svs.com | (708) 983-0889 |
| Tezcat Communications* | info@tezcat.com | (312) 850-0181 |
| ThoughtPort Authority of Chicago* | info@thoughtport.com | (312) 862-6870 |
| Wink Communications* | sales@winkcomm.com | (708) 310-9465 |
| WorldWide Access | info@wwa.com | (708) 367-1870 |
| XNet Information Systems* | info@xnet.com | (708) 983-6064 |

### East St. Louis
see St. Louis, MISSOURI

### Illinois (central)

| | | |
|---|---|---|
| Adams Networks | dley@golden.adams.net | (217) 696-4455 |
| Cen-Com Internet* | info@cencom.net | (217) 793-2771 |
| FGInet, Inc. | admin@fgi.net | (217) 787-2775 |
| ICEnet | icenet@ice.net | (309) 454-4638 |
| Itek* | jasegler@itek.net | (309) 691-6100 |

| State/City/Providers | E-mail | Telephone |
|---|---|---|
| Prairienet, The East-Central Illinois FreeNet | info@prairienet.org | (217) 244-1962 |
| Shouting Ground Technologies | admin@shout.net | (217) 351-7921 |

## INDIANA
### Gary
see Chicago, ILLINOIS
### Indianapolis

| | | |
|---|---|---|
| IndyNet | support@indy.net | (317) 251-5208 |
| Internet Indiana* | info@in.net | (317) 876-5NET |
| IQuest Network Services* | info@iquest.net | (800) 844-8649 |
| Net Direct* | kat@inetdirect.net | (317) 251-5252 |
| surf-ICI | sales@surf-ici.com | (317) 243-7888 |

## IOWA
### Council Bluffs
see Omaha, NEBRASKA
### Des Moines

| | | |
|---|---|---|
| Des Moines Internet, Inc.* | brentf@dsmnet.com | (515) 270-9191 |
| Freese-Notis WeatherNet* | info@weather.net | (515) 282-9310 |
| INS Info Services* | info@netins.net | (515) 830-0110 |
| JTM Multimedia, Inc. | jtm@ecity.net | (515) 277-1990 |

## KANSAS
### Kansas City
see Kansas City, MISSOURI
### Wichita

| | | |
|---|---|---|
| DTC Supernet | info@dtc.net | (316) 683-7272 |
| Elysian Fields Inc. | info@elysian.net | (316) 267-2636 |
| Future Net, Inc. | info@fn.net | (316) 652-0070 |
| SouthWind Internet Access, Inc.* | info@southwind.net | (316) 263-7963 |

## KENTUCKY
### Covington
see Cincinatti, OHIO
### Louisville

| | | |
|---|---|---|
| BluegrassNet* | info@bluegrass.net | (502) 589-INET |
| IgLou Internet Services | info@iglou.com | (502) 966-3848 |
| The Point Internet Services | staff@thepoint.com | (812) 246-7187 |

## LOUISIANA
### Baton Rouge

| | | |
|---|---|---|
| Intersurf Online Inc. | info@intersurf.net | (504) 755-0500 |

| State/City/Providers | E-mail | Telephone |
|---|---|---|
| Premier One* | info@premier.net | (504) 751-8080 |
| *New Orleans* | | |
| AccessCom Internet Providers* | info@accesscom.net | (504) 887-0022 |
| CommNet Information | info@comm.net | (504) 836-2844 |
| Communique, Inc.* | info@communique.net | (504) 527-6200 |
| Cyberlink | cladmin@eayor.cyberlink-no.com | (504) 277-4186 |
| Greater New Orleans Free-Net | info@gnofn.org | (504) 539-9239 |

**MAINE**

*All points*

| | | |
|---|---|---|
| AcadiaNet | support@acadia.net | (207) 288-5959 |
| Agate Internet* | ais@agate.net | (207) 947-8248 |
| Biddeford Internet* | info@biddeford.com | (207) 756-8770 |
| Internet Maine Inc.* | mtenney@mainelink.net | (207) 780-0416 |
| The Maine InternetWorks, Inc.* | info@mint.net | (207) 453-4000 |
| MaineStreet Communications | cfm@maine.com | (207) 657-5078 |
| Midcoast Internet Solutions | info@midcoast.com | (207) 594-8277 |

**MANITOBA**

*Winnipeg*

| | | |
|---|---|---|
| Astra Network, Inc. | sales@man.net | (204) 987-7050 |
| Internet Solutions, Inc.* | info@solutions.net | (204) 982-1060 |
| Gate West Communications | info@gatewest.net | (204) 663-2931 |
| Magic Online Services Winnipeg, Inc. | info@magic.mb.ca | (204) 949-7777 |

*All other points*

| | | |
|---|---|---|
| MTS Internet | registration@mts.net | (800) 280-7095 |

**MARYLAND**

*Baltimore*

| | | |
|---|---|---|
| ABSnet Internet Services, Inc.* | info@abs.net | (410) 361-8160 |
| Charm Net* | info@charm.net | (410) 558-3900 |
| Clark Internet Services, Inc.* | info@clark.net | (410) 254-3900 |
| jaguNET | info@jagunet.com | (410) 931-3157 |

*Maryland (west)*

| | | |
|---|---|---|
| ARInternet Corporation* | info@ari.net | (301) 459-7171 |
| Digital Express Group DIGEX* | info@digex.net | (800) 969-9090 |
| EagleNet | info@eagle1.eaglenet.com | (301) 863-6992 |
| Fred.Net* | info@fred.net | (301) 631-5300 |
| Planetcom, Inc. | info@planetcom.com | (301) 258-2963 |
| Tansin A. Darcos & Company | service@tdr.com | (800) T-DARCOS |

| State/City/Providers | E-mail | Telephone |
|---|---|---|
| **MASSACHUSETTS** | | |
| *Boston/Worcester/Lawrence* | | |
| Blue Sky, Inc.* | info@bluesky.net | (617) 270-4747 |
| CENTnet, Inc. | info@cent.net | (617) 492-6079 |
| Channel 1 | info@channel1.com | (800) 745-2747 |
| COWZ Technologies | beef@cow.net | (617) COW-TOWN |
| CyberAccess Internet Communication, Inc. | info@cybercom.net | (617) 396-0491 |
| North Shore Access | info@shore.net | (617) 593-3110 |
| One World Network* | sales@oneworld.net | (617) 267-2440 |
| Pioneer Global Telecommunications* | sales@pn.com | (617) 375-0200 |
| Software Tool & Die | support@world.std.com | (617) 739-0202 |
| TerraNet Internet Services* | info@terra.net | (617) 450-9000 |
| TIAC | info_ma@tiac.net | (617) 276-7200 |
| Wilder InterNet Gateway* | info@wing.net | (617) 932-8500 |
| The Xensei Corporation | info@xensei.com | (617) 376-6342 |
| *Fall River* | | |
| see Providence, RHODE ISLAND | | |
| *Springfield* | | |
| MAP Internet Services* | info@map.com | (413) 732-0214 |
| **MICHIGAN** | | |
| *Detroit/Ann Arbor/Flint* | | |
| Branch Internet Services Inc.* | info@branch.com | (800) 349-1747 |
| CICNet* | info@cic.net | (313) 998-6703 |
| Gateway Online | accounts@gatecom.com | (313) 291-2666 |
| ICNet* | info@ic.net | (313) 998-0090 |
| Isthmus Corporation | info@izzy.net | (313) 973-2100 |
| Merit/MichNet* | info@merit.edu | (313) 764-9430 |
| Msen* | service@msen.com | (313) 998-4562 |
| O & E On-Line! | info@oeonline.com | (313) 591-2300 |
| *Michigan (central)* | | |
| Arrownet | info@arrownet.com | (800) 999-4409 |
| Sojourn Systems Ltd.* | info@sojourn.com | (800) 949-3993 |
| *Michigan (west and north)* | | |
| Alliance Network, Inc. | info@alliance.net | (616) 774-3010 |
| Freeway* | info@freeway.net | (616) 347-3175 |
| Iserv* | info@iserv.net | (616) 847-5254 |
| Novagate | info@novagate.com | (616) 847-0910 |
| The Portage | fuzzy@portage1.portup.com | (906) 487-9832 |

| State/City/Providers | E-mail | Telephone |
|---|---|---|
| **MINNESOTA** | | |
| *Minneapolis/St. Paul* | | |
| Bitstream Underground | gods@bitstream.net | (612) 321-9290 |
| Digital Solutions, Inc. | info@solon.com | (612) 488-1740 |
| gofast.net | info@gofast.net | (612) 647-6109 |
| GoldenGate Internet Services, Inc. | timmc@goldengate.net | (612) 574-2200 |
| InterNetwork Services* | info@proteon.inet-serv.com | (612) 391-7300 |
| Millennium Communications, Inc.* | info@millcomm.com | (612) 338-8666 |
| MinnNet* | info@minn.net | (612) 944-8660 |
| Minneapolis Telecommunications Network | mtn@mtn.org | (612) 331-8575 |
| Minnesota MicroNet | info@mm.com | (612) 882-7711 |
| Minnesota Online* | sales@mn.state.net | (612) 225-1110 |
| The Minnesota Regional Network* | info@mr.net | (612) 342-2570 |
| Orbis Internet Services, Inc. | info@orbis.net | (612) 645-9663 |
| pclink.com | infomatic@pclink.com | (612) 541-5656 |
| Protocol Communications | info@protocol.com | (612) 541-9900 |
| Sihope Communications | info@sihope.com | (612) 829-9667 |
| SkyPoint Communications, Inc.* | info@skypoint.com | (612) 475-2959 |
| Vector Internet Services, Inc.* | info@visi.com | (612) 288-0880 |
| Vitex Communications | info@vitex.com | (612) 822-1166 |
| WaveFront Communications, Inc.* | info@wavefront.com | (612) 638-9594 |
| WebSpan | info@webspan.com | (612) 333-LINK |
| Winternet (Startnet Communications) | info@winternet.com | (612) 941-9177 |
| *Minnesota (north)* | | |
| Computer Pro | info@computerpro.com | (218) 772-4245 |
| *Minnesota (south)* | | |
| Desktop Media* | isp@dm.deskmedia.com | (507) 373-2155 |
| Information Superhighway Limited | info@isl.net | (507) 289-5543 |
| Internet Connections, Inc.* | info@ic.mankato.mn.us | (507) 625-7320 |
| Millennium Communications, Inc.* | info@millcomm.com | (507) 282-1004 |
| **MISSISSIPPI** | | |
| *All points* | | |
| Aris Technologies* | info@aris.com | (601) 324 7638 |
| Datasync Internet Services | info@datasync.com | (601) 872-0001 |
| EBI Comm, Inc.* | hostmaster@ebicom.net | (601) 243-7075 |
| Internet Doorway, Inc.* | info@netdoor.com | (800) 952-1570 |
| InterSys Technologies, Inc.* | info@inst.com | (601) 949-6992 |
| Southwind Technologies, Inc. | info@southwind.com | (601) 374-6510 |
| TecLink* | info@teclink.net | (601) 949-6992 |

| State/City/Providers | E-mail | Telephone |
|---|---|---|
| **MISSOURI** | | |
| *Kansas City* | | |
| AccuNet, Inc.* | dwhitten@accunet.com | (816) 246-9094 |
| Databank, Inc.* | info@databank.com | (913) 842-6699 |
| Internet Direct Communications | sales@idir.net | (913) 842-1100 |
| Interstate Networking Corporation* | info@interstate.net | (816) 472-4949 |
| Q-Net, Inc. | info@qni.com | (816) 795-1000 |
| SkyNet* | info@sky.net | (816) 421-2626 |
| Unicom Communications, Inc.* | fyi@unicom.net | (913) 383-8466 |
| *St. Louis* | | |
| Cybergate L.L.C. | info@cybergate.org | (314) 214-1013 |
| iCON | info@icon-stl.net | (314) 241-ICON |
| Inlink | support@inlink.com | (314) 432-0149 |
| **MONTANA** | | |
| *All points* | | |
| Avicom, Inc. | avicom@montana.avicom.net | (406) 587-6177 |
| Cyberport Montana* | skippy@cyberport.net | (406) 863-3221 |
| Internet Connect Services | ics@montana.com | (406) 721-4952 |
| Internet Montana | support@imt.net | (406) 255-9699 |
| Internet Services Montana, Inc.* | support@ism.net | (406) 542-0838 |
| Montana Communications Network | info@mcn.net | (406) 254-9413 |
| Netrix Internet System Design, Inc.* | leesa@netrix.net | (406) 257-4638 |
| **NEBRASKA** | | |
| *Omaha* | | |
| Nebraska On-Ramp, Inc. | info@neonramp.com | (402) 339-6366 |
| NFinity Systems | info@nfinity.com | (402) 551-3036 |
| *Nebraska (west)* | | |
| see NATIONAL COVERAGE | | |
| **NEVADA** | | |
| *Las Vegas* | | |
| Access Nevada, Inc.* | info@accessnv.com | (702) 294-0480 |
| InterMind* | info@intermind.net | (702) 878-6111 |
| @wizard.com* | george@wizard.com | (702) 871-4461 |
| *All other points* | | |
| Connectus* | info@connectus.com | (702) 323-2008 |
| Great Basin Internet Services* | info@greatbasin.com | (702) 348-7299 |
| NevadaNet | braddlee@nevada.edu | (702) 784-6861 |
| Sierra-Net | info@sierra.net | (702) 832-6911 |

| State/City/Providers | E-mail | Telephone |
|---|---|---|
| SourceNet* | info@source.net | (702) 832-7246 |
| Tahoe On-Line | info@tol.net | (702) 588-0616 |
| **NEW BRUNSWICK** | | |
| *All points* | | |
| Maritime Internet Services, Inc. | sales@mi.net | (506) 652-3624 |
| **NEWFOUNDLAND** | | |
| *All points* | | |
| Data Bits, Inc. | info@databits.com | (709) 786 5660 |
| Nlnet | slipreq@nlnet.nf.ca | (709) 737-4555 |
| **NEW HAMPSHIRE** | | |
| *All points* | | |
| The Destek Group, Inc.* | info@destek.net | (603) 635-3857 |
| Empire.Net, Inc. | info@empire.net | (603) 889-1220 |
| John Leslie Consulting | info@jlc.net | (603) 673-6132 |
| Mainstream Electronic Information Services | info@mainstream.net | (603) 424-1497 |
| MonadNet Corporation* | info@monad.net | (603) 352-7619 |
| MV Communications, Inc. | info@mv.mv.com | (603) 429-2223 |
| NETIS Public Access Internet | info@netis.com | (603) 437-1811 |
| North Country Internet Access | ed@moose.ncia.net | (603) 752-1250 |
| **NEW JERSEY** | | |
| *Bergen/Passaic* | | |
| Carroll-Net | info@carroll.com | (201) 488-1332 |
| Interactive Networks, Inc. | info@interactive.net | (201) 881-1878 |
| Internet Online Services | info@ios.com | (201) 928-1000 |
| nic.com | info@nic.com | (201) 934-1445 |
| *Jersey City* | | |
| The Connection | info@cnct.com | (201) 435-4414 |
| Mordor International | info@mordor.com | (201) 433-7343 |
| *Middlesex/Somerset/Hunterdon* | | |
| ECLIPSE Internet Access* | info@eclipse.net | (800) 483-1223 |
| Internet For 'U'* | info@ifu.net | (908) 435-0600 |
| Superlink* | info@superlink.net | (908) 828-8988 |
| Texel International | info@texel.com | (908) 297-0290 |
| *Monmouth/Ocean* | | |
| Atlantic Internet Technologies, Inc.* | info@exit109.com | (908) 758-0505 |
| Monmouth Internet | sales@shell.monmouth.com | (908) 389-6094 |

| State/City/Providers | E-mail | Telephone |
|---|---|---|
| **NEW MEXICO** | | |
| *Albuquerque* | | |
| Internet Direct, Inc.* | info@indirect.com | (505) 888-4624 |
| New Mexico Internet Access, Inc.* | info@nmia.com | (505) 877-0617 |
| New Mexico Technet, Inc.* | granoff@technet.nm.org | (505) 345-6555 |
| Rt66-Engineering International, Inc.* | info@rt66.com | (505) 343-1060 |
| Southwest Cyberport | info@swcp.com | (505) 271-0009 |
| Terra Communications | office@terra.com | (505) 256-1676 |
| *Santa Fe* | | |
| Roadrunner Communications* | sysop@roadrunner.com | (505) 988-9200 |
| Studio X | info@nets.com | (505) 438-0505 |
| *All other points* | | |
| Community Internet Access | sysadm@cia-g.com | (505) 863-2424 |
| CyberPort Station | info@cyberport.com | (505) 324-6400 |
| **NEW YORK** | | |
| *Albany/Schenectady/Troy* | | |
| AlbanyNet* | info@albany.net | (518) 465-0873 |
| Automatrix | info@automatrix.com | (518) 372-5583 |
| Global One | info@globalone.net | (518) 452-1465 |
| LogicalNet* | sales@logical.net | (518) 452-9090 |
| NetHeaven | info@netheaven.com | (518) 885-1295 |
| Wizvax Communications* | info@wizvax.net | (518) 273-4325 |
| *Nassau/Suffolk Counties* | | |
| Long Island Internet HQ & Pointblank BBS Ltd. | support@pb.net | (516) 549-2165 |
| Long Island Information, Inc. | info@liii.com | (516) 248-5381 |
| Long Island Net | info@li.net | (516) 265-0997 |
| Network-USA | all-info@netusa.net | (516) 543-0240 |
| North American Internet Services | info@nais.com | (516) 358-8204 |
| Savvy Communications | info@savvy.com | (800) 275-7455 |
| Sestran Industries, Inc. | info@sestran.com | (516) 253-3362 |
| SpecNet | sysadmin@specdata.com | (516) 735-9678 |
| *New York City* | | |
| Angel Networks | info@angel.net | (212) 947-6507 |
| Blythe Systems | accounts@blythe.org | (212) 979-0471 |
| BrainLINK | info@brainlink.com | (718) 805-6559 |
| bway.net (Outernet, Inc.) | info-bot@bway.net | (212) 982-9800 |
| Calyx Internet Access* | info@clyx.net | (212) 475-5051 |
| Cloud 9 Internet* | info@cloud9.net | (914) 682-0626 |
| The Dorsai Embassy, Inc. | system@dorsai.org | (718) 392-3667 |

| *State/City/Providers* | *E-mail* | *Telephone* |
|---|---|---|
| dx.com | info@dx.com | (212) 929-0566 |
| elroNet | info@elron.net | (212) 935-3110 |
| EscapeCom* | info@escape.com | (212) 888-8780 |
| i-2000* | info@i-2000.com | (800) 464-3820 |
| Ingress Communications, Inc.* | info@ingress.com | (212) 268-1100 |
| Internet Channel* | info@inch.com | (212) 243-5200 |
| Internet Exchange* | ksc@inx.net | (212) 935-3322 |
| Internet Quicklink Corp.* | info@quicklink.com | (212) 307-1669 |
| Interport Communications Corp.* | info@interport.net | (212) 989-1128 |
| Maestro Technologies, Inc.* | info@maestro.com | (212) 240-9600 |
| New York Net* | info@new-york.net | (718) 776-6811 |
| The New York Web, Inc.* | nysurf@nyweb.com | (212) 748-7600 |
| NY WEBB, Inc. | gwg7@webb.com | (212) 242-4912 |
| Panix | info@panix.com | (212) 741-4400 |
| PCW Internet Services* | sales@pcwnet.com | (718) 937-0380 |
| PFM Communications* | marc@pfmc.net | (212) 254-5300 |
| Phantom Access Technologies, Inc./MindVox | info@phantom.com | (212) 989-2418 |
| Pipeline New York | info@nyc.pipeline.com | (212) 267-3636 |
| RealNet* | reallife@walrux.com | (212) 366-4434 |
| SenseNet, Inc. | sales@sensenet.com | (212) 824-5000 |
| SILLY.COM | info@silly.com | (718) 229-7096 |
| ThoughtPort Authority of NYC* | info@thoughtport.com | (212) 645-7970 |
| TunaNet/InfoHouse | info@tunanet.com | (212) 229-8224 |
| *Rochester* | | |
| E-Znet, Inc.* | info@eznet.net | (716) 262-2485 |
| ServiceTech, Inc.* | sales@servtech.com | (716) 263-3360 |
| Vivanet | info@vivanet.com | (716) 272-9101 |
| *Syracuse* | | |
| Dreamscape | temerick@dreamscape.com | (315) 446-2626 |
| EMI Communications* | info@emi.com | (800) 456-2001 |
| Syracuse Internet | info@vcomm.net | (315) 233-1948 |

## NORTH CAROLINA
*Charlotte/Gastonia/Rock Hill*

| | | |
|---|---|---|
| Cybernetx, Inc.* | info@cybernetics.net | (704) 561-7000 |
| SunBelt.Net* | info@sunbelt.net | (800) 950-4726 |
| Vnet Internet Access, Inc. | info@vnet.net | (800) 377-3282 |

*Greensboro/Winston-Salem/High Point*

| | | |
|---|---|---|
| Kinetics, Inc.* | info@kinetics.net | (910) 370-1985 |
| Online South | info@ols.net | (910) 983-7212 |

| State/City/Providers | E-mail | Telephone |
|---|---|---|
| Red Barn Data Center | postmaster@rbdc.rbdc.com | (910) 774-1600 |
| SpyderByte | info@spyder.net | (910) 643-6999 |
| *Raleigh/Durham/Chapel Hill* | | |
| Atlantic Internet Corporation* | info@ainet.net | (919) 833-1252 |
| Interpath* | info@interpath.net | (800) 849-6305 |
| NandO.Net | info@nando.net | (919) 836-2808 |
| NC-REN Data Services* | info@ncren.net | (919) 248-1999 |
| Network Data Link, Inc. | staff@nc.ndl.net | (919) 878-7701 |

**NORTH DAKOTA**

*All points*

| | | |
|---|---|---|
| Dakota Internet Access | admin@host1.dia.net | (701) 774-DIA1 |
| Red River Net* | info@rrnet.com | (701) 232-2227 |
| The Internet Connection, Inc.* | tic@emh1.tic.bismarck.nd.us | (701) 222-8356 |

**NORTHWEST TERRITORIES**

*All points*

| | | |
|---|---|---|
| Internet North | stevel@internorth.com | (403) 873-5975 |
| Network North Communications, Ltd. | info@netnorth.com | (403) 873-2059 |

**NOVA SCOTIA**

*All points*

| | | |
|---|---|---|
| Atlantic Connect Inc. | info@atcon.com | (902) 429-0222 |
| Internet Passport Services | sales@ips.ca | (902) INTERNET |
| internet services and information systems (isis) Inc. | info@isisnet.com | (902) 429-4747 |
| North Shore Internet Services | support@north.nsis.com | (902) 928-0565 |
| NSTN Incorporated* | info@nstn.ca | (902) 481-NSTN (6786) |

**OHIO**

*Cincinnati/Hamilton*

| | | |
|---|---|---|
| Exodus Online Services | info@eos.net | (513) 522-0011 |
| horanDATA | info@horandata.net | (513) 241-3282 |
| Internet Access Cincinnati/ M&M Engineering* | info@iac.net | (513) 887-8877 |
| OneNet Communications* | info@one.net | (513) 326-6000 |
| Premiere Internet Cincinnati* | pic@cinti.com | (513) 561-6245 |
| Primax.Net | info@primax.net | (513) 772-1223 |
| *Cleveland/Akron* | | |
| APK* | info@apk.net | (216) 481-9428 |
| BBS One OnLine Service | jimdief@bbsone.com | (216) 825-5217 |

| State/City/Providers | E-mail | Telephone |
|---|---|---|
| CyberGate | info@cybergate.net | (216) 247-7660 |
| ExchangeNet (EN)* | info@en.com | (216) 261-4593 |
| GWIS | info@gwis.com | (216) 656-5511 |
| Multiverse | noc@mail.multiverse.com | (216) 344-3080 |
| New Age Consulting Services* | info@nacs.net | (216) 524-8388 |
| Winfield Communication, Inc. | info@winc.com | (216) 867-2904 |
| *Columbus* | | |
| Global Access Network | info@ganet.net | (614) 766-1258 |
| Infinet, Infinite Systems | info@infinet.com | (614) 268 9941 |
| Internet Concourse | info@coil.com | (614) 242-3800 |
| OARnet* | info@oar.net | (614) 728-8100 |
| *Dayton/Springfield* | | |
| Dayton Internet Services, Inc.* | info@dayton.net | (513) 643-0188 |
| The Dayton Network Access Co. | info@dnaco.net | (513) 237-6868 |
| DONet, Inc. | info@donet.com | (513) 256-7288 |
| EriNet Online Communications* | support@erinet.com | (513) 291-1995 |
| HCST-Net* | info@hcst.com | (513) 390-7486 |
| *Youngstown/Warren* | | |
| CISNet, Inc.* | todd@cisnet.com | (216) 629-2691 |

OKLAHOMA
*Oklahoma City*

| | | |
|---|---|---|
| InterConnect On-Line* | info@icon.net | (405) 949-1800 |
| Internet Oklahoma | info@ionet.net | (405) 721-1580 |
| Keystone Technology | sales@keytech.com | (405) 848-9902 |
| *Tulsa* | | |
| Galaxy Star Systems* | info@galstar.com | (918) 835-3655 |
| OKNET* | oksales@oknet.com | (918) 481-5899 |

ONTARIO
*Ottawa*

| | | |
|---|---|---|
| Achilles Internet Ltd. | info@achilles.net | (613) 723-6624 |
| Channel One Internet Services* | getwired@sonetis.com | (613) 236-8601 |
| Comnet Communications | info@comnet.ca | (613) 747-5555 |
| Cyberus Online Inc. | info@cyberus.ca | (613) 233-1215 |
| In@sec | info@inasec.ca | (613) 746-3200 |
| info.web, A Division of | info@magi.com | (613) 225-3354 |
| MAGI Data Consulting Inc. | | |
| Interactive Telecom Inc. | info@intertel.net | (613) 727-5258 |
| Internet Access Inc.* | info@ottawa.net | (613) 225-5595 |
| Internet Connectivity, Inc. | helpdesk@icons.net | (613) 828-6221 |
| Magma Communications Ltd.* | info@magmacom.com | (613) 228-3565 |

| State/City/Providers | E-mail | Telephone |
|---|---|---|
| NewForce Communications | feedback@newforce.ca | (819) 682-9893 |
| Resudox Online Services, Inc. | admin@2resudox.net | (613) 567-6925 |
| Synapse Internet | info@synapse.net | (819) 561-1697 |
| Trytel Internet, Inc. | dialup@trytel.com | (613) 722-6321 |
| WorldLink Internet Services | info@worldlink.ca | (613) 233-7100 |
| *Toronto* | | |
| 9 To 5 Communications | staff@inforamp.net | (416) 363-9100 |
| All Systems Go | info@asgo.net | (416) 961-7399 |
| CIMtegration Ltd. | info@cimtegration.com | (416) 665-3566 |
| Enterprise Online | sales@enterprise.ca | (416) 932-3030 |
| InfoRamp, Inc. | info@inforamp.net | (416) 363-9100 |
| Interlog Internet Services | info@interlog.com | (416) 975-2655 |
| Internet Front Inc. | support@internetfront.com | (416) 293-8539 |
| Internet Light and Power | staff@ilap.com | (416) 502-1512 |
| Internex Online | info@io.org | (416) 363-8676 |
| ONet Networking* | info@onet.on.ca | (416) 978-4589 |
| Pathway Communications | info@pathcom.com | (416) 214 6235 |
| TerraPoint Online, Inc. | info@terraport.net | (416) 492-3050 |
| UUNorth International | info@mail.north.net | (416) 225-8649 |
| The Wire | info@the-wire.com | (416) 214-WIRE |
| World Wide Wave* | info@wwwave.com | (416) 499-7100 |
| Xenon Laboratories | info@xe.net | (416) 214-5606 |

## OREGON

*Portland/Salem*

| | | |
|---|---|---|
| aracnet.com | info@aracnet.com | (503) 626-7696 |
| Autobahn Internet Services Inc. | info@northwest.com | (503) 775-9523 |
| CenORneT | info@cenornet.com | (503) 557-9047 |
| CyberNet NorthWest | sales@cybernw.com | (503) 256-5350 |
| DTR Communications Services | info@dtr.com | (503) 252-5059 |
| Europa | info@europa.com | (503) 222-9508 |
| Hevanet Communications | info@hevanet.com | (503) 228-3520 |
| Industrial | root@industrial.com | (503) 636-9931 |
| NetRamp | info@netramp.com | (503) 650-8193 |
| One World Internetworking, Inc. | info@oneworld.com | (503) 758-1112 |
| Pacifier Online Data Service | sales@pacifier.com | (360) 693-2116 |
| RainDrop Laboratories | info@agora.rdrop.com | (503) 293-1772 |
| Spire Communications* | info@spiretech.com | (503) 222-3086 |
| Structured Network Systems* | sales@structured.net | (503) 656-3530 |
| Teleport Internet Services | info@teleport.com | (503) 223-0076 |
| Transport Logic* | info@transport.com | (503) 243-1940 |
| A World Locally | thorton@locally.com | (503) 251-2078 |

| State/City/Providers | E-mail | Telephone |
|---|---|---|
| *All other points* | | |
| BendNet | info@bendnet.com | (503) 385-3331 |
| CDS Internet | info@cdsnet.net | (541) 773-9600 |
| Data Research Group, Inc. | info@ordata.com | (503) 465-DATA |
| Empire Net, Inc. | webmaster@empnet.com | (503) 317-3437 |
| InfoStructure | info@mind.net | (503) 488-1962 |
| Magick Net, Inc. | peabody@magick.net | (503) 471-2542 |
| mtjeff.com | info@mtjeff.com | (503) 475-6233 |
| Northwest Internet Services | info@rio.com | (503) 485-7601 |
| Open Door Networks, Inc. | info@opendoor.com | (503) 488-4127 |
| RAINet | help@rain.net | (503) 227-5665 |

**PENNSYLVANIA**

*Allentown/Bethlehem/Easton*

| | | |
|---|---|---|
| Early Access | info@early.com | (610) 770-7800 |
| Enter.Net* | info@enter.net | (610) 366-1300 |
| Internet Tidal Wave | steve@itw.com | (610) 770-6187 |
| Oasis Telecommunication, Inc. | info@ot.com | (610) 439-8560 |
| You Tools Internet* | info@fast.net | (610) 954-5910 |

*Harrisburg/Lebanon/Carlisle*

| | | |
|---|---|---|
| CPCNet | webmaster@news.cpcnet.com | (717) 393-2956 |
| Keystone Information Access Systems | office@yrkpa.kias.com | (717) 741-2626 |
| LebaNet* | office@leba.net | (717) 270-9790 |
| SuperNet Interactive Services, Inc.* | info@success.net | (717) 393-7635 |

*Philadelphia*

| | | |
|---|---|---|
| FishNet | info@pond.com | (610) 337-9994 |
| Micro Control, Inc. | info@inet.micro-ctrl.com | (215) 321-7474 |
| Net Access* | info@netaxs.com | (215) 576-8669 |
| OpNet | info@op.net | (610) 520-2880 |
| RE/COM—Reliable Communications* | sales@recom.com | (609) 225-3330 |
| Voicenet* | info@voicenet.com | (800) 835-5710 |

*Pittsburgh*

| | | |
|---|---|---|
| CityNet, Inc.* | info@city-net.com | (412) 481-5406 |
| Nauticom | info@pgh.nauticom.net | (800) 746-6283 |
| Pittsburgh OnLine, Inc.* | sales@pgh.net | (412) 681-6130 |
| Stargate | info@sgi.net | (412) 942-4218 |
| Telerama Public Access Internet* | info@telerama.lm.com | (412) 481-3505 |
| ThoughtPort Authority of Pittsburgh | info@thoughtport.com | (412) 963-7099 |
| USA OnRamp* | info@usaor.net | (412) 391-4382 |

*Scranton/Wilkes-Barre/Hazelton*

| | | |
|---|---|---|
| The Internet Cafe, Scranton, PA* | info@lydian.scranton.com | (717) 344-1969 |
| MicroServe Information Systems, Inc.* | helpdesk@admin.microserve.net | (717) 821-5964 |

| State/City/Providers | E-mail | Telephone |
| --- | --- | --- |
| **QUEBEC** | | |
| *Montreal* | | |
| Accent Internet | admin@accent.net | (514) 737-6077 |
| CiteNet Telecom Inc.* | info@citenet.net | (514) 861-5050 |
| Communications Accessibles Montreal | info@cam.org | (514) 288-2581 |
| Connection MMIC, Inc. | michel@connectmmic.net | (514) 331-6642 |
| Global Info Access | info@globale.net | (514) 737-2091 |
| Infobahn | info@infobahnos.com | (514) 481-2585 |
| NetAxis Inc. of Montreal | info@netaxis.qc.ca | (514) 482-8989 |
| Odyssey Internet* | info@odyssee.net | (514) 861-3432 |
| PubNIX Montreal* | info@PubNIX.net | (514) 990-5911 |
| ZooNet | info@zoo.net | (514) 935-6225 |
| *All other points* | | |
| ClicNet Telecommunications Inc. | info@qbc.clic.net | (418) 686-CLIC |
| Valiquet Lamothe, Inc. (VLI) | info@vli.ca | (819) 776-4438 |
| **RHODE ISLAND** | | |
| *Providence/Fall River/Warwick* | | |
| IDS World Network | info@ids.net | (401) 884-7856 |
| Log On America | info@loa.com | (401) 453-6100 |
| *All other points* | | |
| Aquidneck Web Inc. | sysop@aqua.net | (401) 841-5-WWW |
| brainiac services, Inc. | info@brainiac.com | (401) 539-9050 |
| **SASKATCHEWAN** | | |
| *All points* | | |
| SaskTel | info@www.sasknet.sk.ca | (800) 644-9205 |
| **SOUTH CAROLINA** | | |
| *Charleston* | | |
| Horry Telephone Cooperative/ Coastal Cruiser Internet Access | htc@sccoast.net | (803) 365-2155 |
| SIMS, Inc.* | info@sims.com | (803) 853-4333 |
| A World of Difference* | sales@awod.com | (803) 769-4488 |
| *Rock Hill* | | |
| see Charlotte, NORTH CAROLINA | | |
| **SOUTH DAKOTA** | | |
| *All points* | | |
| Dakota Internet Services, Inc. | service@dakota.net | (605) 371-1962 |

| State/City/Providers | E-mail | Telephone |
|---|---|---|
| Internet Services of the Black Hills, Inc. | rryan@blackhills.com | (605) 642-2244 |
| RapidNet LLC | gary@rapidnet.com | (605) 341-3283 |
| SoDak Net | info@sodak.net | (605) 582-2549 |

## TENNESSEE
*Knoxville*

| | | |
|---|---|---|
| GoldSword Sys | info@goldsword.com | (423) 691-6498 |
| Internet Communications Group | info@netgrp.net | (423) 691-1731 |
| United States Internet, Inc.* | info@usit.net | (800) 218-USIT |
| World Net Communications | info@wncom.com | (423) 922-2326 |

*Memphis*

| | | |
|---|---|---|
| Magibox, Inc. | info@magibox.net | (901) 452-7555 |
| NetLinx Technologies | sales@netlnx.com | (901) 757-5351 |
| Synapse | info@syncentral.com | (901) 767-9926 |
| World Spice | info@wsp1.wspice.com | (901) 454-5808 |

*Nashville*

| | | |
|---|---|---|
| CoolBeans Network | leblanc@coolbeans.net | (615) 519-6832 |
| Edge Internet Services* | info@edge.net | (615) 726-8700 |
| ISDNet* | info@isdn.net | (615) 377-7672 |
| Last Straw Communications | info@laststraw.com | (615) 519-6832 |
| The Telalink Corporation* | info@telalink.net | (615) 321-9100 |
| United States Internet, Inc.* | info@usit.net | (615) 259-2006 |

## TEXAS
*Austin/San Marcos*

| | | |
|---|---|---|
| Commuter Communication Systems | info@commuter.net | (512) 257-CCSI |
| CyberTects | staff@einstein.ssz.com | (512) 832-4849 |
| The Eden Matrix | info@eden.com | (512) 478-9900 |
| Freeside Communications, Inc. | info@fc.net | (512) 339-6094 |
| i-link | info@i-link.net | (512) 388-2393 |
| Illuminati Online | info@io.com | (512) 462-0999 |
| Moon Tower, Inc. | help@moontower.com | (512) 837-8670 |
| Onramp Access, Inc. | info@onr.com | (512) 322-9200 |
| OuterNet Connection Strategies | info@outer.net | (512) 345-3573 |
| Real/Time Communications* | sales@bga.com | (512) 206-3124 |
| @sig.net* | sales@sig.net | (512) 306-0700 |
| Turning Point Information Services* | info@tpoint.net | (512) 499-8400 |
| Zilker Internet Park | info@zilker.net | (512) 206-3850 |

*Dallas/Fort Worth*

| | | |
|---|---|---|
| CompuNet* | info@computek.net | (214) 994-0190 |

| State/City/Providers | E-mail | Telephone |
|---|---|---|
| Connect! On-Line* | info@online.com | (214) 396-0038 |
| ConnectNet* | info@connect.net | (214) 490-7100 |
| CyberRamp.net | admin@cyberramp.net | (214) 340-2020 |
| Dallas Internet* | manager@dallas.net | (214) 881-9595 |
| DFWNet* | info@dfw.net | (800) 2-DFW-NET |
| DFW VietNet, saomai.org | info@saomai.org | (214) 705-2900 x58 |
| FastLane Communications, Inc. | info@fastlane.net | (817) 589-2400 |
| Galaxy Access Network | info@gan.net | (214) 396-0038 |
| Internet America | info@iadfw.net | (214) 491-7134 |
| National Knowledge Networks, Inc.* | info@nkn.net | (214) 880-0700 |
| On-Ramp Technologies, Inc.* | info@onramp.net | (214) 746-4710 |
| PICnet | info@pic.net | (214) 789-0456 |
| Plano Internet* | manager@plano.net | (214) 881-9595 |
| Spindlemedia | info@spindle.net | (817) 332-5661 |
| Texas Metronet, Inc. | info@metronet.com | (214) 705-2900 |
| UniComp Technologies, Inc. | info@unicomp.net | (214) 663-3155 |
| Why? Internet Services | info@whytel.com | (817) 795-1765 |

*Houston/Galveston/Brazoria*

| | | |
|---|---|---|
| Access Communications | info@accesscomm.net | (713) 896-6556 |
| Black Box | info@blkbox.com | (713) 480-2684 |
| Centurion Technology—Houston | info@cent.com | (713) 878-9980 |
| Compass Net, Inc. | info@compassnet.com | (713) 776-0022 |
| Connections.Com, Inc. | info@concom.com | (713) 680-9333 |
| CyberSim | cybersim@cybersim.com | (713) 229-9992 |
| Digital MainStream, Inc.* | schmidt@main.com | (713) 364-1819 |
| Electrotex | info@electrotex.com | (800) 460-1801 |
| GHG Corporation | info@ghgcorp.com | (713) 488-8806 |
| InfoCom Networks | info@infocom.net | (713) 286-0399 |
| Info-Highway International, Inc.* | info@infohwy.com | (713) 447-7025 |
| Insync Internet Services* | jimg@insync.net | (713) 961-4242 |
| interGate | gcox@intergate.com | (713) 558-7200 |
| IWL Net | info@iwl.net | (713) 992-4082 |
| NeoSoft, Inc.* | info@neosoft.com | (713) 968-5800 |
| NetOne | info@net1.net | (713) 688-9111 |
| NetTap Data Services | helpdesk@nettap.com | (713) 482-3903 |
| Phoenix DataNet* | helpdesk@mailserv.phoenix.net | (713) 486-8337 |
| Sesquinet | info@sesqui.net | (713) 527-6038 |
| South Coast Computing Services, Inc. | sales@sccsi.com | (713) 917-5000 |
| United States Information Superhighway | info@usis.com | (713) 682-1666 |

| State/City/Providers | E-mail | Telephone |
|---|---|---|
| Wantabe, Inc. | ggkelley@wantabe.com | (713) 493-0718 |
| *San Antonio* | | |
| Internet Direct | nerone@txdirect.net | (210) 308-9800 |
| NetXpress | info@netxpress.com | (210) 822-7887 |
| Salsa.Net | info@salsa.net | (210) 704-3770 |
| South Texas Internet Connections | info@stic.net | (210) 828-4910 |
| Texas Networking, Inc. | helpdesk@texas.net | (210) 272-8111 |

## UTAH
*Salt Lake City/Ogden*

| | | |
|---|---|---|
| ArosNet* | info@aros.net | (801) 532-AROS |
| Internet Alliance* | adm@alinc.com | (801) 964-8490 |
| KDC On-Line | support@kdcol.com | (801) 497-9931 |
| ThoughtPort Authority of Salt Lake City* | info@thoughtport.com | (801) 596-2277 |
| Utah Wired | pam@utw.com | (801) 532-1117 |
| X-Mission* | support@xmission.com | (801) 539-0852 |

*All other points*

| | | |
|---|---|---|
| AXXIS Internet Service* | webmaster@axxis.com | (801) 565-1443 |
| CacheNET* | hal@cachenet.com | (801) 753-2199 |
| DirecTell LC* | kathy@ditell.com | (801) 647-5838 |
| Emery Telecommunications and Video | sales@etv.net | (801) 748-2388 |
| Fibernet Corporation* | info@fiber.net | (801) 223-9939 |
| Infonaut Communication Services | info@infonaut.com | (801) 370-3060 |
| InfoWest* | info@infowest.com | (801) 674-0165 |

## VERMONT
*All points*

| | | |
|---|---|---|
| SoVerNet | info@sover.net | (802) 463-2111 |
| TGF Technologies, Inc. | info@together.net | (802) 862-2030 |
| ValleyNet | info@valley.net | (802) 649-2200 |

## VIRGINIA
*Norfolk/Virginia Beach/Newport News*

| | | |
|---|---|---|
| Exis Net, Inc. | support@exis.net | (804) 552-1009 |
| InfiNet* | sales@infi.net | (804) 622-4289 |
| Pinnacle Online | info@pinn.net | (804) 490-4509 |
| *Richmond/Petersburg* | | |
| Global Connect, Inc. | info@gc.net | (804) 229-4484 |
| I 2020* | info@i2020.net | (804) 330-5555 |
| Widomaker Communication Services | info@widomaker.com | (804) 253-7621 |

| State/City/Providers | E-mail | Telephone |
|---|---|---|
| **WASHINGTON** | | |
| *Seattle/Tacoma* | | |
| Access One | info@accessone.com | (206) 827-5344 |
| Alternate Access, Inc.* | info@aa.net | (206) 728-9585 |
| Blarg! Online Services* | info@blarg.com | (206) 784-9681 |
| Compumedia, Inc.* | support@compumedia.com | (206) 623-8065 |
| Cyberspace | info@cyberspace.com | (206) 505-5577 |
| Eskimo North* | nanook@eskimo.com | (206) FOREVER |
| Interconnected Associates, Inc.* | info@ixa.com | (206) 622-7337 |
| Northwest Link* | staff@nwlink.net | (206) 451-1151 |
| Northwest Nexus, Inc.* | info@halcyon.com | (206) 455-3505 |
| NWNet* | info@nwnet.net | (206) 562-3000 |
| NWRAINET, Inc.* | info@nwrain.com | (206) 566-6800 |
| Olympic Computing Solutions | ocs@oz.net | (206) 989-6698 |
| Seanet* | seanet@seanet.com | (206) 343-7828 |
| Seattle Community Network | help@scn.org | (206) 365-4528 |
| TCM Communications | rgrothe@tcm.nbs.net | (206) 941-1474 |
| WOLFE Internet Access, LLC* | info@wolfe.net | (206) 443-1397 |
| *Washington (east)* | | |
| AT-NET Connections, Inc. | support@atnet.net | (509) 766-7253 |
| Blue Mountain Internet | info@bmi.net | (509) 522-5006 |
| Cascade Connections, Inc. | root@cascade.net | (509) 663-4259 |
| Computech* | admin@iea.com | (509) 624-6798 |
| EagleNet* | info@soar.com | (509) 466-3535 |
| Internet Connection | info@eznet.com | (509) 022-0417 |
| Internet On-Ramp | info@on-ramp.ior.com | (509) 624-RAMP |
| One World Telecommunications, Inc.* | info@oneworld.owt.com | **(509) 735-0408** |
| Televar Northwest* | info@televar.com | (509) 664-9004 |
| **WEST VIRGINIA** | | |
| *All points* | | |
| CityNet Corporation | info@citynet.net | (304) 342-5700 |
| IANet | info@ianet.net | (304) 453-5757 |
| Intrepid Technologies, Inc.* | info@intrepid.net | (304) 876-1199 |
| MountainNet, Inc.* | info@mountain.net | (304) 594-9075 |
| Ram Technologies | sales@ramlink.net | (304) 522-1726 |

**WISCONSIN**
*Kenosha*
see Chicago, ILLINOIS

| State/City/Providers | E-mail | Telephone |
|---|---|---|
| *Milwaukee/Waukesha* | | |
| alpha.net* | info@alpha.net | (414) 274-7050 |
| Exec-PC BBS | info@earth.execpc.com | (800) EXECPC-1 |
| Great Lakes Area Commercial | info@glaci.com | (414) 475-6388 |
| Internet Company | | |
| I.Net Solutions, Inc. | info@mke.com | (414) 785-0920 |
| Internet Connect, Inc.* | info@inc.net | (414) 476-ICON |
| MIX Communications | info@mixcom.com | (414) 351-1868 |
| **WYOMING** | | |
| *All points* | | |
| NETConnect* | office@tcd.net | (307) 789-8001 |
| Visionary Communications* | info@vcn.com | (307) 682-1884 |
| wyoming.com LLC* | info@wyoming.com | (307) 332-3030 |
| **YUKON** | | |
| *All points* | | |
| YKNet | yknet@yknet.yk.ca | (403) 668-8202 |
| **NATIONAL COVERAGE: U.S.** | | |
| ACM Network Services | account-info@acm.org | (817) 776-6876 |
| Allied Access, Inc. | sales@intrnet.net | (800) 463-8366 |
| AlterNet/UUNET | info@alter.net/info@uu.net | (800) 488-6384 |
| BBN Planet Corporation* | net-info@bbnplanet.com | (800) 472-4565 |
| CERFnet* | infoserv@cerf.net | (800) 876-2373 |
| Cheney Communications Company | info@cheney.net | (800) CHENEY-1 |
| CICNet* | info@cic.net | (800) 947-4754 |
| Cogent Software, Inc.* | info@cogsoft.com | (818) 585-2788 |
| CyberENET Network (KAPS, Inc.) | access-sales@cyberenet.net | (609) 753-9840 |
| Databank, Inc.* | info@databank.com | (913) 842-6699 |
| Delphi | info@delphi.com | (800) 695-4005 |
| The Destek Group, Inc.* | info@destek.net | (603) 635-3857 |
| EMI Communications* | info@emi.com | (800) 456-2001 |
| free.org | info@free.org | (715) 743-1700 |
| Futuris Networks, Inc. | info@futuris.net | (800) 976-2632 |
| Global Enterprise Services, Inc. | info@jvnc.net | (800) 358-4437 x7325 |
| HoloNet | info@holonet.net | (510) 704-0160 |
| INS Info Services* | info@netins.net | (800) 546-6587 |
| Institute for Global Communications | igc-info@igc.apc.org | (415) 442-0220 |
| Interconnected Associates, Inc.\ (IXA)* | info@ixa.com | (800) IXA-8883 |

| State/City/Providers | E-mail | Telephone |
|---|---|---|
| Internet America | info@iadfw.net | (800) BE-A-GEEK |
| Internet Connect, Inc.* | info@inc.net | (414) 476-ICON |
| Internet Direct Communications | sales@idir.net | (913) 842-1100 |
| Internet Express* | service@usa.net | (800) 592-1240 |
| Internet Online Services, Inc.* | info@ios.com | (201) 928-1000 |
| Internet Texoma, Inc. | info@texoma.com | (800) 697-0206 |
| INTERNExT* | info@internext.com | (703) 502-1899 |
| Interpath* | info@interpath.net | (800) 849-6305 |
| IONet | info@ionet.net | (405) 721-1580 |
| Kallback | info@kallback.com | (206) 286-5200 |
| Midwest Internet | info@midwest.net | (800) 651-1599 |
| Msen* | info@msen.com | (313) 998-4562 |
| National Internet Source, Inc.* | info@nis.net | (201) 825-4600 |
| New Mexico Technet, Inc.* | granoff@technet.nm.org | (505) 345-6555 |
| Nothing But Net* | info@trey.com | (800) 951-7226 |
| NovaLink Interactive Networks | info@novalink.com | (800) 274-2814 |
| OARnet* | info@oar.net | (614) 728-8100 |
| OnRamp, Ltd. | info@theramp.net | (708) 222-6666 |
| Opus One* | info@opus1.com | (520) 324-0494 |
| Pacific Rim Network, Inc.* | info@pacificrim.net | (360) 650-0442 |
| PSI (Performance Systems International) | info@psi.com | (800) 82PSI82 |
| The Point Internet Services, Inc.* | info@thepoint.net | (812) 246-7187 |
| Portal Information Network | info@portal.com | (800) 433-6444 |
| Protocol Communications, Inc.* | info@protocom.com | (612) 541-9900 |
| Questar Microsystems, Inc.* | fbarrett@questar.com | (800) 925-2140 |
| Random Access, Inc.* | marius@randomc.com | (800) 463-8366 |
| Sacramento Network Access, Inc.* | ghall@sna.com | (916) 565-4500 |
| ServiceTech, Inc.* | sales@servtech.com | (716) 263-3360 |
| Synergy Communications* | sales@synergy.net | (402) 346-4638 |
| Traders' Connection* | info@trader.com | (800) 753-4223 |
| Turning Point Information Services, Inc.* | info@tpoint.net | (512) 499-8400 |
| Viper Computer Systems, Inc.* | vipersys@viper.net | (800) VIPER-96 |
| Voicenet* | info@voicenet.com | (800) 835-5710 |
| The WELL | info@well.com | (415) 332-9200 |
| WLN Internet Services* | info@wln.com | (800) DIAL-WLN |
| Zocalo Engineering* | info@zocalo.net | (510) 540-8000 |

| State/City/Providers | E-mail | Telephone |
|---|---|---|
| **NATIONAL COVERAGE: CANADA** | | |
| Focus Technologies* | **info@ftn.net** | (800) FTN-INET |
| HoloNet | **info@holonet.net** | (510) 704-0160 |
| HookUp Communications | **info@hookup.net** | (905) 847-8000 |
| UUNET Canada* | **info@uunet.ca** | (800) 463-8123 |
| see also NATIONAL COVERAGE: U.S. | | |

*Table A-3*   *International Service Providers*

| Provider | E-mail | Telephone |
|---|---|---|
| **UNITED KINGDOM** | | |
| AirTime Internet Resources Ltd UK | sales@airtime.co.uk | 1254 676 921 |
| Aladdin | info@aladdin.co.uk | 1489 782 221 |
| Almac | info@almac.co.uk | 1324 666 336 |
| Atlas InterNet | info@atlas.co.uk | 171 312 0400 |
| BBC Networking Club | info@bbcnc.org.uk | 181 752 4159 |
| Bournmouth Internet | sales@bournemouth-net.co.uk | 1202 292 900 |
| BTnet | internet@bt.net | 345 585 110 |
| Celtic Internet Services Limited | enquiry@celtic.co.uk | 1633 811 825 |
| CityScape | sales@ns.cityscape.co.uk | 1223 566 950 |
| CIX (Compulink Information eXchange), Ltd | cixadmin@cix.compulink.co.uk | 181 390 8446 |
| Demon Internet, Ltd.* | internet@demon.net | 181 371 1234 |
| Direct Connection | sales@dircon.co.uk | 181 297 2200 |
| Dungeon Network Systems | info@dungeon.com | 1473 621 217 |
| Easynet | admin@easynet.co.uk | 171 209 0990 |
| Enterprise PLC | sales@enterprise.net | 1624 677 666 |
| EUnet GB Ltd | sales@Britain.EU.net | 1227 266 466 |
| FastNet | sales@fastnet.co.uk | 1273 675 314 |
| Foobar Internet | sales@foobar.co.uk | 116 233 0033 |
| Frontier Internet Services | info@ftech.net | 171 242 3383 |
| Gaiacom | info@gaiacom.co.uk | 1732 351 111 |
| GreenNet | support@gn.apc.org | 171 713 1941 |
| Hiway | info@inform.hiway.co.uk | 1635 550 660 |
| Internet Discovery | padds@idiscover.co.uk | 181 694 2240 |

| Provider | E-mail | Telephone |
|---|---|---|
| KENTnet | info@kentnet.co.uk | 1580 890 089 |
| Luna Internet | sales-uk@luna.net | 1734 791 900 |
| Magnum Network Services, Ltd. | sales@mag-net.co.uk | 1908 216 699 |
| Mistral Internet | info@mistral.co.uk | 1273 708 866 |
| NETHEAD | info@nethead.co.uk | 171 207 1100 |
| NetKonect | info@netkonect.net | 171 345 7777 |
| Nildram On-Line | info@nildram.co.uk | 01442 891 331 |
| Onyx | onyx-support@octacon.co.uk | 1642 210 087 |
| Paston Chase | info@paston.co.uk | 1603 502 061 |
| Pavillion Internet | info@pavillion.co.uk | 1273 607 072 |
| PC User Group/WinNET Communications | request@win-uk.net | 181 863 1191 |
| Pinnacle Internet Services | info@pncl.co.uk | 1293 613 686 |
| PIPEX (Public IP Exchange Limited)* | sales@pipex.com | 500 646 566 |
| Powernet | info@powernet.co.uk | 1908 503 126 |
| Primex Information Services | info@alpha.primex.co.uk | 1908 313 163 |
| Pro-Net Internet Services | sales@pro-net.co.uk | 181 200 3565 |
| RedNet onLine | orders@rednet.co.uk | 1494 513 333 |
| Sound & Vision BBS (Worldspan Communications Ltd) | world@span.com | 181 288 8555 |
| Technocom | sales@technocom.co.uk | 1753 673 200 |
| Telecall | support@telecall.co.uk | 117 941 4141 |
| Total Connectivity Providers Ltd | sales@tcp.co.uk | 1703 393 392 |
| U-NET Limited | hi@u-net.com | 1925 633 144 |
| Wintermute Ltd. | info@wintermute.co.uk | 1224 622 477 |
| WinNet | info@win-uk.net | 181 863 1191 |
| ZETNET Services | info@zetnet.co.uk | 1595 696 667 |
| Zynet Ltd | zynet@zynet.net | 1392 426 160 |

## AUSTRALIA

| Provider | E-mail | Telephone |
|---|---|---|
| Access One | info@aone.net.au | 1 800 818 391 |
| APANA | propaganda@apana.org.au | 02 635 1751 |
| ASAHi Computer Systems | asahi@asahi.com.au | 03 9429 6011 |
| AUSNet Services Pty Ltd | sales@world.net | 02 241 5888 |
| Australia On Line | sales@ozonline.com.au | 1 800 621 258 |
| Ballarat NetConnect Pty Ltd | info@netconnect.com.au | 53 322 140 |
| BrisNet | dancer@mail.brisnet.org.au | 07 3229 3229 |
| connect.com.au | pty ltd connect@connect.com.au | 03 528 2239 |
| Cooee Communications | sysop@cooee.com.au | 43 696 224 |
| Cynergy | cynergy@cynergy.com.au | 07 3357 1100 |
| DIALix | info@dialix.com | 1902 29 2004 |

| *Provider* | *E-mail* | *Telephone* |
|---|---|---|
| Dynamite Internet | **info@dynamite.com.au** | 06 242 8644 |
| Geko | **info@geko.com.au** | 02 439 1999 |
| Highway 1 | **info@highway1.com.au** | 09 370 4584 |
| iiNet Technologies Pty Ltd | **iinet@iinet.net.au** | 09 307 1183 |
| Informed Technology | **info@it.com.au** | 09 245 2279 |
| Intercom Pacific | **info@ipacific.net.au** | 02 281 1111 |
| InterConnect Australia Pty Ltd | **info@interconnect.com.au** | 03 9528 2239 |
| Internet Access Australia | **accounts@iaccess.com.au** | 03 576 4222 |
| Internet Interface Systems Pty Ltd | **info@webnet.com.au** | 03 9525 0922 |
| Kralizec Dialup Internet System | **info@zeta.org.au** | 02 837 1397 |
| Microplex Pty Ltd* | **info@mpx.com.au** | 02 438 1234 |
| Netcore Pty Ltd | **info@netcore.com.au** | 03 9872 3821 |
| Netro, Your Internet Connection | **info@netro.com.au** | 02 876 8588 |
| OzEmail | **info@ozemail.aust.com** | 02 391 0480 |
| Pegasus Networks | **pegasus@peg.apc.org** | 07 3255 0255 |
| Penrith NetCom | **info@pnc.com.au** | 04 735 7000 |
| Really Useful Communications Company | **info@rucc.net.au** | 03 9818 8711 |
| Stour System Services | **stour@stour.net.au** | 09 571 1949 |
| TMX, The Message eXchange | **info@tmx.com.au** | 02 550 4448 |
| World Reach Pty Ltd | **info@wr.com.au** | 02 436 3588 |
| Zip Australia Pty. Ltd. | **info@zip.com.au** | 02 482 7015 |

INTERNATIONAL/WORLDWIDE COVERAGE

| | | |
|---|---|---|
| GeoAccess Network | **sharpe@cafe.net** | (604) 970-0049 |
| IBM Global Network* | **globalnetwork@info.ibm.com** | *United States:* (800) 933-3997 |
| | | *Canada:* (800) 463-8331 |
| | | *United Kingdom:* 800 614 012 |
| | | *Australia:* 1 800 811 094 |

# INTERNATIONAL NETWORK CONNECTIVITY

*Summary of International Connectivity*
*Country Codes and Connectivity*

Outside the United States, the top-level domains used in Internet addresses are two-letter country codes. The country codes (and their names) are defined in an International standards document called ISO 3166. The bulk of this appendix is a table, distributed by Lawrence Landweber and the Internet Society, that shows all of these codes.* The table also shows what kind of network connectivity each country has. They aren't all connected to the Internet, so services like FTP and TELNET may not be available; but well over half have some kind of international network connectivity (whether BITNET, UUCP, Fidonet, or something else), so you can at least send e-mail.

## ▪ *Summary of International Connectivity*

The total number of entities with international network connectivity is 146. Table B-2 summarizes the countries that have network connectivity, and the kind of connectivity they have.

---

*The official and up-to-date version of this information may be found on the Internet Society Gopher: **gopher.isoc.org/ Internet Information/Charts & Graphs**. The name will be something like *ConnectivityChart;* the actual name varies with the version.

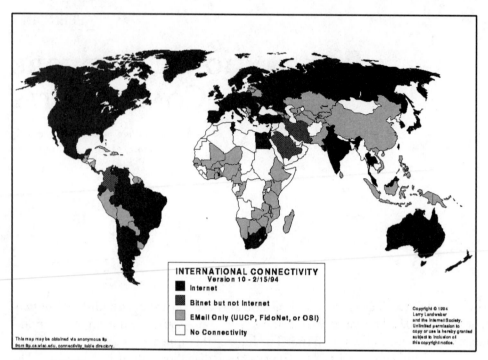

**Figure B-1**    *International connectivity summary*

## Country Codes and Connectivity

Entries in the connectivity table look like this:

```
BIUFO AT        Austria
```

This entry means that **AT** is the top-level domain name for Austria; a domain name like **ffr.syh.at** is probably from an Internet site in Austria. The notation in the left column shows the kind of connectivity each country has, as shown in Table B-1.

**Table B-1**    *Key to Connectivity Table*

| Key | Type of Connectivity |
| --- | --- |
| ---- | No verified connectivity |
| B | Bitnet connectivity |
| I | Internet connectivity |
| U | UUCP connectivity |
| F | Fidonet connectivity |
| O | OSI connectivity |

Lowercase letters indicate minimal connectivity; uppercase indicates widespread connectivity. This entry indicates that Austria has BITNET, Internet, UUCP, Fidonet, and OSI connectivity—i.e., every kind of connectivity that's currently possible.

The information in this list is available from the anonymous FTP site **ftp.wisc.edu**, in the directory *connectivity_table*. It's updated several times a year. We've made a number of modifications to the list to bring it closer to actual usage. For example, Great Britain uses the country code UK, rather than its assigned ISO code (GB). When the Soviet Union was dissolved, the SU code was deleted from the list; we put it back in, because it's still being used, along with the new country codes for the former Soviet states. In the future, this can only get more complicated: When the Virgin Islands get on the Net, will they use their own country codes, or the US and UK domains?

*Table B-2  International Network Connectivity*

| Connectivity | Country | Connectivity | Country |
|---|---|---|---|
| ----- AF | Afghanistan | --Uf- BM | Bermuda |
| ----- AL | Albania | ----- BT | Bhutan |
| ----- DZ | Algeria | --U-- BO | Bolivia |
| ----- AS | American Samoa | ----- BA | Bosnia-Herzegovina |
| ----- AD | Andorra | --uf- BW | Botswana |
| ----- AO | Angola | ----- BV | Bouvet Island |
| ----- AI | Anguilla | BIUFO BR | Brazil |
| -I--- AQ | Antarctica | ----- IO | British Indian Ocean Territory |
| ----- AG | Antigua and Barbuda | ----- BN | Brunei Darussalam |
| BIUF- AR | Argentina | bIUF- BG | Bulgaria |
| --U-- AM | Armenia | --U-- BF | Burkina Faso |
| ---f- AW | Aruba | ----- BI | Burundi |
| -IUFo AU | Australia | ----- KH | Cambodia |
| BIUFO AT | Austria | --u-- CM | Cameroon |
| --U-- AZ | Azerbaijan | BIUFO CA | Canada |
| ----- BS | Bahamas | ----- CV | Cape Verde |
| b---- BH | Bahrain | ----- KY | Cayman Islands |
| ----- BD | Bangladesh | ----- CF | Central African Republic |
| --u-- BB | Barbados | ----- TD | Chad |
| --UF- BY | Belarus | BIUF- CL | Chile |
| BIUFO BE | Belgium | --u-O CN | China |
| --u-- BZ | Belize | ----- CX | Christmas Island |
| ----- BJ | Benin | ----- CC | Cocos (Keeling) Islands |

| Connectivity | | Country | Connectivity | | Country |
|---|---|---|---|---|---|
| B-u-- | CO | Colombia | --u-- | GT | Guatemala |
| ----- | KM | Comoros | ----- | GN | Guinea |
| --u-- | CG | Congo | ----- | GW | Guinea-Bissau |
| --u-- | CK | Cook Islands | ----- | GY | Guyana |
| bIuf- | CR | Costa Rica | ----- | HT | Haiti |
| --uf- | CI | Cote d'Ivoire | ----- | HM | Heard and McDonald |
| -IuFo | HR | Croatia | ----- | HN | Honduras |
| --U-- | CU | Cuba | BI-F- | HK | Hong Kong |
| bI--- | CY | Cyprus | BIUFo | HU | Hungary |
| BIUF- | CZ | Czech Republic | -IUFo | IS | Iceland |
| bIUFO | DK | Denmark | bIUfO | IN | India |
| ----- | DJ | Djibouti | --u-- | ID | Indonesia |
| ----- | DM | Dominica | b---- | IR | Iran |
| --Uf- | DO | Dominican Republic | ----- | IQ | Iraq |
| ----- | TP | East Timor | BIUFO | IE | Ireland |
| bIu-- | EC | Ecuador | BIUF- | IL | Israel |
| bIU-- | EG | Egypt | BIUFO | IT | Italy |
| ----- | SV | El Salvador | --u-- | JM | Jamaica |
| ----- | GQ | Equatorial Guinea | BIUF- | JP | Japan |
| -IUF- | EE | Estonia | ----- | JO | Jordan |
| ---f- | ET | Ethiopia | --Uf- | KZ | Kazakhstan |
| ----- | FK | Falkland Islands | ---f- | KE | Kenya |
| --u-- | FO | Faroe Islands | --u-- | KI | Kiribati |
| -Iu-- | FJ | Fiji | ----- | KP | Korea (People's Republic) |
| BIUFO | FI | Finland | BIUFO | KR | Korea (Republic) |
| BIUFO | FR | France | -I--- | KW | Kuwait |
| --u-- | GF | French Guiana | --U-- | KG | Kyrgyz Republic |
| --u-- | PF | French Polynesia | ----- | LA | Laos |
| ----- | TF | French Southern Territories | -IUF- | LV | Latvia |
| ----- | GA | Gabon | ----- | LB | Lebanon |
| ----- | GM | Gambia | --u-- | LS | Lesotho |
| --UF- | GE | Georgia | ----- | LR | Liberia |
| BIUFO | DE | Germany | ----- | LY | Libya |
| --uF- | GH | Ghana | -I-f- | LI | Liechtenstein |
| ----- | GI | Gibraltar | --UFo | LT | Lithuania |
| BIUFO | GR | Greece | bIUFo | LU | Luxembourg |
| -I-f- | GL | Greenland | ---F- | MO | Macau |
| --u-- | GD | Grenada | --u-- | MK | Macedonia |
| b-uf- | GP | Guadeloupe | --u-- | MG | Madagascar |
| -I-F- | GU | Guam | ---f- | MW | Malawi |

| Connectivity | Country | Connectivity | Country |
|---|---|---|---|
| bIUF- MY | Malaysia | --Uf- PE | Peru |
| ----- MV | Maldives | --uF- PH | Philippines |
| --U-- ML | Mali | ----- PN | Pitcairn |
| --u-- MT | Malta | BIUF- PL | Poland |
| ----- MH | Marshall Islands | bIUFO PT | Portugal |
| ----- MQ | Martinique | BIUFO PR | Puerto Rico |
| ----- MR | Mauritania | ----- QA | Qatar |
| --uf- MU | Mauritius | --u-- RE | Re'union |
| ----- YT | Mayotte | BIuf- RO | Romania |
| BIuF- MX | Mexico | BIUF- RU | Russian Federation |
| ----- FM | Micronesia | ----- RW | Rwanda |
| --uF- MD | Moldova | ----- SH | Saint Helena |
| ----- MC | Monaco | ----- KN | Saint Kitts and Nevis |
| ----- MN | Mongolia | --u-- LC | Saint Lucia |
| ----- MS | Montserrat | ----- PM | Saint Pierre and Miquelon |
| ----- MA | Morocco | ----- VC | Saint Vincent and the Grenadines |
| --Uf- MZ | Mozambique | | |
| ----- MM | Myanmar | --u-- WS | Samoa |
| --Uf- NA | Namibia | ----- SM | San Marino |
| ----- NR | Nauru | ----- ST | Sao Tome and Principe |
| ----- NP | Nepal | B---- SA | Saudi Arabia |
| BIUFO NL | Netherlands | --Uf- SN | Senegal |
| --u-- AN | Netherlands Antilles | --u-- SC | Seychelles |
| ----- NT | Neutral Zone (Saudia Arabia/ Iraq) | ----- SL | Sierra Leone |
| | | bIuF- SG | Singapore |
| --U-- NC | New Caledonia | bIUF- SK | Slovakia |
| -IUF- NZ | New Zealand | -IUFO SI | Slovenia |
| --u-- NI | Nicaragua | --u-- SB | Solomon Islands |
| --u-- NE | Niger | ----- SO | Somalia |
| ---f- NG | Nigeria | -IUFO ZA | South Africa |
| --u-- NU | Niue | bIUF- SU | Soviet Union (former) |
| ----- NF | Norfolk Island | BIUFO ES | Spain |
| ----- MP | Northern Mariana Islands | --U-- LK | Sri Lanka |
| BIUFO NO | Norway | ----- SD | Sudan |
| ----- OM | Oman | --u-- SR | Suriname |
| --U-- PK | Pakistan | ----- SJ | Svalbard and Jan Mayen |
| ----- PW | Palau | --u-- SZ | Swaziland |
| b-uF- PA | Panama | BIUFo SE | Sweden |
| --u-- PG | Papua New Guinea | BIUFO CH | Switzerland |
| --u-- PY | Paraguay | ----- SY | Syria |

| Connectivity | Country |
|---|---|
| BIuF- TW | Taiwan, Province of China |
| --uf- TJ | Tajikistan |
| ---f- TZ | Tanzania |
| -IUF- TH | Thailand |
| --u-- TG | Togo |
| ----- TK | Tokelau |
| --u-- TO | Tonga |
| --u-- TT | Trinidad and Tobago |
| bIUfo TN | Tunisia |
| BI-F- TR | Turkey |
| --u-- TM | Turkmenistan |
| ----- TC | Turks and Caicos Islands |
| ----- TV | Tuvalu |
| ---f- UG | Uganda |
| -IUF- UA | Ukraine |
| ----- AE | United Arab Emirates |
| bIUFO UK | United Kingdom |

| Connectivity | Country |
|---|---|
| BIUFO US | United States |
| --UF- UY | Uruguay |
| --UF- UZ | Uzbekistan |
| --u-- VU | Vanuatu |
| ----- VA | Vatican City State |
| -IU-- VE | Venezuela |
| --u-- VN | Vietnam |
| ----- VG | Virgin Islands (British) |
| ---f- VI | Virgin Islands (U.S.) |
| ----- WF | Wallis and Futuna Islands |
| ----- EH | Western Sahara |
| ----- YE | Yemen |
| --uf- YU | Yugoslavia |
| ----- ZR | Zaire |
| ---f- ZM | Zambia |
| --uf- ZW | Zimbabwe |

# ACCEPTABLE USE

*The NSFNET Backbone Services Acceptable Use Policy*

This is the official "acceptable use" policy for the NSFNET, dated June 1992. As of publication, this is the most recent version of this policy. You can get an up-to-date version of the policy via anonymous FTP from **nic.merit.edu**, in the file */nsfnet/ acceptable.use.policies/nsfnet.txt*. This directory also contains the policies of several other networks.

Though the first paragraph of this policy sounds scary, don't be put off by it. As we said in chapter 3, "support" of research and education is interpreted fairly loosely. And remember that the NSFNET is not the Internet. It's only a part of the Internet, and it has one of the strictest acceptable use policies. As time goes on, the NSFNET's policy is becoming less and less important. A primary goal of the recent efforts toward privatization is to create an Internet without acceptable use policies: i.e., a network where there are no restrictions on commercial use, hobbyist use, or otherwise.

Therefore, the network to which you connect may have a significantly different policy; some branches of the Internet actively encourage commercial use. Take up any questions with your service provider—your provider determines what's acceptable for your connection. If you want an Internet connection for strictly commercial or personal use, it's easy to find a provider who will serve you.

## ■ The NSFNET Backbone Services Acceptable Use Policy

### General Principle

■ NSFNET Backbone services are provided to support open research and education in and among U.S. research and instructional institutions, plus research arms of for-profit firms when engaged in open scholarly communication and research. Use for other purposes is not acceptable.

## Specifically Acceptable Uses

■ Communication with foreign researchers and educators in connection with research or instruction, as long as any network that the foreign user employs for such communication provides reciprocal access to U.S. researchers and educators.

■ Communication and exchange for professional development, to maintain currency, or to debate issues in a field or subfield of knowledge.

■ Use for disciplinary-society, university-association, government-advisory, or standards activities related to the user's research and instructional activities.

■ Use in applying for or administering grants or contracts for research or instruction, but not for other fundraising or public relations activities.

■ Any other administrative communications or activities in direct support of research and instruction.

■ Announcements of new products or services for use in research or instruction, but not advertising of any kind.

■ Any traffic originating from a network of another member agency of the Federal Networking Council if the traffic meets the acceptable use policy of that agency.

■ Communication incidental to otherwise acceptable use, except for illegal or specifically unacceptable use.

## Unacceptable Uses

■ Use for for-profit activities, unless covered by the General Principle or as a specifically acceptable use.

■ Extensive use for private or personal business.

This statement applies to use of the NSFNET Backbone only. NSF expects that connecting networks will formulate their own use policies. The NSF Division of Networking and Communications Research and Infrastructure will resolve any questions about this Policy or its interpretation.

# A UNIX PRIMER

Although you don't need to know UNIX to use the Internet, it can help—particularly if you access the Internet through a public-access UNIX system. Fortunately, though, you really need to know only a dozen or so simple commands. Here's a five-minute UNIX primer.

## Logging In

UNIX is, by nature, a multiuser timesharing system. Whenever you start a UNIX session, you have to start by telling UNIX who you are. This is true whether you are at a terminal in your office or dialing into a huge public-access site. It's not like DOS, Windows, or the Macintosh, which are operating systems with no concept of multiple users. UNIX needs to know who you are to keep you and your property separate from the tens, hundreds, or maybe even thousands of other people who might be using the system.

We've already seen the UNIX login dialog in chapter 5, *Remote Login.* Here's a brief recap:

```
SunOS UNIX (sonne)

login: krol                               type your username
Password:                                 type the password given to you by the sysadmin
Last login: Sat Sep  7 17:16:35 from ux1.uiuc.edu
SunOS Release 4.1(GENERIC) #1:Tue Mar 6 17:27:17 PST 1990
%                                         now you're ready to go
```

The username is the name your account is known by; your system administrator will assign it when setting up your account. The password proves that you are who you say you are and prevents someone else from getting access to your account illegitimately. The system doesn't "echo" your password when you type it, to prevent other people from seeing it. Your system administrator will probably assign you an initial password and then tell you how to pick (and change) your password. Some hints about passwords are given in chapter 4, *What's Allowed on the Internet?* The % is a prompt telling you that UNIX is ready to accept commands. The prompt may not be the same on the system you use; often, the UNIX prompt includes the computer's name.

On some systems, you may need to give a "dial-up password" when you log in through a phone line. The system administrator will give you the dial-up password to use, if you need one.

You may also be asked what kind of terminal you are using. Again, because UNIX is a time-sharing operating system, people can connect all kinds of hardware to it. The way you tell UNIX your terminal type varies, but it usually looks something like this:

```
Last login: Sat Sep  7 17:16:35 from ux1.uiuc.edu
SunOS Release 4.1(GENERIC) #1:Tue Mar 6 17:27:17 PST 1990
TERM=(vt100)?                              prompt for terminal type
sonne%                                     now you're ready to go
```

The line (**vt100**)? is saying, "I think you're using a VT100 terminal. If that's true, press ENTER and you can go on. If it's not, tell me your terminal type." VT100 is a good guess, since most commonly used communications packages support *VT100 emulation*— i.e., they know how to make your computer work like a VT100.

If UNIX is confused about your terminal type, all sorts of things will work incorrectly: You might find that carriage returns don't work, or that characters appear in reverse video, and all sorts of things. If you have problems, contact your system administrator.

To end your UNIX session, give the command **logout**.

## ▉ *Command Basics*

We'll start by showing how UNIX commands work and then go on to list the most commonly used and necessary commands.

### *How Commands Look*

Most UNIX commands look like this:

```
% command options arguments
```

That is, there's a command, followed by some options to the command, followed by some arguments. Arguments are usually names of files. The options all begin with a minus sign. For example, the command below says "execute the command **ls** with the option -l on the file *a.out*":

```
% ls -1 a.out
```

That's 90 percent of what you need to know. Command names are almost always lowercase; options are usually single letters (either uppercase or lowercase). Unlike many other operating systems, UNIX cares about the difference between uppercase and lowercase.

If you use two or more single-letter options, most commands let you stick the options together. For example, these two commands are identical:

```
% ls -1g a.out
% ls -1 -g a.out
```

Some options require arguments of their own. In that case, the option's argument follows the option, and the option can't be stuck together with others. This primer doesn't describe any of these commands.

There are a few commands that don't fit the rules very well, and one of these is important: **tar**. (The others you'll never need.) In the list of commands, I just give a "cookbook" for the three ways you'll need to use **tar**. Follow the cookbook, and you'll be OK.

## Essential Commands

Here's the list of basic commands that I promised. I've shown MS-DOS equivalents in capital letters. Some of these commands are explained further below.

**logout**  Terminate your UNIX session.

**ls**  List the files in your current directory. It's the equivalent of DIR in many other operating systems. **ls -l** gives you more detailed information, including file size, ownership, and creation date. **ls** has many, many options, but -l is the one you'll use most often.

**rm** *files*  DELETE (remove) one or more files. For example, **rm file1 file2 file3** deletes three files named *file1*, *file2*, and *file3*. The command **rm -i** asks you for confirmation before deleting each file.

**mv** *oldname newname*

RENAME (move) a file from *oldname* to *newname*. Lots of people complain about the **mv** command—they have trouble remembering it, because it really means RENAME. They have a good point. However, UNIX users like to think about "moving files around" rather than renaming them. If you think in terms of moving files around, UNIX will make more sense.

**cp** *file1 file2*        COPY *file1* into a new file, called *file2*.

**more** *file*           Display an ASCII file on your screen, a page at a time. Press SPACEBAR to see the next page. Many people use a command called **cat** for this purpose—and they complain, because the name is completely misleading. Well, that's their fault. **cat** wasn't designed to display files; it just happens to work (though not very well). **more** is really a better tool; don't bother with **cat**.* Now, the name **more** isn't exactly intuitive either; it might help to remember the phrase "show me more of this file."

**grep** *pattern file*    Show all occurrences of *pattern* in a file. (I admit: this is about as unintuitive as command names get.) The search is case-sensitive. **grep** is used to find particular text strings in files. For example, if *phones* is a list of telephone numbers and names, the command

```
% grep "John Johnson" phones
```

Finds John's entry in the phone list. Notice that we put quotes around the search pattern; the quotes *never* hurt, and they're necessary whenever you're searching for something with a space or an asterisk in it.

**grep -i** *pattern file* Same as the previous command, except that it's not case-sensitive: uppercase and lowercase letters are the same.

**pwd**                   Show your current working directory.

**cd** *dir*              Change your working directory.

**mkdir** *dir*           Create a new directory called *dir*, with no files in it.

**rmdir** *dir*           Delete (remove) the directory called *dir. dir* must be empty—that is, it may not have any files in it.

**man** *command*         Display the UNIX online documentation about the given *command*.

---

*There is one time **cat** is useful for displaying files. It's a quick-and-dirty way to download a file; just turn on screen capture on your PC and then **cat** the file you want. But be careful: don't **cat** a binary file!

**uuencode** *final-name < file > output*

> Create an ASCII version of a binary file, suitable for shipping in a mail message. *final-name* is the name the file should have when it's unpacked; *file* is the name of the file you're encoding; and *output* is the encoded file that you'll mail off to someone else. The > and < symbols are for standard input and standard output, which we'll discuss briefly below.

**uudecode** *encoded-file*

> The opposite of **uuencode**.

**compress file**  Compress a file so that it takes up less storage. The result is a binary file with the same name as the original, with *.Z* added to the end. The original file is deleted. You can't mail a compressed file, because it's binary; however, you can **uuencode** it. A similar common UNIX program is **gzip**.

**uncompress file**  Given a compressed file, get the original back. A similar common UNIX program is **gunzip**.

**tar**  **tar** was designed for making tapes (the name stands for "tape archive"), but it's also used to create file archives (conglomerates that include several files), like the ones you find on the Internet. Its command structure is weird. Rather than explain how **tar** works, I'll just give you the three commands that do everything you'll need. In these examples, *file.tar* is a **tar** archive. In the first two, we'll work with an archive you got from somewhere else. In the last, we'll create an archive.

```
% tar tf  file.tar        list files in the archive
% tar xf  file.tar        extract files from the archive
% tar cf  file.tar list   create a new archive, including the files in list
```

## Standard Input and Output

Historically, one of UNIX's strengths has been the flexibility of its input and output system. Most commands send their output to your terminal. However, you can save the output of any command in a file by redirecting it. Similarly, many commands take their input from your keyboard; however, you can redirect the input from a file. (The secret behind this is that UNIX treats all I/O operations the same way—everything "looks like" a file. You don't have to understand what that means to use UNIX, though.)

*> file*  Standard output; put the output into a file, instead of sending it to the screen. Anything already in the file is destroyed. For example, if you want

to list the files in your directory, but you want to save the list in a file rather than viewing it, you can give the command:

```
% ls -l > filelist
```

>> *file*          Standard output, append; put the output into a file, following whatever is already there.

< *file*          Standard input; take the input from a file, instead of sending it to the screen. The **uuencode** command listed earlier uses standard input and output; for an example, look back at that.

| *another-command*

Pipe; take the standard output of one program and use it as the standard input of another. This is really one of UNIX's best features; you can use it to create your own commands. Let's say you want a list of all the files that belong to **edk**. You can't do this with any of the **ls** command's many options. However, you can use a pipe to combine **ls -l** and **grep**:

```
% ls -l | grep "edk"
```

**ls -l** lists all the files, including ownership information, and **grep** extracts the entries that contain the string **edk**. If you use UNIX only occasionally, you can get by without pipes. If you start doing anything substantial with pipes, you'll quickly realize how useful they are.

Standard input and output redirectors are generally put at the end of the command, following all the options and arguments.

## ■ *Directory Structure*

Like MS-DOS and the Macintosh, UNIX has a hierarchical (or "tree-structured") filesystem. This means that every file is in a *directory;* directories can include other directories. The Macintosh calls directories "folders"; DOS and Windows systems use the same language as UNIX for talking about files and directories.

UNIX uses a slash (/) to separate the directory names.* For example, */home/john/letters/ mom.txt* means "the file *mom.txt,* in the directory *letters,* in the directory *john,* in the directory *home.* We could also say that *john* is a subdirectory of the directory *home,* and so on.

---

*Note that MS-DOS uses a backward slash, or backslash, (\) for the same purpose. Folklore has it that the developers of DOS were trying to make it look like UNIX, but got it wrong.

You should notice a few other things about this example:

- The name begins with a /. The initial / means "the root directory," which is essentially the point at which all of the system's disk drives are glued together. In UNIX, you never refer to a disk drive itself; you always refer to subdirectories under the root.

- UNIX systems are, by nature, multiuser systems. Every user is assigned a "home directory" to keep his or her own files, even if the system only has one user. */home/john* is probably the home directory for the user "john."

- Users can also create their own directories, just as John has created a *letters* directory.

Our sample filename, */home/john/letters/mom.txt,* is called an *absolute pathname,* because it shows an entire "path" for locating the file, starting from the root, or /. However, you don't need to use absolute pathnames all the time. Here are a few abbreviations:

- At any time, you have a *working directory.* You can give paths that are relative to your working directory, rather than absolute paths from the root. For example, if your working directory is */home/john,* you can use *letters/mom.txt;* if your working directory is */home/john/letters,* you can just use the filename, *mom.txt.* (In fact, that's what you'll do most of the time: refer to a file within your current working directory.)

  The command **pwd** prints the name of your working directory; **cd** *dir* changes your working directory. So, if your working directory is */home/john,* **cd letters** moves you into the *letters* directory. **mkdir** *dir* creates a new directory; and **rmdir** *dir* deletes a directory—provided that it doesn't contain any files.

- You can use the abbreviation ~ to mean your home directory, or ~*name* to mean "the home directory of username." For example, ~*john/letters/mom.txt* is another way of referring to John's letter to his mother. The command **cd** (with no argument) always takes you back to your home directory, regardless of your starting point.

- The abbreviation .. means "the parent directory." It's most often used with **cd** commands; for example, if your current directory is ~*john/letters,* the command **cd ..** moves you back to ~*john.*

You should become familiar with the way UNIX organizes files. Unlike personal computers, which typically have relatively small disks, UNIX systems usually have large disks, and many of them. Gigabyte disk drives are common, and most systems have several disk drives. A large system may have dozens. (By the way, that's why it's good that you never refer to the disk drives themselves. All the information UNIX needs is contained in the directory structure.) The more storage there is, the more important it is to organize it well; and the more important directories become.

## Legal Filenames

UNIX doesn't have very many rules about filenames. On most modern UNIX systems, filenames can have any length. Filenames can also include just about any character—except for the slash (/), which is used to separate directories. However, you're best off limiting yourself to upper- and lowercase letters, numbers, periods (.) and commas (,). Spaces and other special characters can be made to work, but they require special handling. Rather than explaining how, my advice is "just say no."

Don't put a period at the beginning of a filename; the UNIX **ls** command won't list it, unless you give the special command **ls -a**. This is actually a nice feature—it lets you "hide" certain files so they won't clutter up your directory listings. However, if you're new to UNIX, you'll find it confusing.

## Filename Wildcards

The standard UNIX filename wildcards are *, ?, and [ ]. * is by far the most frequently used. Their meanings are:

*          Match anything. For example: * by itself matches any file in your directory; **\*.txt** matches any filename ending in **.txt**; and **gorilla.\*** matches any filename beginning with **gorilla**.

?          Match any single character. For example: **source.?** matches **source.h**, **source.c**, **source.y**, and any other single letter.

[...]      Match any single character that's given inside the brackets. You can list individual characters: for example, [**chyf**] matches **c**, **h**, **y**, or **f**. You can also list ranges: for example, [**a-z**] matches any lowercase letter, and [**a-z0-9A-Z**] matches any alphabetic character or numeral. Note that any single range should not mix upper- and lowercase letters, or letters and numbers. [**a-Z**] or [**A-9**] would have surprising results—they might do what you intended, but only if you're lucky.

You can count on the wildcards listed above no matter what version of UNIX you're using.

Unfortunately, you can't use the filename wildcards in the "pattern" part of a **grep** command. Instead, **grep** uses a more complex feature called "regular expressions," which

I won't describe.* You can, of course, use wildcards in the file part of a **grep** command: for example,

```
% grep "John Johnson" *
```

searches for John's name in all files in your current directory.

## ◼ *Other Books*

There are many introductory books about UNIX. Here are a few that might help you:

- *Learning the UNIX Operating System,* by Grace Todino, John Strang, and Jerry Peek (O'Reilly & Associates): A good general introduction. It's short and to the point, but very accessible to new users.

- *Life with UNIX,* by Don Libes (Prentice-Hall, 1989). Another general introduction that has helped many people.

- *UNIX in a Nutshell* (O'Reilly & Associates) provides a brief summary of all the UNIX commands. There are different versions of this book for different versions of the UNIX operating system.

- *Learning the Vi Editor,* by Linda Lamb, and *Learning Emacs,* by Deb Cameron and Bill Rosenblatt (both published by O'Reilly & Associates). You can't do much with an operating system if you can't edit files. The most commonly used editors for UNIX are **vi** and **emacs**. They are too complicated to describe here, but these books provide excellent introductions.

---

*I've refused to talk about regular expressions elsewhere, and I'm not going to change my mind here! Seriously, they can be complicated; the best detailed discussion available is in the Nutshell Handbook *sed and awk,* by Dale Dougherty. They are also discussed in most UNIX handbooks, including most of the books listed in the following section.

# GLOSSARY

**application**

> (a) Software that performs a particular useful function for you. ("Do you have an electronic mail application installed on your computer?")
>
> (b) The useful function itself (e.g., transferring files is a useful application of the Internet).

**Archie**

> A system for locating files that are publicly available by anonymous FTP. Archie is described in chapter 9.

**ARPAnet**

> An experimental network established in the '70s where the theories and software on which the Internet is based were tested. No longer in existence.

**bandwidth**

> The amount of data that can be transferred over a network connection. (Technically, it is the difference in Hertz between the highest and lowest frequencies of a transmission.) If you think of the network as a sewage pipe, the bandwidth can be thought of as the area of the cross-section: the wider the pipe, the faster "information" will flow. Many use the phrase "wasting bandwidth" to refer to "information" that takes up more flow than it deserves. (That was a better metaphor than the highway, wasn't it?)

**baud**

> When transmitting data, the number of times the medium's "state" changes per second. For example: a 2,400-baud modem changes the signal it sends on the phone line 2,400 times per second. Since each change in state can correspond to multiple bits of data, the actual bit rate of data transfer may exceed the baud rate. Also, see "bits per second." Today, common modem speeds are 14,000, 19,600, and 28,000 bits per second.

**BIND**

The UNIX implementation of DNS (q.v.). It stands for "Berkeley Internet Name Domain."

**bits per second (bps)**

The speed at which bits are transmitted over a communications medium.

**BTW**

Common abbreviation in mail and news, meaning "by the way."

**buffers**

Areas of memory that provide temporary storage for input devices.

**bulletin board service (BBS)**

In online terms, an area where messages can be posted, read, and responded to in a non–real-time discussion. USENET newsgroups are basically bulletin boards. Traditionally, "BBS" has referred to a stand-alone computer or site where users can dial in and exchange messages and files, or access some other types of services (such as chat or mail). These "private" BBSs are self-contained services and are not part of the Internet, although many have gateway connections to the Net.

**cache**

Information saved in memory for later use. For example, Web browsers like Internet Explorer save recently viewed pages in a cache so the exact pages are not downloaded again, thereby saving Internet resources and time.

**chat**

A real-time conversation (in text, usually) among multiple users online. MSN and America Online have chat rooms, with discussions centered on a particular topic. Internet Relay Chat (IRC) is the analogous facility on the Internet.

**CHAP**

Challenge-Handshake Authentication Protocol. An authentication method that enables you to connect to your Internet service provider. It is a reasonably secure way to verify login and password access for dial-up Internet service.

**CIX**

Commercial Internet Exchange; an agreement among network providers that allows them to do accounting for commercial traffic. Although it has been discussed a lot in the press, it's primarily a concern for network providers.

### client

A software application (q.v.) that works on your behalf to extract a service from a server somewhere on the network. Think of your telephone as a client and the telephone company as a server to get the idea.

### COM port

A serial port on a PC. Serial ports have only one transmit line and one receive line. Data is thus sent over the line as a series of bits—hence the name "serial line."

### datagram

A packet (q.v.) of information that is sent to the receiving computer without any prior warning. Conceptually, a "datagram" is somewhat like a telegram: it's a self-contained message that can arrive at any time, without notice. Datagrams are usually used in applications where the amount of information transfer is occasional and small.

### DDN

Defense Data Network; a portion of the Internet that connects to U.S. military bases and contractors; used for nonsecure communications. MILNET is one of the DDN networks. The DDN used to run "the NIC," which coordinated the Internet as a whole. However, the InterNIC (q.v.) has taken over that function; now the DDN NIC is responsible only for the DDN.

### dial-up

(a) A connection to a computer made by calling the computer on the telephone. Often, dial-up refers only to the kind of connection you make when using a terminal emulator and a regular modem. For the technoids: switched character-oriented asynchronous communication.

(b) A port (q.v.) that accepts dial-up connections. ("How many dial-up ports on your computer?")

### DNS

The Domain Name System; a distributed database system for translating computer names (like ruby.ora.com) into numeric Internet addresses (like 194.56.78.2), and vice-versa. DNS allows you to use the Internet without remembering long lists of numbers.

### DOD

The (U.S.) Department of Defense, whose Advanced Research Projects Agency got the Internet started by funding the ARPAnet.

**domain name**

> The name given to a network or site that is connected to the Internet—e.g., ora.com is the domain name for O'Reilly & Associates.

**EFF**

> Electronic Frontier Foundation. An organization founded to address the social and legal issues emerging from the increasing use of computers and their impact on society.

**encryption**

> Encoding information so that only an intended recipient can read it. Encryption is used on the Internet for many things from basic network data packet transfers to the secure exchange of private e-mail. There are several different methods of encryption.

**Ethernet**

> A kind of "local area network." It's a confusing concept, since there are several different kinds of wiring, which support communication speeds ranging from 2 to 10 million bits per second. What makes an Ethernet an Ethernet is the way the computers on the network decide whose turn it is to talk. Computers using TCP/IP are frequently connected to the Internet over an Ethernet.

**FAQ**

> Either a frequently asked question, or a list of frequently asked questions and their answers. Many USENET newsgroups, and some non-USENET mailing lists, maintain FAQ lists (FAQs) so that participants don't spend lots of time answering the same set of questions.

**flame**

> A virulent and (often) largely personal attack against the author of a USENET posting. "Flames" are unfortunately common. People who frequently write flames are known as "flamers."

**followup**

> A response to a USENET posting (q.v.).

**frame relay**

> A data communication technology that is sometimes used to provide higher speed (above 56KB and less than 1.5MB) for Internet connections. Its usual application is in connecting workgroups rather than individuals.

### Free-Net

An organization to provide free Internet access to people in a certain area, usually through public libraries.

### FTP

(a) The File Transfer Protocol; a protocol that defines how to transfer files from one computer to another.

(b) An application program that moves files using the File Transfer Protocol. FTP is described in detail in chapter 9.

### FYI

(a) A common abbreviation in mail and news, meaning "for your information."

(b) A series of informative papers about the Internet; they're similar to RFCs (q.v.), but don't define new standards.

### gateway

A computer system that transfers data between normally incompatible applications or networks. It reformats the data so that it is acceptable for the new network (or application) before passing it on. A gateway might connect two dissimilar networks, such as DECnet and the Internet; or it might allow two incompatible applications to communicate over the same network (like mail systems with different message formats). The term is often used interchangeably with router (q.v.), but this usage is incorrect.

### gif

The Graphic Interchange Format standard; common file format used to exchange graphics over the Internet.

### Gopher

A menu-based system for exploring Internet resources. Gopher is described in detail in chapter 11.

### hostname

The name given to an individual computer attached to a network or the Internet (a host machine).

### HTML

Hypertext Markup Language; the language in which World Wide Web documents are written.

**hypermedia**

A combination of hypertext (q.v.) and multimedia (q.v.).

**hypertext**

Documents that contain links to other documents; selecting a link automatically displays the second document.

**IAB**

The Internet Architecture Board; the "ruling council" that makes decisions about standards and other important issues.

**IETF**

The Internet Engineering Task Force; a volunteer group that investigates and solves technical problems and makes recommendations to the IAB (q.v.).

**IMHO**

Common abbreviation in mail and news, meaning "in my humble opinion."

**Internet**

(a) Generally (not capitalized), any collection of distinct networks working together as one.

(b) Specifically (capitalized), the worldwide "network of networks" that are connected to each other, using the IP protocol and other similar protocols. The Internet provides file transfer, remote login, electronic mail, news, and other services.

**InterNIC**

The combined name for the providers of registration, information, and database services to the Internet. The InterNIC is discussed in the introduction to the *Resource Catalog*. It provides many network resources of its own.

**IP**

The Internet Protocol; the most important of the protocols on which the Internet is based. It allows a packet to traverse multiple networks on the way to its final destination.

**IP address**

A 32-bit number defined by the Internet Protocol that uniquely identifies a resource on the Internet. It is usually shown in dotted-decimal or dotted-quad notation, which is four numbers separated by dots.

**IRC**

Internet Relay Chat. A client/server facility that allows large group conversations over the Internet.

**ISDN**

Integrated Services Digital Network; a digital telephone service. Essentially, with ISDN service, the phone lines to your house carry digital signals, rather than analog signals. If you have the appropriate hardware and software, if your local central office provides ISDN service, and if your service provider supports it, ISDN allows high-speed home access to the Internet (56KB).

**ISO**

The International Organization for Standardization; an organization that has defined a different set of network protocols, called the ISO/OSI protocols. In theory, the ISO/OSI protocols will eventually replace the Internet Protocol. When and if this will actually happen is a hotly debated topic.

**ISOC**

The Internet Society; an organization whose members support a worldwide information network. It is also the governing body to which the IAB (q.v.) reports.

**jpeg**

The Joint Photographic Experts Group standard for encoding and compressing graphic images. A popular graphic file format on the Internet.

**Jughead**

A Gopher (q.v.) service similar to Veronica (q.v.), which searches Gopher menus on a particular set of Gopher servers.

**leased line**

A permanently connected private telephone line between two locations. Leased lines are typically used to connect a moderate-sized local network to an Internet service provider.

**listserv**

A popular software program used to create and manage Internet mailing lists. Mailing lists that run on listserv are usually referred to as "listservs."

**mail reflector**

A special mail address; electronic mail sent to this address is automatically forwarded to a set of other addresses. Typically, used to implement a mail discussion group.

**majordomo**

A widely used software program for creating and managing Internet mailing lists.

**MILNET**

One of the DDN networks that make up the Internet; devoted to nonclassified military (U.S.) communications. It was built using the same technology as the ARPAnet and remained in production when the ARPAnet was decommissioned.

**MIME**

Multimedia Internet Mail Extensions. A protocol that defines a number of content types and subtypes, which allow programs like Web browsers, newsreaders, and e-mail clients to recognize different kinds of files and deal with them appropriately. A MIME type specifies what media a file is, such as image, audio, or video, and a subtype identifies the precise file format.

**mirror site**

A computer that contains an exact replica of the directory structure of another computer to provide alternative access to information at a heavily accessed site. Mirror sites also provide geographically closer site access to save network resources. They are usually updated daily.

**modem**

A piece of equipment that connects a computer to a data transmission line (typically a telephone line of some sort). Most people use modems that transfer data at speeds ranging from 1,200 bits per second (bps) to 28.8 Kbps. There are also modems providing higher speeds and supporting other media. These are used for special purposes—for example, to connect a large local network to its network provider over a leased line.

**Mosaic**

One particular World Wide Web browser that supports hypermedia.

**mpeg**

The Moving Pictures Experts Group standard for encoding and compressing moving video images.

**MUD**

Multi-User Dungeon; a group of role-playing games modeled on the original "Dungeons and Dragons" games. MUDs have also been used in other contexts; they have been used as conferencing tools and educational aids.

**multimedia**

Documents that include different kinds of data; for example, plain text and audio, or text in several different languages, or plain text and a spreadsheet.

**netiquette**

Network etiquette. A loose collection of undocumented rules that is supposed to govern acceptable social behavior on the Internet. Most of netiquette arises from simple politeness to other users, for example, not posting private e-mail without the sender's permission, or reading a FAQ (frequently asked questions) file before joining a USENET discussion on a topic that is new to you.

**Netscape extensions**

A set of HTML tags and HTTP functions that were developed for use with the popular Netscape Navigator Web browser. The extensions exist outside of current HTML and HTTP standards. Many other browsers are able to read them now due to their popular use in Web page design.

**NIC**

(a) Network Information Center; any organization that's responsible for supplying information about any network.

(b) The DDN's NIC, which plays an important role in overall Internet coordination.

**NFS**

The Network File System; a set of protocols that allows you to use files on other network machines as if they were local. So, rather than using FTP to transfer a file to your local computer, you can read it, write it, or edit it on the remote computer—using the same commands that you'd use locally. NFS was originally developed by Sun Microsystems, Inc., and is currently in widespread use.

**NNTP**

Network News Transfer Protocol; the protocol used to transfer USENET news articles between computers on the Internet.

**NOC**

Network Operations Center; a group that is responsible for the day-to-day care and feeding of a network. Each service provider usually has a separate NOC, so you need to know which one to call when you have problems.

## NREN

The National Research and Education Network; a U.S. effort to combine networks operated by different federal agencies into a single high-speed network. Although this transition will be of significant technical and historical importance, it should have no effect on the typical Internet user.

## NSFNET

The National Science Foundation Network; the NSFNET is not the Internet. It's just one of the networks that make up the Internet.

## NTP Network

Time Protocol; a protocol used to synchronize time between computers on the Internet.

## octet

Internet standards-monger's lingo for a set of 8 bits, i.e., a byte.

## OSI

Open Systems Interconnect; another set of network protocols. *See* "ISO."

## packet

A bundle of data. On the Internet, data is broken up into small chunks, called packets; each packet traverses the network independently. Packet sizes can vary from roughly 40 to 32,000 bytes, depending on network hardware and media, but packets are normally less than 1,500 bytes long.

## PGP

Pretty Good Privacy. A freely available program written by Phillip Zimmermann that provides very strong encryption to ensure the privacy and security of communications across computer networks for any user.

## POP

The Post Office Protocol; a mail protocol that allows a remote mail client to read mail from a server.

## port

(a) A number that identifies a particular Internet application. When your computer sends a packet to another computer, that packet contains information about what protocol it's using (e.g., TCP or UDP) and what application it's trying to communicate with. The port number identifies the application.

(b) One of a computer's physical input/output channels (i.e., a plug on the back).

Unfortunately, these two meanings are completely unrelated. The first is more common when you're talking about the Internet (as in "telnet to port 1,000"); the second is more common when you're talking about hardware ("connect your modem to the serial port on the back of your computer").

### posting

An individual article sent to a USENET (q.v.) newsgroup; or the act of sending an article to a USENET newsgroup.

### PPP

Point-to-Point Protocol; a protocol that allows a computer to use the TCP/IP (Internet) protocols (and become a full-fledged Internet member) with a standard telephone line and a high-speed modem.

### protocol

A protocol is just a definition of how computers will act when talking to each other. Protocol definitions range from how bits are placed on a wire to the format of an electronic mail message. Standard protocols allow computers from different manufacturers to communicate; the computers can use completely different software, providing that the programs running on both ends agree on what the data means.

### relevance feedback

The process of using a document you retrieved in a search to further refine your search. WAIS supports relevance feedback, though (currently) only through WAIS clients (and not all WAIS clients). Gateways between the World Wide Web and WAIS servers may support relevance feedback in the future.

### RFC

Request for Comments; a set of papers in which the Internet's standards, proposed standards, and generally agreed-upon ideas are documented and published.

### router

A system that transfers data between two networks that use the same protocols. The networks may differ in physical characteristics (e.g., a router may transfer data between an Ethernet and a leased telephone line).

### RTFM

Common abbreviation in mail and news, meaning "read the ... manual."

**server**

(a) Software that allows a computer to offer a service to another computer. Other computers contact the server program by means of matching client (q.v.) software.

(b) The computer on which the server software runs.

**service provider**

An organization that provides connections to a part of the Internet. If you want to connect your company's network, or even your personal computer, to the Internet, you have to talk to a service provider.

**shell**

On a UNIX system, software that accepts and processes command lines from your terminal. UNIX has multiple shells available (e.g., C shell, Bourne shell, Korn shell), each with slightly different command formats and facilities.

**shortcut**

A feature of Windows 95 that allows you to place an icon on the desktop or in a document and simply click on the icon to access a particular application.

**signature**

A file, typically about five lines long, that people often insert at the end of e-mail messages or USENET news articles. A signature contains, minimally, a name and an e-mail address. Signatures usually contain postal addresses, and frequently silly quotes, pictures, or other things. Some are very elaborate, though signatures of more than five or six lines are in questionable taste.

**SLIP**

Serial Line IP; a protocol that allows a computer to use the Internet protocols (and become a full-fledged Internet member) with a standard telephone line and a high-speed modem. SLIP is being superseded by PPP (q.v.), but is still in common use.

**smiley**

Smiling faces used in mail and news to indicate humor and irony. The most common smiley is :-). You'll also see :-(, meaning disappointment, and lots of other variations. Since the variations are so, er, "variant," it's not worth going into detail. You'll pick up their connotations with time.

**SMTP**

The Simple Mail Transfer Protocol; a protocol that is used to send mail over a TCP/IP network.

## SRI

A California-based research institute that runs the Network Information Systems Center (NISC). The SRI has played an important role in coordinating the Internet.

## subnet mask

An encoding for IP addresses (q.v.) that determines which parts of an IP address identify the network and which part identifies the host machine. It is only used internally on a network; your network administrator will supply you with the appropriate subnet mask if you need it.

## switched access

A network connection that can be created and destroyed as needed. Dial-up connections are the simplest form of switched connections. SLIP and PPP also are commonly run over switched connections.

## TCP

The Transmission Control Protocol. One of the protocols on which the Internet is based. For the technoids, TCP is a connection-oriented reliable protocol.

## TCP/IP stack

The set of programs that connects your desktop to a TCP/IP network. It is composed of the different layers—TCP/IP software, sockets software, and hardware driver software—that data between your Internet application programs and the network must pass through.

## TELNET

(a) A "terminal emulation" protocol that allows you to log in to other computer systems on the Internet.

(b) An application program that allows you to log in to another computer system using the telnet protocol, described in detail in chapter 5.

## timeout

A timeout is what happens when two computers are "talking" and one computer—for any reason—fails to respond. The other computer will keep on trying for a certain amount of time, but will eventually "give up."

## tn3270

A special version of the telnet program that interacts properly with IBM mainframes.

## Token Ring

A technology for creating a local area network that may then be connected to the Internet. Token Ring networks often use the TCP/IP protocols. See also "Ethernet."

## UDP

The User Datagram Protocol. Another of the protocols on which the Internet is based. For the technoids, UDP is a connectionless unreliable protocol. If you're not a technoid, don't let the word "unreliable" worry you.

## UNIX

A popular operating system that was very important in the development of the Internet. Contrary to rumor, though, you do NOT have to use UNIX to use the Internet. There are various flavors of UNIX. Two common ones are BSD and System V.

## USENET

The USENET is an informal, rather anarchic, group of systems that exchange "news." News is essentially similar to "bulletin boards" on other networks. USENET actually predates the Internet, but these days, the Internet is used to transfer much of the USENET's traffic. USENET is described in detail in chapter 8.

## UUCP

UNIX-to-UNIX copy; a facility for copying files between UNIX systems, on which mail and USENET news services were built. Although UUCP is still useful, the Internet provides a better way to do the same job.

## Veronica

A service, very similar to Archie, that's built into Gopher. Just as Archie allows you to search all FTP sites for files, Veronica allows you to search all Gopher sites for menu items (files, directories, and other resources). Veronica is described in chapter 11.

## W3C

World Wide Web Consortium. A consortium of many companies and organizations that "exists to develop common standards for the evolution of the World Wide Web." It is run by a joint effort between the Laboratory for Computer Science at the Massachusetts Institute of Technology and CERN, the European Particle Physics Laboratory, where the WWW was first developed.

**WAIS**

Wide Area Information Service; a very powerful system for looking up information in databases (or libraries) across the Internet. WAIS is described in detail in chapter 12.

**white pages**

Lists of Internet users that are accessible through the Internet. There are several different kinds of white-pages servers and services, described in chapter 11.

**Winsock**

Common term for "Windows Sockets," which is the set of specifications that programmers must use to write TCP/IP software for Windows.

**World Wide Web (WWW)**

A hypertext-based system for finding and accessing Internet resources. The WWW is described in chapter 13.

# INDEX